# AN INTRODUCTION TO
# APPLIED ECONOMICS

# AN INTRODUCTION TO APPLIED ECONOMICS

by

**J. L. HANSON**

M.A., M.Ed., (Leeds), Ph.D., B.Sc. (Econ.) (London)
*Formerly Senior Lecturer in Economics*
*Huddersfield College of Technology*

MACDONALD & EVANS, LTD.
8 JOHN STREET, LONDON, W.C.1
1969

*First published April, 1969*

©

MACDONALD AND EVANS LTD
1969

S.B.N. 7121 0921 8

*Printed in Great Britain by Richard Clay (The Chaucer Press), Ltd.,
Bungay, Suffolk*

# PREFACE

The aim of this book, as its title indicates, is to provide an introduction to a study of some of the more important current problems in applied economics. By its very nature applied economics is a dynamic subject. New developments are taking place all the time. A book on current problems in applied economics, therefore, can deal only with each topic down to the time immediately before it goes to press. By the time of publication of such a book some new developments may already have taken place. For this reason a book on applied economics can never serve as more than an introduction to the subject. It can, however, provide the reader with the historical background to current problems; it can show, too, how recent matters have been dealt with; it can discuss current problems and indicate areas of uncertainty where decisions may have to be taken in the near future. At this point the reader himself must take over from the author and weigh in the balance any further problems which may arise. In order to assist the reader who wishes to bring each topic up to date, a list of recommended sources of further information is given on page xxv.

The book can also be regarded as introductory in another sense. Applied economics covers too vast a field for a comprehensive study of its many problems to be brought within the covers of a single volume. A selection of topics, therefore, has had to be made, but the aim has been to include the most important matters of current interest and those most likely to be chosen by lecturers organising courses in the subject. Since everyone has his own special interests, not everyone will agree with the author's choice. The most obvious omissions are those topics arising directly out of theory and usually dealt with in general economics textbooks to illustrate economic theory. An attempt has been made, even at the risk of a small amount of overlapping, to make each chapter as far as possible complete in itself, so that cross-references from one chapter to another can be kept to a minimum.

The book is primarily intended for students who have already acquired at least an elementary knowledge of economic theory and who are going on to take a course in applied economics for the Higher National Certificate (or Diploma) in Business Studies or in Management Studies. Though advantageous such a preliminary study is not essential and it is hoped, therefore, that the book may also appeal to any reader who takes an intelligent interest in economic affairs and who wishes to have a better understanding of current problems.

The recommendations for further reading appended to each chapter are intended not only to serve as a guide to readers who wish to study a particular topic in greater depth, but also to indicate the author's own general indebtedness to these sources of information.

Grateful acknowledgment is made to the Controller of H.M. Stationery Office for permission to use copyright material taken from government publications such as the *Annual Abstract of Statistics*, various Blue Books and White Papers and the periodic reports of the Department of Economic Affairs. My thanks are also due to the Senate of the University of London and to the Colleges of Commerce and Technology and other examining bodies listed on page vii for permission to reproduce questions from examination papers set by them. I have too to thank those publishers who have allowed me to quote from books published by them. These are duly acknowledged where they occur in the text.

*February, 1969*

Colleges and examining bodies which have given permission for the reproduction of questions set by them at examinations for the Higher National Certificate or Higher National Diploma in Business Studies:

*Colleges:*

Barking Regional College of Technology
Barnsley College of Technology
Bournemouth College of Technology
City of Birmingham College of Commerce
Derby & District College of Technology
Huddersfield College of Technology
Kingston-upon-Hull College of Commerce
Leeds College of Commerce
Liverpool College of Commerce
Manchester College of Commerce
Norwich City College
Sheffield College of Technology
Southampton College of Technology

*Examining bodies:*

Northern Counties Technical Examinations Council, Newcastle upon Tyne
Union of Lancashire and Cheshire Institutes (U.L.C.I.), Manchester

# CONTENTS

## PART ONE. PROBLEMS OF PRODUCTION AND DISTRIBUTION

### *CHAPTER I*

*CHAPTER II*

# LOCATION OF INDUSTRY . . . . . 45

*CHAPTER III*

# COMMERCIAL DISTRIBUTION . . . . . 73

*CHAPTER IV*

## *CHAPTER V*

## PROBLEMS OF INLAND TRANSPORT

# PART THREE. MONETARY PROBLEMS

## CHAPTER IX

## CHAPTER X

### CHAPTER XI

## INTERNATIONAL ECONOMIC RELATIONS

### CHAPTER XII

## INTERNATIONAL MONETARY RELATIONS

# LIST OF ILLUSTRATIONS

# LIST OF TABLES

# GENERAL REFERENCES
(For readers who wish to keep up to date)

Blue Books
White Papers
*Annual Abstract of Statistics*
*Monthly Digest of Statistics*
*The Economist*
*Financial Times*
UN Statistical Yearbooks
Progress Reports of Department of Economic Affairs
*Bank of England Quarterly Bulletin*
Quarterly Reviews of Midland, Barclays, Lloyds, National Provincial,
  Westminster, Three Banks, District
Publications of EFTA, EEC, Institute of Economic Affairs, PEP

For American Affairs:

*Economic Letter* of First National City Bank of New York
US Federal Reserve *Bulletin*

# PART ONE

# PROBLEMS OF PRODUCTION
# AND DISTRIBUTION

## CHAPTER I

# ECONOMIC GROWTH AND THE STANDARD OF LIVING

## *I. INTRODUCTORY*

**Economics—theoretical and applied**

Economics is one of the social sciences, and as such is concerned with a particular facet of human behaviour—the economic aspect. Economic problems have their basic origin in the fact that all things, particularly the resources with which to engage in production, are scarce relative to the demand for them, so that all the time choices are having to be made. The problems that arise in consequence of having to make choices—what to produce, how to produce it, how to distribute the national income, how to dispose of one's personal income, etc.—form the subject-matter of economics.

Economic theory is concerned with the building up of a body of principles. Generalisations can be made and theory developed, however, only if certain assumptions are made with regard to the behaviour of human beings when faced by economic situations, and even then only with the proviso of "other things being equal." Also, for more precise study, economic theory requires that the economic aspect of a problem be isolated from all other considerations. However remote from actuality many of the findings of economic theory therefore may appear to be, some people none the less might still regard it as an intellectual discipline worthy of study for its own sake. On the other hand, to most people the purpose of economic theory is simply to provide a training in the use of the tools and techniques of economic analysis, so that these can then be applied to the practical economic problems of everyday life—the field of applied economics.

Thus, applied economics is concerned with the real world. Unlike economic theory, it cannot therefore be isolated from the other social sciences. As Marshall said as long ago as 1890: "Though the laws of economics are statements of tendencies expressed in the indicative mood, not ethical precepts in the imperative, . . . ethical forces are among those the economist has to take into account."[1]

[1] Alfred Marshall in the Preface to the first edition of *Principles of Economics.*

## Applied economics and economic policy

In applied economics, then, attention must be given to political, social and ethical considerations in so far as these impinge on the economic aspects of problems. In framing economic policy this is even more necessary. Applied economics and economic policy are closely related. Applied economics stresses the economic essentials of a problem without ignoring other considerations but when economic policy is under discussion all relevant factors, both economic and non-economic, must be given attention. It may sometimes even be thought that other considerations are so important as to outweigh the economic. In such a case the economic consequences of the policy should be clearly understood.

Differences of opinion regarding economic theory can be expected to occur only at a high level of study and research; little disagreement is likely on the economics of a practical problem; but sharp and possibly violent differences of opinion arise when economic policy is under discussion. In such a case the benefit of a particular policy to the community as a whole must be weighed and considered. This involves value judgments. Differences of opinion are mainly due to different people attaching varying degrees of importance to the non-economic aspects of a problem. Nevertheless, so far as is humanly possible, practical problems in applied economics should be approached objectively. Economic policy too is influenced by what has happened in the past. Indeed, the historical background to an economic problem, a knowledge of which is essential to a proper understanding of all its implications, will often of itself point the way to its solution, and help in the formulation of policy.

From the time of Alfred Marshall and A. C. Pigou economic welfare has become of increasing importance in economics. According to Marshall, economics "examines that part of individual and social action connected with the attainment of the material requisites of well-being."[1] This definition appears to be of particular relevance to applied economics. It seems logical, therefore, to begin a study of applied economics with a consideration of the problems of economic growth, since the general economic welfare of a community depends in the first place on the size of the real national income. In examining economic growth it becomes necessary to touch on a variety of topics of economic importance that form the subject-matter of applied economics. The principal aim of economic policy then becomes the raising of the standard of living as a prerequisite not merely to the possession of more material things but to leading a more cultured life. Aims such as the permanent maintenance of full employment or the control of inflation then become merely steps to this end.

[1] Alfred Marshall, *op. cit.*, Book I, Chapter I.

## II. THE SATISFACTION OF WANTS

**Economic welfare**

One of the most important problems of applied economics, then, is to consider how the economic welfare of a community can be improved and how the standard of living of people throughout the world can be raised. The total welfare of a people comprises many things outside the scopes of economics. Economic welfare has been defined as "that part of social welfare that can be brought directly or indirectly into relation with the measuring rod of money,"[1] for money is the only means by which economic welfare and the standard of living can be measured and compared. The economic welfare of a people, therefore, will be high or low according to the extent that they are able to satisfy their many and varied wants, and their standard of living, therefore, will be improved if they can satisfy more fully a greater proportion of their wants. Thus, in its economic aspect, a person's standard of living is determined by the quantity of goods and services he is able to enjoy, and this depends mainly on his income.

In the first place, the standard of living of a people as a whole is determined by how much by their combined efforts they themselves can produce. This, the total volume of production of a country, is known nowadays as its national income. It required all the effort and energy of primitive peoples to supply their basic wants of food, clothing and shelter, and for thousands of years they had to make do with a bare minimum of these things, frequently having to go hungry and often suffering from the weather. In spite of the economic progress of recent times there are still large numbers of people in the world who are both ill fed and ill clad. With the passage of time, however, increasing numbers of people have been able to satisfy more and more of their wants. In other words, in many parts of the world over the years the standard of living has been rising, with the result that in countries such as Great Britain and the United States and others with advanced economic systems an increasing proportion of the people are able to enjoy the highest standard of living the world has yet known. For example, in Great Britain today little more than half of total consumers' expenditure goes on food, clothing, housing, fuel and light, the remainder going to satisfy wants which help to make life pleasanter, more comfortable, more varied and, for those who so wish, more cultured.

[1] A. C. Pigou, *Economics of Welfare*.

## Expansion of production and consumption

In the more advanced economies of the world few people nowadays satisfy their wants directly, though some may grow small quantities of fruit and vegetables for their own use, and an increasing number of others in both Great Britain and the United States, in spite of the steep rise in the standard of living in those countries, now find themselves with sufficient spare time on their hands to be able to do more odd jobs in their homes for themselves. The vast increase in output during the past two centuries, however, could not have been achieved without a very high degree of specialisation and division of labour. People thus engage in production—of services as well as of goods—in order to earn the money required for the purchase of other goods and services to satisfy their own particular wants.

Man, however, has always been up against the fundamental problem of economics that wants are many and various while the means at his disposal for satisfying them are limited. Although all the time more efficient methods of employing economic resources are being developed, and the supply of some of these resources increased, people's wants have also at the same time continued to expand, thereby keeping ahead of the means of satisfying them. In the richer societies of the present day, however, there is perhaps a tendency for increasing production not merely to satisfy existing wants but also of itself to create new ones. In the words of J. K. Galbraith:

"As a society becomes increasingly affluent, wants are increasingly created by the process by which they are satisfied. . . . Increases in consumption, the counterpart of increases in production, act by suggestion or emulation to create wants. Or producers may proceed actively to create wants through advertising and salesmanship. Wants thus come to depend on output."[1]

Nevertheless, at no time as yet in the world's history has it been possible for people everywhere to have nearly as much of everything as they would have wished to have. The aim of production, therefore, is to satisfy as many of people's wants as is possible with the economic resources and knowledge available at the time. Once people have satisfied their basic wants to a reasonable degree they then have to choose which of the many other competing wants they will satisfy. In a free economy demand will stimulate the production of those things which the community as a whole most desires, each individual making his choice according to his own particular scale of preferences. In a fully planned economy the State will decide

[1] J. K. Galbraith, *The Affluent Society*, p. 124.

what and how much shall be produced, but, if it provides more than the basic necessaries of life, consumers even so may have to be left to decide for themselves which of their additional wants they will satisfy. In the mixed systems which now prevail in democratic countries some wants are satisfied according to individual choice and some according to what the State regards as good or necessary for the community as a whole.

### Influence of the State on the standard of living

In Great Britain today an individual's standard of living depends, therefore, partly on the range of goods and services he can purchase with the money he earns and partly on the services that the State provides for him. The extent to which a person's standard of living is determined by his own earnings or by the State depends on the size of his personal income. Obviously the larger his income the more personal wants he can satisfy; the smaller his income the greater will be the benefit to him of services provided by the State, since some of them—those of a character that could be supplied privately—he could not have afforded if he had had to pay for them directly himself. State services, of course, have to be paid for, but from taxes raised from the community as a whole, so that where a progressive system of taxation is in operation those in the lower income groups pay less than the full cost of state services whereas those in the higher income groups pay more. In assessing a person's standard of living, therefore, it is necessary to know not only his net personal income after payment of income tax but also what services the State provides for him without further payment or in return for a nominal payment.[1]

The services which the State provides are broadly of three kinds: (*i*) services which can be provided only for the community as a whole and not individually; (*ii*) services which the State regards as necessary for people's physical well-being and which some individuals might neglect if the choice were left to them; and (*iii*) services regarded by the State as being worth while and which might be inadequately provided if their supply was left entirely to market forces. In the first category there are such things as national defence and the administration of justice, both of which have been the responsibility of the State for a very long time. In the second category there are the social and welfare services, some of which a number of people prefer to provide at least partially for themselves. Some of these the State provides directly such as the health service, university education, motorways, trunk roads; some it delegates to local authorities such as primary and secondary education, housing, etc.[2] In the third

---

[1] Taxation is considered in Chapter XIII: "Financing the Public Sector."
[2] The social services are considered in Chapter VIII below.

category are the grants made by the Arts Council of Great Britain to cultural activities such as music, art and drama, where it is clear that these activities are worthy of being fostered, and certain grants to sporting organisations, where it is less clear that the community as a whole should be taxed to assist them. Once, however, the State has decided to widen the scope of its assistance to such activities it becomes increasingly difficult to know where exactly to draw the line. Not all people nor all political parties in democratic countries are agreed on the extent to which the State should attempt to satisfy people's wants and how much should be left to individual choice.

## The standard of living

It is possible now to look more closely at what is meant by a person's standard of living. As already noted this partly depends on how much in the way of services the State provides for him. Apart from this, from a purely economic standpoint, an individual's standard of living depends on *how much* he is capable of buying and not on *what* he buys. From the economic point of view what a person spends his money on does not affect the matter. Many people might consider that Mr A has a higher standard of living then Mr B if, the two men having equal incomes and similar family responsibilities, Mr A indulges in cultural pursuits while Mr B dissipates his income in riotous living. Mr A may have a higher standard of behaviour than Mr B, but to the economist their standard of living is the same. Only if the standard of living is regarded from this purely economic angle can standards of living at different periods of time or in different parts of the world be compared. Thus, a person can improve his standard of living only if he can buy more of the goods and services he wants or if the State or the local authority provides more of these things for him. Nevertheless, it is not strictly true to say that the economic concept of the standard of living is a purely material one, since people do not want money for its own sake but only for the command it gives them over goods and services, an essential prerequisite even of a cultured life. It is merely that in his professional capacity an economist is not concerned with the way in which individuals dispose of their incomes.

## III. THE NATIONAL INCOME

### The importance of measuring the national income

The national income has been defined as "the income which accrues to the inhabitants or normal residents of a country from their participation in world production."[1] Some of this income is received by individuals, some by public or private bodies, and some comes

[1] R. and G. Stone, *National Income and Expenditure* (Bowes & Bowes), p. 13.

from abroad, but only incomes received as payment for services to production are included. Alfred Marshall defined the national income as "the aggregate net product of, and the sole source of payment for, all the agents of production,"[1] thereby linking national income to the total volume of production which the definition of Sir John Hicks emphasises. "The national income," he says, "consists of a collection of goods and services reduced to a common basis by being measured in terms of money."[2]

The size of the national income is the best indicator of economic progress we have. As long ago as 1890 Alfred Marshall said: "The money income, or inflow of wealth, gives a measure of a nation's prosperity which, untrustworthy as it is, is yet in some respects better than that afforded by the money value of its stock of wealth."[3] For a long time, however, estimations of either the national wealth or the national income were merely academic exercises.

The first serious efforts to estimate the national income of the United Kingdom were made during the years between the First and Second World Wars by university departments of economics in an attempt to assess economic progress and to measure more precisely the average standard of living of the people of this country. In making these estimates the universities were handicapped by lack of finance, by not being able to allocate sufficient staff to the task, and by a serious lack of the appropriate statistics. It was not until the Second World War, when for the first time the Government became concerned with the measurement of the national income, that more accurate and more detailed calculations became possible. The State's interest arose out of the exigencies of a war in which professional economists played a greater part than ever before and national income statistics were found to be a useful tool in working out economic policy. A White Paper, *Sources of War Finance*, issued in 1941 to accompany the budget, provided the first official calculation of the national income. Since 1946 it has been customary for the White Paper, *National Income and Expenditure*, along with a number of other White Papers on economic matters, to be published shortly before the budget in order to assist the Chancellor of the Exchequer in framing it to meet the needs of the economic situation. Since 1952 the White Paper has been supplemented each autumn by a Blue Book which over the years has become both more detailed and more accurate. In recent years national income statistics, though continuing to be used in connection with the budget, have acquired even greater importance as a means of measuring economic growth and changes in a people's standard of

[1] Alfred Marshall, *op. cit.*, VI, I, p. 10.
[2] Sir John Hicks, *The Social Framework* (Oxford University Press), Part IV.
[3] Marshall, *op. cit.*, p. 80.

living, a subject in which governments display a much greater interest than ever before. It has become one of the principal aims of economic policy in the modern world to increase the rate of economic growth. A country's success in achieving this objective nowadays tends to be judged by comparison with the rate of growth achieved by other countries, and this is often now taken as the main criterion of a country's economic progress.

## The three aspects of the national income

The first influence on a people's standard of living is the size of the national income or total volume of production. There are three ways of looking at the national income: (*i*) the value in terms of money of all the goods and services produced in a country in the course of a year; (*ii*) the total of all incomes derived from economic activity in that country during the same period; and (*iii*) the total expenditure of consumers and public authorities together with the value of capital formation during that year. These three ways of looking at the national income—output, income and expenditure—account for the method of presenting the national income statistics in the White Papers and Blue Books, and also give an indication of how these figures are compiled.

From whichever of these three angles the national income is regarded, the total must be the same. All costs incurred in the production of a commodity are payments to the factors of production that have been employed in its manufacture and this becomes income in the form of rent, wages and interest in the hands of the owners of the factors, the residue being the entrepreneur's profit. In fact, the price paid for a commodity really comprises a collection of payments for all the services performed by those concerned with its production. The total of all incomes derived from economic activity must, therefore, be exactly equal to the money value of all the goods and services produced, the two totals being in effect the same thing merely regarded from two different angles. The total of incomes derived from economic activity must also be equal to the total expenditure of consumers and public authorities together with the value of capital formation since all income must be spent, paid in taxes or saved. Thus, all three aggregates should be equal. Since, however, the three estimates are based largely on different data there is usually a small residual error, though generally of less than 1%.

## Components of the national income

In recent years the *Blue Book on National Income and Expenditure* has shown the national income accounts built up in the following way to give three aggregates:

(i) *Gross domestic product* (the total value of all goods and services produced in this country), calculated at factor cost, *i.e.* excluding subsidies and indirect taxation of such goods and services. This shows the cost of total output to producers. (If no allowances are made for subsidies and taxes we have the gross domestic product at market prices.)

(ii) *Gross national product*, which is the value of the gross domestic product together with net income from abroad (exports *less* imports).

(iii) *National income*, which the Blue Book now defines as the net national product, *i.e.* the gross national product *less* the value of production required to make good the depreciation of capital assets that has occurred during the year under review, as well as the replacement of obsolescent forms of capital.

## The gross national product

The following table shows the national income as the money value of the total volume of production:

TABLE I

*Gross National Product at Factor Cost*

| Product or service | 1965 | 1967 |
|---|---|---|
|  | £ million | £ million |
| Goods and services produced by |  |  |
| Agriculture, forestry and fishing . . . | 1,056 | 1,121 |
| Manufacturing . . . . . . | 10,747 | 11,385 |
| Mining and quarrying . . . . | 708 | 713 |
| Building and construction . . . . | 2,233 | 2,394 |
| Transport . . . . . . | 2,011 | 2,059 |
| Distribution . . . . . . | 3,596 | 3,759 |
| Insurance, banking and finance . . . | 1,042 | 1,078 |
| Gas, electricity and water . . . | 1,034 | 1,110 |
| Ownership of dwellings . . . . | 1,362 | 1,610 |
| Services provided by public authorities . . | 3,226 | 3,804 |
| Other services . . . . . | 3,419 | 4,849 |
| Net income from abroad . . . | 470 | 410 |
| GROSS NATIONAL PRODUCT . . | 31,310 | 34,292 |
| *Less* capital consumption . . . | 2,697 | 3,144 |
| NATIONAL INCOME . . . . | 28,613 | 31,148 |

Source: *Blue Book on National Income and Expenditure.*

To calculate the gross national product it is necessary to know the value in terms of money of the output of (i) the extractive industries of agriculture, foresty, fishing, mining and quarrying, (ii) the manufacturing, building and construction industries and public utilities, (iii) commercial services such as wholesale and retail distribution, transport, insurance, banking and finance. To this total must be added the value of all kinds of personal and professional services, these being valued at the fees or salaries paid for them. Most of the items in Table I are, therefore, self-explanatory with the exception of the item *dwelling houses*, which includes rents accruing to landlords and the notional income accruing to owner-occupiers of house property, *i.e.* the amount they would probably have had to pay if they had rented their houses. This item, therefore, does not refer to the value of new houses erected during the period, these being included under the heading *building and construction*. Then finally there is *net income from abroad*, the amount by which total receipts from abroad for goods and services exported to other countries exceeds total payments received for all kinds of imports of goods and services.

In calculating the output of an industry care has to be taken to avoid double counting. Thus, where the different stages of production are undertaken by different firms, only the value of the finished product must be included, and not the value of the product as it leaves each separate manufacturer, as this would result in the earlier stages of production being counted more than once. The national income calculated as the gross national product differs from a census of production in that it is reckoned as the value at factor cost (*i.e.* excluding indirect taxes such as purchase tax and excise duties) of total output in terms of money, this being the only way of adding together a heterogeneous mass of things, whereas a census of production records the quantity of each commodity produced—an unwieldy total. The gross national product also includes services, valued at the price paid for them, since production includes both goods and services. To obtain the net national product, *i.e.* the net addition to the existing wealth of a country, it is necessary to deduct from the value of the gross national product a sum for depreciation to cover the cost of replacing obsolete or worn-out capital equipment, since such production adds nothing to a country's stock of capital.

### The national income

Consider now Table II. In this table only income derived from economic activity is included, *i.e.* only from activity for which payment is made. All unpaid services which people undertake for themselves or for others are excluded, as also in Table I. The effect of this is to make the total for the national income slightly less than it really is in real terms. On the other hand, the greater the extent to which division of labour is carried in a country, the greater will appear to be its national income measured in terms of money. In countries such as India most of the people cultivate smallholdings and grow most of their own food, selling only a little of what they

## TABLE II
### National Income

| Type of income | 1965 | 1967 |
|---|---|---|
| | £ million | £ million |
| Wages . . . . . . . | 11,480 | 12,235 |
| Salaries . . . . . . | 7,605 | 8,785 |
| Pay in cash and kind of the Forces . . . | 467 | 524 |
| Employers' insurance and other contributions . | 1,666 | 1,927 |
| Professional earnings . . . . . | 455 | 474 |
| Income from farming . . . . . | 592 | 640 |
| Profits of other sole traders and partnerships * . | 1,471 | 1,509 |
| Profits of companies * . . . . . | 4,820 | 4,694 |
| Profits of public enterprises * . . . . | 1,091 | 1,203 |
| Rent of land and buildings . . . . | 1,831 | 1,891 |
| Net income from abroad . . . . | 470 | 410 |
| | 31,310 | 34,292 |
| *Less* national consumption . . . | 2,697 | 3,144 |
| NATIONAL INCOME . . . . | 28,613 | 31,148 |

* Including depreciation.

Source: *Blue Book on National Income and Expenditure.*

produce and paying for relatively few services provided for them by other people. The national income, therefore, will be low because output per head is small, but it will appear to be even less than it really is because the people perform so many unpaid services for themselves. Thus, Table II shows all forms of income received as payment for services of an economic character that have contributed to production—wages of labour, interest and profit from capital and entrepreneurial service earned by all kinds of business enterprises, public and private, and rent from land. It will be noticed that Table II also shows the item *Employers' insurance contributions*, these sums being regarded as equivalent to additional wage payments since they are made for the benefit of employees. Some forms of income, however, are merely transfers of income from one group of people to another. In this category are benefits paid under the social-security insurance scheme, family allowances, many other government grants, and interest payments on government stocks that comprise the National Debt, since all these are raised by compulsory contributions or taxation. If incomes from these services were included it would result in double counting. The final item in this table, as in Table I, is *net income from abroad.*

Table II shows the respective shares of the various factors of production in the national income, though not as precisely as could be wished since some of the items include returns to more than one factor. For example, it is impossible to distinguish between interest

14    AN INTRODUCTION TO APPLIED ECONOMICS

and profit in the item *Profits of companies*, while *Profits of sole traders* include wages of management and interest on capital as well as profit. The most easily distinguished income is wages of labour, though even this cannot be calculated with absolute accuracy. In 1967 the share of labour in the national income appears to have been just over 39%.

**Expenditure**

Income, whether received by individuals or by private or public bodies, is either spent or saved. The importance of saving is that it makes possible capital formation. Consider now, therefore, the disposal of the national income as shown in Table III. This table gives

TABLE III
*Consumption and Investment*

|  | 1965 | 1967 |
|---|---|---|
|  | £ million | £ million |
| Personal consumption . . . . . | 22,956 | 25,323 |
| Expenditure of public authorities . . . | 5,919 | 7,063 |
| Gross domestic capital formation . . . | 6,331 | 7,145 |
| Other items . . . . . . . | 64 | 562 |
| Net income from abroad . . . . | 470 | 410 |
|  | 35,740 | 39,503 |
| *Less* Indirect taxes . . . . . | 4,430 | 5,211 |
| Gross national expenditure at factor cost . . | 31,310 | 34,292 |

Source: *Blue Book on National Income and Expenditure.*

the same final total as Table I and Table II. It shows that personal consumption accounts for 63% of the total, to which should be added government subsidies. Many consumers' goods and services are subject to indirect taxes such as purchase tax and other excise duties, and these must be deducted since national income and expenditure are calculated at factor cost. The expenditure of the State and local authorities accounts for 16% of the total, with 17% to cover capital formation ("saving"). Some of this is to make good depreciation and to replace obsolescent capital, the remainder representing the net addition to the country's stock of capital.

The amount and quality of a country's capital are one of the main influences on economic progress, economic growth, the size of the national income and the standard of living of its people (*see* below, pp. 36–37). Capital accumulation, however, depends on saving and this involves sacrifice since it requires people to forgo a measure of present satisfaction which otherwise they might have enjoyed, in the hope of being able to enjoy greater satisfaction in the future. Factors of production must be set free from the production of consumer's goods and applied to the production of capital goods. Current consumption can be curtailed by personal saving, by limited companies not distributing the whole of their profits (corporate saving) and by taxation to finance public investment (public or compulsory saving). The rate at which a community is able and willing to save will depend largely on the standard of living the people have already achieved (for the poorer the country the more difficult it will be to save), the extent to which personal saving is required to meet unforeseen contingencies such as sickness and old age, and the general economic, political and social outlook for the future. Thus, the countries with the highest standards of living are the ones that are able most easily to improve their standard of living still further. For a poor country capital accumulation will be both slow and painful—hence the necessity for countries with advanced economies to give aid to developing countries.

## Consumption

Consider now how British consumers allocate their personal expenditure. This is shown in Table IV. Consumers in this country devote 22% of their total personal expenditure to food, only 3% being spent on common foods such as bread and potatoes and no less than $5\frac{1}{2}$% on meat. The low proportion of income spent on food (with the relatively high expenditure on meat, fruit and milk) is an indication of the high average standard of living in the United Kingdom today. Indeed, total expenditure on the basic necessaries of life —food, clothing and shelter–accounts for only 61% of consumers' outlay in this country, no less than 39%, thereafter, being available for other expenditure, with 13% of expenditure going on alcoholic drink and tobacco and 9% on motoring, but only $\frac{1}{3}$% on books.

## IV. THE NATIONAL INCOME OF THE UK AT DIFFERENT PERIODS

### A rising standard of living

In comparing the standard of living of a people at different periods of time, allowance must be made for (i) changes in population and (ii) changes in prices. The first difficulty is overcome by taking average income or expenditure per head of the population. Price changes can be allowed for by recalculating prices in two different years in terms of those ruling in a selected base year, as is now done in the *Blue Book on National Income and Expenditure* for the previous ten years and in the *UN National Accounts Statistics Yearbook*. Over longer periods accurate recalculation of prices is impossible and so

TABLE IV

*Consumers' Personal Expenditure*
At Current Prices

|  | 1965 | 1967 |
|---|---|---|
|  | £ million | £ million |
| Food | 5,112 | 5,522 |
| Alcoholic drink | 1,417 | 1,585 |
| Tobacco | 1,428 | 1,512 |
| Housing (rent, rates, maintenance) | 2,479 | 2,976 |
| Fuel and light | 1,097 | 1,191 |
| Clothing | 2,034 | 2,139 |
| Durable goods (furniture, vehicles, etc.) | 1,829 | 2,021 |
| Other household goods | 640 | 684 |
| Books, newspapers, magazines | 339 | 382 |
| Chemists' goods | 321 | 367 |
| Miscellaneous recreational goods | 455 | 496 |
| Other miscellaneous goods | 317 | 343 |
| Running costs of motor vehicles | 917 | 1,161 |
| Travel (rail, bus, air) | 728 | 809 |
| Postal, telephone, telegraph services | 205 | 240 |
| Entertainment | 355 | 420 |
| Domestic service | 122 | 136 |
| Catering (meals and accommodation) | 1,312 | 1,412 |
| Insurance | 246 | 305 |
| Other services | 1,409 | 1,191 |
| Income in kind | 50 | 52 |
| Consumers' expenditure in the UK | 22,566 | 24,944 |
| Consumers' expenditure abroad | 390 | 379 |
| Total | 22,956 | 25,323 |

Source: *Blue Book on National Income and Expenditure.*

comparisons are less accurate. Further difficulties arise because (*i*) as a people's standard of living improves they allocate their expenditure differently, spending less on food and more on other things, and (*ii*) new commodities may come on to the market. Although the national income total includes public expenditure and capital formation in addition to consumer's expenditure it is usual to compare countries by averaging the national income per head of the population, though this practice is not usually followed in comparing the standard of living over a period of time for a single country. Consumers' expenditure is a better guide to the standard of living of a people, for, although some public expenditure goes to provide "free" services for consumers, much government expenditure—for example, on armaments—however justified it may appear to be, adds nothing to the standard of living and, as already seen, capital accumulation requires present sacrifice for future gain. For a long time the Russian people were compelled to accept a low standard of living in order to make possible rapid capital formation, and during 1933–39 the German people's standard of living was reduced in favour of a rapid programme of rearmament.

In Table V consumers' expenditure is shown in terms of the prices

TABLE V

*The Rising Standard of Living*

| Year | Consumers' expenditure | | Average per head at 1958 prices |
|------|------------------------|----------------|---------------------------------|
| | *At current prices* | *At 1958 prices* | |
| | £ million | £ million | £ |
| 1958 | 15,365 | 15,365 | 298 |
| 1959 | 16,160 | 16,075 | 309 |
| 1960 | 16,963 | 16,724 | 319 |
| 1961 | 17,862 | 17,113 | 325 |
| 1962 | 18,893 | 17,463 | 337 |
| 1963 | 20,049 | 18,282 | 347 |
| 1964 | 21,380 | 18,970 | 351 |
| 1965 | 22,956 | 19,421 | 355 |
| 1966 | 24,296 | 19,811 | 361 |
| 1967 | 25,323 | 20,211 | 367 |

Source: *Blue Book on National Income and Expenditure.*

ruling in 1958. Over this period of ten years consumers' expenditure increased in money terms at an average rate of £1,050 million per year, but in real terms, *i.e.* in terms of what their money would buy, at an average rate of £560 million per year—only a little more than half the rate of money increase. In terms of the standard of living there was an average increase per head of the population in real terms from £298 in 1958 to £354 in 1965, an average improvement rate of 2·7% per year. If children under fifteen years of age and women who do not go out to work are excluded the average expenditure per worker (including people in receipt of pensions, which for tax purposes are regarded as deferred earned income) is as follows:

TABLE VI

*Average Expenditure per Worker*

| Year | In money terms | In terms of 1958 prices |
|------|----------------|-------------------------|
| | £ | £ |
| 1958 | 504 | 504 |
| 1965 | 657 | 550 |

## Longer period comparisons

Comparison of the standard of living in the United Kingdom over longer periods of time is more difficult for several reasons: (*i*) accurate calculations of the national income of this country have been compiled only since 1941; (*ii*) calculations of expenditure in terms of prices ruling in a base year have been undertaken only since 1948. In the following table showing the gross national product for this country over the past hundred years, the figures for 1870 and 1910, therefore, must be regarded as only rough approximations:

TABLE VII
*Expansion of the National Income*

| Year | Total in money terms | Population | Average per head | |
|---|---|---|---|---|
| | | | In money terms | In terms of 1958 prices |
| | £ million | Million | £ | £ |
| 1870 | 929 | 27·4 | 34 | 95 |
| 1938 | 5,175 | 48·0 | 108 | 224 |
| 1948 | 10,520 | 49·5 | 212 | 308 |
| 1950 | 11,740 | 50·0 | 235 | 325 |
| 1952 | 14,012 | 50·4 | 278 | 343 |
| 1954 | 15,923 | 50·8 | 313 | 371 |
| 1956 | 18,420 | 51·2 | 359 | 391 |
| 1958 | 18,605 | 51·6 | 395 | 395 |
| 1960 | 20,857 | 52·4 | 434 | 425 |
| 1962 | 23,353 | 53·3 | 477 | 494 |
| 1964 | 26,821 | 54·0 | 538 | 506 |
| 1966 | 29,921 | 54·7 | 549 | 509 |
| 1967 | 31,148 | 55·0 | 561 | 511 |

The final column shows that during the past hundred years the volume of production per head of the population has increased in this country by more than five times. During the past twenty years there has been an increase of 70 %, *i.e.* an average increase of $3\frac{1}{2}$ % per year. In comparing the standard of living of a people at different periods of time we are faced by two difficulties: (*i*) changes in the value of money; and (*ii*) changes in the distribution of the national income. It has already been seen how the first of these difficulties has been overcome for the period since the Second World War by the recalculation of prices in terms of those ruling in a base year. The second difficulty arises because the only way to make comparisons, in view of population changes, is to take average income per head. This method completely ignores the extent of deviations from the average. Thus, reading from Table VII, to say that in terms of 1958 prices the average income per head in this country was £95 in 1870 and £506 in 1964 gives relatively little information regarding the real incomes of most of the people, especially in 1870, when inequality of income was much greater than in 1964.

## Capital formation

Saving, as already noted, is the prerequisite to capital formation. If a country is to increase its real national income it must increase its stock of capital and replace obsolete and obsolescent capital. Table VIII shows the extent of capital formation in the United Kingdom during the years 1957–67.

TABLE VIII

*Capital Formation*

| Year | Current prices | | In terms of 1958 prices | | Capital formation as % of gross national product |
|---|---|---|---|---|---|
| | Gross national product | Capital formation | National income | Capital formation | |
| | £ million | £ million | £ million | £ million | % |
| 1957 | 19,522 | 3,381 | 20,387 | 3,471 | 17·0 |
| 1958 | 20,385 | 3,485 | 20,385 | 3,485 | 17·1 |
| 1959 | 21,389 | 3,737 | 21,056 | 3,768 | 17·9 |
| 1960 | 22,767 | 4,120 | 22,066 | 4,132 | 18·8 |
| 1961 | 24,363 | 4,615 | 22,897 | 4,524 | 19·6 |
| 1962 | 25,457 | 4,726 | 23,150 | 4,499 | 19·6 |
| 1963 | 27,033 | 4,898 | 24,118 | 4,575 | 19·0 |
| 1964 | 29,062 | 5,828 | 25,488 | 5,347 | 20·9 |
| 1965 | 31,310 | 6,252 | 26,187 | 5,533 | 21·3 |
| 1966 | 32,858 | 6,417 | 26,845 | 5,669 | 19·4 |
| 1967 | 34,292 | 6,793 | 27,156 | 5,994 | 19·9 |

Source: *Annual Abstract of Statistics.*

## Distribution of the national income

The standard of living of a people, as already noted, depends in the first place on the size of the national income in relation to the population, since this determines average income per head. In the second place it depends on the way in which the national income is distributed. In 1870, for example, the wealthiest people in Great Britain enjoyed a relatively higher standard of living than do the wealthiest people in this country today. Vast numbers of the working population, however, in 1870 earned less than £1 per week and few workers received anything—apart, that is, from charity—when they were unemployed. It is clear, therefore, that average income per head gives very little indication of the standard of living of most of the people if the greater part of the national income goes to only a few people. Since 1870 inequality of income has been greatly reduced, and particularly since 1913 the movement towards greater equality has been greatly speeded up. This has been achieved mainly by means of steeply progressive income tax and surtax and a very progressive scale of death duties.

Inequality of income is only to a limited extent accounted for by differences in the rates of pay for different kinds of work and the amount of overtime undertaken. The really wide differences in income are the result of the much greater variations in income from investment, including the ownership of land and property. High taxes on income now make it very difficult to accumulate wealth and so to increase investment income, and a steeply progressive scale of death duties greatly reduces the amount of investment income that can be obtained by the inheritance of wealth. Though slow in their effect death duties, since their introduction in Great Britain in 1894, are inexorably eating into the large accumulation of wealth that existed in this country at the beginning of the nineteenth century, and thereby reducing the inherited incomes to be derived from them, though a few people have found ways and means of building up new accumulations.

Inequality of income has been still further reduced by increasing the range of social services, largely paid for out of taxation, which falls progressively more heavily on people in the higher income groups. Though these services are available to everyone those in the lower income groups derive most benefit from them. On average, state-provided social services are now worth £50 per head of the population. Since family allowances are taxed, their value to recipients depends on the rate of tax paid. On the other hand, social-security contributions are payable at flat rates according to the age and sex of the contributor and not according to income. Some people would like to see all social-security benefits financed out of taxation in order to relate all contributions to ability to pay. They complain too that for those who do not pay income tax there are no benefits corresponding to the children's allowance granted to income-tax payers.

Perhaps in view of the extent to which greater equalisation of incomes has been carried, growth of the national income is now widely regarded as being of greater importance than any further movement towards egalitarianism. An increase in the national income which makes everyone better off, even though inequality of personal income remains, is regarded by many people as preferable to greater equality if this merely means all being poor together. This view was expressed many years ago by A. C. Pigou.[1] Economic welfare, he said, would be increased if the national dividend (*i.e.* national income) were increased, provided that this did not cause a greater inequality of income. At the same time he believed that economic welfare would be increased if inequality of income were reduced but only if this did not entail a reduction in the national income. Equalisation of incomes, therefore, should clearly not be carried to the stage where the effect is to reduce the national income. Indeed, some degree of inequality may be necessary, so long as it is not excessive, to provide an inducement to greater effort and greater output.

## Distribution of personal income

Table IX shows the distribution of personal incomes. Some 17·6

TABLE IX

*Distribution of Personal Incomes*
(1966)

| Range of income | | Number of incomes | |
|---|---|---|---|
| | | Before tax | After tax |
| Not under £ | Under £ | Thousands | Thousands |
| 50 | 250 | 2,480 | 2,480 |
| 250 | 300 | 900 | |
| 300 | 400 | 2,244 | 5,598 |
| 400 | 500 | 2,458 | |
| 500 | 600 | 2,391 | |
| 600 | 700 | 1,892 | 10,391 |
| 700 | 800 | 1,792 | |
| 800 | 1,000 | 3,385 | |
| 1,000 | 1,500 | 6,385 | 5,926 |
| 1,500 | 2,000 | 2,303 | 1,485 |
| 2,000 | 3,000 | 957 | 552 |
| 3,000 | 5,000 | 341 | 210 |
| 5,000 | 10,000 | 151 | 57 |
| 10,000 | 20,000 | 34 | 1 |
| 20,000 and over | | 7 | — |

Source: *Blue Book on National Income and Expenditure.*

million people are in receipt of incomes of less than £1,000 a year *before* payment of tax, but this group includes boys and girls under eighteen years of age, other young workers and a large number of

[1] A. C. Pigou, *Economics of Welfare.*

married women who work only part-time. *After* payment of tax
there are nearly 20 million income-receivers in this group. Thus,
although over 10 million people have incomes in excess of £1,000 a
year before tax, only 8 million have net incomes over that amount after
tax, and, though 1·5 million have incomes of over £2,000 before tax,
only 800,000 have net incomes in excess of that. Again, though there
are now 34,000 people in the country with incomes of over £20,000 a
year, the progressive character of surtax (with a maximum tax rate
of 18s. 3d. in the pound) makes it difficult for many people to have a
net income after tax of much above £6,000 a year. (Even at £100,000
a year net income is only £14,450.) Thus, although there is still
considerable divergence from the average, the present system of
taxation makes it not nearly so great as it once was. Thus in many
countries today average expenditure or average income per head of
the population gives a somewhat better indication of the standard of
living of a people than might have been expected in view of some of
the drawbacks to comparison by means of averages.

## V. THE NATIONAL INCOMES OF
## DIFFERENT COUNTRIES

### Comparing standards of living

The only satisfactory means of comparing the standard of living
in different countries is by taking the average national income per
head of the population. Though the fairest way of making comparisons, it is not free from criticism. In the first place, all countries
do not compile their statistics with the same degree of accuracy.
Drawbacks to the comparison of averages have already been discussed. In international comparisons, however, these drawbacks are
likely to be more serious. Deviations from the average, too, are much
greater in most developing nations than in Great Britain and other
advanced Western countries, the poor generally being very poor
indeed and the rich often being extremely rich, a situation that
redistribution of income can do little to remedy on account of the
overwhelmingly large number of poor people in proportion to the
rich.

In compiling the national income of a country only paid work is
taken into account and in some countries—in general, the poorer
ones—people do much more for themselves than in others, so that the
greater the degree of division of labour the greater the national income is likely to be. As a result national income statistics tend to
exaggerate the differences in the standard of living between different
countries.

Another important factor to be taken into account in using
national income totals as a basis of comparison for standards of

living is that not all production is devoted to consumer's goods. It may be sound policy for a country to employ a large proportion of its resources on the production of capital goods in order to make possible a much higher standard of living in the future, but this requires the acceptance of a lower standard of living in the present, and this fact is not shown by averaging the national income per head of the population. More serious still is the effect on the standard of living of an ambitious armaments programme, however justifiable it may be, since it reduces a people's standard of living without in this case offering any compensation in the form of a higher standard of living in the future. The current standard of living in the country depends, therefore, on the quantity of goods and services produced for present consumption and not on the full total of the national income.

There are great differences too in the living conditions of different peoples, and in consequence considerable differences in the cost of obtaining the same degree of comfort. Even in the United Kingdom the cost of keeping a house warm varies quite considerably between people living in Thurso and those living in Penzance. In hot countries this will be a very small item of expenditure. In the United Kingdom the average amount spent per head of the population on fuel and light is £21. In the West Indies the amount spent under this heading is very small.

## The currency difficulty

Each country naturally calculates its national income in terms of its own currency, so that comparison between different countries is possible only if totals and averages per head are converted into a standard currency, such as sterling or US dollars. If this recalculation is made at the prevailing rate of exchange, the question to be asked is: How far does this rate of exchange represent the relative purchasing power of the different currencies in their home markets? Even when exchange rates are perfectly free to fluctuate, factors other than purchasing-power parity—for example, political events—can influence the rate of exchange. Different peoples too demand different assortments of commodities. As the standard of living of a people rises so does their demand for service in relation to goods, and the prices that have to be paid for them also rise. For example, the cost of domestic service in Great Britain is very much greater than in Italy, and much greater in Italy than in India. Again, differences in costs of transport will affect prices.

Even if exchange rates were free to fluctuate the cost of living would still vary from country to country, but only for brief periods have exchange rates been completely flexible. Though in the last resort the balance of payments is the final arbiter of exchange rates, under the scheme inaugurated in 1944 at Bretton Woods, and since then controlled by the International Monetary Fund, exchange rates have been somewhat arbitrarily determined, and some currencies have been undervalued and others overvalued in terms of others. For example, it seems clear that after the devaluation of 1949 sterling was undervalued though the extent of the undervaluation has gradually declined since then. This difficulty has been overcome in the national income comparisons made by the Organisation for European Economic Co-operation by comparing prices for a range of common commodities and services and weighting them as is done in the case of domestic price indices. Using a selected country as a base, its prices are compared with those in other countries and then, as a check, prices in the other countries are compared with those ruling in the base country.[1] By using this method any undervaluation, *e.g.* of sterling in terms of dollars, can be offset.

In using average income per head of the population as a basis for international comparisons of standards of living it is, therefore, necessary to exercise a good deal of caution. There is no doubt that the average standard of living of a citizen of the United States in 1965 was considerably higher than the average for a person living in the United Kingdom, but it was certainly not as much higher as the average incomes of these two people made it appear if the American's income is converted into sterling at the par rate of exchange then current of $2·80 to the pound. This gave the American citizen with £1,080 nearly twice as much as the British citizen with only £533, whereas a comparison based on relative prices in the two countries gave the American £825 to the Briton's £533, thus making the American only 55% better off.

### Some international comparisons

Bearing in mind the many drawbacks to comparisons of the standards of living of different peoples, it will be of interest to consider Table X, which shows the average income per head in 1964 for a number of countries. In this table conversion of national estimates into sterling as a standard unit has been made at the rates of exchange prevailing in 1964. It was shown above that, if allowance is made for the overvaluation of sterling in terms of dollars and the consequent difference in price levels in the two countries, the total for the United States becomes £825. For more accurate comparison the figures for the other countries should also be similarly reduced. The position of the United Kingdom relative to these other countries is not, therefore, as poor as appears from the table. It is clear, however, that by 1964 in addition to the United States and Canada both Switzerland and Sweden were well ahead of the United Kingdom,

[1] R. and G. Stone, *op. cit.*, pp. 95–96.

TABLE X

*Average Income per Head*

(1964)

| Country | £ sterling (at 1964 rates of exchange) |
|---------|---------------------------------------|
| United Kingdom . . | 533 |
| United States . . | 1,080 |
| Switzerland . . . | 735 |
| Sweden . . . | 726 |
| Canada . . . | 700 |
| Denmark . . . | 588 |
| Germany . . . | 554 |
| France . | 550 |
| Norway . . . | 543 |
| Belgium . . . | 524 |
| Netherlands . . | 450 |
| Austria . . . | 366 |
| Italy . . . | 306 |
| Japan . . . | 234 |

with France, Germany, Denmark and Norway at about the same level
as this country. The average standard of living in Italy is clearly very
much below British standards, as it also is in Japan. In the case of
Italy the north is economically so far ahead of the south that the
average for the country as a whole has little relevance, northern Italy
actually being not far behind the Netherlands, whereas, in spite of
recent development schemes in the region, southern Italy is still among
the more economically backward areas of Europe. Comparison
of different countries, therefore, is possible only in general terms.

## VI. ECONOMIC GROWTH

### Present-day economic policy—growth

Economic growth must be maintained if a people is to improve its
standard of living. During the Great Depression of the 1930s,
neither politicians nor economists were so much concerned with
raising the general standard of living as with reducing unemployment and so raising the standard of living of those previously
unemployed. The achievement of full employment and its general
maintenance for more than two decades in time of peace have led to
its gradual acceptance as a permanent feature of economic life.
This has led politicians and economists to turn their attention from

the problem of maintaining a high level of employment—a problem apparently solved—to the newer problem of sustaining a high rate of economic growth. The persistence of full employment, even though it has been accompanied by varying degrees of inflation, has led people to expect a continual rise in their standard of living. The rate of recovery achieved by the countries which had suffered most severely during the Second World War has helped further to concentrate attention on economic growth. The momentum acquired in achieving recovery carried these countries forward to even greater expansion and roused others to emulate them. The result is that economic growth in consequence has tended to become the be-all and end-all of economic policy.

### The rate of growth

A country's economic growth is measured as the percentage increase in its national income per year. This increase must be measured in real terms and so allowance has to be made for rising prices. Measuring by means of percentages, however, tends to exaggerate the achievements of countries expanding from low levels. Thus, Country A may raise the average income per head by £10 from £500 to £510, giving an increase of 2%, while Country B, although raising its average income by only £8 per head from £200 to £208, nevertheless achieves an increase of 4%. In such a situation some politicians in Country A would complain that the economic growth of their country was at only half the rate of Country B, although actually output had increased by £10 per head in Country A as compared with only £8 per head in Country B.

For a long time economic growth in even the most progressive parts of the world was extremely slow, most centuries until the nineteenth seeing little change in income or output per head. During the latter half of the nineteenth century and the first half of the twentieth the rate of growth for Great Britain and the other economically advanced nations was only a little over 1% per year, and during 1913–38 only 1·5%. It has been estimated that income per head in Great Britain increased by about four times during the century preceding the Second World War. Since the population of the country also increased by four times during that period this meant that in terms of real income people in Great Britain on average were enjoying in 1938 a standard of living sixteen times as great as a hundred years earlier. This statement, however, is inclined to exaggerate the improvement for two reasons: (i) until 1900 at least, inequality of income was also tending to increase; and (ii) during this period a greater proportion of the national income was being given up to the production of armaments, which adds nothing to the standard of living.

The following table shows how the national incomes of countries at different stages of economic progress increased during 1958–64:

### TABLE XI

*National Incomes*
(1958–64)
(1958 = 100)

|  | 1958 | 1960 | 1962 | 1964 |
|---|---|---|---|---|
| World . . . . . . . | 100 | 113 | 124 | 137 |
| Economically developed nations . | 100 | 111 | 121 | 134 |
| USSR and Eastern Europe . . | 100 | 116 | 130 | 146 |
| Developing nations . . . . | 100 | 110 | 119 | 124 |

Source: *UN Statistical Yearbook.*

Thus, for the world as a whole, there was an increase in total production of 37% during this period of six years—the greatest average increase per year in the history of the world. Though the developing nations increased their total output by 24% during this same period, this meant in fact that they fell still farther behind the rest of the world, for they registered not only a smaller proportionate increase but also a smaller percentage of a smaller amount.

During the 1950s, Great Britain, the United States, Canada, Australia and Belgium all experienced annual rates of growth of less than 3%, and, although in the case of Great Britain this was a faster rate of growth than this country had previously experienced, much

### TABLE XII

*Rates of Economic Growth*
(1950–60)

| Country | Average rate per annum % | Average rate of increase per head % |
|---|---|---|
| Japan . . . | 9·1 | 8·0 |
| Germany . . . | 7·9 | 6·7 |
| Italy . . . | 5·6 | 5·0 |
| France . . . | 4·5 | 3·6 |
| Sweden . . . | 3·3 | 2·6 |
| United Kingdom . | 2·8 | 2·4 |
| Australia . . . | 1·8 | 1·4 |
| United States . . | 1·7 | 1·3 |
| Canada . . . | 1·0 | 0·7 |

Source: *UN National Accounts Statistics Yearbook.*

greater rates were enjoyed by Germany, France and Japan. Table
XII shows the rates of growth of a number of countries during 1950–
60. Thus, although during this period the growth rate of the United
Kingdom was well below that of some European countries, it was
relatively high as compared with the United States and the more
economically advanced Commonwealth countries. There is general
agreement too that Great Britain's rate of economic growth in the
1950s and 1960s has been good by historical standards, *i.e.* by comparison with its own growth rates in the past (*see* above, p. 18).

At the time the high rates of growth of countries such as Germany,
France and Japan were thought to be due to the fact that output in
those countries had been reduced to very low levels as a result of the
Second World War. However, even after they had recovered from
the effects of the war they still continued to maintain high rates of
growth during the early 1960s. Table XIII shows the rate of economic

TABLE XIII

*Rates of Economic Growth*
(1960–65)

| Country | Average rate per year % | Average per head % |
|---|---|---|
| Japan | 10·8 | 9·7 |
| Italy | 5·7 | 5·0 |
| France | 5·4 | 3·8 |
| Sweden | 5·3 | 4·7 |
| Germany | 4·9 | 3·5 |
| United States | 4·3 | 2·7 |
| Canada | 5·1 | 3·2 |
| United Kingdom | 3·4 | 2·6 |
| Australia | 2·9 | 2·4 |

Source: *UN National Accounts Statistics Yearbook.*

growth during 1960–65 for the same group of countries. The same
countries as had held the lead during 1952–59 were still at the top of
the table in 1965, though differences in rates of growth were less than
in the earlier period. All those on the lower rungs of the ladder
showed some improvement, stimulated, no doubt, by the success of
those above them, the increased growth rate in the United States
(5¾% in 1965) being probably due to the greater use of automation in
that country since 1960. Over the whole period, however, though far
behind Germany and France, the United Kingdom showed a higher
rate of economic growth than the United States, Canada or Australia.
Figure I (p. 29) shows the relative rates of growth of these countries.

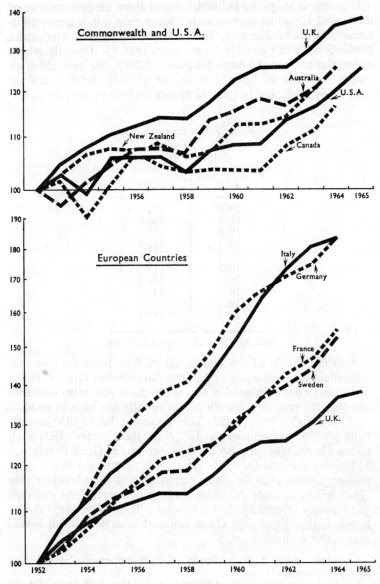

FIG. 1.—Growth Rates
(Gross National Product per head at constant market prices—1952=100)

Reproduced by kind permission of the editor of *Lloyds Bank Review*.

## Industrial production

If growth is judged by industrial output alone the performance of the United Kingdom appears rather better than if it is measured in terms of the national income. Table XIV shows the index of industrial production for this country for the years 1958–65. Over the whole period this averages an annual increase of 3·9% per year although output increased by fits and starts, in 1959–60 by 7% and in 1963–64 by 7·7%, but in 1960–61 and in 1965–66 by only 1·1%.

TABLE XIV
*Index of Industrial Production*
*United Kingdom*
(1958 = 100)

| Year | Index |
|------|-------|
| 1958 | 100   |
| 1959 | 105·1 |
| 1960 | 112·5 |
| 1961 | 113·9 |
| 1962 | 115·1 |
| 1963 | 119·0 |
| 1964 | 128·2 |
| 1965 | 131·9 |
| 1966 | 133·4 |
| 1967 | 133·3 |

Source: *Annual Abstract of Statistics.*

A small minority of economists, indeed, have taken the view that one cannot tell from a study of growth rates whether Great Britain's performance has been good or bad as compared with other countries and that the economic growth of this country has been as good as could reasonably be expected. They point out that in 1950 productivity per head in Germany was 13% *below* that country's 1938 level, whereas in the same year productivity per head in Great Britain was 13% *above* the level for 1938. Again, it is pointed out that if comparison is made over the whole period 1938–60 the advantage over Great Britain of many countries tends to disappear,[1] but this view was strongly refuted by A. Maddison.[2] There seems little doubt, however, that since 1960 Great Britain has tended to fall behind many other countries.

[1] J. Knapp and K. Lomax: "Britain's Growth Performance." *Lloyds Bank Review* (October 1964).
[2] A. Maddison: "How Fast Can Britain Grow?" *Lloyds Bank Review* (January 1966).

## The effect of the "stop–go" policy

One of the complaints of those who favoured more rapid economic growth was the "stop–go" policies of British governments since 1950, *i.e.* alternating policies of credit expansion and contraction. Two consequences of full (or over-full) employment impede growth. In the first place it provides conditions favourable to inflation. This results in an expanding demand for imports of both food and raw materials for a country such as Great Britain which is compelled to import most of these things, and so in the second place creates difficulties with the country's balance of payments, the problem being further aggravated by sterling's role as an international currency. Periods of over-full employment (a condition where the number of unfilled vacancies exceeds the number of people who are unemployed), with wages and prices rising rapidly, have generally culminated in imbalance in the balance of payments and often a run on sterling. Whether they liked it or not, governments have then been compelled to adopt a restrictive policy, sometimes accompanied by attempts to curb rising wages, the effect of which has been a temporary loss of full employment and a fall in production. Fear of the political consequences of failure to maintain full employment has generally led too soon to a reversal of a disinflationary policy with renewed encouragement for inflation followed by a new crisis within a few years' time. In an attempt to rid the economy of inflation once for all the Chancellor of the Exchequer during 1962–63 carried out a more severe deflationary policy than any of his predecessors had dared to do, with the result that production fell while unemployment reached its highest level for fifteen years. In these conditions of "stop–go" a low rate of economic growth was inevitable.

The reflation that followed growth was for a time given priority over protection against inflation, and in the hope of expanding production more rapidly things during 1963–64 were allowed to proceed unchecked until a stage was reached when drastic deflation was required. Even so a growth rate of only 2·6% was achieved. Failure to act quickly and to a sufficient degree in 1964 then led to further runs on sterling so that in the July measures of 1966 inevitably an even more severe deflationary policy than that of 1962–63 had to be imposed. The result was a growth rate in 1966 of less than 1%. By 1967 it was clear that the rate of growth envisaged in the National Plan could not be achieved. Then in November 1967 came the long-expected devaluation of sterling, followed in January 1968 by further measures to restrain consumers' demand, and on this occasion accompanied also by severe cuts in Government expenditure. In these circumstances a high rate of economic growth appeared unlikely to be achieved in the immediate future. A report in *Economic*

*Outlook*, published in January 1968 by the Organisation for Economic Co-operation and Development (OECD), considered that a growth rate of 3% was as much as Great Britain could expect to achieve during 1968–70. Then in January 1968 the United States decided to rectify its balance of payments by reducing investment abroad, and this may well slow down economic expansion throughout the world.

### Efforts to improve the British rate of growth

British economists and politicians have been seriously concerned in recent years at the poor showing of Great Britain in what has come to be known as the "growth league table." Efforts, therefore, have been made to increase this country's rate of economic growth.

(*i*) *NEDC*. In 1961 the Government established the National Economic Development Council (NEDC)—generally known as "Neddy"—to undertake a measure of economic planning in order to increase Great Britain's rate of growth. The Council includes among its members representatives of the Government (including the Minister for Economic Affairs), private industry, the nationalised industries and the trade unions, together with two academic economists and the Director-General of the National Economic Development Office. Since 1964, when the Department of Economic Affairs was established, the NEDC has been under its jurisdiction. At its first meeting in March 1962 its objects were stated to be threefold:

"(*a*) To examine the economic performance of the nation with particular concern for plans for the future in both the private and public sectors of industry.

"(*b*) To consider together what are the obstacles to quicker growth, what can be done to improve efficiency and whether the best use is being made of our resources.

"(*c*) To seek agreement upon ways of improving economic performance, competitive power and efficiency; in other words, to increase the rate of sound growth."[1]

The Council took as its target a growth rate of 4% for the years 1961–66. To consider how different sectors of industry, public and private, could implement this policy a number of sub-committees ("Little Neddies") were set up for seventeen (later increased to twenty) industries. The NEDC quickly got to work and in 1963 produced two reports—*Growth of the United Kingdom Economy to 1966* and *Conditions Favourable to Faster Growth*.[1] In the first of these reports the Council particularly considered the implications of a 4% growth rate for manpower, investment and the requisite level of savings and the balance of payments.

[1] PEP *Growth of the United Kingdom Economy to 1966*, p. viii.

## Economic planning

In a free economy the planning of production is left entirely to individual producers, consumers' demand through the operation of the price mechanism determining what and how much shall be produced. In a fully planned economy, however, it is the State that decides. Even in cases where the maximum amount of freedom has been permitted to private enterprise, the State has found it necessary to impose restrictions to protect the well-being of the community. At the present day, communist countries favour the fully planned economy, while Great Britain and many other countries prefer to follow a "middleway," their "mixed" economies having both private and public sectors. The greatest degree of state planning was achieved in Great Britain during the two World Wars. After the First World War, State controls were dispensed with as quickly as possible; after the Second World War controls were removed more slowly and the public sector was expanded by the nationalisation of a number of industries. Since 1944 too the State has been responsible for the maintenance of full employment. No attempt, however, has been made in Great Britain to introduce overall planning of the economy. Nevertheless, realisation of this country's slow rate of economic growth as compared with many other nations and the adverse effects of "stop–go" policies made the British Government for the first time agree to a measure of economic planning in peacetime, for quite a small difference in the percentage rates of economic growth of two countries will eventually produce a wide gap between them if this difference continues compound for long. Perhaps the example of France was an inducement, that country having adopted since 1946 a greater degree of central planning than any other country pursuing the "middle way."

Thus, it was a Conservative government that set up the National Economic Development Council in 1962, the first step towards greater state planning in Great Britain, the main function of this body being to consider and report to the Treasury whether a greater rate of economic growth was possible. The Labour Party was more strongly inclined towards state planning and on its accession to power in 1964 two new ministerial departments were created to assist towards this end: (i) the Department of Economic Affairs to take over some of the functions previously belonging to the Treasury; and (ii) the Ministry of Technology to be responsible for matters related to economic progress with special interests in scientific and industrial research and in machine tools, computers and electronics. The Department of Economic Affairs is primarily concerned with economic growth and economic planning. To assist economic growth and promote a more balanced economy a higher level of employment and production in the development areas was aimed at, the unemployment rate for these regions being much higher than for the rest of the country (*see* Chapter VII). The first task of this department was to draw up the National Plan. Thus, economic planning became the main responsibility of a government department instead of a government-sponsored body, though the work was largely undertaken by the same staff, who were transferred from the National Economic Department Office to the new Department of Economic Affairs. The Minister became chairman of the NEDC, which became an integral part of the department. Thus, continuity was maintained and the NEDC's report for 1961–66 was followed in due course by the National Plan for 1965–70. These two documents were remarkably similar to one another in their surveys of the British economy and in their recommendations. Whereas, however, the NEDC report had attracted little public attention, the National Plan was announced as a major item of government policy with the promise of a higher standard of living as the reward for supporting it.

The NEDC, the Economic Development Committees (the "Little Neddies") and the newly established Regional Economic Planning Boards and Councils were to assist the carrying out of the plan with the Department of Economic Affairs checking progress. Thus, the report of the NEDC of 1963 was followed by the National Plan of 1965.

## The National Plan (1965)

The National Plan sets out the implications of a more rapid rate of economic growth and the problems to be overcome if this objective is to be achieved. As with the report of the NEDC much of the detail was obtained by direct enquiry of the industries concerned. The target set for economic growth was an increase in the gross national product of 25% by 1970 as compared with 1964, *i.e.* an annual compound rate of 3·8%—a somewhat lower rate than that set out in the NEDC report. At the same time the aim was to bring the balance of payments permanently into balance. The plan outlined the investment that would be required for each industry, the growth rate for each, and the changes that would have to be made in the distribution of labour between different industries.

It was calculated that to achieve a 25% expansion in the volume of production by 1970 an addition to the country's labour force of 800,000 workers would be required. Half of this total, it was believed, would be met by the increase in the working population which statistics of the distribution of population among the younger age groups showed might be expected, allowance being made for the probable raising of the school-leaving age. A further 200,000, it was hoped, might be drawn into employment in the development areas, and more women might be encouraged to go out to work and older people to stay at work longer. This would leave a shortfall of 200,000, and this would have to be made good by increased productivity. The NEDC report too had concluded that part of growth would have to come from an increase in the amount of labour available and part from an increase in productivity. Both the report and the plan suggested that more effective measures might be taken to help older workers to stay at work beyond the normal age of retirement. Both too stressed the need for greater mobility of labour, both occupationally and geographically, to meet the needs of a changing pattern of industry. The NEDC suggested that changes in the demand for labour might make an average of 200,000 workers per year redundant. The plan forecast that during the period 1965–70 the number of workers required in agriculture, mining, transport and textiles would fall by about 600,000, though this would be more than balanced by an increased demand for labour in manufacturing generally and in health and educational services. To increase occupational mobility of labour the plan proposed that more Industrial Training Boards should be set up and more Government Training Centres opened to retrain workers for new forms of employment, with compensation for those becoming redundant.

In industry, both the public and private sectors, management and workers, would have to strive to achieve greater efficiency. It would be necessary, according to the NEDC to increase output per worker more rapidly than ever before, though this was in keeping with the general trend of productivity, output per worker having increased by $1\frac{1}{2}\%$ per year during 1850–1914, by $2\%$ during 1945–55, by $2\frac{1}{2}\%$ during 1955–60 and by almost $3\%$ since 1960. To increase the rate to $3 \cdot 2\%$, therefore, seemed to be a reasonable expectation. Of the planned increase in the gross national product $20\%$ was expected to go to increased consumption and the remainder mainly to public and private investment.

The succession of financial crises which affected Great Britain during 1966–68 made the fulfilment of this carefully prepared and detailed national plan impossible. In 1968, therefore, the Department of Economic Affairs produced a revised and more flexible "assessment" of possible economic development for the period 1969–72 with more emphasis on policy than on the achievement of a specific target.

## VII. INFLUENCES ON ECONOMIC GROWTH

### Natural resources

The size of a country's national income depends on a number of things, but most of all on the quantity and quality of its stock of factors of production. A country may be rich or poor in natural resources. Until well into the nineteenth century the most important of these was coal—till then the main source of power—and before 1914 the countries with the largest national incomes were those with the greatest output of coal. The possession of other minerals only tended to emphasise the industrial preponderance of the coal producers. Agricultural production until fairly recently was almost solely dependent on climate and the fertility of the soil. During the past forty or fifty years, however, things have changed. New forms of power have been developed; raw materials can be imported; agriculture has been mechanised and problems of climate and soil have been surmounted or eased as a result of scientific research or by means of engineering projects such as irrigation schemes. As a result, several countries, as, for example, Norway and Switzerland, not particularly well endowed by nature have in recent years begun to make more rapid progress. Nevertheless, the people of those countries which historically were able to take the lead—Great Britain, the United States, Germany—are still in the forefront as regards their standard of living, even though the gap between them and later developers is now narrowing.

### Capital investment

The most important influence, so most people believe, on the total volume of production is the amount and efficiency of a country's stock of capital. Real capital investment played an important part in the emergence of the industrial economy from the agricultural. The history of the Industrial Revolution in Great Britain is largely a history of the development of new forms of capital. Investment increased productivity, but capital formation depends on saving, *i.e.* on the willingness of a people to forgo some present consumption in order to be able to enjoy greater consumption at some time in the future. In effect, this means being willing to tolerate a somewhat lower standard of living in the present for the sake of a much higher standard of living in the future. The lower a people's present standard of living, the greater, however, is the sacrifice involved in saving. How much people are prepared to save depends, as Lord Keynes showed, on their "propensity to save" and also, under free enterprise, on how keen is their desire for a better standard of living in the future. In a "mixed" economy the State will decide the saving and investment of the public sector, and in a fully planned economy such as that of the USSR it may compel the people currently to accept a low standard of living in order to maximise investment, as did the Russian Government in the 1920s and 1930s. State planning of production makes it possible to take a long-term view of the planning of investment. In programmes for economic growth, therefore, a good deal of attention is paid to the proportion of its national income a country devotes to capital formation. The following table shows the value of gross domestic capital formation for a number of countries in relation to their gross national products:

TABLE XV

*Gross Domestic Capital Formation*
(In terms of 1958 prices except for the USSR)

| Country | Unit | 1960 | | | 1964 | | |
|---|---|---|---|---|---|---|---|
| | | National income | Capital formation | | National income | Capital formation | |
| | | | | % | | | % |
| United Kingdom | £ million | 21,056 | 3,768 | 18 | 25,488 | 5,347 | 21 |
| United States | $ milliard | 511 | 84 | 16 | 639 | 99 | 16 |
| France | Frs. milliard | 288 | 54 | 19 | 355 | 76 | 21 |
| Germany | DM. milliard | 250 | 60 | 24 | 308 | 80 | 26 |
| Netherlands | Fl. million | 41,160 | 10,080 | 24 | 49,370 | 13,350 | 27 |
| Italy | Lit. milliard | 19,607 | 4,408 | 22 | 24,476 | 5,191 | 21 |
| Sweden | Kr. million | 60,902 | 13,285 | 22 | 75,085 | 7,128 | 23 |
| USSR | R. milliard | 145 | 25 | 17 | 182 | 29 | 16 |
| Japan | Yen milliard | 14,592 | 4,738 | 24 | 21,984 | 8,280 | 38 |

Sources: For the UK: *Blue Book on National Income and Expenditure.* For other countries: *UN Yearbook of National Accounts Statistics.*

There are some writers who believe that the role of investment in stimulating economic growth has been exaggerated, since, as the standard of living of a people rises, there is an increasing demand for services as compared with goods, and for the production of services a good deal less investment is generally required. This may be true but as the standard of living rises there is also an expanding demand for consumer durables, particularly motor cars and all the investment that goes with them—greater production capacity, roads, bridges, tunnels, service stations, hotels. Excessive expenditure on defence in relation to the size of the national income, of course, will be detrimental to investment.

The importance of investment in influencing the size of a country's national income has already been stressed. Table XV above shows gross domestic capital formation in the United Kingdom in 1960 to have comprised 18% and in 1964 21% of the national income. Though this compared favourably with both the United States and the USSR for these two years, and was very similar to the achievement of France, it was well below that of Germany (24 and 26%) and the Netherlands (24 and 27%) and considerably below that of Japan (24 and 38%). Although the United States added to its stock of capital only the same proportion of its national income as did the United Kingdom, the amount of capital equipment per worker in that country has been variously estimated at between one and a half and nearly two and a half times the amount per worker in this country. Indeed, during the past twenty years the percentage increase in output per man-hour has been less in Great Britain than in any other Western country. Whenever Great Britain has found it necessary to restrict credit it has invariably meant that investment has been cut, even though not always to quite the extent the Government originally intended. The National Plan of 1965 aimed at increasing investment by 38 % during 1965–70.

## The size of the working population

Since 1945 the growth in the population of the United Kingdom has been mainly concentrated in the lower and the higher age groups, as the following table shows:

TABLE XVI
*Working Population of the United Kingdom*

| Age groups | 1951 | | 1967 | |
| --- | --- | --- | --- | --- |
| | Total per age group | Actual working population | Total per age group | Actual working population |
| | Thousands | Thousands | Thousands | Thousands |
| To 15 | 11,960 | | 13,790 | |
| 16–64 | 33,294 | 23,228 | 34,469 | 25,916 |
| 65 and over | 5,071 | | 6,809 | |
| Total | 50,225 | | 55,068 | |

Although during 1951–67 the total population of the United Kingdom increased by 5 million there was an increase of only 1·17 million in the 16–64 age group. (In view of this fact the increase in investment calculated per head was much greater than its increase reckoned as a percentage of the national income.) In spite of this relatively small increase in the number of people of working age, there was an increase of 2¾ million in the actual working population, mainly as a result of more married women going out to work. Most of the countries that have had higher rates of economic growth than the United Kingdom have had larger increases in their working populations, although only in the United States does a greater proportion of women go out to work. During these years West Germany had the further advantage of a large influx of refugees from the East.

**Education**

The second report of the NEDC, also published in 1963, stressed three things, namely education, technical change and management, as being vital to a more rapid rate of growth:

"Economic growth is dependent upon a high and advancing level of education because of the improvements that education brings in human skills and the greater spread of knowledge" (NEDC: *Conditions Favourable to Faster Growth*).

Modern industry requires an increasing number of scientists and technologists and an expanding army of skilled workers, with a declining demand for the unskilled and semi-skilled. Investment, therefore, in educational building—universities, colleges of technology, schools—is equally important as investment in factories and industrial plant. This fact is now generally realised and in Great Britain since 1947 an increasing proportion of the national income has been devoted to education—$2 \cdot 3\%$ in 1947; $4 \cdot 9\%$ in 1964; $6 \cdot 3\%$ in 1967. The Government now also accepts responsibility for the training or retraining of adult workers who have been made redundant by changes of demand or technical change. Some people have put the blame for Great Britain's slow rate of economic growth on to its educational system, which until recently was inclined to pay insufficient attention to science and technology.

In the field of management, however, it is only quite recently that attention has been given in this country to education and training. Education for management was held back for a long time by the belief that managers were "born and not made," and, though it is true that a manager must possess certain innate qualities, it is nevertheless also true that the efficiency of managers can be increased through education in management studies. On the other hand, the importance of education for management has long been recognised in the United States, where a number of universities established business schools, a policy followed recently by several British universities.

All these things—natural resources, manpower and its quality, investment and technical progress and the quality of management—determine the size of a country's national income, but only if that country's resources are fully employed. Investment is necessary not only to increase future production but also to generate income which stimulates consumption and further investment (*see* Chapter VII).

**The stage of economic development**

A fifth influence on a country's economic growth is its stage of economic development. Great Britain is an example of a country with an advanced mature economy, with only 8% of its working population engaged in primary or extractive production (5% only in agriculture), 44% in secondary or manufacturing occupations and 48% in tertiary employment concerned with the provision of services. (In the United States no less than 60% of the working population is engaged in tertiary employment.) Less mature economies have a greater proportion of people employed in primary production. In 1966 India had 70% of the workers employed in agriculture, Japan over 30% and Italy 27%. As an economy matures more workers are drawn into secondary employment and later into tertiary occupations. Expansion of manufacturing output is a vital element in economic growth but as a country approaches economic maturity it becomes increasingly difficult to draw more labour from agriculture into manufacturing in order to increase manufacturing output. It is significant that the average annual rate of increase of manufacturing output during the ten years 1954–64 was only 2·6% for the United States and 3·2% for the United Kingdom, whereas for Japan it was 13·6%, for West Germany 7·3% and for France 5·6%.[1] Expansion of manufacturing output is generally accompanied by increasing returns to scale, whereas in tertiary occupations opportunities for economies of scale are rare. As already noted, West Germany's supply of labour was reinforced by large-scale immigration of labour of good quality, while the French economy was in process of maturing by the transfer of labour from agriculture to manufacturing industry. In 1938 44% of the working population of France had been employed on the land but by 1965 the proportion so employed had been reduced to 21%. Although in Great Britain the number of people enjoyed in agriculture fell from over a million in 1948 to less than half a million in 1965, this country can expect from this source little further gain to its labour force in manufacturing.

**Preference for leisure rather than further income**

When a certain standard of living has been reached a people may prefer to do less work in order to have more time to engage in enjoyable pursuits. In countries with pleasant sunny climates this stage may be reached at a relatively low standard of living and, provided there is no shortage of food, basking in the sun for long periods every day may yield more happiness than possessing a greater quantity of material things. However, if an easier life is preferred it must be clearly understood that this may mean the acceptance of a lower standard of living than that enjoyed by neighbouring peoples. The fact that British workers appear to expect their real wages to continue to rise regularly seems to indicate that they do want a higher standard of living, and indeed, there are some who will

[1] *UN National Accounts Statistics Yearbook,*

even sacrifice what little leisure they have in order to earn more through overtime. It certainly, therefore, seems economically desirable to accelerate economic growth and raise the general standard of living in terms of real income per head as rapidly as is reasonably possible, but this is not necessarily a desirable thing if it means working such long hours that little opportunity is left to enjoy a higher standard of living.

## Attitude of mind

In Great Britain, in spite of the desire for a higher standard of living, there is a tendency among some sections of the community to look down on money-making, and even to sneer at economics as being "merely a matter of £ s. d." The fact appears to be overlooked that, whatever cultural or aesthetic interests one may have, these are easier to indulge if one has a high rather than low income. Business managers too are said to be held in higher esteem in the United States than in Great Britain. To achieve a more rapid rate of growth in this country may, therefore, require a new attitude of mind to the problem.

## The persistence of over-full employment

Table XVII shows unemployment rates in a number of countries

TABLE XVII

*Unemployment Rates (%)*

|  | 1956 | 1958 | 1960 | 1962 | 1964 |
|---|---|---|---|---|---|
| United Kingdom . | 1·3 | 2·2 | 1·7 | 2·1 | 1·8 |
| United States    . | 4·2 | 6·8 | 5·6 | 5·6 | 5·2 |
| Germany   .      . | 4·0 | 3·5 | 1·2 | 0·7 | 0·7 |
| Italy  .     .      . | 9·4 | 6·6 | 4·2 | 3·0 | 2·7 |
| Netherlands    . | 0·9 | 2·3 | 1·2 | 0·8 | 0·8 |
| Japan .    .      . | 1·7 | 1·4 | 1·1 | 0·9 | 0·8 |

Source: *UN Statistical Yearbook.*

during the period 1956–64. The most striking fact shown by this table is the difference between the unemployment rates for the United Kingdom, where over-full employment has been the rule and shortage of labour a constant problem, and the United States, where for most of the time there has been rather less than full employment.[1] The case of Germany is interesting as showing that shortages of Labour have occurred only since 1960. Not only has over-full

[1] The different methods of calculation adopted in the two countries, however, exaggerate the difference.

employment an adverse effect on mobility of labour and a tendency to encourage firms to hoard labour, but it puts trade unions in an over-strong bargaining position and thereby helps to keep in motion the wages–prices spiral. This, however, is in sharp contrast to experience in West Germany, where the trade unions adopted a more restrained attitude and wage increases have been kept more in line with the rate of expansion of production. In France, too, after that country's entry into the European Common Market, inflation was better kept in check than it was in Great Britain.

## The balance of payments and economic growth

The inadequacy of Great Britain's reserves and the use of sterling as an international currency have meant that very often a deficit in the balance of payments, due to a rapid expansion of demand, has brought on a run on sterling and a crisis that had to be met by a policy of credit restriction which resulted in a curtailment of output. France was able—though only for a time—to ignore its balance of payments in order not to check economic growth, but when Great Britain tried this policy in 1963–64 it eventually led to the most serious sterling crisis for over a quarter of a century. The explanation, of course, lies in the fact that the French franc, not being an international currency like sterling, is less subject to world monetary influences. It has been suggested too that in view of the precarious position of this country's balance of payments too much capital has been exported. The *Finance Act* of 1965, however, attempted to check it. The United States, too, in 1968 found it necessary to discourage the export of capital. In the long term the export of capital is advantageous to a country's balance of payments in yielding "invisible" income, as Great Britain found before 1914, but in the short run it can only increase a country's difficulties on international account unless its balance of payments is in permanent surplus.

## Planning and economic growth

Until quite recently Great Britain made no effort either to plan for economic growth or even to take deliberate action to encourage it. A study, published by PEP[1] in 1960, considered the causes of economic growth, but it was not until 1963 that the British Government began to take an interest in the subject. In that year the newly established National Economic Development Council made a serious study of the British economy's capacity for growth. Then in 1965 came the National Plan, but no sooner had it been published than the Government found it necessary to embark on the most severe policy of restraint as yet imposed, and by January 1967 it reluctantly had to

[1] *Growth in the British Economy*, a report of a project undertaken by PEP (Political and Economic Planning) (George Allen & Unwin).

admit that the plan could not be fulfilled. France had decided on planned economic growth as long ago as 1945, when the French Government established the Commissariat au Plan. The first plan covered the period 1947–50 and the fourth was for the years 1961–65. Those who favour state planning of production attribute the economic progress of France in recent years largely to planning. On the other hand, West Germany while pursuing a policy of free enterprise was even more successful, so much so that its achievement came to be referred to as the "German miracle."

RECOMMENDATIONS FOR FURTHER READING

R. and G. Stone: *National Income and Expenditure* (Bowes & Bowes).
PEP: *Growth in the British Economy* (George Allen & Unwin).
N. Kaldor: *Causes of the Slow Rate of Economic Growth of the United Kingdom* (Cambridge inaugural lecture).
HMSO: *The National Plan* (1965).
NEDC: *Growth of the United Kingdom Economy to 1966.*
NEDC: *Conditions Favourable to Faster Growth* (1963).
J. K. Galbraith: *The Affluent Society* (Hamish Hamilton).
*If available:*
Luc de Nanteuil: "Planning in France." *District Bank Review* (December 1963).
J. Knapp and K. Lomax: "Britain's Growth Performance." *Lloyds Bank Review* (October 1964).
A. Maddison: "How Fast Can Britain Grow?" *Lloyds Bank Review* (January 1966).

QUESTIONS

1. Why do governments at the present time pay so much attention to the national income and the rate of economic growth?

2. What do you understand by the standard of living of a people? How can governments influence the standard of living?

3. Consider the main difficulties to be overcome if comparison is to be made of the standard of living (*a*) of a people at different periods of time, and (*b*) of different peoples at the same period of time.

4. What are the main influences that determine a country's rate of economic growth?

5. "By selecting an unique target growth rate, the authors of the National Plan do more to conceal the economic problem—choice—than they do to clarify it." Discuss. (Degree.)

6. Poor countries typically have a high proportion of their working population in agriculture: rich countries have a high proportion in industry. Should poor countries that want to become richer, then, deliberately accelerate their industrialisation? (Degree.)

7. "It is more important to increase the size of the national income than to worry about redistributing it."

Consider this statement. Are these two objectives incompatible? (Barnsley.)

8. Is economic growth best achieved through national planning? (Birmingham.)

9. "Gross national product is not an ideal measure of economic welfare." Discuss the shortcomings of gross national product as a measure of output. (Leeds.)

10. Present government economic policy faces a conflict of interest between short-term "stop-and-go" and long-term planning for growth. Explain, with examples, why this is so. (Liverpool.)

11. In what sense, if any, was the National Plan a "plan"? (Manchester.)

12. Discuss the ways in which the government of a country whose economic system is based on free enterprise can stimulate economic growth. (Manchester.)

13. Consider the possibility that the standard of living in the United Kingdom might be doubled by 1985. (Northern Counties.)

14. Since 1961 all British governments have given increased importance to economic planning. Account for this. (Northern Counties.)

15. Describe in detail one method of measuring the net national income of a community. Discuss any problems involved and any inadequacies in the result obtained. (Sheffield.)

16. What are Regional Economic Planning Councils and Regional Economic Planning Boards? What contribution are such bodies expected to make that cannot be made by local authorities or government departments? (U.L.C.I.)

## CHAPTER II

# LOCATION OF INDUSTRY

## *I. BEFORE 1914*

### The trend towards localisation

The location of some industries has always been restricted by geographical and geological considerations over which Man has had little or no control. The mining of minerals clearly can be undertaken only in districts where they are to be found. The composition of the soil, range of temperature and distribution of rainfall restrict certain kinds of farming to particular areas. For a long time transport difficulties also restricted the location of manufacturing industries, the processing of raw materials into manufactured goods of necessity having to be carried out close to where the raw materials were found. In early days food supplies were a vital influence on the location of settlements when each small area had to rely on its own efforts to supply its needs. Some degree of specialisation, therefore, was imposed even on primitive self-contained communities by differences in geography and geology. Since at best opportunities for exchange were limited production was almost entirely for the community itself.

For a long time many manufacturing industries were widely dispersed because the raw materials they required were widely dispersed. Thus, wool was spun and cloth woven wherever sheep could be reared, so that in medieval England the woollen industry was carried on in most parts of the country, though the production of the better-quality cloths was restricted to the areas which were more favourably situated.

There could be little competition between different producing areas until transport facilities had been improved. Transport made possible the localisation of industry. Only when commodities could be distributed from their places of production to other regions did it become possible to concentrate production in those areas where goods could be produced most cheaply.

The primary influence on localisation of industry was economic— the cost of production—and this remained so until recent times when this problem first attracted government attention and planned location of industry was introduced. Other factors affecting location of industry all make their influence felt by reducing costs of production in one place more than another. For example, the introduction of water power followed by steam power in the eighteenth century made the production of woollen goods so much cheaper in districts having easy access to these forms of power (after allowing for the cost of transport) that the industry died out in areas that lacked these advantages. Once this stage of development has been reached new firms will set up in the regions where their costs of production will be lowest, and so the industry becomes localised.

### Early influences on localisation

Before 1914 there were strong influences making for localisation of industry. For over a hundred and fifty years the main influence on location of industry was the cost of power. For the greater part of this period coal was the main source of power, and coal was an expensive commodity to transport. Consequently, since coal could be obtained most cheaply near the places where it was mined, industry was attracted to the coalfields. Thus, at the beginning of the twentieth century, all heavy industries and many light industries too were concentrated on the coalfields.

It has already been noted that before the Industrial Revolution the main locating influence was nearness to supplies of raw materials. The importance of coal after the introduction of power-driven machinery lessened the effect of nearness to raw materials except where they formed a high proportion of the total costs of production of a commodity. For example, in iron smelting, nearness to coal outweighed nearness to iron ore because at one time so much more coal was required to smelt iron ore. Changes in the technique of production in recent times have increased the locating influence of iron ore and led to the industrial development of Scunthorpe and Corby. Where raw materials were found near coal this would determine the local industry, as, for example, cutlery manufacture in Sheffield, pottery making in North Staffordshire, the woollen industry in the West Riding of Yorkshire, the iron and steel industry of North-East England and the Black Country, although in the case of most of these industries local supplies of raw materials had to be supplemented before long by supplies from elsewhere.

There are numerous other influences which in varying degrees affected the location of industry in the period before the First World War. Although nearness to power—at first water, then coal—was the principal locating factor for both the cotton and woollen industries, the humidity of the atmosphere of North-West England and nearness to the main port for the imported raw material were other factors that led to the establishment of the cotton industry in Lancashire.

The presence of soft water in the Pennines was of particular advantage to the wool textile industry. Nearness to a supply of water is also important to the chemical industry. Once an industry has become thoroughly established a reservoir of suitable labour begins to develop and this in itself tends to attract new firms to the district. All these influences on location were primarily economic. Industries had to be established where their costs of production were lowest. Though conditions may change, an industry may remain in its original location as a result of geographical inertia, especially if heavy investment has been incurred in fixed capital. Sometimes historical accident may influence the location of an industry, as in the case of the pottery industry in North Staffordshire, though both power and raw material were available in the locality.

### Advantages of localisation

External economies of scale result from the concentration of an industry in a particular area.

The most important of these economies is the greater degree of division of labour that regional specialisation makes possible. Division of labour within the firm, with each worker specialising in a single process, results in a great expansion of output and a lowering of costs of production. Regional division of labour became possible where firms were near enough to one another to enable them to specialise in single processes. Partly finished goods could then be passed on from one firm to another for the next process to be undertaken. The textile industries provided the best examples of regional division of labour. In the cotton industry the two main processes became regionally specialised; the spinning process came to be centred in south-east Lancashire with weaving mainly carried on in the north-east of the county in the Preston–Burnley district. Specialisation of process by firms became a characteristic of the worsted section of the wool textile industry, with separate firms engaged in scouring, combing, spinning, weaving and dyeing. In the wool textile industry there was also regional specialisation of the finished product with fine worsteds in Huddersfield, woollens in Colne Valley, carpets in the Halifax district and heavy woollens in the Wakefield–Dewsbury–Batley area.

Reference has already been made to the existence of a suitable labour supply as an influence making for localisation. This is clearly also a further advantage of regional specialisation. In days when it was common practice for boys to follow in their fathers' footsteps, it was easier for them to acquire the skills required for the local industry than for a totally different form of employment, and this contributed to make the labour in the area of a localised industry more suitable than other labour for that particular industry. With the increasing use of machinery, however, such special skills became of less importance.

Another advantage of regional specialisation is the development of industries subsidiary to the main industry of the district. The manufacture of the specialised machinery for localised industries generally takes place in or near these industries. Thus, machinery for the cotton industry is manufactured in Manchester, for the woollen industry in Huddersfield and Halifax, for the boot and shoe industry in Leicester, and so on. Farming implements are often manufactured in the larger market towns in agricultural areas. Dyeing, including the manufacture of dyes, is carried on in the West Riding and calico printing in south Lancashire. Most accessories for motor cars are manufactured in the areas where the motor cars themselves are produced. The presence of these subsidiary industries in the same localities as the main industries helps to reduce their costs of production.

Where industries are highly localised other services for the main industry will often be found in the same district. For example, highly organised commodity markets may be established. Thus, there are cotton exchanges in Manchester[1] and Liverpool, and a wool exchange in Bradford, though most commodity markets are situated in London (including the principal wool market). Specialised financial services, too, may be developed and bank managers with an intimate knowledge of the local industry are better able to appreciate the problems of local businessmen. Specialised educational facilities also can be provided at local universities, polytechnics and technical colleges where localised industries provide them with a large enough reservoir of students. A close link often exists between these institutions and local industry. All these things are to the advantage of the main industry.

### Disadvantages of localisation

In spite of the many advantages that accrue to a highly localised industry, localisation can have very serious disadvantages. This was seen in the Great Depression of 1929–35. The areas with localised industries suffered the highest levels of unemployment. Even if widespread unemployment resulting from a general trade depression now appears to be a thing of the past, the State since 1944 having been responsible for the maintenance of full employment, changes in demand—a feature of any progressive economy—can at any time affect any industry. If such an industry is highly localised this could result in mass unemployment in a particular locality even though the rest of the country was enjoying full employment. Any situation which adversely affects the demand for the products of the main industry will affect also the subsidiary industries of the area, and the

[1] Closed in 1968.

fall in the purchasing power of these workers will also reduce the incomes of providers of retail and other services.

Thus, even if full employment is generally maintained, unemployment resulting from a change of demand is likely from time to time to affect different industries. At any particular time in a progressive economy there will be some industries that are declining even though most industries are expanding, and the consequences will be more serious if the declining industry is highly localised. If, on the other hand, an industry is widely dispersed, a contraction of the declining industry can take place without causing widespread unemployment, and those thrown out of work can be more easily absorbed into the expanding industries of the area. The more varied the industries of an area, i.e. the less localised a country's industries are, the less serious a problem becomes structural unemployment due to change of demand.

## II. BETWEEN THE WARS (1919–39)

### The new industries

A feature of the period between the two World Wars was the decline in the importance of coal as a localising influence on industry. The old-established industries continued to be carried on near the coalfields, partly as a result of geographical inertia and partly because in the case of heavy industry the cost of power forms a large proportion of a firm's total costs, and for this kind of industry coal generally remained as the principal source of power. The period was characterised by a long and severe trade depression and the old-established industries in Great Britain were the ones most seriously affected. In such conditions there would be few new firms entering these industries, but those that did were drawn into the old centres because costs of production were lower there.

The new expanding industries were generally different in character from the older heavy, mainly capital-producing, industries. The new industries were mainly light, i.e. the cost of power formed only a small proportion of their total costs. In general, too, they were concerned with the production of consumers' goods. In spite of the Great Depression the general standard of living was higher than ever before and there was an expanding demand for consumers' goods. Apart from a few pharmaceutical products, there were few branded goods in 1900, but since that date there had been an enormous extension of branding to a wide range of products, particularly foodstuffs, such as fish, meat, vegetables, and household commodities, such as cleaning materials. These goods were intended primarily for the home market, though small quantities were exported, mainly to British overseas territories. In contrast the older industries exported a large proportion of their output.

The increasing use of electricity stimulated the production of electrical components and accessories of all kinds, and then after 1923 came an expanding demand for radio sets. Another expanding industry was the motor-car industry, producing both goods and passenger vehicles, and the private motor car was soon to become mainly a consumers' good, though an expensive one. Both these industries in time began to fill the gap in British exports caused by the decline in the exports of the older industries.

## New influences on location of industry

(i) *New forms of power.* Before 1914 coal was almost the only form of power; hence the main influence on industrial location was nearness to the coalfields. In the period between the two World Wars new forms of power came into use—gas, electricity and oil. Though the production in Great Britain of both gas and electricity was dependent on coal it was not necessary for either of them to be used near to where supplies of coal were available. Both could easily be transmitted farther afield. Their use as power for industry was, therefore, likely to have the effect of dispersing industry over the country rather than concentrating it in a limited number of areas. In most towns there was a supply of gas, and the development of the grid made electric power available over an even wider area. Though slightly cheaper at the ports, oil could be fairly easily distributed by rail and road to most parts of the country. Industrial concerns using any of these new forms of power were not restricted in their choice of location by the necessity to be near any particular source of supply as had been the case with coal.

Quite early in the twentieth century gas engines were used to drive machinery and this enabled industry for the first time in Great Britain to be carried on away from the coalfields, as happened with the manufacture of boots and shoes, which became a factory industry in Northamptonshire, a county completely lacking coal.

Between the two World Wars first electricity and later oil came to be used as power, both these being particularly suitable for the new light industries that developed during this period and making them independent of coal.

(ii) *New forms of transport.* Another new influence on industrial location was the development in transport that took place during this period. Localisation of industry could never have taken place without the vast improvement in transport—canals, roads, railways —that accompanied the improvement in manufacturing techniques during the Industrial Revolution. Not till near the end of the nineteenth century, however, was there much provision of suburban transport, and up to that time employees in the new factories and workshops were huddled together in dwellings built as close as possible to their place of employment.  Towards the end of the nineteenth century horse-drawn buses appeared on the streets of the larger cities, followed by horse-drawn buses or trams, and finally in the 1890s by electric trams.  In London and the larger conurbations the railways operated suburban services, and in London and Glasgow these were supplemented by underground lines.  The movement of goods, however, was limited to places served by the main-line railways, and factories with their own sidings were often built alongside the railways.

Then, in the 1920s and 1930s, came a return to the roads.  Buses began to compete with the trams and later with the railways, though they also developed a considerable amount of new traffic.  The expansion of road haulage brought a competitor for the railways for the carriage of goods.  Perhaps the most important development to influence industrial location was the growing practice of manufacturing firms of distributing their products in their own vans.  Besides generally being cheaper for both passengers and goods, road transport was more mobile than the railway.  Bus routes could be planned to meet particular needs, and manufacturers' vans could operate as easily from a small town with poor railway connections as from a good railway centre and could reach the village or suburban shop as easily as the retail establishments in town and city shopping centres.

By using electric power to drive the machinery in the factory and employing its own vans to distribute its product to wholesalers or retailers, a firm was no longer bound to one of the existing industrial areas.  These two new developments in power and transport, therefore, operated to disperse rather than to concentrate and localise industry.

## Population as a new localising influence

The new magnet for industry became the large centre of population.  Whereas during the early period of industrialisation people had been attracted to the new industrial centres, which therefore became more densely populated in consequence of their advantages to production, the situation was reversed for the new industries of the inter-war period.  Firms producing mainly for home consumpton found it to their advantage to be near large centres of population as these were the main markets for their products.  Not only was the London area the largest conurbation in the country but also it was the one least seriously affected by the inter-war Great Depression.  In these circumstances London and the South-East probably accounted for more than one-fifth of the entire home market.  Clearly, to be near London would reduce to a minimum the costs of a firm producing mainly for the home market, and London too was available as a port if required.

As a result the period between the two World Wars showed a reversal of the nineteenth-century tendency of population to drift to the coalfields of the Midlands and the North, and instead there was a trend towards the South-East, a movement encouraged by the uneven distribution of unemployment resulting from the Great Depression. South Wales, County Durham and South Lancashire all suffered a decline in the number of insured workers, to the extent of nearly 400,000 in ten years, some of them moving to the expanding industry of the Midlands, more seeking work in the South-East. As a result there was industrial development to the west of London out as far as Slough and also to the east in Essex.

## Uneven distribution of unemployment

The effects of the Great Depression were rendered more serious because the new industries became mainly located elsewhere. If they had established themselves in the old industrial areas instead of seeking new locations, the Great Depression would have been a little less severely felt. In the Midlands, for example, the expansion of the motor-car industry offset the effects of the slump on the older industries of that region. The fact that over most of the country declining and expanding industries were located in different regions resulted in wide variations in the level of unemployment in different areas. Thus, whereas in the Home Counties unemployment among insured workers was as low as 5%, in South Wales, County Durham, West Cumberland, Clydeside and South Lancashire it reached 35% and even 75% in a few particular places such as Jarrow and Merthyr Tydfil.

## Government intervention

Often during the short trade depressions of the nineteenth century local authorities had undertaken public works—generally road building—to relieve distress. On the other hand, following the financial crisis of 1931, many road improvements, only partly completed at the time, were suspended in order to reduce the expenditure both of the State and of local authorities. It was not until 1944 that the State became responsible for the maintenance of full employment and accepted the principle that it must undertake investment—if necessary at the cost of a budget deficit—whenever necessary in order to achieve this objective. Direct state intervention of this kind to get rid of unemployment was contrary to the economic thinking that prevailed down to the 1930s.

The uneven distribution of unemployment during the Great Depression, however, did make the Government believe that something might be done to reduce unemployment in those areas where it was particularly severe. Though the drift of population away from these areas was not on a large scale it was feared that, among younger people at least, it might increase. There was thus a real danger that those parts of the country most severely affected by the Great Depression might become derelict areas with a consequent waste of the social capital—public buildings, schools, public utilities, etc.—that had been invested in them.

In 1934 the *Special Areas (Development and Improvement) Act* was passed. Four areas where there was heavy unemployment, previously known as "distressed" areas, were designated Special Areas. The Act enabled local authorities to obtain financial assistance from the State for public works they were prepared to initiate, and also attempted to make labour more mobile, both occupationally and geographically, through retraining schemes and by assisting removal to another area. Thus, the Act did little more than give a mild degree of support and encouragement to what was already being done—even to the extent of encouraging existing tendencies that were likely to result in congestion and overcrowding in the South-East and the creation of derelict areas elsewhere. However, few of the older workers were willing to move, even though many of them had been continuously unemployed for long periods.

It was, therefore, for these reasons that in 1936 a second Act was passed—the first attempt of any British Government to influence location of industry—the aim being to encourage new firms to set up in the Special Areas. This was done by the State establishing Trading Estates in the various Special Areas and then offering to firms willing to set up there inducements such as low rents, relief of rates and taxes, loans on favourable terms, etc., the Government itself undertaking the task of retraining labour for them. In a time when many firms even in the most favourable locations were finding it difficult to pay their way it was not possible for the Government to apply any sort of compulsion with regard to the location of new firms. In the conditions of the time anyone prepared to employ labour *anywhere* was to be welcomed. No firm would go to a Special Area if it considered that, in spite of the concessions, its costs of production would be higher there than elsewhere. The Government's rearmament programme begun in 1937 enabled it to place orders with firms in the Special Areas and after the outbreak of war in 1939 this policy was extended by the erection of state-owned armaments factories in those areas. It is impossible to say how successful the Government's scheme would have been if war and preparation for war had not ultimately brought a revival to the Special Areas. The point to note is that the revival was almost entirely due to the recovery of the old heavy industry of these areas and not to the new industry that had been tempted to go there.

## III. PLANNED LOCATION OF INDUSTRY

### The Barlow Report (1940)

The Acts of 1934 and 1936 had given some indication of governmental ideas in the 1930s regarding location of industry. Then in 1940 the Barlow Report was published. It was the report of a Royal Commission appointed in 1937 to enquire into the distribution of industry and population in Great Britain. It showed that two-fifths of the population of this country lived in seven large conurbations, London being the largest, but the smallest having over a million inhabitants. The Commission considered that these "sprawling agglomerations of humanity" could adversely affect the economic and social life and development of the country. In the case of localised industries they tended to concentrate unemployment in times of trade depressions, and they produced city congestion. In addition it was feared that these great conurbations might have serious strategic consequences, a point emphasised by the fact that the Commission's deliberations took place on the eve of a great war during which it was expected that the bombing of large cities would be the strategy of all contestants. Densely populated areas were condemned, therefore, on both social and strategic grounds.

The Commission considered that the situation could be remedied only be government action. It recommended, therefore, that the Government should make itself responsible for planning the location of industry and that further expansion of London should be checked and possibly its population reduced by the building of a ring of new towns on the outer fringe of the capital, but separated from it by "green belts."

### Government policy

The outbreak of war postponed any serious attempt at state planning of location of industry, though during the war the Government itself built over a hundred new factories in the Special Areas. In 1944, towards the end of the war, the Government issued its White Paper on employment policy which not only indicated the State's acceptance of responsibility for the maintenance of full employment but also implied that the carrying out of this policy required a more balanced distribution of industry which could be achieved only by state planning of industrial location. Lord Beveridge's book *Full Employment in a Free Society* appeared soon afterwards. Controlled location of industry was regarded by Lord Beveridge as one of the essential conditions for the maintenance of full employment. Thus, the main purpose of planned location of industry was to reduce the effects of structural unemployment due to changes of demand which, even in conditions of full employment, could produce pockets of heavy unemployment where declining industries were highly localised.

The Government's aim, therefore, was to give greater diversification of production to areas with highly localised industries. This meant that new firms in expanding industries should be encouraged (compulsion was not contemplated) to go to those areas where the basic industry was declining. A decline in the demand for its products becomes less serious to an industry that is widely dispersed than to one that is localised, since this spreads the resulting structural unemployment more widely and those who have lost their jobs can more easily be absorbed into the other industries of the area. Socially this policy was regarded as being preferable to organising large-scale migrations of labour from the declining localised industries to the newer expanding industries, since it would prevent the development of derelict areas. Some migration of labour, however, cannot be avoided and may be necessary for economic progress. A coal mine may become uneconomic to operate and it is clearly preferable to transfer the miners to coal mines in other areas where there may be a shortage of suitable labour than to attempt to find alternative employment for the displaced miners in their own area. Where this has occurred the National Coal Board has given financial assistance to those workers who have agreed to transfer to other districts.

In general, the aim of planned location of industry has been to discourage the migration of workers. In other words, the policy has been one of "taking work to the worker" rather than of "taking the worker to where there is work." It should not be forgotten, however, that when new firms are left to themselves to select the sites for their factories they are guided almost entirely by economic motives, *i.e.* they will go where they think their costs of production will be lowest. After all, regional specialisation and localisation of industry were brought about on account of the economic advantages associated with them. Thus, government policy, by encouraging them to go elsewhere, is putting what it regards as the social good before economic considerations.

Diversification could best be applied to new industries, for which generally there were not outstanding advantages of regional division of labour. Some degree of diversification might be possible in the case of an older industry such as the wool textile industry; but the old heavy industries, some of which were declining, would have to remain in their original locations both for geographical reasons and on account of the large amount of capital involved. Complete diversification of industry, therefore, was not possible.

## The Development Areas

Having accepted Lord Beveridge's contention that planned location of industry was an essential condition for the maintenance of full employment, the British Government followed up its acceptance of responsibility for full employment by passing the *Distribution of Industry Act* in 1945.

In effect this was a continuation of the policy first laid down in the Acts of 1934 and 1936 on a rather more ambitious scale. The Special Areas were replaced by Development Areas which were generally wider in extent, and, unlike the Special Areas, included the large towns of the regions. It was to these parts of the country that the Government would attempt to steer new industries. There was, however, a very important difference between economic conditions in these areas in 1934–36 and those in 1945. In the 1930s they were all areas of heavy unemployment with their basic industries severely depressed; in 1945 there was full employment in these areas and their industries, revived by six years of war, were among the most prosperous in the country. Nevertheless, it was widely thought that unless the Government acted in time a post-war slump would occur again as after the First World War.

Under the Act of 1945 four Development Areas were designated, two more being added in 1946, a further two in 1948, and one more in 1953, making a total of eleven:

(*i*) The North-East, comprising most of County Durham together with neighbouring portions of Northumberland (mainly Tyneside and the coal-mining area) and the North Riding of Yorkshire (mainly Tees-side), and including the towns of Newcastle upon Tyne, South Shields, Sunderland, Darlington and Middlesbrough.

(*ii*) The West Cumberland coalfield, with the towns of Maryport, Workington and Whitehaven.

(*iii*) The South Wales and Monmouthshire coalfield, together with a small area round Milford Haven, and including the towns of Swansea, Cardiff and Newport.

(*iv*) The Clydeside and Lanarkshire industrial area in Scotland, together with the Dundee district.

(*v*) The South Lancashire coalfield, comprising the cotton-spinning industry, but excluding Manchester.

(*vi*) The Wrexham coalfield in North Wales.

(*vii*) Merseyside, where unemployment in 1948 was considerably above the national average.

(*viii*) North-East Scotland, mainly the area round Inverness and including the small towns of Dingwall, Tain and Invergordon. For a long time northern Scotland had suffered a drift of population to the south—mainly to the Lowlands of Scotland—and the aim was to check this movement by the development of a new industrial area based on hydro-electric power.

(*ix*) North-East Lancashire, the centre of the cotton-weaving industry, and including the towns of Burnley, Nelson and Colne.

The first four Development Areas in the above list were all extensions of the Special Areas created in the 1930s. All were centres of heavy industry and dependent on the coalfields for power. Areas (*v*) and (*ix*) were the seats of complementary industries and both suffered from the decline of the cotton industry, North-East Lancashire being even more dependent than South Lancashire on this industry. All the Development Areas except two—Merseyside and North-East Scotland were associated with coalfields. In the case of Merseyside it was heavy local unemployment and a lack of industry other than that associated with a port that led to its being designated a Development Area. In North-East Scotland (*ix*) the motive was not to prevent the decline of a previously important industrial area, but to develop a new one; nevertheless this was a policy consistent with the Government's general aim with regard to location of in-

A Inverness District
B Clydeside and Lanarkshire
C West Cumberland
D Durham and North East
E North-East Lancashire
F South Lancashire
G Merseyside
H Wrexham district
I South Wales and Monmouth

Fig. 2.—Development Areas (1945–60)

dustry, namely to achieve a more even distribution of population over the country as a whole.

## Factors favourable to planned location of industry

The attempt before 1939 to encourage new firms to set up in the Special Areas met with very little success. No form of compulsion, direct or indirect, could be applied; only financial inducements could be offered. If, in spite of these, greater advantages could be obtained elsewhere, a firm would not be willing to go to one of the Special Areas, and might have preferred not to set up at all rather than go where it feared its costs might be greater. In such a case, with unemployment at a very high level, the Government was glad for new firms to set up anywhere.

Conditions in 1945 were totally different. There was full employment and the former Special Areas were among the most prosperous parts of the country. After six years of war, during which the production of consumers' goods had been reduced to a bare minimum, there were shortages of all kinds of things in almost every home. Many of the people who had married during the war wanted both homes and all the things necessary to furnish them. Rationing of many things continued. During the war people had been encouraged to save, and they had done so as much because there was so little on which to spend their money as for patriotic reasons. Not only had savings been accumulated but the incomes of wage-earners were higher than ever before. Thus, there was a huge demand for all kinds of goods. For some time at least, manufacturers' profits were likely to be high, and firms, anxious to take advantage of this situation, were willing to accept whatever restrictions the Government might impose if only they could get into production quickly.

These conditions presented the Government with the opportunity it required to introduce planned location of industry. There were other circumstances, too, that contributed to greater success in 1945 than in 1934 and 1936:

(*i*) *Control of Investment.* During the war no new issues of shares had been permitted without the sanction of the Capital Issues Committee of the Bank of England first being obtained. An Act was passed in 1945 to continue this control, which remained in force until 1959. The aim was to control the demand for scarce real resources, so that projects regarded as being in the national interest could be given priority over other schemes. A permit to raise new capital thus became for a time a valuable privilege, and its award could be made conditional on new industrial premises being located in one of the Development Areas designated under the *Distribution of Industries Act.*

(*ii*) *Control of building.* Under the *Town and Country Planning Act* of 1947 an Industrial Development Certificate had to be obtained from the Board of Trade before new premises above a specified size (5,000 square feet) could be erected, and this certificate could usually be more readily obtained if it was required for a site in one of the Development Areas.

(*iii*) *The Supply of labour.* Over most of the country there was an acute shortage of labour. In the former Special Areas, however, there was often more women's and girls' labour available than elsewhere on account of the heavy character of the local industry. This was a further encouragement to many firms to set up in the Development Areas, or open new branches there. During the decade 1945–55 no fewer than 500 firms opened new branches in the Development Areas on account of shortage of labour in the places where they had originally established themselves. Even some firms enjoying external economies of large-scale production and the advantages of regional division of labour in highly localised industries, such as the wool textile industry of West Yorkshire, were impelled by shortage of labour to build new factories in Development Areas.

As a result, therefore, of government policy of planned location of industry, aided by the various circumstances of the time, a large number of new factories were established in the Development Areas, more than half the total number of new establishments being built during the first three post-war years, with a declining proportion during the ensuing seven years. When the post-war boom did not turn into a post-war depression as many people—both economists and politicians—had expected, the pressure on new firms to set up in the Development Areas lessened. From 1954 an Industrial Development Certificate was no longer required. As fewer new firms went to the Development Areas more began to set up in or near small towns in what were predominantly rural areas, such as Banbury and Buckingham, or in seaside resorts, or in places previously regarded as residential, such as Bedford, or in former inland spas such as Bath, Harrogate and Leamington. For industries relying on the newer forms of power—gas, electricity, oil—and road transport these places had most of the advantages of South-East England without the drawbacks of congestion, high rents and rates, with the likelihood of more labour being available. The effect of this development, together with the building of new towns (to be considered below) has been to spread industrial production and population more widely.

### The problem of regional unemployment

A recurrence of pockets of unemployment in the Development Areas during the 1950s and 1960s, even though over-full employment

was the general characteristic of the rest of the country, again
turned the Government's attention to the problem of regional unemployment. The policy of the immediate post-war years was revived and efforts were again directed towards encouraging firms to
go to those areas which were suffering some unemployment. The
Board of Trade, which since 1945 had been responsible for planned
location of industry, again made the award of Industrial Development
Certificates more readily available to those firms which were prepared
to go to the Development Areas.

The *Local Employment Act* of 1960 abolished the Development
Areas and replaced them by Development Districts. Many of the
new Development Districts were merely enlargements of former
Development Areas, but some entirely new districts were designated
(*e.g.* North-West Scotland, North Wales, Cornwall) and some
former areas were excluded (*e.g.* North-East and South Lancashire).
(See Fig. 3.) Any area in which unemployment had been in excess
of 4% for over a year became eligible to be designated as a Development District which then entitled it to receive financial assistance
from the Treasury.

The Act of 1960 empowered the Board of Trade to erect factories,

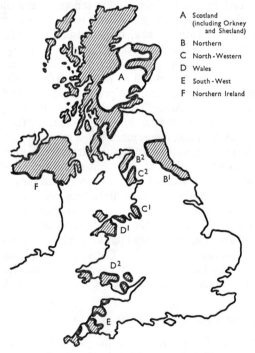

A   Scotland
    (including Orkney
    and Shetland)

B   Northern

C   North-Western

D   Wales

E   South-West

F   Northern Ireland

Fig. 3.—Development Districts (1960–66)

to recommend to the Treasury firms to which grants or loans might be given, and to assist workers who might be transferred to firms in these districts by paying part of their costs of removal. No firm was to erect premises in excess of 5,000 square feet unless it first obtained an Industrial Development Certificate, and this could be made conditional on a firm going to one of the Development Districts. The policy, therefore, was similar to the one pursued in connection with both the Special Areas and the Development Areas.

A further change was made in 1966 by the passing of the *Industrial Development Act*. This Act abolished the Development Districts and revived the Development Areas, most of the former Development Districts being absorbed into the new Development Areas. The Act of 1966 also provided increased grants and investment allowances for firms setting up in these areas. In the same year came further assistance with the introduction of the selective employment tax and the payment of premiums—30s. for men, 15s. for women and boys and 9s. 6d. for girls—to firms in these areas according to the number of their employees. When in 1967 the payment of these premiums to manufacturing firms was abolished, they were, however, to continue in the case of firms located in Development Areas.

FIG. 4.—The New Development Areas (1966)

From the first the Government's aim in supporting planned location of industry had been to reduce regional unemployment. When in the early 1950s there was little regional unemployment it appeared that planned location of industry might be dropped, but the return of regional unemployment in the late 1950s immediately brought about a revival of this policy on a more precise scale, the Development Districts often being much smaller than the former Development Areas.

### The policy of "taking work to the workers"

Throughout the whole period of planned location of industry—indeed, since 1936—the Government has shown a strong preference for the policy of "taking work to the workers," and has made no attempt to encourage workers to move to areas of over-full employment. The adoption of this policy is not entirely due to lack of mobility of labour, which is probably not nearly so geographically immobile as is generally thought. The movement of population away from the "distressed" areas to South-East England in the 1930s has already been considered. During the ten years to 1961 at least as many workers moved into South-East England from other parts of the country as during that earlier industrial depression. At the same time Scotland suffered a net decrease of 100,000 workers, the northern region 59,000, the North-West 43,000 and Wales 41,000. Actual movements of labour, however, were much greater than this, the North-West, for example, gaining 574,000 workers though losing 616,000. It has been estimated that the average movement of employees between other regions was no less than 450,000 a year. Of course, in addition, there was also considerable movement within each region.[1] The extent of occupational mobility is shown by the decline during 1955–64 in the number of workers engaged in agriculture (21%), coal mining (25%), shipbuilding (27%) and the cotton textile industry (19%), and the increased number of workers in engineering, building, the motor-car industry and the service and professional occupations. Many professional people are compelled to move to secure promotion.

There is no doubt, however, that some labour is not very mobile. Some people become very much attached to the places where they have lived for a long time. Local ties are formed and a social position in the locality may have been achieved. To the married, housing is a serious problem. The man who is able to rent a house is in a privileged position and he may be deterred from moving by the difficulty of obtaining a house to rent elsewhere. Many of these people, however, frequently change their jobs where this does not involve moving to another town.

[1] *DEA Progress Report*, No. 3, March 1963.

Mobility of labour is essential to economic progress. The economic advantages of particular areas may change as a result of technological change. Down to the seventeenth century East Anglia was an important centre of the woollen industry, but by the late eighteenth century the centre of this industry had moved to West Yorkshire. Technological improvement has become a continuous and ever-speedier process. The higher the standard of living the greater and more frequent are changes of demand. To meet these dynamic conditions mobility of factors of production, including labour, is essential. In fact, in recent years, there has been a considerable movement of labour between the various regions of Great Britain. During 1966–67 Wales and Scotland each suffered a population loss of over 20,000.

The State in pursuing its policy of taking work to the workers accepts geographical mobility of labour, but it was the passing of the *Redundancy Payments Act*, 1965, which provided for compensation payments to be made to people thrown out of work by technical progress or changes of demand, and the introduction of schemes for retraining workers indicates a realisation of the importance of occupational mobility if economic progress is to be achieved.

Thus, the generally accepted policy, pursued from the 1930s to the 1960s and supported by the recommendations of the Barlow Report (1940) and Beveridge's book *Full Employment in a Free Society* (1944), was to retain a wider distribution of industry and population than would have been the case without state control of location of industry. Throughout a period of thirty years the Government's purpose was mainly to prevent local unemployment and partly to prevent a continuous decline and eventual stagnation of many of the older industrial areas with the possible depopulation of some of them, with the waste of social capital that this would entail. The extent to which there would have been a waste of social capital was probably much exaggerated in many cases, the rebuilding of town centres, schools, hospitals, etc., in many towns in the 1960s indicating that a good deal of this social capital was in need of replacement anyway. Coupled with this second motive to prevent the development of derelict areas went the desire to check the increasing congestion of population in South-East England. How this aspect of the problem was tackled is considered below.

## Some other economic considerations

Reference has already been made to the fact that it was for economic reasons that many industries became localised. Left to itself a firm will select that location where its costs of production— including the distribution of its product—will be lowest. Since 1945 many firms have gone to areas other than those they themselves would have selected if they had been given complete freedom of choice. In the case of dispersal in industry, firms are deprived of the economies of scale associated with the localisation of industry. Thus, it seems probable that many firms which have not been able themselves to choose their location will have higher costs than they might have had. So long as generally inflationary conditions persist—and, with them, over-full employment—the high level of demand and wide profit margins enable them to carry on. A serious check to full employment—not expected, of course, in view of government responsibility for its maintenance—a serious falling off in demand or a narrowing of profit margins as a result of company taxation or other causes might affect these firms more than older-established firms, especially where they are branches of large concerns with their main centres more economically located.

## IV. NATIONAL AND REGIONAL PLANNING

### The problem of regional balance

In September 1965 the National Plan was published by the Department of Economic Affairs, a new government department set up in 1964. Covering the five years 1965–70 its principal aims were to achieve a more rapid rate of economic growth than had previously been achieved. An output target for 1970 was set which required a greater labour force than the country appeared likely to have by that date.

To make up for this expected deficiency of labour not only would greater mobility of labour be required but also it would be necessary to make better use of the existing labour force. Though the emphasis was on increasing the rate of economic growth rather than local unemployment, it meant, of course, that pockets of unemployment should not be permitted to exist in some parts of the country while there was over-full employment elsewhere. Thus, during the 1960s, while the average unemployment rate for Great Britain was 1·5%, in South-East England and the Midlands it was generally below 1·0%, whereas it was 3·0% in northern England (6·9% in Blyth), 3·4% in Scotland and 2·7% in Wales (8·9% in Rhondda), with higher rates in some places. One aim of the selective employment tax, introduced in the budget of 1966, was to encourage greater mobility of labour.

The Department of Economic Affairs considered that one of the main obstacles to the achievement of the production targets set by the National Plan was that in some parts of the country there were economic resources—land and capital as well as labour—that were not being fully used or employed to their best advantage. Since each part of the country had its own particular problems, it was decided to establish regional bodies to formulate and carry out plans for their own areas within the orbit of the National Plan.

1 Scotland
2 Northern
3 Yorkshire and Humberside
4 North-West
5 East Midland
6 West Midland
7 Wales and Monmouth
8 South-West
9 East Anglia
10 South-East

FIG. 5.—Economic Planning Regions

**Economic planning regions**

Ten economic planning regions were eventually delineated, some of them including areas of varying extent designated as Development Districts which were to retain the privileges previously assigned to them:

1. *Scotland.* This region comprises the whole of Scotland, and within its boundaries includes extensive Development Districts to the north and west, the Clyde valley and the Lowlands, most of the east coast (except Edinburgh, the regional capital, and the south-east) and the south-west. Orkney and Shetland also are Development Districts. The main problem of this region is to check the outflow of workers to other regions or abroad, amounting to a net loss of over 10,000 per annum in recent years.

2. *Northern England*, with Newcastle upon Tyne as the regional capital, comprising the four northern counties together with the

North Riding of Yorkshire, with an extensive Development District covering Durham, Tyneside and Tees-side, together with a smaller one along the coast of West Cumberland.

3. *Yorkshire and Humberside*, comprising the West and East Ridings of Yorkshire and most of Lincolnshire, with Leeds as the regional capital. There are no Development Districts in this region.

4. *North-West England*, consisting of the counties of Lancashire and Cheshire, and including the Furness District of Lancashire, with Development Areas in South Lancashire, Merseyside and Furness. Manchester is the regional administrative centre.

5. *The East Midlands*, with Nottingham as its centre, comprising Nottinghamshire, Derbyshire, Leicestershire and Northamptonshire, with part of Lincolnshire near the Wash, but with no Development Districts.

6. *The West Midlands*, another region with no Development Districts and comprising Warwickshire, Staffordshire, Shropshire, Herefordshire and Worcestershire, and with Birmingham as its regional capital.

7. *Wales and Monmouthshire*, comprising the whole of the Principality, together with the county of Monmouthshire and with a number of Development Districts in both North and South Wales— Anglesey and much of Caernarvonshire, a small area in Denbighshire, three areas in Glamorgan and Monmouth and the Milford Haven district. Cardiff is the capital of this region.

8. *South-West England*, comprising the counties of Gloucestershire, Wiltshire, Dorset, Somerset, Devon and Cornwall, with a number of Development Districts in the extreme south-west of the peninsula, in North Devon and Cornwall. Bristol is the regional headquarters.

9. *East Anglia*, with Norwich as its capital, comprises the counties of Norfolk, Suffolk, Cambridgeshire, Huntingdonshire and part of Essex. The region contains no Development Districts.

10. *The South-East* includes the London area, for which there is to be special treatment.

In addition the government of Northern Ireland has set up an Economic Council.

For each of the economic planning regions there have been set up a Regional Economic Planning Board and a Regional Economic Council. The function of the Boards is to co-ordinate the work of different government departments in the regions, their members therefore being civil servants, and their first task was to prepare economic plans for their areas. The Councils have part-time members of local people to provide local views and experience for the regional planners. An important duty for them will be to advise the Department of

Economic Affairs on possible local effects of national economic policies.

Thus, regional development has become equally important as national development. Though the Department of Economic Affairs recognises that some mobility of labour is necessary—indeed, essential—to economic progress, nevertheless the emphasis now placed on regional economic planning, with its encouragement and stimulation of local development, might be expected to discourage movement between regions. This could result in a region with few economic advantages for industrial production being given equal facilities for development as another region with much greater economic advantages. It appears, therefore, that the social implications of regional planning are being given at least as much consideration as the economic, even though the administrative bodies for the region are known as *Economic* Planning Boards and *Economic* Planning Councils. The Board of Trade will continue to give the greatest assistance to the Development Districts, its power to withhold or to grant Industrial Development Certificates being a powerful instrument of control.

## V. THE NEW TOWNS

### The purpose of the New Towns

The period since 1945 has seen the emergence, so far as Great Britain is concerned, of a new idea in industrial location—the deliberate building of new industrial towns. In the past, new towns had grown up at particular places mainly for economic, geographic or strategic reasons—at river crossings, at the intersection of commercial routes, at places that could easily be defended, on the coalfields, or near to sources of raw materials. A few "garden cities" had been build but these were small and mainly residential.

The *New Towns Act* of 1946 aimed to supplement the *Distribution of Industries Act* of the previous year. The purpose of the earlier of these Acts was to discourage new firms going to South-East England, and the purpose of the *New Towns Act* was to disperse industry in order to reduce congestion, particularly in the London area, in accordance with the recommendations of the Barlow Report. This report had suggested that there should be no further factory building in the London area, and that a "green belt" free from further building of any kind should be created round existing urban areas. Congestion in the London area was to be relieved by building a number of new towns on the outer fringe of the metropolis. New towns were also to be built to take overspill population from other densely populated conurbations. The new towns were not to be merely residential "dormitory" towns, a number of which had grown up in the 1930s round the great conurbations, but were to provide work locally for the people living there. Industry, therefore, would have to be attracted to them. Thus, in the London area sites for new towns were selected just beyond the "green belt" which it was hoped to preserve.

### The New Towns of the South-East

During 1947–50 eight places were selected round London to be developed as new towns, in all cases near to existing small places from which they derived their names—Crawley in Sussex, Stevenage, Hemel Hempstead, Hatfield and Welwyn Garden City in Hertfordshire, Harlow and Basildon in Essex, and Bracknell in Berkshire. The original intention was to develop towns with populations between 50,000 and 80,000, but since then the population target has been raised. By 1968 most of these towns were approaching the population originally planned for them:

|  | 1967 *population* | *Target population* |
|---|---|---|
| Basildon       .       .       . | 70,800 | 106,000 |
| Bracknell      .       .       . | 26,000 | 60,000 |
| Crawley        .       .       . | 63,000 | 75,000 |
| Harlow         .       .       . | 71,000 | 80,000 |
| Hatfield       .       .       . | 24,000 | 29,000 |
| Hemel Hempstead        . | 67,000 | 80,000 |
| Stevenage      .       .       . | 59,000 | 80,000 |
| Welwyn Garden City     . | 43,000 | 50,000 |

Under the *New Towns Act*, 1946, a Development Corporation was set up for each new town. Finance for the new undertakings was provided by loans from the Treasury. In 1961 a Commission for New Towns was established to acquire the property of the Development Corporation of each new town when it reached the first stage of its development. As the new towns were intended to provide work for the people living in them, the building of factories went hand in hand with the building of houses and shops, so that housing accommodation could be guaranteed to all employees of firms moving into them from London. In this way it was hoped to remove half a million people from London. The initial difficulties in such projects were considerable: *e.g.* shops can be expected to open only when there is a sufficient number of customers available to them. Once the first stage of development has been reached, however, further progress tends to be fairly rapid.

Since 1963 an attempt has also been made to encourage the movement of offices out of central London. The Government set up the Location of Offices Bureau to give publicity to this policy and to

FIG. 6.—The New Towns

offer information and advice. The Government itself had already given a lead by moving some administrative departments out of London. An important inducement to movement is the much lower rents charged for office accommodation elsewhere. and the saving of the London allowance in the payment of salaries.[1] During its first five years 543 businesses, employing over 48,000 people, decided to move out of central London, approximately a third electing to go to the outer suburbs of Greater London, most of the remainder preferring locations between 20 and 40 miles from London. Under its scheme for regional economic planning the Department of Economic Affairs designated the Greater London area as a region in which office development is to be controlled. It has been calculated that since 1964 office workers have been moved away from London at an average rate of 12,000 to 15,000 a year. Nevertheless, during 1966–67 as many people moved into the regions of East Anglia and South-East England as moved out.

[1] An advertisement of the LOB in 1968 showed these savings per employee to average £315 for office space and £150 for the London allowance, a total per employee of £465 per annum.

## Other New Towns

New towns have also been built in other parts of the country, the first of these being Newton Aycliffe in County Durham, near the trading estate of the same name established in the late 1930s. Also in County Durham are Peterlee and Washington. Killingworth, immediately to the north of Newcastle upon Tyne, was designated in 1962 to take overspill from that city. Corby, which between the two World Wars grew from a village to a town with a population of over 15,000, is also being developed as a new town, so that in this case economic considerations have been mainly responsible for its location—local supplies of iron ore. Other new towns in England include Skelmersdale and Runcorn in Lancashire, Dawley in Shropshire, Redditch in Worcestershire and Cwmbran in Monmouthshire:

|  | 1967 population | Target population |
|---|---|---|
| Corby . . . . | 46,000 | 75,000 |
| Cwmbran . . . | 38,000 | 55,000 |
| Dawley . . . | 21,000 | 100,000[1] |
| Newton Aycliffe . . | 17,000 | 45,000 |
| Peterlee . . . | 20,000 | 30,000 |
| Redditch . . . | 29,000 | 90,000 |
| Runcorn . . . | 29,000 | 90,000 |
| Skelmersdale . . | 13,000 | 80,000 |
| Washington . . . | 20,000 | 80,000 |

[1] In 1968 it was decided to amalgamate Dawley with Wellington and Oakengates to form a single town to be known as Telford, with a population target of 220,000.

Dawley has been less successful in attracting firms from Birmingham than have the new towns of the South-East in attracting new firms from London. It would seem too that Birmingham has been less willing than London to disperse some of its population.

In Scotland there are Glenrothes in Fifeshire, East Kilbride in Lanarkshire and Cumbernauld and Livingston in West Lothian. To these Irvine in Ayrshire was added in 1966. Of these only East Kilbride had reached an advanced stage of development by 1967:

|  | 1967 population | Target population |
|---|---|---|
| Cumbernauld . . | 22,000 | 70,000 |
| East Kilbride . . | 51,000 | 100,000 |
| Glenrothes . . . | 21,000 | 75,000 |
| Irvine . . . . | 30,000 | 85,000 |
| Livingston . . . | 3,500 | 100,000 |

In Northern Ireland, Antrim and Ballymena (both in County Antrim) are to be developed as new towns. It is intended to increase the population of Antrim from its present 6,000 to 30,000 and Ballymena from 16,000 to 70,000.

Thus, by 1968, a total of 27 new towns had been designated, some such as Crawley, Harlow and Stevenage being at that date in an advanced stage of development, while others such as Skelmersdale and Dawley were still only at the preliminary stage. It seems certain that from time to time other new towns will be designated, particularly since some redistribution of population appears to be the policy of the Regional Economic Planning Boards.

Rather more ambitious schemes for the creation of what might be termed new cities have also been put forward. In 1967 a new overspill city for London was designated at Milton Keynes in Buckinghamshire, planned to have a population of a quarter of a million by the year 2000. It will absorb the towns of Bletchley, Wolverton and Stony Stratford. The *New Towns Act* (*Northern Ireland*) of 1965 envisages a new city of Craigavon with a population of between 100,000 and 150,000, and similar new cities have been suggested for north Lincolnshire near the River Humber and Lancashire south of Preston. Consideration is also being given to the building of a new town in Hampshire between Southampton and Portsmouth and another in central Wales, as an overspill from Birmingham.

The plan to reduce congestion in the great conurbations appears to be gaining momentum. To supplement the new towns it is proposed to increase the size of a number of existing towns of moderate extent where these are situated outside densely populated areas. The towns so far selected for aggrandisement are Ipswich, Northampton, Peterborough, Swindon and Ashford (Kent). Similarly, Aylesbury in Buckinghamshire and Thetford in Norfolk are being expanded, the population of Aylesbury increasing by 12,000 in the ten years to 1967 and that of Thetford during this decade doubling to 9,000. All these are to take overspill from the London area. In its first preliminary study of congestion in the Birmingham area the West Regional Economic Planning Council in 1966 suggested that the population of Worcester should be increased during the next fifteen years from 67,000, its present size, to 120,000. Suggestions have been made for increasing some other towns in the region. It seems likely that this policy of expanding towns of moderate size may be used alongside that of building entirely new towns as a means of tackling the problem of urban congestion.

RECOMMENDATIONS FOR FURTHER READING

S. R. Dennison: *The Location of Industry* (Oxford University Press).

W. H. Beveridge: *Full Employment in a Free Society*, Part IV (George Allen & Unwin).

*If available:*

B. J. Loasby: "Location of Industry—Thirty Years of 'Planning.'" *District Bank Review* (December 1965).

H. W. Richardson and E. G. West: "Must we take Work to the Workers?" *Lloyds Bank Review* (January 1964).

"Old and New Industrial Areas in Britain." *Midland Bank Review* (May 1964).

Department of Economic Affairs: Progress Reports (monthly). (For current policy and trends.) From January 1965.

HMSO: Regional Studies.

### QUESTIONS

1. Examine and explain the changes in the aims of government policy towards location of industry during the past twenty-five years.

2. Consider the aim of a "balanced economy" in relation to location of industry.

3. In what ways can the distinction between social and private cost provide criteria for location of industry policy? Compare these with criteria apparently employed in British location of industry policy since the war. (Degree.)

4. Explain the advantages and disadvantages of persuading firms to locate in areas of high unemployment. (Birmingham.)

5. (*a*) What factors should determine government policy on the distribution of industry?

(*b*) Comment on the effectiveness of recent government measures aimed at achieving a balanced distribution of industry. (Bournemouth.)

6. Adam Smith declared that "a man is of all sorts of baggage the most difficult to be transported." Comment on this view with reference to attempted planning of location of industry. (Kingston-upon-Hull.)

7. "The real regional issue is hardly the choice of two extremes: taking the work to the workers or the workers to the work." Do you agree? (Liverpool.)

8. Do you consider government attempts to influence the location of industry to have been in the best interests of economic efficiency? (Liverpool.)

9. Describe the attempts made by successive British governments to influence the location of industry since the Second World War and assess the measures recently announced concerning North-Eastern England and Scotland. (Northern Counties.)

10. Examine some of the major problems associated with government attempts to establish new industries in Development Areas. (U.L.C.I.)

11. Examine the arguments for and against government interference in the location of industry. (U.L.C.I.)

## CHAPTER III

# COMMERCIAL DISTRIBUTION

## I. THE EXPANSION OF COMMERCIAL DISTRIBUTION

### Development of retailing

The marketing of consumers' goods, as we know it, is quite a recent development of economic life. For many centuries people were mainly dependent on their own efforts for the satisfaction of their wants. Even primitive communities, however, developed a degree of division of labour and, until money came into use, exchange took place by barter. With the growth of cities the first shops appeared, but for a long time most retailing was carried on at weekly open-air markets, supplemented by periodic fairs once or perhaps twice a year. Markets and fairs in England date back to the eleventh and twelfth centuries, and for a long time the right of a town to hold a market depended on its obtaining a charter from the Crown.

Although Napoleon contemptuously referred to the England of his day as a "nation of shopkeepers," the gibe was, in fact, far from true. Outside the few cities there was relatively little retailing until the Industrial Revolution of the late eighteenth and early nineteenth centuries had got well under way. The long hours worked in the new factories left the employees little time to do anything for themselves, and the factory owners themselves found it necessary at first to open shops on the factory premises for their workers. The growth of new towns, however, led to the opening of independent shops. Then, with the mass production of many goods and a gradual rise in the standard of living, a wider range and variety of goods began to appear in the shops. Gradually, the number of shops in the country increased so that at the present day Great Britain has one shop to every hundred persons of the population—over half a million shops in all.

### Marketing and production

Thus, the increase in production and the expansion of retailing occurred at the same time, since the marketing or commercial distribution of a commodity is economically the final stage in its production. When a craftsman working alone undertakes the making of an article its production is complete as soon as it has taken its final form and can be handed over to the person for whom it was made.

Large-scale production results in a large output of a commodity being produced in one place, so that the goods afterwards have to be distributed over a wide area. Most goods, however, are no longer made in response to direct orders from consumers and so not only have they to be transported from the place of manufacture to the place of consumption but also consumers must be made aware of their existence, and they must be made available at the time when consumers want them. The advantages of large-scale production are, therefore, to some degree offset by the increased cost of distribution. Thus, the production of a commodity is not complete until it has reached the person who is going to make use of it—the consumer: *i.e.* distribution is the final stage of production. Those who are engaged in commercial distribution—retailers, wholesalers, transport workers, etc.—are just as much engaged in production as those employed on the factory floor. All are performing productive services.

### Increasing amount of labour in distribution

During the present century the number of people employed in commercial distribution has increased much more rapidly than the total population—though, compared with 1913, only slightly more than the working population—and their number continues to increase. At the present day about 12% of the labour force of the United Kingdom is engaged in commercial distribution—a position very similar to that in other countries of Western Europe where the standard of living is high.

The following table shows how the number of people in the United Kingdom employed in the retail and distributive trades increased down to 1965:

TABLE XVIII
*Labour Employed in Distribution*

| Year | No. employed (thousands) |
|---|---|
| 1947 | 2,368 |
| 1950 | 2,571 |
| 1954 | 2,802 |
| 1957 | 2,835 |
| 1960 | 2,850 |
| 1965 | 3,023 |
| 1967 | 2,857 |

The increase during 1947–54 was to some extent accounted for by demobilisation from the Armed Forces in the earlier years and then by the ending of rationing. Of the 3 million people engaged in retailing half a million are self-employed shopkeepers, the remainder being employees of large or medium sized firms.

We have already noticed one reason for the long-term increase—the increasing scale of production and, therefore, of distribution. Two other influences should be noted. First, expanding consumers' demand associated with the general rise in the standard of living not only stimulates the demand for most existing commodities but also encourages the production of new ones. Secondly, though expansion of output in the factories is generally accompanied by economies of scale resulting from mechanisation or automation, so that output per man increases, these industrial techniques cannot easily be appled to retailing, which is a much more personal service. In recent years, however, in some branches of retail trade, attempts have been made to improve efficiency and secure economies through large-scale retailing. Thus, with expanding production, the cost of distribution tends to form an increasing proportion of the cost of most goods entering into retail trade.

In spite of recent changes in retailing, the number of shops in this country has shown little change. The reports of the Censuses of Distribution show that, though the number of retail outlets in Great Britain declined between 1950 and 1961 from 583,132 to 577,307, and between 1961 and 1966 from 577,307 to 497,477.

## II. TYPES OF RETAIL OUTLET

### Channels of distribution

What used to be regarded as the normal channel of distribution was for goods between the manufacturer and the retailer to pass through the hands (or, at least, through the books) of a wholesaler. In the case of goods imported from abroad, more than one "middleman" will be encountered since many imports pass through organised commodity markets so that the specialist services of importers and buyers are needed. Many imports require to be processed in some way and this function is often carried out by the wholesalers in the trades concerned. The wholesaler is also very useful to the small retailers, few of whom have much storage space and so must purchase their stock in relatively small quantities if they are to offer their customers a choice. Such retailers frequently operate on a very small amount of capital and often rely on their wholesalers for credit. The independent retailer of medium size also buys mainly from a wholesaler.

Alternative channels of distribution result in the elimination of the wholesaler. Since the functions of the wholesaler—holding stocks (warehousing), the "breaking of bulk," etc.—cannot be eliminated, this means that either the manufacturer or the retailer, in addition to their normal functions, must also undertake the functions of the wholesaler. Manufacturers of branded goods who "pre-sell" them by nation-wide advertising generally prefer themselves to market them as far as the retailer in order to ensure that supplies are readily available to the maximum number of consumers. Sometimes a manufacturer may also act as both wholesaler and retailer and deal direct with consumers. Some manufacturers, therefore, have opened their own retail shops which sell wholly or mainly their own products. Alternatively, they may concentrate on mail-order business or employ door-to-door salesmen. Large-scale retailers generally purchase their stock direct from manufacturers, undertaking the wholesaling functions themselves. Multiple-shop organisations supply their branches from their own warehouse at headquarters. Department stores also buy most of their stock direct from manufacturers. Both "multiples" and department stores are able to do this because they buy in large quantities to meet a high rate of turnover. To an increasing extent the wholesaler is being by-passed.

Of all the shops in Great Britain today, nearly half are food shops and of these no fewer than 120,000 are grocers. The following table shows the number of shops in each branch of retail trade in Great Britain:

TABLE XIX
*Number of Retail Outlets*

| Type of trade | No. of establishments | |
|---|---|---|
| | 1961 | 1966 |
| Grocers    .    .    .    .    . | 149,548 | 122,366 |
| Butchers    .    .    .    .    . | 44,248 | 38,087 |
| Greengrocers    .    .    .    . | 42,070 | 26,779 |
| Bakers and confectioners    .    . | 17,549 | 17,849 |
| Other food shops .    .    .    . | 25,043 | 20,581 |
| Total food shops .    .    . | 278,458 | 255,632 |
| Clothing, footwear    .    .    . | 92,426 | 81,544 |
| Tobacconists, sweets, newsagents    . | 70,662 | 63,015 |
| Hardware    .    .    .    .    . | 27,560 | 25,795 |
| Furniture    .    .    .    .    . | 21,224 | 19,273 |
| Chemists    .    .    .    .    . | 18,392 | 17,934 |
| Booksellers and stationers    .    . | 6,284 | 5,887 |
| Jewellery, leather, sports goods    . | 19,277 | 18,586 |
| Cycle dealers    .    .    .    . | 5,657 | 3,776 |
| Radio and/or electrical goods .    . | 18,878 | 19,495 |
| Gas and electricity showrooms    . | 2,791 | 3,012 |
| Department stores    .    .    . | 784 | 778 |
| Other general stores    .    .    . | 2,966 | 2,141 |
| Other shops .    .    .    .    . | 11,548 | 11,609 |
| Total .    .    .    .    . | 577,307 * | 498,477 * |

Source: *Censuses of Distribution.*
   * Excluding boot and shoe repairers, hairdressers, laundries, totalling 55,879 in 1961 and 62,634 in 1966.

During the years 1961–66 the number of shops in some branches of retail trade increased, but overall there was a decline of over 78,000. Branches of retailing where the number of establishments seriously declined during this period included grocers (27,000), greengrocers (16,000), clothing shops (11,000), and tobacconists and newsagents (7,600). Increases in numbers occurred in radio and electrical shops. A small amount of retailing is undertaken outside the shops by hawkers, pedlars and "barrow boys" in city streets. Modern versions of some of these are the motor-driven "mobile shops" and direct sale by manufacturers. It is becoming increasingly difficult to classify retailers according to the branch of trade in which they are engaged as the modern tendency is for the range of goods sold by individual shops to widen and thus for shops to become less specialised then they used to be.

## Independent retailers

In numbers the independent retailers still overwhelmingly outnumber their large-scale rivals. Of the total of 498,477 shops in 1966 no fewer than 420,000 (*i.e.* 80%) were independent traders, but their share of total retail was only 49%. This is a much smaller share of retailing than that enjoyed by independent traders in other West European countries. Many of these retail shops are very small, the business sometimes being run as a part-time occupation. Though often grossly inefficient, the independent shop is able to carry on because for a few people it is more conveniently situated—perhaps for the type of smoker who is apt to run out of cigarettes or the improvident housewife who suddenly finds herself short of bread—and open maybe at more convenient hours than neighbouring shops.

The more viable, medium-sized independent retailers are the ones who were formerly responsible for most retailing. Many were family businesses which had passed from father to son, often for generations, their names being household words in their own localities. They set out to offer consumers the maximum amount of service—a wide variety of merchandise, the sort of personal attention that only a well-staffed shop and personal knowledge of one's customers could give, together with a delivery service to suit their requirements. Before 1913 shops were open for long hours, often until midnight in the case of food shops. Knowing his customers personally, the sole proprietor knew to whom credit could be given without undue risk. Both clothes and boots were at one time made to measure and many other things were made to the customer's special order. The customer, of course, had to pay for all these services, for, of necessity, the retailer's mark-up was high.

## Large-scale retailing

It was not until the mid-nineteenth century that the first attempts were made at large-scale retailing. The department store was first in the field, Bon Marché opening in 1852 in Paris. The first successful retail co-operative society—that at Rochdale—had opened in 1844, and so in Great Britain pre-dates the department store by a quarter of a century, but for a long time co-operative societies were very small. The larger co-operative societies have as many branches as many multiple-shop organisations. As large-scale retailers the co-operative societies can be regarded as being second in the field. The first multiples were established in the later years of the nineteenth century. The variety chain store is really a special type of multiple. These are the main forms that large-scale retailing takes in this country.

The movement towards large-scale retailing has been carried farthest in the United States and the United Kingdom as judged by its share in the total volume of retail trade. Although Paris had the first department store, the share of retailing enjoyed by department stores in France is little more than half that of department stores in Great Britain. Similarly, multiples on the continent of Europe have obtained only half the share of retail trade of British multiples.

The aim in all forms of large-scale retailing is to secure economies of scale such as had accrued to large-scale manufacturing. Expansion of the scale of operation makes possible a greater degree of division of labour and greater specialisation enables more efficient, highly skilled workers to be employed at each stage of production. Other economies include the bulk purchase of raw materials, the spreading of advertising costs over a larger output, cheaper borrowing from the bank and generally, in the earlier stages at least, administrative economies too. Some of these economies of scale can perhaps be achieved in large-scale retailing, but, unlike manufacturing, retailing cannot be concentrated in one place, since it involves a personal service and consumers are scattered throughout the country. It does, however, make possible the employment of specialist buyers, and large units justify the appointment of better-paid and more efficient managers.

The departmental structure of department stores, including non-selling departments, lends itself to division of labour and specialisation. Stock can be obtained more cheaply by bulk purchases from manufacturers, but the large-scale retailer must then make provision for warehousing. In the case of a multiple he must also undertake the delivery of stock to the various branches. In order to concentrate its selling all under one roof and attract a sufficient number of customers to make bulk buying worth while, the department store has to be housed in an expensive building on a costly site. All these things reduce somewhat the gain from bulk buying. More effective advertising is open to large-scale retailers on account of their large turnover than to independent traders. It is because economies of scale have not been so easily achieved in retailing as in manufacturing that so many small retail firms have managed so far to survive whereas few small firms remain in manufacturing industry. Present-day developments, however, appear to indicate that recently some large-scale retailers have found more effective ways of achieving economies of scale, so that the small retailer's position has been greatly weakened.

## Department Stores

In the largest department stores almost every branch of retail trade may be carried on, one London store having over 300 departments, so that the shopper has the advantage of being able to make all her purchases, however varied they might be, in one place. The early department stores had fewer departments and developed out of more conventional retail businesses, most frequently starting as drapers. They still vary considerably in size and in the number of their departments.

Generally, each department of a department store is expected to show a profit after it has borne its share—usually based on its turnover—of overhead expenses, including those of the non-selling departments. The buyer is responsible for running his department, but he cannot adopt a policy that might increase the profit of his own department to the detriment of other departments. Thus, he must restrict his stock to the branch of trade undertaken by his department and he must conform to the general policy of the store with regard to the quality of goods, since the customers of one department are expected to be potential customers of others.

An important aim of department stores from their earliest days has been to make an attractive display of their merchandise in order that people who had come in merely to walk round might be encouraged to buy. This was a revolutionary change in retailing, for previously people had been in the habit of entering a shop only for the purpose of making a specific purchase. Previously, too, the price had been a matter for discussion and bargaining between customer and salesman. The department store broke with this tradition by clearly showing the prices of all goods offered for sale. To many people one of the attractions of the early department stores was that the goods offered for sale were cheaper than elsewhere, these shops being the first to practise the principle of "small profits, quick returns." In the old independent shops the rate of turnover had been slow and the mark-up high.

Although the department stores offered their customers rest rooms and reasonably priced meals in their restaurants—to induce them to spend more time in the store—they cut their costs by providing fewer of the services people had previously been accustomed to receive from retailers. In their early days all transactions were for cash, though nowadays most of them allow approved customers to have monthly accounts, whereas regular customers of the independent retailers had always expected to receive credit.

During the nineteenth century there was a general rise in the standard of living, but the rise was greatest among the middle classes, and they were the people for whom the department stores set out to cater. The increasing prosperity of the middle classes was reflected, therefore, in the rapid progress and expansion of department stores in the period down to the outbreak of the First World War. From France the department store spread to Great Britain and then to the United States. Nowadays they are to be found in varying numbers in most of the large towns and cities of the world. Dependent as they are on a large turnover, their location is restricted to large centres of population, especially places with large shopping hinterlands.

Between the two wars department stores continued to make progress but at a slower rate. As their numbers increased in the larger centres of population such as London so did competition between them begin to intensify. This, too, was a period of expansion for the multiples but they and the department stores catered largely for different markets, though where these markets overlapped they became keen competitors. The increase in the range of merchandise subject to resale price maintenance affected both these types of large-scale retailer in reducing the field in which they could cut prices to increase turnover, though the multiples probably suffered more than the department stores on this account. To attract more customers American department stores introduced the "loss-leader," a department deliberately run at a loss.

At one time department stores operated as single units, though one or two of them opened a limited number of branches. Increased competition led to amalgamations though with the retention of the individual names because of the goodwill associated with them. At the present day most department stores in Great Britain are members of large groups, which in several cases also include a number of multiples. For example, in 1964 the House of Fraser controlled 64 department stores while Great Universal Stores and United Drapery Stores each controlled 22 department stores together with a number of multiples.

## Multiple shops

One of the main features of the multiple as a large-scale retail organisation is that it comprises a large number of shops in the same branch of retail trade under a single ownership, all controlled from a central administrative office or warehouse. The second feature of multiples is their policy of cutting prices to increase turnover and their total net profit. The earliest multiples, however, were developed by enterprising retailers who began to expand their businesses by opening branches. In the early period of growth, expansion was often financed out of profits and many of them have continued to finance some part of their expansion in this way. For more rapid and more extensive progress the huge amount of capital required could be raised only by a public company. Expansion was sometimes achieved by acquiring existing shops in other towns, but more generally by opening new branches of their own. More recently amalgamations of multiples have taken place, though in most cases, as with amalgamations between department stores, they have generally continued to operate under their original names.

A multiple must have a large enough turnover and therefore a sufficient number of branches to enable the central buying department with its specialist buyer to make bulk purchases of stock. What this minimum number of branches is will depend to some extent on the branch of trade in which the organisation is engaged. In the Censuses of Distribution a multiple is defined as a retail concern with ten or more branches. It is difficult to decide how many shops must be under a single control to qualify as a multiple, but ten seems to be too small a number. Defined in this way there are over 2,000 multiple-shop organisations in Great Britain at the present day. A great many of them operate in quite small areas, some being organised on a regional basis, and a few being national concerns with branches throughout the country. The regional firms may control 50 to 100 branches, but national ones may have several hundred, the largest number under the same name being 1,300. The largest multiple organisation of all —an amalgamation of several multiples, each still operating under its original name—controls over 3,700 shops.

The variety chain stores—originally fixed-price shops, introduced into this country from the United States by F. W. Woolworth—are of course much larger and offer a much wider range of goods.

The earliest multiples were engaged in the grocery trade though selling only a limited range of goods, often restricting themselves to butter, margarine, cheese, tea and sugar. Even those with a wider commodity range limited their customers to only one or two varieties. Only by doing so could advantage be taken of bulk purchase of stock. In the case of branded goods, however, there has recently been a tendency for shops to widen their range of stock, so that demarcation between different types of food shop, for example, is less sharp. But only commodities for which there is a regular high level of demand will be stocked.

At the present day multiples have invaded almost every branch of retail trade—grocery, fish, meat, clothing, boots and shoes, furniture, bicycles, books and stationery, chemists, even jewellery. Most multiples are solely engaged in distribution, but a few are owned by manufacturers who wish to market their products as far as the consumer. Some of these shops (*e.g.* Manfields) sell only the manufacturer's own products; others (*e.g.* Boots) also sell other manufacturer's products.

Economies of scale have been achieved by multiple shops not only, as already noted, by bulk buying and keeping services to a minimum but also by greater efficiency in retailing as compared with independent shops and in wholesaling as compared with the wholesalers.

(*i*) *Retailing*. All branches of a multiple-shop organisation are under a unified central control from headquarters, their scale of operation making it possible to employ highly qualified specialist staff for all aspects of their work—buyers, accountants, shop designers, publicity and display experts, etc. Local branch managers receive their instructions from headquarters and send back regular reports. Apart from this they do litttle more than supervise the day-to-day running of the shop. The prices of goods are determined by headquarters. Some multiples used to indicate their price policy in their names, as, for example, Thirty or Forty Shilling Tailors, but the long run of inflation since the Second World War has rendered this practice impossible, as the fixed-price variety chain stores have also found. Even if it is not publicised, however, most multiples have a price range, although in recent times it has had to be readjusted periodically to rising prices. The price range selected is the one at which there is a high level of demand. When the first multiples were established in the 1890s this price would be a low one, but as the general standard of living has risen so has the price range of the multiples. The department stores came into existence with the rising standard of living of the middle classes: the multiples appeared when the standard of living of the working classes began to improve. Their price policy, then, is to sell at keenly competitive prices, for, like the department stores, their aim is "small profits, quick returns," this policy being backed up by aggressive publicity. With the help of their design experts, shops are given an efficient and attractive lay-out.

(*ii*) *Wholesaling*. The efficiency of multiples in wholesaling is most marked. Having decided what commodities are to be sold in their shops their buyers can use their expertise to buy in large quantities on favourable terms. Shop fittings and equipment, stationery, etc., are also bought in quantity on good terms. The transfer of goods from warehouse to retail shop is carried out at minimum cost, as many of the independent wholesaler's marketing costs are eliminated. All stock can be disposed of simply by sending it in appropriate lots to the branch shops, all of which must accept what they are offered.

Finance is simplified by invoicing goods to the shops at selling prices, so that credit between wholesaler and retailer does not arise. Costs are still further cut by having regular days for delivery to the shops. Wholesaling risks are, therefore, almost eliminated and further reduced by insistence on branch managers informing headquarters immediately of any change in consumers' demand. Multiples, too, appear to have highly efficient systems of stock control.

Thus, the multiples put themselves in a strong position in competition with independent retailers for the sale of those goods for which there is a large demand, "skimming the cream off the trade," as the independents often complain. Over the past twenty years, the multiples have been the most progressive of all forms of retail trade. Though branch shops are visited periodically by representatives from headquarters—or from regional centres in the case of the larger concerns—an undertaking with so many widely dispersed selling points is in danger of its organisation becoming bureaucratic, with a consequent loss of personal contact between the shops and headquarters. The multiple can do little more than arrange an occasional conference of the branch managers of its larger shops.

## Consumers' co-operative societies

The third form taken by large-scale retail trade is the consumers' co-operative society. In the early nineteenth century a number of attempts were made to establish retail co-operative societies, but most of these early ventures in co-operation failed. The first successful society was that established in 1844 at Rochdale. In the new town that the Industrial Revolution brought into existence some mill owners built both houses and shops. Employees were often compelled to make purchases at the mill shop—perhaps by the part-payment of wages in vouchers which could only be "spent" there—the truck system.[1] Gross overcharging was a common feature of these shops, which often sold inferior goods at high prices to customers who were unable to go elsewhere. The few independent shops in the new industrial towns were very inefficient and in consequence their prices were high. Groups of workpeople, therefore, agreed to co-operate in setting up and running a shop of their own in order to escape exploitation, the profits of the business to be divided among the members in proportion to their purchases. Thus, co-operation in retailing began as a working-class movement. Success at Rochdale stimulated the formation of many more co-operative societies in the industrial north and within twenty years more than 300 societies were operating, with a total membership of 90,000. During the latter half

[1] In some ways, however, this was better than the alternative system prevalent at the time of paying wages at public houses.

of the nineteenth century expansion was rapid, membership increasing to half a million by 1880. By 1901 there were 1,438 societies with a total membership of 3 million. Since that date the number of societies has fallen as a result of amalgamation, so that by 1956 there were 1,066 societies, by 1960 only 875, and by 1968 only 480. The number continues to decline, mainly in consequence of amalgamations, though in a few cases on account of societies being wound up. The Gaitskell Report (1958) recommended that the number of societies should be reduced to 307. Though membership continued to grow it has been at an even slower rate until 1964, when it reached its peak of 13 million. Since then there has been little change in the membership, which in 1966 stood at 12·8 million. Down to 1918 the co-operative movement was heavily concentrated in the north of England, but between the two World Wars expansion was greatest in the Midlands and the South.

Societies vary enormously in size. In spite of amalgamations there were still 117 societies in 1965 each with fewer than 1,000 members. On the other hand, the largest, the London Co-operative Society, had $1\frac{1}{4}$ million members, and there were eighteen others each with over 100,000 members. The central branches of the large societies resemble department stores both in size and in the variety of goods offered for sale, whereas the smallest societies are not unlike the village general store. What might be regarded as a typical co-operative society is one with ten to twenty-four branches—a sort of small multiple. Co-operative societies continued to increase their share of retail trade down to 1957, when it formed $11\frac{1}{2}\%$ of the total. Since then, although their turnover has continued to increase, their share of total retail trade has declined—for the first time in the history of the movement —falling to $10\frac{1}{2}\%$ in 1961. Their total turnover in monetary terms averaged an annual increase of barely $1\%$ between 1960 and 1967, and this represented a decline in real terms of about $3\%$ per year.

From their earliest days the co-operative societies have been most strongly established in the sale of foodstuffs. The smaller the society the greater will be the proportion of its turnover from this branch of trade. Even today half the turnover of retail co-operatives as a whole still comes from foodstuffs. There is, however, great variation in the co-operatives' share in the total market of different foodstuffs—over $33\frac{1}{3}\%$ of the total sale of milk in Great Britain, but only $10\%$ of meat.

The Co-operative Wholesale Society (founded in 1864) and the Scottish Co-operative Wholesale Society were established for the purpose of supplying stock to the retail societies. In their organisation they are generally similar to the retail societies. Just as a member of a retail society receives a dividend in proportion to his purchases, so a retail society receives a share of the profit of the wholesale society in proportion to its purchases from it. There is, however, one important difference: whereas the individual member has only a single vote at meetings, whatever the amount of his purchases, the retail societies vote at meetings of the CWS in proportion to their purchases, thus giving the larger—and generally more efficient—societies a greater measure of control. For a long time the wholesale societies have owned tea plantations, and they also now own over 300 factories. In recent years, too, they have come to take a more direct interest in retailing through their subsidiary, Co-operative Retail Services Ltd., the aim of the CRS being to establish branches in places where it has been found impossible to establish the usual kind of local retail society and also to take over existing societies where this course is felt necessary to save a society from having to close down. In the past, one of the great advantages of co-operative societies over forms of retail trade was the loyalty of members who supported the movement for its own sake. Though less strongly than formerly many members still feel this sense of loyalty. Not all members, however, approve of the political allegiance of the co-operative party. Support came, too, from those who liked the apparent democratic organisation of the co-operative society. In the smaller societies it is possible for most members, if they so wish, to attend and vote at meetings and exercise a small measure of control. In the larger societies individual members have much less influence, and this appears to be to the advantage of these societies. In general they are more efficiently managed and more progressive in outlook than the smaller societies whose policy is subject to greater interference from the ordinary member, who rarely possesses business acumen or experience.

## III. IMPERFECT COMPETITION IN RETAILING

### Perfect and imperfect markets

The perfect market is a concept of economic theory. For a market to be perfect a number of conditions must be fulfilled. In the first place, the commodity offered for sale must be perfectly homogeneous, all units of it being identical, so that it does not matter from whom the buyer makes a purchase. Similarly, the seller must not show any preferential treatment towards any buyers. Secondly, there must be a large number of both buyers and sellers so that each seller can offer only a small fraction of the total amount of the commodity coming on to the market and each buyer similarly must wish to purchase only a small fraction of the total supply available. Thus, there must be no inducement to suppliers to restrict supply in order to keep up the price, nor must any buyer be strong enough to persuade a seller to reduce the price in his favour. Thirdly, all buyers and sellers are assumed to be in complete contact with one another, so that what occurs in one part of the market is immediately known throughout the entire market. If the conditions prevailed for a perfect market a single price (after allowance has been made for costs of transport) would rule throughout at any given time.

Though no example of a perfect market can be found in actual conditions some markets approach more nearly to perfection than others. In the highly organised wholesale markets a degree of perfection is achieved by business being concentrated under one roof in a special building where it is carried on according to a prescribed set of rules. This brings buyers and sellers into close contact with one another. Business is conducted by private treaty or by auction, the former where the commodity can be graded (*e.g.* cotton, wheat) and the latter where accurate grading is not possible and sampling is necessary (*e.g.* wool, tea).

Many markets are very imperfect, as, for example, most retail markets. A tour of all the shops in a town engaged in the same branch of retail trade would reveal quite a wide divergence of price for similar goods. The extent of price variation has been increased by the ending of resale price maintenance (*see* below, pp. 87–89). Large numbers of consumers, however, are still unaware of these price variations and many of those who are aware do not think it worth the time and effort necessary to seek out the low-price shops. There are also many people who are still inclined to look askance at cut prices, especially of non-branded goods. More important in retailing, two articles are not homogeneous even if physically identical, as perhaps with different brands of the same product. Convenience of situation of the shop and the service offered—especially a delivery service—differentiate one shop from another.

## Branded goods

The practice of distinguishing the product of one manufacturer from those of his competitors by a distinctive brand name or trade-mark was first applied to a number of pharmaceutical products some sixty years ago. Gradually, the practice spread, at first to grocery products and more recently to an ever-widening range of merchandise. Bound up as this practice was with resale price maintenance, it had the support of the great mass of small, independent retailers. Branded goods provide an example of a particular form of imperfect competition—imperfect oligopoly—when production of a commodity is in the hands of relatively few producers. The products of the various manufacturers may actually differ from one another hardly at all except in the brand name. The differentiation is stressed by keen competitive advertising, each advertiser attempting to persuade buyers that his brand is superior to all others. As a result one brand is not regarded by consumers as a perfect substitute for another. If a manufacturer is successful in convincing a large enough number of buyers of the superiority of his brand he might be able to insist, when resale price maintenance was permitted, on a higher price for his product.

Branded goods, however have advantages for both retailer and consumer. Such goods are uniformly packed and can be easily identified and handled by people lacking expert knowledge of the commodity. They are sold simply by being passed across the counter and require no weighing out by the retailer. They can be both bought and sold without prior inspection. Since each manufacturer makes himself responsible for advertising his own brand, such goods are in effect pre-sold for the retailer. The consumer who buys branded goods knows their quality from past experience and that they will be of uniform quality wherever he buys them. The main drawback to the independent retailer is that, if he is to provide a satisfactory service for his customers, he has to stock several brands of the same commodity since, as already noted, consumers do not regard one brand as a perfect substitute for another. Formerly, the main disadvantage of branded goods to the large-scale retailer was that they were subject to resale price maintenance so that he was debarred from instituting price competition against his less efficient rivals.

**Resale price maintenance**

Resale price maintenance occurs when a manufacturer is able to insist on all retailers selling his product at a stated fixed price which can be nationally advertised. As already noted, the practice was closely linked with the branding of goods, for it was only to such goods that resale price maintenance could be effectively applied.

The outstanding development of retailing in the late nineteenth century was the emergence of the department store with its policy of "small profits, quick returns" based on cutting prices. Towards the end of the nineteenth century the multiple shop entered the field of large-scale retail trade with a similar policy. A small number of the larger, more efficient independent retailers fought their new competitors with their own weapon—price cutting. Fewer of the independent retailers were adversely affected by the department stores, which were established only in large cities, than were injured by the multiple shops, which were opened in towns of more moderate size. The mass of independent retailers, accustomed to large profit margins, a more leisurely style of business and the provision of the maximum amount of service to their customers, were seriously alarmed at the new development in retailing. This development they hoped to check by persuading manufacturers to insist on fixed prices for their products to protect the small shopkeeper from the price competition of his large-scale rivals.

Thus, the demand for resale price maintenance originally came from retailers and not from manufacturers. Indeed, a good deal of campaigning was required by organised groups of retailers before manufacturers could be induced to adopt the fixed price. It was only later that manufacturers themselves came to favour this practice. The first manufacturers to agree to resale price maintenance were producers of pharmaceutical goods, which were among the first to be branded. As the range of branded goods widened so did resale price maintenance. Though at first opposed to the practice, manufacturers came to see that it could be turned to their advantage since it made available to them a larger number of sales outlets—including the smallest and least efficient shops. This meant that the retailer's mark-up on goods subject to resale price maintenance had to be large enough to yield the least efficient retailers a profit. Though resale price maintenance did not prevent the development of multiples, it deprived them of price competition and so checked their expansion, thereby helping many of the smaller independent retailers to survive. In other words, under resale price maintenance the incentive to improve efficiency was reduced.

Resale price maintenance, therefore, meant that consumers had to pay higher prices for a widening range of goods, estimated at 25% of all consumer spending before this passing of the *Resale Prices Act* in 1964. In return some shops offered them services such as delivery of goods, greater choice and a period of credit; others merely gave convenience of situation. Nevertheless, consumers who did not want credit or delivery had to pay the same fixed price. The consumer who was prepared to purchase in larger quantities could not be given better terms. A retailer who increased the efficiency of his business could not pass on to his customers some of his reduced overhead costs in the form of lower prices. On the other hand, some customers may tolerate the slightly higher price and inefficiency of the small shop in return for the greater convenience of its situation; other consumers may prefer to pay for a delivery service through higher prices rather than spend time and trouble and incur the expense of collecting goods themselves in their own cars. Nevertheless, resale price maintenance had the serious objection that it reduced consumers' choice.

### The end of resale price maintenance

The abolition of resale price maintenance was achieved in easy stages. The Lloyd Jacob Committee, appointed to consider the practice, reported in 1949 largely in its favour on the ground that its abolition would bring greater uncertainty into both the manufacturing of branded goods and their sale. It estimated that about 30% of consumers' goods were subject to resale price maintenance. At this time manufacturers enforced their fixed price on retailers by taking collective action against any retailer who infringed this condition of sale by cutting off all their supplies to him. The Committee recommended that resale price maintenance should be permitted but that joint action against a retailer by a group of manufacturers should be made illegal, only the particular manufacturer whose fixed price had not been adhered to being allowed to cut off supplies. Collective action by manufacturers to enforce resale price maintenance was condemned in 1955 by the Monopolies and Restrictive Practices Commission. This was quickly followed by the *Restrictive Trade Practices Act* of 1956 which carried out this recommendation of the Lloyd Jacob Committee, but for the first time it recognised the legal right, enforceable in court, of an individual manufacturer to take action against a retailer. This Act set up a Restrictive Practices Court which took over from the Monopolies Commission enquiries into cases involving resale price maintenance. One such enquiry concerned the Net Book Agreement which the Court upheld as not being against the public interest. Finally came the *Resale Prices Act* of 1964 which abolished resale price maintenance from 1965 in all cases except those where it could be shown to the satisfaction of the Restrictive Practices Court that its continuance was in the interest of consumers. Though many manufacturers' associations applied to the Restrictive Practices Court to retain resale price maintenance for their products, the summary dismissal of many of the early applications by the court led to many other applications being withdrawn unheard. After the passing of this Act manufacturers could cut off supplies to retailers only when it could be shown that their products were being used as "loss-leaders." Thus, after being operated for over sixty years, resale price maintenance virtually came to an end in 1965, and price competition returned to retailing.[1]

## Excess capacity in the retail trade

Imperfect competition in retailing has resulted in an excessive number of shops. In the eyes of consumers no two shops are exactly alike, the main form of differentiation being difference of location. The fact that almost every shop is more conveniently situated for some people gives it quite an effective, if somewhat limited, degree of monopoly. Other points of differentiation arise because all shops do not give the same range of services.

The retail trade is one of the few remaining types of business in which it is still possible for a person with only a small amount of capital to set up in business for himself. In most cases no special training is required, though some business ability is necessary if a venture is to be successful. In fact, ease of entry has led to many

[1] To the end of 1968 the only successful applicants were book and map publishers.

people with little ability setting up in retailing, with the result that many failures occur.

Many of those engaged in retailing on their own account earn much less than they could earn in other occupations. Evidently they prefer the feeling of independence that being self-employed gives them. Many of them, however, are able to continue only because retailing is not their sole source of income, a wife, for example, sometimes looking after the shop while her husband is away at work, while the prevalence of the five-day week generally makes it possible for the husband to help in the shop on Saturdays.

Resale price maintenance and the widening range of branded goods helped to sustain excess in the retail trade. Branded goods are of equal quality wherever they are bought and resale price maintenance protected the small inefficient shops from price competition from their more efficient, powerful competitors.

The location of two or three small shops within competitive distance of one another will not necessarily benefit consumers. If each shop has only a small turnover its running costs in relation to its sales will be high, and its survival, therefore, will be possible only if its prices are high. In such a case competition will not reduce prices. Competition from a more efficient large-scale retailer, unhampered by resale price maintenance, is a different matter, and may result in the closure of some small shops.

To reduce the number of shops it has been suggested that a system of licensing should be introduced such as that employed during the Second World War. For example, the president of the Co-operative Congress of 1966 declared that it was the duty of the Government to "curb the indiscriminate proliferation of shops." In some towns the number of "fish and chip" shops is restricted by the local authority. In some trades—for example, newspapers—wholesalers restrict the number of retail outlets. To restrict entry into retailing by artificial means such as licensing would only increase the monopoly element of those fortunate enough to secure a licence and so would bring no benefit to consumers. Other influences now appear to be at work that are likely to drive out of business the inefficient shops and so reduce numbers—keener competition following the ending of resale price maintenance and the imposition of the selective employment tax. Thus, consumers by their own actions may be able to decide which shops shall survive.

## IV. CURRENT DEVELOPMENTS IN RETAILING

### The continued expansion of retailing

As the standard of living of a people rises so does consumers' expenditure, but the whole of this extra spending is not devoted to

purchases from retail shops. As the family income rises above a
certain level more money tends to be spent on activities such as
motoring, boating, travel and holidays and probably more will be
saved, but those in the lower income groups spend a large proportion
of their increased pay in the shops, especially on durable goods. The
following table shows the increase in consumers' expenditure in
recent years both in money terms and in real terms:

TABLE XX
*Consumers' Expenditure*

| Year | Consumers' expenditure (actual) | Consumers' expenditure at constant prices (1958) |
|---|---|---|
| | £ million | £ million |
| 1958 | 15,373 | 15,373 |
| 1961 | 17,871 | 17,124 |
| 1962 | 18,892 | 17,461 |
| 1963 | 20,023 | 18,270 |
| 1964 | 21,577 | 19,082 |
| 1965 | 22,956 | 19,421 |
| 1966 | 24,296 | 19,811 |
| 1967 | 25,323 | 20,211 |

Source: *Blue Books on National Income and Expenditure.*

Although consumers increased their expenditure between 1961 and
1967 by £7,452 million, *i.e.* by 41% in money terms or 18% in real
terms, the *proportion* of their expenditure going to retail shops declined as more was spent on housing, fuel, motoring and services.
In fact, in real terms retail trade increased by only about 8% during
these six years.

It is of interest to compare the expansion of sales achieved by the
various types of retail trade:

TABLE XXI
*Expansion of Sales*

| Type of retailer | % increase in sales 1961–67 |
|---|---|
| Independent shops | +19% |
| Multiple shops | +42% |
| Co-operative societies | + 5% |
| Department stores | +21% |
| Mail order business | +88% |

Source: *Annual Abstract of Statistics.*

## Shares of retailing

More significant, however, is the change in the share of each type
of retailing in total retail sales:

TABLE XXII
*Shares of Retail Trade*

| Type of retailer | 1961 | 1964 | 1967 |
|---|---|---|---|
| | % | % | % |
| Independent shops | 54 | $52\frac{1}{2}$ | 49 |
| Multiple shops | 28 | $30\frac{1}{4}$ | $33\frac{1}{2}$ |
| Co-operative societies | $10\frac{1}{2}$ | $9\frac{1}{2}$ | $8\frac{1}{2}$ |
| Department stores | 5 | 5 | 5 |
| Mail order business | $2\frac{1}{2}$ | $2\frac{3}{4}$ | 4 |

Source: *Annual Abstract of Statistics.*

If a longer period is taken the decline of the co-operative societies' share in retail trade is even more striking—falling from $11\frac{1}{2}\%$ in 1957 to $8\frac{1}{2}\%$ in 1967.

Of the long-established forms of retail trade the most successful since the Second World War has been the multiple shop. The expansion of the multiples, so pronounced a feature of retail development during 1950–61, has continued since 1961. Table XXII above shows that multiples increased their share of the greater volume of retail trade from 28 to over 30%. This period also saw an expansion of mail-order business and the rise of the discount house. In spite of a huge increase in turnover, the share of mail-order business in retailing is still small. The discount house, however, appears as yet to be only in its infancy in Britain. These new developments were achieved at the expense of the co-operative societies and independent retailers, though the department stores have only just succeeded in holding their own. Those forms of retailing which have increased their share of trade appear to be the ones that have adapted themselves most quickly to new developments and taken advantage of economies of scale. Let us consider each form of retailing in turn.

## Mail-order business

Most of the department stores and some other large shops have had mail-order departments for a considerable time. Some manufacturers of goods of limited appeal have always preferred to market them in this way. Some wholesalers, too, have developed mail-order retailing. The introduction of c.o.d. (cash on delivery) by the Post Office assisted the growth of mail-order business. The number of firms which made mail-order business their only form of retailing was relatively small before the last war but since the early 1950s, though there has been little change in their numbers, their turnover has increased very considerably. Between 1950 and 1965 mail-order business in Great Britain increased by over eight times from £35 million to over £300 million. Nevertheless, it still forms only $2\frac{3}{4}\%$ of retail trade.

This expansion in mail-order business has been achieved mainly by the specialist mail-order house, three of which, with no other interest in retailing, dominate this form of trading. Orders are mainly secured through a large number of part-time agents, goods being chosen from catalogues. Credit is usually given, payment often being by weekly instalments which the agents collect. The prices charged by mail-order firms are much the same as those of retail shops. The expansion of their turnover is due to the nature of the services they offer, especially useful to housewives who go out to work—orders collected and goods delivered. Credit will be an attraction to many buyers. To overcome the difficulties inherent in buying things from catalogue illustrations a mail-order firm must be prepared to allow customers to return goods which they find unsuitable. Similarly, to retain the goodwill of their customers—and also to reduce to a minimum the volume of returns—it is necessary to maintain high standards of quality. Advertising and delivery costs are heavy for mail-order firms, but they are able to buy in bulk from manufacturers, and the employment of agents, working on a commission basis, is less costly than running a chain of shops.

## Retail discount houses

Of American origin, the discount house is the form of retailing most recently introduced. Since 1950 they have rapidly increased in numbers in the United States. The range of merchandise is similar to that of the department store but, like the multiples, they concentrate on good selling lines both in durables and in foodstuffs. Bulk purchases are made on favourable terms from manufacturers and resold to consumers for cash at a substantial discount—hence their name. Only a minimum amount of service is given: they are generally organised on self-service lines, delivery of goods is rarely undertaken (and, if so, charged for) and no credit is given. On the other hand, they often offer more convenient opening hours than the ordinary shops. Since most customers come in their own cars—of necessity if they are to take away bulky commodities—good parking facilities are required. In Great Britain some discount houses have opened in the suburbs of towns, using former cinemas as premises.

As yet, there are few discount houses in Great Britain, but with the abolition of resale price maintenance their number is likely to increase. After the passing of the *Restrictive Trade Practices Act* of 1956 the multiples and some other shops cut their prices for branded goods, individual manufacturers apparently preferring not to take action against them. However, when the discount houses adopted this policy, they came up against stiffer opposition from some manufacturers who were no doubt urged on by independent traders. Other manufacturers, who recognised the price-cutters as their best customers, ignored what was happening. For the first few years there was something of a running fight between discount houses and manufacturers, which ended in some discount houses undertaking not to sell below the manufacturer's fixed price. In these circumstances the discount houses could make little progress. The *Resale Prices Act*, 1964, however, completely altered the situation and opened the way to an expansion of discount selling.

Another important development in the United States has been the construction of shopping centres just beyond the boundaries of towns where land was cheap and it was possible to make extensive provision for the parking of cars. This has been the retailers' reply to present-day city congestion and the consequent car-parking problem. Two obstacles stand in the way of this kind of development in Great Britain—land is scarcer than in the United States, and the designation of green belts around towns and cities makes planning permission difficult to obtain. Although the use of the motor car for shopping is increasing in Great Britain, most shoppers in this country still shop on foot and buy in small quantities. By 1969 only three out-of-town shopping centres had been opened in Great Britain though several others have been planned.

## Multiple shops

We have already seen how the multiples increased their efficiency by their integration of wholesaling and retailing, and by restricting consumers' choice to the best-selling lines within the price range where demand was greatest. The multiples were quick to take advantage of the *Restrictive Trade Practices Act* of 1956 to cut the prices of many branded goods, knowing that manufacturers could no longer take collective action against them. It was soon clear that individual manufacturers were generally unwilling to take the action open to them under the Act. The ending of resale price maintenance in 1964 put them in a stronger position to compete against their main rivals— the co-operative societies and independent retailers—than they had been in for over sixty years, and the full effect of this has not yet been seen.

To reduce the costs of retailing, self-service was introduced. The first shop of this kind in the United Kingdom was opened as long ago as 1942 by the London Co-operative Society, and, though development of this method of retailing was slow at first, the co-operative societies led the way until 1963, when they were overtaken by the multiples, which also in recent years have forged even farther ahead of co-operative societies in the opening of large self-service supermarkets.[1] The cost of labour in relation to turnover for a super-

[1] The first supermarkets were opened on the Pacific Coast of the United States in the 1930s.

market is only half, and for the small self-service shops about 70%, of that of the ordinary shop. The ever-widening range of packaged and well-advertised branded goods has made self-service possible. It is a method of sale that can be employed most effectively with goods in regular demand for which the customer does not require the shop-keeper's advice. Self-service provides a speedier shopping service to the customer who prefers this and the lower price, at the cost of his own effort, to being served by an assistant. The supermarkets were quick to take advantage of the ending of resale price maintenance, often cutting their prices of some goods before the Restrictive Practices Court had announced its decision.

## Department stores

As already noted, the share of retail trade enjoyed by department stores declined during the period covered by the three censuses of distribution, 1951–61. Table XXII (p. 92) shows that during 1961–67 this decline was checked. However, too much, perhaps, should not be made of this. The multiples have increased their share of retail trade by opening a large number of new branches. On the other hand, few new department stores have been opened, so that their increased turnover has gone almost entirely to the stores already in existence.

Department stores have always made a feature of their service to customers, and so it is no surprise to find that their cost of labour in relation to turnover is higher than in any other form of large-scale retail trade. They have also continued to offer their customers a wide choice and so have not been able to make as large purchases of particular lines as might otherwise have been possible. The main reason for their slower rate of progress, however, is that the market for which from their early days they have catered has not expanded to the same extent as other markets. Their standards of quality and price policy were framed to appeal to customers who were rather more discriminating than most and who were both willing and able to pay for better-quality goods. Taxation in the past twenty-five years has tended to fall more heavily on these people. The huge increase in purchasing power during this period, however, has accrued to people in the lower income ranges, and the multiples have more effectively met this new demand. The department stores that have expanded most are those that have adjusted themselves to these new conditions. If greater economies of scale are to be achieved by department stores it may require more centralised control of buying with a reduction in the status of the former departmental buyers to that of mere depart-mental sales managers.

## Co-operative societies

In Great Britain the share of the co-operative societies in retail trade has been declining since 1951. Nevertheless, only in the Scandinavian countries do co-operative societies have a larger share of retail trade than those in Great Britain, while in the rest of Western Europe they enjoy only 2–3% of retail trade. Though they were the first to introduce self-service and supermarkets, their general adoption of this method of retailing has been slow, owing mainly to the reluctance of societies outside Greater London to adopt it. As a result two-thirds of all self-service shops and supermarkets were by 1966 in the hands of the multiples.

The fact that most co-operative societies still prefer the dividend to price-cutting has handicapped them in competition with the multiples. The ending of resale price maintenance is likely to put the co-operative societies at still greater disadvantage as compared with the multiples.

The principal way in which the multiples have scored over the co-operative societies is in closely integrating their retailing and wholesaling functions. Each retail co-operative society is autonomous and is not compelled to deal exclusively with the CWS. This is due not to a decline in the loyalty of the retail societies to the CWS but to the efforts of the more efficient societies to compete more successfully against their rivals. The efficiency of the CWS as wholesaler is further hampered by its having to operate over 200 factories. Its efficiency might be improved if its manufacturing activities were hived off, so that it could specialise in wholesaling.

It would appear that the traditional loyalty of supporters of the co-operative movement is waning, customers tending to go to those shops, whether co-operative or not, that give them what they want at prices they are prepared to pay. There is, too, a wide difference between the large and more progressive co-operative societies and the smaller ones. Some societies are run most efficiently; others are grossly inefficient, partly because they are below the optimum size for efficient operation, and partly because the members of their committees have little business experience and tend to be narrow in their outlook. Because co-operative societies were able to expand in the past with little conscious effort, they think they should continue to do so. The reduction in the number of small societies through amalgamations with larger ones, however, reduces the number of inefficient directors.

Many of the weaknesses of co-operative societies were high-lighted in the Gaitskell Report (1958), and recommendations were made for improving the efficiency of the societies. For example, it was suggested that their policy should be to sell at the same prices as the most successful competitors whatever effect this might have on the dividend. In fact, some co-operative societies have opened self-service shops or supermarkets in town centres where cut prices replace both the dividend and a delivery service in order to compete more effectively against the multiples. The Report stressed too that reserves were of greater importance than the dividend if societies were to modernise their shops. The recommendation that the smaller societies should merge with larger ones is in process of being carried out, though it is taking some time to accomplish. In many towns, too, many of the less remunerative suburban branches have been closed.[1] Co-operative Retail Services Ltd.—the retail society founded by the CWS—can assist the amalgamation process by taking over small societies, especially where local rivalry is too strong for local mergers to be feasible. Some branches of the CRS offer members, on payment of a small deposit, continuous credit up to £20, or in some cases £40. The Report also criticised the management of both the retail societies and the CWS, and recommended that day-to-day management should be in the hands of paid officials.

Following on the Gaitskell Report the CWS in 1966 for the first time appointed a highly paid executive with high-level business experience to be responsible for the management of the undertaking, the board only to decide policy. A reorganisation of the CWS followed and in 1967 the Co-operative Union outlined plans for a complete reorganisation of the retail side of the movement. It was suggested that throughout the country the shops of the co-operative retail societies should have uniform fascias (a practice which many of the multiples have abandoned), uniformly designed delivery vans, and for the 2,000 products of the CWS a single brand symbol. More attention was to be paid to staff training and to the quality of goods offered for sale. An extensive advertising campaign was proposed. It was recommended that the amalgamation of societies should be accelerated, the aim being to merge the co-operative societies of England and Wales into fifty regional societies—the Gaitskell Report had suggested 300—each based on a town with not less than 100,000 inhabitants. How long this will take it is not easy to say, for many societies have a keen sense of independence and generally only when they are in financial difficulties are they prepared to consider a merger with larger and more efficient neighbouring societies. Nevertheless, since 1960 the number of co-operative societies in the country has been almost halved and each year since then the number of mergers has increased. If the scheme for regional societies is carried out, a number of huge concerns will be created, the largest being the North London, the South London, the Manchester (a merger of 38 societies), the South Yorkshire (a merger of 16 societies) and the Liverpool (a

[1] Between 1960 and 1968 3,000 branches were closed.

merger of 11 societies). These societies will be comparable in turn-over with the largest multiples, and so should be able to take advantage of economies of scale.

There is no doubt that the co-operative movement has failed to keep up with the times and up to now neglected to adapt itself to the changing conditions of retailing in a more affluent society. This is shown by the rising average age of members as fewer and fewer young married couples join, more than 40% of members being over 55 and less than 17% under 35 years of age.

The dividend, which has declined very sharply during the past twenty years, appears no longer to be the attraction that it once was. In the past the policy of co-operative societies was to charge the same prices as the independent shops in the locality, and if this resulted in a society earning higher than average profits the members would benefit by receiving a higher rate of dividend. In a district where prices were low the dividend also would be low. It would appear, however, that, in spite of a rising standard of living, many people have become more and not less price conscious, so that a low price has a greater appeal to them than a dividend payable after a lapse of time. An increasing number of people, too, have come to regard the co-operative as just another shop, caring little about the ideals of the movement or its democratic organisation, and buying there for economic or personal motives and not out of sentiment or loyalty. It seems clear, therefore, that the aura of idealism in which the move-ment started has little or no appeal for the shoppers of today, young or old. This being the case, the co-operative societies can survive only if they can make themselves efficient and commercially viable in competition with other forms of retailing. If this means greater centralisation of authority with all staff responsible to a head office, the recruitment of managers from outside the movement and abolition of locally elected management committees, it would seem to make of the co-operative societies a new giant multiple commercial organi-sation and to be the end of the road for consumers' co-operation.

### Independent retailers

For over sixty years the independent retailer has had to face in-creasing competition from his large-scale rivals—the department store, the co-operative society and the multiple. Further-com-petition has now come from the mail-order business and more recently from the discount house. The ending of resale price main-tenance has made the position of many independent retailers par-ticularly vulnerable.

Not surprisingly, therefore, the share of retailing of the independent trader continues to decline, and it seems likely that in the near future many more small retailers will be compelled to close down. Nevertheless, down to 1967 independent retailers were responsible for almost half total retail business. Those who have tried to withstand the competition of the multiples by offering their customers service in the shop and delivery of purchases have been particularly severely hit by the selective employment tax and the increased cost of operating motor vehicles. Fearing the effect of new developments on their own position, some wholesalers have joined with retailers, more particularly in the grocery trade, to form voluntary chains in order to secure some of the economies of scale enjoyed by the multiples. Retailers who are members of a chain voluntarily agree to purchase their stock from a particular wholesaler. Transport costs to the wholesaler are reduced by making deliveries to retailers only on certain days, and retailers agree to accept larger quantities of lines that the wholesaler can supply at reduced prices. After a slow start more and more retailers have come to see the advantage of belonging to a voluntary chain. Membership of a chain is usually restricted to retailers who are not in competition with one another, and assistance is given to enable members to improve the lay-out and appearance of their shops and reorganise them for self-service. An alternative development has been the emergence of the self-service wholesaler. A retailer can obtain stock more cheaply if he is prepared to use his own transport to collect it from the wholesaler. In these ways some independent retailers are attempting to increase their efficiency, reduce their costs and increase their turnover. These facilities, however, are not open to the very small retailers, especially now that the voluntary chains have become more selective in their admission of new members.

In recent years trading stamps—a sales device actually with a long history—have become more widespread in Great Britain. They were already well established in the United States, where in 1966 over 80% of all retail trade was covered by trading stamps. They can be used as an alternative to price-cutting, but their main purpose is to foster consumers' loyalty to a particular group of shops. Trading-stamp companies produce and sell the stamps to retailers, who are not in competition with one another, and who then give their customers stamps in proportion to their purchases, the stamp-trading company afterwards exchanging the stamps for a wide range of "gifts." Since the passing of the *Trading Stamps Act*, 1964, stamps have had to be exchangeable—at a lower rate—for cash. Opposition to trading stamps has come from many directions—retailers who did not wish to employ them, the Consumer Council and Members of Parliament who considered stamps to be an undesirable means of influencing consumers' choice of retailer.

## V. SOME FURTHER ASPECTS OF MARKETING

### Consumer credit

Consumer credit can take several forms—direct credit between retailer and consumer, instalment buying, hire purchase, a personal loan from a bank, or by means of a credit card. Of these, hire purchase is undoubtedly the most popular. The granting of credit as a retail service has declined in some branches of retail trade with the expansion of cash payment in return for cut prices. With the development of the voluntary chain and self-service wholesaling there has also been a reduction in credit between wholesaler and retailer. Instalment buying has never been very popular, though a good deal of mail-order business is conducted on this system. The bank personal loan is open only to people with accounts at commercial banks. At first credit cards were available only to approved people in the higher income ranges, but the credit card issued by Barclays Bank has extended their availability to a wider clientèle. The credit card, however, is desired as much for convenience as for credit, since payment has to be made monthly.

### Hire purchase

The purchase of the more expensive kinds of consumers' durables has always been a difficult undertaking for many people. Not only those in the lower income groups find it hard to save up in advance; some people prefer to pay out of income so as not to disturb their savings. Hire purchase—another retail device first developed in the United States—makes it possible to do this. Without hire purchase the sale of consumers' durable goods would probably be very small indeed.

The feature of hire purchase that distinguishes it from instalment buying is that goods bought under this system do not become the property of the purchaser until the final instalment has been paid. A deposit is required and then the balance is paid in instalments spread over an agreed period up to two years, or in some cases even longer.

Hire purchase has expanded in Great Britain for a number of reasons: (*i*) the range of consumers' durable goods has widened enormously and with a rising standard of living many of these things—washers, cookers, refrigerators, etc.—have come to be regarded as normal household necessaries; (*ii*) the motor car is a particularly expensive commodity which, but for hire purchase, would be beyond the reach of most present-day car owners; (*iii*) hire purchase has been extended to a wide range of commodities—and even services—which were formerly regarded as unsuitable for this method of retailing, such as clothing, which may be "consumed" before all the instalments have been paid, and even air travel, which may be "consumed" entirely with only the deposit paid; (*iv*) the early prejudice against hire purchase has declined and a generation has grown up that regards it as the normal method of buying many things. A drawback to hire purchase is that it makes buying too easy for some people who in consequence may undertake more commitments than they can fulfil.[1]

On account of the large amount of additional capital required, hire purchase facilities at first were offered only by department stores and other large shops, and many of them continue to do so. Nowadays the finance for hire purchase is mainly provided by finance houses—several of which are subsidiaries of British commercial banks—which obtain their funds partly by borrowing from banks and partly by accepting deposits from investors seeking a high rate of interest on their money. The following table shows how hire purchase has expanded in Great Britain in recent years and also the increasing share taken by finance houses in financing this type of business:

TABLE XXIII
*Hire Purchase*
(in £ millions)

| Financed by | 1962 | 1963 | 1964 | 1965 | 1966 | 1967 |
|---|---|---|---|---|---|---|
| Finance houses . | 569 | 614 | 754 | 836 | 756 | 742 |
| Retailers . . . | 318 | 345 | 361 | 360 | 307 | 276 |
| Total . . | 887 | 959 | 1,115 | 1,196 | 1,063 | 1,018 |

Source: *Annual Abstract of Statistics.*

Thus, between 1962 and 1967, hire purchase increased by 54% and the share of finance houses in this business from 64% in 1962 to 74% in 1967.

### Advertising

Advertising is mainly of two kinds: (*i*) informative, and (*ii*) competitive, though they cannot always be clearly distinguished. The purpose of informative advertising is to "educate" consumers, *i.e.* to make them aware of the goods and services that are available.

The aim, however, of competitive advertising is to persuade consumers to buy one manufacturer's brand of a commodity rather than another's. Thus, competitive advertising is associated with the marketing of branded goods and is a feature of two forms of imperfect competition—oligopoly and monopolistic competition. If a manufacturer can persuade a sufficient number of consumers that his

[1] Consumer protection is considered below, pp. 103–104.

product is superior to all others—even though the differentiation is only in the brand name—it becomes possible to increase sales without reducing price. The effect of competitive advertising therefore, is to keep up prices, so that in the end these "selling costs" are passed on to consumers. In the case of some pharmaceutical products advertising is the largest item entering into their cost. Consequently, to economists selling costs are regarded as one of the wastes of imperfect competition.

The total amount spent on advertising in Great Britain in 1966 was £600 million. Of this sum 46% went on newspaper advertising, 16% on television advertising with the Independent Television Authority, $5\frac{1}{2}$% on outdoor advertising and the remainder on gift coupons, free samples, catalogues, leaflets, etc. In recent years, however, newspaper advertising has been declining. Although the amount spent on advertising is large, it forms only about 2% of the national income, and on average adds at most $2\frac{1}{2}$% to prices. Clearly, individual firms benefit from advertising or they would not spend on it the amount they do. When the advertising of cigarettes on television was prohibited it resulted in an increase in the offer of gift coupons as a means of stimulating sales. Revenue from advertising forms 75% of the income of "quality" newspapers and 46% of the income of the popular journals. Without their revenue from advertising many newspapers would not be able to survive and those that did would have to be considerably increased in price.

If advertising were completely abolished it would not automatically reduce the prices of all previously advertised goods. Indeed, it might reduce the extent of a manufacturer's market, rob him of economies of scale he previously enjoyed, increase his costs and so actually compel him to raise his price. Without advertising it would be extremely difficult to put a new commodity on the market, and so competition would be reduced, thereby checking a possible fall in prices. It is significant that in general it is the most efficient and progressive firms that spend most on advertising. To the extent that advertising encourages competition it is a stimulus to greater efficiency, and this appears to be borne out by the increased advertising of the national fuel and power industries, coal, gas and electricity.

## Taxation and retailing

A variety of taxes has been evolved for taxing consumption (*see* Chapter XIII). In the United Kingdom purchase tax was first imposed in 1940 during the Second World War, mainly for the purpose of reducing demand at a time when almost all kinds of goods were in short supply. It has been retained and now takes its place alongside the excise duties on alcoholic drinks, tobacco and oil as an important source of revenue to the State. Varying the rates of purchase and the other excise duties has been developed as an instrument of fiscal policy, so that to check an inflationary expansion of demand these taxes are increased, and then reduced when it is necessary to stimulate demand. Not only can variations in these taxes be made in the budget or an interim budget but also, since the Chancellor of the Exchequer obtained power to use "the regulator," to a limited extent at any time. Taxes of this type have directional effects since they affect only certain categories of goods. Retailers of commodities subject to purchase tax—mostly consumers' durables—are faced with this arbitrary influence on the demand for their merchandise. The effect is still further exaggerated by changes in hire purchase regulations, such as an increase in the required deposit or a shortening of the period of repayment, which are often made at the same time and affect sales even more than price changes. In this way uncertainty is seriously increased in some branches of retailing.

The selective employment tax, introduced in 1966, is another heavy burden which the retailer now has to bear. Imposed partly for the sake of revenue and partly to discourage labour from entering service occupations, it falls heaviest on those kinds of retailing, such as department stores, where wages form a high proportion of operating costs. In many types of retailing—department stores, the variety chains and the larger independents—most of the shop assistants nowadays are part-time workers and, since the same rate of tax has to be paid for both full-time and part-time employees, the effect in some cases will be almost to double the tax burden. The consequences of this new tax cannot yet be clearly foreseen. It was the difficulty of obtaining full-time employees that led to the employment of so many part-timers in retailing, and so a return to the employment of full-time workers does not seem feasible. The tax may be covered by increased prices or the movement towards self-service may be accelerated and extended to many retailers who would have preferred not to introduce it. Some marginal retailers may find the burden of the tax too heavy for them and so be compelled to close. It seems probable, therefore, that SET will result not only in higher prices but in less service for consumers and eventually a reduction in the amount of labour in commercial distribution.

### Protection of the consumer

It has been found necessary to give consumers protection against some practices formerly associated with hire purchase. At one time the more unscrupulous salesmen often persuaded consumers to undertake too many commitments, with the result that they were unable to keep up with their payments. Even though only a few instalments might be outstanding, the goods could be reclaimed by the seller. An

Act of 1938 for the first time gave protection to consumers buying goods on hire purchase. It provided that, if more than one-third of the amount had been paid on an article, it could be reclaimed by the seller only if he first obtained a court order. The aim being to protect people in the lower income groups, this Act applied only to goods priced up to £100, but successive Acts have raised the maximum to £2000. Further protection was given in 1964 by allowing a consumer in certain cases four "days of grace" in which to change his mind after signing a hire purchase agreement

For a long time, by the principle of *caveat emptor*, the consumer was expected to examine and judge for himself the quality of goods offered for sale. Few consumers, however, have the necessary knowledge and experience to assess the quality of even a small fraction of all the things they buy. The Molony Report, the work of a committee appointed by the Board of Trade to consider consumer protection, was published in 1962. It recommended *inter alia*: (*i*) the introduction of the four "days of grace" into hire purchase agreements noted above; (*ii*) a tightening up of the law with regard to misrepresentation; (*iii*) the setting up of a Consumer Council to watch over the interests of consumers; (*iv*) the abolition of resale price maintenance. The Committee expressed its disappointment that consumers in general, especially those in the lower income groups, showed so little interest in its activities.

All the recommendations of the Molony Report have now been carried out. In 1963 the Government established a Consumer Council, but its functions are too general for it to be of much help to consumers. The Consumers' Association, however, through the reports in its publication, *Which?*, has influenced manufacturers who have hastened to rectify faults noted in their products.

### RECOMMENDATIONS FOR FURTHER READING

C. Fulop: *Competition in Retailing* (George Allen & Unwin).
M. Hall: *Distributive Trading* (Hutchinson).
J. B. Jeffreys and D. Knee: *Retailing in Europe* (Macmillan).
B. S. Yamey: *Resale Price Maintenance* (Weidenfeld & Nicolson).
HMSO: Reports on Censuses of Distribution (1951, 1957, 1961).

### QUESTIONS

1. Consider the various forms that imperfect competition takes in retailing. What legislative action has been or could be taken to reduce imperfection in this field?

2. Account for the success of the multiples in competition with (*a*) other forms of large-scale retail trade, and (*b*) the independent retailers.

3. Is resale price maintenance in the interests of (*a*) manufacturers, (*b*) distributors, (*c*) consumers? (Degree.)

4. "Advertising by firms is evidence that the profit constraint is of less importance than the sales constraint." Discuss this statement with reference to British firms. (Barking.)

5. Consider the social and economic impact of hire purchase on a modern society. (Barnsley.)

6. To what extent is advertising a wasteful use of scarce resources? (Barnsley.)

7. "Consumer acceptance must be gained at an early stage." How would a brand marketing manager carry out this exercise? (Derby.)

8. Compare the management policies and problems of (a) multiple shops; (b) department stores; (c) Marks & Spencers. (Derby.)

9. "Retailing provides the utility of time and place." Explain clearly what part retailing plays in the economic organisation of the country. (Derby.)

10. Write an essay on: Current trends in retail organisation and their impact upon wholesale trade. (Huddersfield.)

11. What are the factors which would influence a manufacturer in determining which middlemen to use when distributing his products? (Norwich.)

12. Do you consider that a reduction in the advertising and sales promotion expenditure on soap and detergents would necessarily cause a reduction in their prices? (Norwich.)

## CHAPTER IV

# MONOPOLY AND ITS CONTROL

## I. THE TENDENCY TOWARDS LARGE SCALE

### The increasing size of firms

Two hundred years ago the typical manufacturing firm was the small one-man business. The proprietor was solely responsible for raising the capital, which of necessity, therefore, was generally small in amount. Only the simplest machines were in use and since only a few men were employed they would be personally known to the owner of the business. The outstanding feature of industrial development since those days has been the increasing tendency towards large-scale production. The raising of the huge amounts of capital required for large-scale operation was made possible by the introduction of limited liability, so that in the private sector of the economy the typical business unit is now the public limited company. The largest firms in Great Britain today number their employees by the thousand, over seventy of them each having over 5,000 employees. Nevertheless, 90% of firms in this country still employ fewer than 200 persons. Firms vary greatly in size, however, between one industry and another, largely because the optimum—the most efficient size—is not the same in all lines of production. Large-scale operation, for example, is typical in the motor-car, iron and steel, and chemical industries, with 55% of the labour (68% in motor-car manufacture) being on the books of the largest firms. Indeed, in many industries, the three largest firms are responsible for 75% of total output. On the other hand, the average firm in boot and shoe manufacture and worsted weaving is small by modern standards. An important influence on the optimun is the size of the most efficient unit of capital, which is large and indivisible in some industries though small in others. As a firm expands towards the optimum it enjoys increasing returns to scale, whereas expansion beyond the optimum will result in diminishing returns.

There are two methods by which firms expand: (i) by natural growth, and (ii) by amalgamation with other firms. In their early days most firms expand by "ploughing back" profits into the business, the owners often submitting, at least temporarily, to a low standard of living to make this possible. Additional capital, however, can be more readily obtained if a business is turned into a limited company. The more progressive of the large limited companies often continue to grow by financing expansion from undistributed profits. Further expansion may be accomplished by "taking over" other firms.

Economic theory assumes that every entrepreneur aims to maximise his profit, and, that being so, he will therefore increase his scale of production if by doing so economies of scale are open to him. This has probably been the main motive for expansion, whether brought about by natural growth or by amalgamation. A second important motive for expansion has been to obtain a larger share in the market for a commodity in order to secure some measure of monopoly power. Even though the primary reason for its expansion may have been to secure economies of scale, the resulting acquisition of a large share of the market may bring with it the temptation to exploit the monopoly power so achieved. For this reason mergers always tend to be suspect, especially when firms that were formerly keen competitors are involved—as when Austin and Morris Motors in 1952 amalgamated to form the British Motor Corporation—even though this motive has often been subsidiary to the desire for economies of scale. The development of the holding company, with control over a large number of other companies, has brought into being the modern industrial giants.

In some cases mergers have taken place between firms at different stages of production in the same industry (*e.g.* Vickers Ltd.)—vertical integration—or between firms engaged on similar work (*e.g.* Lancashire Cotton Corporation)—horizontal integration. More recently there have been examples of a firm taking over another producing a totally different type of commodity in order to give the combine greater diversification of product, as when the Imperial Tobacco Company took over a firm making potato crisps. This provides a firm with a measure of protection against a falling off in the demand for one of its products.

**Economies of scale**

Economies of scale arise when costs of production increase less than proportionately as output increases, *i.e.* when production takes place in conditions of decreasing cost, with production subject to increasing returns. The larger the firm the greater the extent to which division of labour and specialisation can be carried. It then becomes possible to employ highly skilled specialists for certain jobs because in a large firm there is sufficient work for them. Some highly efficient modern forms of capital are large and expensive, so that their installation is economically justified only if a firm's output is large. Since such capital is "indivisible" it cannot be used by the small firm. Marketing economies too are available to the large firm.

Not only can it employ specialised buyers, but by buying in bulk raw materials can be purchased more cheaply. The administrative costs of a firm do not rise—at least, not at first—proportionately to output. Office machinery, too, can be used more effectively by the large firm. However, after a certain point has been reached, administration tends to become more complex, more departmentalised and often more bureaucratic, so that it tends to become an increasing cost to the firm. Other advantages accruing to the large firm include the possibility of its undertaking its own research, the provision of better welfare services for its employees to increase their efficiency, and the ability to raise additional capital more easily and generally more cheaply.

Expansion of output, however, is limited by the extent of the market, though the market may be expanded by reducing the price of the product (made possible as a result of economies of scale), and a particular firm's share of the market by means of competitive advertising. For some commodities the market is of limited extent, especially where quality and variety of product are preferred to standardisation. Another factor which ultimately is likely to check expansion is the increasing difficulty of finding men of the required competence for the management of the very large firm.

### The survival of the small firm

In spite of the tendency towards large scale in industrial production, many small firms still continue to operate successfully. There are a number of reasons why this is so. If the optimum firm in an industry is relatively small, then most firms in that industry will be small. Most worsted-weaving firms in the wool textile industry are small because the success of the industry depends on the production of a wide variety of patterns of high-quality cloth, for the manufacture of which the small firm is better able to organise the necessary "short runs." If there is only a small market for a commodity as, for example, with high-class jewellery, large-scale production is clearly out of the question. When costs of transport are very heavy in relation to other costs of production of a commodity for which there is a widespread demand, and where too the raw material required for its manufacture is widely distributed, as is the case with building-bricks, the average size of the firm in the industry again tends to be small. When personal service is involved it too can generally be provided more effectively by the small firm. Thus jobbing gardeners, plumbers, joiners and electricians often operate one-man businesses. In retailing, many small firms appear to have survived mainly because for a long time they were protected from price competition from their larger rivals by resale price maintenance, the ending of which in 1964 has left many of them with precarious viability, though there are other aspects of retailing that favour the small retailer (*see* Chapter III). It sometimes happens, too, that a large firm puts out a process to a small firm. This may be due to the fact that the optimum technical unit is too large for the optimum administrative unit, so that it is advantageous to reduce the technical unit in this way.

Whether it has been deliberately sought or not, the development of large-scale production has, therefore, had the result of giving some large firms a considerable degree of monopoly power.

## II. THE DEVELOPMENT OF MONOPOLY

### The meaning of monopoly

Neither absolute monopoly nor perfect competition exists in actual conditions. Instead we have imperfect competition, which varies from near-monopoly at one extreme to conditions almost akin to perfect competition at the other. For absolute monopoly to exist there would have to be a single producer of a commodity for which there was no substitute, and the entry of competitors into that line of production would have to be restricted. In conditions of perfect competition there would have to be unrestricted entry to the market.

Near-monopoly occurs when one firm—or a group of firms acting together—produces a large share of the total output of a commodity for which there is no close substitute. An absolute monopolist may maximise his profit by curtailing his output in order to keep up his price, the extent of his power depending on the elasticity of demand for his product. If demand is perfectly inelastic even an absolute monopolist cannot increase his profit by restricting output. The less elastic the demand the greater the power of the monopolist. When we speak of monopoly power, therefore, we mean the extent to which a producer can influence the price at which he sells his product in the market, and he does not have to be an absolute monopolist to be able to do this to some extent. In conditions of perfect competition the price ruling in the market is completely outside the control of any producer.

Thus, though the term *monopolist* in its strict sense means that the output of a commodity is in the hands of a single producer, we have come to think in terms of degrees of monopoly. More accurately, when it is said that a firm enjoys a large measure of monopoly, it really means that competition is very imperfect, and it is this condition that the term *monopoly* is now employed to connote. Indeed, the *Monopolies and Restrictive Practices Act* of 1948 defined a monopolist for the purpose of the Act as a producer of not less than 30% of a commodity, irrespective of whether there were close substitutes for it or not.

Though firms possessing a measure of monopoly power rarely take advantage of it to exploit consumers to the full, nevertheless, when production takes place in conditions where an element of monopoly exists, it generally means that consumers will have to pay a higher price than they would if competition were perfect.

## The achievement of monopoly power

A degree of monopoly power can be achieved in a number of ways. Sometimes natural conditions are favourable to monopoly; sometimes it is technological development that generates monopoly; and sometimes the environment giving rise to monopoly can be artificially created.

(*i*) *Natural monopolies.* These occur when natural resources are found only in a limited number of regions or where conditions of climate and soil restrict the production of a commodity to a particular area of the earth's surface. Many raw materials, especially minerals, fall into this category, *e.g.* diamonds (South Africa producing 90% of world output), nickel (Canada 80%), tin (South-East Asia 60%), silver (Mexico 40%), jute (East Pakistan 99%), natural rubber (South-East Asia 85%), coffee (Brazil 60%). Between the two World Wars some of these natural monopolies were reinforced by commodity restriction schemes as, for example, for tin, the largest producers persuading others to agree to restrict output in order to keep up the price. At one time Brazil produced a sufficiently large proportion of the total output of coffee for the government of that country to be able to control the supply coming on to the world market. More recently the International Coffee Organisation (ICO) has taken over this function, although only 35 of the 58 states that are members of the organisation are coffee producers.

(*ii*) *Technologically induced monopolies.* As already noted, the desire to secure economies of scale has led to a general expansion in the size of firms, partly by growth and partly through mergers. Though the aim has been to achieve greater efficiency, the result has been to give most of these firms increasing shares of the markets for their products and, therefore, some degree of monopoly power. One of the reasons for the increasing size of the business unit is that technological development is leading to the employment of industrial plant of ever-increasing size. This is particularly noticeable in the motor-car industry, where modern methods of production require the entire lay-out of the workshop to be organised on a conveyor-belt system. Not only is a huge amount of capital required before a new firm can set up in this industry but the introduction even of a new model necessitates a long preliminary period of planning followed by a retooling of the workshop, a costly undertaking. Heavy capital costs of this kind severely restrict new entrants to the industry.

Sometimes the expansion of a firm results in its acquiring a monopolistic share of the market. The British Oxygen Co. Ltd., for example, is responsible for 98% of oxygen production in Great Britain, and the merger of Courtaulds and British Celanese gave the combine 85% of the total output of rayon in this country.

(*iii*) *Voluntary associations.* Where no single firm in an industry enjoys a large enough share of the market to give it monopoly power, a group of firms may decide to act together. To achieve this end many different kinds of voluntary associations of producers were formed in the past to fix prices or restrict output, such as price rings, pools, trade associations, cartels. Such associations have now been made illegal in most countries except where they have been instituted by the Government itself. Modern methods of controlling a large share of the market are through holding companies or by means of interlocking directorates. The holding company makes it possible for a group of firms to operate a common policy and yet retain their original names. A group of firms may appear to be independent but because of interlocking directorates, a number of key directors sitting on the board of each company, a common policy can be pursued. The ability of these associations to create monopolistic positions for themselves depends on the proportion of total output under their control and the extent to which the entry of new firms into the industry can be restricted.

(*iv*) *State-created monopolies.* For many centuries in England it was regarded as the prerogative of the Crown to regulate trade, and it was in the exercise of this power that English monarchs granted to their favourites monopolies in the sale of certain commodities. Elizabeth I was particularly prone to this method of rewarding her friends. This type of state-created monopoly was abolished by an Act of Parliament of 1639. During the nineteenth century monopolies were often granted to private entrepreneurs to provide public utilities in towns, since it would clearly have been wasteful to permit rival gas, electricity or water companies to lay pipes or cables down the same streets in order to compete against one another. Similarly, with street tramways it would have been difficult, besides being wasteful, in most cases to allow competition between rival undertakings. On the other hand, it is of interest to note that wasteful competition of this kind between railway companies was actively encouraged in the mid nineteenth century, with the result that alternative routes were constructed between most large towns in Great Britain. Also in some parts of the country in the 1920s and early 1930s rival bus operators were licensed by local authorities, which did not provide public transport themselves, to run over the same routes in order to check any possible development of monopoly practices (*see* Chapter V). However, this did not involve the same amount of wasteful duplication of capital equipment as would have been the case with other public utilities. Often where monopolies of this kind were granted, safeguards against possible abuses of monopoly power and exploitation of consumers were imposed in the agreements with the operators, and often local authorities were given the right to take over these undertakings at an agreed date. In fact, many local authorities did so, and municipal ownership and operation came to be regarded as the best solution for dealing with public utility monopolies.

(*v*) *State monopolies.* In most countries the minting of coins is now a state monopoly, though it was not always so. It is the oldest form of economic activity undertaken by states. In the United Kingdom the Royal Mint is a government department of which the Chancellor of the Exchequer is *ex officio* the Master. It was not until 1660, when the Post Office was founded, that the State took upon itself the operation of a second commercial monopoly. For over three hundred years the Post Office was run as a government department under the Postmaster-General, but in 1969 it became a public corporation. In some countries the State has for a long time had a monopoly of the manufacture of tobacco and matches and, in many more, a monopoly of rail transport. Between the two World Wars the British Government established a number of public corporations including the BBC, which, prior to 1926, had been a public company. During 1945–50, when an extensive programme of nationalisation was carried out, state monopolies were established for coal, gas and electricity production and rail transport, though clearly none of these was an absolute monopoly. Some public corporations—for example, broadcasting—were monopolies from the start, but others were monopolies only when they were brought under state control. State monopolies in manufactured goods are usually protected from foreign competition by import duties.

### Artificial monopolies

There are a number of ways in which monopolies can be created:

(*i*) *Patents.* The inventor of a new machine or process can apply to the Patent Office for its registration, and if the application is granted the owner of the patent then has the exclusive right to its use for a period of sixteen years, with the possibility of renewal for a further five or ten years. The owner of a patent thus becomes the possessor of a measure of monopoly power. The purpose of the Patent Laws is to protect inventors against unscrupulous imitators, but they also make it possible for a manufacturer to patent a minor innovation merely to differentiate his product—as with the manufacturer of branded goods—from those of his competitors, and in order to restrict the entry of other manufacturers into the market.

Somewhat similar to the possession of a patent is knowledge of a secret process of manufacturing as sometimes occurs in the making of drugs.

(*ii*) *Copyright*. The owner of the copyright in a book has the sole right to reproduce it until fifty years after the death of the author. In the case of gramophone records copyright continues for fifty years from the date of issue of the record. Thus, copyright too gives its owner a degree of monopoly power.

(*iii*) *Trademarks*. Brand names and trademarks have to be registered at the Patent Office, and once this has been done they cannot be used by any other producer. Registration holds good in the first instance for only seven years but it can be renewed. Branding gives rise to imperfect oligopoly, *i.e.* the production by a few producers of different varieties of a commodity which are not regarded as perfect substitutes for one another. The aim of branding is to differentiate one's products from those of one's competitors, though the difference between one brand and another may be very slight—often little more than the name itself. Nevertheless, the manufacturer of a branded commodity is its sole producer and he will back up his monopoly by stressing the superiority over others of his particular brand by means of advertising. Thus, differentiation of the product is a means by which a manufacturer may secure an element of monopoly.

(*iv*) *Local monopolies*. Convenience of situation is one of the main advantages that the small independent retailer has over his large-scale rivals. Almost every shop is more conveniently situated than all others for some people, and so enjoys a small measure of monopoly. Improved means of passenger transport, however, have reduced the extent of local monopolies, as the proprietors of many village stores have discovered to their cost. The monopoly of the village shop caused no outcry because the proprietors made no attempt to exploit their position, overcharging being regarded as unfair, and their prices being based on those of shops operating under competitive conditions.

(*v*) *Restriction of entry*. The number of people entering some occupations is restricted—and their earnings thereby increased—by the necessity to pursue a long period of training and pass an examination at the end of it, as is the case with barristers and doctors. Entry to some professions is further restricted by insistence on a qualifying period as an articled clerk. In these cases it is the actual requirements of the occupation—intellectual ability, knowledge, practical experience and training—that impose the restriction on entry. In some other occupations, however, the acquisition of the qualification necessary for entry may be made more difficult by making the qualifying examination competitive. An unnecessarily long period of apprenticeship is another device which some craft unions employ to restrict entry.

(*vi*) *Trade Unions.* The large industrial trade unions, which include within their membership a large proportion of all those engaged in a particular industry, are in a monopolistic position for the sale of labour to that industry. By pursuing a "closed shop" policy they are able to tighten their monopolistic control over the labour the industry employs. The extent to which monopoly power can be exercised will depend on the elasticity of demand for the union's labour, and this in its turn will be determined at any given time mainly by the economic climate. The lower the general level of unemployment the greater the degree of monopoly power a union will generally be able to wield.[1]

(*vii*) *Monopsony.* Under monopoly, if absolute, there is a single *seller* for a commodity or service; under monopsony there is a single *buyer* of a commodity or service. Just as the monopolist has power to influence the price he *charges*, so the monopsonist has power to influence the price he *pays*. In the one case the extent of the power depends on the elasticity of demand for the commodity or service and in the other on the elasticity of its supply. A very large firm which has put out the manufacture of a component to a small firm may increase its orders to such an extent that it results in the small firm having to devote its entire production to this component, so that the large firm then becomes its sole customer with the power of a monopsonist. In a similar way a variety chain store may be able to bring a small manufacturing firm within the orbit of its monopsonist power. A monopolist employer of specific labour also acquires a considerable degree of monopsony. A nationalised industry, itself a monopolist, may also become a monopsonist buyer of certain materials or a monopsonist employer of its specific labour. Thus, the Central Electricity Generating Board is a monopsonist buyer of high-voltage electric cables; the only employer of railway engine drivers and signalmen is British Rail and the only employer of coal miners is the National Coal Board.

### Discriminating monopoly

It is sometimes possible for a monopolist to charge different prices to different customers. Price descrimination of this kind will occur only when two conditions are fulfilled:

(*i*) A customer must not be able to buy at the lower price and then re-sell at the higher price, *i.e.* the markets in which different prices prevail must be separate from one another.

(*ii*) The elasticity of demand for the commodity must not be the

[1] Trade unions are discussed in Chapter VIII.

same in all markets, since, if it were, the most profitable price would be the same in all cases. To maximise his profit the monopolist will charge in each market the price at which his marginal revenue is equal to his marginal cost.

The principle sometimes adopted by transport operators of "charging what the traffic will bear" is an example of discriminating monopoly (*see* pp. 139–40). To make differentiation of charging possible, each group of passengers or category of freight must form a separate market. Freight can be easily classified, and different merchandise charged different rates, but for discriminatory charges to be applied to passengers the markets have to be artificially separated by such devices as restricting cheap travel to certain days of the week, or particular times of departure and return, or travel by special train or aircraft. It is, therefore, usually cheaper to travel midweek by rail or by air and often cheaper still to travel through the night. If the traffic warrants it, passengers may be segregated into different classes—at one time there were three classes on the railways —although in this case there is some difference of service. Thus, airlines issue first-class, tourist, day-tourist, night-tourist and excursion tickets. Railway season tickets, however, are more an example of the economy of bulk buying than of descriminatory prices. An airline may separate business from holiday travel by offering those travelling for pleasure lower fares only when the cost of travel is included as part of a "package" holiday offered by a travel agency. The railways are able to offer particularly cheap fares for travel by special excursion train, since the marginal cost of running an additional train is relatively low and the fixed costs have to be covered whether the train runs or not. However, as was pointed out in the Beeching Report (*see* pp. 161–2), the cost of maintaining rolling stock for seasonal excursions is high in proportion to its use. So far as is possible, lower fares are charged only to those people who otherwise would not have used the service. Clearly, however, passenger travel markets overlap, and so some people who would have been quite willing to pay the ordinary fare will be able to take advantage of the reduced fares.

Similarly, the fact that different prices are charged for different groups of seats in theatres, cinemas and concert halls is due not only to some seats being better located than others but also to an element of discriminating monopoly being present. The first edition of a new novel by an established writer of fiction may be priced at £2 but subsequent editions may be brought out at successively lower prices, with finally a cheap paperback selling for a small fraction of £1. Again, there is clearly a difference in the quality of production of the different editions and some people may be unwilling to wait for the appearance of a cheaper edition, but, as with the theatre seats, an attempt is being made to charge readers as much as they are prepared to pay and so reduce the amount of consumer's surplus accruing to those who would have been willing to pay more. As with travel, there will again be some overlapping of the markets, and expectation of a later cheap edition may deter some people from buying the first edition. A large producer can bring out two or more lines of his product at different prices, separating the markets by offering them under different names and packaged differently, with in effect little, if any, actual difference between them. Similarly, *de luxe* versions of some models of motor cars are priced much more highly than the additional accessories and styling warrant.

Like railways, gas and electricity undertakings have heavy fixed costs relative to their variable and marginal costs. To encourage greater consumption they are prepared to supply gas or electricity at lower rates, and they can effectively separate one market from the other by applying the reduced charge only after a certain level of consumption has been exceeded. This policy appears to be justified on the ground that every consumer should pay a share of the heavy fixed costs. In addition to a measure of discriminating monopoly there is, too, as with railway season tickets, a discount for bulk purchase. The regional electricity boards have also introduced a discriminatory price in favour of people using night-storage heaters and other forms of "off-peak" consumption in cases where the markets can be effectively separated by measuring consumption by different meters.

## III. FOR AND AGAINST MONOPOLY

### In favour of monopoly

Monopoly may in some cases result in greater efficiency than sometimes subsists in competitive conditions. When economies of scale continue to be obtainable expansion of the firm may proceed until the single firm comprises the whole industry and a monopoly has been achieved. If expansion which results in monopoly brings a firm nearer to the optimum, it will then have reached its most efficient size. Between the two World Wars the British Government actively encouraged the amalgamation of firms—in the name of what was then called "rationalisation"—and as a result Woolcombers Ltd. and the Lancashire Cotton Corporation were formed. The aim was to secure greater efficiency by closing the less efficient mills to reduce excess capacity and concentrating production where it could be carried on most efficiently. In 1966 the Government established the Industrial Reorganisation Corporation to encourage and assist the amalgamation of small firms to enable them to benefit from economies of scale and so improve their efficiency; this is, in effect, a continuation of the earlier policy of rationalisation. Similarly, excess capacity in retailing, although increasing competition, does not always result in lower prices for consumers.

It used to be said that monopoly eliminates one of the wastes of imperfect competition—namely, advertising—but recent competitive advertising by the gas, electricity and coal-mining industries shows that this does not necessarily follow the creation of monopolies, though, of course, the three fuel and power industries are not absolute monopolies. As already noted, it was recognised that competition would be wasteful in the case of public utilities and, therefore, their operation had to be left to monopolies. During the Second World War milk delivery in each street was restricted to one roundsman (except for the co-operative society) to reduce overlapping, and though this system was introduced because of the shortage of labour at the time, greater efficiency was achieved.

By production on a large scale and standardisation of products, costs of production and prices to consumers of a wide range of commodities could be considerably reduced. With production in the hands of a monopolist operating factories in different parts of the country, costs of distribution could be reduced by supplying each part of the country from the nearest factory.

Since the nationalisation of the coal industry, householders have not been able to specify the coalfield from which they wish to be supplied, generally having to accept coal from the nearest source of supply, and in recent years the National Coal Board has closed a large number of uneconomic mines in order to concentrate production where it could be carried on most efficiently. The most efficient mines are those where coal-getting machinery can be most effectively employed, and the effect of this reorganisation—only open to a monopolist—has been to raise the output of coal per man-shift. Before the railways were brought under one control by nationalisation, the old Great Central route of the L. & N.E.R. between Sheffield, Nottingham, Leicester and London was in competition with the Midland route of the L.M. & S.R. which also served all these intermediate cities. To operate a single route between these places makes a more efficient railway system. Hence the recommendation of the Beeching Report that the former Great Central line should be closed.

## Against monopoly

The most serious economic objection to monopoly is that it brings about a distribution of economic resources different from that which consumers would have preferred and from what would have obtained under perfect competition. By restricting his output the monopolist employs fewer resources in a particular line of production than consumers would have wished, thereby diverting resources to less desirable uses, so that an optimum distribution of the country's supply of factors of productivity is not achieved. Thus, consumers generally have to make do with smaller amounts of commodities when produced under monopolistic conditions, but have to pay higher prices for these things, so that, though their outlay may show little change, their satisfaction will be reduced.

Though monopoly may sometimes result in greater economic efficiency, as in commercial distribution, it reduces consumer choice. A housewife may wish to be free to choose her own supplier or select the brand of a commodity she prefers; a householder may think he ought to be able to purchase Wallsend coal if he regards it as superior to that from his nearest coalfield. To many people freedom of choice in the economic field is at least as important as political freedom.

Although economies of scale and the achievement of greater efficiency may often be the driving force towards monopoly, nevertheless, once a monopoly has been achieved, the incentive to greater efficiency in some cases may be inclined to weaken. Resistance to change may be encouraged, for example, by the heavy cost of re-tooling a modern industrial plant. In the days when they enjoyed monopolies for local passenger transport, some municipal tramways were content to continue to operate with uncomfortable, old-fashioned vehicles until competition from the motor bus stimulated a belated substitution of more comfortable, more up-to-date and more efficient tram-cars.

The ruthless way in which about the turn of the century some of the American monopolistic giants ground down or swallowed up their small competitors and then proceeded to exploit their monopoly power roused the ire of politicians and others in the United States who regarded the small firm as a desirable economic unit worth protecting and preserving for its own sake. This view might be supported on social grounds, but economically it is untenable unless it can be shown to be the only way to protect consumers from monopolistic exploitation.

Though it is fairly certain that a consumer will have to pay more to satisfy his wants under monopoly than he would under perfect competition, it has been rare for a monopolist to take full advantage of his position. There are two reasons for this:

(*i*) To wield monopoly power too blatantly may attract the unwelcome attention (from the point of view of the monopolist) of the State. Many governments have shown themselves keen to curb monopoly power—especially that of the United States—and to avoid the possibility of state interference monopolists have often tended to show restraint in their exercise of monopoly power.

(*ii*) If it seems clear that a monopolist is charging a very high price for his product and so making a very large monopoly profit other entrepreneurs will be encouraged to enter the industry, with the result that monopoly will then give way to duopoly or oligopoly. The attempt of newcomers to break into the market, tempted by a wide profit margin, often led in the past to cut-throat competition and the employment of most ruthless means of crushing intruders such as few governments would tolerate today. Alternatively, greater competition will come from substitutes, even though generally they may be either much inferior or regarded as not very close substitutes for the monopolist's product. For example, if coffee is very dear the consumption of tea will probably increase or a coffee substitute may be developed, as occurred in many West European countries during the Second World War. Similarly, lead piping may replace copper, or a synthetic form of rubber may be produced as a substitute for rubber.

## *IV. CONTROL OF MONOPOLY*

### American experience

The official attitudes in Great Britain and the United States towards monopoly show wide divergence. The first law against monopoly—the Sherman *Anti-Trust Act*—was introduced in the United States as long ago as 1890, antedating by fifty-eight years the first anti-monopoly legislation in Great Britain—the *Monopolies and Restrictive Practices (Inquiry and Control) Act* of 1948. In the United States the view has always been that monopoly in itself is bad and so should be outlawed. This attitude was based as much on sentimental sympathy for the small firm, which, it was felt, should be protected by the law from being swallowed up or driven out of business by the expanding industrial giants, as on a desire to safeguard consumers against exploitation by monopolists. In so many fields the large firm is technically so superior to the small firm, however, that the trend towards large scale goes on with irresistible force. It was not until the prosecution of the US Steel Corporation in 1920 that it came to be accepted in the United States that size by itself was not necessarily an indication of the misuse of monopoly power.

The Sherman *Anti-Trust Act* of 1890 declared all combinations such as trusts to be illegal, and although it succeeded in breaking up the Standard Oil Company and the American Tobacco Company as then constituted, the Act had not the success its sponsors had hoped

for it. In 1914 came the Clayton Act, which, in addition to prohibiting certain specified monopolistic practices such as local price
discrimination, made both holding companies and interlocking
directorates illegal, if it could be shown that their purpose was to
wield monopoly power. At the same time a Federal Trade Commission was set up to enforce the Sherman and Clayton Acts, with power
to enquire into any suspected contravention of these Acts. The
Commission was also empowered to suppress any method of competition brought to its notice which it regarded as unfair.

The US Congress and the Supreme Court, however, have not
always interpreted the intentions of these Acts as strictly as was
originally intended, since all American administrations have not
shown themselves equally determined to crush monopolies. Action
against monopolies, therefore, tended to be sporadic. From time to
time and for one reason or another exemptions from the anti-
monopoly laws have been granted, as, for example, in 1918, when
combines of exporters were permitted. Although a number of large
industrial undertakings were compelled to reorganise their con-
stitutions, the result was often a change in the way monopoly power
was exercised rather than its abolition. During the world depression of the 1930s there was understandable reluctance to take
action against monopolistic firms when this might increase unemployment.

Nevertheless, the size of American firms continued to expand both
by natural growth and as a result of mergers, although a third of the
largest hundred US manufacturing concerns have never been associated with a merger. To break up a large industrial unit may be
to destroy the optimum and create a number of units each smaller
than the optimum. If this is so, an anti-monopoly policy directed
merely towards the breaking up of large undertakings, even if
socially desirable, may be economically disadvantageous. In fact,
in recent years the main defence of firms accused of monopolistic
size has been that a reduction of size would result in a loss of
efficiency.

Since the end of the Second World War, however, successive US
administrations have taken more vigorous action to curb monopoly.
In 1950 the powers of the Federal Trade Commission and the Inter-
state Commission were enlarged to enable them to deal more effectively with mergers. In the following fifteen years twenty-six mergers
brought before the Commission were approved, including in 1966
that between the Pennsylvania Railroad and the New York Central
Railway, although other proposed railway mergers were turned down.
Since 1950 there have been few examples of the breaking up of
large firms—although American film-producing companies were
divested of the cinemas they controlled—but instead there has been

more action against mergers and restrictive monopolistic practices. Drastic action is not required when firms are found guilty of restrictive practices: all that is necessary is that they shall be compelled to abstain from them with official surveillance to ensure this.

The difficulty of dealing with restrictive practices and other restraints on competition at the present day has increased because it is no longer monopoly but oligopoly that is now the main form taken by imperfect competition. Where the production of a commodity is mainly in the hands of a few firms it is not easy to maintain that competition in the industry no longer prevails, except where it can be shown that they are acting in collusion, in which case the problem again becomes one of monopoly rather than oligopoly.

### British experience: (1) before 1945

Although there was no specific legislation against monopoly in Great Britain until 1948, the British Parliament in the nineteenth century was constantly on the alert to check monopoly whenever it seemed likely to occur.

It was particularly watchful, for example, during the period of railway development. Except where it was considered likely to cause danger to passengers, public opinion favoured the encouragement of competition between railway companies, even where it was clearly wasteful, with the result that by the time it reached its maximum extent the British railway system provided alternative routes between almost every pair of large towns in the country. Parliament interfered with the railways in other ways, and after 1840 hardly a year passed without the setting up of a committee to consider how they could be controlled, especially when lines began to be consolidated into great trunk systems. After 1873 all proposals for amalgamations of railways were examined by the Railway and Canal Commission, and many applications were refused. Railway charges too came under state control, maximum rates and fares being fixed in 1893. Similarly, when public utilities in towns—water, gas, electricity, tramways—were operated by public companies, since of necessity they had to be monopolies, they were restricted in the charges they were allowed to make. The growth of large-scale banking proceeded in much the same way as had the development of the railways, the banks expanding partly by opening new branches and partly be amalgamating with one another. Again fearing the development of monopoly, Parliament through the Treasury intervened in 1918, after the formation of the "Big Five," any further proposals for bank mergers having to be referred to the Treasury and the Board of Trade (*see* p. 128).

Thus, the British Parliament, although not legislating against monopoly as such, took action on a number of occasions to check its development. On the whole, however, Parliament has not generally regarded the mere size of an undertaking as a thing to be opposed, as was the case in the United States. Indeed, there have been occasions—excluding the two World Wars, when special circumstances dictated policy—when the British Government appears actively to have encouraged the development of monopolies. For example, by an Act of 1921 the railways of the United Kingdom were compulsorily amalgamated into four large groups. Then, during the Great Depression of 1929–35, while the United States Government generally turned a blind eye to mergers that might produce monopolies, the British Government and the Bank of England helped to bring about a number of large-scale mergers in the cotton, woollen, shipbuilding and iron and steel industries in order to "rationalise" these industries and increase their efficiency and economic viability. The *Traffic Act*, 1930, regulated road passenger transport, restricting new entrants and in effect giving existing operators monopolies over certain routes, though subject to the control of local Traffic Commissioners with regard to fares and timetables. The *Road and Rail Act*, 1933, introduced a licensing system for road haulage which again gave those obtaining the general "A" and "B" hauliers' licences a considerable measure of monopoly power.

### British experience: (2) since 1945

During the years 1946–51 the British Government nationalised railways, canals, the coal, gas and electricity industries, and in 1967 the iron and steel industry, in all cases creating monopolies where none had existed before. Then in 1966 the Government established the Industrial Reorganisation Corporation for the purpose of assisting the "rationalisation" of those industries where production is mainly carried on by small firms, which because of their small size have a low productivity, can afford little (if any) research and cannot make use of the most efficient modern management techniques. Large-scale operation is essential in the aircraft industry, and in 1966 a merger of the British Aircraft Corporation with Hawker-Siddeley took place at the instigation of the British Government, which obtained a substantial minority interest in the new combine.

Since 1945 the feature of governmental policy towards monopoly in Great Britain has been the passing for the first time of a series of laws directly aimed at controlling monopoly.

As a prelude to later legislation came the pronouncement in the White Paper *Employment Policy* (1944). It accepted the view that monopolies do not always act against the public interest, but, since they are in a position to do so, the Government proposed to obtain powers to enquire into the activities of monopolies with a view to checking any practices which it regarded as undesirable. It was a fear that misuse of monopoly power might make full employment more difficult to maintain, rather than opposition to monopoly as such, that induced the Government to hint that it might have to take action. Even then its intention was to intervene only against those monopolies which after investigation were found to be behaving in a manner contrary to the public interest.

In 1947 the Government set up working parties to study and report on a number of industries not scheduled for nationalisation with a view to improving their efficiency. Some of these enquiries revealed the prevalence of monopolistic practices, as in the manufacture of radio valves and cement, but in neither case did it appear that undue advantage was being taken of monopolistic positions.

Before 1945 neither of the major British political parties appeared to be seriously interested in controlling monopoly: after 1945 both parties became interested in the subject and anti-monopoly legislation was shared between them.

(i) *The Monopolies and Restrictive Practices* (*Inquiry and Control*) *Act*, 1948. The necessity for this Act—the first British Act to be passed against monopoly—was explained in terms of the deleterious effect on the maintenance of full employment of monopolistic practices, which it was alleged had increased in the period between the two World Wars. It was not the intention of the Act to outlaw monopoly, for it was again pointed out that monopoly of itself was not necessarily bad—indeed, a government favouring the creation of nationalised monopolies could hardly think otherwise. The Act, therefore, set up a Monopolies and Restrictive Practices Commission (abbreviated to Monopolies Commission in 1956), at first comprising four to ten members, to investigate the conditions of production of those commodities required of it by the Board of Trade. Thus, commodities and not particular firms, as in the United States, were named for investigation. Nevertheless, the Commission's reports were bound to make reference to particular firms. The criterion for monopoly was laid down in the Act as a firm—or a group operating together—which was responsible for the production of 30% or more of the total output of a commodity. To some people this appeared to be much too small a fraction of a market to be regarded as monopolistic. It has to be remembered, however, that oligopoly, with production mainly in the hands of a few firms, rather than monopoly, is the more typical form of imperfect competition in vogue in Great Britain at the present day. To have fixed the criterion higher than 30% would have allowed many oligopolists to escape investigation, and indeed some supporters of the bill in Parliament would actually have preferred the percentage to have been lower. As indicated by its original title, the Commission was also empowered to deal with restrictive practices, including those having to do with patents.

(*ii*) *The Restrictive Trade Practices Act*, 1956. The Monopolies and Restrictive Practices Commission, as set up in 1948 and enlarged in 1953, was required to enquire into restrictive practices as well as into examples of monopolistic production. Under Section 15 of the Act, therefore, the Board of Trade requested from the Commission a report on the general effects of the restrictive practices which had been brought to light in its earlier reports. In 1955 the general report on restrictive practices was published, the Commission finding that in many cases these practices were contrary to the public interest. Among those so regarded was exclusive dealing (a practice common to many trade associations) supported by discrimination in favour of firms which agreed to this condition, with collective action to maintain resale price maintenance. Finally, the report recommended that there should be further legislation.

The result of this recommendation was the passing of the *Restrictive Trade Practices Act*, 1956, under which the Restrictive Practices Court was set up to take over from the Monopolies and Restrictive Practices Commission all future investigations into restrictive practices. This court was to have all the powers of a court of law and its decisions, therefore, would be legally binding, unlike the Commission's reports, the purpose of which was only to provide information for the Government, which was then at liberty to take whatever action it pleased. The title of the Commission was abbreviated to that of Monopolies Commission to suit its more circumscribed role, and this body was to continue to report on all cases of monopoly referred to it by the Board of Trade. The difference in the powers of the Court and the Commission, the former having compulsive powers to enforce its recommendations and the latter being restricted merely to reporting its findings, is the result of the British attitude towards monopoly that has been prevalent for so long, namely that monopoly is not necessarily a bad thing in itself, whereas restrictive practices are in general presumed to be against the community's interest and, therefore, to be prohibited.

As a preliminary to investigation by the Restrictive Practices Court all agreements by suppliers of goods relating to prices, terms or conditions of sale, etc., together with the full terms of these agreements, have to be registered with a Registrar of Restrictive Practices. It is then for the Registrar to bring each agreement that has been so registered before the Court to determine whether it is in the public interest or not, the defendants of an agreement and the Registrar (as the watchdog of the public interest) leaving their cases to be argued by their counsel. The point to be decided before an agreement can be allowed to continue is whether the restrictions are not unreasonable after balancing the benefits accruing from the agreement against the harmful effects on the community as a whole.

The Act of 1956 also prohibited collective action by suppliers to enforce resale price maintenance upon buyers, as recommended in 1955 in the Report of the Monopolies and Restrictive Practices Commission, but the individual manufacturer was given the legal right to insist that his product should not be sold below a stated minimum price.

(iii) *The Resale Prices Act*, 1964.[1] This Act prohibited both collective and individual enforcement of resale price maintenance, except where it could be shown that it was not against the public interest. Producers who wished to claim exemption from the operation of the Act had to notify the Registrar of Restrictive Practices and in their case resale price maintenance would continue until their claims for exemption had been considered by the Restrictive Practices Court. With these exceptions the Act came into force in April 1965. The criteria for retention of resale price maintenance are: (*a*) if it is necessary for the maintenance of variety or quality; (*b*) if it is necessary to prevent price increases; (*c*) if it is necessary for health reasons; (*d*) if its abolition would seriously reduce the number of retail outlets; and (*e*) if its abolition might lead to the loss of after-sales service when this was required. Though a large number of manufacturers put in applications for exemption many of these were withdrawn when it became clear that the Restrictive Practices Court was going to be difficult to convince of the necessity for any exemption. The summary rejection of the sweet and chocolate manufacturers' application for exemption in July 1967 seemed to support this view. Unless it can be shown that there are special features in the sale of a commodity an application is not likely to succeed. If it can be shown to the satisfaction of the Restrictive Practices Court that the specialist bookseller is essential to the sale of books and that therefore he requires the protection of resale price maintenance the book trade may secure the retention of this practice for books. For most commodities, however, it would seem that resale price maintenance will soon be a thing of the past. It seems fairly certain that the long-run effect of the general abolition of resale price maintenance will be a reduction in the number of retail outlets rather than very large price reductions in spite of drastic price cuts by supermarkets in the short period.

(iv) *The Monopolies and Mergers Act*, 1965. As its title indicates this Act was passed to bring mergers within the purview of the State. Once again the official view was reiterated that monopoly of itself was not necessarily a bad thing. Nevertheless, since monopoly

[1] This Act is dealt with more fully in Chapter III.

power could be achieved through mergers, it was felt that they should be subject to scrutiny. Under the Act the Board of Trade can refer to the Monopolies Commission for its consideration any proposed merger or any merger within six months of its having taken place where the effect would be to create a monopoly (as defined by the Act of 1948) or to increase the monopoly power of an existing monopoly or where the assets of the firm to be taken over exceed £5 million. If the merger is found to be contrary to the public interest it can be either prohibited or dissolved.

## V. ACTION AGAINST MONOPOLY

### The work of the Monopolies Commission: (1) to 1956

Between 1948 and 1956 the Monopolies and Restrictive Practices Commission, as it was then known, was the only body empowered to deal with monopoly and monopolistic practices. The Board of Trade was solely responsible for the selection of the lines of production to be dealt with, and at first the aim was to give the Commission as wide a variety of subjects as possible to consider, so that these early decisions could form a basis for future judgments, although in all cases monopolistic practices were to be reviewed in the specific environment of each industry investigated.

Altogether the Monopolies and Restrictive Practices Commission published twenty reports during its first eight years. These included reports on consumers' goods, dealing with such items as linoleum, certain kinds of rubber footwear and the supply of tea; others concerned goods sometimes bought by consumers and sometimes by producers, such as electric lamps and pneumatic tyres. There were also enquiries touching upon producers' goods such as dental equipment, cast-iron rainwater pipes, imported timber, electrical machinery, electronic valves and cathode-ray tubes; in one case an industrial process, calico printing, and in another a supply problem, building in Greater London, were investigated. The terms of reference for some commodities also included exports, as, for example, with matches, partly manufactured goods made of copper and copper alloys, pneumatic tyres and electrical machinery.

Among the monopolistic practices most frequently met with in the Commission's investigations were common price policies and exclusive dealing, with fifteen examples of each in the twenty industries reviewed.[1] The fixing of common prices was not always found to be detrimental to the public interest, since prices were often set by the most efficient firm in the industry and the one with the lowest costs.

[1] See the Summary Tables on pp. 72–73 of Guenault and Jackson: *The Control of Monopoly in the United Kingdom*.

Nevertheless, it was considered that this practice required to be kept under constant observation and, in the case of electric lamps, periodically reviewed, to prevent harmful effects which might accrue if the practice were allowed to continue unchecked. Somewhat similar to the adoption of the common price is the practice of level tendering, formerly prevalent in building. Exclusive dealing, often supported by a collective boycott—the second of the monopolistic practices most frequently employed—was aimed at restricting the entry of newcomers into an industry. In some instances traders had to sign an agreement to do business only with members of a particular trade association, special discounts or loyalty rebates sometimes being granted as an inducement to do so. This practice the Commission regarded as an unwarranted interference with competition.

Though there were few cases where monopolies restricted output in order to keep up the price of the commodity—as had been the practice of the German *Kartell*—a number of examples were found of quota schemes which restricted each firm's share of the market and so prevented the expansion of the more efficient firm at the expense of the less efficient. The most difficult task for the Commission, in view of the various monopolistic practices prevailing in different industries, was to determine whether prices and profits were "reasonable." In many cases the Commission found it impossible to express an opinion on this matter, but in the manufacture of dental goods, matches, electrical machinery and industrial gases such as oxygen it considered profits to be too high.

### The work of the Monopolies Commission: (2) since 1956

After its reconstitution in 1956 the Monopolies Commission (henceforth known by that name) has continued its work, and during the ensuing ten years issued reports on imported timber, the supply of films to cinemas, household detergents, chemical fertilisers, cigarettes and tobacco, electrical equipment for motor vehicles, wallpaper, petrol sales, colour films and a number of other commodities. In the case of the Imperial Tobacco Company the Commission considered that it had not used its monopolistic position to the detriment of the public interest. On the other hand, it expressed its strong disapproval of agreements between the petrol companies and petrol retailers, whereby retailers were bound to sell the products of only one supplier (the solus system). When the production of colour film came to be investigated in April 1966 it was found that production was oligopolistic, with only five producers in the world, of which two were located in Great Britain. Kodak Ltd. was responsible for more than 75% of the total supply coming on to the British market —not necessarily a bad thing in itself—imports from the three foreign producing groups, which accounted for 20% of the supply, being subject to import duty. The report showed Kodak to be a highly efficient firm, but the Commission considered both the firm's own profit margin and the retailers' mark-up to be much too large, and it recommended that these should be reduced and the import duty abolished. In November 1966 Kodak, therefore, reduced its prices. The Commission's report on household detergents, also published in 1966, stated that the profits of detergent manufacturing were too high, and recommended that Unilever Ltd. and Proctor & Gamble Ltd. should reduce their prices to wholesalers by 20%. At the same time it recommended that these two firms should reduce their selling costs, particularly their expenditure on advertising, by 40%. The presumption behind this recommendation was clearly that, if less was spent on advertising, prices could be reduced, but where there are economies of scale this will be so only if there is no consequent falling off in sales.[1] In 1967 these firms announced reductions in the prices of their products.

In 1965 the Monopolies Commission was given power to consider whether proposed mergers were in the public interest, and since then this function has occupied much of its time. During the following three years some two hundred proposals were considered by the Board of Trade but only eight were referred to the Monopolies Commission. The attempt of the Imperial Tobacco Company to diversify its interests by taking over Smith's Potato Crisps came to naught. On the other hand, a proposed merger between the British Motor Corporation and Pressed Steel and proposed mergers between three dental manufacturing companies, though apparently much more monopolistic than the previous proposal, were stated not to be against the public interest. A proposed merger to bring *The Times* and the *Sunday Times* under one control was brought before the Commission, which in 1967 agreed to this proposal. After the merger of the National Provincial and Westminster Banks had been permitted to take place, a proposed merger of Barclays, Lloyds and Martins Banks in 1968 was referred to the Monopolies Commission, which by six votes to four declared it to be against the public interest. Although the required two-thirds majority was not obtained, the Board of Trade refused to allow this merger to take place, but Barclays was permitted to take over Martins. Yet the purpose of the Industrial Reorganisation Corporation (IRC), set up in 1966 under the aegis of the Department of Economic Affairs, is to encourage mergers in those sections of British industry where it is considered that there are too many small firms and where productivity is regarded as being too low. In the case of the merger between British Motor Holdings and Leyland—both already very large firms —to form British Leyland, no opposition was offered since it was

[1] For a discussion of advertising, *see* pp. 101–2.

realised that the motor-vehicle industry is one where economies of scale are considerable and the optimum size for the industry very large. In 1968 the Monopolies Commission issued its report on man-made cellulose fibres, no less than 98% of the total output of this product being in the hands of Courtaulds. This monopoly, the report stated, was against the public interest in that there was price discrimination in favour of some customers, regulation of imports by arrangement with producers in EFTA, and extensive participation in the textile industry. The Commission recommended that Courtauld's monopoly should be reduced by a cut in the tariff on imports, that price descrimination should be abolished, and that division of the market with EFTA producers should cease. In addition, although the company was forbidden to acquire any further textile concerns without the specific approval of the Board of Trade, there was no suggestion that Courtaulds should divest itself of any of its interests.

Once the Monopolies Commission has issued a report the next stage is for it to be considered by the Board of Trade, and after that for the Minister, if he thinks fit, to take appropriate action. In some of its earlier reports the Commission more often than not reported that prices charged by the monopolies it had enquired into were not "unreasonable." Nevertheless, it had suggested in 1953 that the price of matches should be under government control and in 1957 that the Board of Trade should exercise control over the price policy of the British Oxygen Company. In recent years more drastic and more explicit recommendations have been made, as in 1966–67 in the cases of colour films and household detergents. Industries and firms have generally preferred themselves to put their houses in order rather than wait for government action to be taken against them. The Government, too, has preferred negotiation to direct action even though negotiations have sometimes been prolonged.

## VI. NATIONALISED MONOPOLIES

### Nationalisation and monopoly

The nationalisation of industry and its operation by the State has been advocated over the past seventy years or so for a number of reasons. For a long time "the nationalisation of the means of production" was one of the main aims of socialist policy. Some supporters of nationalisation regarded it as a good thing in itself; others argued that it was in the public interest that basic industries such as coal-mining, iron and steel and transport should be operated by the State. In some countries industries have been run by the State for strategic reasons, as were railways in many countries, or for reasons of prestige, as are many present-day airlines. From the start the production and use of atomic energy in Great Britain has been under the control of the State as it was considered that it might constitute a public danger if left to private enterprise.

As noted earlier in this chapter, public ownership was one of the early methods employed in Great Britain for controlling monopolies set up where competition would have been particularly wasteful, as in the case of public utilities. Thus, public ownership can be invoked to check the misuse of monopoly power, or a highly competitive industry consisting mainly of relatively small firms, such as road haulage or coal-mining, can be turned into a single large concern as a result of nationalisation. For, whatever may be the reasons for nationalisation, the result is the same—the creation of nation-wide monopolies. When the nationalisation of an industry is under consideration the question to be asked should be: will it be run more efficiently if it is brought within the public sector than if it is left to private enterprise? To create a large industrial unit out of a large number of small ones may yield economies of scale and so result in greater efficiency. On the other hand, to bring into being an excessively large concern may mean its expansion beyond the optimum.

**The public sector**

If account is taken of the public services provided in Great Britain by the State, as well as the trading activities of government departments, the public sector is now responsible for 26 % of the national income. Of industrial output in 1965 (reckoned by value in terms of money) the nationalised industries, including the Post Office, were responsible for approximately 12 % of the total. At that date the nationalised industries were responsible for the production of power (coal, gas, electricity), transport (railways, some road-haulage services, London Transport, docks and waterways, the Transport Holding Company and the two state airlines, BOAC and BEA) and the Post Office. In addition there was the Bank of England, which had been nationalised in 1946. To these the iron and steel industry was added in 1967, after previously being nationalised in 1951 and denationalised in 1953. Road haulage was partially denationalised in 1953. The boards responsible for the management of the nationalised industries are appointed by the appropriate responsible ministers.

Mainly for reasons of administrative convenience most of the nationalised industries are operated on a regional basis. Thus, the National Coal Board, the public corporation formed in 1947 to take over the coal-mining industry, is organised in nine regions while the Electricity Council (1948) and the Gas Council (1949) each have twelve area boards. Inland transport was nationalised in 1947 under the British Transport Commission, but in 1963 the BTC undertakings were redistributed among five successor bodies—the British

Railways Board, the London Transport Board, the British Transport Docks Board, the British Waterways Board and the Transport Holding Company. In the case of British Rail there are six operational regions. A point of interest in regard to the brief period of nationalisation of road haulage (1947–53) was that each group—the name given to the operational unit of British Road Services and comprising about 150 vehicles—was expected, *as a spur to efficiency*, to compete with other groups, and in the larger towns there were often two or more groups. Since 1953 the nationalised groups that were not returned to private enterprise under the Act of that year have competed both against one another and against privately owned firms. Transport was further re-organised by the *Transport Act*, 1968 (*see* pp. 164–6).

Except for the Post Office (which became a public corporation in 1969, previously having been a government department) no nationalised industry is free from competition. All the power-producing industries, for example, are in varying degrees in competition with one another, as also against oil, with the result that the structure of this industry is clearly oligopolistic in character. The railways and the state airlines on their domestic routes compete not only against one another but also against the private motor car and the motor bus.

### Price and profit: (1) monopoly and oligopoly

Most of the Nationalisation Acts lay down that the aim of a nationalised industry should be to provide a service in the public interest, and though no Act specifically states that an industry should be run at a profit, it is nevertheless expected to pay its way, taking one year with another. Except in the case of road haulage, where cash payments were made after individual bargaining, compensation in the form of newly issued government-guaranteed stocks, such as Electricity Stock, Transport Stock, etc., was paid to the former owners of nationalised firms, though no compensation was paid to local authorities that had previously owned gas or electricity works. Only in the case of the railways, however, was the nationalised undertaking burdened with a stock redemption fund. On occasions some of the nationalised industries have raised additional capital by the issue of new stocks to the capital market, but since 1956 their new investment has been financed out of revenue or by the Exchequer. In most years the new investment of the Electricity Council has been equal to that of all the other nationalised undertakings together.

In conditions of perfect competition the price a firm can charge is outside its control, being determined by the interplay of the market forces of supply and demand. In these conditions a firm has no inducement to restrict its output, since to do so would reduce its profit. Further, that amount of every commodity will be supplied which consumers as a whole prefer, so that by this criterion an optimum distribution of economic resources is achieved. The monopolist too must take account of market forces, but where the demand for his product is fairly inelastic he has the power, if unfettered by law, to increase his profit above the level that would prevail under perfect competition by curtailing his output in order to keep up his price. The attitude of governments towards monopoly being what it is, and with the possibility that high profits would attract new entrants into his industry, no monopolist, as already noted, would dare to exercise his power to the full. He prefers, therefore, to adopt a compromise policy, and this means that he himself must decide the price at which he will sell his product.

In the case of oligopoly there will be only a few producers, but price and output are again matters to be determined by the producers. Generally, one of the firms—sometimes, but not always, the largest—acts as price leader and, often without any specific agreement among them, the other firms follow. In other cases oligopolists make "information agreements," whereby the participants exchange information with one another regarding prices and other matters of common interest. Thus, oligopolists, like monopolists, decide the prices of their products instead of leaving them to be determined solely by market forces. Each then strives to persuade consumers to buy his product at this price so that, as under monopoly, consumers do not have that distribution of economic resources which they would have preferred.

### Price and profit: (2) nationalised industries

What, then, should be the price and profit policy of a nationalised industry operating in conditions of monopoly or oligopoly? In competitive conditions the capacity of a firm to earn profit is a test of its efficiency. Although in the Acts establishing them it was stated that nationalised industries were expected in the long term to pay their way, they were nevertheless to be operated "in the national interest"—a vague phrase—in order to provide a public service and not to aim at maximum profits if this appeared to be contrary to consumers' interests. It becomes extremely difficult, therefore, to assess the efficiency of a nationalised industry, for a loss can always be explained away as the price paid for rendering a service to the community, and therefore "in the national interest." Thus, there is always strong pressure on the ministers concerned to keep open unremunerative railway services or uneconomic coal mines. Some kind of audit of efficiency by an independent body is clearly required if profit is no longer to serve as a test of efficiency.

Profit in a competitive economy has another function: it is the instrument which, reflecting consumers' demand, determines the relative size of industries. Taking normal profit to mean the level of profit required to keep an entrepreneur in a particular line of production, then if more than normal profit is being earned in an industry new firms will be encouraged to enter and the industry will expand, whereas if less than normal profit is being earned some firms, as opportunity arises, will drop out and the industry will contract. In this way an optimum distribution of resources is achieved. Without the influence of profit it becomes difficult to ensure that each nationalised industry attracts to itself neither more nor less in the way of productive resources than is necessary to bring about an optimum distribution of such resources among all industries competing for them. For, if too much labour or capital is attracted into the nationalised industries, it follows that there will be so much less available for other uses.

Monopoly or oligopoly, therefore, presents a similar problem whether it occurs in the private or the public sector—price cannot be left to market forces but must be decided by those in charge of production. The presumption behind the view that a monopoly can be controlled by letting the State run it is that this will prevent the exploitation of consumers, but, whether a monopoly is in private or public hands, consumers' choice will not be allowed to decide the quantity of a commodity to be produced, and in both cases someone decides for consumers what they shall pay.

In conditions of perfect competition price will be equal to marginal cost, and there are those who believe that this should be the pricing policy of a nationalised industry. In some lines of production this might be a feasible policy, but most of the industries nationalised as yet in Great Britain have heavy fixed costs in the way of capital equipment in relation to their marginal cost. As a result marginal cost is much lower than average cost, and if the price charged were to be equal to marginal cost every one of these industries could not help but operate at a loss. Many people, however, consider that nationalised industries, while not endeavouring to maximise their profits, should not be run at a loss, but should aim to "break even," as appears to have been the intention of the various Nationalisation Acts. Since average cost varies with output the determination of a price that will just cover average cost can be estimated only on the basis of past output and anticipated future output. As already noted, the two-part tariff, where it can be applied, is an attempt to incorporate a charge to cover fixed costs with a charge based on consumption.

RECOMMENDATIONS FOR FURTHER READING

E. A. G. Robinson: *Monopoly* (Cambridge Univ. Press/James Nisbet & Co.).

P. H. Guenault and J. M. Jackson: *The Control of Monopoly in the United Kingdom* (Longmans, Green & Co.).

HMSO: Reports of the Monopolies (and Restrictive Practices) Commission.

## QUESTIONS

1. Account for the different attitude of the State towards monopoly in the United States and Great Britain.

2. Assess the work of the Monopolies Commission and the Restrictive Practices Court in dealing with monopoly practices.

3. On what basis should the pricing policy of a nationalised industry be determined?

4. Is there any need for anti-monopoly legislation in addition to legislation against restrictive practices? (Degree.)

5. Explain the assertion that progress in industry requires that firms should "enjoy a degree of security and at the same time should be subject to active competition." What implications has this statement for monopoly policy? (Degree.)

6. What have been the main causes of amalgamations since 1946? Outline the advantages and disadvantages of such amalgamations. (Birmingham.)

7. What particular problems face nationalised industries in pricing and investment policies? (Birmingham.)

8. Consider the present state of the law on monopoly and restrictive practices. What effects do you expect to follow the gradual implementation of the *Resale Prices Act*, 1964? (Bournemouth.)

9. The *Resale Prices Act*, 1964, came into force 1st May 1965. Discuss its impact on retail price maintenance, tracing the various stages of legislation from 1945 in their marketing aspects. What will be the effect on retail distributive trades now? (Derby.)

10. Is a monopoly the logical outcome of economies of scale? (Liverpool.)

11. The policy of this country with reference to monopolies and restrictive practices is said to be "two-sided" in that it looks with both favour and disfavour on them. Show whether government policy illustrates this or not. (Liverpool.)

12. Critically examine the changes that have taken place in government policy towards monopolies and restrictive practices since 1964. (Manchester.)

13. Monopoly may be contrary to the public interest but restrictive practices are always so. Can this statement be justified? (Northern Counties.)

14. In what circumstances and for what reasons is a monopolist likely to discriminate in his pricing policy? (Sheffield.)

15. Examine the case for nationalised industries operating under a different pricing policy from that in the private sector. (U.L.C.I.)

16. "The Government's major intention, through the Restrictive Trade Practices Court, has been to control restrictive trade agreements in the public interest." Comment upon the success or failure of this intention. (U.L.C.I.)

CHAPTER V

# PROBLEMS OF INLAND TRANSPORT

## I. EARLY DEVELOPMENT

### Economic importance of transport

An efficient, up-to-date transport system is essential for the smooth working of a modern, complex economy. Large-scale production results in the mass production of a huge output of a commodity, in a particular place. The greater the extent to which specialisation of production is carried, the greater will be the volume of goods to be distributed and the greater the demand for transport. The improvement of means of transport, therefore, has gone hand in hand with expansion of production.

Improvements in transport and industrial development have always reacted upon one another. The Industrial Revolution of the late eighteenth and early nineteenth centuries was as much a revolution in transport as in industrial techniques: the one could not have taken place without the other. The present complex system of production was possible only because of the improvements in means of transport that accompanied each stage of industrial development. The problems that beset transport in Great Britain today are to a large extent a consequence of the historical development of transport in this country.

### Transport development, 1760–1850

(i) *Waterways*. Before the Industrial Revolution bulky goods could be transported only by water, with the result that the navigable rivers became the main arteries for traffic in those days. By the end of the eighteenth century the British river system had been supplemented by canals linking the rivers Thames, Severn, Mersey and Trent in England, the rivers Clyde and Forth in Scotland, and the industrial areas of South Lancashire and West Yorkshire. Through traffic on the canals was, however, hampered from the start by differences in width, depth and the size of locks.

(ii) *Roads*. For thirteen centuries the roads of this country received little attention, and though the first turnpike trust was established as early as 1663 this method of financing road improvement did not become widespread for another hundred years. The first half of the nineteenth century was the hey-day of the turnpike road system. Not only were many roads improved but the more progressive trusts also constructed new lines of road to shorten routes or to link up with the roads of other trusts. Road improvements made it possible to run "express" coaches and a new market in passenger travel was developed. The improvement of the roads also made it possible for the first time to carry large quantities of goods overland, new wagons being introduced for the purpose. This expansion of traffic stimulated further road building and improvement. Unlike road construction in France, where the State made itself responsible for planning a unified system, road development in Great Britain was left to local private enterprise. Local initiative was the driving force behind road improvement, local people—merchants, manufacturers, gentry—subscribing the initial capital of the turnpike trusts in the expectation that the tolls paid by road-users would not only cover road maintenance but also yield a profit. Few investors in turnpikes, however, received much financial reward—most trusts continued to accumulate debts until the time of their closure—but a greatly improved road system was achieved.

(*iii*) *Railways*. As had been the case in Great Britain with both canals and roads, the provision of railways, too, was left to private enterprise.

In Great Britain railways were constructed mainly for local needs, at first merely to link neighbouring towns. For a number of reasons their capital cost was high, though the terrain was not generally difficult. Parliamentary bills were expensive to promote on account of the strong opposition that generally had to be faced. Often excessively high prices had to be paid for land. A less direct route was sometimes chosen, either to avoid the heavy cost of a tunnel or to provide a more convenient link for intermediate stations. Such drawbacks were the penalty Great Britain had to pay for being first in the field. Opinion in Britain at first favoured the provision of a way or track rather than full operation. Therefore, as with both canals and turnpikes before them, it was at first expected that the railways on payment of a toll would be open to anyone who wished to run a train over the track. This was soon found to be impracticable but private ownership of goods wagons persisted down to nationalisation in 1947.

The period 1843–47 was one of intense railway development. By amalgamation and extension a national railway system was gradually built up, through-routes to the north being opened by the London and North-Western Railway and by the Midland Railway. In some cases, however, amalgamations led to the development of regional monopolies as with the North-Eastern Railway in North-Eastern England and the Great Eastern Railway in East Anglia. By 1840 Great Britain had 1,857 miles of railway; by 1860 the railways had a combined route mileage of over 10,000. As the railway net spread wider and wider so the coach routes shrank.

### Transport and the State

In some countries the State from the first made itself responsible for the provision of internal means of transport. In France, for example, the State provided a comprehensive plan for road improvement. Napoleon made all French roads free of toll. In France, too, the State planned and constructed a system of canals and after a time these, also, were made free of toll. As early as 1842—only seventeen years after the opening of the first railway in England—a railway system was planned, with a series of main lines radiating from Paris. As with the roads the military aspect was not overlooked. The State, however, built only the bed, bridges and stations and left the laying of the track, the provision of rolling stock and the operation of the railways to free enterprise. By 1860 there were six large companies in France, each with a monopoly in its own area. Although in the United States railway construction was left to private enterprise the companies were assisted by gifts of land from either the Federal Government or the various states which also often helped with loans or by guaranteeing the interest on loans.

As already noted, the development of new means of transport in Great Britain was left to free enterprise. The fact, however, that it was necessary for the sponsors to promote a parliamentary bill before a line could be constructed gave Parliament from the start some control over railway development in this country. As more lines were built Parliament became concerned lest the railway companies should exercise monopoly powers. This had two effects. It led Parliament to sanction an unnecessary number of new lines in order to stimulate competition between railway companies. As a result, a great deal of excess capacity was created. Since in any case competition was bound to be of limited extent, legal controls and restrictions were imposed on the railways.

In the interest of the safety of passengers the Board of Trade in 1840 was empowered to inspect new lines. Two years later railway dividends were limited to 10%. In 1842 the Government was given the option to purchase the railway after a stated period of time, but this option was not exercised and it was not until the *Nationalisation Act* of 1947 that railways in Great Britain came under state ownership.

In 1844 Parliament began to interfere with railway rates. In that year the *Cheap Trains Act* was passed, and British railway companies were compelled to run every day each way on all their lines at least one train with accomodation for passengers at one penny per mile. The following year maximum rates were laid down by Parliament for the carriage of freight. Then in 1854 came Cardwell's Act, which prohibited a railway from giving a preference to one customer as against another. This Act also compelled the railways to provide through traffic. In 1873 there was appointed a Railway and Canal Commission whose main duties were to deal with matters affecting the railways, such as proposed amalgamations, proposals to purchase canals, etc. This became a permanent body in 1888. Railway rates were subject to its approval.

### Railway freight charges

Railway rates for freight were based on the principle of "charging what the traffic will bear." Goods were arranged in twenty-one categories, the lowest charge being levied on goods in Class I and the heaviest charge on those in Class XXI. In general, the cheaper the commodity the lower the class and so the lower the rate of carriage, though other considerations were taken into account, such as the weight of goods in relation to bulk and their liability to damage. In Class I were goods such as coal which were cheap in relation to their weight and bulk. Unless carried cheaply, such goods would not have been carried at all. Smaller and more expensive goods were given a higher classification. Clearly, the more valuable the goods, the smaller the proportion that transport costs (even in the higher classes) would form of the final price.

Railway rates as introduced in the nineteenth century, therefore, provided an example of discriminating monopoly (*see* pp. 114–16), the railways at that time having over most of their routes a monopoly of transport facilities. They could thus make different charges for different classes of goods because at that time there was no competitor to step in to offer to carry those commodities for which the railways made a heavy charge. This was to come later with the revival of transport by road. Discriminatory charges can be made only if it is possible to keep the markets separate as otherwise more goods will be offered in the cheaper market and fewer in the dearer one. This was easily accomplished, however, since the goods in the various categories could generally be easily recognised and classified.

### Rail passenger fares

Apart from the *Cheap Trains Act* of 1844, which as already noted, only insisted on the railways providing a minimum of third-class travel for passengers, the State left the fixing of passengers fares to the railways themselves. If competition between the different railways was encouraged this presumably would keep fares down.

After Thomas Cook in 1850 had shown the railways that discriminatory charges could be applied to passengers as well as freight, the railways themselves began to offer tickets at less than the ordinary fares. This was possible if the markets for railway travel in which different fares were to be charged could be kept separate from one another. It would be profitable only if the elasticity of demand was not the same in all markets. The aim of excursion fares and cheap tickets was to persuade people to travel who otherwise would not have done so. So far as was possible people who would be willing to pay the ordinary fare must be prevented from taking advantage of the cheap fare. For example, in the case of the cheap "workman" return the availability of the tickets was restricted by issuing them only before 8 a.m. and not permitting the return journey to be commenced before 5 p.m. (12 on Saturdays). Similarly, day returns were restricted to people travelling at a later hour than was suitable for those going to business.

When large numbers of people were involved, special excursion trains were run to take people to functions such as sporting events or to holiday resorts. By this means those travelling at cheap rates were segregated from the ordinary passengers and the discomfort often associated with the excursion train would help to keep the markets separate. Nevertheless, there would always be some passengers for whom the cheap fares were not intended who would be able to benefit from them, since it was not possible completely to separate the markets for passenger travel. Since the railways have heavy fixed costs and relatively low marginal costs, the additional cost of running a special excursion train is low, so that net profit can be increased if the revenue it earns only slightly exceeds the marginal cost. The track, stations and signalling would all have to be maintained even if the excursion train did not run. On the other hand, as the Beeching Report was later to show, the cost of maintaining rolling stock throughout the year when only used occasionally was heavy, and might more than absorb the profit on such traffic. The issue of cheap mid-week holiday tickets had another purpose: to spread the load by making better use of train capacity in mid-week and at the same time reducing the demand for weekend travel.

## II. THE RAILWAYS AT THEIR PEAK

### The railways at their maximum extent

During the latter part of the nineteenth century the railways continued to extend their network, as shown in Table XXIV (p. 141).

With one exception—the Great Central Line—all the main lines had been constructed by the middle of this period. The greater part of the later railway extensions comprised branch lines, many of which never yielded a profit although they were regarded as feeders to the main lines. It is not surprising, therefore, to find that railway dividends declined during the last decade of the century. In spite of amalgamations there were still over a hundred separate companies, though the main routes were all operated by the larger companies, of which there were seventeen. London was served by eight main-line companies, the largest of which were the Great Northern, the Midland, the London and North-Western, the Great Western, and the London and South-Western. To these at the end of the century was added the Great Central (formerly the Manchester, Sheffield and Lincolnshire), which in 1899 opened a new route to London. The other larger companies served provincial areas such as the four Scottish companies, the Cambrian in Wales, the Lancashire and

TABLE XXIV

*Railway Mileage*

| Year | Total route mileage |
|------|---------------------|
| 1860 | 10,400 |
| 1870 | 13,600 |
| 1880 | 15,700 |
| 1890 | 17,500 |
| 1900 | 20,314 |

Yorkshire, the North-Eastern, the North Staffordshire, the Furness. The remaining companies mostly operated short local lines, some such as the Cheshire Lines being under the joint control of the larger companies. Amalgamation would have gone much further but for the intervention of Parliament, which refused to sanction some proposals as, for example, in 1854 and again in 1908, a merger of the M.R. and the L. & N.W.R., and in 1909 a merger of the G.N.R., G.E.R. and G.C.R. In order to make through-running possible, therefore, the railways had to enter into operating agreements, as was necessary with all three routes from London to Edinburgh and Glasgow and most cross-country routes in England such as Liverpool to Hull. By the end of the nineteenth century this, then, was the pattern of the railways in Great Britain.

By this time their monopolistic position was almost complete. Long before the end of the century the last of the stage-coaches had ceased to run. To obviate competition from what it was thought might have become a serious rival, the railways bought many canals —about half their total length—not to operate them in conjunction with their main interests but to prevent their development as a rival means of transport. This policy also checked the development of the independent canals, which were often isolated from one another by stretches of railway-owned canals. In either case the canals suffered from competition from the railways. Nevertheless, some canals and rivers continued to carry coal and other bulky goods, especially where they provided connections with important seaports.

### The grouping of the railways

During the First World War the Government took over the operation of the railways. As compensation for the depreciation of their
assets during these years the railways received a grant of £60 million.
Then the Act of 1921 (to take effect in 1923) compulsorily amalgamated them into four groups, thereby reducing the number of railways from more than one hundred to four. Although the grouping
was largely on a regional basis, thus giving large areas of regional
monopoly within each group, a measure of competition between them
was retained.

At long last the L. & N.W.R. (which had taken over the L. & Y.R.
just before the passing of the grouping Act) and the M.R. were
allowed to amalgamate, these two railways being the main constituents of the London, Midland & Scottish Railway, the name
chosen for this group, which obtained through running to Scotland
by the inclusion within it of two Scottish railways—the Caledonian
and the Glasgow and South-Western. The new London and North-
Eastern Railway comprised among others the G.N.R., G.C.R.,
G.E.R., N.E.R. and the Scottish company, the N.B.R. (North
British Railway), this railway thus providing a second route from
London to Scotland in competition with the L.M. & S.R. These two
groups were also in competition with one another in their services
from London to Manchester, Leeds, Sheffield, Nottingham and
Leicester. Similarly, the Great Western Railway (the only railway
to retain its former name) was in competition with the L.M. & S.R.
between London, Birmingham and Liverpool, and with the new
Southern between London and Plymouth. The S.R. competed
with the L. & N.E.R. for continental traffic, and the L.M. & S.R.
with the G.W.R. for Irish traffic.

The route mileage of the four groups was as follows:

TABLE XXV
*Mileage of Railway Groups*

| Group | Route mileage |
|-------|---------------|
| L.M. & S.R. . . | 6,940 |
| L. & N.E.R. . . | 6,380 |
| G.W.R. . . . | 3,793 |
| S.R. . . . | 2,185 |
| Total . . | 20,298 |

The purpose behind this reduction in the number of railways was to
increase their efficiency. It was expected that considerable economies
of scale would result from the amalgamation. However, in spite

of the fact that some degree of competition between railways was retained, their monopolistic position appeared at the time to be strengthened. Consequently, the policy adopted during the nineteenth century was continued, namely control of freight rates and passenger fares. These fares were fixed with a view to limiting their profit. Thus, it was decided that the combined net revenue for the railways should be £50 million per year, apportioned between them as follows:

TABLE XXVI
*Net Revenue of Railway Groups*

| Group | £ million |
|---|---|
| L.M. & S.R.    .      . | 20 |
| L. & N.E.R.    .      . | 15 |
| G.W.R.   .      .      . | 8 |
| S.R..      .      .      . | 7 |
| Total      .      . | 50 |

The railway classification system for freight rates was largely retained though considerably revised. These new rates differed in one very important respect from the rates previously imposed on the railways in that they were not *maximum* rates which the railways themselves could cut if they so wished, but were to be regarded as *standard* rates, to which the railways must strictly adhere, any variation from the standard requiring to be sanctioned by the Railway Rates Tribunal set up under the Act. Passenger fares were to be at a rate of $1\frac{1}{2}d.$ per mile third class and $2\frac{1}{2}d.$ per mile first class. Those who framed the Act of 1921 did not see that the railways had a serious competitor just round the corner. In fact none of the railways ever earned the standard revenue assigned to them. In 1929 the total net revenue came to only £41 million and by 1938 it had fallen to £28 million.

## III. DEVELOPMENT OF ROAD TRANSPORT

**Street tramways**

Just before the close of the century the first indication came of the rise of a competitor to the railways. The street tramway in the larger cities became a rival for suburban traffic or in the developing conurbations for traffic in heavily built-up areas between neighbouring towns. Tramways could not be operated economically unless the density of population was sufficient for a frequent service to be maintained. Horse-drawn trams appeared on the streets of Birkenhead and London during 1860–61. It was something of an anachronism that the first street trams should be horse-drawn when steam-driven railways had been so long in use. There were experiments with steam trams in 1876 in Sheffield and in 1880 in York, but both cities decided to have horse trams on account of the noise and smoke of steam traction in built-up areas. Many other cities, however, persisted with steam until the 1890s when electric traction gradually became general.[1] Electric tramways began to be operated in Leeds in 1891, and in London in 1901. With the introduction of the electric-traction tramways, mileage increased rapidly.

An Act of 1870 enabled local authorities to run tramways and gave them powers of compulsory purchase after twenty-one years of companies operating within their boundaries. In some cases local councils constructed the tracks and then leased them to companies. Ultimately over 150 local authorities took advantage of this Act to operate tramways with, in addition, a further 100 systems in the hands of companies. By 1914 the total route mileage of tramways in Great Britain exceeded 2,000. Much of this development opened up a new market since only in a limited number of cases was the tramway in direct competition with the railway. Most of the people who began to travel to work by tram had previously walked. Some people also began to travel by tram for pleasurable purposes, to local "pleasure gardens," to local "beauty spots," or simply as a means of getting out into the country. For those of slender means this was even cheaper entertainment than the cheap railway excursion, and again, therefore, it was mainly a new market that was being developed. On the whole the railways suffered little competition from the tram, as there were only a few inter-city routes, but instead tramways served as useful feeders to the railway. In most towns where there were tramways the most-used routes were those to the railway station.

The piecemeal growth of the railways of this country has been noted, and a similar complaint has been made of the development of street tramways. It must be remembered, however, that each tramway system was intended to serve mainly local needs, and it was only in the great conurbations such as London and Manchester that the disadvantages of unco-ordinated growth were seriously experienced.

### The return to the roads

Though a few short extensions to street tramways took place during the 1920s and even during the 1930s, tramways had really reached the peak of their development by 1914, and the main concern during these years was to protect them from their first competitor—

---

[1] A few towns continued to operate horse-drawn trams until the coming of the motor bus.

the petrol-driven motor omnibus. Previous to this they had enjoyed local monopolies.

Side by side with the development of the horse-drawn tram had gone that of the horse omnibus. Although the horse omnibus was more costly to operate, since only smaller loads could be carried, it obviated the heavy capital cost involved in laying down rails. Few survived the coming of the electric tram. It continued to be used in central London down to the 1914–18 War as its greater manoeuvrability caused less traffic congestion.

A few motor omnibuses were in operation before 1914, some local authorities using them to supplement their tramway services as early as 1907–8. At this time the petrol engine was very unreliable and breakdowns were frequent, and it was not until its improvement during the First World War that it made the motor omnibus a serious rival to the tram. In 1908 the total number of motor vehicles licensed in Great Britain was 29,000. By 1914 the number had increased to 178,000.

Even after 1918 progress was slow for a time, but after 1921 motor buses appeared on the roads at an ever-increasing rate. The expansion of bus services was carried out by five types of operator: (*i*) small "mushroom" firms which never ran more than a few vehicles; (*ii*) new omnibus companies which often had small beginnings but which developed into concerns of considerable size; (*iii*) existing bus companies which began to extend the range of their activities; (*iv*) small tramway undertakings with only a small route mileage which soon substituted buses for trams in order to operate over a wider area; (*v*) the larger municipally owned tramway undertakings which operated buses only to supplement trams and which fought hard to protect their monopolies and defend them from the new competition. Some of the new operators, especially where village-based, were garage proprietors who took time off from their other activities to run an occasional bus. Others were haulage contractors—perhaps furniture removers—who bought a few vehicles, developed a service at first as a sideline to their main business, eventually turning it into a separate organisation or disposing of it to a larger concern. By expansion and amalgamation many large companies developed, such as the SMT (Scottish Motor Traction), United, West Yorkshire, Yorkshire Traction, Ribble, North-Western, Trent, Midland Red, Crosville, Eastern Counties, Southern National, Western National, Hants & Dorset, East Kent and others. On some routes there was keen competition between different operators.

Not only did many local authorities themselves provide transport but they also acted as the licensing authorities. Those local authorities which owned tramway undertakings tried to protect them by refusing licences to applicants who wished to run buses partly or wholly over their tramway routes. If the local authority provided no public transport its attitude was quite different: it might license several operators in order to encourage competition. When a licence could not be obtained, a go-ahead bus proprietor had to provide his own picking-up and setting-down points, or for intermediate stops he might, as many did, defy the local authority, and regard the fines he had to pay as part of his operating costs. By 1924 the number of motor vehicles licensed in Great Britain had reached 750,000.

With the increase in road traffic of all kinds one great defect of the tram soon became apparent—loading and unloading in the middle of the road. Though some attempt was made to overcome this by laying down special track for trams this was not a feasible solution near town centres, where it was most needed. The report of the Royal Commission on Transport (1931) sounded the death-knell of the tram. Tramways it declared to be obsolescent if not already obsolete, and recommended that (*i*) no further extensions should take place, and (*ii*) existing tramways should be replaced by some other means of transport. The Commission favoured the trolley-bus and some tramway undertakings were converted to the use of this more mobile vehicle. Others began to substitute buses for trams. In two cases in Yorkshire—at York and Keighley—an area bus company came to terms with the local authorities to operate a joint bus undertaking— the York–West Yorkshire and the Keighley–West Yorkshire. By 1936 tramway route mileage had been halved.

### Road haulage

Contemporary with the expansion of road passenger transport was a very similar development of road haulage. As with passenger transport a number of mainly small road hauliers were already in existence. Most of them were engaged in local traffic, a good deal of it to and from the railway stations and goods yards. The railways themselves for a long time had employed horse-drawn vehicles for this sort of traffic. Apart from furniture removers there was very little inter-urban carriage of goods by road. The changeover from horse-drawn vehicles to the motor van or wagon made possible a widening of a firm's field of activity and the more progressive operators were not slow to take advantage of this opportunity. Only a relatively small number of firms developed into large ones, but there was a huge increase in the number of "one-man" businesses. The increasing scale of manufacturing industry had greatly reduced the opportunities of the small man with a little capital who wished to set up in business for himself. For a time the petrol engine again gave him scope as the proprietor of a small repair garage or as the owner-driver of a single motor bus or motor lorry. Throughout the country large numbers of small operators of goods-carrying services came into existence. As on the passenger side—though to a less extent—by expansion and amalgamation a number of haulage firms with large fleets of vehicles came to be established. Even at the time of its nationalisation in 1947 there were over 20,000 separate firms in this country engaged in road haulage, with an average of only three vehicles per firm.

## Road competition and the railways

By 1925 the railways were in a state of serious alarm at the effect on them of the development of inter-urban road passenger services and long-distance road haulage. Although the road operators were in many cases opening up a new market, the railways were by this time beginning to lose traffic and were quick to complain of unfair competition.

The advantages of road transport are as follows:

(*i*) The road operators were not hampered by legal restrictions as were the railways. Since there was keen competition between different road operators Parliament had not considered it necessary to intervene to restrict or fix charges as it had with the railways in their days of near-monopoly.

(*ii*) At law the railways were "common carriers" and so could not be selective in the goods they were prepared to carry. The road-haulage firms could restrict themselves to goods which they regarded as profitable for them to carry—generally those in the higher categories of the railway classification list. These they could usually carry more cheaply than the railways.

(*iii*) Railway charges were based on their average costs for the entire railway system, including their lines running through sparsely populated areas such as north and west Scotland and central Wales, and also their many unremunerative branch lines. Road operators could base their charges on the actual cost of each route or journey.

(*iv*) For short distances road transport was speedier than the railway. Road haulage was speedier for quite long distances owing to the long delays associated with the marshalling of freight trains.

(*v*) For intermediate traffic between towns the motor bus was generally more convenient than a railway route, on which the stations were often at considerable distances from the villages.

(*vi*) Road haulage could offer customers a door-to-door service, thus eliminating the need for loading and unloading at stations. This often also resulted in less expensive packing being required for goods. This feature of road transport was particularly attractive to manufacturers of branded goods, many of whom preferred where possible to make delivery direct to their retail outlets, which in some cases they themselves operated. To such manufacturers the van can itself be made to serve as a very useful advertising medium.

(*vii*) For road transport, whether of passengers or freight, the unit of operation is the single lorry, van or bus, whereas the railway has to work in units of train-loads.

(*viii*) The railways had to incur heavy capital costs in the provision of their own "roads," stations, signalling, etc. Although road operators were taxed—at first by the road-fund licence and later also by a tax on petrol—roads were provided for them and only in the case of the larger towns have they found it necessary to provide themselves with stations.

### The railways obtain road powers

During the nineteenth century the railways had driven the stage-coaches off the roads and a vast industry had been whittled away. Coachmen, ostlers, innkeepers and their staffs, coach-builders and horse-breeders, road-makers, all found their employment taken from them. To many, of course, the railways offered alternative jobs, though often of a very different kind. Now after more than half a century of freedom from competition from the roads, the railways again found themselves having to contend with competition from road transport. The motor vehicle was a much more serious competitor than the old stage-coach. The railways had been so powerful a competitor of the stage-coach that no coach service could be maintained once a railway opened a line over the same route. Though some people complained of the dirt and smoke of the steam engine and the dangers associated with railway travel (this latter charge had been levelled against coaches at an earlier period), there was no doubt that the railway provided a better and more efficient mode of travel, being both faster and smoother, and with its enclosed track also being less of a danger to the community than the "flying" coach dashing madly through the busy streets of towns.

Faced with the new development of road transport the railways sought powers from Parliament to operate road services themselves. It could be argued, therefore, on economic grounds that in the light of history the railways should have been left to fight this new competition in order to discover which forms of transport people really preferred. It would have compelled the railways to look to their own efficiency instead of looking to road operation to offset declining railway receipts on some services. It would probably have led to the closure of many more unremunerative branch lines (easily replaced at that time by bus services) but the rest of the system could have been modernised and made more efficient so that the railways could have concentrated on the sort of traffic for which they were best fitted—express services of all kinds, especially over the longer distances.

However, in 1928 the railways were given permission to operate road services. The Great Western Railway had for some time operated a number of "feeder" bus services, mainly in the West Country, but the new powers were to cover services over the same routes as those offered by the railways. In only a few instances, however, did they actually place their own buses on the road. At a time when there was keen competition between different road operators this was a token of possible competition from a powerful new competitor. Instead, the railways preferred to acquire substantial interests in the larger road-passenger-transport undertakings. The railways co-operated to carry out this policy rather than intensify the road competition by becoming interested in rival companies serving the same route. Where one railway served a particular area it would act alone in relation to bus companies in that area. Where two railways served an area they would both acquire interests in its bus companies.

In four Yorkshire towns—Sheffield, Huddersfield, Halifax and Todmorden—the two northern railways, the L.M. & S.R. and the L. & N.E.R., made agreements with the local authorities to operate jointly owned services over certain routes. Though the agreements differed in detail, the general underlying principle was that entirely local routes (generally defined as those not extending beyond the town boundary) were to be operated by the local authority and other routes by a joint committee comprising representatives of the two railways and the municipality concerned. The railways closed a number of short branch lines and some stations, at least to passenger traffic.

## London Transport

Horse-drawn omnibuses had appeared on the streets of central London as early as 1829, supplemented after 1861 by horse-drawn trams, and in 1861 by the first "underground" with steam traction. With the introduction of electric power there was a considerable expansion of both the tramway system and the underground railways. In addition, some of the suburbs, especially south of the Thames, were served by the main-line railways. As elsewhere, the perfection of the petrol engine led to a huge increase in the number of motor buses. Since the late nineteenth century the London General Omnibus Company had had a near-monopoly of road-passenger transport except over some routes where there was competition from the LCC tramways. Both these concerns had strong vested interests in road transport in the London area and were alarmed in the 1920s by the inrush of "pirate" buses. Traffic congestion was aggravated both by the General Omnibus Company's efforts to fight these new rivals and by the increasing number of private cars. To regulate public transport in London, therefore, a public corporation, known as the London Passenger Transport Board, was set up in 1933 to take over, co-ordinate and operate passenger transport previously provided by the various tramway, motor-bus and underground railway undertakings and by some of the suburban services of the mainline railways. Thus, the LPTB was given a monopoly of public transport in London, and for this reason it was thought best to bring it under public control. Though some such scheme was clearly necessary one cannot help feeling a suspicion that one of the motives of some of its supporters was to protect the tramways from further bus competition.

## IV. THE REGULATION OF TRANSPORT

### Regulation of road passenger transport

As with the earlier development of turnpike trusts and the railways, the growth of motor transport had been haphazard, and, although considerable co-ordination of routes, timetables and fares had taken place after the railways had obtained road powers, there was much overlapping of services. On many routes keen competition still prevailed. This was regarded by many people as a dangerous practice both to passengers and to other road users, and it was widely felt that some kind of control was necessary.

### The Road Traffic Act, 1930

This Act aimed at regulating road passenger traffic. The country was divided into thirteen areas (later reduced to eleven) for each of which Traffic Commissioners were appointed. Their first duty was to license bus operators for each route that was being worked in their area and afterwards to consider applications to provide new services. All timetables and fares came under their control. The Act emphasised the desirability of co-ordinating services and restricting the number of operators over each route. All existing routes were closely scrutinised by the Commissioners. Where two or more undertakings served the same routes these might be distributed among the operators concerned or, where this was not possible, joint services on a single timetable might be introduced. In one or two cases licences were refused to operators of services that had only recently been started. On the whole, these changes were neither revolutionary nor extensive, and often only accelerated tendencies already at work. Nevertheless, the Road Census Returns of 1931 and 1938 show that, the number of buses operating over about two-thirds of the roads, declined between these two dates. The increase in total traffic between these two dates was the result mainly of a large increase in the number of goods vehicles (*see* Table XXVII, p. 153) and an increase in the number of private cars, though the continued increase in the number of people carried by bus shows that the private car was not yet a serious competitor to the bus. The reduction in the number of buses on most roads can, therefore, be attributed to the rationalisation of public transport consequent on the introduction of a system of licensing of passenger road transport.

On grounds of efficiency and safety a monopolistic character had been given to the public carriage of passengers. After the Traffic Commissioners had completed their initial task of rationalisation no new operator could obtain a licence unless he could show either that there was a need for a new route or that an existing route was inadequately served. In deciding whether public transport over any route was adequate not only had the bus services to be taken into account but also the railway services. Before a new licence could be granted objectors were allowed to present their cases. To any new application objection would certainly come from the railways, local authorities if there was to be further competition with municipally owned passenger transport, and other operators over the same or alternative routes. As a result, few new licences were granted. Fares, too, were controlled. Thus, competition between different bus operators was eliminated and to some extent reduced between road and rail.

The Act of 1930, however, also checked the expansion, other than by amalgamation, of the large bus companies. Before the passing of the Act many of the smaller pioneer bus undertakings had already been bought out or driven off the roads. After 1930 the possession of a licence to operate a service became a valuable piece of property for which the large companies were generally willing to pay a good price. The large concerns, therefore, continued to expand and the number of operators to fall. Among road operators the Act of 1930 was of great benefit to the large companies, many of which as a result acquired area monopolies.

The Act also gave some protection to the railways by stabilising road passenger transport and also by bringing to an end fare-cutting by bus companies. The railways continued their policy of buying shares in the larger bus companies, and by 1938 there were few large undertakings in which the railways had not an interest. Since the railways were by this time concerned, directly or indirectly, with the carriage of passengers both by rail and by road, it gave them an opportunity, if they so wished, to co-ordinate these two modes of transport, to which there had been vague reference in the Act of 1930. It would seem, however, that they were more concerned to check the further advance of a rival than to develop the combined potentialities of rail and road transport into an integrated system.

What was required was a much more drastic closure of unremunerative lines and of many more intermediate stations where these were little used, and the substitution of buses on these routes. What perhaps could not be foreseen was that the private car—of which by 1938 there were 2 million on the road—would eventually become the competitor of both the train and the bus.

### Regulation of road haulage

Parliament next gave its attention to the problem of road haulage. The matter was first considered in 1932 by the Salter Committee, which comprised four representatives each of the railways and road interests. The Committee was instructed to consider and devise some basis for fair competition in the field of road haulage for road and rail. As with road-passenger transport the problem was one of keen competition and ease of entry leading to a rapid increase in the number of operators. As when there was competition between bus operators there were complaints of danger to other road users especially, it was said, on account of the excessively long hours worked by drivers. There was again a vague mention of the necessity for co-ordination between road and rail. These complaints were strongly urged by spokesmen from both sides who wished to restrict competition. The aim of the railways was to check the further expansion of the transport of goods by road; the large hauliers complained of the excessive competition they had to face on the roads, especially from what they regarded as the less reliable firms. The Salter Committee, not surprisingly, recommended some form of control and the Act of 1933 followed.

### The Road and Rail Act, 1933

As with road-passenger transport, so with road haulage, a licensing system was introduced. In order to engage in general haulage a firm had to obtain an "A" or "B" licence before it could operate, the "B" licence being for hauliers who proposed either to carry their own goods or to undertake the carriage of goods on behalf of others. The "A" licence was required if the haulier intended only to carry other firms' goods. The "C" licence was available to a firm for the carriage only of its own goods. To obtain an "A" or "B" licence a haulier had to satisfy the licensing authority (the chairman of the Traffic Commissioners of the area from which he proposed to operate) that there was a need for the service he intended to provide. No restrictions were placed on the issue of "C" licences except that the licensee should carry only his own goods. The "C" licence was attractive to retailers who wished to deliver their customers' orders, and it became increasingly popular with wholesalers and manufacturers of branded goods. About half of all "C" licences were issued to retailers and wholesalers. Even though in some cases costs of delivery were higher than if a haulier had been allowed to do the work, there were often other advantages to offset this, such as convenience. Just as the Act of 1930 made it difficult for new entrants to start new bus services, so the Act of 1933 made it difficult for new firms to enter the field of road haulage. It was not regarded as being a sufficient ground for the award of a licence for a firm to offer a more efficient and cheaper service; it had to show that it would meet a need for which existing operators were not already catering. The *Transport Act* of 1953 shifted the emphasis from the applicant's having to show that there was a need for a proposed service to the objector's having to show a lack of need. Although a number of large-scale haulage firms developed, the average firm operating on an "A" or "B" licence had only a few vehicles.

The effect of the Act of 1933, therefore, was to give a degree of monopoly to existing operators through restriction of entry. This greatly reduced the undercutting of charges by firms wishing to break into the market, although competition continued between hauliers and between road haulage and the railways. Restriction on entry to the road-haulage industry was intended also to help the railways, but during the remaining years of the inter-war period the railways continued to lose more and more of their more profitable traffic to the road-haulage firms. Thus, the Act of 1933 restricted the number of vehicles engaged in general haulage, at the same time permitting the number of "C" licensed vehicles to increase.

The following table shows the increase in the number of vehicles on the roads of Great Britain during 1935–38:

TABLE XXVII

*Number of Motor Vehicles in Great Britain* (1935–38)
(Thousands)

| Year | Private cars | Motor buses, coaches, taxis | Goods vehicles | Others | Total |
|------|--------------|------------------------------|----------------|--------|-------|
| 1935 | 1,477 | 85 | 424 | 595 | 2,581 |
| 1936 | 1,643 | 86 | 447 | 593 | 2,769 |
| 1937 | 1,798 | 86 | 465 | 589 | 2,938 |
| 1938 | 1,944 | 88 | 480 | 582 | 3,094 |

Source: *Monthly Digest of Statistics.*

During the 1930s it was a constant complaint of the railways that road haulage competed unfairly against them because road operators were free to fix their own charges and to carry whatever goods they wished and to refuse to carry other goods, whereas the railways had to abide by the goods-classification system. For some years the railways compaigned strenuously for a "square deal." The Act of 1933 allowed them to make "agreed charges" with firms sending all their traffic by rail.

## Nationalisation

As during the First World War so during the Second, the Government took over the control of the railways, which (including London Transport) were guaranteed a yearly revenue of £43 million, the Government taking the entire receipts. This proved to be a very good bargain for the Government as during the war years the railways earned for it a surplus of over £200 million while suffering a severe depreciation of their assets.

Then in 1947 came the Act to nationalise inland transport. It was the Government's intention to nationalise all forms of public transport—railways, road services for both passengers and goods, and waterways. The Act set up the British Transport Commission to acquire the assets of the various transport undertakings, their operation being delegated to five executives: (i) railways, (ii) road transport, (iii) docks and waterways, (iv) London Transport, (v) hotels and catering services. The Railways Executive took over the four main-line railways on 1st January 1948, from which date they became known as British Railways. For operational purposes British Railways were divided into six regions. The London Midland, Southern and Western regions at first comprised respectively the former L.M. & S.R. (shorn of its Scottish lines), S.R. and G.W.R. The Scottish lines of the former L. & N.E.R. were joined to those taken from the old L.M. & S.R. to form the Scottish region and the English portion of this railway was divided into the Eastern and North-Eastern regions. The private ownership of railway wagons—an anachronism from the nineteenth century—came to an end. The railway-owned hotels, station and dining-car catering services, previously run by the railways, were hived off and brought under the control of the Hotels Executive. Canals and other navigable waterways were taken over by the British Waterways Executive. The tramways, buses, trolley-buses, underground and surface suburban lines, operated since 1933 by the London Passenger Transport Board, were taken over en bloc by the London Transport Executive. In the case of all these four executives the transfer to state ownership and operation was easily effected.

The nationalisation of road transport was a much more complicated affair. Road haulage was to be operated by a body known as British Road Services. There were over 20,000 firms engaged in road haulage—a few large, most very small with an average of between only two and three vehicles each. The usual method adopted at this time on the nationalisation of an industry was to base compensation on the value on the stock exchange of the shares of the undertakings concerned and then offer the shareholders government stock to yield the same income. This was not practicable, however, for most road-haulage concerns, few of which were public companies with stock-exchange quotations, and the method adopted was for British Road Services to make individual terms for the purchase of each. The first firms to be bought out were those mainly engaged in hauls of over twenty-five miles. Nationalisation of road haulage applied only to holders of "A" and "B" licences, holders of "C" licences being exempt. British Road Services set up its headquarters in London and the country was divided into eight regions, these being further subdivided into thirty-one districts. To give the industry economies of scale which it previously lacked owing to the small size of most operational units, groups of about 150 vehicles were formed, each under a group manager. Thus in the larger towns there were often two or more groups. As a stimulus to efficiency groups were en-couraged—rather surprisingly—to compete against one another. Most firms lost their former identity when acquired by BRS, but Pickfords, a concern dating back to the days of turnpikes, was per-mitted to retain its name for historical reasons and for the goodwill attached to it.

The work of acquiring and reorganising the administrative struc-ture of road haulage was barely completed by British Road Services when the Act of 1953 repealed those sections of the *Nationalisation Act* of 1947 that referred to road haulage and road-passenger trans-port. The original aim of the Act of 1953 was to return road trans-port entirely to free enterprise, except of course that the State-owned British Railways would retain their wide interest in bus companies. However, the threat to renationalise road haulage made many entre-preneurs reluctant to return to this industry. Consequently, only 54% of the vehicles of British Road Services were disposed of, and in 1956 an Act had to be passed to permit BRS to retain the remainder. The original intention of disposing of vehicles only in groups soon had to be abandoned as few purchasers wished to operate under-takings of this size. Though nearly half the industry remained in the hands of British Road Services, and though there was a greater number of large concerns, road haulage again became to a large extent a small-scale industry with the average firm not a great deal larger than it was before nationalisation.

To effect the nationalisation of road-passenger transport would have taken a long time. Under the Act of 1947 regional schemes had to be drawn up, and local interests, including municipal passenger transport authorities, were to be allowed to put forward their objec-tions. Little progress had been made when denationalisation came in

1953, only two schemes having been formulated, for North-East England and East Anglia, and only in the case of the former had objections begun to be heard. The Transport Commission had been given powers to acquire road-passenger undertakings as well as road-haulage firms and a number of concerns, including in 1948 that of Thos. Cook & Son Ltd., were taken over. As with Pickfords, this firm continued to operate under its own name.

## V. ROAD AND RAIL TRANSPORT SINCE 1953

### Road transport

The Second World War temporarily checked the increase in the number of private cars. For some years after the end of the war it was difficult to meet the expanding demand in the home market. Immediately before the outbreak of war the total reached 2 million. By 1954 it had reached 3·1 million. After 1954 the number of motor vehicles in Great Britain increased rapidly. During the ten years

TABLE XXVIII
*Number of Motor Vehicles in Great Britain (1954–66)*
(Thousands)

| Date | Private | Motor buses, coaches | Goods vehicles | Others | Total |
|------|---------|----------------------|----------------|--------|-------|
| 1954 | 3,100 | 102 | 1,037 | 1,536 | 5,775 |
| 1956 | 3,888 | 102 | 1,179 | 1,751 | 6,920 |
| 1958 | 4,549 | 97 | 1,274 | 1,084 | 7,904 |
| 1960 | 5,526 | 94 | 1,403 | 1,461 | 9,384 |
| 1962 | 6,556 | 93 | 1,476 | 1,480 | 10,505 |
| 1964 | 8,247 | 97 | 1,583 | 1,479 | 12,306 |
| 1966 | 9,513 | 94 | 1,575 | 2,105 | 13,287 |
| 1967 | 10,303 | 94 | 1,624 | 2,075 | 14,096 |

Source: *Annual Abstract of Statistics.*

1954–64 the total number of motor vehicles on the roads of this country more than doubled. The number of buses and coaches slightly increased, but by 1964 only 111 tramcars were running and the number of trolley-buses had been reduced from 3,700 to 984 in ten years. By 1966 the number of trolley buses had been reduced to 435. The number of goods vehicles increased by 50%.

During the decade 1956–66 there was an increase of over 50% in passenger travelling in Great Britain as judged by the increase during those years in the estimated passenger mileage by the different means of transport, as Table XXIX shows.

The actual decline in rail passenger transport was 12·5% but relatively it was much greater than that since in 1956 travelling by train accounted for 19% but by 1966 only 10·5% of passenger travelling. Although air transport increased by nearly four times it still formed less than 0·5% of the total in 1966. The great increase in travelling was due to the increase in the number of private cars.

During this decade the number of private cars increased at an average rate of half a million a year. For the first time the private car become a serious competitor of public transport, both of the railway and of the motor bus. For most owners the private car is more expensive as a means of transport than the bus or the railway if all costs—including depreciation and loss of interest on capital—are taken into account, especially when carrying only the driver. The

TABLE XXIX

*Estimated Passenger Mileage by Rail, Road and Air (Domestic Services)*
(1000 million miles)

| Year | Rail | Road | Air | Total |
|------|------|------|-----|-------|
| 1956 | 24·5 | 108·1 | 0·3 | 132·9 |
| 1957 | 25·9 | 105·8 | 0·3 | 132·0 |
| 1958 | 25·5 | 116·3 | 0·3 | 142·1 |
| 1959 | 25·5 | 126·2 | 0·4 | 152·1 |
| 1960 | 24·8 | 132·8 | 0·5 | 158·1 |
| 1961 | 24·1 | 140·8 | 0·6 | 165·5 |
| 1962 | 22·8 | 146·1 | 0·7 | 169·6 |
| 1963 | 22·4 | 152·0 | 0·8 | 175·2 |
| 1964 | 23·0 | 165·8 | 0·9 | 189·7 |
| 1965 | 21·8 | 172·4 | 1·0 | 195·2 |
| 1966 | 21·5 | 181·4 | 1·1 | 204·0 |
| 1967 | 21·1 | 200·0 | 1·1 | 222·3 |

Source: *Annual Abstract of Statistics.*

attraction of the private car, however, lies in its greater convenience and the fact that it can also be used for pleasure purposes. Since 1954 it has been increasingly used for going to and from work. Since 1954, therefore, the motor bus for the first time has found itself up against a serious competitor. Bus travel reached its peak in 1951. Before that date bus fares had risen relatively little since 1939 compared with other prices, but since then rising costs (especially wages) and falling traffic have led to steep increases in fares, a fact which has still further stimulated demand for the private car. Table XXX (p. 158) shows the effect of competition from the private car on travel by bus.

Thus in ten years travel by bus declined by 10%. During the same period travel by private car increased by more than two and a half times. (1955 was the first year during which travel by private car exceeded travel by bus.) Since during this period there was little

TABLE XXX

*Estimated Passenger Mileage by Bus and Car*

| Year | Motor bus (1,000 *million miles*) | Private car (1,000 *million miles*) |
|------|------|------|
| 1954 | 50·0 | 47·2 |
| 1956 | 48·6 | 59·5 |
| 1958 | 43·4 | 72·9 |
| 1960 | 43·9 | 88·9 |
| 1962 | 42·4 | 103·7 |
| 1964 | 40·3 | 125·5 |
| 1966 | 36·3 | 145·1 |
| 1967 | 34·8 | 165·2 |

Source: *Annual Abstract of Statistics.*

change in rail passenger travel it is clear that the private car greatly increased the demand for travel, total travel increasing by 50%.

In addition to local bus services there are some "limited-stop" services such as the Green Line routes of London Transport and a number of long-distance express services. In general, express coaches are both cheaper and slower than express rail services, though the difference in time is reduced the greater the proportion of motorway on the route.

Buses are operated by London Transport, upwards of 100 local authorities (mostly county boroughs), the State-owned Transport Holding Company (which bought out the large Tilling group and a number of other companies) and upwards of 5,000 other operators, ranging from those under the control of the British Electric Traction Co. Ltd. to small rural concerns with only one or two vehicles. In

TABLE XXXI

*Public Road Passenger Transport—Number of Vehicles*

|  | 1954 | 1960 | 1964 | 1967 |
|------|------|------|------|------|
| (*i*) Buses: |  |  |  |  |
| London Transport . | 8,404 | 7,743 | 8,163 | 7,578 |
| Local authorities . | 14,567 | 16,405 | 17,067 | 16,601 |
| Transport Holding Co. | 14,475 | 14,011 | 14,289 | 14,571 |
| Other operators . . | 37,165 | 36,316 | 36,345 | 35,531 |
| (*ii*) Trolley buses and tram-cars: |  |  |  |  |
| London Transport . | 1,764 | 723 | · — | — |
| Other operators . . | 4,268 | 2,126 | 1,095 | 362 |
| Total . . . | 80,643 | 77,324 | 76,959 | 74,643 |

Source: *Annual Abstract of Statistics.*

ten years the number of public-service vehicles on the roads fell by
$4\frac{1}{2}\%$. These figures show the decline in the tramcar (only 111 in
1964) and the trolley-bus (984 in 1964). They also show, in spite of
the very large number of operators, that, although road passenger
transport has not been nationalised, the state and local authorities
nevertheless directly operated 33% of all public road-passenger
vehicles, and indirectly through the Transport Holding Company a
further 18%, a total of 51%, to which must be added the interest of
British Rail in some road-passenger undertakings. In addition to the
monopolistic aspect given to road-passenger transport by the
licensing system as long ago as 1930, competition between the large
independent area companies is restricted by agreements between
them which define the boundaries of the area in which they operate.

The increase in the number of road vehicles in recent years has been
mainly the result of the increase in the number of private cars (*see*
Table, XXVIII, p. 156). A few motorways have been constructed and
many trunk roads have been modernised by being widened, straight-
ened, provided with dual carriageways, fly-overs, underpasses and
by-passses round towns. The total mileage of trunk roads, however, increased during 1954–64 by only 358, but expenditure on
the roads (trunk, classified and unclassified) during this period increased very considerably.

TABLE XXXII
*Expenditure on Roads*
(in £ millions)

| Year | New con- struction and improvements | Maintenance | Other | Total |
|------|------------------------------------|-------------|-------|-------|
| 1954 | 9·6   | 72·9  | 14·7 | 107·2 |
| 1960 | 81·7  | 97·8  | 33·6 | 213·3 |
| 1963 | 144·5 | 122·6 | 42·7 | 309·8 |
| 1965 | 181·6 | 139·4 | 56·4 | 377·4 |
| 1967 | 202·6 | 154·3 | 62·1 | 419.0 |

Source: *Annual Abstract of Statistics.*

The bus operators, both municipal and company, have found on
their commuter services little demand except in the morning and
evening—and then often only in one direction. This has inevitably
led in some cases to the cutting of services. The Traffic Commissioners, however, expect the more profitable bus routes to subsidise some unremunerative services. Since the percentage of car
ownership is much higher in some areas than in others (especially
those served by municipal undertakings) cross-subsidisation could result in the less wealthy subsidising public transport for the well-to-do.

## Rail transport

The *Transport Act* of 1953 removed the legal restrictions on railway rates and so enabled the railways to compete more nearly on equal terms with road haulage. Nevertheless, although the total volume of internal trade was expanding, railway goods traffic declined by 14% while road haulage increased by 50%. In 1954 road haulage carried 74% (by weight) of all goods transported in Great Britain, but this was to some extent offset by the fact that the average length of journey was much greater by rail than by road (70 miles as against 25 miles). On the basis of ton mileage the traffic was almost equally divided between them. Since then, however, the position of

TABLE XXXIII
*Goods Transport in Great Britain*

| Date | Million tons | | Ton miles (1,000 million) | |
|---|---|---|---|---|
| | Rail | Road | Rail | Road |
| 1954 | 283 | 925 | 22·1 | 21·1 |
| 1956 | 277 | 993 | 21·5 | 23·2 |
| 1958 | 243 | 1,060 | 18·4 | 25·2 |
| 1960 | 249 | 1,192 | 18·7 | 30·1 |
| 1962 | 228 | 1,248 | 16·1 | 33·6 |
| 1964 | 240 | 1,410 | 16·0 | 39·0 |
| 1966 | 214 | 1,450 | 14·8 | 41·5 |
| 1968 | | | | |

Source: *Annual Abstract of Statistics.*

the railways has deteriorated still further. By 1964 the share of road haulage in total internal goods traffic had increased to 85% (by weight) and to 71% (on the basis of ton mileage). During these years, as already noted, the number of road-haulage vehicles increased by 50%. The Geddes Committee, set up in 1963 to enquire into road haulage, recommended the abolition of the licensing system in order to foster competition in the industry. Since 1958 the railways appear to have lost little traffic, though the average length of haul has fallen slightly. Half the freight now carried by the railways comprises coal and coke, but with the appearance of large coal trucks on the road even this traffic is no longer free from competition.

In 1956 British Railways decided upon a scheme of modernisation. Some lines were to be electrified and on others diesel-electric traction was to replace steam, both electric and diesel engines being cheaper to operate than steam. Some further branch lines and stations were to be closed.

The *Transport Act* of 1962 reorganised the nationalised sector of inland transport. The British Transport Commission was abolished, its functions and property being transferred to four boards—the British Railways Board, London Transport Board, British Waterways Board and British Transport Docks Board—and the Transport Holding Company. This meant that in future the railways would have to be judged by their own performance only—deficits could not be offset by profits from other means of transport or other interests such as those of the Transport Holding Company, which in 1965, for example, made a profit of 17·7 million—£8·5 million from road-passenger transport, £7 million from road haulage and £2·1 million from the nationalised travel agency.

## VI. THE TRANSPORT PROBLEM TODAY

### The Beeching Plan

Meanwhile the Government was making a determined effort to discover whether British Railways could be made to pay their way. Dr (later Lord) Beeching was called in by the Minister of Transport to make a thorough study of the railways and to report on the means necessary to make them economic. The result was the Beeching Plan of 1963—*The Re-shaping of British Railways*. The aim was to reshape the British railway system to suit present-day needs.

The main proposals put forward in the Report were as follows:

(*i*) The policy of closing unremunerative branch lines, previously somewhat hesitantly pursued, should be continued more vigorously. The stations on these lines should be closed to passenger traffic and in some cases to all traffic.

(*ii*) On a large number of lines only fast trains should be run, all stopping trains being withdrawn and the intermediate stations closed. In England stopping trains were particularly slow as the average distance between stations was only 2½ miles. The argument in favour of this course was that the demand for short-journey travel by rail had fallen to very small proportions, the bus and the private car by 1962 carrying 90% of this traffic. In spite of this, however, 40% of train mileage continued to be provided for it. At the time of the Report, British Rail had 7,000 stations open to passengers, but half of this number dealt with over 95% of all rail traffic. Here, therefore, there was considerable scope for reducing railway costs in return for little loss of revenue.

(*iii*) It was proposed that for freight a speedy and regular service of "liner" trains should be operated between all large towns where the volume of traffic warranted it. These trains would consist of special trucks to carry road–rail containers, for which speedy loading and unloading mechanism would be provided. Considerable economies could be obtained if the excessive number of railheads for goods traffic throughout the country were reduced, especially for coal, for which there were 3,750 unloading points. If the number were reduced they could be modernised to speed up the transfer from rail to road.

(*iv*) Commuter traffic was costly to operate because of the necessity to provide for relatively brief peak periods in the morning and evening with only light traffic between these times. It was suggested, therefore, that fares to suburban travellers using the service at peak periods should be increased.

(*v*) The encouragement by Parliament of competition between railways during the period of their construction had resulted in the duplication even of main lines. Perhaps the most wasteful example of railway construction had been the extension to London of the old Great Central, which like the former Midland Railway linked Sheffield, Nottingham and Leicester with London, though by a less expeditious route. Similarly, the Midland line from Leeds to Carlisle had been expensive to build and was costly to operate both because of the gradients and also in relation to the small number of trains worked over it at any time. There never had been any justification for this third route between England and Scotland. In addition, there were other pairs of towns served by two (or even three, as, for example, Liverpool to Manchester) alternative railway routes. In all these cases it might be economical to close one or other of the alternative routes, and this course the Report recommended.

(*vi*) Another group of lines which it was suggested might be closed were those serving some holiday resorts and which carried little traffic at other periods of the year. In spite of the relatively low marginal cost of running additional trains there was the heavy cost involved in keeping two-thirds of the rolling stock idle for the rest of the year and the heavy fixed costs of running the service outside the holiday season. Lines in this category included those serving the Lincolnshire coast (except Grimsby), the coast of East Anglia and North-East Yorkshire, most lines in North and some in South Cornwall and Devon, some lines in Wales and those serving South-West Scotland. It was somewhat ironic that among seaside resorts to be deprived entirely of passenger services were some which the railways in earlier days had themselves largely created in their efforts to develop traffic.

If all these recommendations were carried out the passenger services of British Rail would be cut by over 5,000 route miles—a quarter of the entire system; just over half the total of passenger stations would be closed; the number of freight railheads would be drastically reduced. One consequence of these contractions of the

British railway system would be that 70,000 fewer railway workers would be required, though it was expected that normal retirements would keep hardship to a minimum and would reduce considerably the number to whom it would be necessary to make redundancy payments.

The aim of the plan was to enable the railways to cater for the traffic for which they are most suited. The Report concluded that, "if the plan was implemented with vigour, much of the railways' deficit would be eliminated by 1970."

## Problems of today

Since the publication in 1963 of the Beeching Plan, British Rail has carried out many of the closures of lines that it recommended. The process is necessarily slow because objectors have to be heard and in some cases the Minister of Transport has ordered lines to be kept open for further consideration. By 1968 total railway route mileage in Great Britain had been reduced from just over 20,000 to 13,000 miles. The main-line closures, mentioned above (p. 162) had not then taken place. During the same period the number of railway employees fell from over 400,000 to 324,000. Economies in the maintenance of rolling stock were achieved by reducing the number of passenger coaches from 36,000 to 26,000 and of goods wagons from 950,000 to 640,000. The success of the electrification of the Euston to Liverpool and Manchester lines (opened 1966) could lead to further schemes for electrification, though the capital cost of such investment is very heavy. The proposal to run "liner" freight trains met with strong opposition from the trade unions, which insisted that all road transport required to feed and distribute from these trains should be provided by the railways themselves. Nevertheless, the first liner train ran from Liverpool to London in March 1966. The capital cost of providing liner services between all large towns in the country will be heavy and it will take some time to attract the required amount of new traffic.

Thus the position today is that the railways are trying to adjust themselves to the existing situation. Most rail closures—because so much of the traffic has already been lost—have little effect on traffic on the roads, but the closure of commuter lines increases congestion on the road at morning and evening peak periods. Some lines scheduled to close could be made to pay their way if they were run more economically as was shown in 1965 on the Watford–St Albans line, where a previous loss of £24,000 a year was completely wiped out. Most freight is now carried by road, 85% of rail freight comprising coal and other minerals. The reduction of the number of rail depots for coal means somewhat longer journeys for road delivery to customers, though it has been calculated that, even if the number was quite drastically reduced, road delivery need not exceed ten miles. There should thus be little increase in road traffic from this cause and if the liner trains achieve the success expected of them the railways should at least obtain a large share of the increase in total freight transport that may be expected to accompany future economic growth. With regard to the carriage of passengers the position is less clear. All forecasts show that, other things being equal, the number of private cars will continue to increase for at least another ten to fifteen years. The demand, therefore, for public transport can be expected to decline. Greater concentration by the railways on express services should enable them to retain and possibly expand this market, but a decline in bus travel seems to be a necessary corollary of any further increase in the number of private cars, and this means increasing congestion on the roads, especially in city centres, where by 1966 the position was already acute.

### The Transport Act, 1968

*The railways.* During the year 1965–68 the Ministry of Transport undertook on behalf of the Government a comprehensive investigation into the problems of inland transport. A White Paper published in 1966 outlined future government policy with regard to transport, and this was followed in 1967 by a series of White Papers dealing in greater detail with the more important aspects of the problems. These were the prelude to the *Transport Act* of 1968.

As already noted, the feature of passenger transport over the past ten years has been, on the one hand, the continued increase in the number of private cars and the expansion of that form of transport, and on the other, the continued decline in travel by train and by public road transport. Not all the increase in private motoring, however, has been at the expense of other means of transport. As occurred also in the early days of motor-bus development, the private motor car has itself generated new traffic. The decline in railway travel is not confined to Great Britain. Both the United States and Germany have a similar problem. Of the various sections of nationalised transport all except two—British Rail and British Waterways —have in recent years succeeded in making a profit. Lord Beeching was charged with the task of making British Rail show a profit. This required, as already seen, a very considerable contraction of the British railway system. Those people who looked upon the railways as providing a "service" regarded the Beeching Plan as much too drastic a curtailment of the railway system, believing that lines should be kept open, whether a loss was incurred or not, wherever there was a "need" for them.

*Passenger traffic.* The new plan for British railways is something of a compromise between these two points of view. The Government starts from the premise that a transport system has a social as well as an economic function to perform, some lines having a value to the community which outweighs all considerations of profit. Many commuter services are said to fall within this category as also do many cross-country routes. At present the British Railways Board has the statutory obligation to reduce its deficit and "break even" as soon as possible.[1] It is intended that this principle should still apply to a basic railway system, which has been worked out at 11,000 route miles. At their maximum the British railways had a route mileage of 20,300; the Beeching Plan envisaged a route mileage of 8,000. As recently as 1962 British Rail had a route mileage of 17,850. Since British Rail still had a route mileage of 13,000 in January 1968, the new plan will require a further cut of 2,000 miles. This will also necessitate a further reduction in the number of railway employees from the 324,000 of 1967 to 250,000, as compared with 641,000 only twenty years ago. Up to the present the Railways Board has been saddled with the impossible objective of making the railways pay their way in spite of being refused permission to close many non-economic lines. It is now proposed that such non-economic lines that are regarded as "socially necessary" should be separately costed and charged to the Exchequer. It will be for the Minister of Transport to identify the services that are to be treated in this way. The cost of removing surplus capacity on the railways is to be borne largely by the Exchequer, as also is part of the cost of railway police. The capital debt of the railways—£1,262 million—too is to be written down to £300 million. The advantage of this new scheme is that it enables the basic railway system to be judged on strict accountancy principles, while at the same time permitting the continued operation of a selected number of routes that are not commercially viable but which are regarded as necessary on other grounds.

*Freight traffic.* On the freight side a National Freight Corporation is to be set up, the purpose of which is to establish an integrated road–rail system for goods traffic. From British Rail it takes over warehouses, road vehicles and equipment used in its freight-liner service. Thus, the most modern road–rail development is to be under two separate authorities, with British Rail responsible for the trains and the National Freight Corporation for the rest of the service. In effect, British Rail will become merely the agent of the NFC for this service. It is the intention too as far as is possible to divert heavy traffic from the roads to the NFC, and to encourage this the *Finance Act* of 1968 subjected heavy road vehicles to greater taxation. West Germany has also decided to compel heavy long-distance freight to

[1] For the four years 1963–66 the average annual deficit of the British Railways Board was £128 million. In 1967 it was £153 million.

be carried by railway. Mainly on account of the shorter hauls a smaller proportion of the carriage of freight is in the hands of the railways in Great Britain than in Russia, the United States, France or Germany (USSR 80%; USA and France 48%; Germany 35%, as compared with 24% for Great Britain). Some 60% of the freight tonnage carried by British Rail in 1966 was coal, and apart from losses to road haulage this trade is itself declining. From the Transport Holding Company the NFC takes over British Road Services, BRS Parcels Service and Pickfords.

*Road-passenger services.* For road-passenger traffic there is to be a National Bus Company for England and Wales and a separate Scottish transport authority for Scotland. When these are formed they will take over from the Transport Holding Company all its road-passenger interests and some of its shipping. As a preliminary to this development the THC bought—under the threat of compulsory purchase—the bus interests of the British Electric Traction Company, comprising shares in 25 bus companies operating 1,100 vehicles. This left BHC—the division of nationalised transport showing the highest return on its capital—with little more than the Thos. Cook & Son travel agency and a number of shipping services. In each of the larger conurbations there is to be a single passenger transport authority to operate all services. At present there are ten in the Manchester conurbation, each with a large number of routes operated by two or more undertakings. Birmingham, Merseyside, West Yorkshire and Tyneside are other conurbations where road-passenger transport, as yet in the hands of a large number of different operators, may eventually be brought under a single authority. The intention is to give some of these thickly populated areas what London has had in fact since 1933. For the London area the Greater London Council is to be the statutory passenger-transport planning authority, delegating responsibility for day-to-day running to a London Transport Executive. The commuter services of British Rail remain with the Railways Board but these services too come under the GLC as regards their planning. Where necessary public road-passenger transport is to be assisted by subsidies, probably at the cost of the taxpayer though in densely populated areas, such as London, it would seem fairer for the subsidy to be borne by the ratepayer. Bus services will be subsidised by fuel grants, by grants towards the purchase of new buses, and special grants towards the running of uneconomic services in rural areas. Further, the National Bus Company is permitted to borrow £130 million. Uneconomic railway services, as already noted, are to be continued only if it can be shown that they are "socially necessary", but there appears to be no similar safeguard, weak as it may prove to be, in the case of uneconomic bus services.

### City-centre congestion

The first serious proposals to deal with increasing city-centre congestion were put forward in the Buchanan Report of 1963. This took the view that towns should be built so that they could deal with the road traffic of the modern motor-car age. To adapt existing towns in this way could be accomplished only at enormous expense and at a cost possibly of losing some of the attractive features of the older towns. Another way of meeting the problem is to create new shopping centres on the outer fringes of large towns, where accommodation can be provided for large numbers of car-owning shoppers, though this kind of development might be difficult in large conurbations.

Other proposals all involve placing some restriction on the private car. It has been suggested that parking facilities should be provided on all main routes into towns at some distance from the town centre and public transport made available from that point, private cars then being prohibited from entering the congested area. If this plan was widely adopted it is probable that many suburban dwellers who at present travel in their own cars relatively short distances to and from their place of employment would prefer to use public transport for the whole rather than a part of the journey.

A third method of dealing with the problem of city congestion is through the price mechanism. Space in cities is scarce and so, as with other scarce commodities, demand can be brought into equality with supply only at the equilibrium price. This has been applied in many cities to parking in central areas by the use of parking meters. It has been objected that this favours the rich, but the charges are low in relation to the average income of car owners, and in a monetary economy the individual distributes his expenditure to obtain the maximum satisfaction open to him from his income. If a person avoids using parking meters (and thereby reduces town-centre congestion) it merely means that he prefers to spend his money on other things—tobacco, perhaps, or gambling. It has been suggested that this principle should be extended to the running and not merely the parking of a car in a congested area, meters or some electronic "scanning" device being attached to cars to register the time spent or distance covered in such areas, a charge later being made for the privilege. The effectiveness of such a scheme would depend on the elasticity of demand for travel by car in towns. If demand proved to be fairly inelastic the charge might have to be high. This, though not the view expressed in the Smeed Report (1964), which recommended charging vehicles for time spent in congested areas, was the opinion of the Crowther Committee. Nevertheless, this might prove to be more equitable than prohibiting all private cars except those of people who could show "a need" for entering a city centre. Objectors to the scheme might be appeased by reducing the road tax on cars or the petrol tax to make running elsewhere cheaper. There appears to be less opposition to the payment of tolls to use bridges such as that across the Firth of Forth or tunnels such as those under the Mersey and Thames, perhaps because in these cases the user saves both time and the cost of fuel involved in avoiding them.

## Should public transport pay its way?

Since 1945 the British railways have regularly failed to pay their way. This characteristic is by no means peculiar to British railways, for few railways of the Western world now pay their way, the railways of France and Germany both operating at a heavy loss. In 1965 in Western Europe only the Swiss railways made a profit and that a small one and the Dutch lines, which previously had regularly shown a profit, made a small loss. In the case of British railways since 1954 revenue has been insufficient to cover their operating expenses. Down to 1962 the annual deficit was increasing; from 1963 to 1966 the deficit varied between £121 million and £135 million, the economies effected under the Beeching Plan down to 1966 being offset by rising costs, mainly wage increases. In 1967 the deficit again rose sharply to £153 million. The Act of 1947 which nationalised the railways took an optimistic view of their financial viability, since it imposed on them the burden of repaying the compensation stock over a period of ninety years.

The railways, however, cannot be entirely blamed for the size of the deficits, since they are not completely masters over their own affairs. The Transport Tribunal (down to the Act of 1953) and the Minister of Transport have generally been more concerned to keep fares down than to reduce the deficit, and proposals by British Rail to increase fares have on occasions been rejected. Similarly, applications by the railways to close unremunerative lines have sometimes been refused. Several times, too, the railways have been compelled by the Government to grant greater wage increases than they wished in order to avoid the inconvenience of a strike. It would seem, therefore, that if the railways are to be compelled to adopt uneconomic policies the resulting losses should not be taken into account when calculating their operating deficit.

It was competition from road transport in the 1930s that was first responsible for the railways beginning to decline, and the road operators came into the transport business because they thought it would yield them a profit. Since 1955, however, road-passenger operators have faced increasing competition from the private car, and so their profits too have declined. Services have been withdrawn on some routes but they have found it to be in their own interests to continue "cross-subsidisation" of some unremunerative routes in orders to retain the goodwill of the Traffic Commissioners. Nevertheless, the decline in rural traffic, which began in 1952, has steadily continued and many rural services have had to be withdrawn. The Jack Committee reported that by 1960 the route mileage of rural services had been considerably reduced. The decline in rural traffic was attributed mainly to the increase in the number of private cars among people living in the country (who are perhaps more inclined than town-dwellers to give one another "lifts") and, as regards evening traffic, the change in many people's habits from going to the nearest town for evening entertainment to staying at home, most of those who now go out travelling in their own vehicles or in those of friends. The closure of many little-used country stations exaggerates this problem. The smallest bus is often too large and too expensive to operate on many rural services, even if as is sometimes the case higher fares are charged and these are collected by the driver. On such routes the motor car is the most economic unit of transport. If it is impracticable to provide this sort of service, it can better be provided by a small local firm—the owner of the village garage—than a large bus undertaking operating from a distant town centre.

## Transport as a "service"

The rural passenger-transport problem has focused attention on the suggestion that transport is a service which should be provided irrespective of its cost and whether it can be made to pay its way. The Jack Committee adopted this attitude towards rural transport. It recommended that rural bus services should be subsidised by county councils. Two other bodies—the Highland Transport Inquiry and the Council for Wales—made similar recommendations, though both these wanted the subsidy to come from the State. (The bus services linking up with steamer connections to the Western Isles of Scotland have been subsidised in this way since the 1890s.)

It was not the intention of the *Nationalisation Act* of 1947 that transport should be deliberately run at a loss. Revenue, it said, should not be less than what was required to meet all costs properly chargeable to revenue, taking one year with another. It has been suggested, however, in some quarters that the railways too provide a social service for the community and so should be subsidised by the State. Similarly, it has been argued that municipal bus services should not necessarily be expected to pay their way. At least, it is suggested, there should be cross-subsidisation of unremunerative routes by all forms of public transport, as exists with postal services, the charge for sending a letter from London to Stornaway being the same as from London to Windsor.

If public transport is to be run as a social service the first problem to decide is how much of each form of transport to provide. In the past the pack-horse gave way to the horse-drawn wagon and this in its turn had to give way to the railway. However, when the railway had to face competition from the motor vehicle, it was a long time before it began to contract. Until quite recently bus services were superimposed upon an almost unchanged railways system, and though the bus had opened up a new market for transport it had also taken some traffic away from the railways, but, whenever there is a proposal to close a little-used railway line or withdraw an unremunerative bus service, objections are immediately raised. The situation is now aggravated by the increase in the number of private cars. If most people are to run their own private cars public transport must clearly be curtailed, and overlapping of bus and rail services cut out. There still remains the problem of the frequency of the service, and this is difficult to decide unless it is related to demand. One of the dangers, therefore, in operating public transport as a service is that of excess capacity causing too much of the country's resources of land, labour and capital to be absorbed into this industry, with less then available for other services and other forms of production.

In London and other large cities there is, however, a strong argument for subsidising public transport in order to relieve congestion caused by an excessive number of private cars. Even outside these congested areas it might be more economic to subsidise the railways rather than incur heavy expenditure on the construction of new roads.

One of the most serious aspects of running public transport or any other service deliberately at a loss is that once the profit motive is removed it becomes extremely difficult to determine economic efficiency, though it has been suggested that some form of efficiency audit might take its place. A fall in the demand for any publicly provided service, however, is not likely to lead to its immediate contraction since people have a feeling of entitlement to it, so that there is a tendency for excess capacity to develop and so result in a wasteful allocation of productive resources.

## Co-ordination of transport

The railways, after acquiring an interest in road transport during the 1930s, made little attempt to develop co-ordination apart from interchangeability of the return portions of some road and rail tickets. The *Nationalisation Act* of 1947 declared it to be the business of the Transport Commission, set up under the Act, to provide "an adequate, efficient and properly integrated system" of means of transport. Thus, co-ordination of the different means of transport has been the aim of policy since 1947. The denationalisation of road haulage made co-ordination more difficult. When Lord Beeching was given the task of reviewing the railway system with a view to making the railways pay he might have been given wider terms of reference to extend his survey to all forms of inland transport. The change of government in 1964 brought the problem of co-ordination again to the front and in 1966 the Minister of Transport reiterated the determination of the Government to press on with co-ordination. In that year a Transport Co-ordinating Committee was set up to consider transport in London, and also a National Freight Authority was suggested to co-ordinate road and rail freight services.

Co-ordination of transport presumably means assigning to the various means of transport the function each is best fitted to perform. If the railways are to be restricted mainly to express inter-city services for both passengers and freight, road feeder services will be required in both cases. For long-distance traffic rail costs are lower than those of road operators. The railway is better fitted to deal with bulk loads and road transport with small loads. Express pullman services —in some cases, limited to first-class passengers—have been particularly successful. There is, however, a danger perhaps that co-ordination may be taken merely to mean the removal of competition from the railways and there are those who think that more and not less competition is needed. Competition from the private car has made this fear groundless in the case of passenger traffic. Co-ordination of the means of transport is bound to reduce consumers' choice, but this is inevitable if excess capacity, with its waste of economic resources, is to be eliminated.

### Domestic air services

Though there has been a huge increase both in the number of passengers and in the amount of freight carried by domestic air services, nevertheless as a percentage of total internal traffic both remain small. The following table shows the expansion of internal air traffic since 1954:

TABLE XXXIV

*Passenger-miles (Air)*

| Year | (a) As % of total traffic (air, rail and road) | (b) As % of total traffic excluding private cars |
|---|---|---|
| 1954 | 0·15 | 0·26 |
| 1960 | 0·30 | 0·70 |
| 1964 | 0·48 | 1·40 |
| 1966 | 0·53 | 1·87 |
| 1968 | | |

TABLE XXXV

*Expansion of Domestic Air Travel*

| Year | Passengers carried (thousand) | Passenger-miles flown (thousand) | Freight carried (tons) |
|------|------|------|------|
| 1954 | 1,002 | 182,652 | 13,542 |
| 1960 | 2,240 | 477,611 | 19,237 |
| 1964 | 4,216 | 943,855 | 47,639 |
| 1966 | 5,122 | 1,146,213 | 85,036 |
| 1968 | | | |

Source: *Annual Abstract of Statistics.*

Over three-quarters of domestic air traffic is carried by BEA, one of the two state-owned airlines. For a long time BEA was given a monopoly of internal air services. An Act of 1960 set up the Air Transport Licensing Board "to further the development of British civil aviation" by permitting competition without encouraging wasteful duplication of services. No service can be operated without a licence from the ATL Board, and independent airlines are not allowed to operate over BEA routes unless an expansion of demand warrants an increased service. The only serious competition between air and railway occurs on the routes from London to Manchester, Newcastle upon Tyne and Glasgow. The routes with dense railway traffic are in general too short for air travel in view of the time occupied in travelling between airports and city air terminals.

RECOMMENDATIONS FOR FURTHER READING

K. M. Gwiliam: *Transport and Public Policy* (George Allen & Unwin).
J. Hibbs: *Transport for Passengers* (Institute of Economic Affairs—Hobart Papers).
HMSO: *The Re-shaping of British Railways* (Beeching Report).
HMSO: White Papers (1967) on Railways, Freight, Urban Passenger Services.
HMSO: *A Study of the Means of Restraint on Urban Roads.*
HMSO: *Cars for Cities* (Buchanan Report).
G. Walker: *Road and Rail* (George Allen & Unwin).
M. R. Bonavia: *Economics of Transport* (Nisbet/Cambridge University Press).
*If available:*
N. Lee: "A Review of the Transport Bill (1968)." *District Bank Review* (March 1968).

## QUESTIONS

1. Consider the part played by the State in the development of transport in Great Britain before nationalisation.

2. In view of the increasing number of private motor cars consider the future role of public transport in Great Britain.

3. Critically examine government policy towards the railways since their nationalisation.

4. Given that the Government wish to avoid increasing road congestion in cities in the future, what information would you require in order to advise on the balance between restrictions on the use of private cars and the appropriate reconstruction of city centres? (Degree.)

5. Discuss, with special reference to either fuel or transport, the proposition that, if publicly operated industries are to give the public the greatest benefit from the resources they administer, they should set the prices of their products equal to those products' marginal costs. (Degree.)

6. The White Paper on Transport Policy states that "commercial viability is important but secondary." Critically appraise this statement. (Birmingham.)

7. What measures could help to solve the problem of urban road congestion? (Bournemouth.)

8. Examine the proposals relating to rail-passenger traffic in the 1963 Beeching Report, explaining why they were regarded as necessary. (Bournemouth.)

9. Consider the need to make the best use of resources, with special reference to the losses of British Railways. (Huddersfield.)

10. To what extent should the nationalised industries be run as profit-making organisations and how far should they pay attention to "the social approach"? (Liverpool.)

11. "The problem of the railway system is one of size; it has become overgrown and therefore only drastic and speedy pruning will give the industry any chance of growth in the future." Discuss this statement with reference to the Report on the Re-shaping of British Railways. (Liverpool.)

12. Do you think that the nationalised industries should be run on commercial principles? Explain carefully what you mean by "commercial principles." (U.L.C.I.)

# PROBLEMS OF LABOUR
# AND EMPLOYMENT

CHAPTER VI

# POPULATION PROBLEMS

## *I. THE "POPULATION EXPLOSION"*

### The importance of population problems

Population is of economic importance mainly for two reasons: (*i*) people have to be fed; and (*ii*) labour is one of the factors of production. From these two main facts stem the various population problems. Most population problems, however, arise because the population, both of the world and of individual countries, rarely remains stationary for long but is always either increasing or decreasing.

The most serious population problem of all is concerned with the relationship between the rate of population increase and the rate at which food supplies and other necessaries can be expanded. Primarily, this is a problem for the world as a whole, but it can also apply to any densely populated country that cannot produce sufficient other goods to export in exchange for food. The problem of food production is still further aggravated by the fact that throughout history the greater part of the world's people have suffered from malnutrition.

Another important aspect of the population problem is the relation between the size of a country's population and the size of its national income. If the population of a country is increasing at a more rapid rate than its national income, then the standard of living of its people will fall and the Government's efforts to raise their standard of living will be nullified.

The size of a country's population—the basic determinant of its supply of labour—in relation to its stock of the other factors of production will influence the methods of production that will be adopted. Where land is scarce relative to the labour supply, as in Great Britain, Belgium and the Netherlands, farming will be intensive in character. Where, however, labour is very plentiful in relation to land, extensive farming will be carried on if capital, too, is plentiful, as in the United States. In both these cases, though there may be wide divergence between output per acre, average output per man will be high. If, however, capital is scarce in relation to labour, as in densely populated countries such as India, where in consequence labour is cheap, output per man will be low.

Individual countries have their own particular problems of under-population or over-population, and of increasing or decreasing population. Under-population may result in a less than adequate supply of labour and failure to achieve what is regarded as a satisfactory rate of economic growth. Over-population, on the other hand, may make economic growth even more difficult to achieve. The rate of population change too can affect economic growth, which tends to be stimulated by an increasing population and checked if population is static or declining. Special problems, both social and economic, will have to be faced if the population of a country actually begins to decline. In such circumstances the distribution of the population among the different age groups becomes of increasing importance, ex-aggerating as it does the effects of the tendency of the human race towards increased longevity.

It is clear, therefore, that population problems are of a widely varied character and can have far-reaching effects on the welfare both of different peoples and of the world as a whole.

## World population: (1) The present

There are three points to consider: the size of the world's population, the rate at which it is increasing and the probable total in the future. The one thing which it might be expected would be accurately known is the population of the world at the present day, but the greater part even of this total has to be estimated with varying degrees of exactitude for different parts of the world. In Great Britain population censuses have been taken regularly since 1801, and in most Western countries they are now taken at regular intervals. Reasonably accurate population statistics, therefore, are now available for the countries of Western Europe, Russia, the United States, Canada, Australia, New Zealand and Japan. Population statistics for South-East Europe, Mexico and the countries of South America and India are much less reliable, while for the rest of the world only rough estimates of the population can as yet be made.

The following table shows the population of the world by continents in 1965 according to the latest estimates:

TABLE XXXVI
*Population of the World* (1965)

|  | Million |
|---|---|
| Europe . . . . | 654 |
| Asia . . . . | 1,872 |
| Africa . . . . | 281 |
| America . . . | 426 |
| Oceania . . . | 17 |
| Total . . . | 3,250 |

In 1965 the estimated total population of the world, therefore, exceeded 3,200 million.[1] The European countries with the largest populations at that time were as follows:

TABLE XXXVII
*The Largest Populations in Europe* (1965)

|  | Million |
|---|---|
| USSR (including Asian Russia) . . . | 214 |
| West Germany . . | 59 |
| UK . . . . | 54 |
| Italy . . . . | 53 |
| France . . . . | 49 |

In Asia the countries with the largest populations were as follows:

TABLE XXXVIII
*The Largest Populations in Asia* (1965)

|  | Million |
|---|---|
| China . . . . | 657 |
| India . . . . | 434 |
| Indonesia . . . | 103 |
| Japan . . . . | 98 |
| Pakistan . . . . | 94 |

In Africa the only country with a population in excess of 50 million was Nigeria (55 million). In America the United States led with a population of 194 million, followed by Brazil (66 million) and Mexico (40 million).

## World population: (2) The past

The difficulties associated with estimating the population of the world at the present day have already been stressed. How much more difficult then is it to estimate the population of the world for periods in the past, the difficulties increasing and the reliability of the figures decreasing the farther into the past one goes.

It has been estimated that in the time of Christ the total population of the world was under 60 million. By the seventeenth century the total had probably reached upwards of 500 million. Recent estimates of world population growth are shown in Table XXXIX (p. 180). This table shows that the population of the world doubled between 1900 and 1965—a mere sixty-five years, whereas the previous doubling of world population had taken a hundred and fifty years. The rate of increase, however, varies very considerably between one continent and another, even between one country and another, but it

[1] The population of the world in 1967 was estimated at 3,400 million.

180    AN INTRODUCTION TO APPLIED ECONOMICS

TABLE XXXIX
*Expansion of World Population since 1850*

| Year | Population (millions) |
|---|---|
| 1850 | 1,090 |
| 1870 | 1,300 |
| 1890 | 1,470 |
| 1900 | 1,550 |
| 1910 | 1,670 |
| 1920 | 1,810 |
| 1930 | 2,014 |
| 1940 | 2,245 |
| 1950 | 2,521 |
| 1965 | 3,250 |

is clear that in recent times the rate of increase has greatly accelerated. Though for at least 500 years Asia appears to have had the largest population of any of the continents, it has not shown the greatest rate of increase in recent times. The following table shows the increase in world population since 1930:

TABLE XL
*World Population since 1930*

|  | 1930 | 1950 | 1965 |
|---|---|---|---|
|  | Million | Million | Million |
| Europe (including USSR) . | 531 | 595 | 654 |
| Asia . . . . | 1,073 | 1,378 | 1,872 |
| Africa . . . . | 155 | 205 | 281 |
| America . . . . | 244 | 330 | 426 |
| Oceania . . . . | 10½ | 13 | 17 |
| Total . . . | 2,013½ | 2,521 | 3,250 |

Taking the percentage rate of increase between 1930 and 1950 and again between 1950 and 1965 we have the following:

TABLE XLI
*Rate of World Population Increase*

|  | 1930–50 | 1950–65 | 1930–65 |
|---|---|---|---|
|  | % | % | % |
| Europe (including USSR) . | 12·1 | 10·0 | 23·2 |
| Asia . . . . | 18·1 | 24·1 | 58·1 |
| Africa . . . . | 32·3 | 37·0 | 81·3 |
| America . . . . | 35·2 | 28·5 | 74·6 |
| Oceania . . . . | 23·8 | 30·7 | 61·9 |

If Latin America is treated separately from the rest of America, we have:

TABLE XLII
*Population Increase in America*

|  | 1930 | 1950 | 1965 |
|---|---|---|---|
|  | Million | Million | Million |
| USA and Canada . . | 135 | 166 | 213 |
| Latin America . . . | 111 | 162 | 213 |

The percentage increases for these two divisions of America were:

TABLE XLIII
*Rate of Population Increase in America*

|  | 1930–50 | 1950–65 | 1930–65 |
|---|---|---|---|
|  | % | % | % |
| USA and Canada . . | 23·0 | 28·4 | 47·0 |
| Latin America . . . | 44·1 | 31·5 | 90·3 |

Thus, it can be seen that during both 1930–50 and 1950–65 Asia, with an increase of 625 million over the whole period of sixty-five years, showed the greatest increase in numbers of all the continents, while Oceania, with an increase of 4 million in sixty-five years, had the least increase. During the period 1930–50 the greatest percentage rate of increase occurred in America (35·2%), with Latin America (44·1%) far ahead of the rest of the world, and Europe (with 12·1%) —not surprisingly—having the smallest rate of increase. During the years 1950–65 there appears to have been some changes in trends, with the rate of population growth in Africa pushing ahead of the other continents and with Asia, although showing an increase in its rate of population growth, still low down the list. Finally, taking the whole period of sixty-five years and considering the two Americas separately, we find Latin America (90·3%) showing the greatest percentage rate of increase, closely followed now by Africa (81·3%), and with Europe (23·2%) again with the least proportionate increase. Only Europe has shown a smaller rate of increase than America north of Mexico (47·0%), though during the twenty years 1945–65 its population increased by 54 million—from 140 to 194 million. The figures for both Africa and Latin America require to be treated with considerable reserve since statistics for these areas are not very reliable.

## World population: (3) The future

The difficulty of calculating the total population of the world today, great as it is, appears small compared with the difficulty of estimating future population. Projections or extrapolations of future population can be made only on the basis of past and present trends. A change of trend will require a new collection to be made, and, the longer the period ahead for which the estimate is made, the greater will be the possibility of error. The variability of the birth-rate in Great Britain since 1920, for example, has required a revised estimate of the future population of this country to be made almost every decade and has resulted in widely differing forecasts, varying from fear of over-population to the possibility of a declining population. Thus, all estimates of future population must be regarded with caution.

Table XXXIX shows that the population of the world doubled between 1900 and 1965, whereas the previous doubling of the world's population had required a hundred and fifty years. It is thought probable that in prehistoric times it may have taken 10,000 years for the population of the world to double and even in early historic times perhaps as long as 2,000 years. In contrast present-day estimates suggest that world population is likely to double again in a mere thirty-five to forty years to reach a total of possibly 6,000 million by the year 2000. Thus, as the population of the world has become larger, so the time interval between each doubling of the total has shortened. Putting this in another way, it means that in terms of numbers the increment of population for each decade is rapidly increasing. Thus in 1910 there were 120 million more people to feed than in 1900, 200 million more in 1930 than 1920, 300 million more in 1960 than 1950, and it has been estimated that for the decade 1990–2000 the increase may be upwards of 1,000 million. It needs to be stressed that this is not the possible situation in a far-distant future but a situation that appears likely to arise within only half the average lifetime of people living in Great Britain today.

The following table shows the estimated population of the world by continents for the year 2000:

TABLE XLIV

*Estimated World Population in the year 2000*

|  | Million |
|---|---|
| Europe (including USSR) . . | 915 |
| Asia . . . . . | 3,600 |
| Africa . . . . . | 480 |
| North America . . . | 290 |
| Latin America . . . . | 680 |
| Oceania . . . . . | 35 |
| Total . . . . | 6,000 |

This projection is based on a continuance of the existing rate of increase for the world of 2 % per year, though in Mexico, Kenya, Korea and the Philippines population has been increasing for some time at a much greater rate. It assumes, moreover, that within the next thirty-five years there will be no catastrophic occurrence such as a major nuclear war to check the rate of increase. However, it does assume that, with the further spread of medical knowledge, the development of new drugs and improved sanitation, the death-rate will continue to fall, particularly in the developing areas where until recently it was very high. The projection shown in Table XLIV, however, makes no allowance for a possible check to the rate of increase that could result from a more widespread acceptance of family planning, but the period for which the projection has been calculated is too short—a matter of thirty-five years—for this to have any serious effect on the trend.

### The increase in world population

The main reason, then, for the increase in world population has been the fall in the death-rate, though the "population explosion" of recent years has been partly accounted for by a rise in the birth-rate—probably a temporary demographic feature—in the economically more advanced countries where it had previously been falling. For example, in the twenty years 1945–65 the death-rate in Mauritius fell from 30 to 12 per thousand. In many countries the rate is still around 20 per thousand and a future fall in the rate seems certain. In India the death-rate fell from 50·8 per thousand in 1925 to 39·4 per thousand in 1965, and so considerable further improvement can be expected. Over the world as a whole expectation of life has increased to such an extent—in India from 32 to 54 years in the two decades 1945–65—that over many parts of the earth people are living almost twice as long as they did a hundred years ago.

Formerly, the three main enemies of the human race were war, pestilence and famine. In spite of the enormous loss of life in Europe, due directly and indirectly to two World Wars, the population of that continent was greater by nearly 100 million in 1950 than in 1910. Wars in earlier ages, however, when countries were more sparsely populated, were relatively more destructive of human life. The most serious check to population increase in the past, however, was pestilence. A plague such as the Black Death, which swept across Europe in the fourteenth century, wiped out between a quarter and a third of the entire population. The most serious of modern epidemics appears small by comparison. The Black Death attracted the attention of contemporary historians because it was so much worse than the visitations to which all peoples at that time were regularly subjected. On more than one occasion a country's population was decimated. Until quite recently smallpox, typhoid, diphtheria and other

diseases caused large numbers of deaths even in the more economically advanced countries but deaths from these causes are now relatively
few, while in tropical countries yellow fever and cholera have now
been brought under control. Infant and maternal mortality, too, have
been greatly reduced almost everywhere. In Hong Kong, for example,
the infant mortality rate per thousand births fell from 300 in 1935 to
under 10 in 1965. For this modern medicine has been responsible,
and a widening of its influence, even if no further progress took place
(an extremely unlikely eventuality), will lead to further falls in the
death-rate. The sharp fall in the death-rate among children in many
developing nations has brought about a significant change in the
distribution of the population among the various age groups in those
countries, more than half their populations in many cases now being
children under the age of 15. The World Health Organisation (WHO),
a body set up by the United Nations, has already done much to reduce
the death-rate in both Asia and Africa and its work goes on.

Greater care than ever before is taken with the preparation and
handling of food, the general quality of which has been enormously
improved. Famine too was both a more frequent and a more serious
hazard in former times, though war even in modern times can bring
both pestilence and famine in its train. In days when means of com-
munication were poor and when even quite small districts had to be
self-sufficient, a bad harvest often meant famine. The last serious
famine in Great Britain occurred in 1701 when a succession of bad
harvests caused considerable loss of life in Scotland. As is well
known, the failure of the potato crop in Ireland in 1846–47 resulted
in a serious famine in that country. Improved means of transport
and the development of humanitarian ideas, resulting in an increased
willingness of nations to help those in distress, have lessened the
incidence of famine in the modern world. During the twentieth
century, however, serious famines have occurred in Russia, China and
India. As recently as 1943–44 a severe famine occurred in Bengal.
Droughts in 1965–66 again brought some parts of India to the verge
of famine, the situation being only just relieved by large shipments of
wheat from the United States and Canada. But for this timely
assistance India might have suffered another disaster comparable with
that of 1943–44. The Director-General of the Food and Agricultural
Association (FAO) in his report for 1966 expressed his belief that
there is a serious risk of famine in South-East Asia by the mid-
1970s.

## Limitation of family size

The "population explosion" of the past two decades has convinced
many people that something will have to be done to check the rate
of world population growth. In the nineteenth century the expanding

populations of many European countries sought relief in emigration to the more thinly populated areas of the New World. Many of these regions have now themselves become centres of rapidly growing population, and since the 1930s many of them have placed restrictions on immigration, such as the quota system of the United States. For a long time, too, Australia has been selective in its admission of immigrants. Emigration, however, can never give more than temporary relief to countries with rapidly increasing populations, but in any case immigration restrictions prevent the densely populated countries of the world today from seeking this sort of relief.

To consider what might be done international conferences have been called, the last being the World Population Conference held in 1965 at Belgrade. Not unnaturally, the countries of the Far East in the past have resented suggestions that they were the ones mainly responsible for the world population problem.

Primitive peoples, who were brought face to face almost daily with the problem of feeding themselves, had their own methods of keeping down their numbers, such as infanticide and abortion. Though birth control had been practised at various times for over two thousand years it was not until the nineteenth century that a realisation of the seriousness of the population problem led to efforts being made to make knowledge of the practice more widespread. This was the aim, for example, of the Malthusian League, founded in England in 1877, and similar bodies which were established in the United States and in some other Western countries. The activities of these associations often met strong opposition in certain quarters, especially when, as in France in the 1930s, a country's population actually began to decline. In spite of world-wide efforts to bring home to people the dangers of over-population, governments and some religious bodies have actually taken measures to encourage population expansion, either fearing a possible future decline in their population or in order to increase their importance. This was the policy of the Fascist regime in Italy, besides being the basis for the very generous family allowances paid in France since 1939, and since 1946 in the United Kingdom. In 1967, however, the British Government for the first time gave official encouragement to family planning.

Governments in the West have been more inclined to regard their population problem as one of a danger of decline than of too rapid an increase. In other parts of the world many governments which have become concerned for the welfare of their people have come to see in a too rapid expansion of population the frustration of their efforts to raise the standard of living of their peoples. For reasons of their own, therefore, family limitation has been officially encouraged, as in Japan for some time. In recent years the governments of both India and Pakistan—India since 1950—have actually supported policies of family limitation within their borders, though as yet progress has been slow, with only $2\frac{1}{2}\%$ of married couples interested by 1967. In India the Government has established a Department of Family Planning and the aim is to cut the birth-rate by half by 1975, *i.e.* to under 25 per thousand. Family-planning services are free. In 1966 Pakistan mounted a massive family-planning programme—its third "Five-Year Plan," the immediate aim of which is to reduce the birth-rate from 50 to 40 per thousand. In Hong Kong, where $3\frac{1}{2}$ million people are now crowded into an area of less than 400 square miles and where the pressure of population is obvious to every one living there, whether resident or visitor, the practice of family planning has brought about a fall in the birth-rate from 37·1 per thousand in 1960 to 27 per thousand in 1965. In the case of Hong Kong, however, the problem of a high birth-rate has been aggravated by a large influx of immigrants from near-by Communist China. Efforts too are being made in Africa to persuade governments to sponsor programmes of family limitation. In 1966 Kenya decided to launch a national family-planning programme (the population of that country having increased by 55% in seventeen years), and the governments of Nigeria and Ghana have also shown interest in the subject. Family planning can be made to appeal to people only when they can be shown that large families mean greater poverty for them. In Latin America, where the recent "population explosion" has had its most severe impact, there is as yet no serious realisation of the imperative need to check the rate of population increase, though family-planning services are now being developed in Chile. Family-planning programmes, however, as yet make no appeal to Communist China, the country with the largest population.

Though it is a hopeful sign that *in their own interest* many densely populated countries are attempting to slow down their rates of population increase, this will not solve the problem in the short period, since it takes a long time for the effect of a lowering of the birth-rate to influence the total population. It does, however, offer good grounds to hope that the world population problem may be a matter mainly for the short term and may resolve itself in the long term.

An aspect of the world population problem fraught with great danger is that the great difference in rates of increase widens still farther the gap in wealth and the divergence in the standard of living between the economically advanced nations and the developing nations, and the feeling of injustice this tends to foster is aggravated by immigration restrictions which the wealthier nations have found it necessary to impose.

## II. POPULATION AND THE SUPPLY OF FOOD

**Can food output be increased?**

From the dawn of history man has been preoccupied with the problem of obtaining sufficient food to keep him alive. This was his first economic problem. Many peoples have always lived in constant fear that population might outrun food supplies, and there are some parts of the world where this fear has not even yet been lifted.

As we have seen, the estimated population of the world in 1965 was 3,250 million, having doubled in sixty-five years. At that time world population was increasing at a rate of about 2% per annum, so that, if present trends continue, it will probably double again in about thirty-five to forty years. Any changes of trend are not likely to have much effect in the immediate future, and so the world must for some time be prepared to feed an average of 70 million more people each year for many years to come.

It has been estimated that two-thirds of the people in the world at the present day are under-nourished, as judged by Western standards, and so, even if no expansion of population occurs, a considerable increase in food production will be required, since world food supplies are already inadequate. Therefore, to cope with the two problems of meeting the needs of a rapidly expanding population and providing an adequate supply of food for everyone in the world, it would seem to be necessary to produce much more than twice as much food in the year 2000 as the world is producing today, if the short-term population problem is to be resolved. Can this be done? A more optimistic view of the situation is taken today than was held twenty years ago. It seems now to be generally agreed that with the knowledge already at our disposal the huge expansion required in food production can in fact be achieved, provided that better use is made in the world as a whole of existing knowledge and experience.

**More land could be cultivated**

Though there are no longer any new lands waiting to be opened up as food suppliers, as there were in the nineteenth century when the population of Great Britain was expanding more rapidly than food production within its own borders, there are still many areas in the world that are as yet economically either undeveloped or under-developed. Some seven-tenths of the earth's surface is incapable of being used at all for any kind of farming, being under permanent ice and snow or totally lacking in water supply or too rugged or mountainous. It has been calculated that of the remaining three-tenths available for food production only about 29% is at present under cultivation. In Great Britain, Belgium and the Netherlands, as also in India, Japan and Indonesia, there is little usable land that is not in use, but in Canada less than 20%, and in the United States only 58%, of the potentially usable land is actually being used. There is no doubt that the United States, Canada, Argentina and the USSR could all produce considerably more food than they do at present, even though in the case of the United States the domestic problem since the Second World War has been one of over-production of foodstuffs rather than under-production. In South America, where during the past twenty-five years the highest rates of population increase have occurred, even greater increases in agricultural production have been achieved. For example, since 1945 the population of Venezuela has increased at an average annual rate of 3·7% while agricultural production in that country increased at an average annual rate of 4·6%. At the same time Brazil had a rate of population increase of 2·9% while its agricultural output increased at a rate of 3·9%. There are also vast areas in the equatorial regions of almost uninhabited primeval forest, but some of the land regarded as potentially usable could clearly not very easily be brought under cultivation. In some of the more densely populated countries the problem could be eased somewhat if the taboos on certain kinds of food could be removed.

It is probable, however, that any great expansion of food production will be subject to diminishing returns. If it becomes necessary to grow food on inferior land it seems to be essential, therefore, to conserve fertile land for food production. The higher the stage of civilisation reached by a people, the greater the number of competing demands there are for land, though for recreational purposes—climbing, walking, golf—and often, too, for housing, land can be used that is of little value for farming. Expanding population results in the expansion of towns, a development further aggravated by the drift from country to town. A good deal of valuable farmland on the fringes of towns has already been swallowed up for housing development, and many new secondary schools have been built at a distance from town centres so that they can be provided with extensive playing-fields. Likely future developments will be the provision of extensive car parks and the construction of new shopping areas on the outskirts of towns. The motor car has made it possible to commute from farther afield, with the result that villages too are rapidly increasing in size and not only losing their character but also constantly nibbling away at the surrounding farmland, since it is tempting to landowners to sell or lease a little of their land at the higher price it will fetch for building purposes. New roads, particularly excessively wide motorways, and airports, more of which are likely to be wanted in the future, make further inroads into the already shrinking area of farmland in countries such as England, Belgium and the Netherlands.

Up to the present the loss of agricultural land in these countries has been more than offset by increased yields of crops per acre, even though these yields were already the highest in the world, but this process cannot be expected to go on indefinitely. Clearly, therefore, if the output of food is to be increased, greater attention will have to be paid to the conservation of fertile land or this problem will become as serious as that of soil erosion to which it is somewhat similar.

## Improvements in farming

The wide differences in the yields per acre of various crops between different countries is an indication of what might be achieved if more intensive farming methods were applied to those parts of the world where extensive farming is practised today. The Food and Agricultural Organisation (FAO), set up by the United Nations, has done a great deal too to disseminate knowledge of more up-to-date farming methods in under-developed countries. As compared with 1938 almost all countries had by 1965 considerably increased the yield per acre of their basic crops. Over the past ten years, however, India, in spite of the large sums spent on agriculture by the Government, has made little progress in increasing its output of foodstuffs, and this cannot be put down entirely to exigences of the climate such as periodic drought. It has been calculated that the agricultural output of India could be quadrupled, and it has been suggested that the fact that American supplies of wheat have been too readily available may have had a disincentive effect on progress.

In some parts of the world land has been so plentiful that extensive farming has been the rule, and, though the fact that farming is extensive does not necessarily mean that it is inefficient, it is certainly wasteful of land. Where land has been plentiful, short-sighted farming methods have sometimes led to the waste of what was once fertile land. Neglect to maintain the fertility of the topsoil, especially in the United States, was often the result of farmers seeking quick profits in the short run by ploughing up natural grassland, with no consideration for the long-run effects of this policy—soil erosion. As a result, excellent stock-rearing areas in some of the mid-western states, after a brief interval under crops, were turned into bare, rocky deserts. Geographers at one time regarded soil erosion as one of the most serious hindrances to the expansion of food supplies to meet an increasing world population, and in course of time their warnings came to be heeded. Governments, being awakened to the seriousness of the problem, have been encouraged by the FAO since 1945 to pay greater attention to soil conservation, the United States Government having adopted a soil conservation programme ten years earlier.

In other countries where labour was plentiful relative to land, it was so cheap that it was not economic to use any but the simplest forms of capital, and farming was carried on in a most primitive manner. For a long time the peasant farmers of India, for example, were unwilling to give up their traditional ways, but at least they are being made to realise that old methods must give way to new. There is still a long way to go, and in India the output of many crops could probably be at least trebled. In the production of wheat, even allowing for the effects of drought in some years, output has shown very little improvement over the past ten years. Nevertheless, in most of the under-developed and developing countries more modern farming methods are now being employed. Experiments too have been carried out to produce crops that ripen quickly enough to enable them to be grown in regions where the ripening season is short or to permit double-cropping where the season is long enough for this. In many parts of the world land otherwise unsuitable for farming owing to low rainfall has been made fertile by irrigation, and even more ambitious irrigation schemes have been planned. Areas such as the Wash in England could be reclaimed from the sea, for similar schemes in the Netherlands have added considerably to the area of farmland in that country. Though all such developments help to increase food output to some extent, the effect in relation to world output, however, is small.

Throughout the world farming is becoming more mechanised. In many parts of the world the tractor has already replaced the horse and in other parts is now beginning to take the place of the bullock. It has been estimated that for a country with a population increase of $2\frac{1}{2}\%$ per year even to maintain its standard of living requires an annual addition to its stock of capital equal to $10\%$ of its national income. For the most effective use of machines larger fields than have generally been customary in most countries are necessary, and so the structure of farming is beginning to change. The large farm with more machines and employing less labour is becoming the typical unit. As a result, output per man—more important even than output per acre—is increasing. Both Great Britain and the United States have greatly increased their output of farm products though employing ever fewer workers on the land.

Greater use too is being made of chemical fertilisers. Many previously infertile soils—for example, in Australia—have been rendered fertile by being supplied with the small amounts of certain trace elements, such as cobalt, which they lacked. Crop yields have also been increased by the use of insecticides and pesticides. Indeed, research is constantly being pursued into the use of chemical aids in farming as also into both plant and animal genetics. As a result of research, grains with double their previous yield have been developed and dairy cattle have been bred to give almost twice as much milk.

Great strides, too, have been made in preserving and storing food for consumption at a later date. Canning has been extended to a wider range of foodstuffs, deep freezing has been developed as a means of preserving many kinds of food, and as a result its distribution has been greatly simplified. How different is all this from the days when cattle and sheep had to be slaughtered at the onset of winter, and when for six months of the year British people had to make do with salted meat and when green vegetables were non-existent!

Looking to the future, it has been suggested that greater use might be made of the sea as a source of food by the development of "sea-farms," in which not only fish but some mammals might be reared. Recently, too, scientific research has shown that proteins can be obtained from crude oil. There is no doubt that nuclear power is capable of much wider application and solar energy might be developed to replace dwindling stocks of more conventional fuels. Perhaps one of the greatest difficulties to be overcome is how to increase the world supply of raw materials, the demand for which per head, with the general rise in the standard of living, has been expanding for some time, for, if the standard of living of all people is to be raised, the output of raw materials will have to be increased so that a greater supply of consumers' goods of all kinds can be produced. Again, the oceans might provide new sources of supply since there are thought to be abundant oceanic deposits of many metals. Both oil and gas are already being obtained by offshore drilling rigs.

### The crux of the problem

It seems clear, therefore, that in fact the world could support a very much larger population than it does at present, though it will mean the growth of more and larger cities and a more crowded existence for most people. Nevertheless, even if it should prove possible to expand the world's output of food to a much greater extent than until recently was thought possible, food production cannot be expanded indefinitely. There must be a limit to the amount of food that the world can produce. That being the case, unless the expansion of population is checked, over-population of the world is bound to occur at some time in the future, so that all that can be expected of efforts to expand the world's food supplies is to postpone the time when this tragic situation will arise. Some of those who take an optimistic view of the problem believe that the FAO's fears of over-population are unfounded. With more efficient farming (an important proviso) they believe the world could support a population several times greater than the estimated total of 6,000 million for the year 2000. Others place their faith in the proved ability of man to adapt himself to new and changing conditions. Sooner or later he must adapt himself to the situation. The increasing interest shown by governments in many parts of the world in family limitation is perhaps the most hopeful sign for the future. The papal encyclical of 1968 forbidding Catholics to practise artificial means of birth control, if obeyed, can only seriously aggravate one of the most serious economic problems that face the world, especially if it affects the preponderately Catholic countries of Latin America which have the highest *rates* of population increase in the world. The population problem can only be resolved if it is turned into a short-term problem, for it seems that for some time to come the world as a whole can cope with the problem of expanding food supplies to meet the needs of an increasing population. The crux of the matter may lie in the distribution of food among the peoples who are short of it. The standard of living of the world as a whole depends on the success with which the population problem is tackled.

## III. THE POPULATION OF THE UNITED KINGDOM

### The growth of the population

The first census of population was taken in this country in 1801, since when a census has been taken every ten years (with the exception of 1941). It is proposed to take a census every five years from 1966. Between censuses estimates of the population of the United Kingdom are made half-yearly. At the present day, therefore, the population and its distribution within the various age groups of this country is known fairly accurately up to six months back.

For years before 1801 only estimates of population can be given. From the fourteenth century these estimates are based on church records of baptisms and burials or occasional poll-tax returns, and these are far from complete and in some years attempts at tax dodging made the poll taxes very inaccurate. For earlier periods estimates are necessarily very unreliable. The following table gives the estimated population of England at various dates:

TABLE XLV
*Estimated Population of England* (1066–1750)

| Year | Population (in millions) |
|------|--------------------------|
| 1066 | 1·5 |
| 1345 | 4·0 |
| 1350 | 2·5 |
| 1570 | 4·2 |
| 1630 | 5·6 |
| 1670 | 5·8 |
| 1750 | 6·5 |

ꞏ

The table shows that the population of England probably increased by four times in seven hundred years, from a possible 1½ million at the time of the Norman Conquest to perhaps 6½ million on the eve of the Industrial Revolution. During these seven centuries there were two periods when the growth of population was checked: (*i*) during the years 1345–50 as a result of visitations of the Black Death, when the population actually declined, and (*ii*) during 1630–70 as a result of the Civil War and the Great Plague, when the increase in population was small. At the time of the first census in 1801 the population of England and Wales had reached 8·9 million, so that it seems clear that during the second half of the eighteenth century population had increased more rapidly than ever before, possibly by upwards of 36% in fifty years.

The census figures from 1801 onwards show the following increase in the population of the United Kingdom since that date:

TABLE XLVI
*Census Returns for the UK since 1801*

| Date | Males | Females | Total |
|------|-------|---------|-------|
|  | Million | Million | Million |
| 1801 | 5·7 | 6·2 | 11·9 |
| 1811 | 6·3 | 7·1 | 13·4 |
| 1821 | 7·5 | 8·0 | 15·5 |
| 1831 | 8·6 | 9·2 | 17·8 |
| 1841 | 9·8 | 10·4 | 20·2 |
| 1851 | 10·9 | 11·4 | 22·3 |
| 1861 | 11·9 | 12·6 | 24·5 |
| 1871 | 13·3 | 14·1 | 27·4 |
| 1881 | 15·1 | 15·9 | 31·0 |
| 1891 | 16·6 | 17·6 | 34·2 |
| 1901 | 18·5 | 20·3 | 38·2 |
| 1911 | 20·4 | 21·7 | 42·1 |
| 1921 | 21·0 | 23·0 | 44·0 |
| 1931 | 22·0 | 24·0 | 46·0 |
| 1941 | — | — | — |
| 1951 | 24·1 | 26·1 | 50·2 |
| 1961 | 25·5 | 27·2 | 52·7 |
| 1971 | | | |

Source: *Annual Abstract of Statistics.*

The estimated population of the United Kingdom at 30th June 1965 was 54·4 million, of whom 26·4 were males. The census returns show a population increase of 42·5% between 1801 and 1851, of 41·5% between 1851 and 1901, but of only 24% between 1901 and 1951.

Thus, in spite of setbacks, the population of this country continued to grow, though slowly, for seven hundred years, then more rapidly between 1750 and 1911, again very slowly during 1911–31, and rather less slowly since 1951.

## The accelerated rate of population growth since 1750

For several hundred years down to 1750 the birth-rate had been only slightly in excess of the death-rate. The main cause of the upsurge of population in the United Kingdom after 1750 was the falling death-rate. It has been estimated that at that time the United Kingdom death-rate was 31·7 per thousand. By 1820 it had fallen to 25·0 per thousand. The following table shows how the death-rate has fallen since 1870:

TABLE XLVII
*The Death-rate in the UK*

| Year | Rate per 1,000 |
|------|------|
| 1870 | 22·1 |
| 1880 | 19·7 |
| 1890 | 19·6 |
| 1900 | 17·4 |
| 1910 | 14·2 |
| 1920 | 12·7 |
| 1930 | 12·2 |
| 1940 | 13·9 |
| 1948 | 11·1 |
| 1950 | 11·8 |
| 1957 | 11·1 |
| 1960 | 11·5 |
| 1965 | 11·5 |
| 1967 | 11·2 |

Source: *Annual Abstract of Statistics.*

For over a century, therefore, the death-rate has been declining (except in 1940–41), and in 1948 and 1957, at 11·1 per thousand it reached its lowest point ever in this country. Since then it has risen slightly, as the table shows and as might be expected when the proportion of old people is increasing. The most striking feature of the death-rate is the fall in the number of deaths among children. For children under five years of age the death-rate per thousand of the population as recently as 1870 was 64·5, this rate falling to 52·2 in 1900, 20·5 in 1930 and 11·5 on 1960 with 11·3 in 1964. For children between five and ten years of age the rate was 7·9 in 1870, but only 0·4 in 1964. Infant mortality—the number of deaths among infants under one year of age per thousand live births—fell from 150 in 1870 to 20·6 in 1964, in both age groups boys being more vulnerable than girls. In fact, in actual numbers, deaths among children are almost the same today as a hundred years ago, although the population is five and a half times greater. Thus, the chance of survival at birth has improved enormously, and this fall in the death-rate among children was for a long time an important factor offsetting the fall in the birth-rate. The maternal death-rate too has shown a similarly steep fall—from 4·87 per thousand live births in 1870 to 0·25 in 1964.

## Improved health

Large families were uncommon until Victorian times on account of the high death-rate, the large Victorian family being a consequence of a fall in the death-rate among children and not of a rise in the birth-rate. The fall in the death-rate was due to the great strides made in medical progress during the previous two hundred years. More accurate diagnosis of disease was followed by more scientific and more skilful treatment and greater care of the sick in the new hospitals that were built during this period. More attention, too, was paid to sanitation and the general standard of health gradually improved. As a result a great many serious diseases that had previously been widespread became of rare occurrence. Even greater progress in medicine followed during the twentieth century and deaths from many serious diseases were further reduced. Food is now of better quality than formerly and greater care than ever before is taken to keep it clean and free from contamination, this being particularly true of milk, meat and green vegetables.

## Birth-rate changes

The following table shows the decline in the birth-rate in the United Kingdom since 1870:

TABLE XLVIII

*Birth-rate in the UK since 1870*

| Year | Rate per 1,000 |
|------|----------------|
| 1870 | 35·0 |
| 1880 | 33·6 |
| 1890 | 30·6 |
| 1900 | 28·6 |
| 1910 | 24·6 |
| 1920 | 23·1 |
| 1930 | 16·3 |
| 1940 | 14·4 |
| 1950 | 16·2 |
| 1960 | 17·5 |
| 1965 | 18·4 |

Source: *Annual Abstract of Statistics.*

During the fifty years after 1870 the birth-rate in the United Kingdom fell quite sharply. It continued to fall between the two World Wars, but after a temporary rise during the period immediately after the Second World War (as after the First World War) to 20·7 per thousand in 1947, it then, as expected, began to fall again, but it continued to do so only until 1955, when it was 15·4. Between 1955 and 1964 the birth-rate rose again for nine successive years—an unexpected change of trend—as the following table shows:

**TABLE XLIX**
*Birth-rate of the UK since 1955*

| Year | Rate per 1,000 |
|------|------|
| 1955 | 15·4 |
| 1956 | 16·0 |
| 1957 | 16·5 |
| 1958 | 16·8 |
| 1959 | 16·9 |
| 1960 | 17·5 |
| 1961 | 17·8 |
| 1962 | 18·3 |
| 1963 | 18·5 |
| 1964 | 18·7 |
| 1965 | 18·3 |
| 1966 | 17·8 |
| 1967 | 17·5 |

Source: *Annual Abstract of Statistics.*

Thus, the birth-rate in 1964 was higher than at any time since 1920. Whether the fall during 1965–7—the first time for ten years— indicates another change of trend remains to be seen. In 1965 the birth-rate in the United States too was the lowest since 1940. The pattern of birth-rate in that country had been similar to that of Great Britain, with a gradual fall from 1820 to 1940 followed by a rise during 1940–55.

## IV. THE FUTURE POPULATION OF THE UNITED KINGDOM

### "The principle of population"

The so-called "principle of population" was first enunciated by the Rev T. R. Malthus (1766–1834) in his *Essay on Population*, the first edition of which was published in 1798. Though he modified his views somewhat in later editions of the book, it proved to be one of the most influential works written by an economist. Many earlier writers had made reference to the population problem, but Malthus was the first to make it the dominant theme of his writings.

The book was written at a time when the Industrial Revolution was just beginning to get under way. Methods of production which had shown little change for centuries were being replaced by new methods which enabled fewer men, aided by the newly invented machines and assisted by new forms of power, to achieve a greater output than ever before. To some people this seemed to hold out hopes that an extension of the new methods to a wider field would inevitably lead to the achievement of a blissful state where men would find it necessary to work no more than half an hour a day to produce enough to satisfy all their wants—a view of the future that the onset of automation revived a hundred and fifty years later.

It was to refute this view that Malthus was inspired to formulate his "principle of population." He was living too at a time when the population of Great Britain was growing more rapidly than at any previous period of history, although not so fast as it was to do in the ensuing fifty years. It had long been recognised as a fact of life that one of the most serious problems facing any community was the relationship between the growth of its population and the rate at which food supplies could be increased. The accelerated rate of population growth in the late eighteenth century, however, was a new development, and it was this that led Malthus to believe that it was far more likely for vice and misery to be the future lot of many people rather than a carefree happy life with little work to do.

According to Malthus there is a constant tendency for populations to increase more rapidly than the means of subsistence, the reason for this, he thought, being that food production was subject to diminishing returns, since to expand the output of food requires ever less fertile land to be brought into cultivation. To emphasise his point, he alleged that population tended to increase in geometrical progression (2–4–8–16 . . .) whereas the output of food could be increased only in arithmetical progression (2–4–6–8 . . .). This is his so-called "principle of population." Though it was, of course, a gross exaggeration, it would seem that Malthus attached more importance to the arithmetical relationship between these two series than might have been expected. Whether or not he really intended his illustration to be given mathematical precision, it undoubtedly served to stresss his argument that population would continue to increase beyond the means of subsistence unless prevented by powerful checks. These checks, he thought, were all reducible to vice and misery:

"The vices of mankind are active and able ministers of depopulation. . . . Should they fail . . . epidemics, pestilence and plague advance in terrific array and sweep off their thousands and tens of thousands . . . Famine stalks in the rear and with one mighty blow levels the population with the food of the world."

Thus, according to Malthus, war, pestilence and famine are the natural, positive checks by which the growth of population is kept in line with food production. The reason, therefore, why population increased when food supplies increased was that fewer people died of famine or pestilence. In later editions of his book Malthus supplemented his positive checks by the preventive check of "moral restrain," which he explained as meaning later marriage. Early marriage had become a feature of the time in which he lived, since the factory system introduced by the Industrial Revolution made it possible for both husband and wife to go out to work, and children could work in the new factories at a very early age.

It was not a new idea to link population with food production, as this had been the view of Quesnay (1694–1774) and the other French physiocrats. The main difference between Malthus and his predecessors, however, was that they believed serious over-population of the world to belong to the distant future, whereas he considered over-population of Great Britain to be imminent, even going so far as to suggest that it might occur within the space of thirty years, a particularly pessimistic forecast which he modified later.

## An assessment of Malthus

On account of his pessimistic outlook Malthus was greatly reviled by his contemporaries and accused, quite wrongly, of regretting that war, pestilence and famine were no longer the powerful checks on population they had formerly been.

As we have seen, therefore, Malthus believed that, if the population of this country continued to grow at the same rate as in his own day, it must inevitably result in a fall in the British standard of living long before the end of the nineteenth century. Improvements in farming might increase the country's capacity to produce food, but this could do no more than postpone the evil day and could not finally solve the problem if population continued to increase. Malthus was well aware that food output, as a result of new developments, might periodically be increased more rapidly than population, but he saw that it could not be increased indefinitely to supply a population which he thought doubled itself every twenty-five years. Nevertheless, events have shown that the world's output of food could be expanded to a much greater extent than was thought possible by Malthus or even by many people writing more than a hundred years after the publication of his *Essay*. In fact, as Table XLVI shows (p. 193), the population of the United Kingdom did continue to increase and for a time even more rapidly than during the lifetime of Malthus. Further, the general standard of living in this country was much higher at the end than it had been at the beginning of the nineteenth century. The reason for this is well known. During that century many previously undeveloped parts of the world in North and South America, South Africa, Australia and New Zealand were opened up as producers of food and raw materials. Great Britain, therefore, was able to concentrate on the production of manufactured goods and export some of these in exchange for food. Malthus, then, was wrong in thinking, even so far as Great Britain was concerned, that imports of food could have no more than a very minor effect in alleviating the population problem.

Malthus, however, looked at the population problem from the point of view of a single country—Great Britain. If he were alive now he would have been able to write of India today very much what he wrote in 1798 of Great Britain. As we have already noted, the governments of both India and Pakistan have embarked on family-planning programmes mainly because their efforts to raise the standard of living of their peoples were being frustrated by the over-rapid increase of their population. There was indeed plenty of the misery which Malthus associated with those conditions in India in 1943–44 and 1966–67. In thinking that in his own day over-population of the world was imminent, Malthus clearly erred, but both the earlier French physiocrats and Malthus himself in the later editions of his work now appear to us to have been correct in thinking over-population a problem that might have to be faced in the not too distant future. What Malthus forecast for Great Britain in the nineteenth century appears, then, to be a much more likely eventuality for the world as a whole in the twenty-first century unless the rapid growth of population is soon checked. His work, therefore, still appears to have relevance to the problem today. For Malthus was quite correct in thinking that, unless population could be prevented from expanding whenever food supplies were increased, it would be quite impossible to raise the standard of living of a people. It is quite clear that a definite effort will have to be made if the consequences of Malthus's "principle of population" are to be avoided and if the lot of mankind in general is to be improved. Though most of his argument is in terms of an increase in food supplies, Malthus was well aware that man does not live by bread alone, and that an improvement in people's standards of living requires an increase in the output of all kinds of raw materials.

## Forecasts of future population: (1) The forecasts of the 1920s

Earlier in this chapter reference was made to the difficulty of making forecasts of the future population of the world. It might be thought an easier task to forecast the future population of a single country, especially one such as Great Britain where accurate statistics have been compiled for over a hundred and fifty years. Though the world comprises a number of widely differing areas, each with its own population characteristics, an error in forecasting the trend of population growth in one part of the world may be counterbalanced by an offsetting error in the forecast for another region. For a single country the population at a future date depends mainly on trends in the birth-rate, the death-rate, immigration and emigration.

It was easier in 1911 to make a forecast of the future population of Great Britain than in 1967. During the fifty years before 1911 the trends of both the birth-rate (Table XLVIII, p. 195) and the death-rate (Table XLVII, p. 194) were downwards, and both were falling at about the same rate per year. In 1911 it would seem quite reasonable to expect the downward trend of the birth-rate to continue, but by the very nature of things a slowing down in the rate of decline of the death-rate was to be anticipated with the probability of its eventually levelling out on account of the increasing proportion of older people. Thus, in 1911, it seemed fairly clear that for some time the population of this country would continue to increase, though at a gradually declining rate. Excluding the effects of migration (which down to that time represented a small net annual loss), an eventual decline of population was a likely eventuality but only in the fairly distant future.

Estimates of the future population of Great Britain attracted little serious attention until immediately after the First World War when an upsurge in the birth-rate led the late Lord Keynes to suggest that "the devil let loose by Malthus had again become unchained," the assumption being that this high rate indicated the start of a new trend which would result in a rapid increase in the country's population. Such fears very soon proved to be premature. The high birth-rate of the immediate post-war years was not maintained and by the 1930s it was clear that the pre-1914 downward trend had been resumed but at a much faster rate. At 16·3 per thousand in 1930 the birth-rate of the United Kingdom was less than half the rate of 1870 (Table XLVIII). The death-rate was still falling but the crude gap between the birth-rate and the death-rate had been reduced from 12·9 in 1870 to 4·1 in 1930.

Two other factors influencing population changes, and perhaps of more importance than the crude birth-rate, were: average family size and the net reproduction rate. During the period 1870–1930 average family size in Great Britain fell from 5·5 to 2·2 (2·5 for manual workers; 1·7 for others). The net reproduction rate is said to be equal to unity if the number of daughters born to each 1000 baby girls during their lifetime is 1000. Thus, for a population to remain stable a NRR of 1 is required. It was slightly below this figure in 1939 in France, Great Britain and the United States.

It seemed fairly clear, therefore, in the 1930s that before long, unless a further change of trend occurred, the population of the United Kingdom would actually begin to decline, as had already happened in France by 1938, and fear of the Malthus devil of over-population quickly gave way to talk of race suicide.

Based on current trends the forecasts of the mid 1920s suggested that a decline would begin in 1944, when it was estimated that the United Kingdom would have a population of 48 million. A sharp rate of fall was forecast, so that the United Kingdom's population was expected to fall to 45 million by 1956 and to 36 million by 1976. In fact, the population of the United Kingdom was 48·9 million in 1944—an almost correct forecast for that year, but instead of declining after that date the population continued to increase and by 1956 had reached 51·2 million.

### Forecasts of future population: (2) The forecasts of the 1950s

As after the First World War, so after the Second, there was a sharp rise in the birth-rate. With previous experience of the effect of war as a guide, this was regarded as a temporary occurrence. Economic conditions of the two post-war periods, however, were different: the late 1920s saw the onset of the most prolonged and the most severe trade depression in the world's history, whereas in the late 1940s began the most sustained period of full employment the industrial age had ever known. It occasioned no surprise, therefore, that the post-war high birth-rate persisted for a longer time in the late 1940s than it had in the 1920s. Thus, in 1946, the birth-rate in the United Kingdom was 19·4 and in 1947 20·7 per thousand, but in 1948 it fell to 18·1, in 1949 to 17·0, in 1950 to 16·2, and it continued to fall until 1955. In the 1950s, therefore, once again it appeared that the long-term downward trend of the birth-rate had been resumed.

Thus, forecasts made in the early 1950s suggested that the United Kingdom would have a population of 52 million in 1961, 54 million in 1971 and 56 million in 1981. In fact, the population in 1961 was 52·7 million, so that for the short term the demographers were particularly accurate. Present estimates of the future population of the United Kingdom suggest that the longer-term forecasts made in the 1950s underestimate the likely population in 1971 and 1981.

Discussing population figures for the United Kingdom as a whole, however, hides the fact that the rate of increase varies considerably between the four constituents of this political unit. For example, Northern Ireland, like the rest of Ireland, showed a continuous decline in population between the census of 1841 and 1901, and it was not until 1961 that it recovered from this setback to regain its total of 1851. The following table shows the increase in population of England, Wales, Scotland and Northern Ireland since 1921:

TABLE L
*Population of the UK (1921–61)*

| | Census 1921 (million) | Census 1961 (million) | Increase (million) | % increase |
|---|---|---|---|---|
| England . . | 35·25 | 43·5 | 8·3 | 23·6 |
| Wales . . | 2·6 | 2·6 | — | — |
| Scotland . . | 4·9 | 5·2 | 0·3 | 6·1 |
| N. Ireland . | 1·25 | 1·4 | 0·15 | 1·2 |
| Total UK . | 44·0 | 52·7 | 8·75 | 19·9 |

Source: *Annual Abstract of Statistics.*

Thus, England experienced an increase of 23·6% over this period of forty years, whereas the United Kingdom as a whole showed an increase of slightly less than 20%. Wales showed no increase at all, Northern Ireland an increase of only 1·2%, and for Scotland the increase (6·1%) was only approximately a quarter of the rate for England. Wales, Northern Ireland and Scotland all lost population by emigration, a large proportion of these emigrants moving to England, which during the latter part of this period also had a net increase of migrants from other parts of the world.

In the 1950s some difference of opinion began to emerge regarding the possibility of an eventual decline in the total population of the United Kingdom. As already noted, the demographers of the late 1920s had expected a decline to set in by 1944. Projections made in the late 1930s and 1940s had successively put back the estimated date when a decline might be expected to the 1950s, then to the 1970s and even later. There were at this time even some people who were beginning to doubt whether there might be any decline at all—at least during this century. The reports of the Registrar-General were more optimistic that population would continue to increase than had been the Royal Commission on population which issued its report in 1949. The Commission suggested that if the United Kingdom was to maintain its population it required an annual total of at least 700,000 births, and it forecast a fall in the number of births during the ensuing fifteen years. Table LI (p. 203) shows how far from the truth this proved to be.

It would seem, therefore, that there is little possibility of a decline in the United Kingdom's population in the near future, but if the fall in the birth-rate in the United Kingdom in 1965 indicates the onset of a new trend the total number of births may be expected to fall again

TABLE LI
*Number of Births in the UK (1935–65)*

| Year | Total |
|---|---|
| 1935–38 (average) | 722,000 |
| 1950 | 818,000 |
| 1955 | 789,000 |
| 1960 | 918,000 |
| 1965 | 1,000,100 |
| 1967 | |

Source: *Annual Abstract of Statistics.*

below the million mark. The fall in the birth-rate in the United States has already resulted in a fall in the number of births.

### Forecasts of future population: (3) The forecasts of the 1960s

We now come to the most difficult aspect of the population problem —looking forward to the future from our own day. We have seen how population extrapolations made at various dates since the 1920s were one after another proved wrong by events, based as they had to be on the trend existing at the time, for demographers could not be expected to foresee that the trend might change. Experiences of this kind however, tend to make demographers more cautious.

Population projections made in the mid 1960s, for the first time for forty years, indicate the possibility of a considerable growth in the population of the United Kingdom during the remainder of the twentieth century. Previously most demographers still held the view that the population of this country would cease to increase and might possibly decline before the end of the present century.

A population of 61·7 million has been forecast for 1981 and 72 million for the year 2000. In making the forecast the assumption has been made that average family size will rise in this period from 2·2 to 2·4, a change urged as long ago as 1949 by the Royal Commission on Population. As already noted, just about the time this projection was made, the birth-rate in both Great Britain and the United States began to dip downwards (*see* p. 204). It is too early yet to decide whether this indicates another change of trend, but by 1967 there was every indication that this in fact might be the case. A new population extrapolation made in 1967 shows, therefore, a slower rate of increase than the one made in 1964 (*see* Fig. 7). In June 1967 the Government Actuary's Department reduced its estimate of the population of the United Kingdom for 1970 by no less than 588,000.

It used to be thought that a rise in a people's standard of living would lead to a fall in the birth-rate. This appeared to be the experience of Great Britain in the nineteenth century. It is impossible, however, to be certain that the same will be true of the second half of the twentieth century. Conditions are quite different. Today we have a National Health Service, school meals, the provision of milk in schools, family allowances and, perhaps most important of all, governments pledged to maintain full employment. There is no doubt that the birth-rate falls in a trade depression and rises in a trade boom. What will be the effect on the birth-rate of a permanent condition of full employment it is as yet too early to say.

Figure 7 shows some of the population extrapolations made during the past forty years:

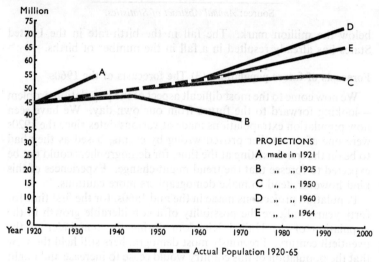

FIG. 7.—Population projection for the United Kingdom

## Migration and the United Kingdom

Population changes can be ascribed to two causes: (*i*) the relation between the birth-rate and the death-rate, *i.e.* the rate of natural increase or decrease; and (*ii*) the effect of immigration and emigration. In general the natural rate is the more important, but for some countries at certain times migration has been the main influence. For example, the United States received over 5 million immigrants during 1880–90, while on the other hand emigration considerably reduced the population of Ireland during the nineteenth century.

Until recently population projections for the United Kingdom took little account of migration, but the most recent forecasts estimate that during the fifteen years 1966–81 this country will receive a net increase due to migration of half a million persons. This is a relatively new development, for until fairly recently Great Britain suffered a net annual loss from emigration, emigrants going mainly to the United

States and the countries of the Commonwealth. The change came in the 1930s when the United States began to restrict the number of immigrants seeking to enter that country. In the later 1930s Great Britain began to receive refugees from Germany and Austria and after 1945 from Poland and Eastern Europe. In the years immediately before and after the Second World War Great Britain received an average of 60,000 immigrants per year. During 1955–62 however, the United Kingdom has experienced a net gain from immigration of about 38,000 persons, in spite of continuing emigration of around 150,000 per year to Australia, Canada, etc. During the twenty years to 1967 1·6 million British people emigrated to Australia, 600,000 to Canada, 350,000 to New Zealand and 220,000 to South Africa. By 1966, however, the number of emigrants from the United Kingdom exceeded immigrants by 83,000, although England and Wales had a net gain of 17,000.

Since 1955 the immigrants to Great Britain have come mainly from the West Indies, Pakistan and India. The *Race Relations Act*, passed in 1965, aimed at limiting the number of immigrants entering Great Britain, restricting the number to 7,500 per year in addition to 1,000 from Malta apart, that is, from families joining husbands who have already taken up residence in this country. An Act of 1968 restricted the immigration of Asians from Kenya after an exceptionally large influx of immigrants from that country had occurred.

Considerable migration takes place between the countries constituting the United Kingdom. Table L (p. 202) shows an increase of population during 1921–61 of 23·6% for England, 6·1% for Scotland, only 1·2% for Northern Ireland and nil for Wales, in spite of the fact that throughout the period the birth-rate in Scotland and Northern Ireland was higher than in England and Wales. During this period a total of about 700,000 people left Scotland for England. There has, too, been a steady influx of people into England from both Northern Ireland and the Republic of Ireland so that, particularly since 1945, immigration has been responsible for a not inconsiderable fraction of the increase in the population of England. There have also, of course, been movements of population within England and Wales between the different regions. It has become government policy to try to check movements of population away from Wales, Scotland and Northern England and also to try and reduce the drift of population from Scotland to England.

## V. FURTHER ECONOMIC ASPECTS OF THE POPULATION PROBLEM

### Changing age distribution

Whether the population of this country continues to expand to the extent shown by the latest population projections or whether in the not too distant future it begins to decline, one thing is certain: as a result of increased longevity, the proportion of elderly people in the community is going to increase still further. In the twentieth century people are living longer than they did in the nineteenth, expectation of life at birth for boys increased from 41 in 1870 to 68 in 1965 and for girls from 45 in 1870 to 74 in 1965.

The following table shows how the number of elderly people in the United Kingdom has increased since the beginning of this century:

TABLE LII

*Age Distribution of the Population of the UK*
(1901–65)

| Age groups | 1901 | 1931 | 1961 | 1965 |
|---|---|---|---|---|
| | Thousand | Thousand | Thousand | Thousand |
| Under 15 . | 12,442 | 11,175 | 12,336 | 12,670 |
| 15–65 . . | 23,977 | 31,446 | 35,244 | 35,210 |
| 65 and over . | 1,818 | 3,417 | 5,119 | 6,555 |
| Total . | 38,237 | 46,038 | 52,709 | 54,435 |

Source: *Annual Abstract of Statistics.*

Over the whole period in actual numbers there has been little change in the number of children, the decline to 1931 being almost exactly balanced by the increase since that date. The number of people in the middle group, which includes "the working population," increased by 31% between 1901 and 1931 but by only 11% between 1931 and 1961. Elderly people, however, almost doubled their numbers between 1901 and 1931 and their number has increased by a further 62% since 1931. The following population projection calculated by the Government Actuary's Department in 1965 shows the expected increase in the number of persons in all three age groups up to the year 2000:

TABLE LIII

*Future Age Distribution of the Population of the UK*
(1970–2000)

| Age groups | 1970 | 1980 | 1990 | 2000 |
|---|---|---|---|---|
| | Thousand | Thousand | Thousand | Thousand |
| Under 15 . | 13,935 | 16,066 | 17,964 | 20,794 |
| 15–65 . . | 35,715 | 37,099 | 40,463 | 45,275 |
| 65 and over . | 7,140 | 8,260 | 8,552 | 8,601 |
| Total . | 56,790 | 61,425 | 66,979 | 74,660 |

Source: *Annual Abstract of Statistics.*

It needs to be remembered that this projection was made before the down-turn in the birth-rate in 1965, so that it assumes a continuing steady rise in the birth-rate to the end of the period. If a change of trend in the birth-rate should occur in the late 1960s, a much smaller increase in population to the year 2000 can be expected. If, however, this population projection proves to be reasonably accurate it means that by the end of this century the number of children in the country can be expected to increase by 65%, the number of those between the ages of 15 and 65 by 27% and the number of elderly people by 34%.

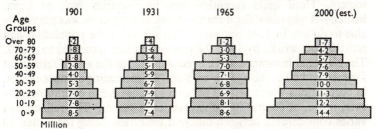

FIG. 8.—Population Pyramids

The population "pyramids" in Fig. 8 show this change in distribution within different age groups. Consider now the changes in the distribution of people between the three main age groups. The main

TABLE LIV

*Proportion of People in Different Age Groups*

| Age group | 1901 | 1931 | 1965 | 2000 (*est.*) |
|---|---|---|---|---|
| | % | % | % | % |
| Under 15 . . | 32 | 24 | 23 | 27 |
| 15–65 . . . | 62 | 68½ | 65 | 62 |
| 65 and over . . | 6 | 7½ | 12 | 11 |
| Total . . | 100 | 100 | 100 | 100 |

Source: *Annual Abstract of Statistics.*

development in population distribution between 1901 and 1965 has been the increase in the proportion of elderly people and the fall in the proportion of children. The extrapolation for the year 2000 shows an increase in the proportion of children.

### The supply of labour

The main determinants of a country's supply of labour are (*i*) the total population, (*ii*) the proportion of the population available for employment and (*iii*) the average number of hours work per year. The size of the working population will depend on a country's standard of civilisation, its stage of economic development and the social attitudes of its people. These are the things which decide the age at which children leave school to join the country's labour force, the age at which they retire from work and the extent to which women go out to work.

In Great Britain the school-leaving age has been successively raised to 15 and is expected to be raised to 16 in 1970. More boys and girls, however, are continuing at school beyond the official leaving age, and increasing provision, too, is having to be made for those proceeding to universities. Retirement is unique to modern industrial society. Until quite recently—even in countries such as Great Britain—it was usual for a man to work as long as he was physically able to do so. In 1901 not more than 1 in 17 of the population had retired from work; by 1965 the proportion had increased to 1 in 7. The National Insurance scheme recognises 65 as the age of retirement for men and 60 as the age for women. An increasing number of men in occupations where private pension schemes are in operation however, retire, at 60 and in some cases even earlier. The retiring age varies considerably between different countries, being for a man 70 in Norway, 67 in Denmark and Sweden, 60 in Russia and 55 in Japan. Before 1914 relatively few women in Great Britain went out to work, but two World Wars have changed the social attitude to this question. After the First World War for the first time it became the usual practice for girls of all classes to take up work on leaving school and to continue at work until they married. The effect of the Second World War has been to increase the number of married women of all classes who go out to work. Since the end of the Second World War the proportion of women going out to work has continued to increase in both Great Britain and the United States. In 1967 the percentage of the female population going out to work was greatest in the USSR (49%) with Great Britain well up the list with 29%, France 27%, West Germany 33% and the United States 24%. About a third of British married women now go out to work.[1] The increased employment of women has more than offset the loss of labour in Great Britain resulting from the longer period of education and earlier retirement.

Thus, the labour force in Great Britain expanded by approximately 54% between 1901 and 1967 although the population increased by only 42%. On the other hand, the length of the average working week has been considerably reduced and holidays increased. In the future both an extension of the period of education and earlier retirement for an increasing number of people can be expected, although there is not likely to be much further increase in the proportion of married women going out to work. On the other hand, it seems reasonable to expect that an extension of mechanisation and auto-

[1] *DEA Progress Report*, February, 1967.

mation will result in further cuts in the length of the working week, though probably not to the extent that some people appear to expect.

## For and against an increasing population

*Drawbacks to an increasing population.* To a country such as Great Britain an increasing population means that it will be necessary to import increasing amounts of food. Since it seems unlikely that the home production of food could be expanded at the same rate as the increase in population, food imports will tend to increase steeply with each increase in population. It will be necessary, therefore, to expand our exports of manufactured goods, and this will require an increase in the import of raw materials. This situation is likely to be aggravated further by the stimulus given to imports by a rising standard of living. Thus, an increasing population will probably add to Great Britain's difficulties with its balance of payments.

Not only will it be necessary to expand the production of goods for export but there will also be a greater demand for all the things necessary to house, clothe and educate an expanding population—houses, house furnishings, clothing, schools, motor cars and the great mass of consumers' goods that go with a high standard of living. The increase in the number of motor cars will bring with it a demand for more roads and more car-parking facilities. Though the increased population might provide the additional labour required for this expansion of output, increased supplies, also, of the other factors of production—land and capital—will be required to go with it. Land in this country is already very scarce in relation to the demand for it, while the production of capital itself requires the employment of factors of production. The industrial and domestic needs of an expanding population will require greater supplies of fuel, the building of more electricity-generating stations and larger imports of oil unless substantial new sources of supply off shore of oil and natural gas can be developed.

Any further considerable growth of the population of England will certainly result in serious overcrowding. For a long time there has been a persistant drift from the country to the towns. Nearly 80% of the people of England and Wales now live in urban areas, and more than half of these town-dwellers are crowded into six great conurbations. Local authorities are already having to fight hard against all kinds of demands to encroach on their fringes of "green belt," and with every increase in population it becomes more difficult to prevent encroachment. England and Wales already have an overall population density of 815 persons to the square mile, with a density in the urban areas of over 4,500 persons to the square mile. In the industrialised parts of the world huge conurbations are already developing (the term *megalopolis* has been applied to these new developments).

For example, the existing conurbations of South Lancashire, West Yorkshire, North Staffordshire, the West Midlands, London and the South East are gradually merging into one huge megalopolis. Similarly, the industrial areas of North-East France, Belgium, the Netherlands, West Germany and Northern Switzerland are beginning to form one huge urban area. In the United States too there is an Eastern megalopolis stretching from Washington to Boston and a Great Lakes megalopolis stretching from Milwaukee and Chicago to Detroit and Pittsburgh with a Canadian extension to Toronto.

*Drawbacks to a declining population.* One of the most serious drawbacks to a declining population is that it increases the proportion of elderly people and may possibly also reduce the proportion of people of working age on whose efforts the output of goods and services depends. This problem has already been discussed above (*see* p. 207). We have seen how an increasing population generates an expanding demand for labour; with a declining population it might prove difficult to maintain full employment, and economic growth would probably be checked, though few people today hold the pessimistic view that in a mature economy such as that of Great Britain economic stagnation would be a consequence of falling numbers. If population were declining, however, it would probably be more difficult to overcome structural unemployment resulting from the changes in demand which occur in any progressive economy, and from the further changes in demand arising from the redistribution of population among the different age groups. With a declining labour force it might be difficult, too, to replace obsolescent capital unless there is labour saving from further developments in mechanisation and automation. If a declining population results in a shrinking of markets, it will become more difficult to secure economies of large-scale production, though a widening of markets through such organisations as EFTA and the EEC might offset this disadvantage. It is feared too in some quarters that a decline in a country's population will reduce its political importance in the world.

## The optimum population

It was suggested at one time that a population of 50 million might be the most advantageous size for the United Kingdom. This level of population, however, has already been passed and it seems certain that it will be considerably exceeded during the next twenty years. Thus, according to this view, Great Britain appears to be heading for a state of over-population. There are some people in the United States who consider that country too to be in imminent danger of being over-populated.

Whether an increasing or a decreasing population is likely to be advantageous or disadvantageous to a country in the long run is a question that cannot be decided from a consideration of mere numbers.

Malthus himself saw that because a country had a large population it did not necessarily mean that it was overpopulated. "A careful distinction," he said, "should always be made between a redundant population and a population actually great." It is widely felt that there is a certain level of population which is the most advantageous to a country, though it might be very difficult to state in figures exactly what that population is. This has been termed the *optimum* population. As with other optima it will vary at different periods of time as circumstances change. Clearly, if Great Britain had had its present population in the conditions of the fourteenth century it would have been grossly over-populated; at the present day it is not easy to say whether it is over-populated or under-populated (the National Plan, published in 1965, envisaged a shortage of labour by 1970 in relation to the planned rate of economic growth).

The optimum population of a country can be defined as the population that will yield that amount of labour which, combined with the supplies of the other factors of production possessed by that country, will yield both the maximum total output and the maximum output per head. If this is so, it makes it possible for the people of that country to enjoy the highest standard of living open to them, provided that the volume of production is distributed among them in such a way as to maximise their economic welfare. Thus, the optimum population of a country depends on the quantity and quality of its economic resources—the extent and quality of its land, the amount and quality of its capital, the efficiency of its labour force—and the state of technical development it has reached. An increase in its stock of capital and in its quality or an improvement in methods of production may enable it to raise total output and so average output per head and therefore also the size of its optimum population.

Taking the optimum, therefore, as the criterion, a country can be regarded as over-populated if its population is in excess of this, or under-populated only if it falls short of it. Thus, a thinly populated country, if poor in economic resources, may nevertheless be over-populated, just as a country apparently rich in economic resources will also be over-populated if its output per head is less than could have been achieved with a smaller population. An under-populated country will be one, whether in numbers its population is large or small, that has an insufficient labour supply to make the best use of its economic resources, so that output per head falls short of what it might be.

Clearly, then, the population to be aimed at is the optimum, since only at that size will a people's standard of living be at the highest possible level compatible with the conditions of that particular time.

## RECOMMENDATIONS FOR FURTHER READING

I. Bowen: *Population* (Nisbet/Cambridge University Press).
E. M. Hubback: *The Population of Britain* (Penguin Books).
United Nations: *Demographic Yearbook*.
HMSO: Report of the Royal Commission on Population (1949).

## QUESTIONS

1. How serious do you consider the world population problem to be?

2. What are the economic and social advantages and disadvantages to a country of an increasing population?

3. "The concept of the optimum as applied to population is of little economic importance since no precise meaning can be given to the term." Discuss this statement.

4. Indicate the main factors which will determine the size and composition of the working population. What factors have governed the deployment of the labour force over the past twenty years? (Bournemouth.)

5. Discuss the population problem in the world today. (Huddersfield.)

6. What are the reasons for stating that the working population will continue to constitute a declining proportion of the total population? What will be some of the economic consequences of this trend? (U.L.C.I.)

## CHAPTER VII

# EMPLOYMENT PROBLEMS

## *I. THE PROBLEM OF UNEMPLOYMENT—BEFORE 1914*

### The incidence of unemployment

The most serious economic hazard that a worker has to face in a modern industrialised society is that of unemployment. A person can be said to be unemployed if he is willing to work but no work that he is *capable* of undertaking is available to him. Thus, at times people may be out of work, not because there are no vacancies at all but because they do not possess the particular skills required for the jobs that are vacant. In other words, the supply of unskilled workers may exceed the demand for them while at the same time there is a shortage of skilled workers. In the reverse—and nowadays less common—situation, however, can unemployment be said to exist if the people out of work are skilled workers who regard the jobs that are vacant as unsuitable because little skill is required to perform them? A more serious problem, and one met with more frequently, arises when skilled workers are unemployed while jobs are vacant requiring skills of a different sort.

Unemployment is associated with the complicated industrial system that has developed since the Industrial Revolution. It was something about which self-sufficient primitive communities had no need to worry. In these conditions, what work had to be done was shared among the members of the community, and if in favourable conditions of soil and climate there was little to do, then all would have more leisure but no one would be out of work. The position was much the same on the medieval manor. Even today in countries that are dependent on the production of primary products the effect of a fall in demand is to cause a reduction in the general standard of living rather than to create unemployment. In medieval times and in early modern times before the Industrial Revolution the only people liable to unemployment were the workers in the towns—where there was greater division of labour—and men returning from the wars. Before the days of the welfare state, when people expected to have to go on working to the end of their days, there were also those who had become too infirm to work. It was, however, the introduction of the factory system, with specialisation and division of labour, that made unemployment the serious problem it became in the nineteenth century. A falling off or a change in consumers' demand or technological changes in production can all cause unemployment in an industralised society.

## Population expansion and unemployment

In Chapter VI it was seen that the population of Great Britain and some other countries has increased during the past two hundred and fifty years at a more rapid rate than at any other time in history. This has meant that throughout this period more and more people have had to find jobs. In general this has not caused an increase in unemployment, for the demand for labour has tended to keep pace with the expansion of population. As population has increased there has been no tendency for unemployment to increase in proportion to the number of workers employed, though during the nineteenth century there was a tendency for the actual number of people out of work to increase at each successive depression. In the under-developed countries an expanding population more often results in a decline in the standard of living than an increase in unemployment.

In fact, in countries with more advanced economies, an expanding population tends to increase the demand for labour through an increased demand for consumers' goods, since, with each increase in population, there are more people to feed and clothe and more of all kinds of things wanted. During the Great Depression of 1929-35 it was the opinion of some writers that depressions of such severity had been avoided during the nineteenth century mainly because the population had then been increasing more rapidly. With an expanding population adjustments to changes of demand can be more easily made too, since in these conditions declining industries may contract only relatively to others and not absolutely. In fact, one of the most feared consequences of a declining population is the probability of an increase in unemployment due to changes in demand together with the possibility of a general fall in consumers' demand.

## Fluctuations in employment

Even with the stimulus of an expanding population the level of employment has been subject to fluctuations. A characteristic of business activity between 1785 and 1913—not only in Great Britain but in other countries too—was the alternation of boom and depression, generally known as the trade or business cycle. Fig. 9 (p. 215) shows industrial activity in Great Britain during 1785–1913. This diagram shows that during this period of 128 years the crests of trade booms occurred in 1792, 1803, 1810, 1818, 1825, 1836, 1845,

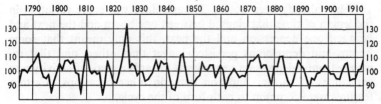

1853, 1860, 1865, 1874, 1882, 1889, 1899, 1906 and 1913, giving the
following series of intervals in years between booms:

$$11, 7, 8, 7, 11, 9, 8, 7, 5, 9, 8, 7, 10, 7, 7.$$

Thus, there was a fairly wide variation in the length of the time interval between the crest of one boom and the next. On two occasions,
1792–1803 and 1825–36, the interval was as long as eleven years, and
on one occasion, 1860–65, only five years. On no fewer than six
occasions the interval was seven years and on three occasions it was
eight years, the average length of the interval for the whole period
being eight years. Since the troughs in the graph alternate with the
crests of business activity the average length of time between depressions is also eight years. There appears, therefore, to be a
sufficient degree of regularity in the ups and downs shown on the
graph to regard this as a cyclical feature of business activity.

A further feature of the business cycle as brought out by the graph
is the tendency for the extent of the fluctuations to decline over time,
with both higher peaks and lower troughs before 1850 than occurred
after that date.

Before 1914 information regarding unemployment is limited to
trade-union returns which relate only to their own members—a total
of not more than half a million workers. Nevertheless, since these
workers were distributed among a wide variety of trades, the trade-
union returns probably run parallel with the general level of employment. The unemployment rate, therefore, appears to have varied
between 2% in the periods when business activity was at its highest
levels and 8% when it was at its lowest. On average this meant that
in only one year of the eight-year cycle was unemployment as low
as 2%, the average rate of unemployment for the period 1860–1913
probably being around 5%. It would seem, then, that in most occupations the supply of labour for most of the time exceeded the demand for it.

### Features of the business cycle

(*i*) *Phases of the cycle*. The regularity with which boom and depression alternated with one another during the 128 years before

1913 has already been noted. Though there was some variation in the length of time that elapsed between one boom and the next and between one depression and the next, this only meant that some booms and depressions persisted longer than others and that recovery from a depression or progress towards a peak of activity was sometimes of shorter duration than on other occasions. Certain features were common to each turn of the cycle.

Four phases can be detected in each turn of the cycle: a period of depression, an upswing, a period of boom and a downswing. At one time it was thought that the upswing was always a gradual process whereas the downswing was usually short and sharp. In fact, the average length of the upswing was less than the average length of the downswing, namely 3·66 years as compared with 4·26 years. During the nineteenth century, however, all the phases of the cycle were of short duration since the average length of a turn of the cycle was only eight years.

(*ii*) *Capital-producing industries.* In all cases the industries to be first affected, whether in the upswing or the downswing of the cycle, were those concerned with the production of capital goods. This feature of the cycle can be explained partly by the acceleration principle and partly in terms of entrepreneurs' expectations. Capital goods are mostly durable goods. Assuming a "life" of seven years for such goods, and that demand is steady for the commodity in the manufacture of which they are to be employed, their production can be evenly spread over the years, with approximately one-seventh of the total supply being renewed each year. A gradual and permanent expansion of demand may be absorbed without upsetting the rhythm of production. A temporary increase in demand, however, will stimulate a temporary increase in the production of capital goods, but when demand falls back to its former level the excess capital equipment that has been accumulated will be reduced by neglecting to renew some of the worn-out capital in a later year. As a result, instead of one-seventh of the supply being renewed each year, production will become irregular with perhaps one-seventh of the total renewed during each of three years, followed by two-sevenths for each of two years and then perhaps two years when no renewals are required. Thus, a temporary change in demand for consumers' goods and in their production transmits an "accelerated" change to the production of the appropriate durable capital goods. This tends to result not only in the cyclical production of capital goods but also in wider fluctuations in the production of such goods than is the case with consumers' goods.

The decision to renew or not to renew capital goods depends on entrepreneurs' expectations of the future demand for their products. If the business outlook is bright and demand is expected to remain strong, capital that is becoming obsolescent may be renewed, but if entrepreneurs feel uncertain of the future they may prefer to be cautious and by postponing the renewal of their capital they help to bring about a reduced production of capital goods. This may happen at the peak of a boom if entrepreneurs from their experience of previous booms feel that it is unlikely to last much longer. Once this has happened some unemployment occurs in the capital-producing industries and in consequence the demand for consumers' goods also begins to fall. The upswing of the cycle similarly occurs when entrepreneurs begin to think, again as a result of past experience, that the slump is likely to end soon and so decide to renew capital while prices are low. The "multiplier" effect then follows upon the expansion of demand, for, once started, both upswing and downswing feed on themselves.

(*iii*) *The price cycle.* The upward and downward swings of the business cycle are characterised by similar fluctuations of prices. At the bottom of a slump prices are low; the rise in demand which ends a slump and starts the upswing also stimulates a rise in prices which reach their peak at the height of the ensuing boom; and the tapering off of demand which marks the end of the boom and the start of the downswing also brings with it falling prices. Just as there was a tendency for each successive boom and slump to occur at a higher level of production and employment than its predecessor, so prices also tended to rise higher with each boom and not to fall as much with each slump. These cyclical price changes were not very great, for it is only after full employment has been reached that a steep, inflationary rise of prices is likely to occur, and before 1913 full employment was an extremely rare occurrence.

The fact that price movements paralleled the fluctuations of the business cycle led some writers to stress the monetary causes of the cycle. In some quarters it was thought that the business cycle was the direct result of fluctuations in bank credit, an expansion of credit stimulating business activity and a contraction of credit checking it. Changes in the volume of bank credit were brought about by varying the rate of interest—a low rate to encourage borrowing, and a high rate to discourage it. Some writers believed that the rate of interest made its effect felt through its influence on the willingness or otherwise of merchants to hold stocks—increasing their stocks and so stimulating production when the rate was low and reducing their stocks and so checking production when the rate was high. Experience, however, seems to show that during the nineteenth century bank credit tends to expand or contract *after* and not before the upswing or downswing of the cycle had been set in motion. It is now generally recognized that the trade cycle cannot be explained in terms of a single cause. Monetary causes are important but so are

218     AN INTRODUCTION TO APPLIED ECONOMICS

psychological factors such as the expectations of entrepreneurs and, to a lesser degree, "real" causes such as the irregularity of economic progress, the acceleration effect induced by the durability of capital and agricultural fluctuations.

## Other cyclical fluctuations

In addition to the eight-year business cycle two other cycles of business activity and employment have been noticed, one with its peak more widely spaced and one with a shorter time interval between peaks. Throughout the whole period of the business cycle from the late eighteenth century to 1913, the level of building activity, and therefore of employment in that industry, alternated between longish periods of great activity and equally long periods of less activity, each of approximately ten years' duration. These changes in the level of building activity do not readily fit in with the ups and downs of the eight-year business cycle, though an expansion of building has often reinforced or even encouraged a resumption of activity in the capital-producing industries, which is a characteristic feature of recovery from a depression. Nevertheless, some peaks of the business cycle must have occurred when the level of building activity was low, while in some general depressions building must not have been seriously affected. Thus, although there was a recession in building during the 1880s, crests of the business cycle occurred in 1882 and 1889, and though during the 1890s the level of building activity was generally high the trough of a general depression occurred in 1893. A greater correlation might have been expected between activity in building and in other industries, since building, whether of houses or business premises, stimulates a demand for a great variety of commodities. On the other hand, house-building is less subject to fluctuation than industry in general. This is especially true of the twentieth century, when house-building is for home-ownership rather than property investment and in general the sort of people who buy their own houses are those whose incomes are least affected by trade recessions.

The least pronounced of the three cycles is the Rostov minor cycle[1] of only four years' duration. This cycle is noticeable only down to 1860, before which time it often provided a minor crest midway between crests of the business cycle. As waves of the eight-year cycle became somewhat less intense after 1860, so the minor cycle too became less noticeable.

## The international character of the trade cycle

The cycle of business activity, so pronounced a feature of the British economy in the nineteenth century, was also experienced in

[1] W. W. Rostov, *The British Economy in the Nineteenth Century.*

varying degrees by other countries. With the passage of time the economies of the various countries of the world have become more and more interlinked with the result that boom or recession is more readily transmitted from one to another. A recession brings with it a shrinking of consumers' demand including the demand for imported consumers' goods. The import of raw materials too is checked because less of these is required as home industry, dependent on imported raw materials, is compelled to reduce its output on account of the falling off in demand. Thus, a recession in one country reduces the exports of others, which then may find it necessary to curtail their production. So the recession spreads. Similarly, a trade boom in one country increases demand in that country for all kinds of imports, thereby stimulating production and demand in other countries. So too a boom spreads. The increased demand for imports associated with a boom may, through its adverse effect on a country's balance of payments, bring in its train the seeds of its own disintegration. On the gold standard, for example, the outflow of gold was thought "automatically" to bring about a contraction of the monetary supply with a remedying of the balance of payments through a reduction of imports. Whatever the monetary system a curtailment of imports will eventually be necessary in order to bring the balance of payments into balance (*see* Chapter XII), and to other countries this will mean a reduction of their exports. During the nineteenth century the ups and downs of the business cycle in Great Britain, the United States, Germany, Belgium and France were very much of a pattern.[1]

## II. CAUSES OF UNEMPLOYMENT

### General deficiency of demand

There are many causes of unemployment, the most serious being unemployment that results from a general deficiency of demand. Since most industries are likely to be affected at the same time it is liable to produce widespread mass unemployment. As general deficiency of demand is a characteristic of the depressions associated with the business cycle, this type of unemployment has been described as cyclical unemployment. Though all industries and all parts of the country may not be equally affected—for even in a depression some of the newer industries will be found to be expanding—only a small number of those who are thrown out of work will be able to be absorbed in other forms of employment so long as the depression persists. As already pointed out, the booms and depressions associated with the business cycle of the nineteenth century were of short duration, and though unemployment did not entirely disappear in a

[1] See Lord Beveridge, *op. cit.*, Chapter VIII, p. 283.

boom, it rarely exceeded 8% in a depression, the severest slump occurring in 1879 when unemployment reached 10%. The inter-war years of 1919–39 provided the most serious example of mass unemployment resulting from a general deficiency of demand (*see* below, pp. 223–6).

## Structural unemployment

This occurs when a change in demand requires the structure of industry to be modified. It is an example of frictional unemployment which occurs because factors of production, including labour, are not perfectly mobile and so cannot easily be switched from one occupation to another. A change in demand merely shifts demand from one commodity to another, total demand remaining unchanged, and with the demand too for labour possibly being unchanged. This is very different from unemployment due to a general deficiency of demand which results in a fall in the total demand for labour. The characteristic of frictional unemployment is that it would not occur if labour could easily be transferred from a declining to an expanding industry. To accomplish this may require both occupational mobility (a change of skill) and geographical mobility (movement to another district). Frictional unemployment can result in the emergence of pockets of regional unemployment at times when there is a generally high level of employment.

A change in demand can occur for any one of a number of reasons. It may simply be due to a change of taste or fashion, or it may occur because a new commodity is preferred to an older one, such as television to the theatre or the cinema, oil to coal as fuel, etc. If, however, structural unemployment occurs as a result of the decline of an industry producing mainly for export, there may be no compensating demand in the short run for the displaced labour.

## Technological unemployment

This is a further example of frictional unemployment, which in this case results from the installation of labour-saving machinery. The immediate short-run effect of a productive change of this kind is to reduce the demand for labour in the industry concerned, though the long-run effect may be to increase the overall demand for labour. Technical progress has been going on, though not always at the same rate, since the Industrial Revolution, and it is obvious to everyone that the increasing use of labour-saving machinery has not resulted in a continuous increase in the number of people unemployed. Indeed, in the early years of the Industrial Revolution there was for a time a shortage of labour—at least in the districts where it was most wanted—and it was partly for this reason that pauper apprentices and other children came to be employed. Though the Industrial Revolution brought about a fundamental change in the techniques of production, it was at first a slow change and opposition to machinery was due to a dislike of working in factories and the loss of independence this brought with it rather than to its effect on the demand for labour. The unemployment and distress of 1815–30 was the aftermath of a great war and not the result of a greater use of machinery. In the case of the woollen weavers the distress resulting from a greater use of machinery in woollen weaving came in the form of low earnings which for a time were regarded as preferable to factory employment.

Mechanisation in industry has proceeded by fits and starts and often the incentive to invention has been a temporary shortage of labour. This was one of the motives that inspired the early inventions in cotton spinning which took place at a time when it required the work of six to eight spinners to provide enough yarn to keep a single weaver fully employed, though, when machinery came to be used in spinning, the situation was reversed. It was the development of a machine-tool industry—machines previously having been made singly and by hand—that speeded up the mechanisation of industry and resulted in the opposition of the workers to machines *per se* and in some cases led to machine-smashing riots. In recent years opposition to labour-saving devices has taken the form of refusals by trade unions to use them, more especially among dock and railway workers, coalminers and others in declining industries. Labour-saving machinery has been installed without opposition in the motor industry, in agriculture, in offices and post-offices, at airports, and in all expanding industries and those where there has been a shortage of labour.

It seems clear, however, that in the past, in spite of some temporary frictional unemployment, technical progress resulting from increased mechanisation has brought about a rising standard of living. Costs of production have been reduced and so have prices, while both the wages of the employees who have been retained in employment and the profits of the entrepreneur (especially if his new machines have been protected for a time by patents) have been increased. The eventual result has been that demand has been stimulated in a number of ways: (*i*) for the products of the industry installing the machinery, thereby causing some of the displaced labour to be re-employed; (*ii*) for consumers' goods in general, thereby increasing the demand for labour in the industries manufacturing these things; and (*iii*) for the production of the new machinery itself, with again an increased demand for labour. Eventually the whole of the redundant labour might be expected to be re-absorbed but, as in the case of structural unemployment, because labour is not perfectly mobile, neither occupationally nor geographically, this process of re-absorption takes time, and in the meantime unemployment will occur.

More recently the introduction of automation has brought with it in many quarters increased fears of redundancy, the effects of automation being similar to those following mechanisation but much more far-reaching. Automation so far has progressed much farther in the United States than in Great Britain but without having any serious effect on unemployment because its introduction has coincided not only with one of the most prolonged periods of continuous economic growth but also with a time of increasing defence expenditure. Many people in Great Britain appear to think that the only way to prevent large-scale unemployment resulting from automation is to reduce the length of the working day, and this has been at the root of trade-union demands for shorter hours. It is true that if automation were too quickly introduced on a very wide scale the immediate effect would probably be a sharp rise in unemployment, but to retain an excessive amount of labour in an automated industry would check economic growth and lessen the beneficial effect of automation on the standard of living. More and not less labour, however, is likely to be required in the future in most service occupations, for it is extremely difficult if not impossible to substitute machines for labour where personal service is involved. The demand too for these services increases as the standard of living rises, and in many of these occupations there is already a shortage of labour—retailing, teaching, nursing and medicine, local government, etc. The branch of automation which so far has made most progress in Great Britain is the use of computers and these have been employed mostly to save labour where there was a shortage or to undertake tasks previously regarded as impossible on account of the huge amount of work involved, so that to some extent the computer has created its own work.

### Seasonal unemployment

In many outdoor occupations, such as the building and construction industries and farming, work has often to be suspended in the winter on account of bad weather. Employment in many occupations at holiday resorts is very limited except for a "season" of four to six months. To offset this, light industries have been encouraged to establish themselves in the larger seaside resorts, and though this development enables more people in these places to obtain all-the-year-round employment, it does nothing to help those employed in hotels, boarding-houses and cafes which remain open for only a part of the year. Though it is sometimes possible to combine related seasonal occupations such as fruit and vegetable growing with the canning of these products or sugar-beet growing with sugar refining, a business firm manufacturing a product unconnected with holiday industry is unlikely to be willing to offer winter employment to people who prefer to work elsewhere in the summer.

## III. THE PROBLEM OF UNEMPLOYMENT—THE INTER-WAR YEARS

### The Great Depression

The Great Depression of 1929–35 was the outstanding feature of business conditions between the two World Wars. This depression was both more severe in its effect on employment and of much longer duration than the depressions associated with the pre-1914 business cycle. It also differed from these earlier short depressions in that it affected not only manual workers but also, especially in the United States, all kinds of non-manual workers.

In the troughs of the pre-1914 depressions, as already seen, the level of unemployment only rarely exceeded 8% (*see* Fig. 9, p. 215). The following table shows the unemployment rate among insured workers in Great Britain in the years between the two World Wars:

TABLE LV
*Unemployment Rate in Great Britain* (1921–38)

| Year | % |
|------|------|
| 1921 | 16·6 |
| 1922 | 14·1 |
| 1923 | 11·6 |
| 1924 | 10·2 |
| 1925 | 11·0 |
| 1926 | 12·3 |
| 1927 | 9·6 |
| 1928 | 10·7 |
| 1929 | 10·3 |
| 1930 | 15·8 |
| 1931 | 21·1 |
| 1932 | 21·9 |
| 1933 | 19·8 |
| 1934 | 16·6 |
| 1935 | 15·3 |
| 1936 | 12·9 |
| 1937 | 10·6 |
| 1938 | 12·6 |

It will be noticed that in only one year—1927—did unemployment fall below 10%. If the table is represented graphically, the rise and fall in the level of employment can be more definitely seen. The graph (Fig. 10, below) shows the post-war depression of 1921–22 giving way to a low "peak" in 1924, then falling slightly but improving again to another rather low peak in 1927. The First World War had clearly upset the rhythm of the business cycle, but during 1921–29 it appeared to be gradually reasserting itself. Then from 1930 to 1935 unemployment dropped to the lowest ever recorded—never below 15·3 % and for 1931–33 averaging no less than 20·9 %, and for 1930–35 18·4 %. In terms of numbers the worst month was January

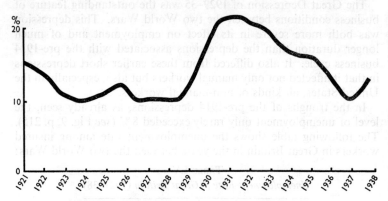

FIG. 10.—Unemployment Rate in Great Britain, 1921–38

1933, when the total number of unemployed persons reached 2,979,000. This was the nadir of the Great Depression. After this date unemployment gradually fell, and once again it began to be thought that the business cycle was re-establishing itself, unemployment falling to 10·6 by 1937. A year later, however, it started to rise again. Thus, the *peak* levels of employment in the inter-war years— 1924, 1927 and 1937—occurred with unemployment around 10 %, *i.e.* with a greater amount of unemployment than was suffered in pre-1914 depressions, and a rate which meant that 1,270,000 people were out of work.

In considering unemployment the length of time people have been out of work is often of more significance, both economically and socially, than the actual number unemployed. Thus, both at the worst period of the Great Depression and in the "peak" year of 1937, though half the total had been unemployed for less than three months, 14 % in 1932 and 26 % in 1937 had been continually out of work for over a year, showing that the longer a person had been out of work the more difficult he found it to get another job.

A further point to be remembered regarding the unemployment rate is that it was the average for the whole country. There were in fact wide deviations from this average both industrially and region-ally. Thus, while the old-fashioned basic industries of coal-mining, iron and steel production and the manufacture of cotton textiles were heavily depressed, several new industries were rapidly expand-ing, such as those concerned with the manufacture of motor cars and all kinds of electrical goods and fittings. The effect of these changes on the regional distribution of unemployment was exagger-ated because the most seriously depressed industries were highly localised on the coalfields while the newer, light industries were attracted to South-East England (see Chapter II: "Location of Industry").

In some parts of Great Britain, therefore, unemployment was re-latively low even in the worst years of the depression. For example, in 1934 the rate of unemployment in some of the more favoured places was as follows:

TABLE LVIA
*County Unemployment Rates* (1934) (1)

| County | % |
|--------|---|
| Bedfordshire . . | 4·6 |
| Middlesex . . | 6·1 |
| Hertfordshire . . | 6·1 |
| Buckinghamshire . | 6·2 |
| Westmorland . . | 6·6 |
| Surrey . . | 6·7 |
| Sussex . . | 6·8 |
| London . . | 9·6 |

At the same time the unemployment rate was much higher in other parts of the country; some of the most seriously affected are listed in the following table:

TABLE LVIB
*County Unemployment Rates* (1934) (2)

| County | % |
|--------|---|
| Glamorgan . . | 36·9 |
| Monmouthshire . | 36·0 |
| Durham . . | 34·2 |
| Lanarkshire . . | 29·4 |
| Cumberland . . | 28·7 |
| Lancashire . . | 21·1 |

There were even wider differences between particular localities. Red-hill in Surrey had an unemployment rate of only 2·0% and Hemel

Hempstead of 2·5% while Blaina (Monmouth) had a rate of 75·5% and Maryport (Cumberland) of 57·5% Even more remarkably Bishop Auckland had an unemployment rate of 53·5% while its neighbour Consett had a rate of only 9·6%.[1]

It seems clear, therefore, that unemployment between the two World Wars was different in character in at least four respects from unemployment before 1914: (i) the rate of unemployment was much higher; (ii) the unemployment rate still remained high even in the years of recovery; (iii) the depression was of much longer duration than the depressions associated with the business cycle; and (iv) individuals were out of work for longer periods at a time, in some cases even for years at a stretch. This type of unemployment had never before been experienced in Great Britain: it was the result of a general deficiency of demand and in consequence an insufficient demand for labour. It might well be described as chronic unemployment.

### A world depression

The Great Depression, like the business cycle, was not confined to any one country. It was a world-wide occurrence and its effects were often aggravated by the actions of countries which sought some slight relief for themselves without regard for any ill effects their policies might have on the economies of other countries. Trade was restricted in all kinds of ways—by tariffs, quotas, bilateral agreements and even barter transactions. Then the general collapse of the gold standard in 1931 led to the introduction of monetary devices that still further hindered trade, such as various methods of exchange control, multilateral exchange rates, and competitive devaluation of currencies. Though a country might obtain a temporary alleviation of its problems, the general effect was only to ensure that all would be poor together.

Unemployment was serious in Great Britain, but it was even worse in the United States and Germany. At the depth of the depression unemployment in the United States reached a rate of 23·4%, which meant that a total of 11·8 million people were out of work.

## IV. THE PROBLEM OF FULL EMPLOYMENT

### Determination of the level of employment

It was not until the nations were suffering from a world-wide trade depression that economists began seriously to enquire into its causes. Throughout the nineteenth century the view of J. B. Say, the French economist, was accepted that supply creates its own

[1] Lord Beveridge, op. cit., Table 36.

demand. If this were so, then nothing could be done in a depression except to wait until demand revived. Down to the 1930s relief works for the unemployed had been regarded solely as acts of charity to assist people in distress and not as a means of stimulating recovery. A study of the business cycle shows that during the nineteenth century it had never been necessary to wait long for the upswing of the cycle, but the experience of the inter-war years showed the utter futility of sitting back and doing nothing—except perhaps injuring one's neighbours—when faced by a severe depression.

Many theories were put forward to explain the trade cycle, as it was usually called, and though some of them contained an element of truth, most erred in regarding the Great Depression as only an exaggerated phase of the trade cycle. It was not until J. M. (later Lord) Keynes in 1936 published his book *The General Theory of Employment, Interest and Money* that it came to be accepted among serious economists that the basic cause of the depression was general deficiency of demand, though this had also been the view of supporters of the earlier under-consumption theories. These early under-consumptionists refuted Say's idea that supply created its own demand, however, with the fallacious argument that some of the money paid out to finance production was, as they said, "lost" and so failed to become purchasing power in the hands of those receiving it. Their crude remedy for this situation was for the State to make periodic distributions of cash to the people in order, to stimulate demand. Keynes, on the other hand, set out to show that investment is the main determinant of employment, income, saving and consumption.

Investment—the actual production of capital goods—generates employment and income, but the extent to which it does so depends on the multiplier effect. A new investment project may perhaps yield direct employment for 2,000 men, providing them with a total income of (say) £40,000 a week. Some of this income may, of course, be saved but what is spent increases the demand for certain goods and services, thereby stimulating the production of these things, and increasing employment (possibly by 1,500) and the total income derrived from it (perhaps by £30,000 a week) in the industries concerned. With each increase in employment and income there will be a further, though at each round smaller, increase in demand, employment and income. The eventual result of £40,000 of investment requiring the employment of 2,000 men may be a rise in employment of 6,000 persons and an increase in total income of £120,000, *i.e.* three times the amount of the original investment. In that case, whether it is regarded from the point of view of employment or of income, the multiplier is said to be 3, the size of the multiplier depending on how large were previous incomes of the people drawn into employment. Thus, the higher the rate of unemployment pay the smaller will be the multiplier effect.

If the total income of consumers was spent on consumer's goods it would require a country's entire economic resources—land, labour and capital—to be devoted to producing goods of this kind, so that no capital accumulation could take place. To enable some economic resources to be engaged in the production of capital goods, the demand for consumers' goods must be curtailed in order to set free some factors of production. Consumers' demand can be reduced by taxation ("compulsory saving") if the Government itself is to undertake investment, or individuals and business enterprises (through undisturbed profits) must be willing to save voluntarily if private investment is to be undertaken. Thus, saving is a necessary prerequisite of investment.

Private investment depends on the expectations of entrepreneurs and the rate of interest in relation to the expected return on the investment; public investment depends on government policy and can be undertaken if necessary to supplement private investment at times when businessmen are chary of investing. Private investment can be encouraged or discouraged by a government's monetary policy, indirect taxation (such as variations of purchase tax), directives to the banks, etc. Saving depends on the level of incomes, the distribution of incomes, the rate of interest and the propensity to save.

For investment to take place there must be an equal amount of saving. Only in a few instances is investment undertaken by those responsible for the corresponding saving, as when a firm finances its expansion out of profits or when a government raises the exact amount of additional taxation required to cover an item of public investment. In most cases, however, investment is undertaken by one group of people—entrepreneurs—while the necessary saving comes from a different group—consumers. At one time it was thought that trade depressions occurred when saving was greater than investment and trade booms when investment exceeded saving. Keynes, however, showed that saving and investment must always be equal, though what people as a whole may plan to save may differ from the actual amount they succeed in saving. Investment, as already noted, generates income, and income determines both the extent of saving and the volume of consumption, and therefore, through its effect on income, the amount of investment undertaken in one period determines the amount that can be saved in the following period. Fig. 11 (p. 229) shows the relationship between these different aggregates. The required amount of investment at any time is that which, through its influence on income, saving and consumption, will yield full employment. If private investment is insufficient for this purpose it must be supplemented by public investment. The difficulty is knowing

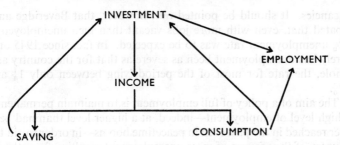

FIG. 11.—Income, Saving and Investment

exactly how much investment at a particular time will give full employment, neither more nor less. Insufficient investment will produce a situation with less than full employment; too much investment will result in a greater demand for labour than the supply, *i.e.* over-full employment and inflation.

### The meaning of full employment

Among economists and politicians there is no general agreement on what precisely is meant by full employment, though all would agree that it does not mean a state of affairs in which there is never any unemployment at all. Such a condition it is impossible to achieve in a progressive economy, in which temporary unemployment of a frictional kind—structural unemployment due to changes of demand or unemployment resulting from technological change— can be expected to occur. A man cannot expect to be continuously employed throughout his working life at a particular job in a particular place. In times, however, when full employment is maintained only those should be out of work who are in process of moving from one job to another.

Writing in 1944 Lord Beveridge defined full employment as a condition of "having always more vacant jobs than unemployed men." At that time full employment was a theoretical concept that had never been tested in actual conditions in peacetime. What Beveridge wanted was to create a sellers' market for labour so that anyone suffering from frictional unemployment would not be out of work for long, in order to keep to a minimum unemployment which is both wasteful and demoralising. For there always to be a shortage of labour, would he thought, stimulate technical progress. What Beveridge regarded as full employment others would consider to be "over-full" employment, and during the twenty years following the end of the Second World War such periods of over-full employment have kept the inflationary spiral in motion. It would seem, therefore, that it would be better to define full employment as a condition where the number of unemployed does not exceed the number of vacancies. It should be pointed out, however, that Beveridge anticipated that, even with more jobs vacant than men unemployed, a 3 % unemployment rate was to be expected. In fact since 1945 only rarely has unemployment been as severe as that for the country as a whole, the rate for most of the period lying between only 1¼ and 2%.

The aim of a policy of full employment is to maintain permanently a high level of employment—indeed, at a higher level than had been ever reached in the past even in peacetime booms—in order to rid the country of the scourge of mass unemployment resulting from the inadequacy of demand. During the period of the trade cycle unemployment had generally varied between 10% and 2%, and so merely to iron out the fluctuations of the cycle would not give full employment but rather a permanent condition of semi-slump with the unemployment rate always between 5% and 6%. Before the end of the Second World War it had become clear that in order permanently to keep demand up to a level that would yield full employment it would be necessary for the Government to ensure that capital investment was always adequate.

It was in 1944 that the State for the first time in Great Britain accepted responsibility for the maintenance of full employment. In that year the wartime Coalition Government published a White Paper in which it declared itself "prepared to accept future responsibility for taking action at the earliest possible stage to arrest a threatened slump,"[1] Similarly, the Government of the United States accepted responsibility for the maintenance of full employment by the *Federal Employment Act* of 1946.

## Unemployment since 1945

At the time it was widely thought that the Second World War would be followed by a depression such as that which occurred after both the Napoleonic Wars and the First World War. In fact, conditions after 1945 have been such that the problem most of the time has been one of trying to contain inflation resulting from over-full employment rather than one of combating unemployment.

Thus, in June 1948, out of Great Britain's total working population of 22¾ million only 282,000 were out of work, *i.e.* a mere 1·2%. Table LVII (p. 231) shows the fluctuations in the level of unemployment in this country since 1948. Even these figures exaggerate the extent of unemployment during these years. Less than half the number given as unemployed had been continuously out of work for eight weeks or more and of these a large proportion, as shown by Ministry of Labour surveys, comprised people unemployed for

[1] Cmd. 6527, Para. 41.

## TABLE LVII

### Unemployment in Great Britain since 1948

| Year (June) | No. unemployed (thousands) | Total working population (thousands) | Unemployed % |
|---|---|---|---|
| 1948 | 282 | 22,780 | 1·3 |
| 1949 | 280 | 22,871 | 1·3 |
| 1950 | 274 | 22,954 | 1·2 |
| 1951 | 188 | 23,228 | 0·9 |
| 1952 | 415 | 23,294 | 1·8 |
| 1953 | 282 | 23,373 | 1·2 |
| 1954 | 358 | 23,465 | 1·5 |
| 1955 | 211 | 23,590 | 0·9 |
| 1956 | 223 | 23,722 | 0·9 |
| 1957 | 265 | 23,859 | 1·1 |
| 1958 | 429 (536 Nov.) | 24,008 | 1·8 (2·2 Nov.) |
| 1959 | 413 (621 Jan.) | 24,196 | 1·8 (2·7 Jan.) |
| 1960 | 305 | 24,526 | 1·3 |
| 1961 | 266 | 25,345 | 1·1 |
| 1962 | 397 | 25,633 | 1·6 |
| 1963 | 516 (878 Feb.) | 25,744 | 1·9 (3·5 Feb.) |
| 1964 | 354 | 25,268 | 1·3 |
| 1965 | 305 | 25,463 | 1·2 |
| 1966 | 292 | 25,583 | 1·9 |
| 1967 | 500 | 25,322 | 2·1 |
| 1968 | 516 (631 Jan.) | 25,400 | 2·2 |
| 1969 | | | |
| 1970 | | | |

Source: *Annual Abstract of Statistics.*
*Monthly Digest of Statistics.*

"personal reasons," such as age, physical or mental incapacity, "lack of financial incentive," and those disinclined to work, euphemistically classed as "voluntarily" unemployed.

This table shows a very different story from that shown in Table LV (p. 223). In only one year between 1921 and 1938 did unemployment fall below 10%, whereas between 1948 and 1966 unemployment (as shown each year by the figures for June) never reached 2%, and only for very brief periods in the winter months exceeded that figure. However, during 1967–68, the unemployment rate gradually rose to 2·6. If Beveridge was correct in thinking that frictional unemployment caused by technical and economic progress would produce a 3% unemployment rate, it would appear that there has been persistent over-full employment since 1945.

As already pointed out, a better test of full employment is to relate the number of unemployed to the number of vacancies, as shown in Table LVIII below. It will be seen that the number of unfilled vacancies exceeded the number of unemployed continuously down to December 1956, with the exception of January–February 1947 (not shown in the table), when the severe weather caused a fuel crisis. By this standard, therefore, over-full employment persisted until late 1956, followed by a condition closely approximating to full employment between October 1956 and November 1957. A recession occurred during 1958–59 with recovery to full employment in 1960, followed by the onset in January 1962 of a further recession which lasted until May 1964. There was then a short period of approximately full employment which was succeeded by yet another recession in 1966–68. In August 1968 the number of unemployed (excluding those temporarily unemployed and school-leavers) exceeded half a million—the highest for thirty years for that month.

## The post-1945 recessions

It must be pointed out, however, that all the periods of recession which have taken place since 1951 have been times when bank rate has been high—6–7%—and generally, therefore, were brought on by a stringent monetary policy deliberately imposed by the monetary authorities for the purpose of checking inflation. The failure of

TABLE LVIII

*Number of Unemployed in Relation to Employment Vacancies (thousands)*

|  | Jan. | Feb. | Mar. | Apr. | May | June | July | Aug. | Sept. | Oct. | Nov. | Dec. |
|---|---|---|---|---|---|---|---|---|---|---|---|---|
| 1949 |  |  |  |  |  | +159 |  |  |  |  |  |  |
| 1950 |  |  |  |  |  | +153 |  |  |  |  |  |  |
| 1951 |  |  |  |  |  | +191 |  |  |  |  |  |  |
| 1952 |  |  |  |  |  | + 82 |  |  |  |  |  |  |
| 1953 |  |  |  |  |  | +103 |  |  |  |  |  |  |
| 1954 |  |  |  |  |  | +120 |  |  |  |  |  |  |
| 1955 | + 40 | + 70 | +101 | +156 | +204 | +232 | +288 | +248 | +242 | +186 | +162 | +166 |
| 1956 | +109 | + 92 | +114 | +138 | +143 | +184 | +159 | + 94 | + 86 | + 64 | + 35 | - 18 |
| 1957 | -127 | -141 | -113 | - 57 | - 30 | - 44 | - 88 | - 44 | + 17 | - 1 | - 65 | - 99 |
| 1958 | -237 | -185 | -208 | -226 | -239 | -216 | -197 | -243 | -297 | -347 | -377 | -369 |
| 1959 | -467 | -428 | -370 | -333 | -271 | -203 | -119 | -164 | -150 | -173 | -185 | -170 |
| 1960 | -180 | -193 | -101 | - 85 | - 14 | + 55 | + 88 | + 35 | + 20 | - 41 | - 42 | - 69 |
| 1961 | -138 | -100 | - 37 | - 3 | + 55 | +117 | +136 | + 55 | + 11 | - 77 | -124 | -115 |
| 1962 | -237 | -241 | -224 | -200 | -229 | -145 | -149 | -234 | -285 | -325 | -383 | -409 |
| 1963 | -672 | -736 | -541 | -414 | -359 | -265 | -266 | -382 | -272 | -259 | -260 | -247 |
| 1964 | -272 | -214 | -128 | -105 | - 42 | + 46 | + 62 | - 12 | - 7 | - 23 | - 31 | - 38 |
| 1965 | - 66 | - 42 | - 14 | + 67 | +113 | +173 | +171 | + 83 | +107 | + 56 | + 34 | + 15 |
| 1966 | - 4 | + 34 | + 91 | +125 | +140 | +191 | +191 | + 93 | + 11 | -135 | -290 | -320 |
| 1967 | -376 | -367 | -313 | -309 | -279 | -219 | -213 | -330 | -309 | -320 | -354 | -359 |
| 1968 | -411 | -388 | -332 | -306 | -262 | -214 | -202 | -275 | -270 | -281 |  |  |
| 1969 |  |  |  |  |  |  |  |  |  |  |  |  |

Compiled from tables of Registered Unemployed and Employment Vacancies in *Annual Abstract of Statistics*.

+ = More vacancies than unemployed.
− = Fewer vacancies than unemployed.

earlier periods of credit restrictions to do more than administer a temporary check to inflation led the monetary authorities to pursue a more severe restrictive credit policy in 1962–63 combined with a not very successful attempt at incomes restraint. Fear of the political consequences of increasing unemployment had previously led to governments reversing their monetary policy before it had really had time to become effective. The reason for making credit restriction more severe in 1962–63 was an attempt to avoid a quick return to inflationary conditions, as had been the experience in earlier recessions. Credit restriction is naturally unpopular and alarm was felt in some quarters when in February 1963 unemployment reached 878,000—an excess of unemployed persons over unfilled vacancies of 736,000 (Tables LVII and LVIII). With unemployment at this level it became a test of the Government's ability to restore full employment when the time came to end credit restriction. By putting the various instruments of monetary policy into reverse—that is, by reducing bank rate, relaxing hire purchase regulations, releasing the Special Deposits of the commercial banks at the Bank of England, abolishing the surcharge applied to purchase tax, and by encouraging the banks to adopt a more liberal lending policy—full employment was in fact restored by mid-1964.

Very often the adoption of a disinflationary policy has been forced on the Government by a sterling crisis. An adverse balance of payments, caused by excessive imports in consequence of too high a level of internal demand and sometimes aggravated by stock-piling, has led on a number of occasions to a severe drain on the Sterling Areas's stock of gold because of the inadequacy of Great Britain's reserves. Sterling crises occurred in 1951, 1955, 1961 (in this case brought on by the revaluation of the Deutschemark) and 1964–66. When action has been taken in good time, the extent of the deflation (and unemployment) required to restore confidence and remedy the situation has not been very great. In November 1964, however, little more was done than raise bank rate to 7%, with the result that inflation increased and the situation worsened in 1965, resulting in extremely severe restrictive measures having to be taken in the summer of 1966 with bank rate again raised to 7% (it had been reduced to 6% in June 1965).[1] In consequence a more serious recession developed during 1966–67.

Both the eight-year trade cycle of the nineteenth century and the Great Depression of the inter-war years were international in char-

---

[1] Cynics may observe that the relaxation of credit to reduce unemployment in the early months of 1964 occurred shortly before the general election of October 1964 and the failure to deal effectively with the situation in late 1964 and 1965 for fear of increasing unemployment also occurred shortly before the general election which took place in May 1966.

acter. To what extent, then, have the recessions since 1945 been international? Beveridge, as already noted, considered that full employment could be successfully maintained only if the main commercial countries of the world were all concerned to achieve it. Several minor recessions have occurred in the United States since 1945, but the government of that country, like many others, having pledged itself to maintain full employment, has taken the measures necessary to keep these recessions both mild and of short duration. Of the American recessions since 1945 only one, that of 1948–49, had a serious effect on the British economy—perhaps only because of the special circumstances of the time—leading as it did to the devaluation of sterling in 1949, though this was due as much to the arbitrary way that exchange rates were decided after the Second World War as to the American recession. During the American recession of 1953–54 Great Britain continued to experience a degree of over-full employment, the excess of unfilled vacancies over the number of unemployed persons actually increasing slightly during the period. The British recssion of 1958–59 came a little later than the American recession of 1957–58, and though to some extent the one may have influenced the other, the British recession was mainly of internal origin and its continuance the consequence of a course of monetary policy deliberately undertaken by the monetary authorities. Great Britain too has had much longer periods of over-full employment than the United States, where the level of unemployment on average has been double the rate of this country, and where, too, fluctuations in employment have also been much greater. The deflationary measures of 1966–67 brought about a serious rise in unemployment during 1966–68.

Italy had heavy unemployment throughout the 1950s in sharp contrast to the other EEC countries, which had relatively little. In consequence of inflation most countries in South America have suffered at least one devaluation of their currencies during the past ten years or so. It would seem, therefore, that since 1945 countries have had their own individual problems, and perhaps because these have been less serious than those of the years before 1939 their effects have generally tended to be kept within the confines of their own boundaries. It might, however, be a very different matter if a serious slump hit one of the major commercial and industrial countries of the world. In such a case it might well spread to other countries, though it might reasonably be hoped that with present-day knowledge of the determination of income and employment and the modern attitude of governments to the problem, such a catastrophe might be avoided if all countries took the necessary action in time.

## Redistribution of labour in Great Britain

The low rate of unemployment in Great Britain since 1945 has been achieved in spite of changes in the demand for labour due to technical progress and also very considerable structural changes in demand, such as the change in the foreign demand for cotton exports and changes in internal demand for different forms of power and transport, all of which have caused some temporary frictional unemployment. The following table shows the changes in the number of persons employed in certain industries between 1950 and 1965:

TABLE LIX

*Changing Employment by industries* (1950–65)
(Number of employees in thousands)

| Year | Mining | Agri-culture | Tex-tiles | Ship build-ing | Transport and com-munications | Con-struction | Vehicles | Engineering and metal manuf. | Distri-bution |
|---|---|---|---|---|---|---|---|---|---|
| 1950 | 852 | 1,161 | 1,004 | 203 | 1,781 | 1,434 | 981 | 2,103 | 2,484 |
| 1954 | 870 | 1,034 | 995 | 205 | 1,701 | 1,411 | 1,132 | 2,290 | 2,676 |
| 1959 | 831 | 642 | 841 | 267 | 1,685 | 1,380 | 860 | 2,483 | 2,697 |
| 1965 | 625 | 486 | 767 | 205 | 1,628 | 1,656 | 862 | 2,892 | 2,962 |
| 1968 | 480 | 418 | 705 | 192 | 1,603 | 1,506 | 817 | 2,896 | 2,798 |
| Change-over period | −372 | −743 | −299 | −11 | −178 | +72 | −164 | +793 | +314 |

Source: *Annual Abstract of Statistics.*

Thus, as can be seen, six industries together lost 1,767,000 and the other three gained 1,179,000 employees. Agriculture, textiles and mining suffered the greatest loss of labour, and engineering and metal manufacturing had the greatest gain. By 1968 the total number employed in mining had fallen to 402,000—less than half the labour force in that industry in 1950—and the number is expected to decline still further. It was a very remarkable achievement to bring about so considerable a redistribution of labour with an unemployment rate for most of the time of less than 2%. In spite of the great reduction in the labour force in farming, agricultural output in Great Britain has continued to increase in consequence of the introduction of greater mechanisation into the industry. An expanding demand for labour in most towns and the higher wages in manufacturing gave further stimulus to the drift from country to town, already encouraged by the greater attractions of town life for younger people, with the result that frictional unemployment among farm workers has been very considerably reduced.

Though unemployment has been heavier in North-West England than in many parts of the country, it has not been nearly so heavy as might have been expected for a declining industry so highly localised as cotton textiles, which first suffered a setback as an exporting industry and then found its home market also beginning to shrink.

## V. MOBILITY OF LABOUR

### The importance of mobility

Mobility of labour is of vital importance, essential if full employment is to be successfully maintained, if economic progress is to be made, and if the rate of economic growth is to be maximised.

Although every item of production requires all three productive resources to be employed, their proportions can often be varied. It is often easier, however, to substitute capital for labour than it is to substitute one kind of labour for another. Obviously, dentists are not interchangeable with accountants, nor are joiners with engineers. On the other hand, the introduction of new machines may often result in less labour being required. Thus, although substitution between different units of the *same* factor may not always be possible, substitution between *different* factors often is. The reason is that some kinds of work can be performed only by those who have a particular aptitude for it or who have acquired the necessary knowledge or skill, perhaps after a long period of training. However, the time required to learn how to do a particular job can be measured in some cases in minutes or in others in years, and, the shorter the period of training, the less specific the labour. Unskilled labour is completely non-specific and unskilled workers, therefore, are not restricted to one particular industry.

Occupational mobility of labour depends on the ease with which it is possible to move from one kind of employment to another, whereas geographical mobility depends on the willingness of workers to move from one district to another. Thus, it is possible for non-specific labour to be very mobile in the occupational sense of the term and yet very immobile geographically, whereas highly specific labour which is quite immobile occupationally may have to be very mobile geographically to obtain the sort of employment for which it is qualified. To obtain promotion most professional people, unless self-employed, have to be willing to move to wherever vacancies occur.

The characteristic of a progressive economy is the ease with which it adapts itself to changing conditions. Down to the eighteenth century conditions changed very slowly, but since then economic and social change has gone on at an ever-increasing rate. The tremendous industrial development that took place during the first half of the nineteenth century made it essential for labour, spurred on by economic necessity, to be both occupationally and geographically mobile. Workers were forced out of the older forms of employment into the new, into the factories and workshops and on to the railways. As time goes on fashions change, new demands develop, and factors of production must be attracted to the new industries. Changes of demand, however caused, may require a redistribution of labour.

## Some obstacles to mobility

Adam Smith declared that "a man is of all sorts of luggage the most difficult to be transported." For many reasons people are often particularly reluctant to move to another country, and yet over the past few hundred years large numbers of people have gone to other lands, often driven, it is true, by persecution or economic necessity. In recent years there has been both emigration from and immigration to Great Britain (see p. 204). The European Common Market encourages mobility of labour between member countries. Nevertheless, the motives for leaving one's native land have to be strong on account of differences of language, culture and climate, in addition to separation from friends and relatives. All these things tend to check geographical mobility. Indeed, quite a number of British emigrants have returned after only a short stay abroad. Some workers even show reluctance to leave a firm where they have been employed for a long time and where they have become accustomed to the routine, fearing the unknown. Then there is the problem of obtaining a new house. With rent control in operation the man who is able to rent a house is in a privileged position which he may be reluctant to give up. The man who owns his house may find the prices of houses higher in other districts, although if movement is away from areas of over-full employment the reverse is more likely to be true. To attract workers to areas short of labour employers may offer to pay costs of removal or themselves provide houses to rent. The National Coal Board has offered these inducements to encourage transfers of miners from coal-mining areas where mines have had to be closed to other coalfields where miners were required.

## Achievement of mobility

Mobility of labour can be achieved in a number of ways. What can be regarded as the normal method is that by which a redistribution of labour between different occupations is accomplished through new entrants and ordinary wastage. Every year some employees reach retirement age and cease work and there are always some who leave for their own private reasons. To some extent this will offset a fall in the demand for labour in a declining industry. Boys and girls leaving school will tend in general to avoid declining industries where in any case there will be fewer openings for them, thus making more labour available for expanding industries. Unfortunately, this method of bringing about a redistribution of labour is very slow to take effect—much too slow in times of rapid economic progress.

Attempts to redistribute labour by artificial means, such as the selective employment tax, are often criticised on the grounds that specific labour cannot easily change occupations. Between some occupations it is extremely difficult and in some cases impossible to transfer labour *directly* from one kind of work to another. Nevertheless, it may be possible to make the transfer *indirectly* by a series of adjustments as, for example, from factory to shop, from shop to office, and from office to profession—or vice versa. Difficulty in securing professional employment will increase the supply of office workers with the result that some who would have preferred employment in an office have to accept work as shop assistants, and some who would have liked to be shop assistants find they have to take factory work. Again, it takes time for such adjustments to work themselves out. Where new work requires quite different skills it will be necessary to retrain workers. The Government's policy with regard to location of industry has not always been consistent (*see* Chapter II), but taking work to the worker has generally been preferred to encouraging workers to move to where work was available—acknowledgment of lack of mobility of labour in the geographical sense of the term. Economic progress becomes impossible, however, unless labour can be made mobile occupationally. Hence, retraining of labour is an essential concomitant of taking work to the worker. Since mobility of labour is an essential condition for economic progress, it is now felt that those who suffer on account of it should be compensated, and this was the reason for the introduction in 1965 of redundancy payments for those people rendered unemployed in consequence of technological changes or because of changes in demand.

## VI. THE MAINTENANCE OF FULL EMPLOYMENT

### Conditions necessary for full employment

Since there are a number of different causes of unemployment no single policy can ensure the achievement of full employment. As shown earlier in this chapter, the most serious cause of unemployment is a deficiency of demand resulting from inadequate outlay. This was the main cause of the mass unemployment of the inter-war years. Total private and public expenditure must be such as will create a demand for further capital goods and for consumers' goods and services, the production of which still stimulate a demand for labour sufficient to yield full employment. Adequate total outlay must then be the first item in a policy for full employment.

Frictional unemployment arises because of changes in the structure of industry which follow from changes in demand or from technological changes, the effect of these changes being aggravated when an industry is highly localised. Economic progress causes some industries to expand and others to decline. Though technological changes may ultimately result in an increased demand for labour, in the short run the effect is likely to be some temporary unemployment. To reduce the incidence of frictional unemployment two things are necessary: controlled location of industry and greater mobility of labour. Government control over the location of industry has been in operation in Great Britain only since the Second World War. During the time this policy has been pursued there have been some changes of aim, but the basic purpose throughout has been to pinch out pockets of regional unemployment. Location of industry is discussed more fully in Chapter II.

To meet the changing conditions brought on by economic progress there must, as already noted, be greater mobility of labour. People who have lost their employment in declining industries must be prepared to be retrained for employment in expanding industries. During the past twenty years a considerable redistribution of labour has taken place, as Table LIX clearly shows (p. 235). The *Industrial Training Act* of 1964 set up a number of Industrial Training Boards to be responsible for training workers for particular industries, the cost being partly borne by the State and partly by a levy on the employers in the industries concerned. Though not solely intended for this purpose, this Act should help to make labour more mobile in the occupational sense of the term. To reduce frictional unemployment may require labour to be mobile too in the geographical sense. Indeed, there has been considerable movement of labour away from the older industrial areas to the Midlands and South-East England, and the purpose of regional development schemes—the latest phase in government policy for planned location of industry—is to check the depopulation of the older centres of industry.

### The accomplishment of full employment

A number of factors have combined to ensure the accomplishment of full employment:

(*i*) *Acceptance of the views of Keynes and Beveridge.* Lord Keynes showed how investment determines the levels of income and employment. Although at first the views put forward by Keynes aroused great controversy they have come in time to be widely accepted. Lord Beveridge stressed too the importance of an adequate level of demand to stimulate production and employment. Governments now accept the view that if unemployment is to be prevented,

or at least kept to a minimum, consumers' demand must be stimulated, in the short run directly, in the long run by undertaking and
encouraging capital investment.

(*ii*) *Government acceptance of responsibility for full employment.*
As already noted, the British Government in 1944 accepted responsibility for the maintenance of full employment. This meant that for
the first time the Government pledged itself to take whatever action
it considered necessary to achieve this objective. Great as was this
innovation it would not of itself have made possible permanent full
employment if the work of Keynes and Beveridge had not shown
what was required to make it successful. This was considered to
mean that the Government would have to undertake public investment if private investment proved to be insufficient to yield full employment, and if faced by an impending slump a deliberate budget
deficit might be required. In fact, the expansion of the public sector
and a general reorientation of opinion with regard to public investment since 1945 have generally resulted in a tendency for total investment to be in excess of the amount necessary to produce full employment. Most of the time government policy, therefore, has been
directed towards checking rather than expanding demand, and a
budget surplus rather than a deficit has more often been the aim.
Over the years since 1951 governments have devised a number of
new instruments to supplement monetary policy in dealing with the
level of employment, such as varying purchase taxes and hire purchase regulations. The problem of pockets of localised unemployment has influenced the Government's aims with regard to planned
location of industry. Emphasis on economic growth, stimulated by
comparison with the achievements of other countries has still further
increased government efforts to keep up a high level of economic
activity. In aiming at maintaining full employment individual governments have been assisted by the fact that other governments were
pursuing a similar aim, a matter of great importance since history
shows that both fluctuations and depressions have generally been
international in their impact.

(*iii*) *The psychological factor.* Expectations of entrepreneurs, as
Keynes pointed out, are an important influence on the level of business activity. There were psychological causes as well as monetary
and real causes of the old trade cycle. In those days entrepreneurs
had come to expect both booms and slumps to be short-lived and
their expectations of what might happen in fact helped to bring
about the change from boom to slump or slump to boom that they
expected. Expectation at the height of a boom of a downturn in
economic activity led some entrepreneurs to delay further capital
investment and this then caused a slackening off in the production
of capital goods and set in motion the multiplier effect. Since 1945

expectations have changed in character. It is true that while the Second World War was still being fought both economists and the Government, remembering what had happened after the First World War, feared the onset of a post-war slump once the expected post-war boom had spent itself. In 1919 both Great Britain and the United States had wished to return as quickly as possible to what the Americans called "normalcy" and this was again the American aim in 1945. In Great Britain, however, this was impossible because the war had dislocated the economy to a much greater degree than had been the case twenty-five years earlier so that physical controls had to be retained for some years. Recovery was more gradual and no post-war slump occurred. Gradually it came to be believed that full employment could be maintained indefinitely and this view was not shaken by the short, mild recessions that occurred. Entrepreneurs expected full employment to continue and acted accordingly. The only serious checks to full employment have come from government measures imposed in attempts to control inflation, but it has always been felt that the Government, having accepted responsibility for the maintenance of full employment, would never permit deflation to go too far. In recent years governments have become concerned with economic growth, and this has reinforced the view of entrepreneurs that a high level of economic activity could be expected to continue indefinitely. Expectations of businessmen since 1945 have, therefore, been radically different from the expectations of businessmen before 1913. Before the First World War the eight-year fluctuations of the trade cycle were expected to continue; at the bottom of the Great Depression between the two wars the outlook seemed hopeless; but since the Second World War expectations have been consistently optimistic, and this attitude of mind has had an important influence on economic activity. Even the more serious recessions of 1962 and 1966–67, because both were government-induced, were regarded as merely temporary checks which no government would permit to last for long. The long-term trend is expected to be one of economic expansion and so it is felt that capital investment can be undertaken with confidence. Entrepreneurs expect full employment to continue and so they act in a way that ensures that it will.

## Full employment and inflation

There are three ways in which full employment encourages inflation:

(i) *The political aspect.* The theory on which full employment is based is that a certain amount of investment will yield full employment. The direct stimulation of consumers' demand will also create employment. The great difficulty is to determine at any particular time exactly how much capital investment is required to achieve this level of employment. Since 1945 the maintenance of full employment has become a political question and governments have found themselves subjected to serious criticism whenever any increase in unemployment has occurred. Consequently, in order to make sure that full employment was achieved, more often than not over-investment has been encouraged, the result being over-full employment and a condition of inflation.

(*ii*) *Uneven distribution of unemployment.* During the 1950s and 1960s pockets of unemployment developed. Even though the average rate of unemployment for the United Kingdom as a whole was only about 1·2%—that is, well below what Lord Beveridge considered would be the likely rate in conditions of full employment—the rate was even lower in the West Midlands, London and the South-East. At the same time, however, the unemployment rate was over 4% in a number of regions—Northern Ireland, Scotland, Northern England, Wales and Cornwall. Within these regions, as during the Great Depression of the inter-war years, there were black spots persistently with even higher rates of unemployment. For example, in the Northern Region Blyth had a rate of 6·9% and the Hartlepools 5·9%; Rhondda in Wales had a rate of 8·9% and Falmouth in Cornwall a rate of 6%. These high rates in particular localities have persisted in spite of all the efforts that have been made to provide more work in the development areas. The effect of this uneven distribution of unemployment has been to raise the average level of unemployment for the country as a whole. A general rise in unemployment in much of the country only reduces the degree of *over-full* employment and, therefore, from the viewpoint of inflation can be regarded as desirable, but in the development areas a rise in unemployment is clearly a serious matter. Whenever a recession has been thought to have gone far enough and a policy has been adopted to stimulate demand, the effect has been beneficial for the development areas, where any reduction of unemployment was to be welcomed, but over the remaining four-fifths of the country the effect of an expansion of demand was to increase the extent of over-full employment and provide a further stimulus to inflation.

(*iii*) *Wage-bargaining.* Lord Beveridge was fully aware that full employment—especially as he defined it—would make the labour market always a sellers' market, and so increase the bargaining power of the trade unions. "There is a real danger," he said, "that sectional wage bargaining, pursued without regard to its effect upon prices, may lead to a vicious spiral of inflation."[1] It was considered, therefore, that full employment could not be assured unless the trade

[1] Beveridge, *op. cit.*, p. 199.

unions were prepared to adopt a responsible attitude to the new conditions. In former times the trade unions had found themselves in a weak position in periods of trade depression and in a strong position in periods of boom. Experience had taught them, therefore, that they had to take full advantage of conditions when they were favourable if they were to improve the long-run position of their members. However, if full employment is permanently maintained conditions are always favourable to the unions. If, in fact, over-full employment occurs there will be a greater demand for labour than the supply, especially in the less attractive occupations. In these circumstances many employers are prepared to pay higher wages in order to secure the labour they require if they think they can pass on their higher costs to consumers in the form of higher prices. In these conditions trade unions and professional associations are quick to suggest that the only way to attract more labour into an occupation suffering from a shortage is to offer the inducement of higher rates of pay—an argument repeatedly put forward by the teachers' and police organisations among others. In conditions of over-full employment this policy, if successful, can only create labour shortages elsewhere.

There is, too, a competitive element in wage-bargaining that still further aggravates the situation. Employees in different occupations do not all receive wage increases at the same time. Success by one union stimulates demands from other unions, and by the time the last group obtain a rise in wages the first group feel that it is their turn again. Thus, in various ways, full employment can stimulate the wages–prices spiral. As a result there has been almost continuous inflation throughout the period during which there has been full employment. The necessity periodically to check inflation, mainly on account of its adverse effect on the balance of payments, has meant that for brief periods full employment has had to be sacrificed —for example, in 1957, 1962 and 1966—to a quite considerable extent. If inflation is to be avoided wage increases must clearly be related to increases in productivity, but if those in manufacturing industry are to receive additions to wages equal to the full amount of the increase in productivity in their particular industries, as they appear to expect to do, increases of wages to those in other occupations based on the "principle of comparability" are bound to be inflationary. A temporary "wage freeze" was imposed in some occupations in 1949, a "pay pause" in 1961 and a more vigorous attempt was made to institute a "prices and incomes policy" during 1964–67. Lord Beveridge considered that for a full employment policy to be successful without its leading to inflation it required the State to adopt a policy of price stabilisation. To date no lasting success has attended upon government-sponsored incomes policies either in Great Britain or in any other West European country.

### International aspects of full employment

The maintenance of full employment in Great Britain is dependent on international trade in two ways. In the first place a high level of internal demand stimulates imports not only of both foodstuffs and raw materials but also of foreign-manufactured goods. This means that as the standard of living of the people in this country rises it becomes necessary to export more and more of our own products and to increase the earnings of our invisible exports in order to pay for these imports. The prices of Great Britain's products, therefore, must be competitive in foreign markets and for this to be so inflation must be no greater in this country than in other countries.

In the second place, the countries of the world have become so interdependent that the prosperity of one is linked to the prosperity of others. The ups and downs of business activity in the nineteenth century were transmitted from one country to another, making the trade cycle international in character. To an even greater extent the Great Depression of the inter-war years became of world-wide extent. A poor country cannot afford to buy from other countries, which, finding their exports shrinking, then begin to cut down on imports, so that all become poor together. Permanently to maintain full employment Great Britain requires other countries to be rich enough to buy its exports. Restrictions on foreign trade—tariffs, quotas, bilateral trading agreements, multiple exchange rates—only serve to reduce the volume of international trade. The greater the degree of international specialisation and the greater the volume of international trade, the richer will be all countries participating in it. To maximise international trade it must be multilateral in character so that countries not only buy from whom they wish but also sell to whom they wish. A falling off in international trade will not only reduce British trade but will also lessen its income from invisible exports. The greater the extent of international trade the easier it will be to maintain full employment.

For the greater part of the time since the Second World War most of the leading commercial and industrial nations of the world have enjoyed full employment. Most of their governments are pledged to take whatever internal measures may be necessary to achieve this objective, and in the international sphere there has been a greater response to a general reduction of tariffs as a means of encouraging international trade. This does not mean that the period since 1945 has not been entirely free from economic crises for individual countries which have often felt compelled to take action to restrict imports for a time. Full employment and a high level of international trade are dependent on one another. World prosperity in international trade is just as much a prerequisite as a consequence of prosperity at home. Thus, the maintenance of full employment within its own borders is not a matter over which Great Britain has complete control, since it depends on the maintenance of full employment elsewhere, particularly in the United States. The government of that country too is pledged to maintain full employment, and since 1945 has adopted a much more liberal attitude than it formerly did to international trade. Another favourable feature of recent origin is the greater readiness nowadays of nations to co-operate to assist a country in temporary economic difficulties—for which Great Britain had good reason to be grateful during 1964–66—as a result of their recognition of their economic interdependence.

### RECOMMENDATIONS FOR FURTHER READING

Lord Beveridge: *Full Employment in a Free Society* (George Allen & Unwin).
G. Haberler: *Prosperity and Depression* (George Allen & Unwin).

### QUESTIONS

1. How do you account for the world-wide depression of the 1930s?
2. "The persistence of full employment since the Second World War has been as much the result of favourable circumstances as of deliberate government policy." Discuss this statement.
3. In the century before the Second World War business cycles occurred regularly in Britain. How do you explain their absence over the last twenty years? (Degree.)
4. Would regional differences in unemployment tend to disappear in the absence of government intervention? How would you expect existing government policy to affect the adjustment process? (Degree.)
5. Account for the changing pattern of employment since 1900. (Bournemouth.)
6. Outline the factors which have led to the unemployment problem in the North-East of England. Discuss the possible measures the Government can take to solve this problem and the economic and social factors they must consider. (Huddersfield.)
7. Discuss full employment as a national policy and examine the contribution attributable to the late Lord Keynes and the late Lord Beveridge. (Kingston-upon-Hull.)
8. Evaluate the importance of the role of the Trades Union Congress in the administration of a national incomes policy. (Leeds.)
9. What is meant by "mobility of labour"? Why is it important—and how might mobility be increased? (Liverpool.)
10. What precisely have been the causes of declining economic activity in the so-called "pockets of unemployment" in this country and what are the measures required to reverse this trend? (Liverpool.)
11. Examine the meaning of "full employment" and the conditions for attaining it. (Manchester.)

12. Regional policy should be understood as a policy for economic growth and not for the relief of unemployment. Discuss. (Northern Counties.)

13. Relate the conception of the durability of products to the problem of trade fluctuations. (Norwich.)

14. What do you understand by the accelerator principle? Discuss its importance in relation to variations in the level of business activity. (Sheffield.)

15. Show how the following measures have helped to improve the vertical and spatial mobility of labour:

(*a*) Ministry of labour grants to workers.

(*b*) Government Training Centres.

(*c*) *Industrial Training Act*, 1964. (Southampton.)

16. "This country's policies for dealing with regional unemployment have concentrated too much on taking work to the worker and not enough on increasing the mobility of labour." Discuss. (U.L.C.I.)

## CHAPTER VIII

# INDUSTRIAL RELATIONS AND SOCIAL SECURITY

## *I. AN OUTLINE OF TRADE UNION HISTORY*

### The origin of trade unions

Like large-scale industry and the emergence of economics as an independent subject of study, the development of trade unions was a consequence of the Industrial Revolution and the rise of the factory system. So long as masters and men were of the same social class with a similar outlook and sharing the same sort of work, there was no conflict of interest between them, so that both could be members of the same organisation, as was the case with the medieval gilds. Since most journeymen in the days of the gilds had reasonable hopes one day of becoming masters themselves they had no incentive to form separate unions of their own. The decline of the gilds in the sixteenth and seventeenth centuries led to a greater degree of state intervention to regulate wages, the *Statute of Artificers*, passed in 1563, making the Justices of the Peace responsible in their own localities for the fixing of wages, and combinations of workers for the purpose of raising wages being forbidden. With the increasing scale and complexity of production (as compared, that is, with earlier periods) this system was gradually discarded as an unwarranted interference with industrial progress. By the late eighteenth century, with a widening acceptance of the principle of *laissez-faire*, wages became a matter which each employer decided for himself. In these circumstances, therefore, it is not surprising to find that workmen, no longer having organisations such as the gilds to protect them, began to combine in separate associations from their employers in order to protect their own interests. Nevertheless, in one trade after another, combinations—whether of employees or of employers—continued to be prohibited by law. Thus, the gilds concerned themselves with the welfare of all of those who were engaged in a particular craft—masters, journeymen and apprentices—whereas the trade unions came into being to support the claims of employees against their employers.

Long before the new industrial development of the eighteenth century, journeymen had combined for mutual assistance in time of trouble, making small weekly contributions to a common fund from which payments could be made to members during sickness or when they became too old to work, or to widows of deceased members. Such associations came to be known as friendly societies, and their number increased considerably during the second half of the eighteenth century. They received legal recognition by the *Friendly Societies Act* of 1793 in spite of the strong suspicion in some quarters that opportunity was often taken at their meetings to discuss ways and means of improving their wages. In other words, some of them began to act as trade unions.

Although the trade union movement received a great impetus from the Industrial Revolution, the first groups of workers to combine were not factory "hands" but skilled craftsmen whose position was already being undermined by social and industrial changes before the onset of the Industrial Revolution proper. The unskilled labourers of the time—the supply always exceeding the demand— were too poor to join any sort of association, whether its purpose was social or economic, where a monetary contribution, however small, had to be paid. The earliest members, therefore, of both friendly societies and trade unions were of necessity skilled artisans.

It was something of a misfortune for the development of trade unions in England that the time of their birth coincided with the outbreak of the French Revolution across the Channel. Fears that combinations of workers in Great Britain might be a prelude to revolutionary violence in this country led to parliamentary action to suppress them. It seems clear that such fears were groundless since at this date it was not those who were "down and out" who combined together but the more conservative artisans who were not fighting *for* change but rather *against* it. The consequence, however, was the passing of the *Combination Acts* of 1799–1800 which made illegal the combination of workmen in any trade for the purpose of raising wages. In spite of the penalties imposed for the infringement of these Acts (they were not nearly so severe or inhuman as those inflicted in 1834 on the "Tolpuddle Martyrs" under an Act of 1797 against the taking of unlawful oaths) men continued to combine. Some employers—perhaps the more humanitarian among them or maybe those who were economically more progressive—were prepared to recognise combinations, possibly realising ahead of their time that it was easier to negotiate with a group than separately with each individual member of it. The widespread unemployment and distress associated with the depression that followed in the wake of the Napoleonic Wars led to demonstrations, such as the one in Manchester that culminated in the "Peterloo Massacre," with the result that the authorities tended to tighten up the application of the *Combination Acts*. However, in 1824, largely as a result of the efforts of Francis Place and Joseph Hume, and with the liberal-minded Sir Robert Peel as Home Secretary, the Acts were repealed, mainly on the grounds that they were ineffective and only inclined to exacerbate relations between employers and employed. The *Combination Laws Repeal Act* of 1824 for the first time gave legal recognition to trade unions. The opponents of repeal appeared to be justified in their attitude when it was immediately followed by the formation of a large number of unions and a spate of strikes which led the Government to pass an amending Act the following year. This Act, though continuing to acknowledge trade unions and recognising the right of workmen to strike, imposed more severe penalties on members found guilty of violence or of interfering with those who did not wish to strike.

## The expansion of trade unionism, 1825–70

After the legal recognition of trade unions in 1824–25 there was, as might have been expected, a huge increase in their numbers. Before 1824 they had to operate in secret, often under the cover of friendly society activities, but after that date secrecy was no longer necessary, and many unions whose operations had of necessity previously been conducted in a clandestine fashion were able to come out into the open. Also, many workmen who would have shrunk from joining a secret society were willing to become members of an association that was not regarded as unlawful. Most of the unions, however, were small and local, for it was not until a railway network had been built up and travel made easy that the organisation of workers on a national scale became a feasible proposition. Nevertheless, during the 1830s several attempts were made to organise large-scale unions. None achieved much success, and even the Grand National Consolidated Trade Union, formed early in 1834, had a very short life. Owing to the influence of the wealthy social reformer, Robert Owen, its aims were wider than those of the small unions, its ultimate objective being a complete reorganisation of society in favour of the workers. Such a policy appealed to few workmen at that time, and it failed to obtain the support its founders expected, and the conviction of the Tolpuddle labourers hastened its end. The truth was that to most workmen the most pressing problem was the level of their wages rather than long-term social improvement. With improved communications independent local unions began to be replaced by national federations, but national unions such as the National Union of Railwaymen and the National Union of Mineworkers did not come into being until quite recent times.

Few of the early trade union leaders regarded the unions primarily as peaceful instruments for collective bargaining between employers and employees round a table, *i.e.* as a means of improving industrial relations. On the contrary, they were generally pugnacious in their attitude to employers and often anxious to employ the strike on every possible occasion in support of their demands. For the next twenty years strikes, often accompanied by violence, became a common feature of industrial life, but after 1843, with the increase in trade union membership, more moderate views began to prevail and the unions became less militant with the result that strikes and disturbances became somewhat less frequent. However, in 1867 a further outbreak of strikes accompanied by considerable violence led to the appointment in 1869 of a Royal Commission to inquire into trade unionism in general.

## Trade union legislation, 1871–76

After the passing of the *Combination Laws Repeal Amendment Act* in 1825 forty-six years elapsed before there was any further trade union legislation. Although after 1825 members of trade unions could no longer be prosecuted on a charge of conspiracy, there was still a possibility of the activities of a union being regarded under the common law as in restraint of trade. The unions were, therefore, in a somewhat anomalous position at law, one consequence of which was that it was impossible for them to prosecute a treasurer who absconded with union funds—a not uncommon occurrence so it would seem. The Majority Report of the Royal Commission of 1869 recommended that trade union funds should be safeguarded and the unions were given this protection by the *Trade Union Act*, 1871. (In the United States trade unions did not obtain legal recognition until the passing of the Wagner Act in 1935.) The Act of 1871 also provided for the registration of trade unions with the Registrar of Friendly Societies, so that at length they ceased to be illegal under the common law. Parliament, however, was greatly concerned at the coercion and intimidation of men who refused to take part in a strike called by a trade union and these practices were made illegal by the *Criminal Law Amendment Act*, also passed in 1871. This roused so much opposition among members of trade unions that a second Royal Commission was called for, and under the *Employers and Workmen Act* of 1875 "peaceful picketing" during strikes was permitted. The *Trade Union Amendment Act*, 1876, defined a trade union as a combination of either workmen or masters, though it is now customary to designate "unions of masters" as employers' associations. These Acts of the 1870s (the first two passed by Disraeli's Conservative Government and the third by the Liberals under Gladstone), which clarified and strengthened the position of the trade unions, would probably not have been passed had it not been for the widening of the franchise in 1867.

## "New Unionism"

Until 1880 trade unions continued to be mainly craft unions, *i.e.* combinations of skilled workers. Most of them were affiliated to the Trades Union Congress (TUC), established in 1868, which down to 1880, therefore, represented skilled workers only and not the great mass of employees. During the last two decades of the nineteenth century attempts were made to organise unskilled workers in trade unions, a movement that came to be known as "New Unionism." Some of the existing unions also widened their membership to include both skilled and unskilled workers. The three trade depressions of 1876–80, 1884–87 and 1892–95 were more severe than any other trade depressions of the nineteenth century—only being surpassed in fact by the depressions of the 1920s and 1930s—and the intervening booms occurred with unemployment never less than 3%. In these circumstances, though strikes were frequent they achieved little, and the development of the trade unions was checked. Down to this time strikes evoked little, if any, sympathy from the general public. Among the first to receive popular sympathy[1] was the dockers' strike of 1889, led by John Burns, and the first to be called by a union of unskilled workers. The success of the dockers gave a great fillip to the "New Unionism" movement and both old and new unions greatly increased their membership. Many of the old craft unions, however, continued to restrict membership to men engaged in a particular craft, their membership usually being small, whereas the new unions of unskilled workers were general unions whose members came from many different lines of production and whose numbers eventually became very large. The large general unions, unlike the small craft unions, did not offer their members friendly society benefits, as it was important to keep the weekly contributions as low as possible for members whose wages were very small. During the last ten years of the nineteenth century, therefore, an increasing proportion of manual workers became trade unionists.

### Trade Union Legislation, 1901–65

Two further Acts of Parliament had their origin in court judgments which threatened the position of trade unions. The right of a trade union to call a strike without being sued for damages for inducing its members to break their contracts with their employers was challenged in 1900 by the Taff Vale Railway in South Wales, at that time a small independent line. The railway company sued the Amalgamated Society of Railway Servants and obtained damages of over £200,000, the judgment being eventually upheld by the House of Lords. It appeared, therefore, as if the position of the trade unions had been seriously undermined. However, the Government appointed a Commission to inquire into the trade union position at law, the report of the Commission being followed by the passing of the *Trade Disputes Act* of 1906. This Act did more than merely reverse the Taff Vale Judgment, for by it trade unions were granted immunity from action in the courts for breach of contract in the case

[1] The success of the match girls' strike the previous year was also largely due to the public sympathy it aroused.

of strikes, and "peaceful persuasion" of non-strikers was to be permitted.

The second judgment that affected the trade unions was the Osborne Case of 1909, the courts upholding W. V. Osborne, a member of the Amalgamated Society of Railway Servants, in his refusal to contribute to trade union funds which were to be used for political purposes, that is, to support Labour candidates at parliamentary elections. It was held that trade unions were not empowered by any of the Trade Union Acts to collect and use money for this purpose. This judgment was reversed by the *Trade Union Act*, 1913, subject to certain safeguards, including the right of a member "to contract out."

After the General Strike, called by the TUC in 1926 in support of the coalminers who were already on strike, the *Trade Disputes and Trade Unions Act*, 1927, was passed—the only Act passed against trade unions this century. Strikes aimed at attempting to coerce the Government (as distinct from strikes in furtherance of an industrial dispute) were declared illegal. The unions retained the right to impose a political levy on their members, but "contracting-in" was to be substituted for "contracting-out." The change in the method of collecting the political levy greatly reduced the income of the Labour Party. The Act of 1927 was bitterly opposed both by the trade unions and, not surprisingly, by the Labour Party—by this time the official parliamentary opposition—and immediately it achieved power in 1945 it was determined to repeal it, as it did in 1946. At the same time Civil Service unions for the first time were permitted to affiliate to the TUC.

The aim of the *Trade Disputes Act* of 1906 had been to give the trade unions immunity from actions for damages for breach of contract in the case of strikes. Therefore, it came as a severe shock when the House of Lords in 1965 in *Rookes* v. *Barnard* found that a threat to strike might in certain circumstances be construed as unlawful. This judgment was quickly followed by the *Trade Disputes Act*, 1965, which amended the Act of 1906 in order to restore the immunity of trade unions from actions of this kind.

## II. CONFLICT OR CO-OPERATION?

### Trade union structure today

At the present day the trade unions of Great Britain vary enormously in both size and character. In 1964 the total number of unions was 591, as against 780 in 1945 and 1,300 in 1900, the reduction in the number of unions being the result of mergers and takeovers. Of the 591 trade unions in existence in Great Britain in 1964, 369 were affiliated to the TUC. Nevertheless, in 1964, at one extreme, there were 109 unions each with fewer than 100 members, one actually having only 24 members. A further 143 unions had fewer than 500 members, and altogether there were 307 unions each with less than 1,000 members. At the other extreme there were 18 unions each with over 100,000 members, two of the largest—the Transport and General Workers' Union and the Amalgamated Engineering Union—with respectively one and a half and one million members. In 1964 for the first time the total membership of trade unions in Great Britain exceeded 10 million out of a working population of 25·9 million (39·3%), an increase of 2 million since 1945. Of the total membership 7·9 million were men and 2·1 million were women. For various reasons women have never been as keen trade unionists as men, mainly because a smaller proportion of them take up work as a career and so are less interested in long-term considerations. In recent times, however, the number of women members of trade unions has increased very considerably, partly because more women now go out to work and partly as a result of pressure from the unions. During the period 1954–64 the number of women members increased by 18%. Even so in 1964 only 23% of women workers were members of trade unions as compared with 46% for men.[1]

Whether it is affiliated to the TUC or not, and whether it is a member of a federation or not, every trade union, large and small, is an autonomous body, fully determined to assert its independence and to exercise its right to decide for itself whether at any time to call upon its members to strike in support of its demands. Trade unions differ too in their methods of calling a strike, the decision more often being left to the executive of the union but in some unions depending on a ballot of all members, in which a majority of a certain size is required. Many people believe that strikes would be less frequent if unions could not decide on this kind of industrial action unless supported by at least a bare majority of members as shown by a secret ballot.

In 1965 the total funds of those trade unions that were registered with the Registrar of Friendly Societies amounted approximately to £115 million. Since, however, this averages only £13 per member it would appear that very few unions could afford a prolonged strike. Trade unions' funds are small because subscriptions have been kept extremely low. Registered trade unions account for about 90% of total trade union membership in Great Britain. Of the total income of trade unions of about £35 million, administration takes over 54%

---

[1] *Annual Abstract of Statistics.* A note indicates that "the statistics relate to *all* [italics are mine] organisations of employees in the United Kingdom—including those of salaried and professional workers, as well as those of manual wage-earners—which are known to include among their functions that of negotiating with employers with the object of regulating the conditions of employment of their members."

and provident benefits 21%. How much goes on "strike pay" depends, of course, on the extent to which resort is made to industrial action, but in 1965 it accounted for less than 2% of the unions' total expenditure.[1]

## The character of British trade unions

Some examples still remain of the oldest type of trade union with its membership restricted to skilled workers all drawn from the same craft and at one time just as keen to assert the importance of their work as to press for an increase in wages. Some of them are old craft unions that have survived from earlier times; others have been established, as new techniques with their new skills have been developed. These are the unions that often tend to insist on over-long periods of apprenticeship, ostensibly to ensure that all members have acquired the necessary skills, but also as a means of restricting entry. In some respects, therefore, the craft unions resemble the professional associations, but with less concern for service to the community. Very often the reason for these small craft unions not amalgamating with a large general or industrial union has been the belief that as a small independent body they will be able to obtain for themselves better conditions of work and higher pay, since the smallness of their numbers means that a rise in their wages will be less costly to employers than would be a rise in wages for members of a large union. Many of these unions are not affiliated to the TUC. Many of them too are quite small, but in some cases larger unions have been formed by the amalgamation of a number of unions covering closely related crafts, though this has often resulted in their members being widely distributed among a number of different industries. In consequence, these unions tend to be less strike-conscious than are the large general unions.

As already noted, some of the early craft unions relaxed their rules during the period of "New Unionism" to admit unskilled workers, thereby considerably increasing their membership. The large general unions draw their membership mainly from unskilled workers engaged in many different kinds of work, with the result that the Transport and General Workers Union has had to organise itself into a number of sections on an industrial basis. Wage-bargaining is the *raison d'être* of the large general union. In the case of an industrial union, such as the National Union of Mineworkers, members are all drawn from the same industry though they may be employed in many different capacities, some being unskilled workers and others skilled. Thus, a good deal of overlapping often occurs both between general and industrial unions and between industrial unions and craft unions, and on occasions rivalry between unions

[1] Reports of the Chief Registrar of Friendly Societies and Annual Abstract of Statistics.

has led to accusations, usually against the larger unions, of "poaching." However, the TUC, at its meeting in Bridlington in 1939, drew up a set of rules—usually known as the Bridlington rules—to restrain competition between unions for membership. The average size of unions has tended to increase as a result of amalgamations or, where unions have wished to retain a greater degree of independence, by forming federations, such as the Confederation of Shipbuilding and Engineering Unions or the United Textile Factory Workers Association. There is clearly great advantage to be derived from the workers in an industry being organised in a single trade union, especially if industrial action is contemplated or if an agreement applicable to the industry as a whole is to be negotiated. One of the causes of labour difficulties in the motor-car industry has been that workers in that industry belong to no fewer than twenty-two different trade unions. This has had two effects. Not only has it made difficult the negotiation of agreements for the whole industry but it has also meant that a strike called by a small union has often brought the entire industry to a standstill.

Trade unions are sometimes classified as "open" or "closed" unions.[1] An "open" union is one that opens its membership to all types of workers, whereas a "closed" union restricts its membership to a particular class of worker. The TGWU (the Transport and General Workers Union) is an example of the former and the NUM (the National Union of Mineworkers) of the latter. It is not surprising to find that "open" unions show the greatest increase in membership. A "closed" union, such as the NUM, by restricting membership to employees in an industry with a declining labour force, is bound to show a decline in its membership.

## Employers' associations

Side by side with the growth of the trade unions has been the development of employers' associations, which like the unions owed their origin to the growing need for an organisation to deal with problems arising between employers and employees as their interests began to diverge during and following the Industrial Revolution. As with the trade unions, some employers' associations are very large and others quite small. In general, however, employers' associations were not formed solely for the purpose of presenting a united front to the trade unions. Most of them are also concerned with matters affecting the prosperity of their particular trades. As has already been mentioned, some of the early craft unions were as much concerned with friendly society activities as industrial relations. On the other hand, large general and industrial unions have concentrated their activities on improving the standard of living of

---

[1] H. A. Turner, *Trade Union Growth, Structure and Policy.*

their members by raising wages and bettering their conditions of work, believing that social security was a matter for the State, the benefits they were able to offer their members being of necessity very small. At the present day trade unions are primarily concerned with industrial relations whereas employers' associations in varying degrees divide their interests between this sort of activity and problems affecting their trades. The general structure of employers' associations is very similar to that of the trade unions, both having an equally diverse collection of organisations: some large, some small; some national, some local or regional; some organised on an industrial basis, some at process level; some associated in federations, others individual. If the specific purpose of employers' associations is to stand up to trade union demands one would expect to find for every union, large or small, a corresponding employers' association as its counterpart. This, however, is not the case. In 1964 the total number of trade unions was 591, whereas at that date there were nearly 1,600 employers' associations. Some employers' associations, especially in the United States, have been as militant in their attitude to trade unions as some trade unions have been to employers. Both trade unions and employers' associations of this kind represent one view of industrial relations—that there must always be a direct conflict of interests between employers and employed. Some employers' associations, more especially perhaps in expanding industries, however, are mainly concerned to improve industrial efficiency, cut down costs, increase output and expand their markets. They regard this policy as conducive to the interests of their employees as well as of themselves, and so are inclined to adopt a conciliatory attitude to the trade unions, seeking their co-operation in aiming at an objective which is to their mutual benefit.

Just as trade unions associate together in a national body, the Trades Union Congress (TUC), so the employers' associations seek national representation in the Confederation of British Industry (CBI), formed in 1965 by the amalgamation of three bodies—the British Employers' Confederation, the Federation of British Industry and the National Association of British Manufacturers. The wide interests of the CBI are shown by its membership, which includes companies, trade associations and commercial associations as well as employers' federations. Although the TUC often debates general political questions, its discussions are mainly centred on labour problems. Both the TUC and CBI frequently negotiate directly both with the Government and with one another. Since 1956 the TUC has had the power to intervene in disputes between unions before strike action has been taken, whereas before that date it could not intervene unless a strike had already been called. For discussion of labour problems at international level there is the International Labour Organisation (ILO), with headquarters at

Geneva. It was set up in 1919 at the same time as the League of Nations by the Treaty of Versailles.

## Weapons of trade unions: The strike

Reference has already been made to the over-keenness of the early trade unionists to strike in support of their demands. This is explained partly by the fact that the right to strike—a decision by a group of workers to withhold their labour at the same time—was the first privilege for which the unions fought, and, having obtained it, they wished to exercise it. There was a feeling too among workers that the strike was a more efficacious weapon than it sometimes proved to be. The basis of the right to strike is that free men, even when acting collectively, have a right to withhold their labour. Strikers, however, expect to get their jobs back when the strike is over, and conditions for a settlement usually include an agreement that there shall be no victimisation of strikers. The aim of a strike is, of course, to try to compel employers to grant the unions' demands for fear of loss of profits arising out of a stoppage of work. In general, strikes occur nowadays only when employers and employees have failed to achieve a negotiated settlement of a dispute. Since it is the strongest weapon a trade union possesses it has tended in course of time to become an instrument of last resort, especially in the view of the more moderate trade union members.

In the 1950s and 1960s, however, there was an increasing number of *"unofficial"* strikes, *i.e.* strikes unsupported by, or sometimes actually in defiance of, a trade union's central executive. An unofficial strike may be due to opposition to a union's policy of moderation or to a feeling that the executive is too remote and out of touch with local affairs. According to the White Paper, *In Place of Strife*, published in January 1969, 95% of all strikes in 1957–68 were unofficial. Though generally of short duration—in many instances lasting no more than a day or two—they are capable of causing great inconvenience and annoyance to the general public besides often being damaging to the economy when they occur in service industries such as air transport, especially when called suddenly and without warning and frequently for what appear to be the most trivial of reasons. It is felt that many of these strikes could be entirely prevented if notice of strike action had to be given, as is required in most other countries,[1] though experience does not show that postponement necessarily makes it easier for the two sides to reach agreement. The most serious strikes have occurred when employees have been faced by wage-cuts, as in the 1920s and 1930s, rather than in support of claims for increased wages when compromise can be more readily

---

[1] In the United States in the case of a strike affecting a large industry the President can seek an injunction to delay it for eighty days.

accepted. On the other hand, unofficial strikes have been known to take place over matters of trifling importance. Occasionally a trade union, with no immediate grievances against employers, may call a strike in support of a union whose members are already on strike, *i.e.* it will engage in a *sympathetic* strike. A *general* strike may occur when a body such as the TUC calls upon all unions affiliated to it to strike at the same time. The only general strike to occur in Great Britain—that of 1926—was in effect a large-scale sympathetic strike in support of a strike of coalminers. In some countries, however, general strikes have been of a more serious kind, inspired purely by political motives and often aiming at nothing less than the overthrow of the Government. The British General Strike of 1926, however, was called off after only ten days. Sympathetic strikes are never popular with the public at large. The term *lock-out* is used (more especially by trade unions than by the general public, who tend to regard all stoppages as strikes) of a situation where the employers refuse to employ their workers unless they agree to new conditions of employment, usually involving a reduction of wages. Lock-outs, indeed, are rare, since they can so easily be made to appear to be strikes.

Strikes result in losses to both sides. Not only do the employers suffer a loss of production—and the greater the boom the greater will be the loss—but during the stoppage they still have to cover heavy overhead costs. If the product sells in a highly competitive world market there may be a permanent reduction in the industry's share of the market. Firms too may suffer in the home market if the strike causes consumers to switch to alternatives as, for example, from rail to bus travel or to the greater use of the private car, or from coal-fired to oil-fired central heating. A reduction in the demand for the product will lead to a contraction of the industry and a reduction in its labour force. In an extreme case some firms may be driven out of business. More than one newspaper has gone out of existence consequent on strikes affecting the newspaper industry. Even if employees obtain higher wages these will be offset for a time by the loss of wages during the strike. Some strikes are more effective than others because their impact on the economy—and the community—is greater. A trade union's power to raise the wages of its members will be greater the more specific the labour of its members and, therefore, the more inelastic the demand for it. It is this that accounts for the survival of many small craft unions. Generally too, in their case, the cost of their labour forms only a small proportion of a firm's total costs. Most trade unions nowadays prefer collective bargaining to strikes but, since the bargaining power of a trade union generally depends to a great extent on the threat of a strike, it has to engage in a strike from time to time to show that it does not just make empty threats. For example, strikes of British seamen have been extremely rare and their strike in 1966 was mainly to show that on occasion they were prepared to engage in industrial action. In times when as at present wages are generally high a strike may sometimes provide a measure of excitement and relief for men in dull and monotonous jobs. When trade unions were weak, employers used to try to avoid shutting down their plant by taking on non-union labour if any were available. Very few employers would attempt to do so nowadays. In any case it would be difficult in conditions of full employment. The effectiveness of a strike depends on the efficiency of *picket ing*. As already mentioned, the unions in the past had a long-struggle to secure the right to employ "peaceful" picketing during strikes.

## Other weapons of trade unions

Not all the other weapons that trade unions have at their command are alternatives to the strike, more often being supplementary to the main weapon. In recent years another method sometimes adopted by trade unionists to enforce their demands, though rarely with other than tacit approval from the trade union itself, is to "work to rule." The phrase is derived from those industries where working rules have been drawn up for the guidance of employees as, for example, on the railways. The term first came into use in these industries to denote the practice of paying such deliberate and meticulously careful attention to carrying out the working rules of a firm that work was greatly slowed down, so that the amount accomplished per man-hour was considerably reduced. The expression is now much more widely used, being applied in any industry where the workers, irrespective of whether or not there are any working rules in their industry, decide to adopt a "go-slow" policy for which the term "working to rule" is clearly a euphemism. In an under-manned employment, such as the Post Office, workers may refuse to work overtime in order to cause dislocation of sorting and distribution. Somewhat similar is the refusal to agree to measures to improve productivity until a wage claim is met.

Most unions favour the policy of the *closed shop*, *i.e.* the employment by employers only of men who are members of the appropriate trade union. Few unions in the past have been able to insist on this. Indeed, for a long time they had to fight employers who refused to employ "union" labour. The long period of full employment since the Second World War has greatly increased the bargaining strength of the trade unions and this power has often been used to insist on the "closed shop." Intimidation has frequently been practised against men who have refused to join a union and on occasions employers have been compelled, albeit reluctantly, to dismiss non-unionists however competent at their jobs they may have been. These men

260 AN INTRODUCTION TO APPLIED ECONOMICS

have, in fact, been driven out of employment in occupations for which they have been specifically trained and for which they have acquired the necessary skills. The argument of the union is that men who are not members should not be able to benefit from better conditions of employment or higher wages secured for its members by the union. For collective bargaining to be effective a large proportion of the employees—though not necessarily all of them—should belong to the union. A worker, however, may not wish to join the union because he objects to its policy, particularly being called upon to strike when he has no wish to do so. The principle of the "closed shop," therefore, restricts the personal freedom of both employers and employees.

As an alternative to the sympathetic strike, union members may support a strike called by another union by *boycotting* any activities which in their opinion might be deemed to be "strike-breaking." Thus, in the case of a seamen's strike, dockers might declare a foreign ship "black" and refuse to load it.

## Collective bargaining

The organisation of employers in employers' associations and employees in trade unions made possible what is known as collective bargaining, representatives of each body acting on behalf of its members. Most employees would be in a weak position if they had to bargain individually with their employers. Most employers too prefer collective to individual bargaining with employees. An agreement between a trade union and an employers' association ensures too that all employees shall receive equality of treatment. A collective agreement will also prevent some employers attempting to cut wage rates in order to reduce their costs and so increase their competitiveness is the market for their goods. In democratic countries collective bargaining has become the recognised method of settling industrial disputes—wage rates, hours of work, general conditions of work, holidays, etc.—but naturally the matter most frequently discussed is wages, either directly or indirectly through a claim for a shorter working week or longer paid holidays. Both trade unions and employers' associations believe all such questions as these should be determined by collective bargaining between the two bodies concerned and resent any interference from outside, such as from a government attempting to carry out an "incomes policy," and yet in times of full employment complete freedom of action for trade unions and employers' associations can lead to the exploitation of the rest of the community.

The success of collective bargaining, however, depends on the willingness of the members of the trade union and the employers' association concerned to accept without question whatever agreement may be made on their behalf by their duly appointed negotia-tors. In general over the years both employees and employers have accepted collective agreements, even though one group or the other has often been disappointed with the terms.

Collective bargaining is an example of what is known as bilateral monopoly—a trial of strength where wages are under discussion between a monopolist supplier of labour (the trade union) and a monopsonist buyer (the employers' association). The success of the large powerful general unions during the past twenty years has led to a widespread belief that the narrowing of wage differentials between skilled and unskilled workers and differences in wages between different occupations are due to the fact that some trade unions are more powerful than others. A trade union's bargaining power, how-ever, depends on a number of factors such as its size, its financial resources, the skill of its leaders in negotiating and the extent to which a strike of its members affects the economy and the community as a whole. More important, however, than any of these things are (*i*) the economic viability of the industry and (*ii*) the prevailing economic conditions. Clearly, it will be more difficult for trade unions whose members are employed in declining industries to improve their position than for a union covering employees in an expanding industry. During recent years the trade unions covering workers in the motor-car industry have been more successful than those representing workers in the cotton industry or on railways. In a time of full employment all trade unions are more powerful than they are during a depression. In conditions of full employment employers are readier to meet union demands (though, of course, every effort will be made to try to reduce them) rather than suffer the dislocation of production and the loss of profit concomitant on a strike. A firm short of labour may even be willing to offer more than union wage rates with a promise too of more overtime. Such local agreements have become more common as a result of the increasing practice of bargaining over wages and conditions of work at shop-floor level—on a practice which has given rise to wage drift (*see* Chapter X). On the other hand, in a slump some employers may actually welcome the opportunity to close down offered by a strike!

## The role of the State

Collective bargaining as a means of obviating strikes has been encouraged by the State, which has attempted to set up machinery to aid the settlement of industrial disputes. During the 1890s many trade union leaders and employers began to favour conciliation and, following upon the recommendations of a Royal Commission, a *Conciliation Act* was passed in 1896. This Act empowered the

Labour Department of the Board of Trade to appoint a conciliator to bring the two sides to a dispute together. The increasing interest of the State in labour problems led to the establishment in 1916 of the Ministry of Labour, which since that date has often taken an active part in attempting to settle industrial disputes, this having become one of the main functions of the Minister. For quite a number of industries Conciliation Boards had been established before the passing of the Act of 1896 but their number increased very considerably during the ensuing twenty years. The Conciliation Act was supplemented by the *Industrial Courts Act*, 1919, under which there were established Joint Industrial Councils—more generally known as Whitley Councils, J. H. Whitley having been chairman of the committee that had recommended the establishment of one for each industry where no such machinery existed. On these councils both employers and employees are represented and their purpose is to provide a vehicle for regular consultation. The *Industrial Courts Act* also empowered the Ministry of Labour to set up a court of enquiry to consider the points at issue in any particular dispute. This Act also provided for arbitration if both sides were agreeable.

A method of settling a dispute where a deadlock has been reached is by arbitration. During both World Wars, when strikes were prohibited, arbitration became compulsory in labour disputes. An independent arbitrator, acceptable to both parties, is appointed to hear arguments put forward by each side. Arbitration, therefore, would appear to be one of the most equitable methods of settling an industrial dispute. However, when arbitration is employed to settle wage disputes, as it mostly is, the arbitrator is apt to consider wages in comparable occupations (though there are few problems more difficult than that of comparing different occupations), so that equity rather than economic efficiency tends to be the criterion for a settlement. The inherent weakness of arbitration lies then in the fact that arbitrators are inclined to compromise, and when this becomes known the result is that exaggerated wage claims are made in the hope that the arbitrator will give a trade union the amount really wanted. But perhaps the main difficulty with arbitration is that there are no generally accepted standards on which decisions can be based.

Thus, for over seventy years the State has attempted to hasten the settlement of labour disputes, and as long ago as 1914 it had acquired the right to appoint a conciliator of an arbitrator or to conduct an enquiry into the causes of a dispute.

*Wages Councils*, which superseded the earlier Trade Boards, were originally set up in industries in which it was considered that trade unions were unlikely to become strong enough to engage in collective bargaining. The *Wages Councils Act*, 1959, consolidated earlier legislation on the subject. Wage Councils already had the power to fix guaranteed wages and such matters as holidays with pay in those industries for which they had been established. Under the Act of 1959 the Minister of Labour[1] can make an order establishing a Wages Council for any industry where he considers that no effective machinery exists for the regulation of wages. In addition to representatives of the employers and employees in an industry each Wages Council has up to three independent members. Proposals made by a Wages Council for the fixing of a minimum wage have to be submitted to the Minister for his consideration, after which, if he thinks fit, he can give effect to the proposals.

The establishment of *personnel departments* by the more progressive firms has helped to settle many minor grievances of individual employees which otherwise might have caused a feeling of discontent.

## Political activities of trade unions

In most countries trade unions have a political link with socialism, with the outstanding exception of the United States. In Great Britain the trade unions did not become politically aligned until 1900 although before 1900 the Trades Union Congress, which had been founded in 1868, had used its influence to harass whatever government might be in power, whether Conservative or Liberal. A few trade union leaders were elected to Parliament as Liberals, but in 1900 the Labour Representation Committee was formed to secure representation of the trade unions in Parliament. Thus, the British trade unions were responsible for the formation of a political party which they expected to safeguard their interests. There was, however, a great difference in outlook between the socialists of those days and the trade unions. Whereas many of the early socialists were inspired by idealism, the outlook of the trade unions was solely materialistic. Most trade unions—especially the older unions of manual workers—in this country are therefore affiliated to the Labour Party, although it has been calculated that nearly one-third of trade unionists do not support that party at election times. Nevertheless, not all trade unions that are affiliated to the TUC are also affiliated to the Labour Party. The TUC itself, in spite of its being the national body representative of the trade unions, claims to be non-political, and this was shown by its attitude to the Conservative Party on the morrow of that party's election victory in 1951. The Labour Party owed its early development to the support of the trade unions but it could never have achieved a parliamentary majority without much wider support. Consequently, the proportion of Labour MPs sponsored by the trade unions has declined over the years. Partly for this reason, and partly because of the differences of

[1] Since 1968 known as the Minister of Employment and Productivity.

functions between a trade union and a political party in power, the trade unions since 1945 have not always seen eye to eye with Labour governments.

Although trade unions in the United States have not gone to the length of founding a political party of their own nor even of aligning themselves permanently with one of the established political parties, the AFL–CIO (the American Federation of Labour and the Congress of Industrial Organisations, which merged in 1955—the American equivalent of the British TUC) from their office in Washington make their views known to the US Congress. Like the British trade unions, the American unions favour the extension of state intervention in the economic life of the nation. For a long time the British trade unions were keen supporters of nationalisation, but, since they discovered that dealing with the managements of nationalised industries was very little different from negotiating with employers in private industry, their enthusiasm for nationalisation has waned somewhat. The year 1966, however, saw the start of an interesting experiment when trade unions and the State both took up shares in the Glasgow shipbuilding firm of Fairfields.

## III. RECENT DEVELOPMENTS IN INDUSTRIAL RELATIONS

### The peak of trade union prestige

During the Second World War the British trade unions showed themselves to be responsible bodies which the Government could consult on labour matters and even on other questions. In return for this privilege the unions gave up—at least for a time—their right to strike, as did American unions after the United States had entered the war, and as British unions had during the First World War. Some of the trade unions leaders accepted high office in the Churchill Coalition Government—notably Ernest Bevin, who had had no previous political experience—and they made it their business to persuade the unions to put national before personal or union considerations, perhaps not too difficult an undertaking in time of war since the vast majority of trade union members are inherently loyal. The unions continued to display this attitude during the difficulties of the immediate post-war period when the Attlee government was in power, and on into the mid 1950s, although the Government's desire for wage restraint following the devaluation of the pound in 1949, though generally supported by the TUC and the leaders of the large unions, did not appeal to the ordinary members. Down to 1955, however, the trade unions continued to enjoy a high degree of prestige—the highest in their entire history—under both Labour and Conservative administrations. The unions secured representation on the National Economic Development Council and on the "Little Neddies." This too was a period that was relatively free of serious strikes, as the following table shows:

TABLE LX
*Incidence of Strikes*

| Year | Number of man-days lost (thousands) | Total trade union membership (thousands) | Average number of days lost per member |
|---|---|---|---|
| Three bad years: | | | |
| 1912 | 40,890 | 3,416 | 12·0 |
| 1921 | 85,870 | 6,633 | 13·0 |
| 1926 | 162,230 | 5,219 | 31·1 |
| (General Strike) | | | |
| Annual averages: | | | |
| 1946–54 | 1,984 | 9,400 | 0·2 |
| 1955–68 | 3,888 | 9,850 | 0·4 |
| 1967 | 2,783 | 10,111 | 0·27 |

Compiled mainly from *Annual Abstract of Statistics.*

The years before 1939 are not strictly comparable with the period since 1945 on the basis of the average days lost per members as a result of strikes, since we find a smaller proportion of workers in membership of trade unions in the earlier than in the later period. In any case 1926, the year of the General Strike, was exceptional. Apart from that year, the worst year between the two World Wars was 1921, with an average number of days lost per trade union member of 13·0, whereas in 1959, the worst year since 1945, the corresponding figure was only 0·55. The average number of days lost per member has been very low since 1945 even though it doubled during the second half of the period. The low incidence of strikes since 1945 has been due partly to employers' being more responsive to the demands of trade unions for higher pay in a period of full employment and partly to increased efficacy of collective bargaining in recent times. Experience in the United States has been very similar, only 23 million man-days being lost in 1964 on account of strikes by 16 million trade unionists, an average of 0·4 days per man, but, even so, rather higher than the British average.

### Declining prestige of the trade unions

Though the trade unions retained their assured position in the country after 1955 they began to lose some of the prestige they had gained during the preceding fifteen years. There were many reasons for this.

*Inter-union disputes.* Three strikes that occurred about the time of the general election of 1955 were responsible for the attitude of the general public towards the trade unions beginning to change. First, there was a strike of dockers over a demarcation dispute and the reputation of the unions was not enhanced by seeing a strong, powerful union compelling men to leave a smaller union. The second strike also was due to conflict between unions. It arose because maintenance men at newspaper printing works who were members of the AEU (the Amalgamated Engineering Union) or the ETU (the Electrical Trades Union) were only able to negotiate indirectly with the newspaper proprietors through the printing union. The third strike affected the railways and again the cause of the trouble was differences in outlook between two unions. The NUR (the National Union of Railwaymen), a large industrial union, accepted the terms offered by the Transport Commission, but the differential offered for skilled men did not satisfy ASLEF (the Associated Society of Locomotive Engineers and Firemen), a smaller craft union. In 1967 ASLEF called a strike because its members objected to "guards" who were members of the NUR travelling on the engine. In the motor-car industry there have been eight times as many strikes as in any other industry, this being due in no small measure to the fact that employees in the motor-car industry belong to no fewer than twenty-two independent trade unions.

*Trade union conservatism.* No body of people has been more opposed to change than the trade unions. Indeed, workers have always been slow to accustom themselves to changed conditions. For a long time after the Second World War their actions were influenced by fear of a serious post-war slump. It took nearly twenty years to convince many of them that full employment had replaced the trade cycle as the normal industrial climate. The most conservative of all in this respect were the large general and industrial unions. When boom alternates with slump the unions rightly feel that they must take full advantage of their power when conditions are favourable to them in order to offset their reduced power when conditions are unfavourable. Thus, there are usually more strikes in a period of trade depression when the unions are resisting wage cuts. In times of boom the unions not unnaturally took advantage of the more favourable economic conditions to improve their position. Full employment, however, means that circumstances are almost always favourable to the unions, thereby requiring them, as Lord Beveridge pointed out, to adopt a more responsible attitude if it was to become a permanent condition of industrial life. This question is discussed below (*see* p. 274). Over the past twenty-five years industrial progress has been rapid, and the changing pattern of industry that has gone with it necessitates a revision of the present lines of demarcation that exist between unions—and which have been maintained unchanged for so long—if there are to be really effective relations between employers and employees.

One important requisite for economic progress is that labour from time to time needs to be redistributed among different industries and occupations to meet changes in demand. To reduce the impact of this policy on those in declining industries who lose their jobs, redundancy payments were introduced in 1965. Nevertheless, unions have fought, though unsuccessfully, for the alternative of work-sharing, although obviously this would do nothing either to assist redistribution of labour or to further economic progress.

*Restrictive labour practices.*[1] The conservatism of the trade unions has led them to adopt restrictive practices the effect of which can only be to check economic progress, though from the point of view of the unions the aim has been to safeguard security of employment or to improve their bargaining strength. Some restrictive practices, however, are due to traditional ways of working that are no longer appropriate to modern conditions and may be accepted or condoned by weak managements. A restrictive practice has been defined as "an arrangement under which labour is not used efficiently, and which is not justifiable on social grounds."[2]

One of the most serious restrictive labour practices is over-manning. This can take several forms. The introduction of new labour-saving devices—even in times of over-full employment—has often been opposed, and there have actually been cases where new up-to-date machinery has lain idle for long periods because of a trade union's refusal to permit it to be used. Frequently agreement to a new machine being used has been obtained only at the cost of employing on it more men than was really necessary. In fact, unions often lay down the minimum number of men to be employed on a particular job—sometimes twice the number actually required.[3] The introduction of freight-liner trains on the railways, an industry struggling to make itself economically viable, was opposed for years and led to strikes at the places affected. Employers have often been compelled to agree not to dismiss any men when more efficient labour-saving equipment has been introduced in return for the privilege of not replacing those who voluntarily leave. When, for example, diesel traction replaced steam on the railways British Rail had to undertake to continue to employ a second man in addition to the engine driver although he was no longer required and had no duties to perform, though again no new men were to be taken on.

---

[1] For a detailed account of restrictive practices, see Research Paper No. 4, prepared for the Royal Commission on Trade Unions and Employers' Associations by the Commission's secretariat.

[2] *Ibid.*, p. 47.

[3] *Ibid.*, Appendix: "Example of Restrictive Labour Practices."

Omnibus workers, faced by a similar problem, in spite of a continuous shortage of labour in the industry, were only persuaded by their employers to agree to the introduction of "one-man" buses on condition that the driver/conductor should be paid a higher rate per hour than a specialist driver, thereby depriving the operators of a good deal of the anticipated reduction in operating costs—again in an industry finding it difficult to pay its way. The traditional employment of craftsmen's mates, many of whom do relatively little work, is a further example of over-manning that cannot be tolerated in present-day conditions when faster economic growth is a national objective.

Other restrictive labour practices include deliberately working slowly—or even wasting time, as do many long-distance lorry drivers—in order to make it necessary for them to work overtime in order to increase earnings, an example of wage drift. This is not a practice of which trade unions approve, nor most employers, but many forms of wage drift have arisen because some employers were prepared to offer their employees higher earnings in order to attract labour. Reference has already been made to inter-union disputes over questions of demarcation, and these have often led to strikes and a disruption of production in industries where different craftsmen are employed.

*Undesirable union practices.* The general public has frequently been shocked at the behaviour of some trade unionists—engaging in unofficial strikes (which only appear to the rest of the community as a manifestation of the weakness of the unions), victimisation of other employees in order to secure a "closed shop," threatening action against men regarded as working too fast, and at least one instance of "ballot-rigging" to ensure the "election" of particular candidates to a union council. A restrictive practice may be imposed on an industry. Agitation from coalminers led the Government to compel the Central Electricity Generating Authority to use more coal in the production of electricity, thereby increasing its cost. Restrictive practices increase costs of production without necessarily permanently increasing the number of workers employed in an industry. Unless the demand for the product is inelastic the higher price will reduce the quantity demanded and a reduction in output may lead to a contraction of the industry. Fear of the consequences of increasing automation in industry has had a great influence on the attitude of trade unions to problems of redundancy which the introduction of redundancy payments has not altogether allayed. To outsiders the adoption of restrictive practices by trade unions appears to be a short-sighted policy. Opposition to the employment of more progressive methods cannot be to the advantage of a trade union in the long run since the level of real wages depends ultimately on the size of the national income. The real interest of all trade unionists—and of everyone else too—must lie in doing everything possible to increase the national income and not to check its growth.

On occasions members of the general public have been inclined to ask whether a strike has been directed against employers or against the community. For example, more than once a railway strike has been threatened at holiday periods both at Christmas and in the summer, and this has sometimes resulted in intervention by the Government, generally to the advantage of the unions. It can only be supposed that the timing of these threats to strike has been selected with this aim in view. All strikes of transport workers cause great inconvenience and often great hardship to the rest of the community, though of course this is not likely to deter a union from calling a strike.

## Productivity bargaining

Most collective bargaining between trade unions and employers' associations has been in connection with wage rates, but more recently productivity bargaining has frequently been linked to wage bargaining. With the speeding up of technological progress restrictive labour practices appear in a more objectionable light as hindrances to progress. Attempts, therefore, have been made by the more efficient employers to make rises in wages conditional on certain restrictive practices being dropped, so that higher wages might be balanced by greater efficiency and higher productivity. In the past employers would have introduced new methods of production entirely on their own initiative. That they now find it necessary to engage in productivity bargaining is an indication of the increasing power of trade unions in present conditions. The fact that for most of the time since 1945 there has been a shortage of labour in many industries has made it all the more necessary for employers to use their labour as efficiently as possible. Productivity bargaining tends to be at workshop level rather than union level—though productivity clauses often find their way into national agreements—since many restrictive labour practices apply more particularly to individual firms than to an industry as a whole, and the development in recent times of workshop organisation, with the increasing importance of shop stewards, has made this type of bargaining possible.

Many restrictive labour practices have proved to be difficult to eradicate, especially excessive overtime, where the additional earnings derived from it have come to be regarded as part of the normal wage. Though a productivity agreement may considerably increase the basic wage, total earnings are unlikely to increase proportionately, but there will be a fall in the number of hours per week worked. It would seem, however, that a large proportion of workers do not value the extra leisure that a shorter working week brings. Nor is it easy to get rid of the practice of employing craftsmen's mates as this is traditional and not a privilege won by the unions. More efficient use of labour will cause a certain amount of redundancy and it was as a protection against this that many restrictive labour practices developed.

## Government of the unions

Superficially trade unions are democratically governed and organised. The basis of trade union structure is the local branch. Every member is entitled to attend branch meetings and the principle of "one man, one vote" is adhered to in electing representatives to the union executive. In practice, however, not more than 5% of members in Great Britain and only a little over 1% of members in the United States attend meetings, not in most cases from lack of desire to support their union but largely because the routine of day-to-day meetings is often dull and uninteresting and impinges upon members' leisure. The result is that trade union government tends to be oligarchic, control being in the hands of a few people—not necessarily the most level-headed. In recent times, however, it has seemed as if shop stewards, who are in closer touch with workers on the shop floor, have become more important when local disputes have arisen. Examples have occurred of shop stewards' organisations usurping functions more properly appertaining to union executives. One of the functions of the union branch is to elect representatives to district and national committees. The oligarchic character of trade union government is further emphasised by the system of "block" voting, representatives not voting as individuals but in proportion to the number of members they represent. Nevertheless, though most members appear to take little interest in union affairs, once a strike has been called they generally show great solidarity in their support of the executive.

## White collar workers

Recent developments in industrial techniques, including the more widespread application of automation, have made possible a huge expansion of production without increasing the number of manual workers employed in industry. For some time the number of manual workers has actually been declining, and so with the total labour force continuing to grow, the proportion of white collar workers has been increasing. In the United States white collar workers already outnumber manual workers, and it has been estimated that by the early 1980s a similar position will have been reached in Great

Britain. The following table shows how the number and proportion of white collar workers has increased in this country since 1921:

TABLE LXI

*White Collar Workers*

| | Number in thousands | | % of total | |
|---|---|---|---|---|
| | 1921 | 1961 | 1921 | 1961 |
| Employers and proprietors . . | 1,318 | 1,139 | 6·8 | 4·7 |
| Manual workers . . . | 13,920 | 14,020 | 72·0 | 59·3 |
| White collar workers . . . | 4,094 | 8,480 | 21·2 | 36·0 |
| Total working population . | 19,332 | 23,639 | 100·0 | 100·0 |

Source: G. S. Bain: *Trade Union Growth and Recognition* (HMSO).

During 1921–61 the number of white collar workers more than doubled with only a very slight increase during this period in the number of manual workers. Since 1931 the number of manual workers has declined by over 750,000.

What has been the effect of this new development on the trade union movement? Since a much smaller percentage of white collar workers are members of trade unions than manual workers the effect has been to check the expansion of trade union membership which over the past forty years has barely kept pace with the growth of the total labour force. More serious for trade unionism is that industries with shrinking labour forces, such as coal-mining and the railways, have been among those where the trade union spirit was strongest. During the years since 1948 the greatest growth was shown by education (teaching and ancillary services), in which the number more than doubled, and professional and business services, insurance, banking, finance and distribution, each with a 50% increase[1] and in all of which, with the possible exception of teaching, trade unionism was not particularly well developed.

There are several reasons why white collar workers have been less willing to take part in trade union activities than manual workers. M any of them have regarded the associations to which they belong as professional bodies with standards different from those of trade unions. Only quite recently, for example, have any white collar unions threatened to strike, and even fewer of them have taken part in one. Among the lower-paid white collar workers there is a high proportion of women, who, as has already been pointed out, are less disposed towards trade unionism th an men. At the other end of the salary scale a large number of men and some women are on the

[1] G. S. Bain, *op. cit.*, p. 16.

threshold of promotion to the lower rungs of management, with whose outlook they tend to sympathise. It is easier too to rouse enthusiasm for trade unionism when firms have a large number of employees. The average unit in retail distribution is small and this makes trade union organisation of shop assistants more difficult. In some occupations—particularly banking and insurance—the managements have formed their own staff associations and consequently have frowned upon independent employees' associations. Nevertheless, the National Union of Bank Employees doubled its membership between 1948 and 1964.

There are a number of reasons for the greater inclination towards trade union membership shown by white collar workers in recent years. With the equalisation of educational opportunity an increasing proportion of them come from homes where membership of an active trade union was a normal feature of an employee's life. The increased militancy of white collar workers is mainly due to the fact that in an inflationary period their members find their real incomes eroded to a greater extent than the wages of manual workers and this they have felt has been because of the greater power and militancy of the manual workers' unions. Some teachers and bank clerks have threatened to strike—and a few have even carried out their threats—and even the doctors on one occasion threatened to leave the National Health Service.

### Reform of the trade unions

As the prestige of the trade unions has declined, so the demand for their reform has increased.

In 1965 a Royal Commission under the chairmanship of Lord Donovan was set up to enquire into trade unions and employers' associations, its finding being published in 1968. Those people who had hoped that it would recommend a curtailment of the powers and privileges of the trade unions were disappointed. With regard to the legal protection of trade unionists who induce other workers to break their contracts of employment (that is, striking without giving notice of their intention to do so), a majority of the Commission favoured permitting the trade unions to continue to enjoy this privilege though only if they were registered. The Report too stressed the dual character of industrial relations that prevail in Great Britain at the present time—negotiations at national level and at factory floor level —resulting in a shift of authority from the union as such to local shop stewards. In wage negotiations this has often resulted in the national agreement being regarded merely as the minimum basis for local agreements for wage rates above the "national" level, resulting in greater wage drift and giving a further stimulus to inflation. The Donovan Commission, however, recommended that these local agreements should form the future basis of industrial relations in this country. A new body, to be known as the Industrial Relations Commission, it was suggested, should be set up to supervise these agreements which should in future be registered with the Department of Employment and Productivity (the former Ministry of Labour). This, it was hoped, would bring to an end the chaotic character that British industrial relations had acquired. The Commission also considered that many trade unions were too small to be effective (nearly 500 of them each had fewer than 10,000 members), and it recommended that where there was overlapping mergers of unions should be encouraged. The Commission rejected both the suggestion that unions should be prohibited from insisting on the "closed shop" and that there should be a secret ballot of members before a strike was called. To many people it appeared that the Commission was more concerned to maintain the *status quo* than to reform the unions.

In a White Paper, entitled *In Place of Strife: A Policy for Industrial Relations*, published in 1969, the Government outlined its proposals for the improvement of industrial relations. Not only was it proposed to reform collective bargaining and reduce the number of unofficial strikes but also (perhaps to make the proposals more palatable to the trade unions) suggestions were made for strengthening the unions. It was proposed to set up immediately a Commission on Industrial Relations (CIR), its main concern to be to improve collective bargaining procedures. The Secretary of State for Employment and Productivity was to have discretionary powers to require a "conciliation pause" of twenty-eight days in the case of unofficial or hastily-called strikes to permit negotiations to take place. An Industrial Board also was to be set up with power to impose fines on anyone acting contrary to an order issued by the Secretary. Employers were not to be allowed to obstruct workers who might wish to join trade unions and they must recognise and be willing to negotiate with the unions. Though many people do not think that the reforms go far enough, the White Paper is important in that it is the first recognition by the Government of the necessity to reform the trade unions.

## The trade unions and inflation

As already mentioned, Lord Beveridge stressed that the successful maintenance of full employment without inflation required the trade unions to adopt a more responsible attitude than they have sometimes displayed in the past. The trade unions have been faced by two difficulties. First, they have felt it to be their duty to protect the standard of living of their members against the effects of inflation, and they have tended to regard inflation as a phenomenon for which they were in no way responsible. Secondly, since the Second World War economic progress has been more rapid than at any previous time in history, and so again they have felt it to be their duty to ensure that their members should enjoy a rising standard of living. To overcome the first difficulty they have pressed for higher wages when prices have been rising, and to overcome the second they have still pressed for higher wages on the few occasions since 1945 when prices have been fairly steady. This has led to the development of the practice of making annual claims for wage increases. Then, too, wage demands of different unions have tended to be competitive: if one union has made a successful claim others have followed in order to maintain their relative positions with one another unchanged. Some economists, many politicians and most businessmen have pointed out that wage increases raise costs of production and so put up prices, thereby helping to keep in motion the inflationary spiral of wages and prices, impetus at one time coming from prices (a "cost–push" inflation) and at other times from wages (a "demand–pull" inflation),[1] but all the time the one influencing the other.

As a matter of principle the trade unions have always been opposed to suggestions of wage restraint. As long ago as 1951 Mr R. A. (now Lord) Butler suggested that wage increases should be related to increased productivity, but the TUC opposed the idea. Only very reluctantly did the trade unions agree in 1949—and then only for a limited period—to Sir Stafford Cripps's proposals for a wage "freeze." There was bitter opposition too to Mr Selwyn Lloyd's "pay pause" of 1962–63. Then in 1964 wage restraint appeared in the guise of a "prices and incomes" policy, and though wage restraint was forcibly imposed, the unions continued to show their detestation of the policy, merely biding their time until its relaxation.

Inflation is too great a problem and too wide in its extent and implications to be dealt with in this chapter: it must, therefore, be left for later consideration (*see* Chapter X).

## IV. SOCIAL SECURITY

### Trade Union "fringe" benefits

Some of the oldest craft unions to be established in Great Britain, as has already been pointed out, provided their members with some social security benefits—unemployment pay, sick pay, pensions—though of necessity on a small scale, and some craft unions continue to do so. In fact, one-fifth of the expenditure of the trade unions at the present day is devoted to "provident benefit" (*see* above, p. 254). Skilled workers until quite recent times were much better paid than

---

[1] A. Rice in *Economics of Trade Unions* argues against this view.

the unskilled and so could afford to pay the small additional contribution, whereas the unskilled workers who joined the large general and industrial unions during the period of "New Unionism" could not. Unable to offer these benefits to their members these unions declared social security to be a matter for the State, a responsibility which during the past sixty years the State has accepted to an increasing extent.

Consequently, British trade unions, unlike their American counterparts, in trying to raise the standard of living of their members, have tended mainly to concentrate on demands on higher wages rather than "fringe" benefits. Nevertheless, during the ten years 1958–68 the monetary value of "fringe" benefits offered by British employers more than doubled. American trade unions, on the other hand, have often been at least equally concerned to secure "fringe" benefits for their members—pensions, life assurance, sick pay, medical attention, etc. To employees the advantage is that these benefits are not taxable as are wages and salaries; to employers the advantage is that such benefits tend to reduce labour turnover; but there is the economic disadvantage that they are inclined to reduce mobility of labour.

## Voluntary efforts

A social service has been defined as one that "provides for those personal and economic needs which arise out of income insecurity and handicaps of poverty."[1] Neither the State nor the local authorities did very much to help people in distress until the twentieth century. Voluntary efforts to provide social services, however, date back to the seventeenth century and possibly earlier. These were of two types. First, there were schemes for mutual aid where a group of people got together for reasons of good fellowship (hence the term "friendly society") to help one another in times of trouble. Contributions were made to a common fund out of which help could be provided in case of sickness or on the death of a member, in the latter case as much to provide for a respectable funeral (hence the name "burial society") as to assist the widow. Many friendly societies, of the type known as "accumulating" societies, accepted deposits and members were encouraged to save, either for a particular purpose or for precautionary reasons. Inability to pay even a modest contribution debarred the very poor from joining friendly societies and this gave rise to the second type of voluntary activity—philanthropic action, the rich helping the poor. The eighteenth century was the great age of philanthropy and it saw the foundation of a very large number of charitable institutions.

---

[1] W. Hagenbuch, *Social Economics*, p. 179.

## Social security and the State

National insurance, organised by the Government, was first tried out by some of the German states in the late nineteenth century, with insurance against accidents and sickness in 1884 and widows' pensions in 1911, though in all cases the benefits were very modest. Apart from benefits paid under the *Workmen's Compensation Acts*, the first of which was passed in 1880, little was done by the State for social security in Great Britain until 1908 when the *Old Age Pensions Act* provided a small non-contributory pension to people of limited means at the age of 70. From this small beginning the present system of social security has developed. In 1911 there followed the *National Insurance Act* associated with the name of Lloyd George. This Act, which provided for the compulsory insurance against sickness of all lower-paid workers, introduced the tripartite system of contribution by employees, employers and the State. Friendly societies, "approved" for the purpose, acted as agents for the scheme. The Act of 1911 provided unemployment pay for workers in only a few industries, so that, although the Act covered nearly 14 million people against sickness, only $2\frac{1}{2}$ million were covered against unemployment. Gradually the British system of social insurance was expanded to cover contributory pensions at the age of 65, unemployment pay and widows' pensions (introduced in 1929 by Churchill). In 1937 salaried workers, provided their incomes did not exceed £400 per annum, were permitted to join the scheme if they wished. Lord (then Sir William) Beveridge in the late 1930s had been working out the details for a more ambitious scheme, and in 1942 he published his *Report on Social Insurance and Allied Services*, generally known as the Beveridge Plan. This recommended a more comprehensive health service, with more generous benefit payments, together with a number of new benefits including family allowances, maternity and funeral grants, all to be paid for by higher contributions.

The scheme of social security introduced in the mid 1940s was covered by a group of Acts passed during 1945–48—after the setting up in 1944 of the Ministry of National Insurance—family allowances in 1945, the National Health Service, National Insurance and insurance against industrial injuries by three Acts in 1946 and National Assistance in 1948. All came into force in 1948. The scheme introduced by these Acts, though very similar to the Beveridge Plan, differed from it in one important respect. Lord Beveridge had wanted national insurance to be based on genuine insurance principles, with benefits related to contributions, but the Act of 1946 did not adhere strictly to this principle, benefits being more generous than the rate of contributions warranted. The health service was to be "free" and family allowances too were to be financed by the Exchequer, as also was National Assistance, which was made available to those in need who were not eligible for benefit under the new scheme or in cases where benefits were considered to be inadequate. Benefits included unemployment pay, sick pay, maternity benefit, death grant, widows' allowances and pensions, and retirement pensions. The new scheme was more comprehensive than any previous one and was intended eventually to cover the whole community, rich and poor alike, including the self-employed.

Since the introduction of the scheme in 1948 the most important innovation has been the inclusion of income-related benefits. Under the *National Insurance Act* of 1959 a graduated pension scheme, with increased contributions, was introduced to operate from 1961. This provided for pensions of up to half average earnings (that is, wages *plus* overtime) during the period immediately before retirement. A more ambitious scheme, expected to operate from 1972, was announced in 1968. Under this scheme most workers would receive half pay on retirement, and during sickness and unemployment. Contributions would be in the form of a percentage deduction from earnings. If adopted such a scheme would be a complete departure from Lord Beveridge's original proposals, *viz.* for the State to provide a minimum standard of living for the old, the sick and the unemployed leaving individuals to decide for themselves whether to make provision for anything above this minimum. The drawback to high rates of unemployment pay is that it may act as a disincentive to work. Such a scheme too might discourage saving. Apart from the introduction of wages-related benefits, the only other changes have been increases in benefits and contributions, mainly to offset the fall in the value of money since the inception of the scheme. In 1966 a Ministry of Social Security[1] was set up to take over the functions of the former Ministry of Pensions and National Insurance and the National Assistance Board. Under this Act a minimum subsistence level was guaranteed over and above the amount to be paid for rent, and supplementary pensions were awarded to those below this minimum. The effect was to add a million to the number of people receiving supplementary benefits. Then in 1967 it was decided to give greater help to families with a large number of children in order to reduce poverty which was found mainly among such people.

## Social security in Western Europe

There are three main differences between the British system of social security and those of other West European countries. In Great Britain, the administration of social security is the responsibility of the Government through the Department of Health and Social Security, whereas in most European countries separate bodies have been set up to administer social security. In Great Britain one

---

[1] In 1968 this ministry was merged with the Ministry of Health to form the Department of Health and Social Security.

contribution covers all benefits instead of there being separate contributions for each benefit. The British scheme too covers everyone, whereas in some countries there are separate schemes for different occupational groups, with a distinction especially between manual and white collar workers. Continental schemes too are much more wage-related than the British system, particularly in regard to benefits, with the result that benefits rise as wages rise, thereby avoiding the time-lag that occurs in Great Britain. It is difficult to compare benefits in different countries just as it is difficult to compare different standards of living. However, it can be said that, although lower-paid workers do rather better in Great Britain than in other countries in Western Europe, standards of social security on balance are somewhat higher on the Continent than in this country. If family allowances are excluded Great Britain spends a smaller percentage of its national income on social security than Germany, Luxembourg or the Netherlands.

## The financing of social security

Most people in Great Britain today have come to favour a state-run system of social security. There is less agreement, however, on how such a scheme should be financed. As already mentioned, Lord Beveridge envisaged a scheme based on sound insurance principles and so really deserving to be called national insurance. Commercial insurance companies conduct their business on the principle of the pooling of risks that are calculable, premiums being related to benefits so that over a period the amount paid into their various funds is sufficient to cover the payments they have to make. In commercial insurance a certain premium entitles the insured in prescribed circumstances to a precise benefit. National insurance, however, is not conducted in this way. Not only do beneficiaries make contributions but employers also are called upon to contribute as well as the State. Although when benefits are improved contributions also have been increased, those already in receipt of pensions have had them increased at no increased cost to themselves. If benefits were actuarially related to contributions of both employers and employees they would have to be reduced to no more than half their present scale. From the start it has been more a scheme of social security rather than of social insurance.

Lord Beveridge considered that social security benefits, such as retirement pensions, sick pay and unemployment pay, should not be greater than necessary so as to ensure that the standard of living of recipients should not fall below subsistence level, but no more, in order to encourage those who wanted something better than this to continue to make some additional provision for themselves. What is subsistence level cannot easily be defined and with the passing of time ideas changed. For upwards of twenty years after the introduction of the present scheme in Great Britain it was found necesssary to supplement the retirement pension of some 2 million people by National Assistance payments related to their needs and financial circumstances, thereby destroying, it has been asserted, the whole basis of social insurance.[1] Even so, social workers calculated that more than half a million people who might have been receiving supplementary payments were not doing so, mainly because national assistance was regarded by many people as a relic of the old Poor Law. The Act of 1967 tried to remove this stigma by bringing national assistance within the scope of the Ministry of Social Security. The cost to the Exchequer of social insurance and the social services has increased steeply since 1945—much more than can be accounted for by the fall in the value of money (*see* Chapter X). A tendency to make excessive demands on the National Health Service, especially for minor and often trivial complaints, leading to many doctors being overworked, was discernible almost from the start and led to the imposition of a nominal prescription (recoverable by those in receipt of National Assistance), and, although this considerably eased the situation, it was for some reason removed in 1964. It is an important insurance principle that an insured person should never receive compensation greater than the value of the loss he has suffered. This principle might well be applied to national schemes of social security. For example, it should clearly never be to the advantage of any beneficiary not to work, but occasional cases have come to light of an unemployed man with a large family being in this situation. However, the more generous scale of family allowances introduced in 1967 should remove this anomaly.

By 1967 according to the more enlightened ideas of the time there was still a considerable amount of poverty in Great Britain, mainly among low-income workers with large families and among old people. At relatively low cost—an estimated £13 million—it would have been possible to raise the standard of living of all those in need to a modest level, a course advocated by many people both inside and outside of Parliament. The main objection to this course appears to have been that it would require the application of a "means test," a phrase still carrying the unpleasant connotation it acquired in the 1930s, although actually employed regularly (but without the term being used) since 1948 in connection with National Assistance. Without some sort of means test benefits are improved for all people entitled to receive them with the result that a large number of people who are not in need receive additions to their incomes whereas the small number who really are in need receive insufficient, in fact leaving more than half of these people still below the officially accepted poverty line—at a cost of over £300 million to the Exchequer, though some of this would be recovered in higher income tax

[1] W. Hagenbuch, *op. cit.*, p. 252.

receipts. Without a means test poor families gain little. Those on retirement pensions gain whether they are rich or poor, though the higher the rate of taxation a pensioner pays the smaller will be his net increase. Thus, too much is given to those who are not in need and too little to those who really are in need. No government has yet found it possible to restrict increases in national security benefits to those who really need them, although there is support for such a change from members of all three political parties. Some people, however, oppose the relating of benefits to need on account of the arbitrary way in which need would probably have to be assessed, so creating other anomalies. They believe that since retirement pensions and family allowances are taxable this will ensure that the poor will derive more benefit from them than the well-to-do. Money payments to the poor, however, do not overcome one of the causes of poverty—the mis-spending of money. Wherever possible, therefore, it is preferable to give benefits in kind as in the National Health Service and with welfare foods, school meals and housing subsidies.

At the present time, then, social security is partly financed by contributions (from employees, employers and the State), partly from local rates, and partly from general taxation, the State being responsible for over two-thirds of the total cost, and contributions less than one quarter.

## Some economic considerations

A national scheme of security must be regarded as being complementary to a progressive system of taxation in reducing inequality of income. In spite of social security benefits being open to all it is nevertheless the people in the lower income groups who on balance derive most advantage. To the extent, therefore, that inequality of income is reduced, economic welfare will be increased, provided that the size of the national income is not thereby adversely affected. In support of redistribution of income by means of taxation and a scheme of social security the principle of diminishing marginal utility can be invoked, since transfers from the rich to the poor reduce income satisfaction to the rich to a less degree than they increase it to the poor.

In fact, the effect of having a comprehensive scheme of social security should have a favourable influence on the national income. The aim in establishing the National Health Service was to provide as good a medical and hospital service as possible that would be available to everyone. It was thought that previous to its establishment a large number of people had often neglected to see a doctor for fear of the expense it might entail and many had continued at work when not really fit to do so because absence from work meant a serious loss of earnings. The purpose of a health service is to raise the general standard of health and aid recovery from illness. This should result in a generally higher standard of physical fitness and in consequence greater efficiency, and so might be expected to assist the maximisation of the national income.

The pursuit of a policy of full employment reduces the amount to be paid in unemployment benefit since widespread mass unemployment is not expected to occur. Economic progress, however, often requires labour to be mobile and is liable, therefore, to cause structural unemployment, the incidence of which is eased when unemployment pay is available, especially when supplemented by redundancy payments.

The more generous the benefits under a scheme of social security the less affected will be the net incomes of many people in a trade recession. Total purchasing power, and therefore total demand, will fall by a lesser amount in any future recession in relation to the extent of unemployment than would be the case if no social security payments were available. This means that in the downswing of a trade recession the multiplier effect will be reduced and production will remain at a higher level so that the recession will be less severe than otherwise. It also means, however, that the multiplier effect will be less too in the upswing from a recession, so that if a very serious recession should after all occur, the government of the day will be called upon to make even greater efforts to stimulate recovery.

In France the granting of family allowances—in that country on a particularly generous scale—was part of a deliberate policy to check a decline in population that had already set in. From the change in population trends since the Second World War in France it would appear that this policy has been successful. Though this motive may have been in the minds of some people when family allowances were introduced into Great Britain in 1945, it is no longer the main motive. When family allowances were increased in 1967 it was primarily for the purpose of reducing poverty which was more prevalent in large families.

On the financial side the employers' contribution to social security is in effect a tax on the employment of labour, which Lord Beveridge thought it was difficult to justify. So long as full employment is maintained its incidence falls on employers. In France the cost of social security bears more heavily on employers than it does in this country. With an ageing population, however, the cost of retirement pensions becomes increasingly heavy, but if measured in relation to the national income this burden may fall if a reasonable rate of economic growth can be maintained. Between 1956 and 1968 the cost to the State of social security (National Insurance, National Assistance, Family allowances) increased from just over £1,000 million to £3,146 million, in addition to over £1,500 million for the National Health Service. Just over half the expenditure on social security is devoted to retirement pensions, the number of people in receipt of these pensions being expected to reach 7 million by 1970.

### RECOMMENDATIONS FOR FURTHER READING

H. Pelling: *A History of British Trade Unionism* (Penguin Books).

A. Rees: *The Economics of Trade Unions.* (Mainly concerned with American experience, but the general discussion is also relevant to Great Britain.) (Nisbet/Cambridge University Press.)

F. Beasley and S. Parkinson: *Unions in Prosperity* (Institute of Economic Affairs—Hobart Papers, No. 6.)

HMSO: *Industrial Relations Handbook.* Research Papers commissioned by the Royal Commission on Trade Unions and Employers' Associations, more especially No. 4, *Productivity Bargaining and Restrictive Labour Practices;* No. 5, J. Hughes: *Trade Union Structure and Government;* No. 6, G. S. Bain: *Trade Union Growth and Recognition*; White Paper: *In Place of Strife: A Policy for Industrial Relations* (Cmnd. 3888).

*For social security:*

W. Hagenbuch: *Social Economics* (mainly Chs. 7–10) (Nisbet/Cambridge University Press). Publications of the Ministry of Health and Social Security.

### QUESTIONS

1. "In times of full employment the power of trade unions is so great that they become a serious hindrance to economic progress." Discuss this statement.

2. How do you account for trade unionism being less developed among (*a*) women, (*b*) white collar workers? For what reasons might trade unionism be expected to expand among these two groups of workers?

3. "The organisation and operation of trade unions in Great Britain is only superficially democratic." Critically examine this statement.

4. Argue the case for and against operating a system of social security according to strict insurance principles.

5. Outline the main features of the British system of industrial relations and show in what ways this system is inappropriate for an economy undergoing rapid economic change. (Bournemouth.)

6. Write an essay on: The changes in trade union power and influence since the General Strike. (Huddersfield.)

7. "Trade union activity takes place in the shop" (George Woodcock). Discuss this statement with special reference to recent discussion on trade union structure. (Leeds.)

8. Argue the case that trade union support for restrictive labour practices is against the best interests of their members. (U.L.C.I.)

9. Discuss (*a*) the objectives of British trade unions, and (*b*) the effectiveness of the policies and practices devised to achieve them. (U.L.C.I.)

# PART THREE

# MONETARY PROBLEMS

## CHAPTER IX

# BANKING AND FINANCE

## I. THE BANKING SECTOR

**Development of banking**

The practice of banking developed very slowly. The first bankers in England were the London goldsmiths, although for a long time banking was only a sideline to their main business. It was not until the great industrial expansion in the North and Midlands in the second half of the eighteenth century that banking began to develop outside the London area. Between 1750 and 1821 the number of provincial banks increased from 12 to nearly 800. All of these were private banks, often at first being merely sidelines to the businesses of merchants or manufacturers.

Next came the development of joint-stock banks. Founded in 1694, the Bank of England was the first joint-stock bank to be established in England and it retained this unique position for over a century. In Scotland, however, the Bank of Scotland, founded only a year later, was but one of a number of joint-stock banks. In the trade depression of 1815–22 the joint-stock banks proved themselves to be stronger than the private banks with the result that few joint-stock banks failed whereas over 200 private banks did so. This gave a great impetus to the development of joint-stock banking.

An Act of 1826 had permitted the establishment of joint-stock banks in England only beyond a radius of sixty-five miles from London, but in 1833 this restriction was removed, and joint-stock banking then developed so rapidly that within the space of a few years more than a hundred new joint-stock banks were established in England. A further stimulus to banking came in 1858 when banks were allowed the privilege of limited liability.

In the development of banking in this country the next stage was the emergence of the large joint-stock bank with many branches, achieved partly by the opening of new branches and partly by the amalgamation of banks. In consequence, during the last thirty years of the nineteenth century, there was a considerable decline in the total number of banks in England, especially private banks. By 1913 the number of joint-stock banks had fallen to 37 and the number of private banks to 60, but whereas the joint-stock banks averaged 165

branches each, the private banks averaged fewer than 7. The amalgamation movement continued until the "Big Five" English banks had
been brought into being, each with a country-wide network of
branches, with only four of the Scottish banks independent of them.
A Committee of Enquiry, set up in 1918, when further amalgamations
were contemplated, recommended that there should be no more bank
mergers without the prior consent of the Treasury, and it soon became known that further amalgamations between large banks was
not favoured.

This remained the situation in banking for some fifty years, with
England having five very large commercial banks together with three
of moderate size, with a total of eleven members of the London
Bankers' Clearing House. In the late 1960s the amalgamation movement was renewed when the District Bank became associated with the
National Provincial. Then early in 1968 the National Provincial and
the Westminster decided upon a merger which was not opposed and
the National Westminster Bank came into being  A merger, however,
of Barclays, Lloyds and Martins was refused, although Barclays was
permitted to take over Martins (*see* p. 128 above). Thus the "Big
Five" became the "Big Four":

| Banks | Total deposits (1968) | No. of branches (1968) |
|---|---|---|
| | £ million | |
| 1. Barclays/Martins . . | 3,037 | 3,300 |
| 2. National Westminster . | 2,924 | 3,000 |
| 3. Midland . . . | 2,186 | 3,400 |
| 4. Lloyds . . . | 1,980 | 2,200 |

The bank amalgamation movement of 1968 was sparked off by a
recommendation of the Prices and Incomes Board that banking in
Great Britain could be conducted more efficiently if there were fewer
and larger units. Economies of scale would include a reduction in
competing branches in less populated areas and more economic use of
computers. In the international field size has become even more
important, and the Barclays/Lloyds/Martins combine would have
ranked fourth—or second if Barclays DCO was included—in the
world to the largest three American banks—the Bank of America
(California), the Chase Manhattan (New York) and the First National
City Bank of New York, if comparison is based on total deposits.
With the increasing size of industrial firms and the increasing scale
of their demands on banks, larger banks to deal with them seem
necessary.

## Types of bank

In Great Britain at the present day banking business of one kind or another is undertaken by four different kinds of bank—savings banks, commercial banks, merchant banks and the central bank. At one time their functions were more distinctive than they are today. During the past twenty years there has been a tendency for each one of them—with the exception of the Bank of England—to widen their activities, so that their functions now overlap to a greater extent than ever before.

*Savings banks.* The main business of these banks, of which there are about eighty, is to accept deposits. They were established to encourage thrift among people with small incomes, but though some people make use of them for short-term saving for holidays, rates, electricity and gas bills, etc., most of their depositors use them to build up reserves of savings. Business accounts, however, are not permitted. The leading bank of this type is the Post Office Savings Bank, which handles more than two-thirds of this kind of banking business. There are over 20,000 post offices distributed throughout the country that conduct savings bank business. In contrast, the trustee savings banks are mostly small and local, only few having more than one or two branches, the average number being seventeen. The statutory rate of interest paid by savings banks is $2\frac{1}{2}\%$. During the long period of "cheap money," 1932–45, and especially of "ultra-cheap money," 1945–47, some of the smaller trustee savings banks found themselves in difficulties and a number of them closed down. In the case of the Post Office Savings Bank the Government guarantees both the interest and repayment. During the last ten years, however, "dear money" has been the rule, and the trustee savings banks have opened Special Investment Departments offering a higher rate of interest on deposits (up to a maximum deposit of £5,000) but subject to notice of withdrawal. Since 1966 a somewhat similar facility has been available to depositors of the Post Office Savings Bank who have at least £50 in their ordinary savings accounts. Deposits in the Special Investment Departments of the trustee savings banks increased from £283 million in 1956 to over £1,100 million in 1966. Depositors of savings banks enjoy the privilege that the first £15 of their deposits are free of income tax. Since 1964 the trustee savings banks have been allowed to offer their customers current accounts and the use of cheques, and in 1968 the Post Office introduced a giro service. The investment of the funds of both the Post Office Savings Bank and the trustee savings banks is in the hands of the National Debt Commissioners. In 1968 the trustee savings banks collaborated in the establishment of a unit investment trust.

*Commercial banks.* These banks undertake a great variety of banking business, but the English ones no longer issue their own bank-notes. Before bank deposits, subject to transfer by cheque, became the principal means of payment, the issue of bank-notes was an important and profitable function of commercial banks. Nowadays their main functions comprise the acceptance of deposits usually subject to notice of withdrawal, allowing customers to open current accounts on which they can draw cheques, lending to customers by overdraft, loan account or personal loan, and accepting and discounting bills of exchange. Commercial banks also undertake many other useful services on behalf of their customers, such as buying or selling stock exchange securities for them, acting as trustees or executors, transacting foreign exchange business, providing safe custody for valuables, etc. In recent years the English commercial banks have considerably increased their hire purchase interests. In addition to lending to finance companies that specialise in this kind of business and offering their customers personal loans as an alternative to dealing with a finance company, all the large commercial banks now have their own hire purchase companies as subsidiaries. In 1967, however, the Prices and Incomes Board recommended that these banks should provide this service directly rather than through subsidiaries. Some of the commercial banks have also gone into the credit card business, either directly (for example, Barclays) or indirectly through a subsidiary (the Westminster), while others such as the Midland and Lloyds have been content to issue bankers' cards guaranteeing the holders' cheques up to a stated amount. The commercial banks too have entered the unit trust field, Lloyds directly, and others by association with existing unit trusts. Another recent change in commercial bank practice has been the granting of loans to business firms for longer periods than was once customary.

*Merchant banks.* The main business of the merchant banks is still in connection with the discount markets (*see* pp. 294–99 below). Often known as accepting houses, since the accepting of bills of exchange was at one time their primary function, these banks owe their name to the fact that their banking business developed out of their trading activities which gave them the opportunity to know something of the financial standing of foreign merchants. As London became the financial centre of the world many of them found it advantageous to have their head offices there. They have frequently too in the past engaged in large-scale lending to governments. The decline in the use of trade bills reduced the demand for acceptance business and in consequence the number of merchant banks declined, while those that continued to operate have tended to develop ordinary banking business in competition with the commercial banks.

*Central banks.* At the present day there is no country in the world of any importance that does not have a central bank, the primary function of which is to accept responsibility for carrying out monetary policy. This is rarely, however, nowadays decided upon by the central bank alone, for a central bank must work closely with the Government. Many central banks have been nationalised, as have been both the Bank of England and the Bank of France. In order to be able to carry out its main function a central bank must have power to control the credit policy of the commercial banks.[1]

## The balance sheet of a commercial bank

The structure of the balance sheet of a commercial bank is best seen from a study of the combined balance sheets of the London

TABLE LXII

*Combined Balance Sheet of the London Clearing Banks*

|  | 1968 | 19— * |
|---|---|---|
|  | £ million | £ million |
| *Liabilities* |  |  |
| Deposits    .    .    .    . | 10,674 |  |
|  |  |  |
| *Assets* |  |  |
| Coin, notes and balances with Bank of England .    .    . | 875 |  |
| Money at call and short notice . | 1,319 |  |
| Bills discounted    .    .    . | 1,216 |  |
| Special Deposits    .    .    . | 194 |  |
| Investments    .    .    .    . | 1,430 |  |
| Advances to customers    .    . | 5,000 |  |

The assets and liabilities in this table do not balance, as some items have been omitted and some of the figures quoted are approximations.

\* This column can be completed with the latest figures.

clearing banks. The principal liability of a bank is deposits.[2] First in the list of assets in order of liquidity is actual *cash* in the form of notes and coin. A bank must always be able to pay cash on demand to all those entitled to ask for it. Experience has shown that the present cash ratio of 8% is ample for this purpose. The item next in order of liquidity is *money at call and short notice*. This comprises short-term loans—repayable on demand or at not more than fourteen days' notice—to members of the market. The item *bills discounted* shows the amount of the bills that the banks have discounted, 53% being Treasury bills and 47% trade bills. These three items comprise the more liquid assets of a bank and it is current practice not to let them fall below 28% of the total. This liquidity ratio is now of

[1] The work of the Bank of England is considered below, pp. 291–94.
[2] Table LXXXVII, p. 351, shows how bank deposits have increased in recent years.

greater importance than the 8 % cash ratio, for it is this that provides the effective restraint on the credit policy of a commercial bank, since any fall in its cash can be made good at the expense of the other liquid assets. *Special deposits* represent the amount compulsorily deposited at the Bank of England in accordance with the central banks' demands. The less liquid assets are *investments* (two-thirds

TABLE LXIII
*Special Deposits*

|  | £ million |
|---|---|
| 1959 | — |
| 1960 | 74 |
| 1961 | 174 |
| 1962 | 159 |
| 1963 | — |
| 1964 | — |
| 1965 | 56 |
| 1966 | 137 |
| 1967 | 194 |
| 1968 | 194 |

in government stocks with less than five years to run) and *advances*. Table LXIV (p. 291) shows the distribution of bank advances.

## The volume of bank deposits

Bank deposits, subject to withdrawal by cheque, form 80% of the money used in Great Britain today. Bank deposits mostly have their origin in bank loans, most loans being by way of overdraft. An overdraft is nothing more than permission from a banker to draw cheques up to an agreed amount in excess of that standing to a customer's credit. Thus, cheques drawn against an overdraft increase the credit balance of the payee with the result that total bank deposits will increase since the drawer's balance cannot be reduced if his account is overdrawn. The importance of bank deposits lies in the fact that they form the principal kind of purchasing power. Thus, bank loans create deposits and increase the supply of money. A curtailment of bank lending on the other hand will reduce bank deposits and the supply of money.

The main restriction on the power of the banks to create deposits comes from the Bank of England and the necessity of the commercial banks to maintain a 28% liquidity ratio. If this liquidity ratio is to be maintained a bank cannot expand its lending unless it increases its

TABLE LXIV
*Distribution of Bank Advances*
(London clearing banks)

| | 1968 | 19—* |
|---|---|---|
| Agriculture . . . . | 446 | |
| Mining and quarrying . . | 23 | |
| Chemicals . . . . . | 102 | |
| Iron, steel and engineering . . | 939 | |
| Cotton . . . . . } Wool . . . . . | 195 | |
| Food, drink and tobacco . . | 205 | |
| Construction . . . . | 305 | |
| Public utilities . . . . | 52 | |
| Transport . . . . | 107 | |
| Shipping and shipbuilding . . | 82 | |
| Retail trade . . . . | 316 | |
| Hire purchase finance companies . | 78 | |
| Other financial . . . . | 355 | |
| Local Government Authorities . | 36 | |
| Personal and professional . . | 1,214 | |
| Other . . . . . | 534 | |
| Total . . . . | 4,989 | |

* For the latest figures.

more liquid assets. If its liquidity ratio is in danger of falling below
28% it must take action to raise it by reducing its advances.

### The Bank of England

The Bank of England is a central bank. The primary function of
this type of bank is to carry out the monetary policy decided by a
country's monetary authorities. Most central banks have been
established specifically for this purpose but the Bank of England,
though founded mainly as a source of borrowing for William III's
government, only gradually accepted the role of central bank. By
the middle of the nineteenth century it was acting as lender of last
resort—an essential function of a central bank—and then it came to
influence the level of bank deposits through its two instruments of
monetary policy—bank rate to make borrowing generally dearer or
cheaper, and open market operations to increase or decrease the cash
basis of the commercial banks and to influence the long-term or short-
term rate of interest. The Bank of England acts as "bankers' bank"
not only to the English and Scottish commercial banks but also to
a total of upwards of seventy banks, including many overseas banks.
By buying or selling securities in the open market the Bank of England
can influence the reserves of the commercial banks held with it and

which these banks regard as cash since withdrawals in cash can be made at any time. The Bank of England regularly intervenes in the market to offset the effects of changes in the public's demand for cash. Heavy tax payments during January–March would otherwise greatly reduce the cash reserves of the commercial banks. Since 1921 the Bank of England has been the sole bank of issue in England.

By the *Bank Charter Act* of 1844 the Bank of England has to publish weekly separate balance sheets—the Bank Return—for its issue and banking departments. The following is a typical return for the issue department:

TABLE LXV
*The Bank Return: Issue Department*
Wednesday, 24th January 1968
*Liabilities*

|  | 1968 | 19— * |
|---|---|---|
|  | £ million | £ million |
| Notes issued: |  |  |
| In circulation . . . . | 2,989 |  |
| In Banking Department . . | 61½ |  |
| Total . . . . | 3,050½ |  |

*Assets*

|  | 1968 | 19— * |
|---|---|---|
|  | £ million | £ million |
| Government debt . . . | — |  |
| Government securities . . | 11 |  |
| Other securities . . . | 3,038¾ |  |
| Coin (other than gold) . . | ¼ |  |
| Fiduciary issue . . . . | 3,050 |  |
| Gold coin and bullion . . | ½ |  |
| Total . . . . | 3,050½ |  |

* This column can be completed with the latest figures.

Since 1937 two important changes have taken place—the huge increase in the note issue, and especially the fiduciary issue, and the almost complete disappearance of gold from the assets of the Issue Department. The country's gold reserves are now held by the Treasury's Exchange Equalisation Account.

The most interesting things to note in the return for the Banking Department are changes in Special Deposits, Discounts and Advances (showing the extent of assistance given by the Bank of England

TABLE LXVI
*The Bank Return: Banking Department*
Wednesday, 24th January 1968
*Liabilities*

|  | 1968 | 196–* |
|---|---|---|
|  | £ million | £ million |
| Proprietors' capital . . . | 14½ |  |
| Rest . . . . | 3½ |  |
| Public deposits . . . | 12 |  |
| Other deposits: |  |  |
| Bankers' deposits . . | 285½ |  |
| Other accounts . . | 122 |  |
| Special Deposits . . | 216 |  |
| Total . . . | 653½ |  |

*Assets*

|  | 1968 | 196–* |
|---|---|---|
|  | £ million | £ million |
| Government securities . . | 484 |  |
| Other securities: |  |  |
| (a) Discounts and advances . | 31 |  |
| (b) Other securities . . | 77 |  |
| Notes . . . | 61½ |  |
| Gold and silver coin . . | 1 |  |
| Total . . . | 653½ |  |

* This column can be completed with the latest figures.

to the money market as lender of last resort) and Securities (which shows the extent of the Bank of England's intervention in the open market). As lender of last resort the Bank of England either lends to members of the money market or rediscounts for them bills which conform to its "eligibility" rule. In addition it operates in the market at what is sometimes known as "the back door" through its own broker, the "Special Buyer."

Since 1945 the Bank of England, the Treasury and the Chancellor of the Exchequer have worked closely together in the formulation of monetary policy. New instruments of policy, such as the Directive and Special Deposits, have been added to the armoury of the monetary authorities, and fiscal policy—the budget surplus, variations in purchase taxes and other excise duties, and hire purchase regulations—have been called upon to supplement purely monetary weapons. By means of "requests" to the commercial banks and some other financial institutions the Bank of England can make known to them the lending policy it considers that they should adopt. By means of Special Deposits the cash basis of the commercial banks can be reduced or raised and their credit policy be influenced accordingly.[1] Special Deposits are a less cumbersome instrument than open-market operations for this purpose. Unlike Bankers' Deposits, Special Deposits bear interest. The Bank of England intervenes in both the securities market and the discount market. Operations are undertaken on the stock exchange nowadays by the Bank of England through the government broker mainly to influence interest rates; its operations in the discount market are through the Special Buyer.

## II. THE MONEY AND DISCOUNT MARKETS

### Financial markets

Since London is the financial centre of the country the main financial markets are to be found there.

There are three pairs of important financial markets in London at the present day, the two members of each pair being closely connected with one another. The first pair comprises the money and discount (or bill) markets which are so intimately related that they are often regarded as a single market. The second pair consists of the capital market and the securities market (that is, the stock exchange), which are complementary to one another. Since borrowers can—and often do—switch their activities from the discount market to the securities market or vice versa, there is in fact a close connection, therefore, between all four of these markets. The third pair of financial markets comprises the foreign exchange market and the London gold market, also very closely linked together, but consideration of these two markets falls outside the scope of this chapter (*see* Chapter XII.) The geographical extent of these six markets varies considerably. The securities market and the gold market are the only ones that are localised in particular buildings, and even they are linked by telephone to dealers outside; the firms doing business in the money and discount markets are all to be found in a small area in the City of London; the capital market is much wider in extent and indeed for some activities world-wide; business too in the foreign exchange market is world-wide, the most important dealings being made between one centre and another by telephone.

### The London discount market

Reference has already been made to the practice of the commercial banks of lending "at call or short notice" to the money market, and of the Bank of England acting as "lender of last resort" to this

---

[1] The work of the Bank of England in connection with monetary policy is considered in Chapter X and its foreign exchange business in Chapter XII.

market. In the strictest sense the money market is a market for very short-term loans, the length of term varying from day-to-day loans (repayment of which can be required almost on demand) to loans for periods of up to fourteen days. More often, however, the money market is given a wider connotation to include also the work of the discount market. The business of the discount houses in these two markets is so closely integrated that it does not seem unreasonable to regard both activities as appertaining to a single market.

The members of the discount market comprise the English and Scottish commercial banks, the London agents or branches of some overseas banks, the twelve discount houses, the seventeen merchant banks that are members of the Accepting Houses Committee, and the Bank of England in its capacity as lender of last resort. The London Discount Houses Association comprises twelve large companies. At one time all of them were private firms, and as recently as 1945 only three were public companies—Alexanders, the National Discount Company and the Union Discount Company of London. By 1947, however, all twelve had become public companies. They require more capital than they formerly did to cover the higher costs and greater risks associated with their newer activities, for the holding of government bonds causes more capital to be locked up for longer periods of time than is the case with bills, and the prices of such bonds are subject to wide fluctuation. During 1946–47, therefore, all the discount houses increased their capital.

## The work of the discount market

The discounting of bills of exchange is the primary function of a discount house, which obtains the funds required for this purpose mainly and normally by borrowing on short terms at a low rate of interest from the English and Scottish commercial banks.

The bill of exchange became a common means of payment between merchants, especially among those engaged in foreign trade, because it often enabled the creditor to avoid having to wait for the term of the bill to expire before being paid. If the bill could be discounted it meant that the merchant could use it to finance the transaction. A bill of exchange, however, is negotiable only if the merchant on whom it is drawn is known to be credit-worthy. Some firms, of course, are known and respected throughout the world while others, though highly thought of within the borders of their own countries, may be almost unknown abroad. It was to overcome this difficulty that some of the larger merchants, with special trading knowledge of the areas in which these lesser-known merchants operated, began to add their own acceptances to their bills, thereby increasing their negotiability by in effect guaranteeing that payment would be met. Bills rendered negotiable as a result of being accepted by a reputable acceptor

could be offered for discounting to a discount house which on selling
the bill would add its own endorsement. For this service they charged
a small commission. Such a bill, complying with the Bank of
England's "eligibility" rule, could be rediscounted at bank rate or
used as security for a loan—the commoner practice—at the Bank of
England. Merchants first, the accepting houses' banking functions
developed out their trading activities. Acceptance business, at first
therefore only a sideline, became for many of them their main business. Many of them were of foreign origin, such as Rothschilds,
Schröder and Kleinwort, but as the volume of sterling bills increased
and a market for dealing in them developed in London these merchant
bankers found it convenient to move their headquarters there too.
Operating in the discount market are the seventeen merchant banks
which are members of the Accepting Houses Committee, membership of which is restricted to those that make the acceptance of bills
an important part of their business.

### The development of the discount market

During the hundred and fifty years of its existence the discount
market has shown itself to be extremely flexible, always ready to
adapt itself to changing circumstances. It came into existence in the
early 1800s when commercial banking was in the hands of hundreds
of small banks and the internal bill of exchange was a common
means of payment in business. At first bill brokers acted merely as
agents between the banks, taking up bills where they were plentiful
and selling them where cash was available. Not until the 1830s did
the bill brokers begin to hold bills on their own account. The final
stage of development occurred when they began to act between the
commercial banks and the Bank of England.

Over the past forty or fifty years considerable changes have taken
place in the character of the business undertaken in the discount
market. Before 1914 the market dealt almost exclusively in trade
bills. Besides being used to quite a considerable extent for domestic
transactions where cheques would be employed nowadays, it was the
normal means of payment at that time in the case of foreign transactions. Inland bills are now comparatively rare, and the use of
foreign bills drawn on merchants too has declined. Payments in
foreign trade are more often made by bank draft or telegraphic
transfer, both of which, like the cheque, enable bank deposits to be
transferred from one bank to another, and although the documentary
credit requires a bill of exchange to be used it is drawn on a foreign
bank rather than the foreign merchant. Over the years, however, the
decline of the trade bill has been to some extent offset by the increasing volume of Treasury bills. Unlike trade bills, which are drawn
for whatever amount is required to cover a particular transaction,

Treasury bills are offered at weekly tenders in round sums of £5,000 and £10,000.

Thus, these changes affected both the accepting houses and the discount houses. The decline in trade bills inevitably meant a decline in acceptance business, the very *raison d'être* of an accepting house. To make matters worse the commercial banks too began to undertake acceptance business. In consequence some accepting houses had to close down and others in order to survive had to develop other sides of their business. The discount houses were rather less seriously affected by these developments. One function they had performed for the commercial banks was much reduced, namely that of arranging the trade bills they acquired in "parcels" of even amounts, varying in value from £100,000 upwards and falling due on the same date. In addition to being issued in round sums, Treasury bills can be dated for any day in the week following the tender to suit the convenience of the bidder. The commercial banks, therefore, could easily have by-passed the discount houses and themselves tendered direct for Treasury bills. In fact, the commercial banks prefer the discount market to continue to operate, and so do not compete against the discount houses at the tender.

The existence of a well-developed money and discount market has for long been a distinctive feature of the British banking system. It serves as a sort of cushion between the central bank and the commercial banks. When they find themselves short of cash British commercial banks never borrow directly from the central bank as do commercial banks in many countries. They prefer instead to call in some of their day-to-day loans to the discount houses, which, to obtain the necessary funds, are then compelled to rediscount some of their bills at the Bank of England or borrow with these bills as security. The members of the discount market are privileged in that it is only to them that the Bank of England acts as lender of last resort. Thus, the London discount market provides the commercial banks with a useful, very liquid asset—"money at call and short notice"—and this enables them to hold less cash than would otherwise be prudent. The advantage of having an intermediary between the central bank and the commercial banks is, in fact, considered to be so great that deliberate attempts with varying degrees of success have been made in some other countries to develop money markets. Since too the commercial banks like to have their assets in more liquid form than the terms of most bills permit—three months for Treasury bills and three to six months for trade bills—the discount houses hold them for a time before rediscounting them with the commercial banks. For these reasons the English commercial banks prefer the discount market to continue to function.

The discount houses can show that in other ways too they are of service both to the Government and to the banking system. Before the weekly tender for Treasury bills, the exact amount to be offered being announced in advance by the Treasury, the members of the London Discount Association meet to decide upon their syndicated bid. Then they agree to cover the tender in full, each discount house taking a quota according to the size of its capital. The Bank of England makes use of the discount market as a means of putting additional cash into the banking system by purchasing bills from the market, or sometimes direct from the commercial banks, through its own broker—the "Special Buyer"—which is one of the smaller discount houses. The Bank of England too may engage in open market operations in bills in order to make short-term borrowing more expensive with the aim of curtailing credit.

## The discount houses today

The decline in trade bills in the inter-war years led the discount houses to take up short-dated government bonds, generally those within five years of maturity. These bonds now have the advantage that they are eligible as collateral security when the discount houses find it necessary to seek accommodation at the Bank of England and the market is "in the bank." The drawbacks to bonds, however, is that they fluctuate in price more widely than bills and are less liquid. During the past few years some of the discount houses have also begun to take up small amounts of stocks issued by local authorities.

The following table summarises the work of the discount market:

TABLE LXVII
*The Discount Market*

|  | Sept. 1967 | 19—* |
|---|---|---|
|  | £ million | £ million |
| *Liabilities* |  |  |
| Bank of England | 39 |  |
| Domestic commercial banks | 1,042 |  |
| Accepting houses | 275 |  |
| Other liabilities | 143 |  |
| *Assets* |  |  |
| Treasury bills | 564 |  |
| Trade bills | 368 |  |
| Government stocks | 452 |  |
| Other assets | 204 |  |

Source: *Bank of England Quarterly Bulletin.*
* For the latest figures.
Note: Liabilities and assets do not balance as some items have been omitted.

This table shows the extent to which British commercial banks are responsible for supplying the discount market with funds—about 69% of the total amount. It is of interest to note that the accepting houses in their capacity as ordinary bankers supplied 18% of the discount market's funds. It also clearly shows that the discount houses use most of their funds to acquire Treasury bills (35%) while trade bills form only 17% of their assets. Bills of both kinds, therefore, nowadays form only just over half of their total assets, their holdings of government stocks having risen to 28% of the total, thus exceeding the value of trade bills discounted.

TABLE LXVIII
*Bills Discounted*

| | Discount houses | | London clearing banks | |
|---|---|---|---|---|
| | Trade bills | Treasury bills | Trade bills | Treasury bills |
| | £ million | £ million | £ million | £ million |
| 1956 | 84 | 523 | 114 | 1,156 |
| 1957 | 84 | 585 | 148 | 1,143 |
| 1958 | 70 | 594 | 110 | 1,167 |
| 1959 | 118 | 635 | 134 | 1,089 |
| 1960 | 117 | 574 | 142 | 1,007 |
| 1961 | 183 | 533 | 233 | 992 |
| 1962 | 189 | 502 | 272 | 933 |
| 1963 | 249 | 529 | 298 | 842 |
| 1964 | 302 | 453 | 365 | 790 |
| 1965 | 339 | 484 | 461 | 653 |
| 1966 | 404 | 424 | 446 | 689 |
| 1967 | 437 | 548 | 492 | 564 |
| 1968 | | | | |

Source: *Annual Abstract of Statistics.*

In recent years, however, there has been quite a revival of the commercial bill of exchange. This is shown by the fact that the value of bills discounted by the discount houses and the London clearing banks rose from £85 million and £114 million respectively in 1956 to £404 million and £446 million respectively in 1966—an increase of upwards of five times. In the case of both the discount houses and the commercial banks there was at the same time some decline in Treasury bills as Table LXVIII shows. A point of particular interest shown by this table is that by 1966 the discount houses for the first time for very many years were doing almost as much business in trade bills as in Treasury bills.

## The accepting houses today

Reference has already been made to the effects on the accepting houses of changes in the money market. Table LXIX shows the liabilities and assets of the accepting houses, and also shows how they have developed their ordinary banking activities, most of the items in their balance sheets being similar to those of the commercial banks. Acceptance of bills, though now comprising only a quarter of their

TABLE LXIX

*Accepting Houses*

|  | 1967 | 19— * |
|---|---|---|
|  | £ million | £ million |
| *Liabilities* |  |  |
| Deposits (on current and deposit account)    .    .    .    . | 1,372 |  |
| *Assets* |  |  |
| Money at call and short notice .    . | 105 |  |
| Loans to Local Authorities    .    . | 302 |  |
| Bills discounted: |  |  |
|    Treasury bills    .    .    .    . | 21 |  |
|    Trade bills    .    .    .    . | 23 |  |
| Acceptances    .    .    .    . | 282 |  |
| Government stocks .    .    .    . | 48 |  |
| Advances    .    .    .    . | 581 |  |

Source: *Bank of England Quarterly Bulletin.*
\* For the latest figures.
Note: Liabilities and assets do not balance as some items have been omitted.

business, is of course much greater than that of the commercial banks. The extent, however, to which they hold bills is quite small. Some of them also act as issuing houses. Dealing in Eurodollars has developed very considerably in recent years. Eurodollars are US dollars held outside the U.S.A. and capable of transfer from one holder to another. Business is largely concentrated in London and undertaken there mainly by the merchant banks.

The financial intermediaries of the discount and capital markets provide alternative sources to the banks for businessmen and others seeking credit. By delaying making payment to their suppliers for as long as their creditors will allow, trade credit can be used as a source of circulating capital. Whenever restrictions have been placed on bank lending the volume and length of trade credit tends to increase. In these circumstances borrowing from sources other than the commercial banks also has increased, a fact of which the monetary authorities have had to take account.

## III. THE CAPITAL MARKET

**Features of the capital market**

Both the Government and industry borrow on short term and long term. To meet day-to-day expenditure and to borrow in anticipation of revenue (a large proportion of which comes in during the fourth quarter of the financial year) Treasury bills are issued to the money market. Merchants too obtain short-term finance from that market, but manufacturers more often obtain at least part of their working capital from the commercial banks or sometimes nowadays from merchant banks that undertake ordinary banking business. Table LXIV (p. 291) shows the wide range of industry, including public utilities, the distributive trades and financial institutions, that obtain working capital from the banks. It used to be said that banks, with their preoccupation with the liquidity of their assets, used to keep even "advances to customers" as liquid as possible by granting loans for periods of only three to six months though making them renewable. This meant that whenever the situation demanded it—fear of deterioration of the borrower's credit or the Government's embarking on a deflationary policy—such loans could be called in. Thus, bank loans, though ostensibly for relatively short periods, were often in practice of quite long duration for more important customers. More recently some banks have been lending for much longer periods.

**The demand for capital**

Thus, as has been seen, the money market is for short-term loans, whereas the capital market is the source from which industry obtains its permanent capital and from which the British and some Commonwealth governments, local authorities and some other public bodies borrow on long term. The length of the period of borrowing varies with the market, the period on the money market being for very short periods varying from day-to-day loans to fourteen days, on the discount market generally for two or three months, and on the capital market varying from a few months (bank loans) to a fixed number of years (dated stocks and debentures) or for an indefinite period (undated stocks) or even permanently (ordinary shares). The Government borrows on the capital market by the issue of stocks. These may be for an indefinite period such as undated $2\frac{1}{2}\%$ Consols (the oldest government stock, dating back to the early eighteenth century) and undated $3\%$ Treasury stock. Some stocks such as $3\frac{1}{2}\%$ War Loan, originally dated "after 1952," and $2\frac{1}{2}\%$ Treasury stock after 1975, give the Government the option of redeeming them *at any time* after the date indicated, so that in fact they are regarded as irredeemable. Dated stocks are for a fixed term, the Government generally having the option of redeeming them between two stated dates as, for example, 3% Savings Bonds 1965–75, 5½% Funding Loan 1982–84 or 5¼% Treasury stock 2008–12. On occasions nationalised industries have entered the capital market on their own account, their stocks being government guaranteed, for example, 3% Gas stock 1990–95, 3% Transport stock 1978–88, and 3½% Electricity stock 1976–79.

As stocks fall due for redemption new ones are issued to obtain the necessary funds. When the volume of Treasury bills is considered to be over-large for a floating debt (*see* p. 469) the debt may be funded by the issue of a new stock. At any time, therefore, there will be stocks nearing maturity and others with short, medium or long periods to run. New stocks are issued for varying periods, twenty or thirty years being the commonest choice. The length of period chosen depends largely on the prevailing rate of interest, a short period being preferable when the rate is high and so expected to fall, and a longer period being chosen when the rate of interest is low. Among Commonwealth governments, Australia and New Zealand have eleven and nine stocks respectively outstanding on the London capital market. The larger local authorities too borrow by issuing stocks to the capital market, London (the former LCC, the GLC and the Corporation of London) having no fewer than seventeen such stocks outstanding. Most local authorities also borrow by mortgage loans. Numbers of foreign governments—literally from China to Peru—have at various times made use of the London market to raise funds.

In general—though there have been recent exceptions—British industry goes to the banks only for working capital. For the renewal of its fixed capital it depends very largely on itself. Reserves, accumulated out of undistributed profits, can be employed either as working capital to avoid or lessen bank borrowing or for the replacement of worn-out or obsolescent capital equipment. Expansion too is more often than not financed by "ploughing back" profits into the business. For the small firm this has been the usual method of expansion, and indeed many large businesses have developed from small beginnings in this way. It is, however, a very slow method, and if more rapid expansion is aimed at, recourse will be had to the capital market which is the main source from which industry obtains its fixed capital. This can be done by issuing ordinary or preference shares to the market or raising a long-term loan by means of an issue of debentures. Trade credit is a means by which some firms supplement their working capital, though this usually means for the debtor the payment of a higher price through loss of discount and for the creditor the necessity to obtain additional capital through the normal channels.

Consumers may borrow on short term from the banks by over-draft or in some cases by personal loan, repayment of the latter possibly being spread over two years. Alternatively, a consumer may take advantage of hire purchase, financed either by a retailer or a hire purchase finance company. For the purchase of houses individuals can borrow from building societies by mortgaging their property.

## The supply of capital

Since saving is a prerequisite of capital formation and investment, the supply of new capital depends on savings. Most savings now come from the undistributed profits of companies but there is still a considerable amount of private saving, as the following table shows:

TABLE LXX
*Net Saving* *

|  | 1956 | 1960 | 1965 | 1967 |
|---|---|---|---|---|
|  | £ million | £ million | £ million | £ million |
| Personal saving . . | 730 | 1,164 | 1,959 | 2,092 |
| Companies . . . | 1,757 | 2,268 | 3,351 | 2,580 |
| Public corporations . | 188 | 288 | 644 | 623 |
| Central government . | 416 | 202 | 890 | 1,073 |
| Local authorities . . | 126 | 246 | 293 | 415 |
| Total . . | 3,217 | 4,168 | 7,137 | 6,783 |

Source: *Blue Book on National Income and Expenditure.*
* That is, after allowing for depreciation and stock appreciation.

Thus, although in 1967 at a record total of £2,092 million, personal saving formed only 30% of the total. Since 1915, when War Savings Certificates began to be issued, the Government has encouraged "small" savers by the issue of National Savings Certificates, Defence Bonds (since 1940) superseded in 1964 by National Development Bonds and in 1968 by British Savings Bonds, and Premium Savings Bonds (since 1956). Other small savings are collected by the Post Office Savings Bank and the trustee savings banks. Table LXXI shows the distribution of small savings among different forms of investment in 1968.

Other institutions that cater for small savers are the large commercial banks (savings accounts), building societies (deposit and share accounts), assurance companies (endowment policies), and investment trusts and unit investment trusts (for widely spread investment in stock exchange securities).

## Building societies

These are institutions that collect funds from investors and then use them to lend on mortgage to people who wish to buy houses or certain

TABLE LXXI
*Distribution of Small Savings*

|  | 1957 | 1968 | 19—* |
|---|---|---|---|
|  | £ million | £ million | £ million |
| National Savings Certificates (including accrued interest) . . | 2,433 | 2,610 | |
| Defence Bonds, National Development Bonds and British Savings Bonds . . . . . | 742 | 934 | |
| Premium Savings Bonds . . | 66 | 676 | |
| Post Office Savings Bank . . | 1,706 | 1,790 | |
| Trustee savings banks . . . | 1,118 | 2,377 | |
| Total . . . . . | 6,065 | 8,387 | |

Source: *Annual Abstract of Statistics.*
* For the latest figures.

kinds of other property. Most building societies offer three different rates of interest according to the type of account. These in ascending order of the rate of interest are deposit accounts, paid-up share accounts and subscription share accounts (for those agreeing to save a fixed sum regularly). Depositors being creditors would receive priority over those holding share accounts in the case of a society being wound up and generally too enjoy greater ease of withdrawal. Paid-up shares usually require notice of withdrawal, though they are the more popular form of investment. Building societies have an arrangement with the Department of Inland Revenue, under which they pay an agreed lump sum as income tax, so that individual accounts are not subject to this tax, although where appropriate the interest is grossed up and subject to surtax. For people who pay income tax at the standard rate, deposit or share accounts are an attractive investment. Through the Building Societies Association the societies pursue a common policy with regard to both interest rates and mortgage rates. The interest rates offered have to be high enough to attract sufficient funds to meet the demand for mortgages and so must keep in line with the yields on other similar investments. Thus, their interest rates and mortgage rate depend on the prevailing rate of interest.

Until 1874 building societies were registered under the *Friendly Societies Act*, but since that date they have been registered with the Registrar of Building Societies. As compared with banks and insurance companies the amalgamation of building societies has been less rapid, though the number of societies fell from nearly 3,000 in 1890 to 576 in 1966. This reduction in numbers was only due in part to amalgamations. In the early days of the movement there were many "terminating societies," established by small groups for the limited purpose of providing each member with a house. Of the societies in existence in this country in 1966 most were still local institutions. Where expansion has taken place it has been in most cases by the opening of new branches. The two very large societies, however, were themselves amalgamations of two large societies, the largest, the Halifax, being formed from the Halifax Permanent and the Halifax Equitable, and the second largest, the London-based Abbey National, from the Abbey and the National. The assets of

TABLE LXXII
*Building Societies*

|  | 1956 | 1967 | 19—* |
|---|---|---|---|
|  | £ million | £ million | £ million |
| *Liabilities* | | | |
| Deposits . . . | 193 | 321 | |
| Shares . . . | 1,909 | 6,665 | |
| *Assets* | | | |
| Mortgages . . . | 1,879 | 6,037 | |
| Investments . . . | 275 | 1,198 | |

Source: *Annual Abstract of Statistics.*
* For the latest figures.
Note: Liabilities and assets do not balance as some items have been omitted.

each of these—standing at £1,246 million and £1,001 million respectively in 1967—are more than double those of the third largest society. Table LXXII shows how building societies have expanded during recent years. The investments of building societies are in trustee securities.

**Assurance companies**

Some insurance companies engage only in non-life insurance against such risks as fire, accident, marine, etc. In addition to the non-life business undertaken by insurance companies, some also—particularly, marine—is in the hands of Lloyd's underwriters. Other companies restrict their activities to life assurance, and the largest undertake both insurance and assurance. Through their life assurance business the assurance companies collect individual savings, for most life assurance nowadays is combined with personal saving by the endowment policy which yields the assured a stated sum, usually "with profits," at a certain date in addition to providing him with life assurance cover until the date of maturity of the policy. The companies collect savings in the form of premiums from a large number of people, with the result that assurance companies have huge funds at their disposal for investment. As with most other financial institutions their income and assets have enormously increased in recent times, and as a result the assurance companies have become one of the most important sources of supply to the capital market. For example, in 1966 the life premium income of the Prudential Assurance Company was £113 million, with the Legal and General second with £81 million, out of a total of £493 million for all assurance companies and friendly societies undertaking this type of business. The introduction in recent years by many large companies of private pension schemes for employees has led to further accumulations of funds. Some of these schemes are operated by assurance companies or friendly societies and some are independently operated.

The assurance companies and the managers of pension funds invest their funds in such a way as to obtain the highest return consistent with safety. Particularly in the case of pension funds there is also the motive of trying to secure an income for beneficiaries that will offset to some extent the falling value of money. This means that a proportion of the available funds must be invested in ordinary shares (equities). In the case of the British assurance companies this forms 25% of their total investments, which in 1964 were distributed as follows:

TABLE LXXIII
*Investments of British Assurance Companies*

| Investment | £ million |
|---|---|
| British government stocks . . . | 1,267 |
| Commonwealth government stocks . | 254 |
| Foreign government stocks . . | 261 |
| Debentures and preference shares . | 1,733 |
| Ordinary shares . . . . | 1,620 |
| Mortgages . . . . . | 891 |
| Total . . . . . | 6,026 |

The assurance companies invest in fixed interest securities or equities according to the state of the market and the economic outlook. On occasion a new issue of debentures has been issued direct to an insurance company.

In 1967 there were over 400 funded pension schemes with estimated funds of over £600 million operated by friendly societies. In that year, however, the total assets of all funded pension schemes stood at nearly £5,000 million. An increasing number of public companies offer their employees pensions additional to the retirement pensions of the Ministry of Health and Social Security. In the different branches of the public sector and for local government employees too there are superannuation schemes. Contributing to all these schemes has become an important form of saving, and the funds in many cases an increasing source of capital for the capital market.

## Investment in Equities

Small investors are generally reluctant to invest in ordinary shares, though individual investors with larger sums at their disposal can purchase existing shares or subscribe to new issues either through their banks or through stockbrokers. However, many people who would never think of buying equities (ordinary shares) directly do so indirectly by taking out life assurance policies, for, as already noted, assurance companies invest part of their funds in this way. For the small investor ordinary shares are too risky, as both the dividend and the capital value are liable to fluctuate. For this kind of investment it is essential to spread the risk over as many shares as possible, so that if one company suffers misfortune only a part of the investor's assets will be affected. Only a relatively small number of individuals have sufficient resources to spread their investments over a wide enough range, as it is costly to make a large number of very small purchases of different ordinary shares. Even then there is the risk inherent in share prices generally rising or falling. During 1966, for example, share prices on average fell by nearly 30%, though this ground was more than regained during the following two years. The large investor in ordinary shares needs to watch regularly what is happening on the market in order to vary his holdings to suit changing conditions. He can, of course, employ a stockbroker to advise him or he can hand over the entire responsibility to the investment department of a commercial bank. Thirty years of inflation and rising prices have made people aware as never before that the value of money can fall, and that investment in equities can offer them some protection. As already stressed, the small investor can do none of these things. He can, however, invest indirectly in equities through either an investment trust company or a unit investment trust. Only about half of all ordinary shares dealt in on the stock exchange are held by individuals, the remainder being held by institutions.

## Investment trusts

Most of the investment trust companies in the United Kingdom were formed in the mid nineteenth century, many in Scotland. Except when new issues are made to the market—generally in the form of debentures—their shares, as with other public companies, can be bought and sold only on the stock exchange. These companies, of which there are some 300 with quotations on the London stock exchange, invest their capital mainly in the shares of other companies. Therefore, every share in an investment trust is in fact an investment in a large number of independent companies. Thus, an investment trust is a company formed for the express purpose of acquiring and holding investments. Dividends depend on the returns from the trust's investments, but profits from the sale of securities are re-invested.

## Unit investment trusts

The unit investment trust is operated on somewhat different lines. A company manages a unit trust—or more often a group of unit trusts—and units are generally on offer at any time, supplemented periodically by block offers. Units too can be resold to the managers at any time at the prevailing market price which is determined by the current prices on the stock exchange of the underlying securities. A unit trust must be authorised by the Board of Trade before it can commence operations. Though some unit trusts restrict their invest-ments to particular fields such as banking, insurance, consumers' goods, mining, etc., or to particular types of investment, stressing either the income yield or capital growth, the main purpose, as with the investment trust company, is to reduce risk by spreading invest-ment over a large number of companies. Most unit trusts are "flexible," *i.e.* the managers are permitted to vary the trust's holdings of securities to meet changing conditions.

First established in the early 1930s, unit trusts did not attract much attention in Great Britain until the mid 1950s when restrictions on new capital issues, imposed during the Second World War, were eased. During the 1960s, following a period when units had appre-ciated to an exceptional degree—90% of the underlying securities being in equities—most existing unit trusts greatly expanded and many new ones were formed. At 31st December 1966 the value of the total assets of British unit trusts was £484 million, an increase during the year of £37 million. Unit trusts are even more popular in the United States, where they had their origin. There were fewer than a dozen unit trusts in the United Kingdom in 1939, but by 1968 their number had increased to over two hundred under upwards of fifty different managements. Prices of units vary between a few shillings and forty or fifty shillings, most being between 6s. and 9s. There is usually a certain minimum initial purchase, but for as small an outlay as £25 investment might be spread over more than a hundred companies. By 1968 the total assets of the British unit trusts exceeded £600 million—half this total being held by Save and Prosper, the largest group—as compared with over £3,000 million for the invest-ment trusts. By that date there were upwards of a million people in Great Britain with holdings in unit trusts. As already noted in con-nection with banking, British banks have recently begun to take an interest in unit trusts, Lloyds being first in the field in 1966. Then Westminster joined with Hambro to form one, and in 1967 Martins took over the Unicorn Group to form Martins Unicorn. In 1968 the trustee savings banks combined to form a unit trust. Most of the large groups of unit trusts have made agreements with insurance companies whereby life assurance can be linked with the holding of units in order to provide the assured with some protection against inflation. It has been suggested too that the Government should establish a unit trust. It would seem that considerable further expansion of unit trusts can be expected.

## Medium-term capital

The Report of the Macmillan Committee on Finance and Industry, published in 1931, provided the most detailed survey of the British banking and financial system until the publication of the Radcliffe Report in 1959. On the banking side the Macmillan Report considered among other things the practice of the English commercial banks of calling in loans immediately before compiling their weekly statements to show a somewhat higher cash ratio (10%) than they normally maintained (8%). This practice the Report condemned but it was not until 1946 that it was abolished. The Report also considered the effects of this country's return to the gold standard in 1925 at the pre-1914 parity, but it favoured remaining on this standard. Looking back most economists would regard this view as mistaken. In fact, later that year, Great Britain had to leave the gold standard. Bank rate, the Report considered, was a delicate instrument which influenced the internal economic situation. Nevertheless, only a year later, bank rate was discarded as an instrument of monetary policy and was not used again for that purpose for nineteen years. The Report recommended that the burden of the National Debt might be alleviated by a reduction in the rate of interest paid on government stocks. The opportunity for doing so occurred in 1932 when many stocks were converted to a lower rate of interest. London was also considered to have too large a volume of short-term liabilities. In fact, "lending long and borrowing short" was an important cause of Great Britain's difficulties in 1931. One of the principal recommendations of the Report was that an institution should be established to provide medium-term lending to industry.

## Finance corporations

There were, however, two finance corporations already in existence in this country. The Agricultural Mortgage Corporation—to make loans to farmers for longer periods than banks were willing to do—had been established as long ago as 1928. Shortly before the Macmillan Report was published the Bankers' Industrial Development Company was set up to assist industry, more particularly to help carry through rationalisation schemes (as, for example, for the cotton industry) or to assist large firms the existence of which was endangered by the Great Depression. In both cases the capital was provided by the Bank of England and the commercial banks. Neither of these corporations, however, was intended to fill the gap in bank lending.

No further attempt was made to implement the recommendation of the Macmillan Committee until 1945. As already noted, it has long been customary for British industry to depend mainly for its fixed capital on issues to the capital market of shares with no date of redemption or long-term debentures, relying for its circulating capital on short-term borrowing from the banks. Thus, there appeared to be a need for capital to be provided for periods intermediate between these two extremes. One particular case is that of the private or close company, with its shares in only a few hands. Death duties payable on the death of a very large shareholder could put such a company in a position of extreme difficulty. Without criticising existing methods by which industry raised its capital, the Macmillan Committee considered that many businesses, both large and small, might occasionally find it advantageous to be able to obtain medium-term credit for periods of up to five years, and might prefer this to raising additional permanent capital by a new issue to the capital market. Even longer-term credit would be useful to the smaller and lesser-known public companies which might find it difficult to make new issues, and of particular benefit to close companies to which this course of action was not available.

In 1945, therefore, the Industrial and Commercial Finance Corporation (ICFC) and the Finance Corporation for Industry (FCI) were established. The main difference between the two institutions is in the amount of assistance each can offer to industry. Thus, the ICFC will consider loans for sums between £5,000 and £300,000, whereas the FCI concerns itself only with loans in excess of £200,000. The capital of the ICFC was provided by the Bank of England and the English and Scottish commercial banks, while the capital of the FCI came from the Bank of England, insurance companies and investment trust companies. In 1959 the ICFC and the FCI became public companies, previously having been public corporations. It was also expected that these two corporations would have an important part to play in assisting firms to switch over from wartime to peacetime production.

The ICFC and the FCI operate on similar lines, giving assistance only to firms where a searching enquiry into their past records and present positions appears to warrant it. In some cases assistance takes the form of a loan for ten to twenty years, supported by collateral security acceptable to the particular corporation concerned as with an ordinary bank advance. In other cases the corporation may provide a company with capital by taking up debentures, preference shares or occasionally even ordinary shares. At 31st December 1967 the assets of the ICFC included loans to industry and investments in industry to the value of over £80 million. Whereas a large proportion of the loans granted by the ICFC are for amounts of less than £20,000, the FCI on one occasion in 1964 made a loan of no less than £25 million.

A number of other financial corporations have been established during the past twenty-five years, often of a more specialised nature to help specific industries. These have included the National Film Corporation, the Commonwealth Development Finance Company, and more recently the Industrial Reorganisation Corporation to assist schemes of industrial rationalisation and mergers regarded as being in the national interest.

Thus, capital is supplied to the capital market by the institutional investors—banks, insurance companies, investment trust companies —in two ways. They do so directly when they lend or take up stocks or shares; they do so indirectly through their interest in the financial corporations. Thus, the Bank of England and the commercial banks, through a number of subsidiaries, have taken an increasing interest in recent times in providing additional capital to industry. By taking up Treasury bills and investing mainly in government stocks the banks lend large sums to the Government—£2,868 million in 1968. The Government, though primarily a borrower in the capital market, also sometimes acts as a supplier of capital to the market. It has sometimes compelled local authorities, instead of themselves borrowing directly from the capital market, to do so indirectly—and often on better terms—by borrowing from the Government. On a number of occasions nationalised industries have sought additional capital by direct appeals to the market—hence the various Gas, Electricity and Transport stocks—but more recently they too have been supplied by the Government. Then some government departments accumulate funds which they invest in government stocks.

### The stock exchange

The stock exchange is essentially a market in which dealings take place in *existing* stocks and shares. The capital market, on the other hand, is the source from which *new* capital is obtained. The two markets are closely connected nowadays, and as a result of new developments more so than ever before. In the first place the existence of a stock exchange—a place where buyers and sellers of stocks and shares can be brought together—means that there is a daily price for all marketable securities, varying from day to day according to conditions in the market, and this makes more liquid many securities which otherwise might be very illiquid. Shares and some government stocks have no date of redemption while debentures and some government stocks are very long-dated. Not many people would be prepared to hold shares or long-dated stocks if there were no stock exchange. Thus the stock exchange performs the important function of stimulating the flow of new capital to the capital market. Secondly, the stock exchange has a part to play when new issues are made (*see* below, pp. 316–19).

Though dealings in stocks and shares had taken place for some years previously, the first stock exchange was opened in London in 1773. In addition there are now a number of stock exchanges in other important commercial centres in the United Kingdom, such as Birmingham, Manchester, Leeds, Glasgow, Belfast, Cardiff. Stockbrokers are to be found too with offices in most provincial towns of any size. A number of them formed the Northern Stock Exchange. Since all are connected by telephone the price of a particular security on any day will be approximately the same throughout the country. The London stock exchange differs from the provincial ones by having jobbers in addition to brokers as members. Jobbers deal on their own account with the brokers who act on behalf of their clients. Jobbers of necessity specialise in particular groups of stocks or shares. Altogether on the London stock exchange upwards of 10,000 securities, with a market value in 1968 of over £82 million, are dealt in. The turnover in 1967 came to over £32 million from over 4,000 separate transactions, gilt-edged accounting for 75% of the turnover and 55% of the transactions, dealings in gilt-edged clearly being much larger in amount than dealings in shares.

TABLE LXXIV
*Value of Stock Exchange Securities*

| Year | Gilt-edged, etc. | Company securities | Total |
|------|------------------|--------------------|-------|
|      | £ million | £ million | £ million |
| 1958 | 14,485 | 17,141 | 33,102 |
| 1959 | 14,778 | 22,588 | 39,020 |
| 1960 | 14,287 | 29,149 | 45,068 |
| 1961 | 14,900 | 34,450 | 50,951 |
| 1962 | 14,251 | 34,359 | 50,224 |
| 1963 | 16,306 | 37,108 | 55,309 |
| 1964 | 16,257 | 41,469 | 59,841 |
| 1965 | 15,202 | 57,359 | 75,155 |
| 1966 | 15,220 | 60,095 | 78,164 |
| 1967 | 17,720 | 61,222 | 82,033 |
| 1968 | 1,7089 | 85,242 | 103,331 |
| 1969 | | | |

Source: *Annual Abstract of Statistics.*

Consider now Table LXXIV. During the period covered by the table the volume of gilt-edged stocks increased by £2,500 million. The increased value of company securities was partly due to new issues (accounting for approximately £8,000 million of the increase), the balance of £60,000 being due to capital appreciation. As a result by 1968 gilt-edged formed only 16% of the total as against 45% in 1958.

## Security yields

The London stock exchange is a good example of a highly organised market, only jobbers and brokers who are members being allowed to deal and business being conducted according to a prescribed set of rules or accepted custom. The market in stocks and shares too is as nearly perfect as any market in existence, business being largely concentrated in a particular building and buyers and sellers being in such close contact with one another so that what is happening in one part of the market is quickly known throughout the market. Prices, as in other markets, depend on the demand for particular commodities, in this case stocks and shares, in relation to the keenness of their holders to sell. An increased demand to buy a share immediately puts up its price, just as an increased desire to sell will cause the price to fall. The prices of gilt-edged stocks too are especially susceptible to changes in bank rate. A rise in bank rate will cause falls in the prices of these stocks in order to raise their yield to new buyers.

Inflationary tendencies in the economy or fears of devaluation will make many people switch from fixed interest securities of all kinds to equities, with the result that the prices of the former will fall while the prices of the latter will rise. At one time the yield on gilt-edged was always less than the return of equities—perhaps $2\frac{1}{2}\%$ or $3\%$ as against $5\%$ or more—on account of the greater risk in holding ordinary shares. The long period of inflation experienced in recent times and increased awareness of a persistent tendency for the value of money to fall has led to a greater proportion of investors than ever before putting savings in equities, either directly or through unit trusts, with the result that the gap between the yield on ordinary shares and on fixed interest stocks has narrowed and on many occasions actually been the reverse of what used to be the case, the difference being known as the "reserve yield gap." For example, on 9th February 1968, the prices and yields of a few representative stocks and shares were as shown in Table LXXV.

At the date when these prices prevailed bank rate stood at $8\%$—hence the high yields on government stocks. Another influence on these fixed interest stocks is their date of redemption, the yield generally nowadays being higher the longer the period they have to run. The equities in the list have been chosen from the main section of the market. Most of them, it will be noticed, have yields considerably below the yields of gilt-edged stocks. Many factors influence the prices of ordinary shares, some of which affect the whole market,

TABLE LXXV

*Stock Exchange Prices and Yields*

|  | Price | Yield |
|---|---|---|
|  | £ | % |
| *Fixed interest stocks* |  |  |
| 2½% Consols . . . . | 35½ | 7·1 |
| 3½% War Loan . . . | 49⅝ | 7·2 |
| 6¾ Treasury, 1995–98 . . | 94¾ | 7·3 |
| 3% British Gas, 1990–95 . . | 52½ | 7·0 |
| 6¾% Greater London, 1976 . | 95½ | 7·1 |
| *Equities* | *s.  d.* |  |
| Midland Bank . . . | 70  9 | 4·0 |
| Prudential . . . . | 50  0 | 2·9 |
| ICI . . . . . | 54  6 | 4·6 |
| English Electric . . . | 57  0 | 3·8 |
| Unilever . . . . | 48  3 | 2·5 |
| Dunlop . . . . . | 39  0 | 4·1 |
| Marks & Spencer . . . | 39  1½ | 4·0 |
| Vickers . . . . . | 38  0 | 5·2 |
| Schweppes . . . . | 18  10½ | 3·7 |
| Cunard . . . . . | 13  0 | 7·7 |
| Courtaulds . . . . | 24  0 | 5·2 |
| Shell . . . . . | 57  3 | 3·5 |
| Calico Printers . . . | 7  7½ | 8·2 |

such as the general economic climate, expectations of future business trends, political events, the international situation, economic policies of other countries; individual share prices will be influenced additionally by the past performance of the companies concerned and their future prospects judged by the policies of their boards.

Table LXXVI shows the relationship between the average yields on gilt-edged and ordinary shares.

**Speculation**

Many people buy stock exchange securities for the sake of the income they yield and probably pay little attention to day-to-day fluctuations in their prices so long as dividends or interest payments are maintained. Some people, however, buy shares which they believe likely to rise in price, hoping to resell them some time in the future at a profit. Such people may be content in the present with a small return on their investment. Before the introduction of taxes on capital gains, investment for capital growth was more attractive to high taxpayers than investment for income.

Speculation takes place on all highly organised markets—the

foreign exchange market, commodity markets—as well as the stock exchange. Those who buy shares in anticipation of a rise in their price are known as "bulls" and those who sell in expectation of a fall in price are known as "bears." The market is said to be "bullish" when there is a general keenness to buy and so for the prices of shares to rise, and "bearish" when there is a general keenness to sell so that there is a tendency for prices to fall. The system of fortnightly settlement on the London Stock exchange makes it possible for speculators to hold securities for short periods without becoming the registered owners and pay on settlement the difference between purchase price

TABLE LXXVI
*Security Yields* (1958–68)

| Year (Jan.) | Equities | Bank rate (Jan.) | Gilt-edged % |
|---|---|---|---|
| 1958 | 6·88 | 7 | 5·27 |
| 1959 | 5·36 | 4 | 4·73 |
| 1960 * | 4·00 | 4 | 5·15 |
| 1961 * | 4·81 | 5 | 5·75 |
| 1962 * | 5·59 | 6 | 6·52 |
| 1963 * | 4·65 | 4½ | 5·67 |
| 1964 * | 4·32 | 4 | 5·83 |
| 1965 * | 5·22 | 7 | 6·28 |
| 1966 * | 5·36 | 6 | 6·44 |
| 1967 * | 5·86 | 7 | 6·61 |
| 1968 | | 8 | |
| 1969 | | 7 | |

Source: *Annual Abstract of Statistics.*
* Years in which there was a reverse yield gap.

and selling price. It may be said that this practice encourages speculation, but the presence of speculators in the market is of advantage to the small investor. It means that it is almost always possible for him to sell some of his shares if at any time he finds himself in need of cash. It means too that he is generally able to buy shares at any time. In either case, of course, he will have to be prepared to accept the price ruling in the market at that time for the shares in which he is interested. If there were no speculators in the market there would be times when it might be very difficult to buy or sell particular shares.

Thus, speculation tends to make stock exchange securities more liquid, *i.e.* more readily turned into cash. Speculation also tends to steady the prices of securities since speculators enter the market to buy when prices are low owing to other people selling, the result being that prices do not fall as much as otherwise they might have done.

Similarly, speculators begin to sell when the prices have risen sufficiently for them to make a profit, with the result that the rise in prices is checked. In this way speculation reduces the extent of price fluctuations. If he is to make any profit from his activities a speculator must be an expert in the section of the market in which he operates, for it is essential for him always to be just ahead of the market.

Some other activities of speculators are more open to question. Their intervention in the market becomes reprehensible if, with large funds at their disposal, they attempt directly to influence prices merely for their own profit, thereby exaggerating or instigating price fluctuations instead of ironing them out. Though members of the general public are not likely to be able to enter the market quickly enough to profit from short-term speculation, their activities if widespread can have an unsettling effect on the market, a condition more likely to be met with in the United States, where shares are more widely held than in Great Britain. It is not, however, always easy to distinguish between the different kinds of speculation. The most satisfactory test as to whether speculation at a particular time is unobjectionable or objectionable is its effect on market prices. It can be regarded as unobjectionable—perhaps, even desirable—if it tends to reduce price fluctuations and objectionable if it causes wider variations in the market prices of securities. British banks are not very willing to lend for speculative purposes, and in 1968 outstanding loans to stockbrokers came to only £6 million.

The institutional investors—insurance companies, pension fund managers and investment trusts—all of which are constantly accumulating funds for investment, nowadays set the tone for the securities market since (i) they deal in very large sums, and (ii) their investment policy is determined by expert advisers who attempt to time their buying to occasions when prices are low and appear, in their opinion, likely to rise. Also in keeping with economic circumstances they distribute their available funds between the various forms of investment they favour.

## Capital issues

In 1966 capital issues to the value of £1,072 million were made to the capital market. These were made up as shown in Table LXXVII. The table indicates the principal methods by which new capital is raised at the present day. The first point of interest is that the London capital market continues to attract borrowers from overseas, most of these—both public authorities and companies—being from the Commonwealth. The amount raised by overseas borrowers in 1966, however, was rather less than had been the case in earlier years.

When a new public limited company is to be launched a Memorandum of Association must first be drawn up and signed by seven sponsors. The Memorandum gives the basic facts about the company, such as the name under which it intends to trade, the address of its registered office, the amount of its authorised capital and the way in which it is to be divided into shares, and a statement showing whether its liability is to be limited. The Memorandum also indicates the field of activity in which the new company proposes to engage. It has become common practice for this "objects clause" to be drawn in wide terms, as nowadays companies often like to have a variety of

TABLE LXXVII
*Capital Issues*

| Borrowers | 1967 | 19—* |
|---|---|---|
| | £ million | £ miilon |
| *Local authorities* | | |
| Stocks . . . . . . | 136 | |
| Bond (placings) . . . . | 182 | |
| *Public companies* | | |
| Public issues and offers for sale . | 164 | |
| Tenders . . . . . . | 2 | |
| Placings . . . . . | 356 | |
| "Rights" and bonus issues to shareholders: | | |
| (*i*) Ordinary shares . . . | 117 | |
| (*ii*) Preference shares and debentures . | 76 | |
| *Overseas borrowers* | | |
| Public authorities: | | |
| (*i*) Public issues . . . | 12 | |
| (*ii*) Placings . . . . | 12 | |
| Companies: | | |
| (*i*) Public issues . . . . | 1 | |
| (*ii*) Placings . . . . | 15 | |
| Total . . . . | 1,071 | |

Source: *Bank of England Quarterly Bulletin.*
* For the latest figures.

products as a safeguard against changes of demand. The Articles of Association must then be framed, their purpose being to set out the rules that are to govern the internal working of the company. Next a statutory declaration must be made that all the legal requirements of the *Companies Acts* have been complied with. When these formalities have been completed the new company is entitled to receive from the Registrar of Companies a Certificate of Incorporation which in effect recognises the company's legal existence.

A company may raise capital on the capital market by an issue of shares, ordinary or preference, or by an issue of debentures (loan capital). The dividend on preference shares is limited to a stated amount, though less than this sum might be paid if the profits in any year are insufficient to cover the full amount, no dividend at all being paid on the ordinary shares in such a case. Preference share holders may receive the unpaid balance at a later date if they hold cumulative preference shares. The relation between the total amount of dividend payable on a company's ordinary shares and the amount payable on preference shares and loan capital (if any) is known as its "capital gearing." A company is said to be high-geared if the amount payable on the ordinary shares is high in relation to prior charges and low-geared in the reverse situation.

The public company has become the typical form of business unit in conditions of free enterprise. There are two reasons for this: (*i*) all its members can enjoy limited liability; and (*ii*) it provides an organisation that can raise the large amount of capital required for modern large-scale production.

### Issuing houses

The new company is then ready to appeal to the capital market. The new issue of shares can be offered directly to the market by the company itself if it so wishes. Unless the company is very well known —a most unlikely event unless it is being formed to take over an old one—it might take a considerable time or it might prove impossible to dispose of the shares in this way or even to raise the minimum amount necessary to make a start. The usual practice nowadays is to employ an issuing house. This function is undertaken by specialist institutions as well as by some of the merchant banks and accepting houses. It is thought that some of the commercial banks too are considering entering this field. An Issuing Houses Association represents most of the institutions undertaking this kind of business. A third of the members are also members of the Accepting Houses Committee. The whole business of floating a new company or making a new issue can be handed over to an issuing house. In return for an agreed payment an issuing house will buy the shares from the company and then offer them at a slightly higher price to the market, this procedure being known as an "offer for sale." Alternatively, it may act as agent for the company in finding subscribers to the new issue.

Table LXXVII, however, shows that public issues and offers for sale account for only 23% of new issues. An existing company requiring additional capital may be able to obtain it by offering a "rights" or "capitalisation" issue to its present shareholders only. Since such shares are issued on favourable terms all shareholders will generally take up their allotment (a proportion of their present holding) even if they do so only to resell at a profit. Alternatively, a company may decide to capitalise some of its reserves and finance expansion from undistributed profits accumulated during past years. In such a case shareholders may receive "bonus" shares (again in proportion to their present holdings) for which no payment will be required. After a bonus issue the value of the company's shares on the stock exchange, however, will fall, though not always proportionately to the increase in the number of shares, so that shareholders are not necessarily any better off financially than they were before.

Table LXXVII, however, shows that approximately half the new capital going to companies is raised by the methods so far considered, the remainder nowadays being raised by placings. In this case the issuing house first applies to the stock exchange through a stockbroker for a quotation and then, the stock exchange being satisfied regarding the issue, it seeks out institutional investors—particularly insurance companies and investment trusts—that might be expected to be interested in the shares in question. Most of the shares are then sold privately to the institutions that are agreeable to taking them, the remainder being offered to smaller investors in the market.

The issuing house can thus perform a very useful service to a company. In return for a payment a company is assured of the capital it requires quite quickly. The issuing house can also give expert advice —of particular value to the smaller companies—regarding both procedure and the timing of the issue. In return the issuing house expects to make a profit as payment for its services. Its business, however, is not without risk. The price selected for a new issue will be the highest at which it can be expected that the securities concerned can be fully disposed of, and here there is margin for error. It is essential, therefore, in its own interests for an issuing house to make a thorough investigation into the affairs of any company requiring its services. This, together with the further enquiries made by the Quotations Committee of the stock exchange before a quotation is granted, provide a considerable measure of protection to subscribers to new issues.

### RECOMMENDATIONS FOR FURTHER READING

R. S. Sayers: *Modern Banking*, Chapter 3 (Oxford University Press).
HMSO: *The Radcliffe Report* (1959), Chapter 4.
Institute of Bankers: *The Bank of England Today*.
Institute of Bankers: *The London Discount Market Today*.
F. W. Paish: *Business Finance* (Pitman).
Sir O. Hobson: *How the City Works* (Dickens).

### QUESTIONS

1. Show why the 28% liquidity ratio is of greater importance than the 8% cash ratio.

2. "The survival of the London discount market over the past hundred years has been due to its great flexibility." Amplify this statement.

3. From what sources can British industry obtain the finance it requires?

4. "British banks provide only about one-tenth of the financial requirements of industry." Does this mean that their role is, therefore, unimportant? Explain clearly the importance of bank advances to industry. (Derby.)

5. Explain the place of the issuing house in the provision of long-term capital to industry. (Derby.)

6. Discuss the importance to industry of finance houses, building societies and insurance companies. Of what value are they in the national economy? (Huddersfield.)

7. Write an essay on: The economic functions of the stock exchange, and the effects of current trends upon these functions. (Huddersfield.)

8. "A unit trust is merely a poor man's equivalent of an investment trust." Discuss. (Manchester.)

9. Write brief notes on *two* of the following:
   (a) Holding companies.
   (b) Merchant banks.
   (c) The function of the council of the stock exchange.
   (d) The jobber's turn. (Manchester.)

10. "It would not be beyond human ingenuity to replace the work of the discount houses; but they are there and they are doing the work effectively . . ." (Radcliffe Report, 1959). Examine the functions of the discount houses in the light of this statement. (Liverpool.)

11. What limits are there to the ability of the joint-stock banks to engage in the process of creation of credit? (Liverpool.)

12. The ability of a joint-stock bank to lend depends upon its holding of Treasury bills rather than upon its cash position. Explain. (Northern Counties.)

13. Describe the part played by the merchant banks of the City of London. Has their importance increased or decreased in the post-war years? (Northern Counties.)

14. What part do institutional investors play in the capital market? Do any disadvantages to the market result from their activities? (U.L.C.I.)

## CHAPTER X

# INFLATION AND ITS CONTROL

## *I. THE SPREAD OF INFLATION*

### Changes in the value of money

The value of money is decided by what can be bought for it. Changes in the value of money can be seen, therefore, only through changes in the general price level. If a given assortment of goods which could be bought at one time for £4 now costs £5, then clearly the value of money has fallen. All price changes, however, do not indicate changes in the value of money. Individual prices may change as a result of changes in the supply of, or the demand for, a particular commodity or service. For example, a rising standard of living will increase the demand for many things and, unless supply can be readily expanded to match this increased demand, there will be a tendency for the prices of those commodities to rise, even though the general level of prices remains unchanged. Similarly, an expansion of production may result in some prices falling at a time perhaps when the general price level is rising. Individual prices can thus move contrariwise to the general price trend.

The value of money has never been stable for very long. Over the centuries there has been a long-term tendency for the value of money to fall, *i.e.* for the general price level to rise. Down to 1913 the main cause of this was increased production of the monetary metals which until the nineteenth century tended to outrun the production of other commodities. At certain times the value of money fell more rapidly than at others as, for example, during the sixteenth century, largely in consequence of the great inflow of silver from the New World to Europe during that period, but also partly owing to the mid-Tudor debasement of the coinage. There was a further sharp fall in the value of money during the middle years of the eighteenth century, for which no satisfactory explanation has been offered. In both these cases the effect on the value of money was permanent. Great wars are always periods of inflation and this was so for the Napoleonic Wars as well as for the two World Wars of the twentieth century. However, during the depressions that followed the Napoleonic Wars and the First World War the pound very nearly recovered its pre-war purchasing power, so that the effects of wartime

inflation were in both cases only temporary. In contrast the inflation of the Second World War has persisted in varying degrees ever
since. Exceptions to the long-term downward trend in the value of
money occurred in the fifteenth century when the value of money
remained remarkably steady, and in the seventeenth century when
for most of the time the value of money was actually rising. Apart
from these two exceptions the long-term trend has been for the value
of money to fall.

During the nineteenth century there are discernible medium-term
fluctuations in the value of money associated with changes in the
relationship between the output of gold and the production of other
goods. For example, new discoveries of gold were made around
1847–51 in Australia, California and Russia, and again during 1884–
96 in South Africa and the Klondyke in the Yukon, and these emphasised the general upward trend of prices. There were other
periods, such as 1820–40 and 1874–95, when the output of gold
failed to keep pace with the production of other goods with in consequence a tendency for prices at least temporarily to fall.

During the nineteenth and early twentieth centuries there developed a short-term variation in the general price level associated
with the ups and downs of the trade cycle—the price level rising
during the upswing of the cycle and falling during the downswing.
Similarly, during the Great Depression between the two World Wars,
there was a tendency for the value of money to rise somewhat and
then for it to fall slightly again after 1935 with the onset of recovery.

It has been calculated that between the years 1300 and 1500 prices
rose by no more than 18%, between 1500 and 1700 by over 400%
and between 1700 and 1900 by a further 200%, representing a total
increase of about sixteen times over the whole period of six hundred
years. During the twentieth century prices have risen more rapidly than
ever before, being in 1968 approximately six times the level of 1900.

In earlier periods when the quantity of money was directly related
to the amount of monetary metal available its value depended
directly on the relationship between the output of gold or more
usually silver and the output of other goods. With the development
of banking and the maintenance of gold reserves only fractional to
the note issue and the use as money first of bills of exchange and
then bank deposits, the value of money over long and medium
periods of time continued to be generally influenced by the rate at
which the quantity of monetary metal could be increased in relation
to the rate of expansion of output of other goods, though less
directly than formerly. Nevertheless, although the gold standard
restricted an individual country's power to inflate by the necessity to
check outflows of gold whenever these occurred, it did not prevent
all countries on that standard inflating together.

## The velocity of circulation and the demand for money

In the short run another influence on the value of money makes itself felt—the velocity of circulation, *i.e.* the average number of times each unit of money is used during a period. Thus, an increase or decrease in the velocity of circulation will have a similar effect to an increase or decrease in the quantity of money. It is theoretically possible that a change in the velocity of circulation might offset a change in the quantity of money, but in practice it appears more likely to exaggerate such changes. Over the long period it is probable that the velocity of circulation changes only very slowly, but in the short period it is liable to vary considerably, and indeed it may increase quite sharply if the value of money is falling rapidly. On a system of fluctuating exchange rates the link with gold is completely severed and in consequence checks on monetary expansion and inflation are very much weakened, so that runaway inflation becomes possible. In these circumstances, with prices rising every day, goods of any kind become preferable to money, which then tends to be spent as quickly as possible after being received. The rise in the velocity of circulation then of itself becomes an additional influence on the value of money, which then begins to fall at an even more rapid rate.

In recent discussions of the value of money, more attention has been paid to the demand to hold money as distinct from investing it than to the velocity of circulation. If the symbol $V$ is used to represent the velocity of circulation and $k$ the proportion of the total stock of money at a particular time being withheld from investment, it will be seen that $V$ and $k$ fluctuate inversely. As the demand for money increases, so does $k$ but $V$ falls. In a severe inflation $k$ will fall but $V$ will increase. It was Lord Keynes who first developed the theory that changes in the value of money were more likely to be brought about by changes in investment than by changes in the supply of money. Changes in investment depend on changes in the demand for money and this in its turn is influenced by the rate of interest. Thus, another factor that influences the value of money is the prevailing rate of interest.

## Types of inflation

Inflation is the condition which results from an expansion of the monetary supply on a scale sufficient to raise the general price level. On the gold standard the central bank of a country experiencing an inflow of gold in consequence of a favourable balance of payments was expected to take measures to expand bank credit, *i.e.* to adopt an inflationary policy just as in the case of an outflow of gold a deflationary policy was required. In either case on the gold standard the extent of the inflation or deflation was strictly controlled by the size of the gold movements, and during the years before the First World War no more than quite a moderate amount of inflation or deflation was required to restore equilibrium to the balance of payments.

At the other extreme there is uncontrolled inflation, variously known as a "runaway" or "galloping" inflation or *hyperinflation*. In the years immediately following the First World War hyperinflations occurred in Germany, Austria, Russia and some other countries, while after the Second World War Hungary, Rumania, Greece and China, to name only a few sufferers, all experienced hyperinflation. Two of the earliest historical examples of hyperinflation occurred in France. The first was in 1720 when John Law, a Scottish banker, persuaded the French Government to found a national bank to issue notes. The second example occurred later in the same century when the French Revolutionary Government began to issue *assignats* to supplement the monetary supply, a huge over-issue of this paper money leading to a steep rise in prices with the result that the value of the *assignats* declined almost to nothing.[1] After the great German hyperinflation of 1923–24 the Mark had to be replaced by a new currency unit—the Reichsmark—at a rate of 1,000,000 M to 1 RM, the Mark having declined to $\frac{1}{50000}$ of its former value. In Austria about the same time the schilling replaced the krone, and in 1946 Hungary had to replace the pengö by the forint after an even more stupendous increase in the note issue. More recently the inflations in Chile, Argentina, Brazil and Bolivia have all been serious enough to warrant being described as hyperinflations. In Brazil, for example, the value of money in 1966 was only a mere $\frac{1}{200}$ of its value in 1952. Inflations of this kind are always accompanied by tremendous increases in the supply of money. Huge increases in prices follow and prices are pushed still higher by the rise in the velocity of circulation due to the increasing unwillingness of people to hold money.

The type of inflation, however, experienced by most countries over the past twenty years or so has been mainly of the kind known as "persistent" or "creeping" inflation. It should be stressed that because present prices are higher than they were previously it does not necessarily indicate the presence of inflation. Equilibrium can be achieved at any level of prices, high or low. Inflation is a dynamic condition where the general price level is persistently rising as a result of a constant tendency for purchasing power to run ahead of the output of goods and services.

---

[1] *Assignats* in denominations of 10 francs were redeemed in 1796 at a rate of 300 in exchange for one gold franc, that is, at $\frac{1}{3000}$ of their face value.

## The declining value of the pound sterling

The following graph shows how the value of the pound sterling has fallen during the present century:

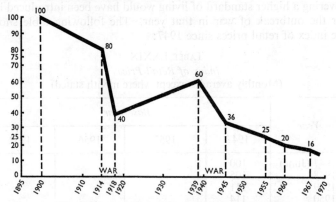

FIG. 12.—The fall in the value of the pound since 1900 (1900 = 100)

The effects of two World Wars are clearly shown. It is clear too that the value of the pound had already been falling for thirteen years or so before the outbreak of the First World War. During that war its value halved. Between the wars, however, the value of the pound had been rising but the effect of the Second World War was to reduce its value by approximately 40%. There is a sharp contrast between the two periods following the two wars. During the great inter-war depression the pound increased in value by about 50%, but since the Second World War the value of the pound has continued to fall—fairly rapidly until about 1956 and generally more slowly after that date until at least 1968 when the effects of devaluation began to be felt.

The index of retail prices shows in greater detail the rise in prices to the consumer. The first index to be compiled was the Cost-of-Living Index with 1914 as base year. During the time this index was in operation it fluctuated as follows:

TABLE LXXVIII

*The Cost-of-Living Index* (1914–45)

| Year | Index no. |
|------|-----------|
| 1914 | 100 |
| 1921 | 240 |
| 1929 | 100 |
| 1933 | 85 |
| 1939 | 96 |
| 1945 | 312 |

This index gives a rough approximation only of changes in a limited range of retail prices as it was based on the pattern of expenditure of manual workers at a time when their standard of living was very low. By 1939 it was clearly very much out of date and a new index covering a higher standard of living would have been introduced but for the outbreak of war in that year. The following table shows the index of retail prices since 1947:

TABLE LXXIX
*Index of Retail Prices*
(Monthly averages except where month stated)

| Year | Base year | | | |
|---|---|---|---|---|
| | 1947 | 1952 | 1956 | 1962 |
| 1947 (June) | 100 | | | |
| 1948 | 105 | | | |
| 1949 | 111 | | | |
| 1950 | 114 | | | |
| 1951 | 125 | | | |
| 1952 | 136 | (Jan.) 100 | | |
| 1953 | | 105·8 | | |
| 1954 | 143 | 107·7 | | |
| 1955 | 149 | 112·6 | | |
| 1956 (Jan.) | 153 | 115·8 | 100 | |
| 1956 | | | 102·0 | |
| 1957 | | | 105·8 | |
| 1958 | | | 109·0 | |
| 1959 | | | 109·6 | |
| 1960 | | | 110·7 | |
| 1961 | | | 114·5 | |
| 1962 (Jan.) | | | 117·5 | 100 |
| 1963 | | | | 103·6 |
| 1964 | | | | 107·0 |
| 1965 | | | | 112·1 |
| 1966 | | | | 116·5 |
| 1967 | | | | 119·4 |
| 1968 (June) | | | | 125·4 |

Source: *Annual Abstracts of Statistics.*

With a rising standard of living frequent revision of an index number of retail prices becomes necessary. This is particularly the case with food, expenditure on which forms a smaller proportion of total outlay as one's standard of living improves. The weight in the index for food has been successively reduced from 60% in 1914 to 39·9%

in 1952, 35% in 1956, 31·9% in 1962 and to 29·8% in 1966. Between 1947 and 1962 the index was revised no fewer than four times, and since 1962 the weighting of the items covered by the index has been revised annually.

## World Inflation

During the years 1952–67 the average annual rate of depreciation of the pound sterling was 2·9%, which gave Great Britain a higher degree of inflation than such countries as the United States, Germany and Switzerland, but less than that experienced by France or Japan and considerably less than that of some Latin American countries. Table LXXX shows how money depreciated during

TABLE LXXX
*Monetary Depreciation* (1952–62)
(1952 = 100)

|  | 1962 | Average rate per year |
|---|---|---|
|  |  | % |
| Canada       .       .       . | 90 | 1·1 |
| Switzerland .       .       . | 88 | 1·3 |
| United States       .     . | 88 | 1·3 |
| West Germany       .     . | 86 | 1·5 |
| Australia       .       .       . | 79 | 2·4 |
| United Kingdom .       . | 75 | 2·9 |
| Japan .       .       .       . | 72 | 3·5 |
| France       .       .       . | 70 | 3·5 |
| Brazil .       .       .       . | 9 | 21·5 |

Source: *Monthly Economic Letter of the First National City Bank of New York.* (Reproduced by kind permission of the Editor.)

1952–62 in the leading countries of the world. This table shows that during the ten years 1952–62 Canada, Switzerland, the United States and West Germany all managed to keep inflation fairly well under control; Australia, the United Kingdom, Japan and France were rather less successful; Brazil and some other Latin American countries suffered quite severe inflations, Brazilian money depeciating to only 9% of its previous value ten years before. During the ten years 1956–66 inflation continued to show very much the same pattern as Table LXXXI indicates. Guatemala is the only country in the list to maintain the value of its currency over the whole of this period. It is clear that with this one exception inflation continues to be a monetary feature common to all countries of the

TABLE LXXXI
*Monetary Depreciation* (1956–66)
(1956 = 100)

| | 1961 | 1966 | *Average rate per year* |
|---|---|---|---|
| | | | % |
| Guatemala | 102 | 100 | 0·0 |
| United States | 91 | 84 | 1·8 |
| Canada | 91 | 82 | 2·0 |
| Australia | 90 | 82 | 2·0 |
| Greece | 91 | 81 | 2·1 |
| Belgium | 93 | 80 | 2·2 |
| Union of South Africa | 91 | 80 | 2·2 |
| West Germany | 92 | 79 | 2·3 |
| Portugal | 92 | 78 | 2·4 |
| Switzerland | 94 | 78 | 2·4 |
| New Zealand | 88 | 77 | 2·6 |
| Austria | 90 | 75 | 2·8 |
| United Kingdom | 89 | 74 | 2·9 |
| Italy | 92 | 72 | 3·2 |
| Ireland | 89 | 72 | 3·2 |
| Norway | 88 | 72 | 3·2 |
| Netherlands | 88 | 71 | 3·4 |
| Pakistan | 84 | 70 | 3·5 |
| Denmark | 93 | 69 | 3·6 |
| Mexico | 78 | 69 | 3·6 |
| Sweden | 85 | 68 | 3·8 |
| Japan | 88 | 66 | 4·0 |
| France | 74 | 62 | 4·7 |
| India | 83 | 57 | 5·5 |
| Spain | 73 | 49 | 6·9 |
| Turkey | 58 | 45 | 7·7 |
| Bolivia | 31 | 25 | 13·0 |
| Chile | 38 | 10 | 20·6 |
| Argentina | 20 | 6 | 24·5 |
| Brazil | 29 | 2 | 31·0 |

Source: *Monthly Economic Letter of First National City Bank of New York.*
(Reproduced by kind permission of the Editor.)

world. Where countries differ, however, is in the extent of the inflation they have suffered. Of the leading nations the United States
experienced the smallest amount of inflation. Quite a number of
countries kept inflation under reasonable control with average rates
of depreciation for their currencies of around 2–2½%. The United
Kingdom with an average rate of 2·9% stands midway between
those with fairly good records in keeping inflation under control and
those such as Japan, France and India with rather high rates of

monetary depreciation. Latin American experience has been of a much more severe form of inflation.

## Full employment and inflation

Although inflation is much too serious a condition to be capable of being explained in terms of a single cause, the fact that it has been of world-wide occurrence during the past quarter of a century or so seems to indicate that its main causes too must have been of world-wide implication. A characteristic of the economies of most countries since the Second World War has been the generally high level of employment. When full employment has been reached, further increases in demand can result only in higher prices since in this condition there are no unused resources that can be drawn into production to increase output.

The governments of the United Kingdom, the United States and some others pledged themselves to maintain a permanent condition of full employment. One of the factors making for the persistence of inflation since 1945 has been this long period of full employment. On no question have successive British governments or the electorate been more sensitive. Since 1945 the unemployment rate in Great Britain has rarely, and only then for very short periods, fallen below an average of 1·5% for the country as a whole.[1] In consequence of having accepted responsibility for the maintenance of full employment British governments have often shown great reluctance to pursue an anti-inflationary policy as far as the situation demanded and reversed this policy almost at the first indication of its being effective in order to prevent a serious rise in unemployment. To make sure that full employment was achieved it appeared to be necessary to have over-full employment, a condition where the demand for labour exceeds the supply and consequently an inflationary situation.

In these conditions the bargaining power of the large trade unions is greatly increased. Their demands are more likely to be met since employers are reluctant to have production interrupted by strikes, and also because generally they expect to be able to pass on their increased costs in the form of higher prices. Wage drift, i.e. payments in excess of agreed wage rates, special bonuses, increased overtime, etc.—largely due to competition for labour from employers, and the shortening of the normal working week—also tends to be greater in these circumstances. Even during the brief periods since 1945 when prices have been fairly steady, claims for higher wages to improve the standard of living have continued to be made.

[1] The highest unemployment rates occurred (*i*) during the severe winter of 1947, and (*ii*) during 1966–68 as a result of a severe bout of deflation aimed at saving sterling from devaluation, a result it failed to achieve.

330 AN INTRODUCTION TO APPLIED ECONOMICS

In conditions of full employment wages rise periodically but never fall, so that the trend is always upwards. Increases in wages run ahead of productivity and so prices rise. It would appear, therefore, that full employment of itself creates a potentially inflationary situation, a fact recognised by Lord Beveridge as long ago as 1944,[1] when he pointed out that full employment required organised labour to adopt a more responsible attitude to questions of pay.

Attempts have been made to distinguish between "cost–push" and "demand–pull" influences. If the main influence in keeping an inflation in motion is excessive demand, then the situation is described as being that of a demand inflation, whereas if the main influence is rising costs it is regarded as a cost inflation. The older term of "inflationary spiral" refers to the effect of excessive demand raising prices, then being followed by wage increases and higher production costs, followed again by higher prices and a continuance of the spiral effect. It may be that at one time the main influence on prices is excess demand and that at another it may be rising costs of production (wages, raw materials, power, taxes on the employment of labour, etc.). More probably both influences are at work at the same time, the one affecting the other, wage rates like other prices being mainly influenced by excess demand.

### The persistence of inflation since 1945

A great war provides the environment which most frequently gives rise to inflation—stupendous government expenditure only part of which is offset by taxation or saving—but it is generally during the immediate post-war period that the danger of inflation getting out of hand is greatest. At such times all kinds of goods—both consumers' goods and producers' goods—are both in short supply and in great demand, with a mass of purchasing power accumulated during the war. After the First World War inflation was soon replaced by deflation and unemployment. After the Second World War, however, wartime physical controls were continued in an effort to contain the inflation. The Government, too, attempted to do too much in too short a time. As a result, public investment was excessive, while at the same time private investment was so over-stimulated by the cheap money policy in vogue at the time that it had to be restricted and controlled. The maintenance of full employment in these conditions, therefore, presented no difficulties.

In the interdependent world of the twentieth century inflationary tendencies are easily transmitted from one country to another, so that inflation has been a world phenomenon. To a country such as Great Britain with a fairly inelastic demand for imports, rises in the

---

[1] Lord Beveridge, *Full Employment in a Free Society*, p. 199.

prices of imports can have a strong influence on the internal price level.

Once in being, an inflation tends to be self-perpetuating unless drastic action is taken to bring it to an end, as happened in the 1920s. No such extreme measures were taken after the Second World War—at least not until 1966–67. The situation since 1945 too has been aggravated by a number of mainly extraneous events of an economic or political nature which from time to time gave further impetus to inflationary pressures. For example, in 1949 sterling had to be devalued. There is no doubt that at the rate of $4·03 to the pound, arbitrarily agreed after the war, sterling was over-valued. The new rate of $2.80 to the pound was clearly more realistic. For devaluation to be successful the internal or domestic value of the currency had to be aligned with its external value, *i.e.* price rises resulting from dearer imports had not to become the basis for higher incomes. In conditions of full employment trade unions are unwilling to tolerate a "wage freeze" for long, so that whatever benefits the economy derives from devaluation tend to be short-lived. The eventual result of devaluation, therefore, is likely to be a further stimulus to inflation. Then, in 1950, came the Korean War and, though the United States bore the brunt of the cost, its inflationary effects soon percolated from that country to others. Another effect of this war was that it led to the rearmament of the Western Powers with further public investment unaccompanied by the necessary saving, for which the low rate of interest was to some extent responsible.

By the early 1950s there was a fairly wide consensus of opinion that inflation in most parts of the world had been brought under control. During 1950–52, however, Great Britain was feeling the delayed effects of the 1949 devaluation and in two years retail prices rose at an average rate of 9% per year (Table LXXIX, p. 326). During 1953–54 prices steadied down, the rise being only 1·9% according to the revised index. Then in 1956 there came the Suez affair with its repercussions, both political and economic, and further stimulus was given to the inflationary process. After a brief lull during 1958–59 when the price index rose by barely half a point, from 109·0 to 109·6, the position of sterling was further aggravated in 1961 as a result of the revaluation of the German Deutschemark and the Dutch guilder.

Another lull occurred during 1961–63, and in spite of the braking effect of the Prices and Incomes Policy, announced in October 1964, the measures taken to deal with the external sterling crisis included the usual increases in indirect taxation which pushed up some prices. Although purchase taxes have been raised in most times of monetary crisis—1955, 1957, 1961, 1965–67—and, in the earlier ones at least, lowered in the ensuing reflations, there has been a general tendency over the past twenty years for indirect taxation to increase and so influence the general price level in an upwards direction. Since 1950, too, Chancellors of the Exchequer have resorted to the budget surplus as a means of curtailing the volume of purchasing power in the hands of consumers, and this has meant a higher level of taxation than would otherwise have been necessary. Because of the disincentive effects of high taxation the tax increases have been mainly in indirect taxes which increase the cost of living and so lead to demands for higher wages. Thus budget surpluses—rather to the surprise of those who first advocated this kind of fiscal policy—can have inflationary effects.

In fact, on capital account there have been deficits regularly during recent years. Another contributory cause (a primary cause according to some writers) to the persistence of inflation in this country, therefore, has been heavy spending in the public sector of the economy in excess of the amount raised by taxation or covered by saving. This has resulted in an exceptional increase in the National Debt, unprecedented in peacetime. In the ten years to 1967 the National Debt increased by almost £5,000 million, an average of £500 million a year, in consequence of government expenditure (formerly shown "below the line") exceeding revenue, though some of it has been in the form of loans to state enterprises, some of which might reasonably be expected to be repaid. The result has been a faster rate of expansion in the public sector than in the private sector, owing to some extent to the public sector being less influenced by credit restriction.

The inflationary situation in the years 1965–67 was again affected adversely by political events. First there was the war in Vietnam, which stimulated inflation in the United States though it had less effect on Great Britain than had the Korean War, and then in 1967 came the war in the Middle East with the closing for a time of the Suez Canal and in consequence the heavier cost of transporting oil and other goods by the Cape route. Finally, in November 1967 came the second devaluation of sterling in a quarter of a century, the value of the pound in terms of US dollars being reduced from 2.80 to 2.40. It seems fairly certain that sooner or later the effect of the devaluation of 1967 will be to increase prices by from 10 to 15%. In any circumstances—except of severe depression—it is difficult to convince trade unions of the necessity for wage restraint, least of all during periods of rising prices. In 1967 the trade unions were already chafing against two years of wage restraint,[1] and so not surprisingly they were strongly opposed to a continuance of this policy. During

---

[1] In fact, during these so-called years of restraint, hourly earnings rose more than twice as fast as output per man hour. During the first six months of 1966 over 5 million workers obtained wage increases.

1967, therefore, there was considerable opposition to the Government's policy, some increases in wages having to be granted to end strikes or threats of strikes, and often, where increases were postponed, employers having to agree to backdate them. So that although the devaluation of 1967 was only of the order of 14% as compared with 30% in 1949, and in spite of "productivity" agreements, a further impetus to inflation appears to be certain, as was the case with the earlier devaluation.

## II. EFFECTS OF INFLATION

### Inflation and production

Rising or falling prices influence production. When the general price level is falling, perhaps as a result of the adoption of a deflationary policy by the monetary authorities, all prices do not fall to exactly the same extent. In these circumstances wages for a long time have tended to be "sticky" and some other costs of production fall more slowly than the general price level. In any case, since production takes place in anticipation of demand, costs of production are incurred at a time when the general price level is higher than when the final product comes to be marketed. As a result the entrepreneurs' profit margin will be less than was anticipated when production was first undertaken. If the fall in the general price level is fairly considerable only the most efficient firms may succeed in making any profit at all while the less efficient will suffer varying degrees of loss, and if these conditions persist the least efficient may be forced into bankruptcy. Falling prices, therefore, add to the uncertainty that an entrepreneur has to bear and so influence his expectations. In these conditions he tends to take a pessimistic view of the future. He will tend to become less enterprising and to safeguard himself against possible loss he may curtail output. Thus, there is a tendency for business activity to be checked and for unemployment to increase when the general price level is falling.

In contrast a mild degree of inflation acts as a stimulus to production. In these conditions costs of production rise more slowly than the general price level, entrepreneurs have high expectations of the future, investment is encouraged, there is an increased demand for labour, unemployment falls, the demand for consumers' goods is stimulated and further expansion of production takes place until full employment is reached. This then becomes the danger point. Up to this point quite a mild degree of inflation will have been sufficient to stimulate production, but if demand continues to expand after full employment has been reached the full impact will henceforth be on prices since there is now no unused capacity to be drawn into production.

It might be thought, therefore, that the most desirable condition would be one of stable prices. Both international trade and internal trade can be carried on with less risk to traders and producers if prices are reasonably stable. Confidence is promoted and forward contracts can be entered into with safety. Stable prices too are more equitable than either rising or falling prices for consumers in general, since price changes have an arbitrary influence on the distribution of incomes. A stable price level, however, does not mean that individual prices would not change in response to changes in demand or supply. A fall in price as a result of an improvement in conditions of supply would benefit all consumers equally if the general price level was stable. Money too can effectively fulfil its functions as a medium of exchange, a measure of value and a store of value only if its value remains fairly stable. This would make the role of money in the economy a neutral one.

Though stable prices appear to have some theoretical advantages they do not necessarily indicate that an economy is sound. A stable price level may be achieved, for example, at the bottom of a depression. It may seem to some to be incompatible with its historic functions for money to play a dynamic role in the economy, but this is necessary if monetary policy, whether of a deflationary or inflationary character, is to achieve the objective sought by the monetary authorities. Nor does it seem as if full employment can be permanently maintained without the stimulus of at least a mild degree of inflation, while in its turn full employment creates conditions in which inflation flourishes. In any case, it would be extremely difficult for the authorities to ensure that the volume of investment was just sufficient and no more than sufficient to keep prices stable. Rising, falling and stable prices all have their particular drawbacks, but mildly rising prices have the great advantage of stimulating production and assisting the maintenance of full employment. Indeed, many people consider a mild degree of inflation to be a small price to pay for this. The important proviso is that the degree of inflation should be small and kept within strict control.

For upwards of twenty years after the Second World War, governments lectured their electorates on the dangers of inflation, but never succeeded in quite getting rid of it. Many, however, have now come round to the view that a little mild inflation is good for the economy. How much this should be it is not easy to decide, but it has been suggested that a maximum annual price rise of 2% might be considered acceptable. If so, few countries, as Table LXXXI (p. 328) shows, have succeeded in controlling inflation sufficiently. The fear used to be that even a small degree of inflation was dangerous since it might spark off a serious hyperinflation. Sometimes, of course, this does happen, as in the hyperinflations that followed the two World

Wars and those more recently suffered in Latin America, but periodic bouts of deflation have kept inflation at least within bounds in most countries, though on occasion at the expense of economic growth.

## Effects of a rise in the value of money

One of the strongest arguments against inflation is that it brings about an arbitrary redistribution of incomes. The same too, however, can be said of a period of falling prices, *i.e.* when the value of money is increasing. Periods when the value of money has been rising have been rarer and generally of shorter duration than periods when the value of money has been falling. The last occasion when there was a substantial increase in the value of money—50% in ten years—was immediately before and during the worst part of the Great Depression between 1925 and 1935 (*see* Fig. 12, p. 325). Previous to that the value of money had varied in the short run with the ups and downs of the trade cycle, though the general long-term tendency had been for its value to fall.

When analysing the effects of changes in the value of money it is usual to consider separately the consequence for each of three groups of people: (*i*) those who derive their incomes mainly from business profits; (*ii*) those who receive wages; and (*iii*) those in receipt of fixed money incomes. It has already been pointed out that when prices are falling profit margins are squeezed and in some cases turned into losses, so that there is a tendency for production to be curtailed. In these circumstances total profits will fall, and so those whose incomes depend on business profits will find that their incomes fall by a greater proportion than does the general price level, so that their real incomes in terms of what money will buy will be reduced. Consider the position of wage-earners. Since with the increasing power of trade unions wages tend to be "sticky" they will not fall to the same extent as prices, and in any case there is likely to be a time-lag between the fall in prices and the fall in wages. Though some wage-earners as a result may be slightly better off, many in manufacturing industry in consequence, however, of the curtailment of production will find themselves out of work and others will be put on "short time." Only those wage-earners who remain in continuous employment, therefore, will benefit from the falling price level. Among agricultural workers there will be less unemployment but farm incomes and, therefore, the wages of farm workers will fall again to a greater extent than the general price level. The third group comprises people with fixed incomes, and these will be mainly salaried workers and people who have retired from work. Those whose incomes are irrevocably fixed in terms of money will clearly be better off as a result of falling prices. Those in receipt of pensions—not a very large proportion of the retired population before the Second World War—will be in this category, as will those whose retirement income is derived from annuities purchased out of past savings. In general, this group will also include those who have invested their savings in gilt-edged securities. Those who have invested in company ordinary shares, however, will be in similar straits to the businessmen. While wages and profits fluctuated in the trade cycle salaries generally remained unchanged and so could be regarded as a form of fixed income, what was gained on the swings when prices were falling being lost on the roundabouts when prices were rising. When the value of money was rising they were clearly better off.

What was true of downswings of the trade cycle was not wholly true of conditions during the Great Depression, which was both longer and deeper than earlier recessions. As a result business profits fell to lower levels than previously and more bankruptcies occurred. Unemployment was higher and more prolonged than ever before, but hardship was mitigated to some extent by a higher rate and much wider incidence of entitlement to unemployment pay since this benefit had been provided under the national insurance scheme. Many workers, however, had been out of work so long that they had exhausted the benefit to which they were entitled, and after 1931, when the rate of benefit was reduced, further assistance depended on a family means test. Salaried workers too fared worse than before. Many clerical workers lost their jobs when factories closed down and many more had to submit to reductions of pay. Those in public service enjoyed the advantages of fixed money incomes until the autumn interim budget of 1931 when 10% cuts were decreed in the salaries of all civil servants, local government employees, teachers and the armed services.[1] Even some of the people with investments in gilt-edged suffered a reduction of income. It just happened at this time that several government stocks of very large amount were due for redemption and in 1932 this enabled a great funding operation to be carried out to substitute low-interest stocks for the maturing stocks that had been issued at high interest during the First World War. Since the commercial banks were paying only $\frac{1}{2}$% interest on deposits and building societies only $1\frac{1}{2}$%, holders had no option but to accept this cut in their incomes. Relatively few people, therefore—those with fixed pensions or annuities and holders of unredeemable fixed interest securities such as Consols—found falling prices to their advantage. Nevertheless, some arbitrary redistribution of income occurred.

[1] These salaries were restored to their former levels in two annual instalments after 1935.

## Inflation and incomes from profits

The effect of inflation on the three different sections of the community might be expected to be the reverse of the consequences of falling prices. For businessmen producing in anticipation of demand production takes place at a lower general price level than that expected to prevail when the product comes to be sold. Profit margins, therefore, tend to be wider than had been anticipated, so that even the less efficient entrepreneurs achieve a satisfactory profit, while the efficient entrepreneurs cannot fail to make a substantial profit. In these circumstances profits tend to rise to a greater extent than do prices in general, and so those people whose incomes are derived from business profits find themselves better off when prices are rising than when prices are falling. This was true of the upswing of the trade cycle and it has been generally true of the prolonged period of inflation experienced since the Second World War. In its efforts to check inflation, however, a government may try to persuade the trade unions to agree to a pay pause by taxing business profits and capital gains more heavily or by imposing other taxes—such as the selective employment tax—on employers. An attempt too may be made to limit distributed profits and capital gains. Depending on the extent to which the demand for the product is inelastic, producers may be able to pass on some of their increased costs to consumers in the form of higher prices, but some entrepreneurs will find taxation cutting into their profit margins. In the past taxes on profits have generally been condemned by economists as penalising, and therefore, checking enterprise. Provided such taxes are not excessive there appears, however, to be more justification than formerly for their imposition since a government, pursuing a full employment policy, sets out to create conditions permanently favourable to entrepreneurs. In spite of increased taxation, however, it would seem that in general incomes from profits in an inflationary period do more than merely keep pace with the rise in the general price level.

## Inflation and the wage-earner

How, then, do wage-earners fare in times of rising prices? During the short-term fluctuations of the trade cycle in times of both rising and falling prices there used to be a time-lag before any adjustments were made in wages, so that when prices were falling wage-earners were a little better off and when prices were rising they were worse off. Since both the upswing and the downswing of the cycle were short, these alternating conditions offset one another over each period of seven years or so. If, however, wage increases had continued to lag behind price increases during the prolonged period of inflation since 1945, wage-earners would have had no period of falling prices to offset this. Their position, however, has been altered by the equally prolonged period of full employment, throughout which the bargaining power of the trade unions has been strong. The time-lag between a rise in prices and an increase in wages tends to be longer if there is serious unemployment at the time, but once full employment has been reached both prices and wages begin to increase more rapidly. The result is that wage rates first catch up with prices and eventually overtake them. Of course, economic growth makes possible a higher standard of living for all, and since economic growth does not appear to be possible without some degree

TABLE LXXXII

*Wage Rates and Retail Prices*

| Year | Index of wage rates | Retail price index | |
|---|---|---|---|
| 1956 (Jan.) | 100 | 100 | |
| 1957 | 110·7 | 105·8 | |
| 1958 | 113·4 | 109·0 | |
| 1959 | 116·8 | 109·6 | |
| 1960 | 119·9 | 110·7 | |
| 1961 | 125·0 | 114·5 | 100 |
| 1962 | 129·3 | 117·5 | 103·6 |
| 1963 | 134·1 | | 107·0 |
| 1964 | 140·7 | | 112·1 |
| 1965 | 146·3 | | |
| 1966 | 153·7 | | 116·5 |
| 1967 | 157·6 | | 119·4 |
| 1968 (June) | 168·6 | | 125·4 |

Sources: *Annual Abstract of Statistics.*

of inflation, it is not altogether surprising, therefore, to find real wages increasing during a period of persistent inflation. Table LXXXII shows, however, that wage rates have increased more rapidly than retail prices since 1956. The change in the base year for the index of retail prices makes comparison over the whole period less easy to see. However, it is clear that between 1956 and 1962 wage rates increased by 29·2%, while retail prices increased by only 17·5%. Between 1962 and 1968 wage rates increased by 30%, whereas prices increased by 24%. Over the whole period there was an increase in wage rates of 68·6% as compared with a price increase of 43·1%. In fact, these figures under-estimate the improvement in the position of wage-earners, since owing to wage drift, actual earnings have increased much more than wage rates. These wage rates, too, are the average for all wage-earners. In addition to variations between one industry and another other variations have been noticeable. For example, unskilled workers have generally done rather better than the skilled, women better than men, and young workers under 18 years of age better than adults.

## Fixed incomes and inflation

Finally, the position of people with fixed incomes remains to be considered. Those people whose incomes are fixed in terms of money will, of course, find the real value of their incomes eroded as prices rise. Most of these are retired people who were over 55 years of age in 1948 when the present scheme of national insurance came into operation. They were thus too old to qualify for a State retirement pension. Those of them who derive their entire incomes from gilt-edged securities bearing fixed rates of interest, or from annuities or from fixed pensions awarded by private employers, have all suffered a declining standard of living in their later years. What was an adequate income in 1948 or even 1955 may today be very much below the amount that would give them the standard of living which they had reasonably expected to enjoy on retirement. To make matters worse, direct taxation has not been adjusted sufficiently to take account of the fall in the value of money, the tax-free personal allowance in real terms being much less than it was a few years ago. The number of such people is small and by 1968 they were all over 75 years of age, but suggestions that these people should be allowed the State retirement pension have so far met with no response.[1] If some people gain in a period of inflation, then others must lose. These are the people who have suffered most.

## Inflation and the salaried worker

However, many of those whose incomes used to be considered to be fixed are no longer so. At one time, for example, salaries were regarded as fixed. For a long time after prices began to rise in 1935 most salaries remained unchanged until the later years of the Second World War. Even in 1950 when the value of money was little more than half of what it had been fifteen years earlier many salaried workers, including graduate teachers in grammar schools, bank employees and those employed in local government, had obtained no more than a 16% increase in their salaries. Table LXXXIII (p. 340) shows the share of wages, salaries and incomes of professional persons in the national income since 1951.

[1] Even though, as was pointed out in Chapter VIII, contributions of employers and employees together actuarially only cover half the retirement pension, the remainder being paid for out of taxation.

TABLE LXXXIII
*Wages and Salaries*

| Year | Wages | Salaries | National income |
|------|-------|----------|-----------------|
| | £ million | £ million | £ million |
| 1951 | 5,095 | 2,580 | 11,946 |
| 1952 | 5,450 | 2,780 | 12,762 |
| 1953 | 5,760 | 2,925 | 13,509 |
| 1954 | 6,160 | 3,130 | 14,289 |
| 1955 | 6,765 | 3,445 | 15,514 |
| 1956 | 7,330 | 3,785 | 16,836 |
| 1957 | 7,660 | 4,100 | 17,831 |
| 1958 | 7,785 | 4,340 | 18,594 |
| 1959 | 8,040 | 4,665 | 19,545 |
| 1960 | 8,600 | 5,110 | 20,834 |
| 1961 | 9,240 | 5,580 | 22,298 |
| 1962 | 9,575 | 6,015 | 23,259 |
| 1963 | 9,920 | 6,410 | 24,710 |
| 1964 | 10,685 | 6,925 | 26,593 |
| 1965 | 11,480 | 7,605 | 28,613 |
| 1966 | 12,085 | 8,265 | 29,921 |
| 1967 | 12,235 | 8,785 | 31,148 |
| 1968 | | | |

Source: *Blue Books on National Income and Expenditure.*

Between 1951 and 1955 the total amounts paid out in wages and salaries increased by 30 and 33% respectively, so that, after lagging behind wages for more than a decade, salaries began to push ahead. During the next five years, 1956–60, wages increased by 17% as compared with a 32% increase in salaries. Salaries were thus making up some of the ground lost prior to 1951. The tendency for salaries to increase more rapidly than wages was continued during the next period of five years, 1961–65, when salaries increased by 34% as against 22% for wages. Over the whole period, 1951–67 the total paid out in wages increased by 140% and salaries by 240%. Increases, it should be stressed, refer to the total amounts paid out in wages and salaries and not to increases in the rates of payment of individuals. The present trend is for the number of wage-earners to fall and the number of salaried workers to increase. If account is taken of this trend the overall increase of 140% in wages underestimates the increase in individual earnings, while the increase of 240% in salaries exaggerates somewhat individual increases. Over the years many of the professional organisations of the various groups of salaried workers have tended to concentrate more and more on trade union activities and less on maintaining professional standards, to the extent of adopting the aggressive tactics of the more militant of the manual workers' trade unions. It would seem, therefore, that in a prolonged period of inflation salaried workers can no longer be regarded as having fixed incomes since generally they are now able to secure increases in pay that more than compensate them for the rise in prices.

## Inflation and the pensioner

The remaining people in the former group of fixed-income receivers are those who have retired on pensions. It has become customary to increase State retirement pensions periodically either on account of rising prices or to give retired people a share in the rising standard of living. Thus, the pension for a married couple, which was £109 a year in 1950, had become £254 by 1961 and £378 by 1968, a rise of 270% as compared with a rise in wages of 120% and in the prices of consumers' goods and services of about 85%. (In Germany state pensions are geared more directly both to the cost of living and to the standard of living.) Retired persons, however, who have previously been in public employment—the Civil Service, Armed Forces, teaching—can have their pensions increased only by special Act of Parliament. Acts of 1944 and 1947 granted small increases. Since then a number of further Acts have been passed. The basis of the awards made in the later Acts was a graduated scale of percentage increase according to the length of retirement. For example, in 1966 those who had been retired only two years received an increase of 2% while those who had been retired nine years received 16%. In the case of most of the large banks and insurance companies increases are often, though not always, given to those in receipt of pensions shortly after their present employees have received increases. As with those previously in public employment, increases are usually greatest for those who have been retired longest. For example, some past employees of banks received six increases in their pensions in the ten years to 1966. Many pensions, therefore, now almost keep pace at least with the rising cost of living—though with a time-lag—though a few unfortunate people depending on private pension schemes are still in receipt of rigidly fixed incomes.

A long experience of persistent inflation has taught an increasing number of people to try to protect their future income. The huge rise during the 1950s in the value of equities and also in consequence in the value of units in unit investment trusts drew the attention of savers to these forms of investment, though experience in the 1960s did not match that of the 1950s. The linking of life assurance with unit trusts has also provided protection against the erosion of savings.

With the passage of time, therefore, fewer people tend to be quite as severely hit as formerly by persistent inflation. In addition in inflationary conditions all debtors—and the Government is the largest debtor of all—gain at the expense of their creditors. Nevertheless, in spite of all the efforts made to alleviate the position of many of those who are adversely affected, and the fact that persistent inflation today involves rather less injustice than it once did, some arbitrary redistribution of incomes still takes place. If redistribution of income is thought to be desirable it should obviously be effected on equitable principles, for an arbitrary redistribution of incomes is almost certain to be inequitable by increasing inequality of income.

## III. CONTROL OF INFLATION

### Monetary policy and its aims

During the past quarter of a century or so the Government has constantly been trying to reconcile two apparently incompatible policies: (i) to maintain full employment, and (ii) to keep inflation in check. Monetary policy, therefore, has aimed at checking demand through a reduction in purchasing power wherever inflation has become excessive and the economy has appeared to be "overheated," and has aimed at stimulating demand through an expansion of credit whenever it has thought that full employment was in danger. Thus, deflation has alternated with reflation—a mildly inflationary stimulus—policies which have earned the derisive appellation of "stop–go." This term emphasises one of two other factors associated with monetary policy—economic growth. Full employment is not an end in itself but a concomitant of economic growth, which has become the prime objective of economic policy among the nations of the West. Deflation clearly checks economic growth. Full employment, however, engenders inflation, and this then stimulates the demand for imports and injects imbalance into the balance of payments, followed by a threat to the country's gold and convertible currency reserves—the second of the two other factors associated with monetary policy. Thus, the monetary authorities are constantly faced by the extremely difficult problem of balancing the different effects of any policy they decide to adopt on the level of employment, internal monetary stability, the rate of economic growth and the balance of payments.

The impact of monetary policy is, therefore, on the pressure of demands for goods and services. Changes in the pressure of demand are brought about through changes in interest rates and in liquidity. Spending is not limited by the quantity of money in existence at a particular time since money is only one aspect of liquidity. There are many liquid assets that are close substitutes for money, these often being termed "near-money." As the Radcliffe Report says: "The decision to spend thus depends on liquidity in the broad sense, not upon immediate access to money."[1] Monetary policy affects liquidity through changes in interest rates, so that the structure of interest rates becomes of greater importance than the quantity of money.

## Instruments of monetary policy

It may be said that the function of monetary policy is to offset the adverse monetary effects arising out of the complexities of a modern economic system. In such an economy money has a dynamic influence and variations in the availability of credit can be used to stimulate or damp down demand and so influence the economy. In the strictest sense monetary policy comprises the use of bank rate as an instrument of policy and such measures as open market operations to make it effective.

During the nineteenth century the Bank of England developed the use of these two instruments of policy. On the gold standard excessive internal demand led to an adverse balance of payments and an outflow of gold. This situation, both internally and externally, was rectified by raising bank rate in order to increase prevailing rates of interest generally, and this was supported by appropriate open market operations—in this case the Bank of England would sell securities on the open market in order to reduce the credit basis of the commercial banks and so compel them to contract credit, that is to say, a deflationary policy was pursued. In the event of an inflow of gold bank rate would be lowered and open market operations through a purchase of securities on the open market would be undertaken by the Bank of England to encourage an expansion of credit and through that of demand, the Bank therefore pursuing an inflationary policy. Thus, it was primarily the needs of the external situation—whether the balance of payments was favourable or adverse—that determined the form that monetary policy should take, though it was rare that the internal and external policy requirements did not coincide.

At this time the Bank of England always regarded bank rate as its main instrument of monetary policy, open market operations being undertaken merely to make bank rate "effective." More recently, it has been thought that in those days open market operations were the more efficacious, at least in the short run, as it takes a change in bank rate longer to make its influence felt, although it is admitted that bank rate is important as a signal of the intentions of the monetary authorities. In the early 1930s it came to be felt in some

[1] Report of the Committee on the Working of the Monetary System, para. 390.

quarters, however, that bank rate was a quite ineffective instrument of policy. In an effort to get out of the depression bank rate was reduced in 1932 to 2% and an era of cheap money was inaugurated. In the generally pessimistic climate of the Great Depression—the severest in history—the future appeared to most entrepreneurs to be so black that cheap money offered them little inducement to expand production. The fact that recovery from the Great Depression was so very slow seemed to support the contention that bank rate was an ineffective instrument of policy. Arguing on the same lines it was suggested that in an inflationary period bank rate would be equally ineffective since in an optimistic atmosphere with high profits to be earned even a high bank rate would not deter most entrepreneurs from seeking bank loans. Indeed, most businessmen admit that the rate of interest at which they borrow is insignificant in relation to their other costs. As a result bank rate as an instrument of policy became discredited.

Nevertheless, the first intimations of recovery from the Great Depression, though much delayed, came in the form of the development of a building boom in the middle 1930s. House building being particularly interest-sensitive, it could be traced to cheap money. This gave support to those who retained their faith in bank rate, especially those who thought that all that could be said against it was that it was slow to take effect. Psychologically, too, bank rate can influence business activity, as movements in the rate indicate the policy of the monetary authorities. This is particularly so in the case of a rise in the rate since knowledge of the onset of deflationary conditions is likely to make many entrepreneurs more cautious. Similarly, with open market operations a reduction in the credit basis of the commercial banks is bound to be effective in restricting borrowing from them if they are to maintain their recognised liquidity ratio, whereas an expansion of the liquid assets of the banks, although it makes possible increased bank lending, cannot compel businessmen to borrow.

The belief that bank rate was an ineffective weapon for influencing business activity led to its falling into disuse as an instrument of monetary policy. This being the accepted view, bank rate, it was believed, should be kept as low as was practicable if only to enable the Government, the country's biggest borrower, to borrow as cheaply as possible. Thus, bank rate was reduced to its recognised minimum of 2% in 1932 in the hope that it would assist a business revival, retained at 2% during the Second World War in the knowledge that a huge amount of government borrowing would have to be undertaken (cheap money in time of war was a new departure, borrowing during the First World War being at 5%), and still kept at 2% from 1945 to 1951, in spite of its inflationary effects in a time of over-full employment, again in order to permit the Government to borrow cheaply and also because some members of the government of the day looked upon the payment of interest very much in the same light as the medieval Church regarded usury.[1] The efforts of the Chancellor of the Exchequer, however, to use the means at the Treasury's disposal to bring down interest rates still further failed.

As a substitute for monetary policy physical controls, introduced of necessity during the Second World War, were continued well into the peace. The British economy had been so orientated to the sole purpose of prosecuting war, and the economic effects of the war had been so great and so far-reaching, that this course would have had to be pursued at least for a little by any government in power in those days. The Labour Government which took office in 1945, however, favoured the retention of physical controls, regarding them as instruments for furthering the extension of State planning. Consumers, therefore, had to submit to the continuance of rationing for six years or more after the war had ended. Imports were restricted, the allocation of raw materials for building and other purposes was subjected to a system of licensing, and investment was again controlled by the Capital Issues Committee of the Bank of England. By these means it was possible to ensure that priority of investment was given to projects which the Government favoured, such as housing, road construction, the building of new factories in the development areas, etc. However, the drawback to physical controls is that, instead of getting rid of inflation, they merely suppress it.

There is, moreover, also some opposition to monetary policy on theoretical grounds. Since in effect its impact is made through an expansion or contraction of the monetary supply its effectiveness depends on the extent to which the quantity theory of money is accepted. Lord Keynes, for example, believed the main effects of a change in the quantity of money to be on investment with only a weak effect on demand in the markets for consumers' goods. As already pointed out, however, the modern view is that liquidity is of greater importance than the quantity of money. The cash ratio, too, is considered to be of less importance than formerly as a means of controlling the volume of bank deposits, since the Bank of England now keeps the market supplied with the amount of cash necessary to maintain the customary 8% cash ratio. The role of the cash ratio has been taken over by the banks' liquid assets ratio, for long maintained at 30%, but since 1964 at 28%. Then, the Radcliffe Report of 1959 stressed that the main influence on spending, whether

---

[1] Interest, of course, is a payment for a service, the price to be paid for the use of money in the present instead of at some future date. Lord Keynes regarded interest as a payment for parting with liquidity.

on consumers' goods or producers' goods, is the general liquidity of the economy and not merely the supply of money. A number of other financial institutions besides the commercial banks can influence general liquidity, such as insurance companies, managers of pension funds, building societies, investment trust companies, unit investment trusts and hire purchase finance companies. The actions of these institutions can to some extent offset any action the commercial banks may be compelled to take. Recent "requests" regarding credit policy from the Bank of England, therefore, have been addressed not solely to the commercial banks but also to some of these other financial intermediaries.

### The revival of monetary policy

In 1951 monetary policy was restored as an instrument of economic policy. Many writers had regarded cheap money as one of the main causes of the persistence of inflation and for some time they had been advocating higher interest rates. Revival by the British monetary authorities of bank rate as an instrument of policy was not, however, solely due to a reappraisal of its effectiveness in Great Britain. Interest rates were rising in other parts of the world too and it was necessary for this country to fall into line. It should be pointed out that excess liquidity in the banking system would have nullified any attempt to employ monetary policy during the immediate post-war years. A degree of excess liquidity persisted down to 1955 and this to some extent reduced the effectiveness of higher interest rates internally. In fact, since it is customary for the rate charged on bank loans to be 1% above bank rate with a minimum rate of 5%, it was not until 1955, when bank rate had been pushed up to $4\frac{1}{2}\%$, that it became dearer to borrow from the banks, *i.e.* not until four years after the revival of bank rate as an instrument of policy. Table LXXXIV shows the changes in bank rate that have been made since 1951. This table shows the rise in interest rates that has taken place since 1951. Since 1955 bank rate has never fallen below 4%.

It is now fairly generally agreed that the prevailing rate of interest as indicated by bank rate is of greater economic importance than was at one time thought. Though a change in the rate of interest may have little or no effect in the short term, it does appear to have a long-term influence on investment, its effect being mainly on the future plans of entrepreneurs rather than on their present attitude to holding stocks. It would certainly appear that changes in bank rate have considerable influence abroad, particularly in the case of a rise, which is regarded as an outward sign of the intention of the monetary authorities to adopt severe anti-inflationary measures to improve the balance of payments and protect the pound sterling. Bank rate too is a general market influence, whereas some of the

TABLE LXXXIV

*Changes in Bank Rate since 1951*

| Year | High | Low | No. of changes |
|------|------|-----|----------------|
| 1951 | 2½   | 2   | 1 |
| 1952 | 4    | 2½  | 1 |
| 1953 | 4    | 3½  | 1 |
| 1954 | 3½   | 3   | 1 |
| 1955 | 4½   | 3   | 2 |
| 1956 | 5½   | 4½  | 1 |
| 1957 | 7    | 5   | 2 |
| 1958 | 7    | 4   | 4 |
| 1959 | 4    | 4   | 0 |
| 1960 | 6    | 4   | 4 |
| 1961 | 7    | 5   | 3 |
| 1962 | 6    | 4½  | 3 |
| 1963 | 4½   | 4   | 1 |
| 1964 | 7    | 4   | 2 |
| 1965 | 7    | 6   | 1 |
| 1966 | 7    | 6   | 1 |
| 1967 | 8    | 5½  | 6 |
| 1968 | 8    | 7   | 2 |

Source: *Annual Abstract of Statistics.*

more recently introduced instruments mainly affect certain sectors only of the economy.

## Modern instruments of policy

During the past twenty-five years, therefore, a number of new instruments of monetary policy or adjuncts to it have been tried and developed.

(*i*) *Physical controls.* As already pointed out, the main instruments of policy adopted during the years following the end of the Second World War were non-monetary physical controls. At first these controls were accompanied only by a policy of cheap or ultra-cheap money. For a time after the revived use of bank rate in 1951 physical controls were continued but over the ensuing few years they were gradually dismantled and eventually abolished. In 1966, however, restrictions were again imposed on expenditure on foreign travel. In a sense too the precise limitation of bank advances is a physical control, though it is better to restrict this term to non-monetary measures.

(*ii*) *Fiscal policy.* Since 1949 the budget has become an important instrument of policy. Fiscal policy takes two forms: (*a*) the creation of a budget surplus as a disinflationary measure; (*b*) variations in the rates of particular indirect taxes such as purchase tax and the excise duties on tobacco, alcoholic drink and petrol.

Before the outbreak of the Second World War some economists, who regarded bank rate as an ineffective instrument had suggested that monetary policy should be replaced by fiscal policy. In the conditions of those days—a high level of persistent unemployment—what they desired was an inflationary budget to stimulate demand, *i.e.* the deliberate creation of a budget deficit by increasing government expenditure above the level of revenue yielded by existing taxation. Such a policy (except in time of war) was anathema to all orthodox financiers and indeed British Chancellors of the Exchequer, to whichever political party they were aligned, and so "deficit financing," as it was called, was never attempted in this country. Failure to get rid of inflation in the immediate post-war period led some economists to suggest that if a budget deficit was suitable to slump conditions, then *mutatis mutandis* a budget surplus might be appropriate to an inflationary situation. A budget surplus, it was suggested, would cream off the excess of purchasing power. On a number of occasions quite substantial budget surpluses were obtained by successive Chancellors of the Exchequer. Since, however, most of them found for one reason or another little scope for achieving a surplus by reducing government expenditure, the only course open to them was to increase taxation. Since further it was generally thought desirable to avoid the distinctive effect of increasing direct taxation, the additional revenue required had to be obtained mainly from indirect taxation. As this increased the cost of living it gave further impetus to trade union claims for higher wages. A budget surplus, therefore, by the very manner of its creation appeared as likely to encourage as to check inflation in conditions of full employment. The earlier budget surpluses were achieved after all government expenditure had been taken into consideration, both "above the line" (expenditure on current account) and "below the line" (expenditure on capital account). Arguing from business practice, it was suggested later that, in calculating a budget disinflationary surplus, capital expenditure should be ignored.

(*iii*) *The regulator.* The demand for certain commodities can be checked or stimulated by raising or lowering, as the case may be, purchase tax or similar excise duties. This device has been employed regularly since 1951 on all occasions when the Government has wished to influence the level of demand, but until 1961 changes in these taxes were restricted to the April budget and the occasional interim budget. In 1961, however, the Chancellor of the Exchequer obtained powers to vary these taxes by up to 10% in either direction at any time, since to be effective it was necessary for action to be taken promptly to meet a changing economic situation. This instrument of policy came to be known as the regulator. Apart from the fact, already noted in connection with the budget surplus, that to check demand by raising prices and the cost of living can itself have inflationary effects by further stimulating demands for wage increases, variation of the rate of taxation of commodities can have yet another serious drawback. Purchase tax affects only a limited range of commodities, as also do the other excise duties. The greatest effects, therefore, of variations in purchase tax have been on consumer durables such as motor cars, furniture and most kinds of electrical goods, an increase in the rate of tax quickly checking demand and a reduction in tax stimulating demand. However, in the case of the duties on alcoholic drink, tobacco and petrol, there has been a tendency for increases in these duties, once imposed, to remain. The demand for all these commodities is inclined to be inelastic, for the effects of higher prices for alcoholic drink and tobacco have been only temporary, demand generally returning to its pre-tax level within a few months. In fact, with a rising standard of living, consumption of alcoholic drink has tended to increase over the years, while consumption of tobacco has declined only slightly, more as a result of anti-smoking propaganda than because of increasing prices.

TABLE LXXXV

*Consumers' Expenditure*
(at 1958 prices)

| Year | Alcoholic drink £m. | Tobacco £m. |
|---|---|---|
| 1955 | 879 | 973 |
| 1957 | 914 | 1,012 |
| 1959 | 969 | 1,053 |
| 1961 | 1,080 | 1,101 |
| 1963 | 1,115 | 1,084 |
| 1965 | 1,170 | 1,042 |
| 1967 | 1,229 | 1,063 |

Source: *Blue Book on National Income and Expenditure.*

(*iv*) *Hire purchase.* Over recent years there has been a large increase in the volume of hire purchase business, as Table LXXXVI (p. 350) shows. In spite of checks during periods of credit restriction hire purchase business has clearly shown a tendency to increase. About two-thirds of hire purchase business is financed by finance houses, the remainder mostly by retailers and some by personal bank loans. The commercial banks are involved in three ways: (*i*) through their own subsidiaries since they acquired interests in finance houses; (*ii*) through their lending to finance houses; and (*iii*) through direct

TABLE LXXXVI

*Hire Purchase Debt*

| Year | Financed by finance houses | Total amount outstanding |
|------|-----------------|------------------|
|      | £ million       | £ million        |
| 1961 | 618             | 934              |
| 1962 | 569             | 887              |
| 1963 | 614             | 959              |
| 1964 | 754             | 1,280            |
| 1965 | 836             | 1,386            |
| 1966 | 756             | 1,261            |
| 1967 | 742             | 1,226            |

Source: *Annual Abstract of Statistics.*

personal loans to customers. The volume of hire purchase business is now so great that changes in hire purchase regulations—the amount of the initial deposit and the length of the period of repayment—can have an important influence on demand. Variations in purchase tax and in hire purchase regulations, however, have both affected the same range of commodities—mainly consumer durable goods. The result, therefore, has been that changes in demand have tended to be concentrated only on certain sections of the economy which, in consequence, have been subjected to severe fluctuations both in output and in employment. Thus, these directional effects can be harmful to economic growth.

(v) *The directive.* The revival in 1951 of bank rate as an instrument of monetary policy was accompanied by a Treasury directive to the commercial banks to restrict their lending to purposes that could be regarded as being in the national interest—a vague phrase incapable of precise definition. This was the qualitative directive. When this did not bring about as great a restriction of bank credit as the authorities desired, a quantitative directive was issued to the effect that, irrespective of the purposes for which loans were required, bank credit should be reduced by a stated amount. In 1964 and again in 1966 the commercial banks were requested not to increase their advances by more than 5%. In earlier days a rise in bank rate had been accomplished by open market operations to reduce bank cash and therefore bank credit. Open market operations are undertaken nowadays mainly for the purpose of influencing the long-term or short-term rate of interest, intervention for the former purpose being in the securities market and for the latter in the discount market. Until 1955 there was excess liquidity in the British banking system and in such conditions open market operations of the kind employed in the past would have had little or no effect. Then, it is generally acknowledged too that bank rate is slow to take effect.

whereas in the case of the directive action can be taken at once, that is so far as new loans are concerned. Whereas, however, bank rate is general in its application, in the case of the directive the onus is placed on bank managers to decide to whom it shall be applied.

Action by the monetary authorities to restrict credit has been directed mainly against the London clearing banks. This appeared to be justifiable since banks are the principal lenders and have the widest range of borrowers. Nevertheless, both bank deposits and advances continue to expand, as the following table shows:

TABLE LXXXVII
*Bank Deposits and Advances (1959–68)*

| Year | Bank Deposits £ million | Bank Advances £ million |
|---|---|---|
| 1957 | 6,432 | 1,868 |
| 1960 | 7,236 | 3,123 |
| 1964 | 8,550 | 4,328 |
| 1966 | 9,376 | 4,732 |
| 1967 | 9,772 | 4,725 |
| 1968 (June) | 10,278 | 5,089 |

Frequent restrictions of bank lending have had the effect of making frustrated borrowers look to other sources to meet their requirements, such as finance companies, acceptance houses, discount houses and insurance companies. In fact the London clearing banks in 1967 held only 59% of total deposits. Clearly, to be effective, credit restrictions must be extended so far as is possible to all financial institutions that accept deposits. In fact, recently the Bank of England has widened the scope of its "requests" to embrace the non-clearing banks.

(*vi*) *Special Deposits.* In 1961 yet another instrument was added to the "package deal," namely, Special Deposits. The Bank of England can now ask the commercial banks to make Special Deposits with it for the purpose of reducing their liquidity, since Special Deposits, unlike Bankers' Deposits, cannot be regarded as cash, and can be released only when the monetary authorities agree to this course. The effect of this action is to reduce the commercial banks' liquidity ratio below the 28% which since 1964 has been customary. To restore the ratio to this level the commercial banks have to curtail their lending. The amount required in the way of Special Deposits is expressed as a percentage of a commercial bank's deposits. Thus, in 1960, the amount asked for by the Bank of England was 2% in the case of the English banks and 1% for the Scottish. A further call was made in 1961 but in 1962–63 Special Deposits were released in order to support a reflationary policy. Two years elapsed before

## 352 AN INTRODUCTION TO APPLIED ECONOMICS

the Bank of England in 1965 again called for Special Deposits from the commercial banks. There was a further call for Special Deposits in 1966.[1] Special Deposits are a less clumsy device than open market operations. When first introduced in 1961 it was thought they might also supersede the directive, but in fact in recent years these two instruments have generally been used as part of the same "package."

### The "package deal"

It is, moreover, difficult to assess the effectiveness of the various instruments of monetary policy employed since 1951 as particular measures have not been used entirely alone, instead always being employed in conjunction with one another. The application since 1951 of a group of restrictive measures at one and the same time came to be described as the "package deal," a popular term to which the Radcliffe Report gave respectability. The principle underlying this policy is that each of the measures comprising the "deal" affects different sections of the economy, even though in some cases only to a limited degree, but taken together their effects are thought to be more far-reaching. As the Radcliffe Report says:

"This 'package deal' approach has been based partly on the view that the coincidence of measures would enhance the shock effect on would-be spenders, and partly on the associated belief that the outside world (of relevance to the balance of payments) would be favourably impressed by a comprehensive programme of this kind."[2]

The Report goes on to say, rather cynically, that "there may also have been a disposition to try everything once when there was no great confidence in the efficacy of any one measure." Another factor in the situation has been the necessity—especially where the balance of payments was concerned—to achieve a quick response, and some measures, such as bank rate, are known to be slow to take effect. Apparently, however, bank rate impresses the outside world, a matter of some importance when an outflow of gold has to be checked. The "package deal" has been most frequently employed to check demand. A government might voluntarily adopt a restrictive policy in order to bring an inflationary situation under control, but more often the adoption of such a policy has been forced on the Government by the necessity to take drastic action on account of a particularly large deficit in the balance of payments and a serious outflow of gold. In either case the aim has been the same—to reduce internal demand and to check imports. When the position has improved and recession has threatened, government policy has not

[1] See Table LXIII, p. 290, for variations in Special Deposits.
[2] Report of the Committee on the Working of the Monetary System (1959), § 434.

merely taken the form of a new "package deal" with all the various measures reversed. Generally, reflation has been undertaken cautiously and so restrictions have tended to be relaxed one by one and not altogether.

The "package deal" makes it possible to take account of the fact that monetary policy affects some people more than others. By employing a number of instruments simultaneously the net is more widely cast. It also makes it possible to employ changing degrees of emphasis as well as to adapt to changing circumstances. It is said that the "package" has often impressed foreign governments and financiers, but to do so it is essential for a bank-rate change to be included, even though it may be regarded as little more than a symbol and indication of the seriousness of the intentions of the monetary authorities. Thus, bank rate is likely to continue to be employed as an instrument of policy though it has become at the present day primarily a weapon for the external situation.

## IV. GOVERNMENT POLICY IN ACTION

### Monetary policy, 1951–64

*1951.* Apart from a brief period in September 1939 on the outbreak of the Second World War, bank rate had remained unchanged at 2% from 1932 to 1951—a period of nineteen years. When at length it was raised in 1951 it was by the smallest of margins, a mere ½%. In fact, the change in bank rate was intended to be nothing more than an announcement of the future intention of the monetary authorities to make use once again of bank rate as an instrument of policy.

*1952–55.* In 1952 the "package deal" was applied for the first time, although in 1950 physical controls had been combined with fiscal policy and a strong recommendation for a wage freeze. The "package deal," however, implies the use of bank rate as one of the items of the package. When in 1952 bank rate was raised, some physical controls were still in operation, and to these were added the directive—at that time issued by the Treasury—that bank advances should be restricted. When these measures were beginning to check demand, the slight increase in unemployment that they induced led to fear of a recession and of failure to maintain full employment, experience of which as a permanent feature of the economy was at that time limited. Once lost it was feared full employment might prove difficult to restore, both the Government and the trade unions still being very conscious of the Great Depression of the inter-war years. The restrictionist policy, therefore, was quickly reversed just as it was beginning to take effect. At the same time the remaining

physical controls were swept away. Consequently the ensuing reflation of 1953–54 soon led to a sharp expansion of demand and a
return to inflationary conditions.

*1955–57.* To meet this new inflationary situation and the associated balance of payments and sterling crisis a more comprehensive
package was employed. Bank rate, the symbolic weapon, was raised
first to $4\frac{1}{2}\%$ in 1955, then to $5\frac{1}{2}\%$ in 1956 and eventually to what came
to be regarded as the crisis level of $7\%$ in 1957. The directive to the
commercial banks this time was more strongly applied. After an
attempt had been made to compel the commercial banks to restrict
their loans to purposes considered to be in the national interest—
often a particularly awkward decision for individual bank managers
to make—the banks were given a definite instruction to bring about
a "positive and significant" reduction in advances. Thus, the quantitative replaced the qualitative direction. In 1956 the Chancellor of
the Exchequer called a meeting of leading bankers for the purpose
of impressing on them that a contraction of bank credit was imperative. Fiscal policy was now orientated to checking demand through
higher prices following increases in purchase taxes and excise duties,
this aim being regarded as at least as important as achieving a large
budget surplus. For the first time increases in indirect taxation were
accompanied by a tightening up of hire purchase regulations to
check easy buying. Control of investment by the Capital Issues
Committee was revived. At the same time efforts were made to
stimulate private saving by offering more attractive terms for
National Savings Certificates and by the issue of Premium Bonds,
the latter soon to become very popular. Internal difficulties at this
time were aggravated by the revaluation of the Deutschemark, and
it was to check the resulting outflow of gold that bank rate had again
to be raised to $7\%$. The result was a recession. As was becoming
customary, fear of increasing unemployment—as much a political
issue as an economic problem—led to a swift switch from disinflation to reflation. Bank rate was quickly brought down to $4\%$, all
restrictions on bank lending were removed, hire purchase terms were
eased and in the budget of 1959 there were considerable reductions in
taxation, both direct and indirect.

*1961–64.* During these years the economic pattern was again one
of disinflation to meet a sterling crisis followed by reflation. Again
the "package deal" was employed, all the usual instruments being
used, but this time together with the new device of Special Deposits.
Bank rate again touched $7\%$. As compared with earlier crises there
were two important differences. In previous attempts to rid the
economy of inflation it had always appeared that anxiety lest full
employment should be lost had led to policy being reversed too
soon, reflationary measures to overcome any tendency towards re-

cession being generally over-employed, so that before very long inflation was again rife. On this occasion a more severe disinflationary policy was pursued and it was allowed to proceed until its impact on the level of employment, with 497,000 people wholly unemployed in June 1963, began to give serious cause for alarm. At the same time an attempt was made to impose a "pay pause," which had no more success than the "wage freeze" of 1949–50. The Chancellor of the Exchequer was, however, only carrying out a policy which a number of distinguished economists had been advocating for some time. It had been suggested that, if wages in the United Kingdom could be held for a short time, costs of production would be reduced relative to the costs of foreign competitors with beneficial permanent results for the British balance of payments. There was, moreover, a growing opinion too that wage increases should be related to productivity.

The reflation that in 1963–64 followed this severe bout of deflation —it was too serious to be described as disinflation—also differed from previous reflations in that it was permitted to run unchecked in spite of increasing difficulties with the balance of payments. Again this was a course that some economists had recommended as a means of obviating the harmful effects of "stop–go" on economic growth— a new factor in the situation. In a courageous attempt to try to ensure a sustained and adequate rate of economic growth the inflationary effects of expansion on the balance of payments were ignored. When it seemed that this policy might have to be reversed on account of the 30% liquidity rule of the commercial banks, these banks were authorised by the Bank of England to lower their liquidity ratio to 28%, the ratio which has now become customary. This looked like an attempt to secure economic growth whatever might be the cost. What was being tried out was the theory that the conditions created by expansion would eventually of themselves restore equilibrium to the balance of payments. The experiment was interrupted by a general election. Maybe the change of government before this policy had had sufficient time fully to work itself out, and the frightening proportions of the deficit which by this time had accumulated in the balance of payments, made it impossible to persevere further with this policy. Or maybe, by its very nature—at least without an effective incomes policy—it was doomed to failure in any case from the start.

## Monetary policy, 1964–68

By the autumn of 1964, therefore, it was clearly necessary to take action to end the mounting deficit in the balance of payments. The interim November budget did little more than announce in advance proposed tax increases for the 1965 budget. The rise in bank rate which the situation demanded was unduly delayed, and when it did take place it was regarded abroad more as a sign of weakness than as an indication of the Government's intention to take stern measures, especially since the change in the rate was made on a Monday instead of the customary Thursday. It seemed too to foreign observers that the wrong moment had been chosen to increase the salaries of Members of Parliament and retirement pensions, however much these increases may have been justified. The tax increases—a rise in income tax and the new capital gains tax and corporation tax—were announced but delayed until the 1965 budget, and they would be slow to take effect. Discussions were opened with the TUC with regard to an incomes policy, and agreement "in principle" was reached, but it would clearly take time before any such policy could be implemented. Actually, therefore, little was done to meet the immediate situation. Instead, long-term plans for future economic growth were adumbrated in the National Plan.

There was, however, a slight improvement in the country's balance of trade late in 1965, and by March 1966 it appeared to some people that balance of payments difficulties had been resolved for the first time without any serious rise in unemployment. Almost immediately afterwards, however, there was a sharp deterioration in the situation, and unemployment began to increase. The budget of 1966, delayed until May, again displayed a lack of urgency. For example, the new selective employment tax (SET) was not to operate until the following September, the surcharge on surtax would not be payable for over a year, and there would also be a lapse of time before the effect of dividend restriction was felt. The "freeze" on wages and prices, it was announced, was to be strictly applied. The rapid deterioration of international confidence in sterling made it necessary to take drastic action on lines similar to that taken in previous sterling crises. The July measures of 1966 were, indeed, the most severe taken to meet any crisis since 1931. Bank rate was immediately raised to the crisis rate of 7% and the other measures in the package included a strict instruction from the Bank of England that bank advances were to be reduced, and this "request" was made to other banks and financial institutions and not merely to the London clearing banks. Special Deposits were increased from 1 to 2%, hire purchase regulations were tightened, purchase tax and other excise duties were increased by 10%, and a limited foreign travel allowance was again introduced. The Government had resigned itself to a steep rise in unemployment as the price to be paid for recovery. However, as an ex-Governor of the Bank of England pointed out, little was done to curtail government expenditure. On the contrary, investment in the public sector had increased by no less than 45% during 1963–66.

It might have been expected that a package as severe as the July measures would have resolved both the external problem of the balance of payments and internal inflation, though at the cost of high unemployment and a serious check to economic growth. Indeed, unemployment did rise to an unprecedented height for the post-war period—exceeded only during the brief dislocation caused by the severe weather of 1947—reaching over 583,000 in December 1967, and the economy suffered actual stagnation instead of the improved rate of economic growth outlined in the National Plan of 1965. Unfortunately, however, the improvement in the external situation was both slight and short-lived, though enough, unfortunately, to induce the authorities to indulge in a little premature reflation. The improvement apparent in the early months of 1967 was not maintained, however, and bank rate, which had been reduced to 5½%, had to be increased again. The protracted seamen's strike of 1966 and the "unofficial" strikes of dockers in 1967 harassed the Government and aggravated balance of payments difficulties. Moreover, in spite of efforts to impose an incomes policy, wages had continued to rise, and in the space of two years increases in retirement pensions had been awarded to all pensioners irrespective of their total incomes. Many people both at home and abroad, economists as well as politicians, had by this time come to believe that sterling's troubles were the result of a fundamental disequilibrium in the British balance of payments, *i.e.* due to over-valuation of the currency. Once this fact is widely recognised, devaluation becomes inevitable. Overseas buyers begin to safeguard themselves by holding back their orders in expectation of lower prices; holders of sterling begin to get rid of some of it; and speculators increase their activities in the foreign exchange market. In November 1967, therefore, the value of the pound in terms of US dollars was reduced from 2·80 to 2·40.

It is just possible that if action on the lines of the July measures of 1966 had been taken eighteen months earlier the sterling crisis of the mid-1960s might have been successfully surmounted as had the similar crises that had occurred over the previous two decades. Alternatively, if devaluation had come earlier, the severe deflationary measures of 1966 might not have been necessary. Recurring crisis of this nature, however, only hinder economic progress. If the cause was to be found in the over-valuation of the pound in relation to other currencies, then clearly devaluation was the remedy. A currency tends to become over-valued externally when on account of inflation its internal value is falling more rapidly than the internal value of other currencies. Table LXXXI (p. 328), however, shows that during 1952–62 only a few countries had suffered less severely from inflation than had Great Britain, while many countries had suffered more severely. Further inflation following the devaluation of 1967 could, of course, eventually erode all the advantage to be derived from it and so bring a return of troubles with the balance of payments—the first sterling crisis after the devaluation of 1949 occurred in 1952! To support the devaluation of 1967 another package of measures was announced, headed by a rise in bank rate from $6\frac{1}{2}$ to 8%—an unprecedented figure for modern times. Other measures included restrictions on bank lending, abolition of the SET premium except for firms in development areas, and advance warning that corporation tax would be increased from 40 to $42\frac{1}{2}$% in the 1968 budget. The pros and cons of devaluation are discussed elsewhere.[1]

## Attempts to secure wage restraint

As already pointed out, one of the consequences of a prolonged period of full employment is for wage rates (and, more particularly, earnings) to increase more rapidly than productivity, with the result that there has been a continuous rise in prices. This has been the experience not only of Great Britain but also of most Western countries during the past twenty-five years. It is this situation that has led to demands for wage restraint. Not all economists, however, are agreed that this is the right way to tackle the problem. To some the root cause of the problems is a demand for goods and services—and, therefore, for labour—in excess of the supply. They argue that if equilibrium were restored to this situation an incomes policy would be unnecessary. It is quite true that over the past twenty-five years wage increases have been greatest at times when there has been the greatest number of unfilled vacancies, but in the economic climate of the mid 1960s rising unemployment has not always seriously checked wage increases.

In many West European countries, especially the Netherlands, Sweden and Denmark, serious attempts at wage restraint have been made by governments in order to check rises in prices.[2] Even in the United States the Government's economic advisers make an annual recommendation of a "guide-post" for wage increases, for example, 3·2% in 1965 and 1966. The aim in most cases had not been to try to stop prices rising altogether—an impossibility anyway—but to prevent prices rising more than in other countries with which they have commercial relations. When the British Government in 1964–65 put forward suggestions for wage and price restraint it was stressed that it wished only to delay certain price increases, as there was no intention to control all prices. Thus, the aim has not been to rid an enonomy entirely of inflation as such but to prevent inflation having an adverse effect on the balance of payments. This too has been the objective of all attempts at wage restraint in Great Britain. In this country the problem has been rendered more difficult to resolve on account of the greater freedom enjoyed by trade unions and em-

[1] Chapter XII, pp. 422–23.
[2] See Report of United Nations Economic Commission for Europe, 1966.

ployers' associations in collective bargaining. Most union leaders and employers still consider wage bargaining a domestic matter to be decided among themselves without government interference, not accepting the view—at least where wages are concerned—that it is the duty of a government to watch over the interests of the community as a whole. In some other countries governments have been accustomed to exercising varying degrees of control over wages, and this has made the pursuit of incomes policies easier for them than has been the case in Great Britain. Automatic "cost-of-living" adjustments in this country and so-called "escalator" clauses in American wage agreements make wage restraint more difficult to impose.

The history of wage restraint in Great Britain really goes back to the Second World War. Experience of inflation during the First World War led to the introduction of rationing and price controls at an early stage during the Second World War, in the hope that by checking the increase in the cost of living, trade union demands for increased wages would be moderated. As a result both prices and wages during the Second World War rose less than had been the case during the First World War.

However, wage restraint as generally understood dates back to the devaluation of sterling in 1949. With the aim of allowing the country to obtain some competitive advantage from devaluation, an attempt was made to operate a "wage freeze" during 1949–50 and with the co-operation of the TUC this was accepted for a brief period, though trade unions with wage agreements which included automatic increases in line with increases in the index of retail prices refused to forego this privilege. The period of restraint, however, was short-lived. The rise in prices in the years immediately following 1949—partly in consequence of devaluation and partly due to external events such as the war in Korea—led to a widespread upward movement of wages.

Further attempts were made during the 1950s to relate wages more closely to productivity. Firms were exhorted voluntarily to refrain from increasing prices whenever possible in the hope that this might check demands for wage increases—a forlorn hope in conditions generally favourable to trade unions. In 1957 the British Government set up an independent body known as the Council on Prices, Productivity and Incomes—very similar to the American Council of Economic Advisers—to advise it on matters connected with inflation. It comprised three economic experts, often referred to derisively as "the Three Wise Men." Their pronouncements were mainly to the effect that the persistence of inflation was largely due to excessive wage increases in relation to productivity. Not unnaturally the trade unions refused to accept this diagnosis of the situation.

In 1961 there came another attempt at wage restraint, this time under the name of a "pay pause." Unfortunately, it was timed to take effect just when applications for higher wages were being made by several groups of workers, such as nurses, whose earnings over the years had fallen considerably behind those of members of the more militant trade unions. The decision to defer consideration of these claims made the pay pause appear particularly inequitable, a fact which those with less justifiable claims were not slow to stress. In spite of trade union opposition the Government persisted in its policy and in 1962 set up the National Incomes Commission with the function of considering and commenting on any wage agreements that might be made between unions and employers. The trade unions were suspicious of this body from the start and it had no more success than the Council on Prices, Productivity and Incomes.

## Prices and incomes policy since 1964

The Government inaugurated its prices and incomes policy by agreement with the TUC and the CBI in a "Declaration of Intent on Productivity, Prices and Incomes," signed on behalf of these two organisations and the Government in 1964. To secure the agreement of the unions to wage restraint it had to be shown that restraint would be applied to all incomes as well as to prices. It was announced in advance that a corporation Tax and a new capital gains tax would be introduced in the 1965 budget.

The aim of an incomes policy is the very desirable one of relating increases in incomes to the rate of increase in productivity in order to make wage increases non-inflationary so that economic growth should not be jeopardised by the periodic necessity to cut back consumers' demand. In calculating productivity the rate has to be that for the economy as a whole. The method to be employed is to estimate in advance the rate of productivity that can be expected to be achieved in the ensuing twelve months, and this—since 1964 known in Great Britain as the "norm"—then determines the average rise in income per head (with certain exceptions) that can be permitted during the year. This means that workers in industries which show high rates of productivity cannot *ipso facto* be allowed to permit to their workers a greater rise in wages than those employed in less progressive industries, unless it can be clearly shown that increased productivity has been the result of employees undertaking more exacting work and not the consequence of technological advance. Before a productivity increase in wages can be allowed, a prior firm assessment must be made of the improvement in productivity on which it is based. In its report of December 1966 on this difficult question the National Board for Prices and Incomes said such increases in incomes were to be regarded as "a means of offering rewards to workers for their co-operation in the more effective use of resources." It needs to be stressed that the criterion for an increase in incomes was to be an increase in *productivity* and not an increase in *prices*. An incomes policy cannot save the country from the inflationary effects of a boom. It cannot, therefore, provide a safeguard against some rises in price. If workers in some of the more progressive industries cannot obtain wage increases there will be a tendency for profits in these industries to rise unduly. Hence, the necessity also, so the argument runs, to restrict profits by taxation or some other means.

In 1965 the Prices and Incomes Board was established, and a norm of 3–3½% was announced. In fact hourly wage rates rose by much more than that—nearly 7% between November 1964 and November 1965—with an even greater increase in earnings, since the "shorter working week" results in more overtime being worked. During this period prices rose by only 4%, much of the increase being acounted for by increases in indirect taxation. The greater degree of price stability (excluding the tax element) was largely due to the efforts of the Prices and Incomes Board. One difficulty in persuading trade unions as a whole to restrict wage increases to a government-fixed norm is that workers in industries showing above-average improvement in productivity are inclined to feel themselves entitled to the full benefit of this in their wages, however much above the norm it may be. If accepted the effect could not be otherwise than inflationary, since those in "comparable" occupations, irrespective of productivity—particularly service occupations—would demand equal treatment. Though trade unions often point to rising prices and profits when making claims for higher wages, there appears to be no certainty that if a measure of control is exercised over prices and wages this will serve to check demands for higher wages. An incomes policy too requires to take account of wage drift, a factor of increasing importance as more and more negotiations with employers take place at shop-floor level. A rise in wage rates to the full extent of the norm will result in a much greater increase, therefore, in earnings if at the same time the union concerned obtains a reduction in the length of the normal working week without an actual reduction in the number of hours worked.

The feature of the incomes policy introduced during 1965–66 was its voluntary character. The Act of 1965 set up the National Prices and Incomes Board, the members of which comprise employers, trade unionists, academics and politicians. It functions under the auspices of the Department of Economic Affairs. In 1966 the so-called "early warning" system was introduced. The choice before the trade unions was whether to allow the Government to interfere in what they regarded as their own affairs or to concede some of their powers to the TUC. Of the two possible infringements of their power they preferred the latter. Policy is the Government's responsibility. The Prices and Incomes Board can consider and report on any price increases, wage claims or conditions of service of any group of workers if these matters are referred to it by the Government acting through the Ministry of Labour, but not otherwise. While a question is under consideration a standstill operates for three months or up to the time of publication of a report. The Board, however, has no power to enforce its recommendations. The vetting committee of the TUC also considers any wage claims that may be submitted to it, and the TUC's norm need not coincide with the Government's. The Ministry of Labour receives notifications from employers; the TUC is prepared to offer advice to its affiliated members and help them frame their claims before any action is taken; and the CBI is informed by its members of all national claims. The TUC is of the opinion that its members are generally anxious to accept its advice, that is so far as their own members will allow them. The Ministry has two weapons at its command: ($i$) it can check industry passing on the cost of excessive wage increases in higher prices; and ($ii$) it can refer any case that comes before it to the Prices and Incomes Board. Some indication of the part played by the TUC is shown by the fact that down to December 1967 of over 300 claims put before it only 93 received unqualified approval. Nevertheless, there was an average increase in hourly wage rates of $12\frac{1}{2}\%$ between the establishment of the Prices and Incomes Board in 1965 and January 1968.

Part IV of the Act of 1965 which established the Prices and Incomes Board gave the Government wide powers for a period of one year to make its prices and incomes policy compulsory, this section of the Act requiring an Order in Council to bring it into effect. The Government at first hoped that its objective could be achieved by voluntary means, but an Order had to be made after the July measures of 1966. For prices and wages the norm for the next six months was to be nil, this to be followed by a period of severe restraint. The devaluation of sterling in November 1967 made a successful prices and incomes policy essential if the potential advantages to be derived from devaluation were not to be thrown away.

As already noted, an exception from the norm was to be made in the case of workers making a direct contribution towards increasing productivity. A further exception was to be made in the case of low-paid workers. Wages in low-paid occupations tend to lag behind wages in general for two reasons: ($i$) in these occupations the supply of labour tends to exceed the demand for it (most of such labour being unskilled); and ($ii$) such workers also tend to be less well organised. Exceptions too were to be made where it was considered necessary to offer higher wages as an inducement to attract labour into expanding, undermanned industries, though experience appears to suggest that wage differentials are not the most important influence on mobility of labour. The more exceptions that are allowed to an order, however justifiable they may be, the more difficult it becomes to apply it.

### RECOMMENDATIONS FOR FURTHER READING

HMSO: *Report of the Radcliffe Committee on the Working of the Monetary System* (1959).
A. J. Brown: *The Great Inflation* 1939–51 (Oxford University Press).
F. W. Paish and J. Hennessy: *Policy for Incomes?* (Institute of Economic Affairs: Hobart Papers).
*The Economist.*
*Bank of England Quarterly Bulletin* (opening commentary on the economy).

### QUESTIONS

1. What have been the main causes of the persistence of inflation since 1945?
2. "The main objection to inflation is that it brings about an arbitrary redistribution of incomes." Discuss this statement.
3. With trade unions well established it is really possible to operate a successful prices and incomes policy?
4. "If fiscal and monetary policies are appropriate, an incomes policy is unnecessary; if they are not, it cannot work." Discuss. (Degree.)
5. Consider the relation of "wage drift" to the success or failure of an incomes policy. (Degree.)
6. Outline the aims of the prices and incomes policy. Would you consider it a useful addition to the armoury of economic controls available to the Government or is it an indication of the failure of these controls? (Barking.)
7. "A gradual inflation is not only inevitable, but is necessary in a modern society." Discuss, with special reference to the United Kingdom. (Barnsley.)
8. What are the main difficulties for the successful continuation of a national incomes policy? (Bournemouth.)
9. Contrast the aims and results of post-war monetary policy. (Huddersfield.)
10. Discuss the view that full employment, fixed exchange rates, a stable price-level, full collective bargaining, and a satisfactory rate of economic growth are mutually incompatible. (Kingston-upon-Hull.)
11. What difficulties hinder a prices and incomes policy in conditions of full employment and free collective bargaining? (Liverpool.)
12. Examine the conflicts that might arise between economic policies aiming at a high rate of growth and policies aiming at price stability. (Manchester.)
13. A high bank rate is likely to have more impact upon the strength of the pound in the foreign exchange market than upon the level of effective

demand in the home market. Explain and discuss. (Northern Counties.)

14. What are the main causes and effects of inflation? (Norwich.)

15. For what purpose was the National Board for Prices and Incomes constituted? Give a critical analysis of the work of this board since its inception. (Southampton.)

16. "In controlling the economy monetary policy can play a part—but only a part" (Radcliffe Report). Discuss. (U.L.C.I.)

## CHAPTER XI

# INTERNATIONAL ECONOMIC RELATIONS

## *I. INTERNATIONAL TRADE*

### The development of international trade

People of different nations first began to trade with one another because some countries were able to produce certain goods which others, on account of climatic and geological dissimilarities, could not. Differences of soil and climate restrict the cultivation of many crops to particular regions, while for geological reasons some minerals are found only in a few areas of the world. These geographical differences provided a basis for international trade once satisfactory means of transporting goods had been developed. Since for a long time costs of transport were very high, partly because of the heavy losses often incurred in transit, the commodities that were the first to enter into international trade generally possessed the further attribute of being fairly valuable articles. For a long time, therefore, only the well to do could afford to buy imported goods.

As means of transport improved and transit risks decreased—and those that remained came to be covered by insurance—international trade gradually expanded. In time its character changed as countries began to import increasing amounts of commodities which they were already producing themselves in order to supplement home-produced supplies.

The greatest expansion of international trade occurred, however, when countries began to find it to their advantage to specialise in the production of a more limited range of goods, even though this meant reducing their output of some things or ceasing altogether the production of some commodities which they had shown themselves capable of producing. Division of Labour and specialisation in the international field, as in the domestic, results in a vast increase in total output and production at lower *real* cost. Since any country's stock of factors of production is limited—that is, since factors are scarce in relation to the demand for them—the employment of more in some lines of production requires the withdrawal of some from other uses. Consequently, when specialisation is introduced, a choice has to be made of how factors of production shall be employed.

According to the theory of international trade this choice will be made in accordance with the *principle of comparative cost*, so that each country specialises in the production of those goods for which it has the greatest *comparative* advantage over others, that is to say, it will undertake those forms of production in which it requires to employ the fewest factors of production as compared with others.

International specialisation makes it possible for the world output of all commodities to be maximised, but for all countries to derive the greatest possible benefit from international specialisation it must clearly be followed by unrestricted international trade. In the same way that internal division of labour and specialisation within a country increases the amount of distribution required to enable people in all areas to enjoy the increased production, so international division of labour and specialisation enlarges the volume of international trade and increases the national incomes of all countries that take part in it.

The following table shows how British imports and exports (excluding "invisible" items) have increased *in monetary terms* in recent years:

TABLE LXXXVIII

*Expansion of British Trade*

| Year | Imports | Exports | Total |
|------|---------|---------|-------|
|      | £ million | £ million | £ million |
| 1954 | 3,359 | 2,748 | 6,107 |
| 1955 | 3,461 | 2,993 | 6,454 |
| 1956 | 3,324 | 3,377 | 6,701 |
| 1957 | 3,538 | 3,509 | 7,047 |
| 1958 | 3,378 | 3,407 | 6,785 |
| 1959 | 3,640 | 3,522 | 7,162 |
| 1960 | 4,141 | 3,733 | 7,874 |
| 1961 | 4,045 | 3,892 | 7,937 |
| 1962 | 4,098 | 3,994 | 8,092 |
| 1963 | 4,370 | 4,287 | 8,657 |
| 1964 | 5,016 | 4,471 | 9,487 |
| 1965 | 5,065 | 4,784 | 9,849 |
| 1966 | 5,262 | 5,110 | 10,372 |
| 1967 | 5,660 | 5,023 | 10,683 |

Source: *Annual Abstract of Statistics.*

Allowing for changes in the value of money during this period this represents an increase in real terms in the volume of British trade of just over 50%; of British imports in 1967 31% came from the Commonwealth, 22% from the EEC, 16% from EFTA and 14% from the United States. Of British exports in that year 26% went to the

Commonwealth, 19% to the EEC, 14% to EFTA and 12% to the United States.

## Restrictions on international trade

The theoretical argument in favour of free trade appears to be so convincing that one might reasonably have expected that all countries by now would have accepted it. In fact, the exact opposite has been the case. At no time in history has any country ever completely implemented a free trade policy. Although Adam Smith had advocated free trade as part of his *laissez-faire* policy as long ago as 1776, the nearest Europe as a whole came to it was during the third quarter of the nineteenth century when both France and Great Britain sought to persuade other nations to reduce their tariffs. The statesmen who brought Great Britain nearest to free trade were Huskisson, Peel and Gladstone. In two of his budgets Gladstone abolished import duties on no fewer than 400 articles. The great expansion in British trade that occurred during this period convinced most of those who had previously been opposed to free trade, though it is important to note that during the latter part of the nineteenth century both Germany and the United States prospered behind the shelter of tariff walls. Disraeli, for example, who had gone to the length of opposing and eventually overthrowing his own leader, Sir Robert Peel, on this question, made no attempt whatever when he came to power himself to reverse Gladstone's free trade policy. When Joseph Chamberlain attempted to restore a modified form of protection in the guise of imperial preference his party suffered an overwhelming defeat in the ensuing general election of 1906, as also did Baldwin in 1923 when he offered the electorate protection as a means of reducing unemployment. Nevertheless, the McKenna duties imposed in 1915 on a select range of imported manufactures (including motor cars) were an important step away from free trade taken by a Liberal Chancellor of the Exchequer.

The peace settlement after the First World War brought into existence many new small nations which were intensely nationalistic in outlook and, aiming at self-sufficiency, built up their industries behind high tariff walls. Great Britain too took further small steps away from free trade under Baldwin during the year 1924–29—as, for example, the duties on key industries in 1921 and the artificial silk duties of 1925—but it was the length and severity of the Great Depression that eventually caused Great Britain in 1932 to forsake its traditional free trade policy, all other nations except the Netherlands previously favouring free trade already having introduced tariffs while many others had greatly increased their duties on imports. During the Great Depression world trade had shrunk to very small proportions and every country had been reduced to adopting courses—often described as "beggar my neighbour" policies—that might safeguard a little of its own trade however unfortunate the effect might be on others. In 1932, therefore, Great Britain introduced a general import tariff, though by international standards most duties were only moderate in amount and foodstuffs were either lightly taxed or exempt. Later in the same year the Ottawa Agreement was negotiated whereby preference in the form of lower duties was given to imports from British territories overseas.

### The changing attitude to tariffs

Restrictions on foreign trade, whatever form they may take—tariffs, quotas, bilateral agreements—reduce the volume of international trade, divert production from areas where it can be most advantageously carried on, with the result the world *as a whole* is poorer than it otherwise might have been. It was the realisation that the high tariff barriers erected during the Great Depression of the inter-war period had checked recovery from that depression and hindered the expansion of world trade that led to efforts being made after the Second World War to secure greater liberalisation of trade. By this time countries were more aware of the harmful effects of narrow economic nationalism than they had been during the years following the First World War. Even while the Second World War was still being fought and its end not yet in sight plans were already being formulated to avoid a return to the stagnation of production and trade that had characterised the 1930s. This was in sharp contrast to the general attitude after the First World War when the great desire had been to return to what the Americans called "normalcy." Thus as early as 1943 Benelux was in embryo and in 1944 the first meeting to discuss international monetary relations took place at Bretton Woods. Eventually efforts to secure greater liberalisation of trade took two forms: (*i*) the formation of regional free trade areas, of which the European Economic Community (EEC) and the European Free Trade Association (EFTA) were the outstanding examples, and (*ii*) the general lowering of tariffs through the General Agreement on Tariffs and Trade (GATT), culminating in 1967 in the Kennedy Round.

## II. THE EEC AND EFTA

### Towards European unity

Until comparatively recent times the economic development of both France and Germany was hindered by the existence of a large number of separate customs areas within their frontiers. With the strengthening of the Paris Government's control over the provinces,

France, already united politically, was able to make the whole country into one economic entity. Germany, however, until the second half of the nineteenth century, consisted of some thirty-nine separate states, but in 1833 Prussia took the lead in forming the *Zollverein*, a customs union, which assisted the economic development of Germany as well as paving the way for the political union of that country. The success of the *Zollverein* showed how beneficial to economic progress a regional customs union could be.

After the Second World War it came to be realised more than ever before that the fragmentation of Europe—more especially Western Europe—into a number of relatively small states (as compared with the United States and Russia) was a source of weakness, both politically and economically. Within one year of the end of the war Sir Winston Churchill in a speech in Zürich urged reconciliation between France and Germany and suggested the formation of a "kind of United States of Europe." Supported enthusiastically by the United States a "European" movement developed in Western Europe, and General Marshall, the US Secretary of State, proposed that American aid be given to Europe. The Council of Europe, established at Strasbourg in 1949, was the outcome of this wide outlook. Perhaps as a result of British influence the Council of Europe became an association of governments, each of which retained its full sovereignty. Though its ultimate aim is European unity, it has made little progress in this direction mainly on account of the large number of states involved and their reluctance to surrender their political sovereignty.

Greater success came in the economic field—though on a smaller scale—with the formation in 1947 of Benelux, a customs union comprising Belgium, the Netherlands and Luxembourg. Then the establishment of the Organisation for European Economic Co-operation (OEEC) in 1947 brought the nations of Western Europe together in a new organisation, but the communist countries of Eastern Europe refused to take part. Though the primary purpose of the OEEC was to supervise the distribution of American aid to Europe under what came to be known as the Marshall Plan, it was hoped that it might also assist the co-ordination of economic development in Western Europe. This latter aim foundered because of the difficulties of securing unanimity among a large number of sovereign states. Co-operation, however, in the economic sphere resulted in the lowering of some tariff barriers, and co-operation in the monetary field was achieved by the setting up of the European Payments Unions (EPU) in 1950 to facilitate financial clearings between the members of the OEEC. The EPU was a regional version of the International Monetary Fund (IMF) and it was replaced by the European Monetary Agreement (EMA) in 1959 when sterling and some other currencies at length became convertible for US dollars. The OEEC was then replaced by the Organisation for Economic Co-operation (OECD). Both the United States and Canada became members of the OECD and in 1964 Japan also joined.

## The establishment of the European Common Market

The European Economic Community (EEC)—better known in Great Britain as the European Common Market—developed out of the European Coal and Steel Community (ECSC). M. Robert Schuman proposed in 1950 that the French and German coal and steel industries should be brought under a single authority to overcome the difficulties arising from the fact that the geographical frontiers of the two countries had been determined by political and not by economic considerations, thus endangering relations between them. The ECSC was established in 1951 and, with headquarters in Luxembourg, began operations in the following year. In addition to France and West Germany[1] it included the three Benelux countries —Belgium, the Netherlands and Luxembourg—together with Italy, and in 1954 Great Britain signed an agreement of association with the new organisation. For the country whose prestige in Western Europe had stood highest at the end of the Second World War this was a somewhat inferior role. In 1945–47 Great Britain could easily have taken the lead in the formation of the European Common Market as it did in the founding of the Council of Europe. Although economic integration was provided by the ECSC only over a very limited field, involving no more than a single group of industries, its success encouraged those who desired the formation of a wider organisation.

The six countries that had co-operated to form the ECSC, therefore, began negotiations in 1955 at Messina and these culminated in the signing in March 1957 of the Treaty of Rome, which established the European Economic Community (EEC) or Common Market. By a second treaty, also signed in Rome, Euratom also was established to promote the peaceful use of nuclear power in the EEC.

## Common Market institutions

The principal institutions set up to manage Common Market affairs are as follows:

(*i*) The *Council of Ministers*, comprising one representative of each member state. The Council is responsible for basic policy.

(*ii*) The *Commission* of nine members, appointed by agreement of

[1] Officially the Federal German Republic.

the member governments. The Commission can formulate proposals which are then put before the Council, but its main functions is to take responsibility for the day-to-day management of the affairs of the EEC.

(*iii*) *Joint Committees*, set up to consider particular aspects of Common Market policy such as, for example, the committee comprising the governors of the EEC central banks which deals with monetary policy in the Common Market. Another committee comprises the finance ministers of the EEC and concerns itself with financial matters. There are also special committees that deal with the economic policy of the Common Market. Before taking action the Commission must consult the appropriate committee.

(*iv*) The *European Investment Bank* which, among other activities, has helped to finance projects in Southern Italy (the "Mezzogiorno"), the most economically backward region in the entire Common Market.

(*v*) The *European Social Fund* which was established to assist the movement of redundant workers to other areas in the Common Market and to new jobs.

(*vi*) The *European Court of Justice*, set up to deal with any complaints of unfair trading practices that might arise or other matters affecting trade between members of the EEC. It also deals with matters arising under the ECSC treaty.

(*vii*) The *European Development Fund*, the purpose of which is to provide aid for overseas countries that have been admitted as associates of the EEC.

(*viii*) The *European Parliament*. The ultimate aim of the European Common Market is political as well as economic union. Eventually it is hoped to have a democratically elected parliament with full powers, but as yet its powers are very limited as little progress has been made in the political field.

The immediate concern of the European Common Market after its establishment was to reduce tariffs between the members by easy stages with the aim of bringing about free trade between them by 1970 (later brought forward to 1968). The second aim was to harmonise the tariffs of the "Six" so that by 1970 (again brought forward to 1968) there would be a common tariff between the Common Market members and the rest of the world. There were also to be common agricultural and transport policies. The Treaty of Rome stressed the fact that political union was the ultimate aim of the signatories (hence the establishment of the European Parliament) and it was hoped that the EEC might form the basis and eventual nucleus of a future United States of Europe, as in the past economic association had often been the forerunner of political union. There were also provisions in the Treaty of Rome for the admission to membership of other countries willing to accept the provisions of the treaty. Other economic aims included the free movement of labour and capital within the Community, co-ordinated economic policies and formulation of rules against unfair competition. In addition social policies too were to be co-ordinated.

The first tariff reduction took effect on 1st January 1959 and with the further acceleration of this process 1st July 1968 became the date for the complete abolition of all tariffs between members with at the same time the establishment of a common external tariff. By this date, therefore, the EEC's customs union had been accomplished. Since 1st July 1967 all duties on imports have been paid into the Community's budget, no longer to be received by the individual members.

## The agricultural policy of the EEC

One of the objectives of farm policy in the European Common Market—as also in Great Britain and in the United States since 1945 —was to give workers on the land a better standard of living than had been their lot in the years before the Second World War. In those days farming had been characterised by wide fluctuations in output and during the Great Depression extremely low prices and incomes. Farm policy in Great Britain was laid down in the *Agriculture Acts* of 1947 and 1957. The aim was to secure stability by offering farmers guaranteed prices for the main agricultural commodities and an assured market for their produce, lower prices to consumers being achieved through government subsidies in the form of "deficiency" payments to farmers where necessary to maintain the guaranteed prices, which are kept in line with world prices, and subject to annual review. The cost to the Exchequer of government support to farming was £237 million in 1965–66. In the United States the Government helped the farmers by price supports, agreeing to buy surpluses that could not be sold at the fixed prices.

The policy of the EEC is to fix prices (also as in Great Britain reviewed annually): (*i*) a "target" price which it is hoped the farmers will obtain in the market; (*ii*) a slight lower "intervention" price, below which prices are not allowed to fall and at which institutional buying begins. Levies are imposed on imported farm products to raise their prices to the level of the "target" prices, these levies being paid into a European Agricultural Guidance and Guarantee Fund out of which payments are made to assist the modernisation of farms and to subsidise certain exports. In order to attract farm products to areas where they are most needed higher regional target prices can be set.

The six members of the Common Market had found it relatively easy to agree on their common policy for manufactured goods. In the case of agricultural products, however, agreement was reached only after prolonged negotiations. Nevertheless, by late 1964 a common agricultural policy was accepted for the production of beef and dairy products, and early the following year the agreement was extended to include cereals, pig-meat, poultry, eggs, vegetables, fruit and wine.

The date fixed for effect to be given to the common agricultural policy was 1st July 1967, but failure at first to agree on the method of financing it led to a boycott by France of the Community's institutions for a period of seven months before negotiations were resumed. Agreement was eventually reached in 1966, common prices being agreed for a number of commodities, with free trade within the Community in agricultural products to operate from 1st July 1968.

## The establishment of EFTA

Largely owing to the influence of Sir Winston Churchill, Great Britain had been one of the first nations to perceive the advantages of a Western Europe united both economically and politically, and yet Britain has held aloof, mainly on political grounds, when it might have played a prominent part in the formation of the European Common Market.

Though the initiative came from Sweden, nevertheless Great Britain took an active part in November 1959 in the establishment of a second customs union and free trade area in Europe in which the political aspect was to be less prominent—the European Free Trade Association (EFTA). This comprised Great Britain, Austria, Denmark, Norway, Portugal, Sweden and Switzerland—the "Seven." Later Finland was admitted as an associate member.

The European Free Trade Association was established in January 1960 by the Convention of Stockholm. It had two aims: (i) to provide a free trade area in industrial products for those countries in Europe which were not members of the European Common Market and which at the time of the formation of EFTA desired the economic advantages of association without the political implications of the EEC; (ii) ultimately it was hoped that the two European trade groups would find it possible to combine to form one large economic unit. Unlike the Common Market, however, EFTA has no common external tariff, and the lack of this means that its members receive less protection than do the members of the Common Market from competition from non-members. It also makes it necessary for EFTA countries to prevent goods from non-members entering the area through member countries with the lowest tariffs. Agricultural and marine products were expressly excluded from the EFTA agreement, though rather surprisingly bilateral agreements between members were encouraged.

EFTA based its tariff cuts on the programme laid down by the EEC, the original intention being to achieve complete freedom of trade within the area by 1st January 1970. In fact, like the Common Market, the timetable was speeded up and this objective was accomplished by 31st December 1966, *i.e.* three years ahead of schedule and indeed one and a half years ahead of the EEC. Quotas and other quantitative restrictions on imports are no longer permitted, except temporarily, and only then if a member is in difficulties with its balance of payments. When Great Britain found itself in this situation in 1964 it did not avail itself of this article in the Stockholm Convention but, as already noted, preferred instead a temporary import surcharge which was in fact contrary to the rules of the Association.

As compared with the Common Market, only a few administrative institutions were set up for the governments of EFTA—a *Council* with one representative from each member country, a *Consultative Committee* representing economic groups such as employers and trade unions, and an *Economic Committee.*

### The EEC and EFTA compared

The European Common Market forms a more compact and homogeneous area than does the European Free Trade Association. It is a geographical unit that could easily become a political one, whereas EFTA is aptly described as the "Outer Seven," actually comprising four geographical units—the United Kingdom, Scandinavia, Switzerland/Austria and Portugal—separated from one another by intervening non-member countries, by seas or by both.

The population of the European Common Market is almost double that of EFTA—184 million as against 98 million. In 1965 the total value of the gross national product of the six members of the European Common Market was £105,000 million and of the seven members of EFTA £60,000 million, thereby giving an average per head for the Common Market of £570 and for EFTA of £600. Thus, the standard of living is slightly higher in EFTA than in the European Common Market. However, the rate of economic growth since 1960 in the Common Market has been 45% as against 30% for EFTA, and so it might not be long before the position is reversed.

The trade between members of the Common Market forms a much higher proportion of their total trade than does the trade between members of EFTA. The three main Scandinavian countries are the only ones with a large proportion of their trade with EFTA members—an average of 45% for the three of them, the remainder of their trade being almost equally divided between the Common Market and the rest of the world. In contrast, Switzerland and Austria—not surprisingly, in view of their geographical situation—

trade mostly with the EEC (40% and 47% respectively as against 18% and 19% with other EFTA members). The pattern of Great Britain's trade is quite different from that of either of these two groups, no less than 60% of its trade being with the rest of the world and only 21% with the other EFTA countries and 19% with the EEC. In fact, only 25% of the trade of EFTA as a whole is between its members, at least as much being with the EEC.

In spite of the occasional intransigence of France and the fact that the Benelux countries have retained their organisation, thus preserving their loyalty to one another, the members of the European Common Market appear to be more strongly bound to one another than do the members of EFTA. The common external tariff of the EEC may have been one factor helping to bind them more closely together. The EEC appears too to have a greater sense of single purpose, probably inspired by political motives and the hope of eventual political unity. On the other hand, signs of apparent disunity have been discernible in EFTA. The fact that it was formed as an alternative—and in the case of Great Britain a second-best alternative—to the European Common Market weakened its prestige from the start. Great Britain's application to join the Common Market, though supported by the other EFTA countries which were prepared to follow its lead, was not welcomed by all members of EFTA.

There is, too, a wide divergence of opinion among EFTA members of what their relationship to the EEC should be, varying from those such as Great Britain that desire full membership and those such as Sweden which desire only some sort of association with that organisation.

## Enlargement of the Common Market

Other countries were quick to appreciate the benefits that the members of the European Common Market were beginning to enjoy, particularly their greater than average rate of economic growth. The Common Market widened its scope by admitting as associate members Greece (1961) and Turkey (1963). In both these cases association covered membership of the customs union with a transition period of twelve years (longer for some commodities) during which duties on imports would be gradually reduced. In 1963 by the Yaoundi Convention eighteen independent African states—formerly colonies of France and other Common Market countries and with a total population of 65 million—became asssociated with the Common Market. Discussions also took place with Algeria, Tunisia and Morocco, and in 1965 Nigeria became an associate—the first member of the Commonwealth to do so. Though all associates agree gradually to reduce their tariffs to the EEC they are permitted to retain duties that can be shown to be for the protection of "infant" industries. From 1st July 1968, however, the products of associates can enter the Common Market free of duty.

About the time of Great Britain's first application to become a member of the European Common Market there came a spate of applications from other countries for either full or associate membership, the other members of EFTA being among the applicants. Protracted negotiations took place during 1961–63 between Great Britain and the Common Market, but largely owing to opposition from France—and in particular from President de Gaulle—negotiations had to be broken off. The French President declared that Great Britain was insular and maritime, and differed greatly from the continental countries that were already members of the Common Market. Great Britain, too, he asserted was inclined to emphasise economic considerations to the exclusion of the political. When Great Britain failed to obtain entry to the Common Market the other applicants allowed their applications to lapse with the exception of Austria.

Application for association with the European Common Market came from Spain in 1964, from Israel in 1966 and from the five members of the Arab Common Market in 1967, and in the same year also from Malta. When Great Britain made its second application in 1967 applications for full membership were also made by the Republic of Ireland, Denmark and Norway, while Sweden applied for association. As in 1963 Great Britain's application was blocked by opposition from France.

Disappointment has been felt in some quarters regarding the lack of progress in the political field and an expansion of the Six to the Ten or the Twelve is felt to be likely still further to delay steps towards political integration. For this reason there were others besides President de Gaulle who might well have preferred the smaller membership.

### Great Britain and the EEC—advantages

In 1967 Great Britain made a second application for membership of the Common Market. This time the application was unconditional though negotiations were expected to take place on such matters as agriculture (although in principle the common agricultural policy of the Common Market was accepted), capital movements and trade relations with the Commonwealth. Since the breakdown of the negotiations that accompanied its first application for membership in 1962–63 public opinion in Great Britain has become more favourable to this course, mainly on account of the Labour Party's change of attitude. Indeed, it would seem that by 1967 a majority of the supporters of each of the three main political parties wished Great Britain to enter the Common Market, though substantial minorities in all three parties were against entry. The TUC too gave its qualified support. There will be both advantages and disadvantages to Great Britain if this country succeeds in joining the Common Market.

The outstanding advantage to all members of an organisation such as the EEC is the *wider "home" market* it provides for each country's products. The British home market at present contains a population of 55 million, while the population of the EEC is 184 million. This, while opening its own market to the other members of the European Common Market, British goods would gain entry into a market three and a half times as great in terms of population (rather less in terms of purchasing power). The addition of the United Kingdom to the European Common Market would produce a market of 239 million people—about the same size, therefore, as the USSR but slightly larger than the United States. With total external trade of over £17,000 million (nearly double that of the United Kingdom) the EEC is a close second only to the United States in foreign trade. The addition of the United Kingdom would make the European Common Market the world's greatest trader. This would undoubtedly bring some advantage to Great Britain and perhaps help it to increase its share of the carrying trade.

For many manufactured goods *economies of scale* extend far beyond the present size of many British firms. Only by considerably increasing the scale of production is it possible to take full advantage of recent technological advances, and by keeping equipment fully employed keep down costs of production to a minimum. British firms cannot, therefore, hope to compete successfully in foreign markets if they are geared to a small market while their competitors have all the advantages of producing for a much larger market. The increased competition which must inevitably follow from the necessity to compete on equal terms with other firms in the European Common Market should not be regarded as a disadvantage, since competition is a great spur to efficiency and to the adoption of the most up-to-date techniques in production. With the increased regional specialisation that must inevitably follow, some industries indeed will decline relatively or perhaps even absolutely while others will expand to an extent that will more than offset the decline of others. The old-established industries are the ones most likely to suffer, but a great opportunity for expansion will be provided for the already growing newer industries. On balance, therefore, there should be a gain to all members, including Great Britain, from the greater degree of specialisation that the wider market makes possible, though in the transition period economic frictions may arise on account of lack of mobility on the part of some factors of production.

The rapid rate of *economic growth* achieved by the European Common Market during the first eight years of its existence—exceeding that of Great Britain by 50%—holds out hopes that this country's rate of growth might be improved if it became a member of the Common Market. Although the EEC's rate of growth has slowed down somewhat since 1965 the rate is again expected to increase once the effect is felt of the final removal of tariff barriers in July 1968. Though the spectacular rate of economic growth in the European Common Market down to 1965 cannot be ascribed entirely to increased trade between its members following upon a reduction of customs duties, this nevertheless appears to have been at least a contributory factor making for growth. Expansion may also have been assisted by the character of the harmonised tax system of the Common Market with its concentration of taxation on consumption, with enterprise and investment only lightly taxed. Great Britain may find it necessary to modernise its tax system on similar lines.

## Great Britain and the EEC—disadvantages

Probably the greatest adverse effect for Great Britain from entering the European Common Market will arise from having to accept the EEC's common agricultural policy. The immediate consequence will be a *rise in the cost of living* for the British people, calculated to be in the range of $2\frac{1}{2}$–$3\frac{1}{2}\%$, as a result of the higher prices that will have to be paid for many foodstuffs. For example, even before the devaluation of sterling in November 1967, the price of butter in the Common Market was double the price in Great Britain, the price of beef was $33\frac{1}{3}\%$ higher, and wheat too was dearer. On the other hand, some foodstuffs—for example, eggs—were cheaper in the Common Market than in Great Britain. If, however, the Republic of Ireland and Denmark (both of which devalued their currencies in 1967 to the same extent as Great Britain) enter the Common Market at the same time as Great Britain, as appears to be likely, this would have a considerable effect on food production in the EEC, both countries being important producers of dairy products with Denmark one of the greatest exporters of the agricultural produce of temperate latitudes. The rise in the cost of living, however, is not likely to be greater than the rise suffered by British people in many years since 1945 as a result of inflation, and with a more rapid rate of economic growth and a general and more rapid rise in the standard of living it should be possible for most people to meet the extra cost of food without undue hardship.

Assuming that at the time of Great Britain's entry to the Common Market inflation in this country was under control, a sudden rise in the cost of living, however, might spark off another round of *inflation* through stimulation of the wages and prices spiral.

As already pointed out, duties imposed on foodstuffs imported into the European Common Market are paid into a *common fund*, and, since Great Britain is the largest importer of food in the world, this would mean a heavy payment from this country into the Common Market's coffers. Loss of revenue by the abolition of customs duties between members, however, can be made good by non-discriminatory taxes on both imported and home-produced goods.

Since the agricultural policy of the European Common Market has been framed, as is British farm policy, to give farmers a standard of living more comparable with that of industrial workers, it would seem that the more efficient British farmers—that is, mainly those with large farms—are not likely to suffer adversely from a change from one form of guaranteed prices and government subsidies (the British method of assisting farmers) to another form of price support (the Common Market method). Nevertheless, as has been the experience of small farmers in Brittany and other fringe areas of the Common Market, some small farmers in Great Britain may find it difficult to carry on in the new conditions, and amalgamations of small farms may be necessary to achieve a viable size.

There are fears too that when Great Britain joins the Common Market the bonds between this country and *the Commonwealth*—especially with the older members—will be weakened. For a long time, however, Canada has been economically more closely linked with the United States than with Great Britain, receiving 72% of its imports from that country as compared with a mere 7% from the United Kingdom and selling 55% of its exports to the United States as compared with 13% to this country. Australia too now buys only 25% of its imports from the United Kingdom and sells to this country only 20% of its exports (a fact emphasised by the increasing proportion of its reserves held in US dollars), its trade each year becoming more orientated towards the United States and the Far East. Of the old Commonwealth countries New Zealand has the closest trading relations with Great Britain, sending 75% of its exports over here and purchasing 50% of its imports from this country. With the exception of New Zealand, trade bonds with Great Britain are already weakening and for some time this country has been having to seek new markets for its products. In the case of New Zealand (which in 1967 devalued its currency by 19% as against 14% by Great Britain), this country's entry into the Common Market could be more serious, and, in the short period at least, special arrangements would be both desirable and necessary.

By expanding some industries and causing others to contract entry into the Common Market would aggravate one of the *economic frictions* associated with the maintenance of full employment and economic progress—the redistribution of labour. Unless labour can be made more mobile structural unemployment is likely to increase. In the Common Market there is free movement of labour between the member countries, none of which is now permitted to show any preference for its own labour.

Most serious of all is the problem of the British *balance of payments*. This problem is considered more fully below (*see* Chapter XII). Whenever any one member of the European Common Market has suffered a greater degree of inflation and of over-full employment than the other members, the high level of demand, coupled with inability to expand supply to match it, has resulted in a huge inflow of imports from its neighbours. The effect of this has been to cause the country concerned to incur a serious temporary deficit in its balance of payments. The correction of this situation has often led in its turn to a substantial credit balance. Such wide fluctuations in the balance of payments would be further aggravated for Great Britain by capital movements, the consequence of sterling being a reserve currency, and sterling balances, withdrawable at short notice, being held in London. The weakness of sterling in fulfilling this role, especially since 1964, has made some members of the European Common Market less enthusiastic to welcome Great Britain into the EEC. The Brussels Commission, appointed by the EEC to consider the implications of Great Britain's entry, reporting in October 1967, stressed what it regarded as the ineffectiveness of sterling as a reserve currency, thereby supporting President de Gaulle, who is opposed to this role of sterling also on political grounds. The Commission was concerned as to the adverse effects on the other members of the European Common Market if it were to admit a new member whose economy was subject to periodic monetary and financial crises. It remains to be seen what effect the devaluation of sterling in 1967 will have.

## III. THE GENERAL AGREEMENT ON TARIFFS AND TRADE

### The aims of GATT

The harm done to international trade by high tariffs was realised by most nations even during the Great Depression of the 1930s, when restrictions on trade had reduced world trade to small proportions. Nevertheless, the World Economic Conference of 1935, called in the hope that the nations of the world might agree to at least some reduction of tariffs, turned out to be a complete failure. In the unfortunate conditions of the time far too many countries took the view that, though greater liberalisation of international trade might be beneficial to the world as a whole, their own particular interests were best served by high protective tariffs.

In the very different climate that prevailed after the Second World War much greater success was achieved. Nevertheless, in 1964, Great Britain imposed an import surcharge, which it thought to be justified as a temporary measure to rectify an exceptionally serious adverse balance of payments, though neither EFTA nor GATT approved of this action. In 1968 France introduced import quotas and export subsidies. In both cases there were strong protests not only from other members of EFTA and the EEC but also from other countries, including France in the former instance and Great Britain in the latter!

When the International Monetary Fund and the World Bank were established after the Second World War a third international institution, the International Trade Organisation (ITO), was planned. The nations failed to reach agreement on the scope of the ITO and the General Agreement on Tariffs and Trade was signed instead. Not originally intended to be a permanent trade organisation, that in fact is what it has become. Since its establishment its membership has grown from 23 to 76. All members must accept its code of conduct. The members of GATT include most of the leading trading nations of the world; non-members include the USSR and China.

GATT is a trade treaty based on four important principles: (*i*) that trade between nations should be non-discriminatory; (*ii*) that the tariff should be the only instrument employed to influence foreign trade; (*iii*) that nations should consult with one another before taking action that might harm another's trade; and (*iv*) that means should be provided for the negotiation of tariff reductions. The aim of GATT, therefore, is to secure a liberalisation of world trade through a general reduction of tariffs with the object of increasing the volume of international trade and encouraging the general economic development of the signatories to the agreement. Between 1948 and 1962 five international conferences were held under the auspices of GATT, and at each one of them agreement was reached to reduce a large number of import duties. The first of these conferences, held at Geneva in 1947, achieved most—not surprisingly since at that date many tariffs were extremely high—but the conferences at Annecy (1949), Torquay (1951) and Geneva (1956 and 1962) all achieved some further tariff reductions. GATT too has given help to developing nations anxious to expand their export trade. Most of the concessions concerned manufactured goods. Few countries were prepared to make tariff concessions in the case of agricultural products.

## The "Kennedy Round"

The establishment of the two regional free trade areas in Europe—the European Common Market and the European Free Trade Association—and their success in spite of many difficulties, led to the United States in 1963 under President Kennedy suggesting an all-round reduction of tariffs, with the object mainly of reducing tariffs between the United States and the two European free trade organisations, more especially the Common Market. Down to the Second World War the United States had been one of the strongest believers in protection, principally as a means of safeguarding the standard of living of its people against cheaper labour in the rest of the world. The effect of two World Wars, and the huge increase in its productive capacity, had been to make the United States for the first time the leading country in the world both as exporter and as importer, and the effect of this development has been to make that country somewhat less protectionist than it formerly used to be. As a member of GATT the United States had agreed at each of the five conferences held down to 1962 to a number of tariff concessions, but none of these compared in scope or depth with those agreed during what came to be known as the "Kennedy Round." This was largely due to the fact that the initiative came from the President himself with more support from Congress than at previous conferences on account of a growing fear lest US exporters should find it difficult to sell to the EEC countries on account of their common external tariff. The sixth GATT conference, held at Geneva during 1964–67 and attended by fifty nations, was responsible for the "Kennedy Round" of tariff reductions. The US Government's report, issued in 1967, showed that the United States had agreed to reduce its duties on two-thirds of its imports, the extent of the reductions on average being about 35%, although in some cases the reductions were of the order of 50% or even more. The reductions were not to come into effect immediately but were to be gradually introduced over a period of five years. When the Kennedy Round has been fully implemented the duties on manufactured goods imposed by the leading industrial countries will only be of the order of 5–15%, so that by then the barriers to the export of goods of this kind will no longer be a serious deterrent to trade. It would seem, therefore, that the way has been opened to the complete abolition by those countries of duties on imported manufactured goods. Similar tariff cuts were agreed by the other leading industrial nations. Smaller tariff reductions were agreed by Canada, Australia, New Zealand and South Africa, for, although these countries are now all highly industrialised, they are still as exporters mainly concerned with primary products.

The Kennedy Round was a most remarkable achievement. There are, however, other hindrances to world trade besides tariffs—quotas, taxation, subsidies, levies such as road duties, etc.—but these were not considered in the Kennedy Round negotiations. It would be a matter for regret if their continued retention could offset some of the gains achieved in the Kennedy Round. More serious was the development in 1967–68 of a movement in the US Congress for the imposition of quotas on a range of US imports. The economic difficulties of the United States and the measures to be taken during 1968 to strengthen its balance of payments may make the next few years a critical period for GATT.

## Expansion of trade and economic growth

Another reason why most industrial countries have tended in recent years to adopt a more liberal attitude to freer trade is their increased concern with economic growth, and this depends to a considerable extent on a corresponding expansion of international trade. Then in the production of some commodities maximum economies of scale can be enjoyed only if production is geared to a wide market. As already pointed out, expansion of production requires a corresponding expansion of trade and distribution, both home and foreign. In the interests of economic growth, therefore, it has become advantageous to remove or at least reduce hindrances that exist to the expansion of international trade, and this created a favourable climate in which the Kennedy Round negotiations could take place. Even so, the negotiations at Geneva extended over nearly four years owing mainly to opposition from the Common Market countries, since the Kennedy Round reduced the effect of their common external tariff which was one of the strongest ties binding them together. There were also serious fundamental differences between members of the European Common Market and non-members with regard to agricultural policy. The Common Market favours high prices for farm products and is, therefore, unwilling to admit imports of cheap agricultural products. Protection of agriculture has much deeper roots than protection of manufacturing, and farmers tend to be more conservative in outlook than manufacturers. Governments too are inclined to consider home production of food as important as expenditure on weapons for defence, a view strongly supported by Great Britain's experience in two World Wars. Stability of prices rather than low prices (unless achieved by subsidies) has been the aim of governments since 1945, so that farming has tended to become regulated, with the result governments have found it necessary to place checks on imports of many farm products.

## Great Britain and the Kennedy Round

All the countries—and there were over fifty of them—taking part in the Kennedy Round negotiations can be expected to gain something from the tariff reductions agreed upon. The theory of international trade supports this view. All countries, however, will not make equal gains. Since the concessions are almost entirely restricted to manufactured goods, *ipso facto* the greatest gainers will be the leading manufacturing countries, in other words, those which already have the highest standards of living. In contrast, the developing nations gained relatively little.

Since the tariff cuts were reciprocal all the leading industrial nations can expect to gain from them, concessions by one country being balanced by similar concessions by others. Great Britain, however, imports mainly foodstuffs and raw materials (mostly unaffected by the agreements) and only a relatively small quantity of manufactured goods (£1,908 million out of £5,016 million in 1964), whereas its exports consist almost entirely of manufactured goods (£3,973 million out of £4,471 million in 1964). For a long time too British "visible" imports have exceeded "visible" exports, the balance being made good by "invisibles," which, of course, are unaffected by the Kennedy Round. It would appear, therefore, that Great Britain's gain from reduced tariffs on its exports should more than offset the concessions made with regard to its imports, though it can be expected that imports of manufactured goods will tend to increase in the future. Thus in 1964 (the latest year for which full statistics were available and the basis on which the arrangements were calculated) Great Britain in relation to the United States reduced its tariff on £268 million of imports in return for tariff concessions on £322 million of exports, and in relation to the European Common Market £417 million of imports as against £520 million of exports. About half Great Britain's exports go to the Commonwealth and EFTA countries (tariffs between members of the latter group having already been completely abolished) and these are not affected by the 1967–72 arrangements. However, exports form a greater percentage of the national income for Great Britain than for any other country (15% as compared with 12% for Japan, which comes second in this respect, and compared with only 4% in the case of the United States). Clearly, the greatest gains go to the countries which are the greatest overseas traders. Another important point is that the tariffs to be cut are in Great Britain's most important markets—those that are already expanding and likely to expand still more. The British industries which appear to be most likely to benefit are the motor-car industry together with bicycle and motor-cycle manufacture, the makers of high-quality woollen goods, machine tools and probably also the chemical industry.

#### RECOMMENDATIONS FOR FURTHER READING

J. F. Deniau: *The Common Market* (Barrie & Rockcliff).

D. H. Hene: *What the Common Market Really Means* (Jordan).

EEC Information Service: *The European Community—The Facts.*

*EEC Bulletin.*

*EFTA Bulletin.*

HMSO: *Britain and the EEC—The Economic Background* (Dept. of Economic Affairs).

*If available:*

E. Wyndham White: "The Role of the General Agreement on Tariffs and Trade." *National Provincial Bank Review* (November 1967).

#### QUESTIONS

1. Account for the changed attitude to tariffs since the Second World War as compared with the general attitude to tariffs immediately before that war.

2. What advantages might Great Britain expect to derive from becoming a member of the European Common Market? What disadvantages might this country suffer from taking this course?

3. "In view of the Kennedy Round Great Britain now has little to gain and much to lose by joining the European Common Market." Discuss this statement.

4. What factors do you consider determine the terms of trade between primary and manufactured products? (Degree.)

5. Examine the case for and against Britain's entry into the European Economic Community. (Barking.)

6. What do you understand by "The Law of Comparative Costs"? Why has Britain applied for membership of EEC and what economic difficulties must be overcome? (Birmingham.)

7. What advantages accrue to a country from membership of a Free Trade Area? Why should Britain seek to join other industrial countries in Europe rather than develop a closer economic union within the Commonwealth? (Huddersfield.)

8. "However unquestioned may be the advantages to all countries together of free trade, the imposition of tariffs is often in the national interests of individual countries." Discuss. (Kingston-upon-Hull.)

9. What economic factors might a company consider in supporting or opposing an application by the United Kingdom to join the European Common Market? (Liverpool.)

10. Despite the advantages of international trade based on the principle of comparative costs, countries do in fact impose restrictions on trade. Why is this? (Liverpool.)

11. Examine the British system for fixing prices of agricultural products. What changes might be made? (Northern Counties.)

12. Outline the theory of comparative cost in international trade. Explain the expression "terms of trade." (Norwich.)

13. In 1954 the UK share of the world export of manufactured goods was about 20%, but in 1964 it was only about 13%. What factors have been suggested as being responsible for this decline? What measures have been taken in recent years to increase the UK share of exports? (Southampton.)

14. Examine the function of the discount houses as (a) financial units, and (b) instruments of the Government's monetary policy. (Southampton.)

15. Compare the tariff and the quota as a means of protecting the home market of a country. (U.L.C.I.)

CHAPTER XII

# INTERNATIONAL MONETARY RELATIONS

## I. INTERNATIONAL PAYMENTS

**Payments between nations**

If comparison is to be made between the value of a country's exports and its imports a difficulty immediately arises because the value of exports is calculated in terms of its own currency whereas imports are priced in a wide range of different currencies. Before any comparison can be made, the value of imports will have to be recalculated at the prevailing rate of exchange in terms of the country's own currency. Even more important, imports will have to be paid for in the currencies of the various supplying countries or by some means of payment that can be readily converted into those currencies. Transactions between people using different currencies can take place, therefore, only if one currency can be exchanged for another, since each—whether in the form of inconvertible bank-notes or bank deposits—can usually be spent only in the country of origin. A country's demand for foreign currency comes then from its demand for imports, and so foreign currency is wanted, therefore, only for the purpose of making purchases from the issuing country.

When primitive forms of commodity money were in use, such as cattle or salt, transactions between different peoples could take place only on a system not far removed from barter, for what was money in one country was merely an ordinary commodity in another. However, when gold or silver coins of full face value came into use, merchants were willing to accept them, whatever their country of origin, assessing their value by the weight of the precious metal they contained. Nowadays, payment in commercial transactions is more likely to be made by one of the following means: (*i*) a foreign bill of exchange, (*ii*) a documentary credit requiring the opening of a credit at a bank in the exporter's country, (*iii*) a bank draft drawn on the importer's bank in terms of the seller's currency or (*iv*) the telegraphic transfer of a bank deposit from one country to another. Many banks, both British and foreign, have overseas branches (or local banks which act as their agents where the amount of business does not warrant the opening of a branch), and balances in the local currency have to be maintained, these supplies of foreign currency being mainly earned by exports from the home country.

For international trade to be maximised it must be multilateral, *i.e.*, each country must be able to buy from, or sell to, whatever country it wishes. This means that currency earned by the exports of Country A to Country B must be capable of being spent by importers of Country A on goods from Country C, D or E or any other country. Failing the existence of an international currency, this requires all currencies to be freely convertible. Although the world has been unable to provide itself with an international currency, sterling and in recent years the US dollar have to some extent fulfilled this role. Convertibility further requires there to be rates of exchange at which currencies can be exchanged for one another and this poses the problem: how are these rates of exchange determined?

## Foreign exchange—the gold standard

How rates of exchange are determined depends on the system of foreign exchange in operation at the time. The present system has been developed out of experience of systems employed in the past. To understand present-day problems associated with international payments it is necessary, therefore, to recall how the present system evolved.

Throughout the greater part of the time that money has been in use in the world—that is, until little more than fifty years ago—it had to take as its standard unit a commodity regarded as being of value for its own sake, silver and gold soon being found most suitable for this purpose. At quite an early period of history it was found that transactions between peoples using silver or gold coins minted by different authorities and differing in size and weight— and perhaps also in shape and fineness—could easily be used as means of payment simply by weighing them. However, with the expansion of world trade, a more efficient method of making international payments was required.

The gold standard—it could just as easily have been a silver standard—was essentially only a more sophisticated version of primitive money-changing techniques. On the gold standard the standard unit of each country's currency comprised a definite amount by weight of gold, and generally coins of exactly this weight were minted and put into circulation. This was the essential feature of the gold standard, under which therefore there was a fixed price for gold. Thus, the rate of exchange between two currencies depended as in earlier times on the amount of gold in each. Under this system it was essential that other forms of money such as banknotes should be freely convertible for gold and that the use of token coins should be restricted. Since, too, customers had to be permitted on demand to withdraw bank deposits in gold, the total amount of money in a country on the gold standard was dependent on its stock of gold. Thus, reserves of gold had to be held for two purposes: (*i*) as a backing for the note issue, and (*ii*) to cover payment for any excess of imports over exports. The fact that a single gold reserve was made to serve two purposes meant that any loss of gold due to an excess of imports over exports at the same time reduced the backing for the note issue and made necessary a contraction in the domestic supply of money. In other words, a policy of deflation had to be pursued. Similarly, an inflow of gold from abroad, resulting from an excess of exports over imports, made possible an expansion of the internal supply of money.

Thus, monetary policy in the domestic sphere depended on the external situation. If the appropriate policy was always followed—that is, if the so-called "rules" were always obeyed—then, it was said, the gold standard was "automatic" in its operation, an adverse balance of payments correcting itself as a result of the internal deflationary policy that of necessity followed in its train, by reducing incomes and demand and so checking imports, by reducing costs and prices and so stimulating exports, and so in time ending the outflow of gold. Exactly the reverse process would be set in motion by a favourable balance of payments, so that in either case a country's internal payments would be brought into balance. This was the system that operated in Europe and over a large part of the world before 1914, the years 1900–13 being the heyday of the system.

### Foreign exchange—flexible exchange rates

During the years immediately following the First World War few currencies were convertible into gold, few had a gold backing and fewer still had gold coins in circulation. Most countries during that period operated flexible exchange rates. Under this system money, whether coin or notes, comprised merely tokens that could be used as purchasing power only in the country of issue. Money in the foreign exchange market was exchanged as in other markets at rates (or prices) in response to supply and demand, a country's demand for foreign currencies being derived from the demand for imports and the supply from the sale of its exports. Thus, when rates of exchange are free to fluctuate, the rate of exchange depends on the relation between a country's imports and its exports, the rate at any time being that which equates the demand for a currency with its available supply. An increase in imports or a fall in exports will cause the rate to depreciate; an increase in exports or a fall in imports will cause it to appreciate.

As with the gold standard, so with flexible exchange rates disequilibrium in the balance of payments was "automatically" rectified. Thus, an adverse balance would cause a currency to depreciate, and as a result imports would become dearer to domestic buyers and exports cheaper to foreign buyers. Therefore, the demand for imports would be checked and the sale of exports stimulated until a balance was again achieved. Whereas, however, the gold standard provides an effective check on inflation (though all countries can inflate together), with flexible exchange rates there is no such brake. The more stable exchange rates of the gold standard too are better for trade than exchange rates that are liable to fluctuate. On the other hand, on the gold standard a country's monetary policy is dictated by inflows and outflows of gold, whereas if its exchange rate is not linked to gold a country can pursue whatever monetary policy suits its internal situation, and indeed, it need never adopt a deflationary policy.

### The revived gold standard, 1925–31

In effect Great Britain and the other belligerents left the gold standard on the outbreak of the First World War in 1914. Makeshift expedients were employed during the war and when it came to an end few countries would have found it possible immediately to return to the gold standard. For some years, therefore, exchange rates were free to fluctuate. In many cases inflation during the war was succeeded by even more severe inflation after the war was over. In Great Britain it was generally expected that there would be a return to the gold standard when world economic conditions returned to "normal," and this view was supported by the Report of the Cunliffe Committee (1918) which recommended a return to the gold standard as soon as conditions allowed. The monetary chaos in Europe during the immediate post-war years appeared to emphasise the need for stability of exchange rates which only the gold standard could provide.

During the 1920s a number of countries returned to gold—Austria in 1922, Germany in 1924 (in both cases following runaway inflations), Great Britain in 1925 and France in 1928. The form of gold standard adopted was the gold bullion standard under which notes were exchangeable for gold only in large quantities so that the expense of a gold coinage was avoided. Some other countries adopted the gold exchange standard, holding their reserves in securities issued by countries on the gold bullion standard.

The economic position of many countries had been greatly weakened in consequence of the war. Some, therefore, returned to the gold standard at a lower parity, but in Great Britain concern for the prestige of sterling led to the pound being given its pre-war parity of 4·86⅔ US dollars. This greatly over-valued the pound, whereas France returned to gold at a parity of 125 francs to the pound (as compared with 25 francs to the pound in 1914), which undervalued the franc. It is now generally admitted that the British choice of parity was mistaken, but at the time it appeared to the monetary authorities to be the only way to get back to "normal." To be workable, over-valuation of sterling required deflation on an impossible scale, and the result was that Great Britain ran into a trade depression ahead of the great world depression.

There was, too, an inherent weakness in the gold exchange standard. Fear that the "parent" country might be compelled to leave the gold standard led to heavy withdrawals from that country whenever it found itself in difficulties with its balance of payments, and because sterling was often chosen for the gold exchange standard Great Britain suffered most in this way. Experience of inflation in the post-war years made investors more concerned for the safety of their money rather than the rate of interest. This "hot money," as it was called, would be moved away from any country at the first sign of danger, aggravating thereby that country's difficulties. Perhaps most serious of all was the apparent unwillingness of many countries to carry out what were regarded as the "rules" of the gold standard, namely to inflate in the case of an inflow of gold and to deflate in the case of an outflow, on the grounds that inflation would raise the prices of exports and deflation would lead to an increase in unemployment.

Then in 1930, when the United States, faced by the trade depression, ended the financial assistance it had been giving to Germany, the weakness of Great Britain's position became apparent—long-term lending to Germany on the one hand while holding short-term foreign funds. Heavy withdrawals of these funds were the immediate cause of Great Britain being forced off the gold standard in September 1931. Some other countries left gold at the same time as Great Britain, and others followed later.

The difficulties of the 1920s and the ensuing world trade depression cannot be laid upon the gold standard itself, for it had worked quite well in the easier conditions that prevailed before 1914. It had, however, two serious drawbacks: (i) its rigidity, and (ii) the fact that it restricted increases in total purchasing power to the rate at which the gold supply could be increased. After their dismal experience of flexible exchange rates what many countries wanted more than anything else was the advantage of stability of exchange rates, but without the disadvantages of the gold standard. The gold standard as operated in the 1920s was a very different system from the one that prevailed before 1914. After 1925 it became much more of a managed system, since measures that would have been effective before 1914 proved to be quite inadequate in the changed conditions of the 1920s. Actually the circumstances of the time were against the restored standard. Maldistribution of gold among the leading countries of the world resulted in many of them having inadequate reserves, whereas, as a result of the rise of prices, debits and credits in balances of payments were greater in terms of money (and, therefore, gold) even though no greater in volume than in pre-1914 days. Thus, when Great Britain was compelled to leave the gold standard, its gold reserves were actually three times larger than during the twenty years before 1914.

### Exchange control

By 1931 neither the gold standard in its revived form nor flexible exchange rates were regarded as satisfactory systems of foreign exchange. After leaving the gold standard Great Britain's aim was to maintain a reasonably stable rate of exchange. First, sterling was allowed to find its market level and by March 1932 it had depreciated by about 30% in relation to currencies still linked to gold such as the US dollar and the French franc. The Treasury established an Exchange Equalisation Account to operate in the foreign exchange market, buying sterling when other countries wished to sell in order to keep up its exchange rate and selling sterling in the market when other countries wished to buy in order to keep down the rate. By this means fluctuations in the exchange rate for sterling were reduced to a minimum. The British monetary authorities would have liked to restrict their intervention to offset capital movements, since these have the most serious disturbing influence in the foreign exchange market, permitting the sterling rate to fluctuate only in response to changes in supply and demand arising out of changes in the volume of trade transactions. In practice, however, it is very difficult to distinguish between the demand for sterling arising from current transactions and demand owing to capital movements. In the end British policy came to be directed primarily towards maintaining a stable rate of sterling.

As the Exchange Equalisation Account acquired foreign exchange this was converted into gold, and with the gradual improvement in Great Britain's position during the 1930s it built up a not inconsiderable gold reserve of its own. The success of the British system led to both France (which left gold in 1936) and the United States (which left gold temporarily in 1933 in order to return almost immediately at a lower parity) setting up similar equalisation accounts.[1] From 1936, when these three countries signed the Tripartite Agreement, they began to operate a sort of regional gold

[1] That of the USA was known as an Exchange Stabilisation Fund.

standard, but with more flexible exchange rates than the gold standard offered. In somewhat similar fashion the Bank of England intervenes at the present day to restrict fluctuations of sterling to the narrow limits of 2.42 and 2.38 in relation to the US dollar.

When Germany left the gold standard in 1931 fear of another runaway inflation similar to that of 1923 led to the adoption of a restrictive system of exchange control. The German monetary authorities pegged the rate of exchange for the Reichsmark at its gold-standard parity with the US dollar. The features of the German system of exchange control became familiar to the nationals of many other countries after 1945, foreign currency being obtainable by Germans only through the Reichsbank with no allowance for personal use.[1] Payment due to foreign merchants who had exported goods to Germany was made to "blocked" accounts in that country. During the Second World War Great Britain adopted a system of exchange control of a very similar kind. However, in the 1930s, Germany went on to develop a system of multiple exchange rates—the rate varying according to the Government's assessment of the importance of the purpose for which the foreign exchange was required—which in recent times some other countries have copied.[2] The effect in the 1930s of Germany's excessively restrictive and rigid system of exchange control was to reduce that country's trade almost to the level of barter, with a consequent strangulation of its foreign trade.

## II. INTERNATIONAL FINANCIAL INSTITUTIONS

### The Bretton Woods Conference

As the Second World War was drawing towards a close the statesmen of many countries became concerned to prevent a return to the pre-war conditions that had resulted internally in industrial depression instead of economic growth and externally in a shrinkage instead of an expansion of world trade. While the war was still in progress plans were already being formulated in several countries for the maintenance of full employment after the war. In the realm of international trade, too, discussions were proceeding to secure a reduction

[1] As recently as 1966 the British Government reintroduced restriction in the form of a small basic travel allowance.

[2] Although the Bretton Woods conference had condemned multiple exchange rates they proliferated during the decade following the end of the Second World War. During 1945–50 the practice was prevalent among the countries of South America, but by 1955 it had become more widespread, with 36 out of the 58 members of the IMF being guilty of it. Since 1955, however, the practice has declined and by 1962 only 15 out of 82 members of the IMF were operating multiple exchange rates.

of tariffs, the eventual outcome of which was the establishment of GATT. Further discussions also took place on the problem of international monetary relations.

In 1944 a conference was called at Bretton Woods in the state of New Hampshire in the United States with a view to working out an international monetary system that would facilitate international transactions and so encourage and not hamper world trade. What was wanted was a system that would encourage multilateral trade. The Conference, therefore, began by condemning the restrictive practices associated with exchange control indulged in to an increasing extent by many countries in the 1930s, such as bilateral agreements, blocked accounts, multiple exchange rates, and indeed, in principle most forms of exchange control.

A prerequisite for multilateral trade is that different currencies should be freely convertible to enable exporters to sell to wherever there is a market for their products and to encourage importers to buy in the cheapest markets wherever they might be in order thereby to maximise world trade. Stable exchange rates, too, are generally regarded as desirable if international trade is to be encouraged. It could be pointed out that the gold standard offered all these advantages. There was, however, one serious drawback to the gold standard: under it the external situation determined what internal monetary policy a country should pursue, and on occasion this might conflict with the policy necessary to maintain full employment. On the other hand, a system of flexible exchange rates would have given control over internal monetary policy together with external convertibility, but fluctuations in exchange rates are not generally regarded as being conducive to the expansion of international trade. What was wanted was the best of both worlds— usually an unattainable objective. What in fact was worked out was a scheme that had many features of the gold standard but which was less rigid in its operation.

In the preliminary discussions Lord Keynes, who represented Great Britain, had suggested the establishment of an international institution with a world function somewhat similar to that of a commercial bank in the domestic sphere, i.e. with power to grant overdrafts. However, this idea did not find favour with the Americans, who were afraid that it might lead to an over-expansion of credit. If Keynes' plan had been adopted some of the difficulties of the mid 1960s, particularly those due to insufficient international liquidity, might have been alleviated.

The scheme adumbrated at Bretton Woods included the establishment of the International Monetary Fund (IMF) and the International Bank for Reconstruction and Development (IBRD) or World Bank, both with their headquarters in Washington, D.C.

The work of these two institutions is supplemented by the Bank for International Settlements (BIS), established in Basle in 1930.

## The International Monetary Fund

The purpose of the IMF was officially stated to be:

"To facilitate the expansion and balanced growth of international trade, and to contribute thereby to the promotion and maintenance of high levels of employment and real income and to the development of the productive resources of all members as primary objectives of economic policy."

First, all members of the IMF had to select the gold parity for their currencies (as on the gold standard). In practice, since the US dollar was already linked to gold, parities with the dollar were generally chosen, the United Kingdom selecting a rate of $4.03 to the pound. In contrast to the gold standard the rate of exchange was not rigidly fixed, a change of parity of up to 10% being permitted simply by notifying the IMF. For a change of over 10% the permission of the IMF had first to be sought and if the proposed change did not exceed 20% a decision had to be given within the space of seventy-two hours, but if a change in excess of 20% was desired the IMF was not to be bound by any time limit before making its decision known.

The IMF was to be provided with funds of its own, all members contributing to a pool in accordance with quotas assigned to them. The original quotas of some of the leading members were as follows:

TABLE LXXXIX

*International Monetary Fund Quotas* (1945)

|  | $ *million* |
| --- | --- |
| United States . . . . | 2,750 |
| United Kingdom . . . | 1,300 |
| France . . . . . | 450 |
| India . . . . . | 400 |
| Canada . . . . . | 300 |
| Netherlands . . . . | 275 |
| Belgium . . . . . | 225 |
| Australia . . . . | 200 |
| Brazil . . . . | 150 |
| Argentina . . . . | 100 |
| Union of South Africa . . | 100 |

In 1959 these quotas were increased to the levels shown in Table XC.

TABLE XC
*International Monetary Fund Quotas* (1959)

|  | $ million |
|---|---|
| United States . . . . . | 4,125 |
| United Kingdom . . . . | 1,950 |
| France . . . . . | 787·5 |
| West Germany . . . . | 787·5 |
| India . . . . . | 600 |
| Canada . . . . . | 550 |
| Netherlands . . . . | 412·5 |
| Belgium . . . . . | 337·5 |
| Australia . . . . | 400 |
| Brazil . . . . . | 280 |
| Argentina . . . . | 280 |
| Mexico . . . . . | 180 |
| Union of South Africa . . | 150 |
| Spain . . . . . | 150 |
| Yugoslavia . . . . | 120 |

In 1965 further increases in members' quotas were agreed. It will be noticed that the list for 1959 includes a number of countries which were not members of the IMF in 1945. Of each member's contribution to the pool not more than 75% had to be in its own currency, the remainder being in gold or US dollars.

The main function of the IMF is to give a strictly limited amount of assistance to any member country with a temporary debit in its balance of payments. A member is permitted to purchase from the IMF in any year any foreign exchange it requires to the value of not more than 25% of its contribution quota, but, if the IMF already has a supply of a member's currency equal to double its quota, that member can then obtain foreign exchange only in return for gold of equivalent value. These restrictions were imposed because it was to be the purpose of the IMF to assist a country in temporary difficulties and not with a fundamental disequilibrium in its balance of payments. In such a situation it must have recourse to other means as, for example, internal deflation or external devaluation.

## The International Bank for Reconstruction and Development

As its full name implies, the function of the World Bank (IBRD) is to provide loans to countries in need of assistance to cover reconstruction or capital development. Loans are made primarily to governments and only to companies or corporations if the loans are government-guaranteed. In 1956 the International Finance Corporation (IFC) was established to supplement the work of the World Bank in providing assistance to developing countries.

## The Bank for International Settlements

Founded in 1930 with its headquarters in Basle, Switzerland, to assist the payment of reparations arising out of the First World War, the Bank for International Settlements (BIS) is essentially a central bankers' bank. It was the first *permanent* organisation to be established for the co-operation of central banks, though for upwards of a quarter of a century its activities were restricted to a somewhat limited field. It seemed to the delegates at the Bretton Woods conference that the establishment of two new international financial institutions—the IMF and the IBRD—would make the BIS redundant. In July 1944, therefore, the conference proposed that the BIS should be liquidated. However, when the war was over this decision was rescinded on the ground that the BIS would be complementary to the new institutions and would not merely duplicate their functions. There is one important difference between them: the IMF and the IBRD are world-wide in their activities while the BIS is primarily a European institution, although until 1953 Japan was a member. There is co-operation between the BIS and the IBRD, each being represented at the other's annual meeting. In procedure too there is a difference: the work of the IBRD is conducted more publicly than that of the BIS.

The very character of its work tends to make the BIS avoid publicity, although a good account of its activities is given in its annual report. Since 1945 the BIS has again been the custodian of part of the reserves of European central banks. Its assets, therefore, are similar to those of the IMF, consisting partly of gold and partly of the principal world currencies. Though the BIS is not empowered to lend to governments it can take up short-term government securities. Its main activities comprise direct transactions with central banks, but it never operates in a currency without the consent of the central bank of the country concerned, while its gold operations are undertaken only on instructions from central banks. In recent years it has adapted itself in quite a remarkable fashion to new situations which have required it to widen and expand its activities considerably (*see* below, pp. 419–21).

## III. STERLING AND THE STERLING AREA

### The convertibility crisis of 1947

The Bretton Woods conference expected that a transition period of five years would be required after the end of the war before the new scheme could be put into operation. During this period most countries would find it necessary to continue with some form of exchange control until their economies had been put on a sounder basis. However, under the Washington Loan Agreement of 1945, Great Britain, in return for a loan of $3,750 million from the United States, had to agree to make sterling freely convertible by July 1947, *i.e.* only two years after the end of the war. Within five weeks of sterling being given convertibility it had to be withdrawn to save further depletion of the gold reserves, the American loan already having been almost completely exhausted. The conditions of the time were clearly against the restoration of convertibility so soon. The countries of Europe, their economies shattered by the war, had as yet made little progress on the road towards recovery, so that the only country at the time capable of exporting on any scale was the United States. Any sterling they acquired, therefore, was immediately exchanged for US dollars—hence the run on sterling.

The immediate consequence of Great Britain's failure to maintain the convertibility of sterling was the announcement of the Marshall Plan, under which the United States proposed to give assistance to Europe to speed up its economic recovery. Of the $4,800-million worth of goods given by the United States under the Marshall Plan Great Britain received $1,200-million worth. To administer "Marshall Aid" the Organisation for European Economic Co-operation (OEEC) was established. To encourage intra-European trade the United States gave additional aid to countries willing to make amounts of their currencies available to one another, and under the auspices of the OEEC a European payments scheme was worked out to facilitate payments between West European countries and so to encourage multilateral trade between them. The BIS became banker to the new European Payments Union (EPU) on its establishment in 1950. The EPU was in effect a regional version of the IMF and operated on somewhat similar lines. By promoting multilateral transactions between its members it brought to an end a good deal of bilateralism in Europe and paved the way for the more successful working of the IMF nine years later.

### Towards convertibility, 1947–59

The main effect of the convertibility crisis of 1947 was that it delayed for twelve years the general convertibility of the principal currencies of the world, an essential prerequisite for the full working of the Bretton Woods scheme. The failure of 1947 too made Great Britain more cautious—possibly over-cautious—in restoring convertibility to sterling. The devaluation of the pound in 1949 should have paved the way towards convertibility since one cause of Great Britain's difficulties was that the arbitrary parity of $4.03 to the pound given to sterling in 1945 overvalued the pound and so produced a fundamental disequilibrium in Britain's balance of payments. The new rate of $2.80 to the pound was more realistic than the former rate.

However, several more years were to elapse before the European economies could be considered to be on a reasonably sound basis. The restoration of convertibility of sterling was further hampered by the inadequacy of Great Britain's gold reserves, the effect of which was to exaggerate the seriousness of any deficit that occurred in the balance of payments.

Restrictions on the convertibility of sterling, therefore, were relaxed gradually. Agreements were made with a number of countries which were admitted one by one to what was known as the Transferable Account within which sterling was freely convertible. Sterling was also made freely convertible between countries in the dollar area—the American Account—and, as it was already freely convertible within the sterling area, it thus became convertible *within* each of three areas, but convertibility *between* the three areas continued to be restricted until 1st January 1959, when the three areas were combined and sterling was given non-resident convertibility, the acquisition of foreign exchange, particularly for foreign investment, continuing to be restricted for British residents. Another step towards convertibility had been to allow sterling to fluctuate within the narrow limits of $2.78–$2.82 to the pound, the Bank of England intervening in the market through the Exchange Equalisation Account—both spot and forward—only when one or other of these limits was under pressure. Then in 1954 the London gold bullion market was reopened.

## The sterling area

*Before 1914.* During the nineteenth century sterling became a convenient means of international payment in consequence of the predominating position occupied by Great Britain both in world trade and in the carrying trade. Most of the British possessions overseas were economically as well as politically dependent on the home country. Most of their trade was with Great Britain; they were dependent too on Great Britain for most of their investment; and in monetary affairs they relied on Great Britain for their banking and other financial institutions. In most British territories overseas British banks were established, generally with their head offices in London. Since, however, Great Britain, the most economically advanced country in the world at the time, also enjoyed the largest share of the trade of most other countries and undertook investment throughout the world (British companies, for example, owning and operating railways in Argentina and tramways in Lisbon), most foreign countries as well as British overseas territories found it convenient for purposes of trade to maintain balances in London, which in consequence became the banking centre of the world. Since too sterling was linked to gold, with its value never in doubt, the monetary standard of pre-1914 days was in fact as much a sterling standard as a gold standard. Thus, during the nineteenth century, there was little to mark off the sterling area from the rest of the world.

*The inter-war years.* During the 1930s after the collapse of the gold standard, the sterling area took on a different character. Though sterling was no longer linked to gold there were many countries, both within and without the old sterling area, which preferred the stability which the link with sterling was able to give them—a clear indication of the success of the British Treasury's exchange intervention. Eventually the sterling area comprised not only British territories throughout the world (except Canada) but also several European countries, such as, for example, Norway, Sweden, Finland and Portugal, together with Egypt, Japan, Argentina and some others. Except, of course, for Great Britain itself and South Africa, all these countries held their reserves in sterling. The sterling area, however, was a purely voluntary association of countries, without any kind of formal organisation, which in a period of rising tariffs and declining international trade wished to protect their economies against the world trend by permitting freer movement of goods, services and capital among themselves than other countries were willing to allow. The result was that the sterling area at this time provided a sort of oasis of less severe depression in a world of severe depression. Throughout the inter-war period and "despite the weakening of the relative position of Great Britain, sterling remained throughout the world by far the most popular and convenient means of making international payments."[1]

*Since* 1945. In consequence of the Second World War the character of the sterling area again changed. In 1940 it had become for the first time a legally defined unit. It also came to be officially known as "the scheduled territories." It had lost many of the members it had gained in the 1930s but others joined it. The members' practice of pooling their resources of US dollars, introduced during the war, was continued. This and a common policy of exchange control, together with increasing co-operation between the monetary authorities of the members, periodic meetings of their finance ministers and the setting up of a liaison committee, have given the sterling area a greater degree of cohesion than it ever had before. Great Britain's main role, however, is as banker and adviser to the area.

[1] B. S. Karlstroem, "How Did They Become Reserve Currencies?" *Fund and Bank Review* (September 1967).

The sterling area remains a voluntary association of independent members who remain attached to it because they have found it in their own interest to do so, and this in spite of a weakening of the ties holding the area together. The advantages of belonging to a group with greater freedom of trade between its members have lessened with the gradual reduction of tariffs that culminated in the Kennedy Round. As a result the amount of intra-sterling area trade has declined, and some members now have gold and dollar reserves as well as sterling reserves. Therefore, in view of Great Britain's economic difficulties since 1945, it is indeed remarkable that the sterling area has survived at all. Whereas Great Britain during the years 1956–66 averaged a credit balance on current account of only £31 million, its average credit balance with the sterling area has been £226 million. With the rest of the world the sterling area during these years had an average credit balance of £515 million. Some writers, however, saw in the devaluation of sterling in 1967 signs that the end of the sterling area might be in sight. The more important members of the sterling area—Australia and South Africa, for example—and some of the less important members, such as Malaysia and Libya, decided not to follow the United Kingdom in devaluing their currencies. Australia now keeps 20% of its reserves in US dollars, for half the foreign capital coming into that country now comes from the United States and a third of its exports go to that country. The declining role of sterling as a reserve currency was emphasised in 1968 when twelve of the world's central banks, meeting at Basle, offered the United Kingdom a standby credit of $2,000 million to be used if it should prove necessary to offset withdrawals from sterling balances.

## IV. STERLING AND THE BRITISH BALANCE OF PAYMENTS

### The balance of trade

The British balance of payments comprises three main elements: (*i*) the balance of trade, the "visible" balance, *i.e.* the relation between payments for imports of goods and receipts from the export of goods; (*ii*) the "invisible" balance, *i.e.* the relation between payments for services provided by foreign firms, people and institutions and receipts from services provided by British firms, people and institutions; (*iii*) capital movements into and out of the United Kingdom. The balance of trade and the invisible balance together give the balance of payments on current account. When capital movements also are taken into consideration this gives the overall balance of payments on current and capital account.

It is extremely rare nowadays for the United Kingdom to have a credit (or favourable) balance of trade, though in fact this did occur in 1956 and 1958. It was, however, a regular occurrence during the nineteenth century. In recent times this country has generally had a deficit in its balance of trade as the following table shows:

TABLE XCI
*The Balance of Trade*

| Year | Imports | Exports and Re-exports | Balance |
|------|---------|------------------------|---------|
|      | £ million | £ million | £ million |
| 1956 | 3,324 | 3,377 | + 53 |
| 1957 | 3,538 | 3,509 | − 29 |
| 1958 | 3,378 | 3,407 | + 29 |
| 1959 | 3,640 | 3,522 | −118 |
| 1960 | 4,138 | 3,732 | −406 |
| 1961 | 4,043 | 3,891 | −152 |
| 1962 | 4,095 | 3,993 | −102 |
| 1963 | 4,362 | 4,282 | − 80 |
| 1964 | 5,003 | 4,466 | −537 |
| 1965 | 5,049 | 4,777 | −272 |
| 1966 | 5,244 | 5,108 | −136 |
| 1967 | 5,660 | 5,023 | −637 |
| 1968 |       |       |       |

Source: *Balance of Payments* (HMSO).

The *terms of trade* have a great influence on the visible balance. This is the relation between the prices to be paid for imports and the prices of a country's exports on the world market. Thus, if during a period the prices of its imports rise by a smaller percentage than the prices of its exports, it will clearly be able to obtain a greater volume of imports in exchange for a particular volume of exports. In such a case the terms of trade would be said to be moving in that country's favour. This occurred in the case of Great Britain during the 1930s when the prices of primary products were very low in relation to the prices of manufactured goods. The reverse situation occurred in the years following the Second World War when Europe was short of both food and raw materials, its own production having been reduced to small proportions. Between 1956 and 1962 the terms of trade were again moving in favour of this country. The terms of trade as shown in Table XCII are calculated by taking the export price index as a percentage of the import price index. With rising prices over the period covered by Table XCI the debit balance might be expected to increase in terms of money even though there was no

TABLE XCII
*Great Britain's Terms of Trade*
(1961 = 100)

| Year | Index no. |
|------|-----------|
| 1956 | 87 |
| 1957 | 89 |
| 1958 | 96 |
| 1959 | 96 |
| 1960 | 97 |
| 1961 | 100 |
| 1962 | 102 |
| 1963 | 101 |
| 1964 | 99 |
| 1965 | 102 |
| 1966 | 103 |
| 1967 | 105 |
| 1968 | |

Source: *Annual Abstract of Statistics.*

change in the volume of trade. The huge debit balances of 1964 and 1967 occurred with exports at record high levels as a result of huge increases in imports.

### The invisible balance

For a long time the United Kingdom achieved a balance on current account by having a sufficiently large credit balance on invisibles to offset its debit (or adverse) balance of trade. The main invisible items comprise receipts and payments for shipping and air transport, insurance and banking services, the receipt and payment of interest and dividends on British investments abroad and foreign investment in this country, the expenditure of foreign tourists in Great Britain and of British tourists abroad. Since the Second World War, however, the United Kingdom has had a relatively smaller balance (allowing for the fall in the value of money) than it generally had in the period between the two World Wars. With rising prices the credit balance might be expected to rise to offset the increasing cost of the excess of imports over exports in the trade balance, instead of which there has actually been a tendency for the invisible balance to fall, the average for 1962–67 being only £188·9 million as compared with an average for 1956–61 of £209·8 million and this in spite of rising prices. Here appears to lie the cause of the United Kingdom's difficulties with its current balance of payments. It is necessary to

TABLE XCIII

*The "Invisible" Balance*

| Year | Payments | Receipts | Balance |
|------|----------|----------|---------|
| | £ million | £ million | £ million |
| 1956 | 1,754 | 1,909 | +155 |
| 1957 | 1,759 | 2,021 | +262 |
| 1958 | 1,771 | 2,089 | +318 |
| 1959 | 1,821 | 2,088 | +267 |
| 1960 | 2,046 | 2,196 | +150 |
| 1961 | 2,112 | 2,270 | +158 |
| 1962 | 2,158 | 2,389 | +231 |
| 1963 | 2,297 | 2,496 | +199 |
| 1964 | 2,534 | 2,672 | +138 |
| 1965 | 2,711 | 2,892 | +181 |
| 1966 | 2,769 | 2,920 | +151 |
| 1967 | 2,892 | 3,125 | +233 |
| 1968 | | | |

Source: *Balance of Payments* (HMSO).

consider the individual items in the invisible balance if the cause of the decline is to be diagnosed.

### The invisibles: (1) Transport

During the nineteenth century Great Britain enjoyed 70% of the world's carrying trade so that for a long time shipping was an important source of invisible income. As recently as 1952 it yielded a credit of £105 million and it remained a credit item until 1960, but since 1961 it has become a debit. The decline in the importance of this item in the British invisible balance began with the building by other countries of their own merchant fleets, necessitated partly by Great Britain's inability to provide this service for them during two World Wars and owing also to this country's heavy shipping losses during those two wars. Not only, however, had British shipping to meet foreign competition on the seas of the world but since the Second World War there has also been increasing competition from air transport for the carriage of both passengers and freight. By 1965, for example, airlines were carrying more passengers across the Atlantic than were the shipping companies. In air transport Great Britain has never enjoyed the overwhelming advantage it once possessed on the sea. Almost every country in the world now has its own airline, generally state-owned and often operated more to maintain national prestige than to make a profit. Most of these countries never have many ships and some of them are even without coastline and harbours. Income from abroad to UK airlines has rarely exceeded by very much British payments to foreign airlines. Consider the following table:

TABLE XCIV
*Transport*
(Net receipts)

| Year | Shipping | Civil aviation | Overall balance |
|------|----------|----------------|-----------------|
|      | £ million | £ million | £ million |
| 1952 | +105 | | |
| 1956 | −48 | − 1 | −49 |
| 1957 | + 7 | − 3 | + 4 |
| 1958 | +45 | + 8 | +53 |
| 1959 | +14 | +18 | +32 |
| 1960 | −34 | +18 | −16 |
| 1961 | −26 | +23 | − 3 |
| 1962 | −21 | +22 | + 1 |
| 1963 | −26 | +27 | + 1 |
| 1964 | −43 | +27 | −16 |
| 1965 | −10 | +27 | +17 |
| 1966 | −15 | +30 | +15 |
| 1967 | + 1 | +29 | +30 |
| 1968 | | | |

Source: *Balance of Payments* (HMSO).

Thus shipping, once the source of considerable invisible income to the United Kingdom, is now often a debit item, and not always completely offset by a credit balance on air transport.

## The invisibles: (2) Investment

Another important invisible item is income from investment abroad. During the nineteenth century Great Britain helped to finance investment all over the world. This export of capital was made possible by this country's almost permanent credit balance of payments at that time. By 1913 British investment abroad had reached upwards of £4,000 million. There was relatively little foreign investment in this country in those days, and so interest and dividends yielded a very considerable net invisible income to the British balance of payments. In each of the two World Wars British investment abroad was run down to pay for imports and between the wars painfully built up again. How British investment abroad has again been accumulated since 1945 is a matter to be considered in connection with the balance of payments on capital account (*see* below, pp. 412–14), but, as Table XCV shows, foreign investment has again become an important source of invisible income to this country. Investment includes not only dividends and interest paid by foreign businesses or governments to British individuals, companies or institutions, but also the earnings of foreign branches or subsidiaries of British firms. Included too are the overseas earnings of British oil companies. Table XCV shows the extent to which foreign

TABLE XCV
*Investment Income*

| Year | Receipts | Payments | Balance |
|------|----------|----------|---------|
| | £ million | £ million | £ million |
| 1956 | 571 | 342 | +229 |
| 1957 | 583 | 334 | +249 |
| 1958 | 683 | 389 | +294 |
| 1959 | 662 | 396 | +266 |
| 1960 | 678 | 438 | +240 |
| 1961 | 685 | 422 | +263 |
| 1962 | 766 | 420 | +346 |
| 1963 | 845 | 443 | +402 |
| 1964 | 899 | 490 | +409 |
| 1965 | 1,025 | 555 | +470 |
| 1966 | 990 | 568 | +422 |
| 1967 | 1,013 | 603 | +410 |
| 1968 | | | |

Source: *Balance of Payments* (HMSO).

investment in Great Britain has increased. By 1968 the United States had over $5,600 million of investment in Great Britain as compared with $3,000 million in West Germany and $1,750 million in France. In the ten years to 1966, therefore, although income to Great Britain from foreign investment increased by 63%, payments from foreign investment increased by 66%.

### The Invisibles: (3) Travel

Foreign travel, whether undertaken for business reasons or for purposes of tourism, also gives rise to receipts and payments that affect invisible income. This has always been a debit item to Great Britain. In spite of great efforts by the British Tourist Board to attract more foreign visitors to this country, the number of British people taking holidays abroad has increased more rapidly than the number of foreign tourists coming into Great Britain. For some countries, especially Italy (+ £428 million net balance in 1966) and Spain (+ £368 million), tourism has become an important source of invisible income, but for the United States (− £620 million net) and West Germany (− £277 million), as well as for Great

Britain, it is a debit item. In comparison with the United States and West Germany the British debit of £78 million net in 1966 is quite small (Table XCVI). Two-thirds of British expenditure on travel abroad goes, as might be expected, to Western Europe, whereas Great Britain's main source of income from tourism comes from North America (£78 million in 1966) with Western Europe (£61 million) coming second. Table XCVI shows the extent to which the expenditure of British people abroad is offset by the expenditure of foreign visitors to this country.

TABLE XCVI
*Travel*

| Year | Receipts | Expenditure | Balance |
|------|----------|-------------|---------|
|      | £ million | £ million | £ million |
| 1956 | 121 | 132 | −11 |
| 1957 | 129 | 146 | −17 |
| 1958 | 134 | 152 | −18 |
| 1959 | 143 | 164 | −21 |
| 1960 | 169 | 186 | −17 |
| 1961 | 176 | 200 | −24 |
| 1962 | 183 | 210 | −27 |
| 1963 | 188 | 241 | −53 |
| 1964 | 190 | 261 | −71 |
| 1965 | 193 | 290 | −97 |
| 1966 | 219 | 297 | −78 |
| 1967 | 236 | 275 | −39 |
| 1968 |     |     |     |

Source: *Balance of Payments* (HMSO).

Since 1963, it will be noticed, the debit balance on travel has increased, partly in consequence of rising prices and partly as a result of the rising standard of living which has led to more and more people taking holidays abroad. However, whatever may be the motive for which foreign travel is undertaken, it may be expected to have at least some cultural value. The re-imposition in 1966, therefore, by the British Government of restrictions on foreign travel for purposes of holidays and tourism—the only economically mature country at the time to do so—appears, therefore, to be particularly short-sighted, especially since it might lead to retaliatory measures by other countries.[1]

## The Invisibles: (4) Government expenditure

The following table show the expenditure of the British Government abroad and the amount spent by foreign governments—

[1] The year 1967 had been declared "International Tourist Year"!

particularly the United States—in this country. It will be noticed that throughout the period the balance was always a large debit.

TABLE XCVII
*Government Expenditure*
(Net)

| Year | Expenditure | Receipts | Balance |
|---|---|---|---|
| | £ million | £ million | £ million |
| 1956 | 267 | 92 | −175 |
| 1957 | 250 | 106 | −144 |
| 1958 | 276 | 57 | −219 |
| 1959 | 270 | 43 | −227 |
| 1960 | 327 | 45 | −282 |
| 1961 | 378 | 46 | −332 |
| 1962 | 398 | 39 | −359 |
| 1963 | 421 | 40 | −381 |
| 1964 | 477 | 45 | −432 |
| 1965 | 492 | 46 | −446 |
| 1966 | 503 | 43 | −460 |
| 1967 | 489 | 36 | −453 |
| 1968 | | | |

Source: *Balance of Payments* (HMSO).

Government expenditure abroad comprises a wide assortment of items—military expenditure, economic grants to developing nations, the cost of the diplomatic and consular services abroad, and the United Kingdom's subscriptions or contributions to certain international organisations such as the United Nations and the South-East Asia Treaty Organisation (SEATO). Total government expenditure of £489 million in 1967 was distributed as follows:

TABLE XCVIII
*Distribution of Government Expenditure Abroad*

| Purpose | % |
|---|---|
| Military expenditure . . . | 54½ |
| Diplomatic and consular services . | 9½ |
| Economic grants . . . . | 19½ |
| Subscriptions and contributions . | 5 |
| Other expenditure . . . . | 11½ |
| Total . . . . . | 100 |

Source: *Balance of Payments* (HMSO).

TABLE XCIX
*Financial and Other Services*

| Year | Receipts | Payments | Balance |
|------|----------|----------|---------|
|      | £ million | £ million | £ million |
| 1956 | 379 | 200 | +179 |
| 1957 | 405 | 215 | +190 |
| 1958 | 413 | 209 | +204 |
| 1959 | 438 | 221 | +217 |
| 1960 | 467 | 245 | +222 |
| 1961 | 505 | 250 | +255 |
| 1962 | 525 | 254 | +271 |
| 1963 | 518 | 271 | +247 |
| 1964 | 568 | 296 | +272 |
| 1965 | 600 | 324 | +276 |
| 1966 | 647 | 345 | +302 |
| 1967 | 713 | 366 | +347 |
| 1968 |  |  |  |

Source: *Balance of Payments* (HMSO).

## The invisibles: (5) Other services

Under this heading are included the earnings from business overseas of British commercial and merchant banks, insurance companies, issuing houses and other financial institutions, as also their profits from their overseas branches and subsidiaries. Also included are royalties on books, patents and films, together with rents from cinema and television films. Table XCIX shows that over a long period these items have consistently earned a substantial credit balance for the British invisible balance.

## The invisibles: (6) Private transfers

These are mainly gifts sent to people abroad or received from them. At one time this formed a large debit item in the balance of payments of the United States when immigrants, especially from Ireland and Southern and Eastern Europe regularly used to send sums of money out of the country to help their poorer relatives at home. In the case of Great Britain this was until recently almost a self-balancing item with a negligible effect on the British balance of payments, but since 1964, as Table C shows, it has become an increasingly important debit item as a result of the influx of immigrants from the West Indies and Pakistan, reaching a net debit of £62 million in 1967. Although in effect private transfers are capital

TABLE C
*Private Transfers*

| Year | Receipts | Payments | Balance |
|------|----------|----------|---------|
|      | £ million | £ million | £ million |
| 1956 | 91 | 109 | −18 |
| 1957 | 90 | 110 | −20 |
| 1958 | 103 | 99 | + 4 |
| 1959 | 100 | 100 | Nil |
| 1960 | 104 | 101 | +3 |
| 1961 | 109 | 102 | +7 |
| 1962 | 111 | 111 | Nil |
| 1963 | 114 | 128 | −14 |
| 1964 | 131 | 154 | −23 |
| 1965 | 131 | 165 | −34 |
| 1966 | 134 | 183 | −49 |
| 1967 | 135 | 197 | −62 |
| 1968 |    |    |    |

Source: *Balance of Payments* (HMSO).

movements it is usual to regard them as current transfers arising from an earlier transfer of the personal capital the immigrants have brought with them.

### The changing invisible balance

Though some invisibles continue to yield substantial credits to the British balance of payments on current account, these have not been sufficient to offset the decline in others. Consider Table CI, which summarises the position for the five years to the end of 1966. This

TABLE CI
*Average Invisible Balance (1962–67)*

|  | £ million |  |
|------|-----------|---|
| *Credits* |  |  |
| Investment | +397 |  |
| Financial services | +280 |  |
| Transport | + 10 | +687 |
| *Debits* |  |  |
| Government expenditure | −421 |  |
| Travel | − 52 |  |
| Private transfers | − 32 | −505 |
| Net balance | | +182 |

Source: *Balance of Payments* (HMSO).

compares unfavourably with the average net balances for earlier
periods—£231 million for 1957-61 and £293 million for 1952-56.
It is clear, therefore, that Great Britain no longer has the great advantage in invisible earnings over other countries that it once had.
As its invisible earnings have declined, those of the United States,
France, Italy and Germany have increased—mainly in the case of
Italy as a result of tourism. It is, therefore, of paramount importance
that Great Britain should at the very least maintain its income from
foreign investment and from the services of the City of London,
particularly if sterling continues to decline as a reserve currency.
One might reasonably expect a country such as Great Britain to
have a credit balance for transport or be able to ensure that this is at
least a self-balancing item.[1]

### The balance on current account

Consider the balance of payments on current account. In the first
place there has been a tendency for the debit balance on visible
trade to widen, mainly on account of the huge increase in the import
of manufactured goods—from 27% of total imports in 1958 to 45%
in 1967—a consequence of the rise in the British people's standard
of living and of inflation. Secondly, as Table CII (p. 412) shows,
the widening of the trade gap has not been balanced by a similar
expansion of the invisible balance.

It seems clear, therefore, that during the past twenty-five years a
fundamental change has occurred in the general structure of the
British balance of payments and it is this that has been largely
responsible for the increased difficulties this country has had to face
in achieving a balance on current account. The main cause of the
trouble has been the severe decline in such invisibles as transport and
the huge increase in others such as government expenditure abroad.
It would seem, therefore, that in framing measures to deal with the
problem of the balance of payments successive British governments
have not been fully aware of the root cause of the trouble. Assuming
that no structural changes are taking place a deficit is most likely to
occur as a consequence of domestic inflation running ahead of the
average level of world inflation, with as a result an increase demand
for imports. There is no doubt that such conditions have on occasion
aggravated Great Britain's difficulties, but since 1951 the measures
taken to deal with them have invariably been deflationary in character. Such measures have certainly been necessary from time to
time to damp down inflation, but they mainly affect the balance
of trade, whereas it would seem that what was even more urgently

[1] See Report of the Clark Committee on Invisible Earnings.

TABLE CII

*The Balance of Payments on Current Account*

| Year | Visible balance | Invisible balance | Net balance |
|------|-----------------|-------------------|-------------|
| | £ million | £ million | £ million |
| 1956 | + 53 | +155 | +208 |
| 1957 | − 29 | +262 | +233 |
| 1958 | + 29 | +318 | +347 |
| 1959 | −118 | +267 | +149 |
| 1960 | −406 | +150 | −256 |
| 1961 | −152 | +148 | − 4 |
| 1962 | −102 | +231 | +129 |
| 1963 | − 80 | +199 | +119 |
| 1964 | −537 | +138 | −399 |
| 1965 | −272 | +181 | − 91 |
| 1966 | −136 | +151 | + 15 |
| 1967 | −637 | +233 | −404 |
| 1968 | | | |

Source: *Balance of Payments* (HMSO).

required was action of some kind to improve the invisible balance.

Since every payment to a buyer is also a receipt to the seller, all countries of the world cannot at the same time achieve credit balances. For world-wide stability all should balance their payments over a period. By this criterion, as Table CII shows, Great Britain's balance of payments could be regarded as reasonably satisfactory, at least down to 1963. In spite of a total debit of over £800 million in 1964–67 there was a credit balance of £39 million over the whole period, 1956–67. The invisible item that has shown the greatest growth in recent years is income from foreign investment, but this has been accomplished only at heavy cost to the balance of payments on capital account.

**Capital movements**

Finally, then, the balance of payments overall is influenced by capital movements into or out of a country. Capital movements can take several forms—long-term capital investment comprising inter-governmental loans, investment by British companies in their overseas branches or by foreign companies in Great Britain, capital taken out of the country by emigrants or brought in by immigrants, and short-term capital movements. Net long-term capital investment is normally made possible by achieving a credit position in the current balance of payments, and it was in this way that Great Britain built up its huge total of foreign investments during the nineteenth century. Table CIII shows that during recent years large capital transfers have taken place far in excess of credit balances on current account and, indeed, often even when debit balances have occurred. Although in five years out of seven between 1956 and 1962 the current balance was more than sufficient to cover the net export of capital, this has not been so since 1963.

There is, however, a very vital difference between a debit on current account and a debit on capital account. The former indicates an inability to pay one's way, and the debit balance can be covered only by a loss of assets. In contrast a debit on capital account, to the extent that it arises from long-term investment abroad, represents an increase in foreign assets from which further invisible income to the current balance can be expected to flow. In fact, at the cost of these debits on capital account, the United Kingdom with net investment income of over £400 million had by 1963 recovered its status as a creditor nation. During the five years to 1967 this item averaged £422 million per year. Very often foreign loans too stimulate the export of real capital and so benefit the trade balance.

TABLE CIII

*Long-term Capital Transfers and the Balance of Payments*

| Year | Current balance | Capital transfers | Overall balance |
|------|----------------|-------------------|-----------------|
|      | £ million | £ million | £ million |
| 1956 | +208 | −187 | + 21 |
| 1957 | +233 | −106 | +127 |
| 1958 | +347 | −196 | +151 |
| 1959 | +149 | −255 | −106 |
| 1960 | −258 | −192 | −450 |
| 1961 | + 5 | + 68 | + 73 |
| 1962 | +127 | − 98 | + 29 |
| 1963 | +111 | −148 | − 37 |
| 1964 | −399 | −370 | −769 |
| 1965 | − 91 | −203 | −294 |
| 1966 | + 15 | −104 | − 89 |
| 1967 | −404 | − 86 | −490 |
| 1968 |  |  |  |

Source: *Balance of Payments* (HMSO).

In addition to long-term capital transfers undertaken largely for permanent investment there are short-term capital movements to take into account. At the present day the US dollar and sterling serve as reserve currencies since payment for most international transactions is made in one or other of them. Many countries, therefore, both within and without the sterling area, find it both necessary and convenient to hold sterling and/or dollar balances. In 1968 the sterling balances stood at £7,100 million, of which £3,000 million was held by countries within the sterling area. In addition there are balances held for purely speculative purposes, and these are the more volatile and so more likely to be withdrawn if a higher rate of interest with safety can be obtained elsewhere or on the slightest fear for the soundness of the currency in which it is invested. It is here that a crisis of confidence makes itself felt. A lack of confidence abroad in sterling creates a critical situation for the British balance of payments. To check withdrawals by members of the Sterling Area from their balances in London it was agreed in 1968 that a portion of these balances should be guaranteed in terms of US dollars.

When all international payments and receipts—on both current and capital account—have been taken into consideration, the deficit or surplus that arises must be covered in some way or other. Under the present system a limited amount of assistance in the form of drawing rights can be obtained from the IMF, but after these have been exhausted the balance requires to be paid in gold. Ultimately, therefore, gold is still, as on the gold standard, the means by which a deficit is covered, just as a surplus leads to an influx of gold. As will be seen shortly, neither of these means has proved sufficient to meet Great Britain's needs during the most severe sterling crises of the past quarter of a century. On some of these occasions Great Britain has had to have recourse to borrowing from foreign banks (*see* below, pp. 419–21).

### International economic aid

One item of government expenditure abroad in the British balance of payments is aid to the developing nations. All countries of the world with advanced economies nowadays make contributions to assist the economic progress of those until recently described as under-developed and now regarded as developing nations. Outstanding in providing such assistance is the United States, economically the richest country in the world. In fact, about two-thirds of total economic aid has come from that country.

During the nineteenth century Great Britain had taken the lead in supplying capital to economically undeveloped countries, including at that time the United States. Investment abroad at that period was mainly undertaken by companies established for the purpose or by individuals who were encouraged to risk their savings in foreign enterprises or by subscriptions to foreign government loans (generally floated on the London capital market) by the prospect of a greater yield on their investments than they could have obtained at home. Not only did the United States benefit from an inflow of

capital from Europe but British capital also flowed out to British overseas territories and to many countries in South America and in
Asia. Since those days the character of international aid has
changed. It is now a matter mainly for international institutions and
national governments.

Foreign aid has been provided by the International Bank for
Reconstruction and Development (IBRD), the International
Finance Corporation (IFC) and the International Development
Association (IDA). The IFC supplements the activities of the
IBRD by assisting private enterprise in the developing countries,
whereas the IBRD offers aid only to governments. Also set up under
the auspices of the United Nations are the Economic Committee
for Asia and the Far East (ECAFE) and the United Nations Conference on Trade and Development (UNCTAD), a body similar to
GATT except that its specific aim is to help the developing nations.
Assistance of a different kind is provided by the World Health
Organisation (WHO). The motives that have inspired national
governments to offer aid to the developing nations have been
various—economic, political, humanitarian, or a mixture of all
three. For example, since 1962 political assistance in the form of
military aid has formed about 25% of American help.

International aid has taken the form of either grants (in money or
in kind) or loans. Down to 1957 about 75% of American economic
aid was by means of grants with only 25% by way of loans. Since
that date, however, the proportion of loans has increased, so that by
1967 loans comprised 56% of the total. Though recently reduced,
US foreign aid for economic purposes has averaged upwards of
$5,000 million per year since 1961—a very considerable sum, but in
view of the high national income of the United States only a relatively small average amount per head of the population. In addition
the US Government has sold some of its food surpluses[1] at low
prices to those parts of the world where food shortages exist.

Table CIV (p. 416) shows how economic aid provided by the
United Kingdom for developing nations has increased since 1957–68.
Of the total amount devoted by the United Kingdom to economic
aid in 1965–66 £91 million was in the form of grants and the rest in
loans. As with the United States the proportion of the total formed
by loans has been increasing in recent years. Nearly half of British
aid, both grants and loans, has gone to former British territories in
Africa. Per head of the population British aid works out at about
half the average for the United States.

[1] Under the U.S. Government's agricultural scheme farmers are guaranteed
high prices which stimulate production beyond the amount that can be sold in
the open market at those prices. The surpluses are bought and stored by the
Government.

TABLE CIV

*UK Economic Aid*

| Financial year | Amount (£ million) |
|:---:|:---:|
| 1957–58 | 65 |
| 1958–59 | 88 |
| 1959–60 | 113 |
| 1960–61 | 147 |
| 1961–62 | 170 |
| 1962–63 | 156 |
| 1963–64 | 173 |
| 1964–65 | 191 |
| 1965–66 | 204 |
| 1966–67 | 194 |
| 1967–68 | 178 |

Source: *Annual Abstract of Statistics.*

## Economic effects of foreign aid

One immediate adverse effect of providing aid is obvious—its influence on the balance of payments of the country providing the assistance. In the case of grants these are debits without any balancing credits either in the present or in the future; in the case of loans these are similar to other exports of capital and yield invisible income from abroad for a period in the future, but at the time the loans are made they are debits on capital account. Foreign aid, therefore, has increased somewhat Great Britain's difficulties with its balance of payments. The effect on the United States of foreign aid and investment abroad has been stupendous, turning credit balances on current account, in both visible and invisible items, into an overall debit balance on current and capital account. The result has been a continuous drain on the US gold reserves, which eventually of necessity it decided must be checked.[1] On the other hand, the more rapid economic development of the developing nations is to the advantage of the trade of all economically advanced countries. Characteristics of the developing countries are low average income per head—in many cases a mere fraction of the American average—a low level of education, poor standards of health, a grossly inadequate supply of capital (what they have being of poor quality), lack of electric power and insufficient and generally inefficient exploitation of natural resources. In these conditions capital accumulation, which depends

---

[1] US gold reserves fell from $21,000 million in 1958 to $15,000 million in 1966. During the same period the EEC countries increased their combined gold reserves from $10,500 million to $21,000 million.

on a curtailment of consumption, would be both slow and painful without foreign aid. To the extent that loans and grants are spent in the lending country that country receives a stimulus to production and employment. A more rapid rate of economic progress hastens the day when the standard of living in the developing nations reaches the stage when the people are able to satisfy a wider range of wants and so makes possible increased international specialisation which, as the theory of international trade shows, is to the advantage of all countries taking part in it.

## V. STERLING UNDER PRESSURE

### Sterling crises

The years since the Second World War have been punctuated by a series of sterling crises, the first occurring in 1949. Immediately after the war it was difficult to determine the true value of sterling in relation to the US dollar, and the rate of $4.03 to the pound was more or less arbitrarily decided. After the failure to maintain convertibility of sterling in 1947 it was felt, at least in the United States, that the sterling rate was simply being bolstered up by American assistance under the Marshall Plan. This was taken by many Americans to be proof that the pound was over-valued and that Great Britain's difficulties, therefore, were very largely the result of a fundamental disequilibrium in its balance of payments.

Expectation that the pound would be devalued led to foreign importers holding off buying from Great Britain and to the withdrawal of short-term funds from this country. As a result Great Britain found itself running a heavy deficit in its balance of payments during the first eight months of 1949. Deflation might have been a remedy appropriate to the situation, but it would have had to be on a very severe scale. Deflation, it was feared, would have imperilled full employment and so such a policy was at this time ruled out. The Government too would have liked to have avoided devaluation but circumstances forced its hand. Looking back, therefore, there seems little doubt that, at $4.03 to the pound, sterling had been over-valued and consequently a revision of the rate was required. The new rate agreed upon was $2.80 to the pound. The extent of the devaluation came as a greater shock to many people than the devaluation itself. Several other countries followed Great Britain's example and also devalued their currencies in terms of US dollars, though not all to the same degree as Great Britain. The effect on the British balance of payments was immediate. The backlog in exports, due to fear of devaluation, was quickly made up and the demand for British exports increased, and the year ended with a credit balance of £31 million on current account. The long-run effect of devaluation is, however, less certain.[1]

Further sterling crises occurred in 1951, 1955 and 1961 and then in 1964–67 a particularly severe one supervened. In all cases the crises were aggravated by heavy withdrawls of foreign funds from London due to fear that the pound might be devalued again. The crux of the matter was that Great Britain's reserves of gold and convertible currencies were only barely sufficient to meet temporary difficulties with its balance of payments and quite inadequate in face of heavy withdrawals of foreign-held sterling. The IMF was established to provide assistance to countries in temporary difficulties

TABLE CV

*Great Britain's Gold and Convertible Currency Reserves*

| End of year | £ million |
|---|---|
| 1956 | 799 |
| 1957 | 812 |
| 1958 | 1,096 |
| 1959 | 977 |
| 1960 | 1,154 |
| 1961 | 1,185 |
| 1962 | 1,002 |
| 1963 | 949 |
| 1964 | 827 |
| 1965 | 1,073 |
| 1966 | 1,107 |
| 1967 | 1,091 |
| 1968 | |

Source: *Annual Abstract of Statistics.*

with their balances of payments. Great Britain's original quota was $1,300 million (£464 million), but this was increased to $1,950 million in 1959 and to $2,440 million (£871 million) in 1966. Each country's drawing rights are determined by its quota. Thus, almost without formality, a country can draw in exchange for its own currency a sum equal to one quarter of its quota (the equivalent of £218 million in the case of Great Britain). There are four further credit tranches that can be drawn, but these are subject to increasingly severe scrutiny by the IMF, which may require the borrower to give details of the policy it is proposed to adopt to get rid of its balance of payments deficit. Thus, the maximum drawing limit is

[1] For a consideration of the case for and against devaluation, *see* below, pp. 422–23.

125% of the quota—£1,089 million, therefore, in the case of Great Britain. The amount of assistance a member can obtain from the IMF has thus been considerably enlarged. In the early years of this institution the amount had been quite inadequate.

In the severe crises of 1964–65 and 1966–67 Great Britain took full advantage of the assistance it could obtain from the IMF. In addition it attempted to reinforce its reserves of gold and convertible currencies in February 1966 by transferring to these reserves £316 million from the portfolio of dollar securities which the Treasury's Exchange Equalisation Account had acquired on the British Government's behalf during the Second World War. Actually, American equities were sold and US government securities bought with the proceeds. The sale of these securities will mean a reduction in invisible income of upwards of £20 million, thus adding to future balance of payments difficulties. A debtor who draws on past savings to balance current income and expenditure only makes things more difficult for himself in the future. In the case of Great Britain, however, it could reasonably be argued that there had been too much saving in previous years in relation to its balance of payments on current account. Clearly, neither an individual nor a nation can make a regular practice of drawing on past savings in this way.

## Central bank co-operation

A feature of international finance during recent years has been the increasing co-operation between the central banks of Western Europe. This is not an entirely new departure as a certain amount of co-operation between central banks took place during the years 1924–31 in an effort to prevent the collapse of the gold standard.

The Bank for International Settlements (BIS), to which reference has already been made (*see* p. 397), has become the main instrument of central bank co-operation, the promotion of which has become one of its primary functions. Set up in 1930 for the specific purpose of dealing with German reparations after the First World War, the BIS—which, as already noted, came near to being liquidated in 1944—has shown itself to be an institution with a quite remarkable capacity for adapting itself to new circumstances and changing conditions. Thus, it became banker in 1948 to the OEEC, in 1950 to the European Payments Union (EPU) and in 1954 to the European Coal and Steel Community (ECSC). Since 1960 it has concerned itself to an increasing extent with problems of international liquidity and with co-ordinating the financing of balance of payments deficits. In its recent developments it has contributed greatly to monetary stability. It also undertakes analytical studies on particular aspects of international finance.

It would appear to have fully justified its continued existence independent of the IMF. It holds regularly monthly meetings at its head office in Basle, at which a representative of the US Federal Reserve System is usually present, and it is because these meetings provide opportunities for the informal exchange of ideas between the governors of the various central banks that it has come to be referred to as the "Basle Club." In the sterling crisis of 1961 the BIS took action, known as the "Basle Arrangements," to check speculative activity against sterling at a time when Great Britain was suffering a deficit in its balance of payments on current account. Except when it intervenes directly in the market in support of central banks, it is not always easy to assess the extent of the intervention of the BIS as most of its operations are undertaken under a cloak of secrecy. The BIS operates as a commercial bank, buying and selling gold both on its own account and on behalf of central banks, lending to and borrowing from them, as well as making advances to governments. Whatever action the BIS takes, it must always be in harmony with the policies of its members.

In addition to its intervention in foreign exchange markets the BIS acts as agent for the gold pool and also engages in what are known as "swap" transactions with central banks. When a central bank seeks the aid of other central banks it is the BIS that acts as intermediary and negotiator. In "swap" transactions gold or securities are transferred for three months, and the "swap" may be for gold or dollars or some other currency. "Swap" facilities, too, take place with the Federal Reserve System. The first line of defence of the BIS against short-term capital movements is to offer a central bank gold against dollars. During the serious sterling crisis of 1964–65 operations were undertaken to support sterling. It helped again in 1966 when confidence in sterling once more declined and, with higher interest rates elsewhere, stimulated an outflow of sterling from Great Britain. In June of that year further Basle arrangements were made whereby a number of central banks, known as the "Group of Ten," together with the BIS came to the assistance of the Bank of England. The Group of Ten comprises the central banks of seven European countries—the United Kingdom, West Germany, France, Italy, the Netherlands, Belgium and Sweden—together with the United States, Canada and Japan. The group makes *ad hoc* arrangements, preferring not to form any permanent association. The Ten have agreed to increase international liquidity by lending agreed sums to the IMF, whenever required, to increase its resources, the amounts ranging from $2,000 million for the United States to $1,000 million each for the United Kingdom and West Germany and $100 million for Sweden. The original agreement was for ten years but it has been extended to 1970. Amounts are lent to the IMF for four years but if a lending country finds its balance of payments in deficit it can be repaid earlier. The BIS and the Group of Ten have made possible massive short-term lending on an unprecedented scale. During 1961–68 central banks also co-operated to operate the "gold pool" in the London gold market.

**Difficult years for sterling**

The 1960s have been a difficult time for sterling, culminating, as already noted, in the exceptionally severe crisis of 1964–67 with a second devaluation of sterling in twenty years. The situation was probably aggravated by too little being done at the onset of the crisis —both by the Conservative Government before the general election of 1964 and by the Labour Government immediately after that election—so that even a most severe deflation, accompanied by a very high level of unemployment, was slow to take effect, other than to check economic growth. The attempt to impose a "prices and incomes" policy achieved a temporary degree of success, but throughout it was bitterly opposed by the trade unions, and by late 1967 appeared likely to be imperilled by a spate of wage claims and rising prices.[1] Difficulties with the balance of payments, however, persisted and 1964–65 had left a huge legacy of foreign debt to be paid off in the immediate future. In these circumstances it might well be asked what could be done to restore equilibrium. Deflation, on account of its deleterious effect on economic growth and the level of employment, appeared to be a discredited policy. Something might possibly have been done to modify the structure of the balance of payments itself, perhaps by a further stimulation of exports and by improving invisible earnings, possibly from transport or maybe by an expansion of earnings from foreign tourists. It was, however, the balance on capital account that required most attention, and some attempt might have been made to check the outflow of capital.

**The devaluation of sterling, 1967**

Ever since 1964 there had been a growing feeling abroad that Great Britain's difficulties with its balance of payments were of a fundamental nature and so could be overcome only by a change in the exchange rate, *i.e.* by devaluation of sterling. The July measures of 1966 had failed to restore foreign confidence in sterling and by November 1967 another substantial deficit in the British balance of payments seemed to be inevitable.

A number of factors contributed to the weakness of sterling at this time. During 1966–67 the rate of growth of world trade had begun to slow down and this had made it more difficult for Great Britain to

---

[1] Inflation is discussed in Chapter X.

increase its exports. The Middle East war of 1967 with the closing of the Suez Canal aggravated Great Britain's difficulties, as also did prolonged dock strikes. Then, too, French opposition to Great Britain's application to join the European Common Market was ostensibly based on the weakness of sterling and the necessity for its devaluation. Though to the last the British Government tried to avoid devaluation the fact that further foreign loans could be obtained only by accepting what were regarded as harsh conditions made devaluation inevitable. In November 1967, therefore, the value of sterling in terms of US dollars was reduced from $2.80 to $2.40 to the pound.

When sterling was devalued in 1949 most other countries in the sterling area and in Western Europe also devalued by a similar amount, so that at that time it was in effect a revaluation of the US dollar. In 1967, however, only a few countries followed Great Britain's lead—Ireland, New Zealand, Malta and Bermuda in the sterling area and Denmark, Spain and Israel of non-sterling countries. Thus, sterling area countries which did not devalue included Australia, the Union of South Africa, India and Pakistan. The members of the EEC and the other members of EFTA (with the exception of Denmark) all decided not to devalue.

**The case for and against devaluation**

If there is a fundamental disequilibrium in a country's balance of payments it means that its currency is being pegged at a higher external value than its real internal value. In such circumstances devaluation would appear to be the appropriate course to adopt. The theory of devaluation is that it raises the prices of all imported goods and services, thereby reducing imports, while at the same time exports are cheapened to foreign buyers with the result that exports are increased. By reducing imports and increasing exports equilibrium is restored to the balance of payments. Even so it will be necessary, if equilibrium is to be maintained after devaluation has taken place, to ensure that net investment abroad does not exceed the surplus earned on current account.

In practice, however, the problem is not so easily resolved. Imports will certainly become dearer but the extent to which the quantity demanded will fall will depend on the elasticity of demand for them. Since British manufacturers depend very largely on imported raw materials, exports of manufactured goods cannot be expanded without increasing imports unless demand in the home market can be reduced. Indeed, the effect of devaluation may be to increase imports of raw materials. Great Britain's second main group of imports comprises foodstuffs, the demand for which, especially in an affluent society, also tends to be fairly inelastic. It would seem that devaluation is not a policy to be recommended unless there is a reasonable degree of elasticity in a country's demand for imports as also in foreign demand for its exports. The effect too of devaluation is to increase the burden of government expenditure abroad, already the largest debit in the current balance of payments and one of the main causes of imbalance. Then the higher prices that have to be paid for imports will raise the index number for retail prices, and in consequence trade unions will put in claims for wage increases. The success of devaluation depends on its reducing demand in the home market but this will not occur if wages are allowed to rise, and in conditions of full employment it will be very difficult to prevent a general rise in wages. If wages rise, then the higher costs due to this and to raw materials being dearer will eventually make exports dearer and so reduce the demand for them, and so with little change in imports the pre-devaluation situation in the balance of trade will return. Any gain from devaluation is bound to be short-lived unless it is accompanied by severe wage restraint, and experience of devaluation in 1949 showed that this is difficult to achieve for long. While sterling remains an important reserve currency devaluation appears to some people to savour of sharp practice and as likely to reduce the future prestige of sterling. Devaluation reduces the burden of the National Debt at the expense of holders of Government stocks. In certain quarters it was regarded as a matter of honour not to devalue the pound. Whether a government wishes to devalue or not, this course could be forced on a country by foreign traders and holders of the currency taking action for fear this should happen.

## The case for and against flexible exchange rates

The foreign exchange system established at Bretton Woods in 1944 and developed since then is much less rigid than the gold standard but ultimately a country in trouble with its balance of payments is still dependent on gold. Difficulties arise with this system on account of the fixed rate of exchange, even though in certain circumstances it is subject to modification.[1] The consequence has been that the monetary authorities of some countries have tended to become preoccupied with gold movements and the necessity to trim internal monetary policy to meet the needs of the external balance, as, for example, Great Britain deflating in 1966–67 in a time of serious unemployment and with growth at a standstill. This has led to the suggestion in some quarters that "floating" rates should be

[1] During the twenty years to 1968 no fewer than 96 countries found it necessary at one time or another to devalue their currencies, 45 of them making three or more devaluations. In Latin America devaluations have been of almost regular occurrence.

adopted—*i.e.* that exchange rates should be "unpegged and more flexible rates adopted."

Earlier in this chapter (*see* pp. 389–90) flexible exchange rates were considered as an alternative to the gold standard. There it was seen that a currency that was free to fluctuate appreciated or depreciated in terms of others according to the relation between a country's demand for imports and foreign demand for its exports. Experience during the inter-war years of flexible exchange was not a particularly happy one, at least in the period before the return to the gold standard. Many countries returned to the gold standard in 1925–26 with feelings of relief after suffering hyperinflation on a scale they had never previously known, an experience, however, which some were to repeat after the Second World War. Freely fluctuating exchange rates were so thoroughly discredited that on the collapse of the gold standard in the 1930s exchange control was preferred, though exchange control distorts the pattern of international transactions. Sterling, however, was allowed to depreciate to its equilibrium price on the foreign exchange market before the Treasury began to intervene in 1932 through the Exchange Equalisation Account in order to maintain a more stable rate of exchange. Those who favour more flexible rates than those provided by the present system point out that circumstances have completely changed since flexible exchange rates were previously in operation. Full employment has replaced mass unemployment and today most nations are concerned to maintain a satisfactory rate of economic growth.

With rates of exchange fully free to fluctuate there can be no imbalance in the balance of payments and no need for a gold reserve, but even if in present circumstances hyperinflation appears to be a somewhat more remote contingency, a change of system might merely replace concern for an outflow of gold and fear of devaluation by concern for the depreciation of a currency. Fear, for example, for the loss of prestige that would follow a severe depreciation of sterling—as would have occurred in 1964–65 if at that time sterling had been free to fluctuate—might impel the Government to take restrictive measures. One argument against flexible exchange rates is that they increase uncertainty in the international field and so are disadvantageous to trade. Clearly, the rate of exchange must not be allowed to fluctuate to such an extent that international trade will be hindered. Some people, therefore, would prefer sterling to be given greater flexibility only within set limits, considerably wider perhaps than the present range of $2.38–$2.42 to the pound, with intervention by the Bank of England at these points to prevent wider fluctuations. It has been suggested, for example, that variations should be restricted to (say) $\frac{1}{6}\%$ per month. At present, however, there appears to be too wide a difference of opinion on this matter

for a return to flexible exchange rates to appear likely in the immediate future. Most systems, including the present one, have both
advantages and disadvantages.

## VI. INTERNATIONAL LIQUIDITY

### Reserve currencies

Since there is no international currency as such national currencies
have had to fulfil this role. As has been seen, sterling at one time
held an unassailable position as a reserve currency and an international means of payment. At the present day, however, the US
dollar has taken its place alongside sterling, so that nowadays international payments are generally made either in sterling or in US
dollars. Many countries too keep a part of their reserves in one or
other or both of these currencies. It was during the nineteenth
century that sterling became an international currency, whereas the
US dollar has come to share this function only during the past half
century or so and more particularly since 1945. Both the pound and
the dollar have become accepted means of international payment
solely because the people who had to make such payments found it
convenient to use them for the purpose. This being so it becomes
natural to hold reserves of these means of payment.

The rise of the dollar as a reserve currency dates from the First
World War, during the course of which the United States changed
from a debtor into a creditor nation. Whereas restrictions were
placed on the convertibility of most currencies, the US dollar remained convertible. So what the pound sterling lost the US
dollar gained. The currency difficulties of the 1920s revolved
round Great Britain's return to the gold standard and still further
weakened the position of sterling and increased the importance
of the US dollar as an international means of payment. Though
sterling improved its position again after 1932 it suffered another
severe blow as a result of the Second World War. By the end of that
war there was a striking difference between Great Britain and
the United States. For the United States the position was the exact
reverse. For many years after 1945 the foreign demand for dollars
greatly exceeded the supply. Ten years later, as a result of American
aid to the rest of the world, increasing American foreign investment
and European recovery, foreign holdings of dollars increased and
by the 1960s the US dollar had become the more important of the
two reserve currencies. By 1965 foreign holdings of sterling and
dollars exceeded the gold reserves respectively of Great Britain and
the United States. An indication of the decline of sterling as a reserve
currency was provided by the fact that the Group of Ten found it

necessary to grant Great Britain a large stand-by credit to enable it to withstand withdrawals from the sterling balances.

### International liquidity

During the later 1960s increasing difficulty was experienced as a result, it was thought, of the amount of international means of payment failing to keep pace with the increasing monetary value of world trade. Not only did the volume of world trade double during 1958–66 but its value in terms of money, owing to the continuous rise in prices, increased even more rapidly still. For the same reason increased international liquidity too is required to provide assistance to countries in difficulties with their balances of payments.

One hindrance to an expansion of international liquidity is that since 1934 the price of gold has remained unchanged at \$35 per ounce. Over the past twenty years the world's output of gold has been increasing at a rate of only $1\frac{1}{2}\%$ per year, and not all this newly mined gold has found its way into the world's monetary systems. All suggestions for raising the price of gold as a means of expanding gold reserves, however, have been firmly resisted by the United States. In view of the rise in prices of other commodities the relative value of gold in terms of goods had been declining. Consequently gold reserves have been tending to become insufficient to meet the current needs of international trade. In many countries it was thought that a corresponding rise in the price of gold would rectify this situation. France, for example, suggested that the price should be doubled.

With a view to increasing international liquidity—and also to enable the quotas of some members to be readjusted—the quotas of members of the IMF were generally increased in 1959 and again in 1965. The result was that the gold holdings of the IMF increased during 1951–65 at an average rate of $8\frac{1}{2}\%$ per year,[1] which was a quite inadequate rate to meet the increasing demand for international means of payment.

Reserve currencies such as sterling and the US dollar were clearly necessary, therefore, to fill the gap in international liquidity. Although since 1951 foreign holdings of sterling have actually shown an average decline of $1\frac{1}{2}\%$ per year, holdings of US dollars have been increasing at an average rate of $9\frac{1}{2}\%$ per year. This is an indication of the decline relative to the US dollar of sterling as a reserve currency. The dollar has achieved this position at a cost to the United States for many years of a massive balance of payments deficit, caused partly by its foreign aid programme and partly by the extent of American investment abroad. The United States was able

---

[1] B. S. Karlstroem, *op. cit.*

to carry this huge deficit because of the large gold reserves—nearly two-thirds of the world total—it had accumulated by the end of the Second World War. For sterling the position is very different. With inadequate reserves and, unlike the United States, frequently having difficulty even with its current balance, every crisis in connection with its balance of payments has resulted in a sterling crisis due to withdrawals of short-term foreign holdings of sterling. It would seem that at the present day no single country—not even the United States—is strong enough economically to bear the strain of providing the world with a reserve currency. At their meeting at The Hague in 1966 the Group of Ten, however, declared that the American balance of payments deficits could not be considered to be a satisfactory means of increasing international liquidity. The two reserve currencies between them have helped, however, to overcome the world shortage of gold for monetary purposes, but it seems extremely doubtful whether further expansion of international liquidity can be obtained from this source. In 1967 gold (valued at US $40,000 million) comprised only 57% of the world's total monetary reserves (valued at US $70,000 million). The balance was mainly made up of US dollars ($15,000 million), sterling ($6,000 million) and the IMF reserves ($6,000 million). The importance of the US dollar and sterling in international payments is clear.

### The need for further international liquidity

Not all countries, however, are even agreed that the world does require an increase in international liquidity. For example, France and some of the other members of the European Community believe that there is no shortage of liquidity. Even as recently as 1966 the Group of Ten too considered that at the present time there is no general shortage. France dislikes the use of sterling and the US dollar as reserve currencies and would prefer to replace them by a European reserve unit. The Group of Ten, however, believed that an increase in international liquidity might be required in the near future and in order to be prepared for this contingency proposed that a scheme should be worked out in advance. The decision by the United States to bring its balance of payments into balance if possible during 1968–69 in order to end the drain on its gold reserves makes the provision of alternative international means of payment a matter of urgency.

One of the great difficulties in planning an increase in world liquidity is to decide the amount to provide. In general terms an adequate level of liquidity would be one sufficient to enable governments to achieve balances in their balances of payments without having recourse to a harmful degree of deflation, but not so much that countries with deficits were able to avoid taking action against inflation. As long ago as 1943 Lord Keynes said:

"We need a *quantum* of international currency, which is neither determined in an unpredictable and irrelevant manner as, for example, by the technical progress of the gold industry, nor subject to large variations depending on the gold reserve policies of individual countries; but is governed by the actual current requirements of world commerce, and is also capable of deliberate expansion and contraction to offset deflationary and inflationary tendencies in effective world demand." [1]

## A new reserve unit

The question as to what form any increase in international liquidity should take had been debated for many years before early in 1967 the Group of Ten was able to agree upon the scheme which was ratified at the annual meeting of the IMF at Rio de Janeiro later in the same year. The United States wished the new medium to be as near to money as possible. Lord Keynes in the preliminary discussions that preceded the establishment of the IMF and the IBRD had wanted something in the international sphere more akin to the overdrafts of commercial banks than at that time the United States would accept. The Group of Ten insisted that any new international means of payment should not be directed towards the financing of particular balance of payments deficits but should be based on the reserve needs of the world as a whole.

A compromise solution of the problem was agreed upon. The IMF was to be given power to issue Special Drawing Rights (SDRs), to be determined in accordance with the existing quotas of members. SDRs are to be issued only if in the opinion of the IMF the need for them should arise, *i.e.* if a further increase in world trade should require an increase in international means of payment. Their issue is to be unconditional and they are to be regarded as part of a country's reserves, transferable only between central banks. SDRs are definitely not to be considered as borrowings from the Fund. They will, however, carry a modest rate of interest in order to discourage holders from disposing of them too quickly. It is expected that when the scheme is put into operation there will be agreed annual distributions of SDRs in a pre-determined ratio to members' quotas. Thus, the United States will receive 22% of each distribution, Great Britain 10%, Germany and France each 5%. SDRs are expected to form a permanent addition to international reserves, whereas of course the ordinary drawings on the IMF do not. It has also been suggested that all SDRs should be guaranteed in gold.

[1] Introduction to his proposals for an International Clearing Union, 1943.

At the meeting of the Group of Ten at Stockholm in March 1968 it was decided to press on with the scheme, though France refused to participate and it was agreed that any other member of the IMF that wished to opt out should be allowed to do so. This would appear to be a potential weakness in the scheme.

## The international monetary crisis, 1968

The principal central banks—the Group of Ten and the members of the gold pool—had co-operated to assist Great Britain to withstand the pressure on sterling during 1964–67 in an effort to avoid the devaluation of that currency. In spite of this assistance sterling again came under such severe pressure in November 1967 that devaluation of the pound appeared to be unavoidable, and once dealers in foreign exchange realised it this course became inevitable.

No country was more anxious than the United States that sterling should not be devalued. Since 1945 the US dollar had shared with sterling the role of reserve currency and it was thought to be in the interests of both countries that the values of these two currencies should be maintained. Devaluation of sterling, as expected, brought the US dollar under pressure, and in March 1968 this culminated in heavy buying of gold for US dollars. In 1961 eight central banks—those of the United States, Great Britain, France, Germany, the Netherlands, Belgium, Italy and Switzerland (all members of the Group of Ten)—formed the gold pool for the purpose of giving assistance to one another in case of necessity to protect their gold reserves. In 1967 France withdrew from the gold pool, the French Government being opposed to the international monetary system then in operation, the use of sterling and the US dollar as reserve currencies and the determination of the United States not to raise the price of gold—maintained since 1934 at $35 per ounce—being particularly disliked. Nor did France care for the International Monetary Fund's scheme to increase international liquidity by the issue of Special Drawing Rights.

By 1968 the US dollar had become particularly vulnerable on account of the huge mass of dollars that had accumulated over the years in many parts of the world though especially in the form of Euro-dollars. Unlike the British balance of payments that of the United States on current account, both for visible and for invisible items, has throughout the period since 1945 been in credit. It is on capital account that the US balance of payments has run into deficit as a result of over-investment and excessive government spending abroad. Europe's problem after 1945 had been its shortage of dollars, and this had led to the introduction of foreign aid under the Marshall Plan in late 1947, and continued and expanded since that date. The United States did a great deal to speed up economic recovery in Europe and after that turned its attention to giving assistance to under-developed or developing nations, especially those thought to be in danger from communism. In recent years American firms have invested heavily in Western Europe, a development not altogether liked by some West European governments as, for example, that of France. In addition the United States became increasingly involved in Vietnam. All this was much more than that country's surplus on current account would pay for. The result latterly has been a drain from the United States of over $20,000 million a year and a fall in its gold reserves from $21,000 million to $11,000 in eight years. Dollars, once scarce, had become too plentiful.

Speculators began to feel that the price of gold would soon have to be raised. To buy gold in anticipation of a rise in its price, therefore, seemed to be an attractive proposition. Some banks bought gold on their own account as well as on behalf of financial, commercial and industrial undertakings and in some cases on behalf of private individuals where, as in France, Mexico and Canada, they were permitted to buy gold. A joint statement by the seven members of the gold pool, after a meeting in Basle, that the price of gold would not be changed did nothing to stem the demand for gold in preference to US dollars or sterling, and the Bank of England had difficulty in maintaining the exchange rate even at the recently devalued level. The gold markets—except for the one in Paris—had to be closed while a meeting of the seven central banks that were members of the gold pool met in Washington to decide how the international monetary system should function. France was not represented either at Basle or at Washington.

It was agreed to operate a "two-tier" system. For all transactions between central banks the price of gold was to remain at $35 per ounce, and central banks were to deal in gold only with one another. For all other dealings in gold there was to be a free market. Thus, the gold pool came to an end. There would clearly have to be safeguards to prevent gold being bought in the cheaper official market and sold at a profit in the free market. At the same time the other central bankers urged on both Great Britain and the United States, as suppliers of reserve currencies, the necessity of bringing their balances of payments on both current and capital account into balance. In Great Britain there soon followed the stiff deflationary budget of 1968 which involved an increase in taxation of over £900 million.

By many people the two-tier system is regarded as only a temporary expedient until a better scheme can be agreed upon. To some people the only solution is either to raise the price of gold or to demonetise gold completely. There are those who believe that gold cannot effectively serve as a means of settling international debts unless its value is realistically determined. If the price of gold were raised the value of gold reserves everywhere would be increased proportionately, and there would be an increase too in the output of new gold from the mines, and if as a result the US balance of payments was brought into equilibrium the problem of international liquidity would be eased. To other people it seem illogical to have international means of payment dependent on gold since supplies of the metal cannot be closely related to the needs of expanding world trade, and these people regard the two-tier system merely as a step towards the ultimate complete demonetisation of gold. Nevertheless, there are still large numbers of people in the world who have a high regard for gold not only in economically advanced nations such as France but also in many backward countries. It cannot be said, therefore, that the world is ready yet to dispense with gold. The great drawback to a monetary system independent of gold is that motives for checking unrestricted expansion of monetary supplies are weakened so that the danger of a runaway inflation is increased, for however remotely a monetary system is linked to gold it still forms a useful brake.

RECOMMENDATIONS FOR FURTHER READING

IMF and IBRD: *The Fund and Bank Review* (quarterly).
HMSO: *Balance of Payments* (Central Statistical Office) (published August each year) supplemented by quarterly White Papers, *Economic Trends*.
HMSO: *Radcliffe Report on the Working of the Monetary System*, Chapter 8.
HMSO: *Annual Abstract of Statistics*.
P. Einzig: *Foreign Exchange Crises*.
R. Aubin: *The Bank for International Settlements*, 1930–55 (published by the BIS).
Annual Reports of the Bank for International Settlements.
*If available:*
J. E. Meade: "Exchange-Rate Flexibility." *Three Banks Review* (June 1966).

QUESTIONS

1. Account for the continued survival of the Bank for International Settlements.

2. What would be the consequences for the United Kingdom of sterling ceasing to be a reserve currency?

3. "The only countries that regard international liquidity as being inadequate for present-day needs are those that are unwilling to take the measures necessary to give stable values to their currencies." Discuss this statement.

4. "Devaluation is an unsatisfactory remedy for Britain's balance of payments difficulties, because its effects would soon be offset by inflation." Discuss. (Degree.)

5. What evidence would you require in order to judge whether or not there were a shortage of international liquidity? (Degree.)

6. "The post-war international monetary system is merely the gold standard in another guise." Discuss. (Barking.)

7. Discuss the proposals put forward to increase international liquidity. Consider how the position of reserve currencies like sterling and the US dollar would be affected. (Barnsley.)

8. Describe and evaluate the main weapons available to a country seeking to remove an adverse balance of payments. (Birmingham.)

9. How might we solve our balance of payments difficulties in the short run and in the long run? (Bournemouth.)

10. Write a short essay on the transition, in Great Britain, from the international gold standard system, as it worked before 1914, to the managed currency system of the present time. (Huddersfield.)

11. Consider the relative merits of deflation and devaluation as a means of eliminating a deficit in the balance of payments. (Liverpool.)

12. Current debates concerning the urgency of the need to increase world liquidity would be needless if the world were to adopt a system of flexible exchange rates. Do you agree? (Manchester.)

13. Define fixed and flexible exchange rates. Consider, with reference to British interests, their relative merits. (Northern Counties.)

14. "Gold is no longer necessary for internal transactions. It should no longer be necessary in international transactions." Explain the first statement and suggest, with reference to the international monetary fund, what machinery is likely to supersede the use of gold in international transactions. (Norwich.)

15. Compare and contrast the advantages and disadvantages of fixed exchange rates with those of variable exchange rates. (Sheffield.)

16. Show that the internal value of the pound sterling is directly related to its external value. What action may be taken by the Bank of England when the external value falls to a critical level? (Southampton.)

17. "Devaluation and deflation are commonly regarded as alternative policy measures to rid the economy of the effects of inflation; but in fact they are complementary measures." Discuss, bringing out the undesirable consequences that may follow either measure used by itself. (U.L.C.I.)

## CHAPTER XIII

# FINANCING THE PUBLIC SECTOR

## I. PUBLIC FINANCE

### The character of public finance

Public finance has to do with the raising and spending of money by public authorities. In most countries the individual taxpayer is compelled by law to make the payments demanded of him to more than one public body. In all countries taxes have to be paid to the central government. A citizen of a country with a federal constitution, such as the United States, Canada or Australia, will also have to pay taxes to his state government, and probably too to a local authority. In Great Britain taxes have to be paid to the central government at Westminster and rates (the British term for local taxes) to the local authority of the place where the ratepayer lives. In addition, under the *National Insurance Acts*, regular contributions to the insurance funds have to be made by employers and employees, the State also making a contribution from its own revenue. Since these payments are compulsory they are of the nature of taxes even though, unlike taxes, they entitle contributors to certain benefits.

At one time the State demanded services rather than money payments of its citizens, as, for example, the duty of performing so many days' labour a year on road repairs. Some taxes were paid in kind, as, for example, one-tenth of a farmer's annual produce. Though houses and their contents are sometimes accepted in lieu of death duties, taxes at the present day are money payments. Taxes and rates are levied to enable public authorities to cover the expenditure on which they have previously decided, although almost invariably both national and local authorities find it necessary to supplement their current revenue by borrowing. The amount a person pays in taxes and rates is not directly related to any benefits accruing to him. A heavily taxed parent is not entitled to a better education for his children than a lightly taxed parent. A householder who is heavily rated cannot expect to have better lighting in the street where he lives than a ratepayer who is less heavily assessed. Many people, however, believe that taxes on motoring—the vehicle licence and petrol duty— should be entirely devoted to road improvements. It would be just as logical to say that the revenue from the tobacco duty should be used to provide amenities for smokers. Taxes and rates are merely sources of revenue for public authorities, being raised to cover general expenditure and not to provide specific benefits for those who pay them.

Public finance is related to both politics and economics, not only in the wider sense that public finance is an important part of government but also in the narrower sense that decisions regarding the expenditure of the State and the taxation required to finance it are made and put into effect by the political party in power at the time. Thus, political as well as economic considerations will influence both the form and amount of State expenditure and the structure of the tax system. With local rates the political influence, though present, is less marked. In the case of national insurance the amount of both contributions and benefits can be varied by the government of the day. For example, benefits can be increased for those already receiving benefits without their having to pay increased contributions. The motive for changes may be social or economic or it may be political. In public finance, therefore, it is often as necessary to take account of political or social considerations as of economic or financial.

### Parliament as public financier

The system whereby grants are voted by Parliament to cover government expenditure on the various supply services dates from 1688. Before that time the entire cost of governing the country as well as the personal expenses of the king and his court had to be met from royal income. On the accession of William III and Mary royal expenditure was separated from administrative expenditure, the former to be covered from an annual grant, known as the Civil List, granted to the monarch for life on his (or her) accession to the throne. Nowadays, the parliamentary grants for the supply services are consolidated in an *Appropriation Act* which authorises the expenditure on each of these services as indicated in the budget which precedes it. More often than not government departments find it necessary to put supplementary estimates before Parliament later in the financial year to enable them to exceed the expenditure allotted to them in the budget. Sometimes too an interim budget is submitted to Parliament. An important feature of national finance is that money raised by taxation shall be used only for the purpose for which it has been voted by Parliament, though the "block" grants made by the central government to local authorities since 1959 have not been earmarked for particular purposes.

When the king was responsible for national finance he could distribute the royal income as he pleased. Apart from his personal needs the only other items of expenditure were to cover the general administration of the country—comprising mainly the salaries of state officials, judges, etc.—and defence, including the maintenance of internal law and order. Some monarchs were parsimonious in their expenditure on all these items, others were extravagent in personal expenditure, often at the expense of national defence. In Great Britain the royal income came partly from personal property and partly from revenue from taxes, the granting of which to the king came over the centuries more and more under parliamentary control. Generally, the king managed to make ends meet in peacetime, but in time of war his income was inadequate, but attempts to raise taxes other than those agreed by Parliament invariably aroused opposition. If the king had recourse to borrowing—whether to cover personal extravagence or to finance a foreign war—it was a personal undertaking in the king's name, and all monarchs were not honourable debtors.

When Parliament took over national expenditure after the Revolution of 1688 it was still limited to covering the cost of general administration and national defence. The country at the time being engaged in a European war—and wars were becoming more expensive—the Government's expenditure exceeded its revenue. The establishment of the Bank of England in 1694 brought into existence the National Debt at the same time and made available to the Government an easier method than had been available to any royal financier of spending in excess of income.

Apart from the demands of war, government expenditure during the seventeenth, eighteenth and early nineteenth centuries remained relatively small. Revenue came mainly from customs and excise, and the tax on tea at one time reached 120%. Towards the end of the seventeenth century a tax on the annual value of land was imposed and in the following century taxes on carriages, racehorses, menservants and windows followed. The tax on windows was an oversimplified attempt to tax houses in proportion to their size. Income tax was first imposed in 1799 as a temporary measure during the war against France, as the huge cost of the wars required new sources of taxation to be found.

## II. STATE EXPENDITURE AND REVENUE

### The widening field of government expenditure

A century and a half ago—in 1816 to be precise—the budget showed government revenue and expenditure to be £66 million, as against £18 million in 1780. The increase was partly accounted for by the fall in the value of money and partly by the increased cost of the National Debt.

During the nineteenth century it was widely held that taxation should be kept to a minimum. Nevertheless, government expenditure —and therefore taxation—began to increase, though only slowly at first. In the twentieth century—especially since the Second World War—the increase in government expenditure has proceeded at an ever-increasing rate. For long government expenditure had been restricted to general administration, external defence and internally the administration of justice and the maintenance of law and order. Public expenditure on social services was negligible until a hundred years ago, increased slowly during the second half of the nineteenth century and has expanded rapidly during the last twenty-five years. Over the five years to 1968 government expenditure increased at an average rate of 8·1% per year. (10% in 1968–69, the year for which the Government announced cuts in public expenditure as part of its deflationary policy!)

(*i*) *Poverty*. The first social problem with which the State had to concern itself was that of poverty and unemployment, taking over this function from the Church in the sixteenth century. From the *Poor Law Act* of 1601 until the *National Assistance Act* of 1948 the cost of relief of the poor was borne mainly by local authorities. The increasing burden of poor relief in the early nineteenth century led to the passing of the *Poor Law Amendment Act* of 1834, the aim of which was to discourage the poor from seeking relief. The *National Insurance Act* of 1911 made it compulsory for certain groups of workers and their employers to contribute to a fund from which payments could be made to them during periods of sickness or unemployment and in old age. The State also contributed to this fund. The high level of unemployment during the Great Depression of the 1930s proved too much for the insurance principle, just as the amount of Poor Law relief that had to be paid in those places where unemployment was most severe proved to be beyond the resources of the local authorities of those areas. National Assistance replaced the Poor Law in 1948 and the cost was transferred from local authorities to the State. Family allowances were introduced by an Act of 1945. More humanitarian ideas of what constitutes poverty have resulted in increased expenditure on National Assistance,[1] and National Insurance, which in 1957–58 cost the State £925 million (£131 million for National Assistance) and in 1967–68 £2,128 million (National Assistance £409 million).

(*ii*) *Education*. Expenditure by the State on education too has increased enormously. A meagre grant of £20,000 in 1833 to assist the Church of England and the British and Foreign Bible Society in the building of schools was the beginning of the State's direct interest in education in Great Britain. Gradually, the cost of education increased as elementary education was made compulsory (1880) and

[1] Now known as Supplementary Benefits.

free (1891), and these developments together with the raising of the
school-leaving age necessitated the building of more schools. Late
in the century grants too were made towards secondary and technical
education. The *Education Act* of 1944 (the Butler Act) made secondary education free for all. In recent years an ambitious programme
of school rebuilding has been carried out and many new universities
and technical colleges established and existing ones expanded. By
1958 education was costing the State £740 million and by 1968
£1,986 million—a stupendous increase even after allowing for the
fall in the value of money—and with every prospect of the cost
continuing to rise in the future.

(*iii*) *Health*. It was not until 1848 that the State began to take a
serious interest in the health of the nation, the first *Public Health Act*
being passed in that year. Then, under an Act of 1875, medical
officers of health and sanitary inspectors were appointed. Other
*Public Health Acts* followed and the State's duties in this sphere
increased to such an extent that in 1919 a Ministry of Health was
established. Between the two World Wars the work of this ministry
continued to expand, but it was not until the introduction of the
National Health Service in 1946 that public health became a serious
charge on the Exchequer. Every year since its introduction the cost
of the National Health Service has increased. By 1958 it had reached
£694 million and by 1966 £1,162 million. The abolition of the
nominal prescription charge in 1964 added over £50 million per year
to the cost of the service. To this should also be added expenditure
on services such as child care, welfare foods, school meals, milk, etc.,
bringing total expenditure on health and ancillary services in 1968
to over £1,855 million.

(*iv*) *Housing*. During the nineteenth century the State also began
to take an interest in housing. Improved water supplies, drainage
and sanitation resulting from the *Public Health Act* of 1848 reduced
the death rate and the incidence of disease in the slums of large towns.
An Act of 1868, however, gave local authorities power to demolish
property regarded as not fit for human habitation. It was not until
the years immediately following the First World War, when there
was a great shortage of small houses, that heavy expenditure began to
be incurred by the State and local authorities on the erection of
houses. Subsidies too were paid to private builders. Council houses
were usually let at uneconomic rents, so that losses had to be made
good from the rates. This policy was again pursued after the Second
World War and continued through the 1960s as slum clearance was
intensified. By 1958 the cost of housing to the public sector had
reached £447 million and by 1968 had further increased to £1,106
million.

(*v*) *Subsidies*. During the Second World War the State introduced subsidies to keep down the prices of many consumers' goods as a check on inflation. Most of these subsidies were removed in the early 1950s. To improve agriculture and to encourage an increased output of home-produced foodstuffs subsidies are paid to farmers. In 1954 subsidies cost the Exchequer £422 million and ten years later £520 million.

Total public expenditure on the social services, on both current and capital account, was £567 million in 1938, £3,164 million in 1958 and £7,931 million in 1968. The increase in public expenditure under this heading is clearly one of the main causes of the rise in government expenditure over the past thirty years.

(*vi*) *Defence.* Some services provided by the State could be—and used to be—left to individuals to provide for themselves. Other services can be provided effectively only by the State. In the latter group is defence. The defence of the country against foreign enemies has always been the concern of the State and it is clearly a service which the State must undertake for the community as a whole. The provision of up-to-date weapons of war has become an increasingly costly business. Standards of comfort required to attract recruits into the Armed Forces too have become much higher than formerly with the continuance of full employment. In 1967–68 defence accounted for around 24% of all government expenditure.

(*vii*) *Economic services.* Services of an economic nature provided by the State have also increased. Much of the work of the Board of Trade, especially the Department of Overseas Trade and the Exports Credit Guarantee Department, is for the benefit of British trade. At one time regarded as a local matter, roads too have become of increasing concern to the State. Before 1936 the State contributed to the cost of roads according to their classification as "A" or "B" roads, local authorities bearing the rest of the cost. Since 1936 the more important roads have been designated as trunk roads and for these the State is solely responsible. The huge increase in road traffic in recent years has led to the building of motorways by the State, though tolls are charged to vehicles using some bridges and tunnels. Among other items of state expenditure of an economic nature are forestry, atomic energy, new towns and loans by way of the Public Works Loans Board to local authorities. Since 1945 losses incurred by nationalised industries—especially the railways—have had to be covered. Other items of government expenditure have all increased in terms of money if only in consequence of the continuous fall in the value of money that has taken place since 1939.

In times when state expenditure is high there appears to be less inclination to scrutinise carefully individual items of expenditure. In times of war a government cannot afford to consider costs but this attitude tends to extend for a time into the post-war period until checked by deflation and an economy drive, as occurred after 1815 and 1919. Since 1945. however. there has been no serious deflation but only a number of brief disinflationary episodes, during which there has never been anything more than a temporary check to rising government expenditure. Public opinion too has generally favoured expansion of the social services during the past twenty-five years and in such conditions an increase in expenditure—for example, on education—is often taken of itself to indicate the government's increased concern for the service. When State expenditure is high not only is there likely to be more waste but also a possibility that public money may be frittered away on dubious or trivial projects such as appeared to many people the establishment of a Ministry of Sport in 1964 and the grant of £500,000 to football in 1965–66. Local authorities often pay closer attention to their expenditure than does the central government but much of their expenditure is forced on them in carrying out functions delegated to them by the State.

The increasing part taken by the State in most forms of economic activity means that State expenditure is likely not only to increase in the future, but also to require an increasing proportion of the national income to finance it. Actually, as the following table shows, government ordinary expenditure fell slightly between 1955 and 1965 as a proportion of the national income:

TABLE CVI
*Government Expenditure and the National Income*

| Year | Government expenditure | National income | Column (2) as % of (1) |
|---|---|---|---|
| | £ million | £ million | |
| 1954–55 | 4,304 | 15,500 | 27·7 |
| 1959–60 | 5,244 | 20,834 | 25·3 |
| 1964–65 | 7,307 | 28,613 | 26·0 |
| 1967–68 | 10,878 | 31,148 | 35·1 |

If the expenditure of local authorities is also taken into account public expenditure now takes 30% of the national income.

### The financial statement

This is the White Paper which the Chancellor of the Exchequer lays before the House of Commons when opening the budget. It shows proposed expenditure and the taxation required to cover it and also the outturn for the preceding year compared with the previous budget estimate. It is the practice of governments first to decide how much to spend and then impose taxes to meet this expenditure, whereas the prudent individual adjusts his expenditure to his income.

Rather illogically, therefore, the White Paper deals first with taxation and secondly with government expenditure.

Governments, like both businesses and individuals, incur expenditure on current account and on capital account. The distinction is important in that orthodox accounting would require all current expenditure to be met from current revenue, but would permit capital expenditure to be covered by borrowing. At one time the budget showed mainly current expenditure and it was regarded as balanced if this expenditure was covered from current revenue even though there might be a deficit on capital account, which was not shown, the budget, therefore, at that time not giving a complete picture of government expenditure. By the late 1940s it was felt that the budget should show all government expenditure and revenue. Some economists would have liked the Chancellor of the Exchequer to copy the Swedish practice of drawing up two separate budget statements, one on current account and the other on capital account. In fact, the device was adopted of dividing the budget into two parts with some expenditure and revenue "above the line" and some "below the line," current items being mainly "above" and capital items mainly "below," though this distinction was not fully maintained. Since 1965 these terms have not been used. Instead, a statement is given of the estimated cost of the various supply services together with what are now known as Consolidated Fund Standing Services (*see* Table CVII, p. 442), the total comprising largely what was previously designated as "above the line" expenditure (though including Post-War Credits, previously shown "below the line"). This total can still be regarded as government ordinary expenditure, which is shown under a number of broad general headings, so that details of particular items of expenditure have to be sought elsewhere. It shows total defence expenditure in 1967–68 to have been £2,205 million, that local government, housing and social services accounted for 51% of the £7,740 million spent on the other supply services, while the servicing of the National Debt cost £654 million. What was previous to 1965 shown as "below the line" expenditure is shown in two tables (*i*) Consolidated Fund Loans to Industry and (*ii*) Other Consolidated Fund Loans. These are all capital items which the Government can expect to be repaid, although in the past this expectation has not always been realised, especially in the case of the British Railways Board. Over the years loans to public bodies tend to increase, so that repayments fall short of new borrowing, with the result that the amount outstanding is continually increasing. Consequently, on capital account an excess of expenditure over income—that is, a deficit—is to be expected. In effect, therefore, the budget statement distinguishes between expenditure on current and that on capital account.

## Purposes of taxation

The aim of taxation was originally simple—merely to raise revenue to cover state expenditure. During the twentieth century taxation has assumed a more far-reaching role. The following are some of the purposes for which taxation is now imposed:

(*i*) *To cover expenditure of the public sector.* In early days taxes were imposed to cover services which the community as a whole could provide more effectively than could any individual for himself —external defence and internally the maintenance of law and order and the administration of justice. During the nineteenth and twentieth centuries in building up the welfare state as seen earlier in this chapter, the State began to provide for the community as a whole many services which individuals might have been able to provide for themselves. Taxes, therefore, have to be levied to cover this expenditure.

(*ii*) *To curtail consumption of harmful commodities.* Sometimes taxes have been imposed to reduce the consumption of commodities the excessive consumption of which is regarded as harmful. The most quoted example of this is the stiff increase in the tax on gin in 1736— when it was possible "to get drunk for a penny and dead drunk for twopence"—the newly developed taste for gin having caused a sharp rise in mortality and crime among the poorer classes of London and other cities. The heavy duty imposed on spirits at the present day— over £14 per proof gallon—is also of this character. In the case of a tax of this kind, therefore, the revenue it yields is not a prime consideration, since a reduction of the tax might actually increase its yield if the demand for the commodity over a lower range of price is fairly elastic. Over the higher price range, however, demand appears to be very inelastic, an increase in the duties on spirits, wine and beer in 1965 yielding an extra £50 million of revenue. In spite of propaganda on the dangers of smoking the duty on tobacco appears to be imposed mainly for the sake of the huge revenue obtained from it— over £1,000 million a year since 1965. It would require a very strong-willed Chancellor of the Exchequer to raise the duty sufficiently to curtail consumption of a commodity the tax on which provides him with 11 % of his total revenue.

(*iii*) *To redistribute labour.* The Selective Employment Tax, first introduced in 1966, has a dual purpose—to increase government revenue and to encourage labour to move from "service" occupations to manufacturing industry. It was felt too that service occupations could be more heavily taxed as previously they had been less heavily taxed than manufacturing industry. All employers have to pay the tax (25*s.* per week for men, 12*s.* 6*d.* for women, with lower rates for

## TABLE CVII
### Government Expenditure

| | 1967–68 | | 1968–69 |
|---|---|---|---|
| | Original budget estimate | Outturn | Estimate |
| | £ million | £ million | £ million |
| *Supply Services* | | | |
| *Defence Budget* | | | |
| Defence—(Central) . . . | 21 | 24 | 24 |
| (Navy) . . . | 620 | 649 | 656 |
| (Army) . . . | 592 | 621 | 604 |
| (Air) . . . . | 544 | 537 | 557 |
| Ministry of Technology . . | 245 | 241 | 227 |
| Ministry of Public Buildings and Works . . . . . | 177 | 184 | 198 |
| Atomic Energy Authority . . | 6 | 4 | 5 |
| *Total Defence Budget* . . | 2,205 | 2,260 | 2,271 |
| *Other Supply* | | | |
| I Government and Exchequer | 199 | 203 | 181 |
| II Commonwealth and foreign | 277 | 305 | 264 |
| III Home and justice . . | 207 | 222 | 231 |
| IV Transport, trade and industry | 1,640 | 1,881 | 1,993 |
| V Agriculture . . . | 367 | 389 | 392 |
| VI Local government, housing and social services . . | 3,882 | 3,955 | 4,335 |
| VII Education and science . | 409 | 409 | 433 |
| VIII Museums, galleries and the Arts . . . . | 14 | 14 | 15 |
| IX Public buildings and common governmental services | 231 | 234 | 265 |
| X Smaller public departments. | 8 | 9 | 16 |
| XI Miscellaneous . . . | 110 | 119 | 152 |
| *Total Other Supply* . | 7,344 | 7,740 | 8,277 |
| *Total Supply Services* . | 9,549 | 10,000 | 10,277 |
| *Consolidated Fund Standing Services* | | | |
| Interest on and management of National Debt . . . | 595 | 654 | 515 |
| Northern Ireland . . . | 185 | 194 | 219 |
| Other services . . . . | 30 | 30 | 30 |
| *Total* . . . . . | 10,359 | 10,878 | 11,312 |

## TABLE CVIII
### Government Loans

| | 1967–68 | | 1968–69 |
| --- | --- | --- | --- |
| | Original budget estimate | Actual outturn | Budget estimate |
| | £ million | £ million | £ million |
| *Loans to Nationalised Industries* | | | |
| Post Office . . . . | 170 | 193 | 230 |
| National Coal Board . . . | 10 | 85 | 26 |
| Electricity Council . . . | 411 | 336 | 237 |
| North of Scotland Hydro-electric Board . . . . . . | 8 | 3 | 6 |
| South of Scotland Electricity Board | 39 | 40 | 39 |
| Gas Council . . . . . | 225 | 262 | 292 |
| British Steel Corporation . . | 75 | 175 | 100 |
| British Overseas Airways Corporation . . . . . | −3 | −3 | −3 |
| British European Airways . . | 18 | 19 | 52 |
| British Airports Authority . . | 6 | 2 | 7 |
| British Railways Board . . | 10 | 5 | 10 |
| Other Transport Boards . . | 43 | 83 | 45 |
| *Less:* estimated shortfall on borrowing . . . . | −100 | — | −120 |
| | 912 | 1,200 | 921 |
| *Loans to other Public Corporations* | | | |
| New towns . . . . . | 85 | 76 | 90 |
| Other bodies . . . . | 42 | −2 | 56 |
| | 127 | 74 | 146 |
| *Loans to Local Authorities* . . | 515 | 369 | 505 |
| *Loans to the Private Sector* | | | |
| Ship credit scheme . . . | −6 | −6 | −6 |
| Housing associations and building societies . . . . . | 3 | 1 | −1 |
| | −3 | −5 | −7 |
| Northern Ireland Exchequer . | 25 | 25 | 24 |
| Other loans . . . . | 190 | 85 | 155 |
| | 215 | 110 | 179 |
| *Total* (net lending) . . | 1,766 | 1,748 | 1,744 |

boys and girls), the tax being refunded together with a bonus in the case of manufacturing firms. The Government's aim was to encourage a reduction of staffing in shops, professional offices, etc., to set free more labour to work in factories in order to increase industrial production and the rate of economic growth.

(*iv*) *To reduce inequality of income.* If it is accepted that the economic welfare of a community will be greater if inequality of income is not excessive, it follows that to lessen inequality of income will increase economic welfare provided that this does not reduce the national income through its disincentive effect. In Great Britain those with very high incomes were not heavily taxed until the First World War when the standard rate of income tax was raised to 6*s.* in the pound, with surtax on the highest incomes of a further 6*s.* making a total of 12*s.* in the pound on marginal income. The rate of taxation was much higher during and immediately after the Second World War, the maximum rate of income tax with surtax being 19*s.* 6*d.* Though there has been some reduction in income tax and in surtax on earned incomes under £5,000 a year, the fall in the value of money since 1939 has brought lower and lower real incomes within the surtax range. For example, when sterling was devalued in 1949, no change was made in the level of income at which surtax was imposed. The total yield from surtax is only 2% of total government revenue and the higher rates of tax affect only 14,000 people (those with over £20,000 a year before tax), so the retention of the higher rates in peacetime can be explained only as deliberate action to reduce inequality of incomes. As a result a net income of £6,000 a year after tax is possible to a married couple without children only if their gross income is over £10,000 in the case of earned income or £21,000 if all their income is derived from investments. A gross income of £100,000 yields only just over £14,000 after tax. Out of 27 million incomes in Great Britain only 58,000 people have £5,000 or more a year after payment of tax. Thus very high incomes are no longer possible in this country. Inequality is still further lessened by the fact people in the lower income groups benefit more than the well-to-do from the social services provided by the State.

Table CIX (p. 445) shows the distribution of personal incomes in 1964–65 after tax. Thus, over 69% of income receivers had incomes within the range £250–£1,000 a year after tax.

(*v*) *As an instrument of economic policy.* It was during the Great Depression of the early 1930s that the first suggestions were put forward for using the budget as an instrument of economic policy. A budget deficit, whether arising from unwillingness to raise enough revenue to cover expenditure (*i.e.* a dislike of heavy taxation) or from a deliberate reduction of taxation, or from an expansion of state investment, will have an inflationary effect and so stimulate consumers' demand and through that encourage production. Deficit financing, as it is called, might, therefore, be a means of ending a slump. Roosevelt's New Deal policy, inaugurated in 1932, involved budget deficits which added $20,000 million to the National Debt of the United States. The depression at that time was so severe that the effect of this huge amount of government expenditure on unemployment was not very great. This policy, however, was quite successful in ending the mild British recession of 1958. In Great Britain the first indication that taxation might be used as an instrument of government policy was given in the White Paper *Employment Policy* issued in 1944 when the Government accepted responsibility for the maintenance of full employment. Fiscal policy, at first as an alternative to monetary policy and later to supplement it, was first employed in Great Britain as a means of checking inflation. The theory

TABLE CIX

*Distribution of Personal Incomes*

| Income after tax Not under £ | Under £ | No. of incomes (thousands) | % of total incomes |
|---|---|---|---|
| 50 | 250 | 2,480 | 8·9 |
| 250 | 500 | 6,598 | 23·9 |
| 500 | 1,000 | 10,391 | 37·5 |
| 1,000 | 2,000 | 7,411 | 25·6 |
| 2,000 | 3,000 | 552 | 2·0 |
| 3,000 | 5,000 | 210 | 0·8 |
| 5,000 | 10,000 | 57 | 0·2 |
| 10,000 and over | | 1 | 0·1 |
| | | 27,700 | |

Source: *Blue Book on National Income and Expenditure.*

is that a budget surplus (used to reduce the National Debt) would reduce demand, though this would follow only if the increased taxation, resulting in higher prices, did not stimulate successful claims for higher wages. To enable the Government to act quickly it was given power to vary purchase taxes and other excise duties by up to 10% at any time—a device known as the regulator—if this course was considered to be necessary. For greater tax changes an interim budget is required. The aim of fiscal policy, therefore, is to influence the aggregate income of the community through variations in taxation. An inflationary situation at home is likely to stimulate imports of all kinds of goods without any comparable increase in exports, with the result that a deficit occurs in the balance of payments. Loss of confidence in sterling as an international currency resulting from the Government's failure to check internal inflation will aggravate the situation. Necessity to take action to improve the balance of payments may, therefore, compel an unwilling government to adopt a deflationary fiscal policy.

## The purpose of the budget

The drawing up of the budget, then, is no longer the relatively simple matter it once was of trying to make the two sides balance. Orthodox finance, to which the principal Chancellors of the Exchequer were faithful for so long, dictated that an attempt to balance the budget should be made each year. If, then, the estimated budget surplus (except in wartime, Chancellors always budgeted for a small surplus) was exceeded in the outturn, taxpayers could confidently look forward to a reduction in taxation in the following budget; if the outturn showed a deficit, an increase in taxation could confidently be expected. Hence, the main general interest in the budget is in the announcement of tax changes. There are still some people who believe that though the budget need not be balanced each year—a year being only an arbitrary period of time—it should balance over a period of years. This would apply only to current expenditure and revenue, for there is nothing unorthodox in meeting capital expenditure by borrowing, though the orthodox financier would expect a loan to be repaid within the lifetime of the asset for which it was borrowed. Since 1945 Chancellors of the Exchequer more often than not have been forced by the economic situation to budget for a surplus and so a reduction in the National Debt might have been expected. Instead, since the end of the Second World War, the National Debt has increased by no less than £11,000 million (50%), as much as it did in monetary terms during the First World War—an unprecedented increase in peacetime. This means, of course, that in most years budget surpluses on current account have been more than offset by deficits on capital account.

The budget a Chancellor of the Exchequer is likely to frame nowadays depends mainly on the economic situation. Though neither the outturn of expenditure and revenue nor the estimates of the various government departments may offer much guidance to the forthcoming budget, there are other indicators of its possible character. Something can be learnt of the country's economic situation from a series of White Papers published shortly before budget day—the *Economic Survey* from 1947 to 1961 and since 1962 the *Economic Report* (the work of a department of the Treasury), the preliminary national income and expenditure figures (full details do not appear until the publication of the Blue Book on national income in late summer), and the balance of payments. The Economic Survey gives a review of production, distribution of labour, investments, etc., for the past year with a comparison with preceding years, together with a statement of prospects for the coming year. The White Paper on national income and expenditure shows the national income in terms of the money value of the goods and services produced the previous year and also in terms of different forms of income—wages, salaries, profits—and in both cases comparison is made with earlier years, first with no allowance for price changes and then in terms of the prices ruling in a particular year. The White Paper on the balance of payments shows the country's financial relations with the rest of the world and the state of the reserves. These documents enable an assessment to be made of the sort of budget the economic situation requires. How all this information is interpreted depends on which political party is in power. The general character of the budget will be decided by the Cabinet and the details by the Chancellor of the Exchequer, both of whom will be influenced by political as well as economic considerations.

### Sources of government revenue

Table CX (p. 448) shows government revenue from taxation, together with miscellaneous receipts such as broadcast receiving licences. It shows that the Government derives its revenue almost entirely from taxation. National Insurance (social security) contributions from employers and employees are not shown in this table since they are regarded as being paid into an insurance fund.

From this table it can be seen that direct personal taxation (income tax, surtax, death duties) account for about 47% of total revenue; with company taxes (corporation tax and selective employment payments) this brings total direct taxation to just over 50%. A century ago less than one-third of the State's revenue came from direct taxation. In 1913 taxation was almost equally divided between direct and indirect. With increasing state expenditure there was a gradual shift (speeded up by the First World War) to direct taxation, which in the inter-war years accounted for 60% and in 1945 to 65% of government revenue. In recent years there has been some reversal of this trend and receipts from the two main groups of taxes are again approximately equal. The relative merits of these taxes are considered below. For the moment it is sufficient to note that high direct taxes have a deleterious effect on production through their disincentive effect. One effect, too, of inflation is to extend income tax to lower incomes since, although the tax-free allowance for a married couple has been increased to £340, this in real terms is worth less than half the married allowance of 1939. Similarly, as already noted, surtax too now operates at a lower level of real income than formerly, especially on investment income.

Of the indirect taxes those on tobacco and alcoholic drink now yield 17% of the total revenue of the State. Taxes on motoring (in-

TABLE CX
*Government Revenue*

| | 1967–68 | | 1968–69 |
| --- | --- | --- | --- |
| | *Original budget estimate* | *Outturn* | *Estimate* |
| | £ million | £ million | £ million |
| *Taxation* | | | |
| *Inland Revenue* | | | |
| Income tax      .      .      . | 3,807 | 3,817 | 4,401 |
| Surtax      .      .      . | 250 | 232 | 320 |
| Death duties   .      .      . | 300 | 330 | 346 |
| Stamp duty  .      .      . | 81 | 98 | 105 |
| Corporation tax      .      . | 1,280 | 1,257 | 1,441 |
| Capital gains tax      .      . | 5 | 16 | 44 |
| *Total Inland Revenue*   .      . | 5,723 | 5,750 | 6,657 |
| *Customs and Excise*      .      . | | | |
| Tobacco  .      .      .      . | 1,020 | 1,038 | 1,045 |
| Purchase tax      .      .      . | 735 | 747 | 887 |
| Oil  .      .      .      .      . | 950 | 959 | 1,101 |
| Spirits, beer and wine   .      . | 718 | 736 | 723 |
| Betting and gaming  .      .      . | 70 | 67 | 100 |
| Other duties   .      .      . | 108 | 143 | 156 |
| *Total Customs and Excise*   . | 3,601 | 3,690 | 4,012 |
| Motor vehicle duties .      .      . | 255 | 266 | 413 |
| Selective employment tax (gross) . | 1,100 | 1,064 | 1,393 |
| *Total taxation*   .      .      . | 10,679 | 10,770 | 12,475 |
| *Miscellaneous Receipts* | | | |
| Broadcast Receiving Licences   . | 75 | 81 | 82 |
| Other Receipts .      .      .      . | 339 | 326 | 318 |
| *Total .      .      .      .      . | 11,093 | 11,177 | 12,875 |

cluding road haulage and public service vehicles for the carriage of passengers) have become an increasing source of revenue in most countries, though motoring is nowhere more heavily taxed than in Great Britain. Taking together the tax on oil and motor-vehicle duties motoring taxes in this country yield 10% of total revenue. Another 8% of the revenue comes from purchase taxes.

**Covering a deficit (or surplus)**

Table CX shows what is still often known as "above the line" revenue or government ordinary revenue. Since Table CVIII (p. 443) shows government loans net (*i.e.* new loans less repayments) there is no longer need of a table to show "below the line" revenue. By comparing Tables CVII and CX it is possible to see whether a surplus or a deficit was achieved in the actual outturn of expenditure and revenue in 1967–68, and the size of the surplus budgeted for in 1968–69. In fact, in 1967–68 there was a surplus of £299 million on current account. If this surplus is deducted from the government loans shown in Table CVIII, this gives an overall deficit of £1,449 million to be covered by borrowing. Most years one or more government stocks fall due for redemption and these repayments are usually covered by the issue of new stocks. In addition there is the borrowing to cover the excess of government expenditure over revenue. If the borrowing for this purpose is not to be inflationary it must come from savings and so mean a reduction in spending. It is for this reason that the Government is constantly urging people to save by purchasing National Savings securities—National Savings Certificates, National Development Bonds and Premium Savings Bonds. In some years repayments for some of these securities exceed new savings, the balance having to be raised mainly by Treasury bills, thereby increasing the floating debt portion of the National Debt. If there had been a surplus overall this would have resulted in a reduction of the National Debt.

## III. PRINCIPLES OF TAXATION

### Adam Smith's views

The first attempt to lay down a set of principles on which a state should base its system of taxation was Adam Smith. He put forward four general maxims with regard to taxation:

(i) The amount each person has to pay should be certain and the time of payment should be clear.

(ii) Taxes should be levied at times most convenient for tax-payers to pay them.

(iii) The cost of collecting a tax should be as low as possible.

(iv) The subjects of every state should contribute to the cost of government as nearly as possible in proportion to their respective abilities, for only if this maxim is carried out can there be "equality" of taxation.

The first three maxims enumerated above are now widely accepted. When taxes were farmed out the tax-gatherers squeezed as much as they could from taxpayers. The PAYE method of tax collection fulfils the second maxim to perfection. It is clearly uneconomic to impose a tax the revenue from which is largely absorbed by its cost of collection since this results in a waste of economic resources. To these maxims might be added a fifth—that taxes should be imposed without distinction of class and no privileged group be given exemption.

It is Adam Smith's fourth maxim (actually he put it first) that is the main subject of discussion nowadays. Ability to pay depends partly on a person's income and partly on his family commitments. There is no doubt that equity demands that those with high incomes should pay more in taxes than those with low incomes, and that those with greater family commitments should pay less than those with less responsibility of this kind. Adam Smith, therefore, would probably have approved of the system of allowances built into the British income tax so that after the deduction of these allowances each taxpayer should pay an amount *as nearly as possible* proportional to his taxable income. This, he considered, would make for equality (*i.e.* equity) of taxation. Later, in his book *The Wealth of Nations*, he went farther than this by saying that the rich should contribute something more than in proportion to their incomes. In most countries at the present day the proportional system is not regarded as bearing heavily enough on people in the higher income ranges.

### Other principles of taxation

At different times a number of different principles of taxation have been enunciated. According to the so-called benefit theory, the amount a person should pay in taxes should be related to the benefit he might expect to receive in return. This argument has sometimes been applied to local rates, but in general it falls down since it would result in the impossible situation that those in the lowest income groups would be called upon to pay most. Somewhat similar and equally impracticable is the "cost of service" principle, according to which a person's liability to taxation would be based on the cost of the public services of which he takes advantage.

On grounds of equity it has been suggested that a tax system should be based on a principle of equal sacrifice or ability to pay. Both are difficult to define precisely and different people have different ideas of what is equitable. In France before the Revolution the tax system was most inequitable, the rich paying very little and the poor a great deal. As a result of the influence of the philosopher Locke, many people in eighteenth-century England thought that for political and moral reasons all people, rich and poor, should pay something towards the cost of government, but this view was opposed on both humanitarian and economic grounds. In England the rich have paid more than the poor since the seventeenth century but it was not until the introduction of Pitt's income tax in 1799 that a more precise relationship was established between the amount payable and ability to pay. From the time of Adam Smith until the First World War ability to pay was taken to mean that taxation should be proportional to income. Since the war of 1914–18 taxation in most countries has become more progressive, *i.e.* the amount payable in taxation as income increases becomes more than proportional to income. Since the late nineteenth century there has been a gradual development of opinion in favour of progressive taxation, though recently there has possibly been some reaction against it. That taxation should be on a progressive scale, however, appears to be the generally accepted modern conception of equity as applied to taxation. How progressive a tax system should be is more open to argument.

## The theoretical basis of progressive taxation

The theory of declining marginal utility is now generally accepted as a satisfactory subjective theory of value, though it is usual to point out that there are some exceptions to it. As applied to income it shows that an extra £1 of income would give less satisfaction to a millionaire than to a man whose sole income is derived from a retirement pension from the Ministry of Health and Social Security. At these extremes few people would question the validity of the theory, but does it hold good between people whose incomes are not quite so far apart? People differ very widely in their range of wants. With £1,200 a year one man, A, may be able to satisfy most of his wants, whereas another man, B, with £2,500 a year may have many wants which he can satisfy only very inadequately. A's tastes may be simple, with music, the theatre, books and travel all having little attraction for him, while B may greatly appreciate these things but finds his income insufficient to give him a proper enjoyment of them. The marginal utility of a further £100 a year might, therefore, actually be greater for B than for A. Thus, the marginal utility theory does not appear to provide a satisfactory theoretical basis for a progressive system of taxation. Nevertheless, most economists agree that if taxation is to be related to the ability to pay there must be some degree of progression in taxation, though some believe that perhaps it need not be as progressive in an affluent society as in one where there is widespread poverty. Few people would deny that everyone should be assured of an adequate standard of living, but transfers of income from the moderately well-to-do to the less well-to-do appear to be more difficult to justify.

A further theoretical point with regard to progressive taxation is that where very high incomes accrue they almost invariably include large elements of rent. This is particularly the case with entertainers of unique or exceptional talent who are in consequence able to command high fees for their services. Economic rents are regarded as unearned and therefore a good object of taxation, and since no adverse economic effects follow, however high the tax on such

452 AN INTRODUCTION TO APPLIED ECONOMICS

rents, a steeply progressive rate of taxation of them appears to be justified.

## IV. SOME TAXES

**Types of taxes**

Taxes can be classified as direct and indirect. Alternatively, a distinction can be drawn between income and outlay taxes. Direct taxes have been defined as those involving a direct personal relationship between the tax-levying authority and the taxpayer. Income tax, surtax and death duties are levied directly on individuals (in the case of death duties, on an individual's estate after death), and corporation tax directly on companies. Social security contributions also are paid direct. Since the introduction for those assessed under Schedule E of the PAYE method of paying income tax, under which employers deduct the tax from the wages and salaries of their employees, the direct relationship between the taxpayer and the Inland Revenue has become somewhat blurred. Those who are assessed under Schedule D (the self-employed) still pay their income tax direct to the tax collector, while surtax in all cases is paid direct. Other features of direct taxes are said to be: (*i*) they cannot be shifted on to someone else by the person or persons on whom they have been imposed; (*ii*) they cannot legally be avoided. In general direct taxes cannot be shifted, nor can they be completely avoided though legally it is perfectly legitimate for a taxpayer so to arrange his affairs to reduce his liability to tax. Tax evasion is, of course, illegal.

Indirect taxes are those on outlay, thus being paid only when taxed commodities or services are purchased. These are among the oldest taxes, especially customs duties on imports, on account of the ease of their assessment. Customs and excise duties (the former on imports, the latter on home-produced goods) were greatly increased during the Second World War with the introduction of purchase taxes on a wide range of goods. They were imposed to check consumption but have been retained as revenue yielders and, as already noted, have become an instrument of fiscal policy. It was thought at one time that indirect taxes could be avoided since there is no compulsion to buy the commodities on which they are imposed. Thus, the non-smoker avoids the tax on tobacco and the teetotaller the taxes on alcoholic drink. The first principle of indirect taxation, however, is that in view of the great differences of taste among consumers the tax net should be cast as widely as possible, so that no one can escape. No particular indirect tax, therefore, can be singled out for criticism. It would, then, be better, when a change of taxation, whether upwards or downwards, is announced in the budget, if it could be made to apply equally to all forms of indirect taxation, so that it should not appear that discrimination was being practised for or against particular groups of consumers. This suggestion, however, is impracticable for two reasons: the required change in taxation may be small; the elasticity of demand is not the same for all commodities.

Though small indirect taxes on some common necessary foodstuffs were retained until the 1920s, it was considered as long ago as the seventeenth century that luxury goods were the most suitable objects of taxation. As the standard of living rises former luxuries, however, tend to become present necessaries, and if indirect taxation was limited to luxuries the yield would be small. From the standpoint of maximising revenue goods most suitable for taxation are those in wide and inelastic demand. Unfortunately, these include many necessary foodstuffs. The main criticism of indirect taxes, therefore, has been that they tend to be regressive, bearing most heavily on large families in the lower income groups. It is probably true too that individual expenditure on tobacco varies inversely with income and possibly this may also be true, though to a lesser extent, of the consumption of alcoholic drink.

The degree to which indirect taxes are regressive depends on whether they are *ad valorem* or specific. The taxes on beer, tobacco and petrol are specific, being in 1969 nearly £10 per 36 gallons on beer and over £4 per lb on tobacco. The purchase taxes are based on the value of the commodity, *i.e.* they are calculated *ad valorem*, and also the percentage rates of tax vary between different commodities, being higher, for example, on jewellery than on clothing or furniture. In some cases the cheaper ranges of goods are exempt from tax. Thus, these taxes tend to fall more heavily on the well-to-do than on those of more moderate means. The advantage of *ad valorem* taxes in inflationary times is that the yield from them increases as prices rise.

Hence, for long it was argued that direct taxation was the more equitable since it could be more precisely related to ability to pay, whereas indirect taxation was often regressive. This was true during the nineteenth century when indirect taxes fell heavily on foodstuffs and there was little direct taxation. By 1910 the Government's revenue came in almost equal parts from direct and indirect taxes and by 1945 approximately 60% of total revenue was obtained by direct taxation. Since 1945 indirect taxation has increased more than direct and by 1966 the two groups of taxes were each again yielding about half the revenue received by the Exchequer. During the past twenty years it has been felt that direct taxes have a greater disincentive effect on workers than indirect taxes and thereby tend to check the rate of economic growth. As for the indirect taxes of the present day, these are much less regressive than formerly. The removal of most taxes on food and the imposition of a wide range of purchase taxes have been responsible for this, particularly since purchase taxes are on an *ad valorem* basis so that in general the people who buy more expensive things—generally those in the higher income groups—pay more tax than people who always buy cheap goods.

## Income tax

The most important direct taxes are those on income. Income tax was first imposed in Great Britain in 1799 by William Pitt. Taxes on income were not imposed earlier partly because of the difficulty of accurately assessing people's incomes. By granting certain concessions—an exemption limit of £60 a year, a graduated scale for incomes between £60 and £200 a year and an undertaking that in no case should the tax exceed 10% of a person's gross income—Pitt was able to persuade people to declare their incomes. The graduated tax started at 2d. in the pound on incomes of £60 and rose to 2s. on incomes of over £200. Thus, in its earliest form, it had two progressive features—exemption of small incomes from tax and higher rates on the larger incomes. Imposed only for the duration of the Napoleonic Wars, the tax was repealed in 1816. It was revived by Sir Robert Peel in 1842. Again it was expected to be only a temporary measure but the loss of revenue to the Exchequer resulting from the abolition of several hundred import duties by Peel and Gladstone led to its retention, though always on a temporary basis (as late as 1874 Gladstone was promising to repeal it), until finally in 1907 Asquith made it a permanent feature of the British tax structure. Two years later Lloyd George, as Chancellor of the Exchequer, supplemented the ordinary income tax by an additional levy on incomes over £5,000 (the equivalent of at least £30,000 today), reduced to £3,000 in 1914 and to £2,000 in 1918, known at the time as supertax but since 1929 as surtax.[1] During the second half of the nineteenth century income tax varied between 7d. and 1s. 4d. in the pound, the highest rates occurring in 1855 and 1899 as a result of the Crimean War and the Boer War respectively. During the twentieth century income tax rates have soared, with a maximum rate of 6s. during the First World War and of 10s. during the Second World War with in addition in the latter case of 9s. 6d. surtax, making a rate of 19s. 6d. on the highest incomes. Two World Wars helped to make income taxes, always at least mildly progressive, in Great Britain the steeply-progressive taxes they are today. This has been achieved in two ways—by an extensive system of allowances to suit taxpayers with differing family responsibilities, and discrimination in favour of earned income as against investment ("unearned") income—and

[1] On *earned* income the exemption rate for surtax was raised to approximately £5,000 in 1961. On *unearned* income the exemption rate remained at £2,000.

increasingly higher rates of tax the higher the income especially in the case of surtax. Table CXI below shows the progressive character of income tax in Great Britain today for a married man with one child under eleven years of age.

One objection to subjecting small incomes to income tax used to be the heavy cost of collecting it. In days when the tax was collected in half-yearly instalments there was the further objection that people with low incomes would find it extremely difficult to save up to pay the tax in two lump sums—though many had to do so in the case of their local rates. The introduction of the system whereby tax is deducted from an employee's pay before he receives it appears to overcome these objections, though it should not be forgotten that most of the cost of collection now falls on employers and for a large firm this can be a quite considerable sum.

TABLE CXI

*A Progressive Income Tax*
(1967–68)
For a married couple with one child under 11 years
of age (all earned income)

| Annual income £ | Income tax and surtax £ | Tax as percentage of income % |
|---|---|---|
| 800 | 40 | 5·0 |
| 1,000 | 89 | 8·9 |
| 1,200 | 153 | 12·7 |
| 1,500 | 249 | 16·6 |
| 1,800 | 346 | 19·2 |
| 2,000 | 410 | 20·5 |
| 2,500 | 570 | 22·6 |
| 3,000 | 731 | 24·3 |
| 4,000 | 1,051 | 26·2 |
| 5,000 | 1,418 | 28·3 |
| 10,000 | 4,111 | 41·1 |
| 15,000 | 8,020 | 53·4 |
| 20,000 | 12,449 | 62·2 |
| 25,000 | 17,011 | 68·0 |
| 50,000 | 39,824 | 79·6 |

The extension of income tax to lower incomes, begun during the Second World War and continued afterwards on account of the increasing cost of services provided by the State—mainly for the benefit of people in the lower income groups—has changed the character of the tax. As recently as the late 1930s it was a tax that fell mainly on the middle classes and the well-to-do, so that only a small proportion of wage-earners paid it. Largely in consequence of the rise in the standard of living during the past twenty-five years, it has now become a widely based tax, falling on 89% of income-receivers. The yield from income tax and surtax rose from £400 million in 1938–39 to over £4,000 million twenty years later in 1968–69, as a result (*i*) of the declining value of money; (*ii*) the rising standard of living; and (*iii*) higher rates of tax.

In most of the economically advanced countries of the world a stiff rate of personal income tax is imposed and not only in Great Britain as many people in this country suppose.

Where personal taxation in Great Britain falls more heavily than in these other countries is on high incomes. Below the equivalent of £1,500 a year people in this country are less heavily taxed than elsewhere, but above that level up to £10,000 a year taxation is heavier on personal income in Great Britain, and above £10,000 a year very much heavier. At £10,000 a year the marginal rate of tax is 74% in Great Britain, 48% in the United States and only 32% in France. In Great Britain the highest rate of income tax (including surtax) in 1968 was 18*s*. 3*d*. and this rate became effective at £19,000 a year. In contrast, the highest rate at that time in the United States was 14*s*. but this did not become payable until one's income reached £140,000. Comparable figures for France and West Germany were 13*s*. 7*d*. and 10*s*. 7*d*. respectively for the highest rate and £15,000 and £17,000 respectively for the level of income to which these rates applied.

A more serious criticism of British income tax is that its progressiveness is not sufficiently graded, but tends to increase by a number of steps. Thus, it is steeply progressive up to the point where the standard rate is payable (about £750 a year in the case of a single person) and then becomes gradually less progressive until surtax has to be paid (that is, at £2,000 or £5,000 a year according to whether income is from investment or earned). After the onset of surtax it then again becomes steeply progressive until income reaches £20,000 a year. Tax reformers have suggested that a more evenly graded rate of progression would reduce the disincentive effect of the tax at particular levels of income.

### Estate duty

Estate duty—more generally known as death duty—was first imposed in its modern form by Sir William Harcourt in 1894. Payable from the start on a graduated scale, though with a maximum rate of 8% in 1894 as compared with 80% today, the tax has been made steeply progressive as Table CXII (p. 457) clearly shows. It is levied on all property possessed by the deceased at the time of death, but the duty on agricultural land is reduced by 45% and gifts *inter vivos* are exempt only if made within five years of death. Estate duty supplements income tax in lessening inequality of income. One of the causes of differences of income is that income is derived from property (real estate, stock exchange securities) as well as from work, and property can be inherited. Estate duty together with income tax have made it more difficult for people to accumulate property. The progressiveness of estate duty is increased by the whole of a large

TABLE CXII

*A Progressive Scale of Estate Duty*

| Value of estate £ | Tax (% of whole estate) |
|---|---|
| Less than 5,000 . . . | Nil |
| 5,001–6,000 | 1 |
| 6,001–7,000 | 2 |
| 7,001–8,000 | 3 |
| 8,001–10,000 | 4 |
| 10,001–12,500 | 6 |
| 12,501–15,000 | 8 |
| 15,001–17,500 | 10 |
| 17,501–20,000 | 12 |
| 20,001–25,000 | 15 |
| 25,001–30,000 | 18 |
| 30,001–35,000 | 21 |
| 35,001–40,000 | 24 |
| 40,001–45,000 | 28 |
| 45,001–50,000 | 31 |
| 50,001–60,000 | 35 |
| 60,001–75,000 | 40 |
| 75,001–100,000 | 45 |
| 100,001–150,000 | 50 |
| 150,001–200,000 | 55 |
| 200,001–300,000 | 60 |
| 300,001–500,000 | 65 |
| 500,001–750,000 | 70 |
| 750,001–1,000,000 | 75 |
| More than 1,000,000 | 80 |

estate being taxed at a higher rate than a small estate, and not like income and surtax with different rates on different tranches of income. Thus, on estates up to £5,000, no tax is payable, whereas, on an estate of £10,000, £400 has to be paid and on £15,000 tax amounts to £1,200. Tax at 80% on very large estates approaches confiscation. An inheritance tax appears to be more equitably based, with the tax varying according to nearness of kinship to the deceased so that a widow pays less than a son, and a son less than a niece. The amount payable, however, is somewhat reduced when an estate is subjected to duty more than once within a short period of time.

## Capital Gains Tax

Great Britain, unlike many other countries, has had a capital gains tax for only a very short time—in fact, only since 1962. In that year a short-term capital gains tax was introduced covering capital gains accruing within six months in the case of stock exchange securities or within three years in the case of land. An Act of 1965 extended the incidence of the tax to gains on stock exchange securities, however long they might have been held, and also to many other kinds of property (for example, for personal chattels if sold for over £1,000), though not to owner-occupied houses. Capital losses can be offset against capital gains. Tax at the rate of 30% was imposed, but gains up to £50 are exempt.

The argument for capital gains taxes was that such gains were equivalent to income. Against these taxes it was argued that much of so-called capital gains were the result of a fall in the value of money and not due to an increase in the real value of the asset. Part of the increase in the stock exchange prices of equities during an inflationary period arise for this reason. However, to exempt from taxation capital gains due to this cause and tax only real capital gains would be impracticable. Another argument in favour of capital gains is that such gains tend to increase inequality of income since they are likely to accrue only to a small, if increasing, section of the community and mainly to the well-to-do. This was particularly true of people with substantial interests in companies more interested in "growth" (*i.e.* in the accumulation of assets) than in increasing dividends, capital gains when not taxed being preferred to income subject to tax. Now, however, that a wide range of capital gains is taxed it seems inequitable that huge winnings on football pools should be exempt from capital gains tax even though the chance of winning is open to rich and poor alike.


## Company taxation

For over fifty years various forms of profits taxes, excess profits taxes and income tax have been imposed on companies in Great Britain. In 1965 these taxes were replaced by corporation tax, a tax on the profits of companies. The rate of tax is decided annually by Parliament and for the first year was at a rate of 40%.[1] There are allowances for capital expenditure and there is provision for relief for trading losses.

It is now generally recognised that on grounds of equity companies as such should be taxed as well as individuals.

---

[1] Increased to 42½% in 1967.

## Payroll taxes

In a number of countries businesses have to pay taxes on the people they employ. In Australia, for example, the Government levies a payroll tax on all employers whose wage bill exceeds $20,800 a year, any sum in excess of this amount being subject to a tax of $2\frac{1}{2}\%$. Such a tax has been advocated in Great Britain in order to discourage employers from retaining more labour than they require, as often happens in the minor recessions that periodically occur in times of over-full employment, the aim being to attract labour to industries where there is a shortage of workers. In 1966 a selective employment tax was introduced in this country as a result of which all employers have to pay a poll tax on the labour they employ. One argument put forward to support it was that it would fall on some sections of the community that were less heavily taxed than others— professional businesses such as those of accountants, solicitors and shopkeepers. Another argument for it was that it would assist the transfer of labour from "service" to "productive" occupations and this was further encouraged by refunding the tax together with a small bonus to employers in manufacturing industry.[1] In the case of nationalised industries, building and construction, farming, central and local government employees, the tax is refunded. The distinction drawn between service and productive occupations is completely out of date (the idea goes back to Adam Smith, but was refuted over a hundred years ago) and it encourages rather than discourages the only likely hoarders of labour—manufacturers in the more prosperous industries and the central government itself. Then, too, in the more highly developed economies the numbers in service occupations tend to increase because these occupations are of a personal nature and so cannot be mechanised to any great extent, whereas in manufacturing industry an inceasing amount of automation can be expected. The assertion, therefore, in the SET White Paper that it is upon the manufacturing sector that the growth of the economy depends appears to be contrary to the facts. More than half of all employed persons in the United States are engaged in service occupations. When it was introduced, SET created many anomalies and, though some were eliminated after the first year's experience of the tax, many still remain. For example, employees of manufacturing and service industries are often engaged on similar work and yet in one case they are regarded as "productive" and in the other as "non-productive" workers for tax purposes. As a tax, however, it is an important producer of revenue for the State, yielding £1,064 million in 1967–68.

[1] Since 1968 the bonus has been payable only to manufacturers in development areas.

## Sales taxes

Various forms of sales tax have been imposed by different countries. A sales tax can be made to cover the whole field of retail sales as in the Republic of Ireland or some classes of goods can be exempted as in Australia. Different groups of commodities can bear different rates of tax. A sales tax imposed at the retail stage is more difficult to collect than the British purchase tax, which is collected at the wholesale stage and applies to only a limited range of commodities. Another variant is the turnover tax, which can be applied to the total sales of any kind of business at any stage of production, or the value-added tax, which is imposed only on the value of the particular process carried out by a firm. These are all outlay taxes, whether imposed on the manufacturer, wholesaler or retailer. The value-added tax is imposed in the E.E.C. countries, but as yet has found little support in Great Britain.

## V. EFFECTS OF TAXATION

### Economic effects of taxation

(*i*) *The general level of taxation.* Including local rates and national insurance contributions taxation in the United Kingdom in 1964 reached about 35% of the national income. For over half a century there have been complaints about the high level of taxation with hopeful hints that the limit of taxable capacity had been reached. It has been pointed out that this limit depends on how the Government spends its revenue. The more the State does for the people in reducing inequality of income and in providing welfare services, the greater the amount of taxation the people are able to bear. Nevertheless, there are those who believe that heavy taxation of itself produces harmful results. It has been suggested, for example, by Colin Clark[1] that if taxation exceeds 25% of the national income the effect will be inflationary. Certainly since 1939 the level of taxation in relation to the national income has increased everywhere, and in all countries there has been inflation, in varying degrees of severity, and the high level of taxation may have been a contributory factor in pushing up incomes, costs and prices. A high level of taxation tends to make people look for loopholes for tax avoidance through tax-free perquisites such as the provision of a car or lunch vouchers.

(*ii*) *The disincentive effect* (*labour*). Direct taxation of current earnings through the PAYE system of tax payment exaggerates the tax effect on marginal earnings, especially where, as in Great Britain, income tax is progressive and not as smoothly graded as might be.

[1] Colin Clark: *Taxmanship* (Institute of Economic Affairs).

Tax-free allowances reduce the average rate of tax payable per pound of income and the marginal rate of tax is very much higher, especially at points where the rate of tax increases. In the case of low incomes the marginal rate of tax may be two to three times as great as the average rate of tax. A high marginal rate might be expected to act as a disincentive, though the Royal Commission on Taxation (1954) found little evidence to show that taxation has a serious disincentive effect. Not all economists agree with this but perhaps the disincentive effect is less than was supposed. Nevertheless, workers are often given bonuses as an incentive, and since most of them are interested only in the amount they take home and not their gross pay they might be expected to regard an increase in income tax as the equivalent of a reduction in wages. Absenteeism will be encouraged if it is found that to stay away from work occasionally for a day only reduces their "take-home" pay very slightly.

(*iii*) *The disincentive effect* (*the entrepreneur*). It used to be asserted that taxes on profits were economically unsound because they were a tax on enterprise. The main function of the entrepreneur is the bearing of risk or uncertainty. To penalise him through taxation when he is successful and to leave him to bear his losses when unsuccessful, it was argued, would make entrepreneurs less willing to take risks and so check economic progress. The fact that in so many countries the State has made itself responsible for the maintenance of full employment, thereby ensuring a high level of demand and providing conditions in which the earning of profit is less risky, has considerably reduced the economic drawbacks to taxes on profits. In inflationary conditions, too, firms tend, so far as they are able, to regard such taxes as a cost of production and aim at a level of profit after tax. The fact remains that in most countries taxes on business provide a large part of the State's revenue, forming a particularly high proportion of total revenue, for example, in France.

(*iv*) *The effect on saving.* By reducing the proportion of income at one's disposal, taxation clearly makes saving more difficult, though some people may continue to save by curtailing consumption. To the extent, however, that the revenue received from taxation is used to provide services—social security, national health—there will be less personal need to save. If, to reduce inequality of incomes, a steeply progressive system of taxation is introduced, saving will probably be reduced still further. Those who formerly were responsible for most personal saving may save little (or there may even be dis-saving—*i.e.* they may begin to live on capital) since they are likely to try to maintain the standard of living to which they have become accustomed. Most of those who benefit from redistribution of income have of necessity been in the habit of spending and are more likely to increase their spending than to become savers. Transfers of purchasing power by means of taxation thus tend to be from savers to spenders. By reducing the demand for consumers' goods and thereby freeing economic resources for the production of capital goods, saving is an essential prerequisite of real investment and therefore of paramount economic importance. The decline in personal saving, however, has been more than balanced by corporate saving by companies in the form of undistributed profits. Clearly, if corporation tax is at a high rate companies should be granted investment allowances. If personal and corporate saving fall short of what is necessary for the required amount of investment the State will be compelled to have recourse to compulsory saving, reducing consumption by taxation and using the proceeds to finance investment itself.

(v) *Effect on the structure of production.* Taxation of commodities and services, other things being equal, will reduce the demand for these things. How much effect any particular tax will have will depend on the elasticity of demand for the commodity on which it is imposed. The effect, however, may be to cause consumers to redistribute their expenditure. Wide differences in taxation and in elasticity of demand may result in economic resources being transferred from one form of production to another. A serious criticism of the British purchase tax is that it applies only to a limited range of goods. Variations in the rate of tax by the budget or the regulator are apt, therefore, to have serious directional effects through the fall in the demand for goods subject to this tax and increased demand for other things. A broadly based sales tax would not have these directional effects.

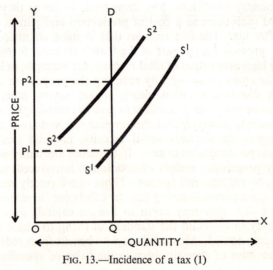

FIG. 13.—Incidence of a tax (1)

### Incidence of taxation

The incidence of a tax is on the person who ultimately pays it. The announcement by the Chancellor of the Exchequer in his budget speech of an increase in the tax on a commodity generally results in an immediate rise in the price of that commodity by the amount of the tax. This may lead one to assume that the incidence of indirect taxes is entirely on the buyer. Whether the price remains at this higher level will depend on the elasticity of demand for the commodity. Only if demand is perfectly inelastic will the incidence of

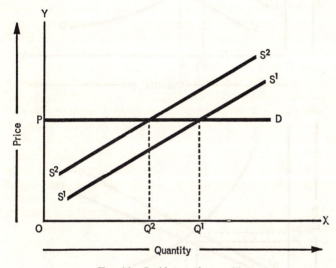

FIG. 14.—Incidence of a tax (2)

the tax be wholly on the buyer. Fig. 13 (p. 462) shows that in this case the price rises from $OP^1$ to $OP^2$, *i.e.* by the full amount of the tax. The curve $S^1$ shows the condition of supply before tax and $S^2$ after tax.

If demand were perfectly elastic the incidence of the tax would be entirely on the seller. Figure 14 above shows that no increase in price takes place but the quantity supplied falls from $OQ^1$ to $OQ^2$.

In all other cases the incidence of the tax will be shared by buyer and seller. Fig. 15A (p. 464) illustrates the effect of a tax on a commodity in fairly inelastic demand and Fig. 15B on a commodity in fairly elastic demand. In both cases the price rises by less than the amount of the tax, the greater share of the tax being borne by the buyer the more inelastic the demand, and the greater share by the seller the more elastic the demand. When the demand for a commodity is very

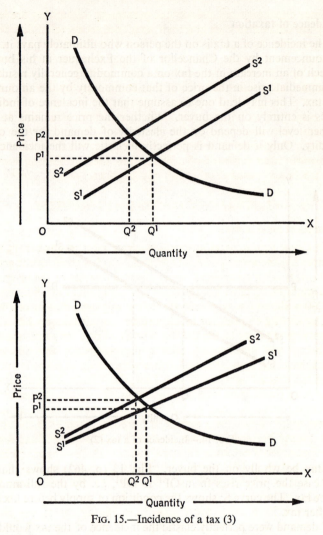

FIG. 15.—Incidence of a tax (3)

elastic to increase the rate of tax on it may so reduce the quantity demanded that the revenue from the tax may fall.

Similarly, the incidence of social security contributions depends on the demand for labour. In a trade depression, when the demand for labour is low, there will be a tendency for the incidence of employers' contributions to be on labour, but when the demand for labour is high, with shortages of labour in some lines of production, the incidence of the employee's contribution tends to be on the employer.

Since direct taxes are paid by the persons on whom they are levied they are difficult to shift and their incidence seems to be directly on these people. In general, one pays one's own income tax and surtax (if any). Nevertheless, some large firms pay their executive directors exceptionally high salaries solely in order that these men may receive a certain salary after tax. To some extent, therefore, in such cases the tax is being shifted from the employee, on whom it is levied, to the employer, to whom it ranks as a cost of production. As has already been noted above, the producer of a commodity in fairly inelastic demand in an inflationary period might aim to earn a certain profit after payment of a profits tax, thereby shifting some of the tax on to consumers through higher prices.

## VI. FINANCE OF LOCAL AUTHORITIES

### Sources of local finance

In Great Britain local authorities derive their revenue from three sources: (i) the levying of a rate or local tax; (ii) government grants; and (iii) trading enterprises. Only about a quarter of the revenue of local authorities comes from rates—£1,132 million in 1965–66 as against £1,260 million in government grants out of a total income of £4,690.

The levying of rates for local purposes in this country has a long history, going back to the twelfth century. For a long time the local authority was the parish. During the eighteenth and nineteenth centuries many new local authorities were set up to provide and administer specific services—Poor Law Guardians, School Boards, etc. As a result there was a large number of local authorities with different functions, often with different boundaries, each having the power to levy a rate for a particular purpose. After 1888 the county and county borough councils gradually took over the functions of the specialised local authorities on their abolition—for example, the School boards in 1902 and the Poor Law Guardians in 1929.

At first the revenue from local rates was expended on purely local services, mainly of their own choosing, but a succession of Acts of Parliament have made local authorities the agents of the central government for an increasing number of new services which they are now compelled by law to provide. Rates are still only partly a tax and partly a payment for services, though expenditure by local authorities for purely local purposes at the present day absorbs only about 35% of the total or 40% if the cost of the police is included. Table CXIII (p. 466) shows the income and expenditure in 1965–66 of local authorities in the United Kingdom. Before the nationalisation of electricity and gas supplies these services were sources of considerable income to many local authorities (mainly county boroughs), as at an earlier period, before competition came from the private

TABLE CXIII

*Income and Expenditure of Local Authorities*
*in the UK (1965–66)*

|  | £ million |
|---|---|
| **Expenditure** (both current and capital) | |
| Education . . . . . | 1,557 |
| Housing . . . . . . | 1,285 |
| Highways . . . . . . | 311 |
| Police . . . . . . | 208 |
| Trading services . . . . | 370 |
| Other expenditure . . . . | 219 |
| Interest on debt . . . . | 740 |
| Total . . . . . . | 4,690 |

Of this total £943 million comprised capital expenditure.

|  | £ million |
|---|---|
| **Income** | |
| Rates . . . . . . | 1,132 |
| Government grants . . . . | 1,260 |
| Trading services . . . . | 290 |
| Rents from housing . . . . | 370 |
| Other income . . . . . | 487 |
| Borrowing . . . . . | 1,151 |
| Total . . . . . . | 4,690 |

car, had been local passenger transport. Even if capital expenditure
is excluded, trading services of local authorities show a deficit. If
some of the country bus services are to be maintained in thinly
populated areas it may be that the local authorities of the areas in
which they operate will have to pay the subsidy required.

Table CXIII shows that only 26% of the expenditure of local
authorities comes from rates, 35% from government grants, and no
less than 23% from borrowing. The total debt of the local authorities
in 1968 amounted to nearly £13,000 million, of which the central
government through the Public Works Loan Board had provided
£3,010 million.

### The character of local rates

Rates are based on property—houses, shops, factories, etc.—the
owner or occupier paying according to the rateable value, which in
principle corresponds to the estimated annual rent of the property,
churches and agricultural buildings, however, being exempt. In
1948, in an attempt to standardise assessments, the Inland Revenue

was made responsible for determining rateable values. Revaluations of property take place periodically, the last in 1963, the next probably in 1973. Many objections have been made to rates as a local tax. As the Allen Report (1965) showed, rates tend to be regressive since it is not possible to relate payments closely to ability to pay. Though in general people in the higher income groups live in houses with the higher rateable values, this is not always so. Similarly, people with low incomes do not all live in houses with low rateable values. As income increases, the proportion spent on housing tends to fall. Some privileged people who live in council houses enjoy not only subsidised rents but also low rates. People of widely differing incomes often live next door to one another in similar houses. Another objection is that people who may be earning high wages escape the payment of rates if they are living with parents. Not only may rates be regressive within the area of one local authority but there is also a tendency for rates to be regressive between one place and another. A rate of one penny in the pound yields much less in an industrial town with a large proportion of small houses than in a mainly residential town, so that to cover the same expenditure a higher rate will be required in one than in the other. Large differences in rates between different localities can influence the location of industry, especially in times of trade depression, and in the places with the highest rates the rate is double that in places with the lowest rates. To lessen the regressive effect of rates, equalisation grants (known since 1958 as Rate Deficiency Grants) have been paid by the Government to places where the product of a penny rate is low. Then, in 1966, some relief of rates in the form of a rebate was given to people in the lower income groups and those with large families.

In favour of rates as a local tax there is the fact that they are locally based. It is said too in their favour that the revenue from rates is not subject to wide fluctuations. After each of the two World Wars, however, rateable values were hopelessly out of date and rates appeared to be exorbitantly high because, in consequence of the low rateable values, they often exceeded 20s. in the pound. Local rates could be supplemented by other local taxes—receipts from motor vehicles licences or a small local income tax proportionate to income, or the central government might be persuaded to share one of its taxes with local authorities. None of these suggestions has received very much support. A local income tax would have the merit as compared with rates of being more closely related to ability to pay.

The extension of national services administered by local authorities has led to increased government grants to help to finance them. This has led to suggestions in some quarters that the central government should take them over completely, especially education, which accounts for a third of the expenditure of local authorities. In reply to this it is pointed out that local administration, based so far as possible on local finance but of necessity supplemented by government grants, is the main safeguard of democracy. Local authorities cannot, then, be left to manage only minor matters. The main argument in favour of local administration is clearly political rather than economic. It is argued, therefore, that a degree of regressiveness in rates—provided central government taxation is progressive—is a small price to pay for political freedom.

## VII. THE DEBT OF THE PUBLIC SECTOR

### Types of public debt

The debt of the public sector comprises (*i*) the debt of the central government (commonly known as the National Debt), (*ii*) the debt of local authorities and (*iii*) the debt of the nationalised industries.

The National Debt dates from 1694, when the newly established Bank of England lent the government of the day £1,200,000. Table CXVI (p. 471) shows how the National Debt has increased during the past 275 years. Since the debt has increased mainly as a result of wars, most of it is not balanced by any corresponding assets and so it is sometimes known as "deadweight" debt. The debt of local authorities, however, has all been accumulated to finance some kind of investment—roads, local passenger transport undertakings, waterworks, schools, houses, etc.—and so there is something tangible to show for most of this debt, which in consequence is sometimes known as "reproductive" debt. The third type of debtor in the public sector is the nationalised industries. On the nationalisation of the railways and coal, gas and electricity production, compensation was paid to the former shareholders in newly created government-guaranteed stocks, some of which bear the distinguishing name of the industry concerned—Transport Stock, British Gas Stock, etc. These are clearly reproductive debts.

### External and internal debt

(*i*) *External debt*. Until quite recent times the British Government had no debts to other countries. In time of war it had often financed its allies and in fact it has never had to borrow on its own account for the prosecution of a war. During the First World War it lent more to France and Italy than it borrowed from the United States. During the Second World War the operation of the "lend–lease" system obviated borrowing between Great Britain and the United States, but imports were obtained on credit from a number of countries. After the Second World War, however, the British Government found it necessary to borrow from the United States and

Canada in order to speed up the country's recovery from the effects of that war, and repayment of this debt, principal and interest, will not be completed until the year 2001. In addition, the foreign debt increased in consequence of the outstanding debits when the European Payments Union ceased to function in 1959. During 1964–6 Great Britain incurred short-term debts from both international institutions and foreign central banks to support the pound sterling.

(*ii*) *Internal debt.* The British National Debt is, therefore, mainly an internal debt. It consists partly of short-term debt—the floating debt, consisting mostly of three-months Treasury Bills together with a little in the form of direct Ways and Means Advances from the Bank of England. Before 1914 the floating debt formed only 5% of the total debt whereas today it forms 15%. The remainder of the debt comprises the funded debt and national savings securities. In its strict sense the term "funded" is taken to mean stocks with no definite date of redemption, and before 1914 nearly 95% of the debt was in this form, mainly in Consols. During the past fifty years or so, the practice developed of issuing dated stocks generally giving the Government the option of redeeming them between two specified dates, and these also sometimes are referred to as funded stocks. National savings securities were first issued during the First World War and now include National Savings Certificates, Defence Bonds, National Development Bonds, British Savings Bonds and Premium Savings Bonds. Table CXV (p. 470) shows how the National Debt is made up.

## Other debt of the public sector

Local authorities borrow from the Government through the Public Works Loan Board, or by the issue of redeemable stocks to the market, or by the issue of bonds direct to investors. The nationalised industries also sometimes borrow by the issue of redeemable stocks to the market, or by borrowing from the Government or from

TABLE CXIV
*Debt of the Public Sector* (1968)

|  | £ million | £ million |
|---|---|---|
| The National Debt . | | 34,193 |
| Debt of local authorities . . . . | 12,950 | |
| *Less* borrowing from Public Loan Board | 4,867 | |
|  | 8,093 | 8,093 |
| Debt of public corporations . . . | | 12,509 |
| Total . . . . . . | | 54,795 |

the banks. Table CXIV (p. 469) shows the total debt of the public sector. It is necessary to deduct borrowing from the Government from the debt of local authorities in order to avoid double counting.

TABLE CXV
*Composition of the National Debt* (1968)

|  | £ million | £ million |
|---|---|---|
| Marketable stock exchange securities: |  |  |
|    Redeemable within 5 years . . . | 7,041 |  |
|    Redeemable in 6–15 years . . . | 4,685 |  |
|    Redeemable over 15 years . . . | 10,118 | 21,844 |
| Terminable annuities . . . . . |  | 562 |
| National savings securities: |  |  |
|    National saving certificates (principal only) . . . . . . . | 2,074 |  |
|    Defence bonds, National Development bonds, British Savings bonds . . | 972 |  |
|    Premium savings bonds . . . | 636 | 3,682 |
| Tax reserve certificates . . . . | | 308 |
| Other debt . . . . . . . | | 263 |
| | | 26,159 |
| Floating debt: |  |  |
|    Treasury bills . . . . . | 5,455 |  |
|    Ways and Means advances . . . | 278 | 5,733 |
|     TOTAL INTERNAL DEBT . . . | | 31,892 |
| External debt . . . . . . . | | 2,301 |
|     TOTAL NATIONAL DEBT . . . | | 34,193 |

Source: *Annual Abstract of Statistics.*

### Growth of public debt

Table CXVI shows how the National Debt has increased since 1694. Down to 1914 the aim was to reduce the debt whenever possible. As early as 1725 Walpole had established a Sinking Fund and, though it was invariably raided whenever a Chancellor of the Exchequer found himself in difficulties, it was re-established first by Pitt and then by Disraeli, and in spite of the setback due to the Crimean War it appeared in 1899 as if the debt might eventually be paid off. The two World Wars ended all such ideas. Nowadays it is regarded as being of great importance to the operation of monetary policy.

TABLE CXVI
*Growth of the National Debt*

| Year | £ million | Influences |
|------|-----------|------------|
| 1694 | 1·2 | |
| 1697 | 21 | After wars with France (William III) |
| 1701 | 16 | |
| 1714 | 49 | End of wars of Marlborough. |
| 1742 | 45 | Retirement of Walpole |
| 1748 | 78 | After Peace of Aix-la-Chapelle |
| 1756 | 72 | |
| 1785 | 244 | End of War of American Independence |
| 1798 | 530 | End of French Revolutionary Wars |
| 1815 | 878 | End of Napoleonic Wars |
| 1841 | 886 | Budget deficits 1830–41 |
| 1853 | 771 | Before Crimean War |
| 1856 | 831 | After Crimean War |
| 1899 | 635 | Before South African War |
| 1902 | 798 | After South African War |
| 1914 | 617 | Before First World War |
| 1920 | 7,800 | After First World War and before Second World War |
| 1945 | 23,000 | After Second World War |
| 1968 | 34,193 | Budget deficits on capital account |

More important perhaps than the increase in the debt of the public sector as a result of past wars is its increase in recent years in a time of peace, as the following table shows:

TABLE CXVII
*The National Debt*

| Year | Total £ million | Annual increase £ million |
|------|-----------------|---------------------------|
| 1954 | 26,583 | — |
| 1956 | 27,039 | 228 |
| 1958 | 27,232 | 96½ |
| 1960 | 27,732 | 250 |
| 1962 | 28,674 | 471 |
| 1964 | 30,226 | 781 |
| 1966 | 31,340 | 537 |
| 1968 | 34,193 | 1,428 |

TABLE CXVIII

*Debt of Local Authorities*
(including loans from Public Works Loan Board)

| Year | Total £ million | Annual increase £ million |
|------|-----------------|---------------------------|
| 1954 | 3,947 | — |
| 1956 | 4,879 | 466 |
| 1958 | 5,742 | 431½ |
| 1960 | 6,555 | 406½ |
| 1962 | 7,661 | 553 |
| 1964 | 8,800 | 579 |
| 1966 | 10,752 | 976 |
| 1968 | 12,950 | 1,099 |

Source: *Annual Abstract of Statistics.*

**Holders of the National Debt**

Before 1914 almost the whole of the funded part of the National Debt was held by individuals, whereas today individuals directly hold only 15% of it, though through the Post Office and trustee savings banks, insurance companies and friendly societies they are indirectly interested in a further 12%. About 20% is held by banks though in recent years they have reduced their investments in order to expand loans (except during times of credit squeeze). About 21% is held by non-residents—some by individuals, but most by financial institutions. Most interesting of all is that no less than 16% is held by government departments. Not only is this important for debt management but also it means that in effect the debt is not really quite as large as it appears.

**The burden of the National Debt**

(*i*) *External Debt.* It is important to distinguish between internal and external debt. The latter is always a serious burden on a country since the payment of the interest and repayment of the principal become debit items in the balance of payments and, in effect, have to be paid by the export of goods or the provision of services to other countries. Foreign loans too are usually made in terms of the lender's currency and so, unlike the internal debt, the burden cannot be reduced by inflation—action which, in any case, savours of sharp practice. The purpose for which the external debt was incurred is of great importance with regard to its burden. A developing or under-developed country may borrow in order to speed up its economic development and the resulting gain may outweigh the burden of repayment and interest payments. Even an economically advanced country suffering from a temporary dislocation of its economy at the end of a great war would find it economically advantageous to borrow from abroad to speed up its recovery. Thus, the British Government's borrowing from the United States in December 1945 was justified because the burden of the debt was to some extent offset by the speedier increase in the British national income. A loan to aid the prosecution of war is more difficult to justify on economic grounds unless it shortens the war.

(*ii*) *Internal debt.* Clearly, if government departments hold some of the National Debt, this part of it cannot in any sense be regarded as a burden. In considering this aspect of the National Debt it seems justifiable to deduct the £4,800 million held by government departments, leaving then in 1965 a net total of £25,644 million.

An internal debt makes a country neither poorer nor richer since the interest is paid to one section of the community out of the proceeds of taxes raised from the community as a whole, *i.e.* they are merely transfer payments. These transfers, however, affect the distribution of income. Before 1914, when the greater part of the debt was held by individuals, most of whom were wealthy, and when taxation was much less progressive than it is today, transfers tended to be from the poor to the rich. Since then the position has changed in three ways: (*a*) as we have seen, a great deal of the debt is held by banks and other financial institutions; (*b*) the individuals who hold government debt nowadays include most of the people with small savings, the well-to-do usually preferring other forms of investment; and (*c*) taxation at the present day is steeply progressive. As a result, transfers now tend to be mainly from the rich to those of moderate means.

The burden of the debt will be affected by changes in the prevailing rate of interest. Changes in bank rate will have immediate effect on the cost to the Government of issuing Treasury Bills and the rate at which new government stocks can be put on the market. A stock with wide redemption dates, such as 4% Funding Loan 1960–90, enables the Government to redeem it at a time when a more advantageous rate of interest can be obtained on a new issue.

The burden of the debt, for purposes of comparing different periods, can be calculated in a number of ways: the interest can be shown as a percentage of the national income or of government revenue or it can be averaged per head of the population. In all cases changes in the value of money must be taken into account.

In 1816 the interest on the National Debt formed 47% of government expenditure, in 1938 22% and in 1966 less than 10%. This is largely explained by the huge increase in government expenditure.

Calculated as an average per head of the population, interest, on the National Debt came to £4 in 1816, 9*s*. in 1914, £7 in 1920 and

£14 in 1966, but, if allowance is made for the fall in the value of money, the average per head today is only two-thirds of what it was in 1920 and only half of what it was in 1816.

In relation to the national income the interest on the National Debt in 1870 was about 4%, in 1938 it was under 5%, in 1946 about 8% and in 1966 about 4%. This is probably the fairest method of calculating the burden of the debt. It shows that in relation to the ability to pay of the community as a whole the debt is no more serious a burden now than it was a hundred years ago in spite of two World Wars. It also shows that although the debt has increased very considerably since 1946 two factors have reduced its effect: (a) the rise in the national income, both in real and monetary terms, and (b) the fall in the value of money. If some degree of inflation is to be a regular feature of economic life in the future as it has been since 1939, the burden of the National Debt will tend to decline unless the Government's expenditure is regularly allowed to exceed its revenue by an amount that offsets the fall in the value of money.

### Management of the National Debt

According to the Radcliffe Report (1959) the management of the National Debt has become a vital adjunct to monetary policy. That being the case there is no longer any need to think, as did Gladstone and Disraeli, in terms of eventually paying off the National Debt, even if such a course was practicable. To say that a National Debt is essential to monetary policy is merely to emphasise that the National Debt can be made to serve monetary ends.

As has already been seen, a large part of the National Debt is made up of stocks that can be bought and sold on the stock exchange. Table CXV (p. 470), for example, shows that in 1968 over £7,000 million of the debt was in stocks due to be redeemed within five years—an average of £1,400 million per year. The usual procedure when a stock is due for redemption is to offer a new stock to the market so that those holders who so wish can convert from the old to the new stock, and also to raise money to repay holders who prefer a cash payment. To achieve its object the new stock must have a yield at least as good as that given by existing government stocks with a similar period to run.

The opportunity is provided by the fact that 16% of the National Debt is held by government departments. The government broker—officially he is broker to the National Debt Commissioners—goes into the market to buy stocks that are approaching maturity, and when a new stock is issued he enters the market again as a buyer, later releasing the stock gradually to the market. Thus, if the terms of the new issue are not particularly attractive, the issue will be fully subscribed. The 2½% unredeemable Treasury stock issued in

1947 when Mr (later Lord) Dalton was Chancellor of the Exchequer (popularly known as "Daltons") was an outstanding example of a new issue that proved so unattractive to the market that most of it had to be taken up by government departments. Heavy purchases by the government broker can be used too to push up the prices of stocks in order to reduce their yield and the prevailing long-term rate of interest.

To influence the short-term rate of interest operations in Treasury bills are undertaken by one of the discount houses acting as special buyer on behalf of the Bank of England.

It is clearly to the Government's own advantage for the prevailing rate of interest to be low in order to reduce the interest burden of the National Debt, but this does not mean that debt management is always directed towards keeping down the rate of interest. A high rate may be necessary to support a disinflationary policy.

Thus, the character of the securities that comprise the National Debt enables the monetary authorities to influence both the long-term and the short-term rate of interest through their management of the debt.

### RECOMMENDATIONS FOR FURTHER READING

U. K. Hicks: *Public Finance* (Nisbet/Cambridge University Press).
A. R. Prest: *Public Finance* (Weidenfeld & Nicholson).
Colin Clark: *Taxmanship* (Institute of Economic Affairs).
H. Dalton: *Public Finance* (Routledge).
HMSO: *Annual Financial Statement.*
HMSO: *Annual Report of Commissioners of Inland Revenue.*

### QUESTIONS

1. Examine the principles on which the British tax system is based at the present day.

2. Show how public finance has become an instrument of social and economic policy.

3. "The budget has widespread and complex effects on the economy, and yet only the most elementary propositions of macro-economic theory are used in its formulation." Discuss. (Degree.)

4. "The purpose of the budget today is to keep the economy on an even keel." Explain and discuss. (Barnsley.)

5. What is the National Debt? In what ways is there a "burden" on the community from this debt? (Bournemouth.)

6. To what extent is it desirable for a tax system to discriminate against distributed profits? (Huddersfield.)

7. With its short-term rates of interest the floating debt should be a cheap source of government borrowing. It has proved otherwise. Discuss. (Kingston-upon-Hull.)

8. The rates system for local authority income receives considerable

criticism. Give the case for and against this form of tax and suggest methods of reform. (Kingston-upon-Hull.)

9. "The real purpose of taxation is not to raise revenue but to reduce consumption. Therefore the best taxes are those that fall on expenditure." Discuss. (Leeds.)

10. Compare the relative merits of monetary and fiscal measures as devices which governments may use to maintain full employment together with a stable level of prices. (Leeds.)

11. Discuss the budget as an instrument of economic control, indicating in what ways it might be regarded as preferable to the use of monetary measures. (Liverpool.)

12. Discuss budgetary policies which can be used to curb inflation. (Northern Counties.)

13. "As higher indirect taxes result in higher prices, the consumer always pays in the end." Consider this statement. (Sheffield.)

14. By an analysis of the following two taxes, show that the government need for revenue may be of only minor importance:
   (a) Capital gains tax.
   (b) Selective employment tax. (Southampton.)

15. The principles of taxation might be summarised in three words: equity, incentive, efficiency. Discuss. (U.L.C.I.)

16. Discuss the advantages and disadvantages of a general sales tax, indicating in your answer what limitations to its incidence you consider advisable. (U.L.C.I.)

# INDEX

inflation, 4, 31, 229, 232–3, 241–3, 273–4, 321–63, 411
 control of, 342–53
 cost-push, 274, 330
 creeping, 324
 demand-pull, 274, 330
 effects of, 333–42
 fixed incomes and, 339
 full employment and, 329–30
 income from profits and, 337
 pensioners and, 341–2
 persistent, 324
 production and, 333–5
 salaried workers and, 339–41
 spread of, 321–33
 types of, 323–4
 wage earners and, 337–9
 world, 329
information agreements, 132
Inland Revenue, 304, 466–8
instalment buying, 100
insurance companies, 278
interest, 10
International Bank for Reconstruction and Development, see World Bank
International Development Association, 415
International Finance Corporation, 396–7
International Labour Organisation, 256
international liquidity, 25–31
International Monetary Fund (IMF), 24, 369, 381, 394, 395–6, 414, 426–8
international trade, 244–5, 365–85
 development of, 365–7
 restrictions on, 367–8
 theory of, 366
International Trade Organisation, 381
investment, 20, 36–8, 227–9
 as item in balance of payments, 405–6
 control of, 58
 private, 228, 330
 public, 228, 240, 330
 trusts, 307–8
iron and steel industry, 46, 130
irrigation, 190
issuing houses, 318–19
Issuing Houses Association, 318

Jack Committee, 169
joint stock banks, 285–6

Kartell, 127
Kennedy Round, 368, 383–5
Keynes, Lord, 36, 200, 227, 323, 345, 394, 428
Kodak, 127–8
Korean War, 331, 359

labour,
 division of, 6, 47, 365
 migration of, 55
 mobility of, 35, 236–8
 non-specific, 236
 redistribution of, 235
 specific, 236
 supply of, 59, 177, 207–9
Labour Party, 264, 376
labour relations, 247–74
Labour Representation Committee, 263
laissez-faire, 247, 367
large-scale production, 74
 tendency towards, 106–9
Law, John, 324
League of Nations, 257
leisure, 40–1
"lending long and borrowing short," 309
level tendering, 127
Leyland Motors, 128
limited liability, 285
liner trains, 163, 268
liquidity ratio, 289–90, 345, 346, 351
Lloyd George, David, 276, 454
Lloyd Jacob Committee, 88
Lloyd, Selwyn, 274
local authorities, 7, 14, 145–6, 209, 465–8, 469
Local Employment Act (1960), 59
location of industry, 45–72
 advantages of, 47–8
 disadvantages of, 48–9
 early influences on, 46–7
 new influences on, 50–1
 trends towards, 45–6
Location of Offices Bureau, 68
Locke, John, 450
lock-outs, 258
London Bankers' Clearing House, 286
London Co-operative Society, 84
London Discount Association, 295, 298
London General Omnibus Company, 150
London Transport, 130, 149–50, 158
 Board, 131, 150
"loss leaders," 80, 89

McKenna duties, 367
Macmillan Report, 309
mail order business, 92–3
Malthus, Rev. T. R., 196–9
Malthusian League, 185
Manfields, 82
manufacturing industries, 11
marginal cost, 133
market,
 forces, 7
 imperfect, 85
 perfect, 85

markets, 73
mark-up, 88
Marshall, Alfred, 3, 9
Marshall, Gen. George, 369
Marshall Plan, 369, 398, 417
mass production, 73
means test, 279
mechanisation, 221–2
megalopolis, 209–10
Memorandum of Association, 317
merchant banks, 288–9
mergers, 110
"middle man," 75
migration, 204–5
Minister of Transport, 165, 168
Ministry of Health, 437
Ministry of Labour, 230
Ministry of National Insurance, 276
Ministry of Social Security, 276, 277, 306
Ministry of Technology, 33
mixed economy, 6, 36
"mobile shops," 77
Molony Report, 104
monetary policy, 342–58
aims of, 342–3
instruments of, 343–6, 347–52
revival of, 346–7
money,
at call and short notice, 289, 297
demand for, 323
market, 294–300
value of, 321–3, 335–6
*Monopolies and Mergers Act* (1965), 125–6
*Monopolies and Restrictive Practices Act* (1948), 109, 119, 123
Monopolies and Restrictive Practices Commission, 123, 126–9
monopolistic competition, 101
monopoly, 106–33
absolute, 109
action against, 129
artificial, 112–14
control of, 119–26
development of, 109–16
discriminating, 114–16
for and against, 116
local, 113
meaning of, 110
nationalised, 129–33
natural, 110
near, 109
oligopoly and, 131–2
power, 110–12
state-created, 111–12
technologically induced, 110
voluntary associations and, 111
monopsony, 114
motor car industry, 157
motorways, 159
multiple retailing, 82

multiple shops, 76, 80–3, 87, 92
multiple wholesaling, 82
multiplier, 217, 227

Napoleon, 73
Napoleonic Wars, 230, 436, 454
National Assistance, 276
*National Assistance Act* (1948), 436
National Bus Company, 166
National Coal Board, 55, 117, 130, 237
National Debt, 309, 332, 435, 468–75
burden of, 472–4
Commissioners, 287, 474
"deadweight," 468
external, 468–9, 472–3
growth of, 470–1
holders of, 472
reproductive, 468
internal, 469, 473
National Development Bonds, 303, 449, 469
National Economic Development Council (NEDC), 32, 33, 265
National Freight Corporation, 165
National Health Service, 276, 279, 280, 437
national income, 5, 8–25
distribution of, 19–21
population and, 177
statistics, 22–3
three ways of looking at, 10
*National Income and Expenditure* (Blue Book), 9, 10
National Incomes Commission, 360
National Insurance, 208, 276, 436
*National Insurance Act* (1911), 276, 436
*National Insurance Act* (1959), 277
National Plan, 31, 34–5, 64, 211
National Savings Certificates, 303, 449, 469
nationalisation, 33, 122, 129–33
*Nationalisation Act* (1947), 138, 155, 170
nationalised industries, 132–3
natural resources, 35–6
Net Book Agreement, 89
net national product, 11
new towns, 67–71
*New Towns Act* (1946), 67, 68
*New Towns Act (Northern Ireland)* (1965), 71
"New Unionism," 251
Northern Stock Exchange, 312

"offer for sale," 318
oil, 50
*Old Age Pensions Act* (1908), 276
oligopoly, 101, 131–2
omnibus,
horse, 145
motor, 145, 157–8
one-man, 268